PORTLAND COM
LEARNING RES(

D0407368

WITHDRAWN

ALSO BY STEPHEN E. AMBROSE:

Halleck: Lincoln's Chief of Staff

Upton and the Army

Duty, Honor, Country:
A History of West Point

Eisenhower and Berlin, 1945

Rise to Globalism:
American Foreign Policy 1938–1990

The Supreme Commander:
The War Years of General Dwight D. Eisenhower

Crazy Horse and Custer:
The Parallel Lives of Two American Warriors

Ike's Spies:
Eisenhower and the Espionage Establishment

Eisenhower:
Soldier, General of the Army, President-Elect
1890–1952

Eisenhower: The President

Pegasus Bridge: June 6, 1944

Nixon:
The Education of a Politician 1913–1962

Nixon:
The Triumph of a Politician 1962–1972

Eisenhower: Soldier and President

NIXON

VOLUME THREE

Ruin and Recovery 1973–1990

STEPHEN E. AMBROSE

SIMON & SCHUSTER

NEW YORK • LONDON • TORONTO
SYDNEY • TOKYO • SINGAPORE

SIMON & SCHUSTER
Simon & Schuster Building
Rockefeller Center
1230 Avenue of the Americas
New York, New York, 10020

Copyright © 1991 by Stephen E. Ambrose
All rights reserved
including the right of reproduction
in whole or in part in any form.
SIMON & SCHUSTER and colophon are
registered trademarks of Simon & Schuster Inc.
Designed by Edith Fowler
Manufactured in the United States of America

10 9 8 7 6 5 4 3 2 1

Library of Congress Cataloging-in-Publication Data

Ambrose, Stephen E.
    Nixon.

(Revised for volume 3)

    Includes bibliographical references and index.
    Contents: v.   1. The education of a politician, 1913–
1962—v.   2. The triumph of a politician, 1962–1972
—v.   3. Ruin and recovery, 1973–1990.
    1. Nixon, Richard M. (Richard Milhous), 1913–
2. Presidents—United States—Biography.   3. United
States—Politics and government—1945-   . I. Title.
E856.A72 1987   973.924'092 [B]   86-26126
ISBN 0-671-52836-X (v. 1)
ISBN 0-671-52837-8 (v. 2)
ISBN 0-671-69188-0 (v. 3)

A leatherbound signed first edition of this book
has been published by The Easton Press.

To the women in my life:
Moira, Stephenie, Grace, Celeste, Edie,
and Corina

CONTENTS

FOREWORD

THIS IS the political story of the century. It is a story of high drama and low skulduggery, of lies and bribes, of greed and lust for power, of abuse and misuse of power. It features attack and counterattack, vicious infighting, and constant psychological warfare. It includes high-minded appeals to basic constitutional doctrine along with base attempts to rewrite the Constitution. It involves fundamental questions of democracy, freedom, justice, and just plain decency.

At stake is the Presidency of the United States, as it was in 1973–74 and as it would be in the future.

The central character is Richard M. Nixon. The drama revolves around him. He is not only the lead actor but also the author, director, and producer of the play. All Presidents command attention, as did Nixon from 1969 through 1972, but from January 1973 through August 1974, he became a national obsession.

Most of what happens in the following narrative happened because Nixon so willed it, although not the climax. Still, at almost any time between January 1973 and August 1974 he could have brought down the curtain—by confessing, by resigning, by burning the tapes, by defying the Special Prosecutor, the courts, and the Congress, or through a number of other possible actions.

Instead, he chose to try to save all by risking all. He tiptoed on the edge of the precipice, buffeted by storms, trying not to look down, striving to maintain his balance and hold his job. He was heroic, admirable, and inspiring while simultaneously being dishonorable, despicable, and a horrible example. It was a role only Richard Nixon could have invented or played.

The supporting cast is a kaleidoscope of American life and politics. There is a loving family, a wife of strength and courage and loyalty, daughters and sons-in-law who provide support. Then there are the judges, the bureaucrats, and most of all Nixon's fellow politicians. Like him, they seldom rise above their milieu. Self-serving actions appear far more often than high-minded ones. Partisanship almost always comes before principle. There is precious little that is edifying in their behavior, and much that is dismaying.

This is a play that does not edify or enlighten or uplift. There is no moral lesson to be learned from a play in which many of the characters, much of the time, are rotters.

Yet there is a hero. Justice does prevail, virtue does triumph, despite the shortcomings, human failings, selfishness, and mendacity that all but overwhelm. That hero, much battered and abused throughout the play, rises in the end to achieve vindication. That hero is the American system of justice, as embodied in the Constitution.

But this is no simple morality play, with good conquering evil at the climax. If it were, it would not be so compelling a production. Justice wins, and the American system triumphs, but at a heavy cost. The United States and the world had to pay—and are still paying—a price for Nixon's resignation. Within less than a decade of his disgrace, many who had clamored loudest for his head found themselves, to their utter amazement, wishing they had Dick Nixon back again, so unhappy were they with his successors and with the consequences of the repudiation of Nixonian Republicanism.

Incredibly, unbelievably, he does come back. Were this really a play, instead of real life, the story would end with his resignation. But Nixon is Nixon. There is no one else like him for refusing to quit, for plotting and executing comebacks, for winning redemption, for self-resurrection. Within a decade and a half of his resignation, he had not only become America's elder statesman but was threatening to become America's beloved elder statesman.

I have loved writing this book.

PORTLAND COMMUNITY COLLEGE
LEARNING RESOURCE CENTERS

CHAPTER ONE

THE NEW AMERICAN REVOLUTION AND TROUBLES IN VIETNAM

November–December 1972

ON NOVEMBER 7, 1972, Richard Milhous Nixon won a landslide victory in the presidential contest by a staggering 60 to 40 percent. This was the climax to twenty-six years of campaigning. His re-election, however, was a personal triumph only. The Republican Party lost, as the Democrats held onto and even expanded their control of both houses of Congress.

The two victories, by the Republicans in the presidential race and by the Democrats in the congressional races, dominated American politics over the following twenty-two months, a period characterized by more bitterness, divisiveness, and pure hatred than any since Reconstruction. The unanticipated, the unwelcome, and the unimaginable became the norm.

This unhealthy situation came about: Because of the way Nixon had conducted his re-election campaign, which left his opponents furious; because of ethically questionable and possibly illegal acts carried out by his men during his first term, which left him vulnerable; because of the long-drawn-out retreat from Southeast Asia, which left the hawks with no incentive to defend him and the doves with feelings of bitterness over the death and destruction that had marked the period 1969–72 in Vietnam; because of Nixon's determination to take on not only the Democrats but the basic structure of American government; and because of Nixon's deep-rooted, long-standing anger at his opponents, real and imagined, which led him to ill-considered and ill-tempered outbursts, which in turn goaded his opponents into extremism, thus raising the stress on the already badly battered body politic.

His anger was exacerbated because he knew that in the war that lay ahead, he had some serious weaknesses. Although he had that 60–40

11

vote, and although he had done a magnificent job on the politics of his problems in the 1972 campaign, all the problems remained. He did not have peace in Vietnam, and the 93d Congress was not going to give him any funds to continue the war. The Central Intelligence Agency (CIA) had refused his order to help him cover up the June 1972 break-in by men working for his re-election committee at the Democratic National Committee offices in the Watergate complex in Washington. The Federal Bureau of Investigation (FBI), the courts, and some reporters were pressing various investigations into Watergate, and the Democrats in control of the 93d Congress could hardly wait to get organized and begin investigations of their own.

Nixon, on election night 1972, could anticipate that despite his overwhelming victory, the Democrats, the bureaucracy, the media, and the courts were all going to go after Watergate and other issues from his first term as hard as they could. And Nixon knew, better than any other individual in the country, how much there was in the Watergate break-in affair and other first-term activities for them to find.

So, on election night 1972, Nixon could not enjoy his triumph. He was not planning how to bring people together, to create a consensus behind his program, but rather how to destroy his enemies before they destroyed him. In his own immortal phrase, "They are asking for it, and they are going to get it."

That was going to be the real theme of his second term, if Nixon could get his way.

NIXON's announced program for his second term was so ambitious he dared to call it nothing less than the "New American Revolution." Although the phrase contained some element of typical Nixonian hyperbole, what he proposed to do was certainly sweeping, even breathtaking. He gave an outline in an interview with Garnett Horner of the Washington *Star-News* on the Sunday before the election; it was published the day after the election.

In some places, Nixon sounded like a leader rallying his people for a protracted war. He called for a return to the rigors of self-reliance to replace the "soft life" and said he hoped to use his second term to lift the nation out of a "crisis of the spirit." He vowed to work to end "the whole era of permissiveness" and to nurture "a new feeling of responsibility, a new feeling of self-discipline."

Nixon believed the nation had become pampered and indulged, that its character had been weakened. "The average American," he said, "is just like the child in the family. You give him some responsibility and he is going to amount to something. He is going to do something.

"If, on the other hand, you make him completely dependent and pamper him and cater to him too much, you are going to make him soft, spoiled, and eventually a very weak individual."

In explaining his thoughts, Nixon drew on the comparison he saw between himself and the nineteenth-century British Prime Minister, Benjamin Disraeli. He had been reading Robert Blake's biography of Disraeli, recommended to him by Professor Daniel Patrick Moynihan of Harvard. "My approach," Nixon explained, "is that of a Disraeli conservative—a strong foreign policy, strong adherence to basic values that the nation believes in and the people believe in, and to conserving those values, and not being destructive of them, but combined with reform, reform that will work, not reform that destroys."

His "strong foreign policy" was designed to ease tensions in the post-Vietnam War world. He had begun the process in his first term, with the Strategic Arms Limitation Talks (SALT I), the opening to China, and the movement in the Paris peace talks toward a cease-fire in Vietnam. He intended to follow up vigorously. His first priority was SALT II, "which will be more important than SALT I" because it was going to establish tighter limitations on strategic weapons. Next came a European Security Conference and, in a parallel channel, the Mutual Balanced Force Reduction (MBFR) talks, designed to reduce conventional forces in Europe. Equally important was to "continue the dialogue with the People's Republic of China [the PRC]." He intended to work for peace not only in Vietnam but also in the Middle East.

In a word, détente, or an easing of tensions, around the world. Whether he could develop a constituency for such fundamental changes remained to be seen. He had failed to do so in the preceding four years. Liberals and left-wingers continued to regard *anything* Nixon proposed with the greatest skepticism, while conservatives and right-wingers were deeply suspicious of détente in general and Nixon's specific proposals in particular. He had not consulted with the military before signing SALT I, which made the Joint Chiefs unhappy. They were also upset by Nixon's proposed peace settlement in Vietnam, because Nixon had dropped his demand that the North Vietnamese Army (NVA) withdraw from South Vietnam.

On the domestic side, Nixon's plans were equally ambitious. He told Horner he intended to reduce drastically the size and scope of the federal government, which he said, "is too big and it is too expensive." The bureaucracies were "too fat, too bloated." He intended to "shuck off" or "trim down" the Great Society programs of the 1960s, and to carry out a major reorganization of the executive branch of the government.[1]

In three words, a "New American Revolution." Like any revolution, it was sure to arouse opposition. Lyndon Johnson's Great Society programs, especially those designed to help poor and minority kids, had their defenders; indeed, they constituted a majority in the Congress. Entrenched interests, headed by Congress and supported by the congressional staffs, the lobbyists, the corporations that did business with the government and the federal bureaucracy, regarded any attempt to reorganize the government with skepticism and suspicion.

Nixon, with a mandate from the people, was ready to take them all on—the Joint Chiefs, the right wing, the left wing, the entrenched interests. He knew it would be the biggest battle of his political career. He intended to win it, and thereby reshape the nation, its government, and its foreign policy.

He was in good physical shape to do battle—fifty-nine years old and in excellent health. Although he was constantly chiding himself, rightly, for not getting sufficient exercise, he kept his weight down. He had not missed a day's work due to illness in his entire first term (and very few throughout his career). He took no vitamins nor any medication. He went to Bethesda, Maryland, for a post-election physical examination; emerging from the hospital, he said jokingly, "They told me I feel fine."[2]

Mentally, he was gearing himself up. In his own view, he had too often been weak in his first term, had too often allowed the bureaucrats to subvert or sabotage his program, had too often accepted compromises proposed by his department heads rather than insist on his bold initiatives. He resolved, in the second term, to take control, to act tough, to be tough.

He got started the day after the election. At 11 A.M. he met with the White House staff. The members were still a bit groggy from the victory celebrations of the night before. Nixon had a toothache. To his National Security Adviser, Henry Kissinger, he appeared withdrawn, "grim and remote." Kissinger sensed his mood accurately: "It was as if victory was not an occasion for reconciliation but an opportunity to settle the scores of a lifetime." Nixon gave perfunctory thanks to the staff, before announcing that the first order of business was to reorganize. "There are no sacred cows," he declared, then changed the metaphor: "We will tear up the pea patch."

He gave his thinking. He told them that while rereading Blake's *Disraeli,* he had been struck by Disraeli's description of Gladstone and his Cabinet as "exhausted volcanoes." He was not exhausted, he went on; he was determined to avoid the "lethargy that had characterized [President Dwight] Eisenhower's second term. . . ." Then he strode out of the room.

His chief of staff, H. R. "Bob" Haldeman, took over. He passed around mimeographed forms on which he told the staffers to list all the documents in their possession. Then he said that each man present was to submit his resignation immediately.[3] At noon, Nixon and Haldeman repeated the performance in a meeting with the Cabinet.

Had Nixon waited, the resignations would have come in over the next month or so, voluntarily, as was customary. As it was, his actions and his obvious anger bemused and confused his closest associates, men who had worked diligently and enthusiastically for his re-election. They had expected to be thanked; instead, they got slapped. Director of Communications Herb Klein, who had been with Nixon on mornings after election day since 1946, knew him well enough to expect a letdown of some kind, but even Klein was appalled: "I found this post-election act the most disheartening, most surprising, and most cruel of all. . . . It was ungrateful and it was bitterly cold."[4] Kissinger was bothered by "the frenzied, almost maniacal sense of urgency about this political butchery," and by the way Nixon conveyed "in his hour of triumph an impression of such total vindictiveness and insensitivity. . . ."[5]

That afternoon, Nixon flew to his vacation retreat at Key Biscayne, Florida. Accompanying him on *Air Force One* were his wife Pat, his daughters Julie Eisenhower and Tricia Cox, his sons-in-law David and Edward, his friend Bebe Rebozo, his secretary Rose Mary Woods, and Kissinger, Haldeman, and his domestic adviser John Ehrlichman. For the next few days, while the others swam and soaked up the sun, Nixon, Haldeman, and Ehrlichman worked on the details of the reorganization.

That was a small group for such a big task. Nixon's isolation bothered some of his supporters. Robert Finch, an old friend and former Secretary of Health, Education and Welfare (HEW) in the first Nixon Administration, was one. He called Woods and asked her to tell the boss not to announce or leak any decisions he made without first at least pretending to consult with the Cabinet and party leaders. As Woods put it in a memo for Nixon, "He said even if you have decided exactly what you are going to do he feels it is imperative that nothing be put out until it appears that you have given the people concerned 'their day in court.' "[6]

Leaks came anyway. At the end of the first full day in Key Biscayne, a "high Administration source" told Robert Semple of *The New York Times* that Nixon's restructuring of the federal government would "further increase the authority of his own Executive Office and accelerate a long-term decline in the power of the Cabinet."[7] A few days later the same newspaper, citing "senior officials," said the goal was to decentralize the machinery of government while centralizing the policy-making process, which would be taken "out of the departments and moved to the White House, where it is much more difficult for Congress and the public to trace how the decisions are made."[8]

Charles Colson, a special assistant to the President, was one of those slated to have his resignation accepted, primarily because of his close association with E. Howard Hunt and G. Gordon Liddy, who were under indictment for their role in the break-in to the Democratic National Committee (DNC) headquarters at the Watergate apartment complex in June.

Colson, typically, was blunt about what was going on at Key Biscayne: "Haldeman and Ehrlichman are in a major power grab."[9]

NIXON'S most immediate problem was not reorganizing the government, or taming the bureaucracy, or promoting SALT II, but Vietnam. On the eve of the election, Henry Kissinger had announced that as a result of his negotiations in Paris with North Vietnamese envoy Le Duc Tho, "Peace is at hand." But although the North Vietnamese had indicated they were ready to sign the agreements worked out in October—which provided for a "National Council of Reconciliation" composed equally of Communists and anti-Communist members, a cease-fire, the return of the American prisoners of war, and the right of 160,000 members of the North Vietnamese Army (NVA) to remain in place in South Vietnam— President Nguyen Van Thieu of South Vietnam had protested bitterly over what he regarded as a sellout, even a surrender, and refused to sign or accept the agreements. The fighting went on.

Nixon wanted to stop it, for many obvious reasons. He, or at least Kissinger, had promised that the fighting was all but over. Détente could not be fully implemented until the war ended. The war was a major drain on the budget. It exacerbated the divisions among the American people; it threatened to tear the country apart. And it could not be won. Nixon had withdrawn all ground combat troops in his first term. The Army of the Republic of Vietnam (ARVN) was incapable of driving the NVA out of South Vietnam. Nixon's options were to increase the level of bombing in North Vietnam and extend the target list to include the Hanoi-Haiphong complex, or persuade/force Thieu to accept the agreement.

The bombing option, however, had little appeal, especially after "peace is at hand." How could Nixon explain to the American people a bombing campaign against North Vietnam when it was South Vietnam that refused to accept the agreement? Bombing Hanoi was not going to get the NVA out of South Vietnam. Escalation on the ground via the reintroduction of American combat units might work, but that was unthinkable, because of domestic politics, and in fact was never considered.

So Nixon turned on Thieu, whose objections to the agreement he regarded in any case as unfounded. Thieu said that the National Council represented the coalition government the Communists had always demanded; Nixon thought that was poppycock. He called the Council a facade, a consulting body without power or purpose. Thieu wanted the NVA out of his country; Nixon knew that was impossible. Thieu wanted guarantees that no North Vietnamese would cross the Demilitarized Zone (DMZ, which ran along the 17th parallel that divided the two Vietnams); Nixon doubted that he could get North Vietnamese acceptance of such a demand.

Above all, Thieu wanted a guarantee that the United States would support his country with air cover and military supplies. That guarantee Nixon was willing to give. But the pledge had to be made secretly, because of the mixed results of the election. In the presidential contest, the people had rejected Democratic candidate George McGovern. But in the congressional contest, the people had sent more doves to Washington than hawks. The doves had picked up three seats in the Senate, which meant that when the 93d Congress convened in January 1973, there was a real possibility that it would cut off all funds for South Vietnam.

Nixon had seven weeks in which to end the war. He made it his first order of business. On November 8, he wrote a letter to Thieu. He gave it to Kissinger's deputy, General Alexander Haig, to hand-deliver in Saigon. It contained threats if Thieu did not consent to the agreement, promises if he did. Nixon expressed disappointment at Thieu's characterization of the October agreement as a surrender. He promised to improve the agreement, for example, by ensuring that the Vietnamese translation of the phrase "administrative structure" in the description of the National Council was changed to remove any implication that it was a governmental body, and by strengthening the provisions to respect the DMZ. The letter concluded: "I wish to leave you under no illusions, however, that we can or will go beyond these changes in seeking to improve an agreement that we already consider to be excellent."

Thieu was unmoved. He told Haig he must insist on the removal of the NVA from his country. Nixon responded in a letter dated November 14. He charged that Thieu was being "unrealistic," then held out the bait: "But far more important than what we say in the agreement on this issue is what we do in the event the enemy renews its aggression. You have my absolute assurance that if Hanoi fails to abide by the terms of this agreement it is my intention to take swift and severe retaliatory action."[10]

Kissinger began his preparations for a return to Paris and one last negotiating session with Le Duc Tho. The North Vietnamese were ready to sign the accord that had been reached in October; Kissinger planned to ask for the changes Thieu was insisting on. The meeting was scheduled for November 20.

NIXON saw enemies not only in Hanoi, but among the Democrats and the media. Down at Key Biscayne, he went after both. On November 10, he instructed Haldeman to send out an "Action Memo" to the staff: "Be sure we have established a total embargo on *Time* and *Newsweek* and especially no background material to [Hugh] Sidey [*Time* columnist]." The memo ordered a "complete freeze on the *Washington Post*, the *New York Times*, and CBS."[11] Two days later, in another "Action Memo," the orders were "to follow up on all major Democratic contributors and financial backers. We need a plan set for this to be put into motion as soon as the personnel changes have been made [in the White House staff]."[12]

On November 15, Nixon sent his own memo to Haldeman. He was not in a mood to be a gracious winner; he wanted to rub the noses of his defeated enemies in the dirt. He told Haldeman to get together with one of his speechwriters, Pat Buchanan, to prepare a monograph on "Things They Would Like to Forget." He wanted to begin with the things columnists and television commentators wrote and said "at the time of Cambodia" (in the spring of 1970 Nixon sent U.S. troops into Cambodia to hit the Communists along the Ho Chi Minh Trail) "when they predicted World War III." The monograph should also point out what they wrote and said after Nixon's May 8, 1972, decision to bomb Hanoi and mine the harbor at Haiphong.

In addition, Nixon wanted to throw back at the media "the predictions that were made in 1971" about the imminent collapse of South Vietnam. Further, the monograph should reprint the predictions that were made "with regard to McGovern's inevitable appeal to youth, the prairie populist, and all that sort of thing."

Nixon ordered the preparation of a second monograph, to be called "Dirtiest Campaign in History Against a President." It would quote the worst McGovern charges, plus "You might go back and pick up some of the smears on RN through the years." Beyond that, it should highlight the campaign tactics of the Democrats, the way "we were unmercifully heckled and our meetings disrupted by violent demonstrators." Nixon wanted these tactics contrasted with his own, which he called "one of the cleanest campaigns in history. . . . Never engaged in name calling. . . . Stuck to the issues."

A third monograph should be called "RN Won It!" and point out that Nixon won "against overwhelming odds." That monograph should make the point that Nixon never shrank from the "tough decisions," that he ran the campaign his way, and that "it wasn't just the case of McGovern losing it, it was the case of RN winning."[13]

Consumer advocate Ralph Nader did not see it Nixon's way at all. He charged that Nixon had run a campaign of half-truths and full lies while the White House press corps served as a "mimeo machine" for Nixon's propaganda. In Nader's view, the trouble was the publishers, "who like to have dinner at the White House," and who paid for it by telling their reporters not to criticize the President.

When Nixon saw that comment on his News Summary, he scribbled in the margin, "B [for Buchanan]—should Knock this bull—RN has worst press of any President in this century."[14] This *idée fixe* of Nixon's had spurred him to attempt to woo some of the media executives, as Nader noted; others he tried to intimidate. Colson later recalled the night Nixon called in the network executives, "all three of them, and afterwards Nixon and I sat there and chortled over how he had twisted their tails and backed them into corners and how they were cowards and how he would lower his voice when he really wanted to make a point to them. We would sit there and laugh after we had them in on how we had put the screws to them. . . . We got them to back off of some stories frequently. Got Bill Paley [of CBS] to back down on some of his reporting."[15]

Public intimidation was another technique. On November 12, Colson told the New England Society of Newspaper Editors that *The Washington Post, The New York Times,* and CBS News were guilty of "McCarthyism" in their reporting on the Watergate break-in. He singled out Benjamin Bradlee, executive editor of the *Post,* and Eric Sevareid, commentator on CBS News, for special criticism; in a phrase reminiscent of Vice President Spiro Agnew's speeches, Colson said that Bradlee and Sevareid were "self-appointed leaders of a tiny fringe of arrogant elitists."[16]

Nixon was a man whose mind never rested. Even as he was dealing with the Vietnam negotiations, reshuffling his Cabinet and White House staff, taking on the Democrats and the media, planning his revolution, he found time immediately after the election to send Haldeman a three-page, single-spaced memo on thank-you notes to contributors to his campaign. He got down to details. As one example, he said he felt "we went a bit overboard [in 1968] when we sent pen sets to major financial contributors. These fellows are pretty perceptive; they know that this had to come from campaign funds and not from me personally. . . . It looks as if we were being too extravagant and wasting campaign funds."[17]

AFTER a week at Key Biscayne, Nixon flew to Washington, then took a helicopter to Camp David, the presidential retreat in the Maryland mountains. Haldeman and Ehrlichman joined him; in the following two weeks they brought up other top players, one by one, to explain the reorganization and their new roles, or to fire them.

The first target in the reorganization was the bureaucracy. Nixon chided himself for failing to take control of it in his first term; he was determined to rectify that in his second term. He made this clear, and explained his rationale, in his meetings with his appointees. To George Shultz, whom Nixon was retaining as Secretary of the Treasury, he complained that the "IRS [Internal Revenue Service] was a walking disaster under Ike and me." The agents were "biased against our friends. They hate those with money." Besides, there were "too many Jews." Therefore, he wanted Shultz to "clean the house." While he was at it, Nixon wanted Shultz to go after "Ford, Brookings, and other foundations," because they had been used "for partisan, left-wing purposes."[18]

In a meeting with Ehrlichman, Nixon asserted that the "big law firms and companies get the best of the conservatives," while the top liberals "go into government or teaching." Meanwhile the FBI was reduced to accepting its new agents from the bottom half of the law school classes. In the State Department, more than half the career people came from the Ivy League, where, according to Nixon, "they were playing together those frilly games—squash, crew."

It was standard Republican philosophy to assert that what the government needed was a few businessmen who had met a payroll to run it. Nixon had outgrown that belief. He told William Simon, an investment banker at Salomon Brothers whom he was appointing Deputy Secretary of the Treasury, that "most businessmen are a disaster in government." The reason was that the average businessman came in "and is a patsy for the brown-nosers in the bureaucracy." He also told Simon to get to know Wilbur Mills (D.-Ark.), Chairman of the House Ways and Means Committee, and Russell Long (D.-La.), Chairman of the Senate Finance Committee. Nixon characterized them as "brilliant and unreliable, much smarter than Republicans." He told Simon to treat them with a combination of "tender loving care and ruthlessness." Another piece of advice was, "Don't live in the District. Get out into Virginia or Maryland."[19]

To John Dean, who was being retained as counsel to the President, Nixon declared, "I'm one of the most hated Presidents by the Washington establishment," and explained the reason: "They know I'm one of them but I'm not captured by them." (After the meeting, Nixon told Ehrlichman that Dean was a "superb young man.")[20]

That Nixon had enemies in the bureaucracy was true. The career people in the State Department were especially furious with him, because of his shoddy treatment of Secretary of State William Rogers, because of the way he had excluded the Department from the most basic decisions of his first term (the opening to China, the SALT talks, Vietnam, among others), because he so often expressed his contempt for the Department, and because so many of them were Kennedy Democrats.

That his enemies in the bureaucracy could subvert his orders was also true. Back in the campaign, for example, he had issued an executive order that was designed "to lift the veil of secrecy" from needlessly classified official documents. He directed a freer flow of information to the public from secret and confidential papers over ten years old. He had more than an open government in mind; as he confessed to Haldeman, his aim was to reveal the origins of American involvement in the Korean and Vietnam wars and to expose the Kennedy blunders in the 1961 Cuban Bay of Pigs invasion.

Despite his partisan purpose, Nixon was eloquent in promulgating his order for openness: "Fundamental to our way of life," he said, "is the belief that when information which properly belongs to the public is systematically withheld by those in power, the people soon become ignorant of their own affairs, distrustful of those who manage them, and—eventually—incapable of determining their own destinies." (Seventeen years after he left office, Nixon was still using the legal system to block access to the basic documents of *his* Administration.)

The State Department made a shambles of his order. Historians who submitted requests for documents relating to Korea, Vietnam, and the Bay of Pigs complained that they got a run-around. *The New York Times* submitted thirty-one requests for documents; some months later the newspaper got partial answers to three of them (according to the *Times,* the "least consequential" of the requests). No new Kennedy material was made available; the State Department simply buttoned up.[21]

Nixon could be as devious in his methods as the bureaucracy. Charles Colson was the first aide summoned to Camp David. Haldeman told him he should be flattered, because Nixon wanted to talk to his aides "in the order of importance of the individual to him in the second term." Actually, Nixon wanted to fire Colson, but he was bothered by the timing. Haldeman's handwritten notes for November 15 state: "Re Cols[on's] departure—inev. prob. w/H[unt] trial etc. Can't go under fire, can't be sure what come out [of the Hunt trial]."[22]

Nixon attacked the problem in his own convoluted way. He began by inviting Colson to have a pre-dinner drink with him at Aspen Lodge. The President asked Colson's plans. Colson said he wanted to return to his law practice. Nixon asked him to stay on as counselor to the President, in charge of legislative affairs. Colson demurred: "I don't think that's my thing."

"Come to think of it," Nixon eagerly responded, "you're probably right. You can probably do more good on the outside." He said he would fix it up so that Colson could be the chief lawyer for the Republican National Committee (RNC) "and you'll be part of a 'Kitchen Cabinet.' . . . You can advise me, and then you can practice law and make all the money you want at the same time."

The two men finished their drinks, then went in for dinner with Haldeman and Ehrlichman. After dinner, Nixon said he had had second thoughts. Perhaps Colson ought to stay on for a few months. Colson agreed, and it was left at that.[23]

Nixon's convolutions and little games aside, he had big matters on his mind up at Camp David, much bigger than exposing Kennedy's Bay of Pigs and Vietnam policies, or forcing the IRS to bend to his will. He was deadly serious about imposing from the top a "New American Revolution." It would affect not only the bureaucracy but the judicial system, the relations between the federal and state governments, the tax base, the executive branch, Congress, and the American character.

On November 18, Haldeman sent out one of his Action Memos. Nixon had instructed him to write it, on the basis of a conversation the President had held with his most trusted adviser, former Secretary of the Treasury John Connally, who had handled the national Democrats for Nixon Committee in the campaign. Haldeman's memo opened: "John Connally recommends consideration of Administration supported amendment to the Constitution requiring Congressional reconfirmation of all federal judges every eight years on an automatic basis." The purpose, the memo said, was to "make these judges answerable to someone, while at present they are answerable to nobody, and have acquired great autocratic and arrogant attitudes as a result."

Nixon's acceptance of that idea reflected his anger at the Supreme Court for such decisions as mandating busing as a means to end segregation (1971), refusing to block publication of the Pentagon Papers by *The Washington Post* and *The New York Times* (1971), and rejecting in a unanimous opinion the Justice Department claim of an inherent power to wiretap without warrant domestic groups suspected of being subversive (1972).

Obviously, anything as major as a constitutional amendment designed to change the bedrock basis of judicial independence through lifetime tenure would take time. Meanwhile, Nixon pledged to appoint more conservative judges, while planning to see to it, in Haldeman's words, that they not "sit unchallenged for life."[24]

In his meeting with Shultz, Nixon spelled out another fundamental change in the American system he was determined to foster. The President said that "aid to private schools" was the "highest priority," while number two was "property tax relief." Support for private schools was a way to avoid busing. The middle class was groaning under the weight of property taxes; Nixon planned to help his constituents by gutting the Great Society ("flush Model Cities," he told Ehrlichman, "and Great Society along with it. It's failed. Do it, don't say it") and using the savings for revenue sharing, a program that he had gotten started in his first term. It returned federal tax money to the states for general purpose revenue. The supposition was that the states would use the income to reduce property taxes.[25]

Private school aid and property tax relief were old issues that had established and enthusiastic support. There was no such base from which to launch a major change in the executive branch. Quite the contrary; there was massive opposition to changing the way things worked, from the Congress, the lobbyists, the bureaucracy, and the contractors. Nixon plunged ahead anyway.

"I was gripped by this sort of sensation that all of a sudden the Presidency has changed," Colson said of his visit to Camp David. He had the "eerie sensation . . . that the Presidency was in exile up at Camp David . . . while it was being totally restructured." In his view, the motivation came from Haldeman and Ehrlichman, "two guys wanting to become sort of super deputy Presidents."[26]

Colson was wrong. The idea and the impetus came from Nixon. He wanted to take command of the federal government while simultaneously turning back some of that government's power and income to the states.

The heart of the reorganization was to reduce the number of Cabinet departments from twelve to eight. Nixon proposed to keep State, Defense, Treasury, and Justice substantially intact, while cutting in half the remaining eight, which would be reorganized by function into four: Human Resources, Community Development, Natural Resources, and Economic Development. The proposal envisioned eliminating duplication, always a nightmarish problem in government, and reducing the number of officials reporting directly to the President.

Structural changes of the magnitude Nixon proposed had to await congressional approval. Meanwhile Nixon tried to achieve his goal administratively by designating four Cabinet members as "super-secretaries" for Natural Resources (Earl Butz of Agriculture), Human Resources (Caspar Weinberger of HEW), Community Development (James Lynn of Housing and Urban Development or HUD), and Economic Affairs (George Shultz).[27]

On November 27, Nixon met with a dozen newsmen in the helicopter hangar at Camp David to explain some of his plans and announce personnel changes. He noted speculation "to the effect that there is a move here on the top of this mountain to, as a result of the rather significant victory of November 7, to reach out and grasp a lot of power and draw it into the White House. . . ." He asserted that "exactly the opposite is the case." His aim, he said, was to make "our Government more responsive to people" by delegating power to others.[28]

Personnel changes included the acceptance of the resignations of George Romney at HUD and Melvin Laird at Defense. Elliot Richardson would leave HEW to replace Laird at Defense, while Weinberger would leave the Office of Management and Budget (OMB) to take over HEW. Roy Ash, president of Litton Industries and author of the plan to restructure the executive branch, would take over OMB. Ehrlichman would take on added responsibilities as assistant to the President. Nixon said nothing about Kissinger's status, or Rogers's future. He did say that neither Connally nor Governor Nelson Rockefeller of New York would be members of the Cabinet, although Connally would be available for special assignments.

Behind Nixon's relatively bland and benign words lay some tough reality, as the Cabinet members learned when Ehrlichman passed out to them a mimeographed "Rationale of New Organization." In the new setup, "A Cabinet Secretary should not anticipate either free access or frequent consultation with the President." Instead, he would be expected "to seek the advice and accept the recommendations of the Assistants to the President with respect to the operation of the Departments." Cabinet members would submit to the President's assistants all congressional testimony and public statements "for clearance prior to release." Bluntly, the form declared, "Cabinet meetings will be rare."

"The essence of the new organization," the form declared, "is the concept that the [Cabinet] secretaries . . . are the President's men and not the creatures of their departments. . . . Every appointee of Cabinet rank will be expected to be the President's man in the Department and not the Department's advocate to the President." There was a space beside each point for the Cabinet member to check off to show that he accepted the orders.[29]

"George, be King," George III's mother is supposed to have told him. One can almost hear Nixon saying to himself, "Richard, be President."

As to what Nixon planned to do with his new, more efficient and more tightly controlled executive branch, Haldeman gave some of the details in an Action Memo. Four key goals, he wrote, would be: "1) to destroy and discredit the old liberal establishment—keep fighting them like they fought us, 2) to build the New Majority, 3) to build the President as he is—the compassionate side, and 4) to re-write the history by building a new establishment across the board."[30]

Nixon's first-term experiences had, in his words, "confirmed and deepened" his "fears about the American leadership classes." He believed that "in politics, academics, and the arts, and even in the business community and the churches, there was a successful and fashionable negativism which . . . reflected an underlying loss of will, an estrangement from traditional American outlooks and attitudes. The Vietnam war had completed the alienation for this group by undermining the traditional concept of patriotism."[31]

But the people—the people were solid. They were patriotic. They retained traditional values. They were Nixon's real constituents.

To show that he was not only their leader but one of them, Nixon had taken to wearing an American flag in his lapel. He got the idea from Haldeman, who had seen it done in a movie called *The Candidate*. Nixon was never one to do things by half-measure. When he put the flag pin on his lapel, he had aide Clark MacGregor pass the word to the staff "that since the President wore a flag many of them might want to do so also to show their support of the President and their support of the country."

Small changes and big ones. None had been mentioned in the campaign, few had been anticipated. What was the point to them all? Nixon explained that his reading of history had taught him "that when all the leadership institutions of a nation become paralyzed by self-doubt and second thoughts, that nation cannot long survive unless those institutions are either reformed, replaced, or circumvented."[32]

Beyond those goals, Nixon at Camp David indulged himself in a fantasy that had appealed to Teddy Roosevelt and Dwight Eisenhower, the creation of a new political party. He had come to distrust big businessmen—"they don't really like us," he told Ehrlichman[33]— and was indulging himself in a love affair with the hard-hats, the ethnics, the housewives in Dayton, all those members of the Silent Majority who had voted Democratic in the congressional races but overwhelmingly for him in the presidential contest. He felt, as he told Connally, that the Republicans were too inhibited, too restrained, too proper, while "the Democrats let it all out and love to shout and laugh and have fun. The Republicans have fun but they don't want to let people see it."[34]

Much more than fun was involved. Nixon was upset with the Republican Party because its lackluster candidates had done so badly in the election, and because the elected congressmen failed to give him their total support. He much preferred the Southern Democrats, men like Russell Long and John Connally (in this he was at one with Ike). Worse, the Republicans were blaming Nixon for their losses, which struck him as both wrong and ungrateful. A series of memos came to Nixon in the post-election period that emphasized the same point: Republicans were "mad as hell" at Nixon's "pallid efforts" to help their candidates. William Timmons, responsible for White House–Capitol Hill liaison, warned that the discontent was widespread and "could result in an independent attitude toward the President's legislative proposals."

Nixon's response was to instruct Timmons and others to "get the record out" and "knock this down." He insisted that he *had* supported Republican candidates (which was simply not true; see chapters 25 and 26 of volume two of this work) and that their defeats were due to "local issues."[35]

But however tempted Nixon was by the thought of a new party, he realized it was hopeless and quickly dropped the idea. He did not, however, abandon his ambitious program to restructure the government and restore American values.

Yet he proposed to bring such changes about in the teeth of the bureaucracy, the courts, the Congress, the Cabinet, the lobbyists, big business, the media, and his own party. The political philosopher Hannah Arendt once commented that the American President is simultaneously the most powerful man in the world and the national leader with the least power. Nixon wanted to eliminate that paradox, using his election mandate as his base. He had persuaded the people to vote for him overwhelmingly; now his problem was to lead the nation in the direction he wanted it to go.

BEFORE he could accomplish any of his goals, Nixon had to put the Watergate break-in problem behind him.

On June 17, 1972, a team of burglars led by G. Gordon Liddy and E. Howard Hunt, working for the Committee to Re-Elect the President (CREEP), had broken into the offices of the Democratic National Committee in the Watergate complex. They had been caught and identified.

The Democrats and some Washington- and New York–based reporters had attempted to make the break-in a major campaign issue, but without success. Nixon dismissed the affair as a "bizarre business" and a "third-rate burglary." His White House Counsel, John Dean, had managed to keep Liddy and Hunt from naming the people for whom they had worked. Federal Judge Charles Richey had postponed hearings on the Democrats' civil suit until after the election. Federal Judge John Sirica had postponed the trial of the burglars until January 1973. House Minority Leader Gerald R. Ford (R.-Mich.) had played a critical if hidden role in getting the House Banking Committee to postpone hearings on the sources of the money found on the burglars. The FBI had conducted one of the most intensive investigations in its history but had directed it down instead of up. As a result of all this help, Watergate had hardly hurt Nixon.

The various postponements, however, had only put off the problems, which were certain to return to haunt him. His enemies would organize the House and Senate, select the chairmen of the regular and special committees, decide what to investigate (the Democrats had already made it clear they intended to appoint a special committee to investigate the Watergate break-in). From his own days as a congressman, when the Democrats were in the White House but the Republicans controlled the Congress, Nixon knew full well how powerful the subpoena was, how far afield an investigating committee could roam in the pursuit of its inquiries, how easily an ambitious congressman could play to the press in public hearings, and how ineffective White House attempts to cover up would be. He had made himself into a national figure as a freshman congressman in 1947–48 by using the subpoena power and the publicity potential in the investigation of Alger Hiss.

Nixon also knew that the Democrats would find a great deal more than the June 17 break-in to investigate and condemn. His people had placed telephone taps on National Security Council (NSC) staffers and on newspaper and television reporters, in order to find and plug leaks. E. Howard Hunt had attempted to rewrite history by concocting fake cables placing responsibility for the 1963 assassination of South Vietnamese President Diem on the Kennedy Administration. Liddy and Hunt had attempted to break into George McGovern's office, and had broken into the office of Daniel Ellsberg's psychiatrist in an attempt to get damaging information on the man who had leaked the Pentagon Papers. People working for Nixon had played a series of dirty tricks on Senator Edmund Muskie of Maine when he was the front-running Democratic candidate. They had tried to use the IRS to get at their political enemies. Most of all, there was the cover-up of Watergate, which had begun the instant Nixon learned the burglars had been caught.

Never mind that Franklin Roosevelt, John Kennedy, and Lyndon Johnson had indulged in illegal activities; as Nixon knew (and said hundreds of times), *they* could get away with things he could not. This was partly because their party controlled Congress, more because the public had an affection, even a love for them. (Truman and Johnson had lost that sentiment in their last years in office, which was one reason why neither one stood for re-election.) For Nixon, it was the case that while many people admired him, few loved him. In this, he was the opposite of one of his GOP successors, Ronald Reagan.

Nixon's inability to bring enough Republican congressional candidates along on his coattails, coupled with his inability to inspire warm personal feelings toward himself, made him vulnerable even at the moment of his greatest triumph. Further, he had been involved in a whole series of activities that were not necessarily illegal, but which, if exposed, would look just terrible. His half-million-dollar tax deduction for his vice presidential papers; the ITT settlement; the use of federal money to improve his personal residences in Florida and California; the millions in unreported cash contributions to CREEP; the use of the Justice Department to harass and intimidate antiwar protesters; and more.

McGovern had charged that the Nixon Administration was the most corrupt in American history. Considering the competition, that was too sweeping a generalization. It would have been more accurate to say that despite the deplorable record of some of Nixon's Democratic predecessors, no Administration in American history was more ruthless, more partisan, more personal, or more reckless in its disregard not only for the law but for the decent opinion of mankind as that of Richard Nixon. His methods in striving for and achieving and using power had created countless enemies and given his foes the ammunition to ruin him.

Nevertheless, in mid-November 1972, Nixon in his own words "felt sure that [Watergate] was just a public relations problem that only needed a public relations solution."[36]

It was characteristic of Nixon to so believe. As President, indeed throughout his political career, Nixon had put more emphasis on PR than any of his predecessors. An astonishing number of his memos to Haldeman and others, and of Haldeman's memos to the staff, and of Nixon's scribbled comments on his News Summaries, were concerned solely with PR. James Reston, columnist for *The New York Times,* once observed that Nixon was much better at handling the public relations of a problem than he was at handling the problem itself. Nixon believed that the way the public perceived a problem was the critical factor in solving it, which is a defensible point of view for the leader of a democracy to hold, but dangerous when it gets down to using PR to assert that black is white.

In this case, Nixon's real problem was not the break-in itself. He had not given a direct order to go into the DNC offices in the Watergate and plant a bug on Chairman Larry O'Brien's telephone, and he almost certainly did not know of the operation in advance. But he had ordered

Haldeman, on June 23, to use the CIA to limit the investigation of the burglary; his exact words were to instruct the CIA director, Richard Helms, to "call the FBI in and say that we [the CIA] wish for the country, don't go any further into this case, period!"

With those words, Nixon had ordered the CIA to commit an illegal act. The CIA is prohibited by statute from operations of any kind within the United States. Nor did the President have the authority to order one federal agency to interfere with another federal agency as it carried out its responsibilities.

He could claim that his motive was national security, on the grounds that Hunt and some of the Cuban members of the burglary team were former CIA agents who had been deeply involved in the Bay of Pigs. The difficulty with that line was that Helms vehemently denied there was any CIA involvement in Watergate, and it was not Hunt's activities as a CIA agent in the early 1960s that had to be kept secret, rather his activities as one of the "Plumbers" (a secret intelligence unit in the White House) for the Nixon Administration in the early 1970s.

Nixon's PR problem was to convince the public that he had no direct role in the break-in, which was true; his real problem was to prove that he had played no role in a cover-up of a crime, and that he had no idea as to who had ordered the break-in, or why, which was not true. Bill Rogers exposed the weakness of his position with crystal clarity in a telephone conversation with Haldeman in March 1973. Haldeman's notes summarize Rogers's point: "Why cover up if we don't know real story. Just isn't believable. The attempts to cover up make the basic alibi of non-involvement inconceivable."[37]

Despite that obvious truth, Nixon's tops aides continued to use questionable practices to maintain the cover-up. On November 13, Hunt talked to Colson on the telephone. Hunt and his burglary team had already received $187,000 from CREEP officials for bail money, legal fees, and "family support." Hunt wanted more, and he set a deadline of November 25 for receiving it. "After all," he told Colson, "we're protecting the guys who were really responsible. . . . But this is a two-way street . . . we think that now is the time when some moves should be made and, uh, surely your cheapest commodity available is money. . . ."[38]

Colson tape-recorded the conversation. His reason, he later explained, was that "I maneuvered Hunt into the position of saying that I didn't know anything about it in advance. I saved that tape as my ticket that I wasn't involved in the Watergate." (Hunt gave a "Yeah, I know" answer to Colson's strong assertion that he was uninvolved.)[39] Colson gave the tape to Dean, who on November 15 took it to Camp David, where he played it for Haldeman and Ehrlichman. They told Dean to have former Attorney General and head of CREEP John Mitchell take care of Hunt's demands.

Haldeman and Ehrlichman were not convinced about Colson's innocence. They told the President that Colson "might be more involved than he was acknowledging." Colson said the same about both of them.[40] Ehrlichman urged Nixon to get rid of Colson, at once, but Nixon did not want "to leave the impression that he is leaving under fire." In his diary on November 18, Nixon wrote: "It is a very sad commentary that an individual can be bruised and battered and maligned and libeled and then become expendable. But in politics I fear that is the case." He added that he disagreed with Ehrlichman, who wanted to fire "anybody who has even the appearance of wrongdoing. I would never take this approach because of the human equation." Besides, "backing off of people when they come under attack could simply encourage the piranha fish to go to with a vengeance and leave nothing but the skeleton."[41]

When Dean went to Mitchell to get the money for Hunt, Mitchell stalled. Hunt extended his deadline to November 27. Mitchell then told Dean to get the money in cash from Haldeman's secret fund in the White House; he did so, then passed it on to Fred LaRue, a CREEP official from Mississippi, who in turn passed it on to Hunt's lawyer.[42]

Whether Nixon knew about the payment or not is unclear. Whether the payment constituted blackmail, or was a perfectly legal way to provide support for the men under indictment, is perhaps debatable. That the intent was to buy the silence of the accused is obvious. The hope was that Hunt and his men would plead guilty without revealing who they worked for and serve their sentences in prison (presumably short sentences, as these were first offenses by men who had not taken anything out of the DNC offices, only left telephone bugs behind).

Dean's job was to deal with what Nixon liked to call "problem areas." It kept him busy. On the day Nixon demanded the resignations of all the top officials in the government, for example, Dean called Haldeman: "Bob, I've been thinking about those resignations. There's one guy we can't afford to piss off. One guy we need, who's been helpful, concerned, and who's been watching out after our interests. And that's Henry Petersen [head of the Criminal Division in the Justice Department; he had been supplying Dean with information as the investigation went forward]. I don't think we should let Henry worry about his future."

Haldeman agreed, and assented to Dean's request that he be authorized to call Petersen and assure him his job was safe.[43]

Despite these efforts, the problem areas continued to grow. On December 4, Judge Sirica said during pre-trial hearings (the trial was scheduled to begin January 8) that the motives behind the bugging were "one of the crucial issues" in the case. "What did these men go into the headquarters for?" he asked. "Was their sole purpose political espionage? Were they paid? Were there financial gains? Who started this? Who hired them? A whole lot is going to come out in this case."[44]

That was ominous. More bad news followed. On December 8, Hunt's wife Dorothy, who had acted as a courier distributing money to the accused, died in an airplane crash near Midway Airport in Chicago. Policemen searching through the wreckage found her purse stuffed with hundred-dollar bills, a total of $10,000. Despite intensive investigations, no evidence that the plane was sabotaged was ever found. Still, the event threw Hunt into a depression that made him even more unpredictable, as well as raising suspicions that the White House was paying blackmail money.[45]

That same day, *The Washington Post* revealed for the first time the existence of the White House Plumbers. It identified Hunt and Liddy, and said their function was to stop national security leaks. White House press secretary Ron Ziegler confirmed the existence of the Plumbers but said the unit had been closed down after January 1972, and had no involvement in the Watergate break-in.

So Watergate was not quite over. Neither was the Vietnam War. And just as one of the Watergate problems was intrigue and power plays among the courtiers, so too with the Vietnam War.

Just before the election, Nixon, Kissinger, and Haldeman had discussed the Rogers problem. Kissinger had insisted that Rogers had to go, because according to Kissinger, Rogers and the bureaucrats in the State Department "keep stabbing me in the back." Nixon hated to fire Rogers, who had been a close adviser since 1952, but he had agreed to appoint Laird's deputy at Defense, Kenneth Rush, as Secretary of State.

Kissinger doubted Nixon's resolve. He had taken Haldeman aside to say, "I won't believe it until I see it, Haldeman. That Rogers will never quit. He'll be with me until I die."[46]

After the election, Nixon summoned Rogers to Camp David. He designated Haldeman to deliver the blow. "I had the enviable task," Haldeman later wrote, "of telling Richard Nixon's closest personal friend in the government that Richard Nixon had decided it was now time for him to leave." But Rogers would not cooperate. He said he would leave in six months or so, after the Vietnam War ended, but would not go now, when all the others were leaving. Nor would he accept dismissal from Haldeman; the word had to come from the man himself.

Nixon backed down. When he met with Rogers, the President acquiesced in the Secretary of State's demand to be allowed to stay on for six months. He told Haldeman to inform Kissinger. The National Security Adviser was furious. "You promised me, Haldeman," Kissinger exploded. "You gave me your *word!* And now he's hanging on just like I said he would. Piece by piece. Bit by bit. He stays on and on and on." Lowering his voice, Kissinger said resignedly, "There is a price you must pay, I suppose. Mine is Rogers. He will be with me forever—because he has this President wrapped around his little finger."[47]

Actually, Kissinger's own position was in jeopardy. There was, first of all, Kissinger's "peace is at hand" news conference just before the election; the phrase had already caused Nixon considerable embarrassment, especially after President Thieu had rejected the terms of the October agreement. In addition, on November 16 a Kissinger interview with Italian reporter Oriana Fallaci, in which he had described himself as the cowboy who rode into town alone to restore law and order, was published in *L'Europeo* magazine. He had also said "independence" was very important to him, and that "I've by no means decided to give up this job yet. . . . You see, when one wields power, and when one has it for a long time, one ends up thinking one has a right to it."[48]

Nixon was furious. Although Haldeman told Kissinger, the day after the election, that his resignation would not be accepted, Nixon changed his mind. On November 20, he took Colson for a walk outside the main presidential quarters at Camp David, and told him, "It's time for Henry to go back to Harvard, Chuck. It's the best thing for him. He needs to do it." Colson thought that the purpose of the walk was to get away from a hidden tape recorder.[49]

Before Kissinger could return to Harvard, however, Nixon needed him to complete the peace agreement in Vietnam. Kissinger was scheduled to go to Paris for a last meeting with Le Duc Tho on November 20. Before leaving, he met with Nixon. Kissinger, in Nixon's words, "began to rumble around to the effect that we have a very good record" on the negotiations.

"We're not concerned about being right on the record," Nixon responded. "What we are concerned about is to save South Vietnam and that's why we had to temporize with Thieu as much as we did, because our interest is in getting South Vietnam to survive and Thieu at present seems to be the only leader who could lead them in that direction."

He added that if Thieu would not go along, "we shall simply have to make our own deal, have our withdrawal . . . and then say that Vietnamization has been completed and Thieu then can do what he likes."[50]

In Paris, Kissinger opened his meeting with Le Duc Tho by giving him a picture book of Harvard and offering him a post teaching a seminar on Marxism there. But Le Duc Tho was no more interested in leaving power for pedagogy than Kissinger was. Kissinger then presented a list of changes in the October agreement requested by Thieu. It amounted to sixty-nine in all; it was, as Kissinger later confessed, "preposterous."[51]

Many of the proposed changes were minor, most of them over wording and translations. But two were substantive: a demand that at least some of the NVA in South Vietnam leave the country; and a demand that the accord spell out in detail that there be no movement across the DMZ. The latter amounted to a demand that North Vietnam recognize South Vietnam as a sovereign nation and the 17th parallel as a legal boundary, thus undercutting Hanoi's contention that Vietnam was one country.

Le Duc Tho rejected these changes and came back the next day with some demanded changes of his own. He withdrew the critical concession that American POWs would be released without the release of civilian Viet Cong prisoners held by Saigon. He also insisted that all American civilian technicians would have to leave along with the military forces.

Nixon was incensed. Kissinger described him: "Ensconced at Camp David, surrounded only by public relations experts, Nixon was still deep in the bog of the resentments that had produced the darkest and perhaps most malevolent frame of mind of his Presidency."

The President fired off a tough set of instructions for Kissinger. He wanted Le Duc Tho told that unless he showed "the same willingness to be reasonable that we are showing, I am directing you to discontinue the talks and we shall then have to resume military activity until the other side is ready to negotiate." He wanted the North Vietnamese "disabused of the idea they seem to have that we have no other choice but to settle on their terms." Kissinger should threaten them. "We do have another choice," Nixon said, "and if they were surprised that the President would take the strong action he did prior to the Moscow summit [when he bombed Hanoi and mined Haiphong Harbor] . . . they will find now, with the election behind us, he will take whatever action he considers necessary to protect the United States' interest."[52]

These instructions ignored such obvious facts as : it was the Americans who first demanded changes in an agreement Le Duc Tho had been eager to sign; the United States was currently conducting bombing missions in North Vietnam (although not against Hanoi) so it could hardly "resume" such activity; it was not U.S. interests the President was trying to protect, but those of South Vietnam.

After another meeting with Le Duc Tho that produced no progress, Kissinger sent Nixon a message containing two options. Option One was to break off the talks and dramatically increase the bombing; Option Two was to decide upon a fallback position on Thieu's demands and present them as a final offer. According to Nixon, Kissinger recommended Option One. According to Kissinger, he did not.[53]

Nixon replied that the October agreement "was one which certainly would have been in our interest." He wanted Kissinger to continue to try to improve it, "but most important we must recognize the fundamental reality that we have no choice but to reach agreement along the lines of the October 8 principles."[54]

Almost immediately, however, the President changed his mind. He did not want to appear reluctant to increase the bombing, and did not want to deprive Kissinger of this "bargaining chip." So he sent another message, authorizing Kissinger to "suspend" the talks for a week. He said that he was prepared to order a massive bombing strike on North Vietnam in that interval.

"I recognize that this is a high-risk option," Nixon wrote, but he assured Kissinger that "our aim will continue to be to end the war with honor. And if because of the pursuit of our strategy and the accident of the timing of the election we are now in a public relations corner, we must take our lumps and see it through . . . even though the cost in our public support will be massive."[55]

The following day, November 25, Nixon had another change of mind. He ordered Kissinger to keep the talking going. But Kissinger had already arranged a recess. He flew back to Washington, where he met with the President. Nixon told him to "back off the position that we really had a viable option to break off the talks with the North and resume the bombing for a period of time. It simply isn't going to work. . . . We must have no illusions that we now have no option except to settle." And instead of increasing the bombing, he directed that it be reduced.[56]

Nixon's back-and-forth posture showed serious indecision on his part, but it also showed what an awkward position he was in. The President was ready to sign and claim victory, just as he had been since October 8. It was not the enemy who kept him from doing so; it was his ally in Saigon. Although he never referred to it, there was a parallel to his dilemma. Back in 1953, negotiators in South Korea had reached an agreement that was satisfactory to Eisenhower and to the Chinese, only to be rejected by South Korean leader Syngman Rhee. Vice President Nixon had served as Ike's envoy to Rhee, informing him that he had to either accept the armistice or face a complete cut-off of American aid. Rhee had reluctantly given in.

In 1972, Nixon tried to repeat the performance. On November 29 he met in the Oval Office with Nguyen Phu Duc, Thieu's personal representative at the Paris talks. Nixon gave Duc a "brutally tough presentation." He said that if the war did not end at the next negotiating session in Paris, scheduled for December 4, the 93d Congress, coming to power in January, would end the war by cutting off the appropriations.[57] That added to a threat Nixon had already sent to Thieu in a November 23 letter: "If . . . you fail to join us in concluding a satisfactory agreement . . . you must understand that I will proceed at whatever the cost."

But, just as Ike had done with Rhee, Nixon held out some bait. He outlined for Duc a U.S. contingency plan to keep North Vietnamese targeting information updated even after the cease-fire. He promised to enforce the agreement and to retaliate swiftly and forcefully in the event North Vietnam violated the agreement.[58]

According to Kissinger, "all this fell on the stolid Duc without any noticeable effect." Nixon told Kissinger that Thieu was playing "chicken" and that "we had probably no choice except to turn on him."[59]

That was a meaningless threat. Although Kissinger's staff had apparently raised the possibility of assassination, the United States had been down that route before, with Ngo Dinh Diem in 1963, only to make a bad situation worse. Besides, there was no reason to suppose that Thieu's successor would be more cooperative, for the good reason that it was not personality or personnel or PR that was the problem, but the reality of the agreement. If Thieu's characterization of it as a surrender was an exaggeration, so was Nixon's claim of victory.

No matter how brilliant the American diplomacy, it was never going to get the NVA out of South Vietnam, or force Hanoi to respect the sanctity of the DMZ. The agreement was not going to end the war; it was merely going to provide a cease-fire while the POWs came home and the American armed forces withdrew.

Everyone knew this. Under the circumstances, what Nixon could provide Thieu was his personal promise to unleash the American Air Force when Hanoi resumed the fighting. But Thieu and his advisers knew the American political system well enough to realize that Nixon was not in a position to make such a promise meaningful; after all, it was Nixon himself who had warned them that if they did not accept the agreement, Congress would cut off the funds and leave them isolated.[60]

Nixon nevertheless made the promise, and worked to give it meaning. On November 30, he met with the Joint Chiefs of Staff (JCS) in the Oval Office. Kissinger and Haig were present.

Admiral Elmo Zumwalt, Chief of Naval Operations, felt like he was on "a strange planet." Nixon wanted JCS support in the PR effort to convince the American people that the agreement was the equivalent to a victory, but he spent most of his time asking for JCS support in forcing Thieu to accept it. This involved reassuring Thieu that the Americans would continue military assistance and resume bombing if (when) Hanoi started shooting again. But the American people could not be told about these critical, albeit secret, promises, because Nixon wanted them to believe that the agreement "meant the end of any kind of American involvement in Vietnam no matter what happened there after the cease-fire was agreed to."

Zumwalt was disgusted at Nixon's duplicity: "Not even the JCS were informed that written commitments were made to Thieu." He commented bitterly, "There are at least two words no one can use to characterize the outcome of that two-faced policy. One is 'peace.' The other is ' honor.' "

Zumwalt's notes indicated the importance Nixon attached to PR. "The President insisted he must have JCS support—the left will debunk his deal—which he expects to have by the end of next week—DOD [Department of Defense] must support it—he compared the solution to that of Korea—after all the blood, the sacrifices, the military must be for it . . . he urged that we not worry about the words, we will keep the agreement if it serves us."

Then the President got down to cases. He wanted the chiefs to prepare contingency plans for bombing Hanoi and mining Haiphong again. He wanted to use B-52s. The chiefs should not plan to use ground forces.[61]

That last point was the fact that mattered. The NVA was in South Vietnam in force, and nothing Nixon could do, short of reintroducing ground combat units (and quite probably not even that), would get the NVA out. The North Vietnamese had, in effect, already annexed the two northernmost provinces of South Vietnam.

Nixon's diplomacy, Nixon's warmaking methods, the facts of the situation, and above all the determination on the part of an ever-growing majority of the American people to just get out and be done with it, combined to put the American point man, Henry Kissinger, in an impossible position. Nixon summed it up accurately: in Paris, Kissinger had "not only to convince the North Vietnamese that we would stay in and continue fighting unless they agreed to a settlement, but to convince the South Vietnamese that we would stop fighting and get out unless they agreed to one."[62]

Kissinger claimed to be optimistic, but told Nixon that if he did not reach an agreement within two days, he would have to resign. That was a power play he had used effectively before. Nixon, who two weeks earlier had said Kissinger should go back to Harvard, bent with the pressure. On December 2, he announced that Kissinger would stay on through the second term as his National Security Adviser.

On December 3, as Kissinger flew to Paris, Nixon noted in his diary that the "great forces of history" were moving in the direction of a settlement. But he ominously added, "Only insanity and irrationality of some leaders may move us in other directions."[63]

In Paris, Le Duc Tho rejected all Kissinger's demands while making some new ones of his own. A furious Kissinger recommended that the talks be broken off and that the President commence massive bombing raids against Hanoi. He wanted Nixon to go on national television to explain his actions and enlist the support of the people: "I believe that you can make a stirring and convincing case to rally them as you have so often in the past with your direct appeals."

Nixon knew better. That card had been played out. After "peace is at hand," after all the promises in November that "one more session" would bring peace, for him to go on television and announce a major escalation while confessing that there was no end in sight "is simply going to be a loser."[64]

On December 5, at Camp David, Nixon discussed the situation with

Haldeman and Ehrlichman. He said Kissinger was in a weak bargaining position because of the "peace is at hand" statement and because of the Fallaci interview, which Nixon characterized as "debilitating to a negotiator." He feared Le Duc Tho had concluded that Kissinger "must make a deal or lose face." He complained that "there are no good choices," but vowed, "We won't let them humiliate us." He ordered Haldeman to have DOD send up bombing renewal contingency plans, while repeating that "there is no point going on TV to ask the American people to support more of the same."[65]

That same day, Kissinger reported a stalemate and offered two options: "To yield or to rally American support for one more effort which I do not believe the North Vietnamese can withstand." If Nixon chose to increase the bombing, Kissinger again recommended that he go on television to rally the people.[66]

Nixon replied on December 6, in a message that was unusual even for Nixon in its confusion, contradictions, complexities, and convolutions. "We must try to reach an agreement," he began. But Kissinger should "attempt to get some reference to the troop withdrawal principle." But this "should not be an absolute condition." But he should try to get something the South Vietnamese could accept. But if "this turns out to be impossible, we will have to go it alone."

If Kissinger could not reach an agreement, he should try "to keep the talks alive," because if he broke them off, "we will exacerbate our relations with the Russians . . . likely lose the essential Congressional support for continued assistance to South Vietnam and be faced with the bitter POW issue hanging over our heads."

If Kissinger could not reach an agreement, he should "return for consultation." In that case, "we would escalate the bombing and the mining and I am prepared to do so immediately." But there would be no prime-time television address by the President.

To sum up: Kissinger should present minimum demands, but not as an ultimatum; he should keep the talks going; he should break off the talks for a recess, during which time Nixon would escalate the bombing; he should bring Thieu along on the agreement; he should prepare to go it alone.[67]

In reply, Kissinger said Nixon's orders were understood "and will be followed." He would not, however, raise Nixon's first point first (withdrawal), but would wait until Le Duc Tho had rejected the other minimal positions.[68] But Le Duc Tho said no to everything.

Nixon's response got to the point. Le Duc Tho evidently was still willing to sign off on the October 8 agreement, which Nixon and Kissinger had considered satisfactory and had indeed called a victory. But to accept it now was impossible, not just because of Thieu's objections but because of the PR problem. "We must get some improvement over Oct. 8," Nixon instructed Kissinger. But he knew he could not expect much improvement, and realized Thieu would continue to be difficult. "However, I believe the risks of the other option of breaking off the talks and escalating the bombing are far greater." Therefore he wanted Kissinger to press for a settlement rather than a recess. "There must be no turning back and no second guessing. The decision has been made."[69]

Le Duc Tho would not give on the NVA and DMZ issues. Kissinger told Nixon the conduct of the North Vietnamese was "composed of equal parts of insolence, guile, and stalling." Still he kept trying, but on December 13 Le Duc Tho broke off the talks. He said he needed to return to Hanoi for consultation.

Kissinger flew back to Washington, where he met with Nixon. Gritting his teeth and clenching his fists, Kissinger said, "They're just a bunch of shits. Tawdry, filthy shits." Nixon agreed that they were guilty of "cynicism and perfidy."[70]

Saigon would not cooperate. Hanoi would not cooperate. Nixon was having a terrible time extracting the United States from the war so that he could get on with détente and the New American Revolution. Because he was a frustrated President, he was a dangerous President.

CHAPTER TWO

THE CHRISTMAS BOMBING;
THE SECOND INAUGURAL;
CEASE-FIRE
December 14, 1972–January 31, 1973

ON DECEMBER 13, Kissinger flew back to Washington from Paris, where his negotiations with Le Duc Tho were deadlocked and in recess. The following morning, he met with Nixon and Haig to discuss the options.

The one being urged on them by the doves was to make a separate deal with Hanoi for the release of the POWs in return for a total American withdrawal. President Thieu could then either sink or swim on his own. It had almost no appeal to Nixon and his aides. To abandon South Vietnam now, after all the blood that had been shed, all the money that had been spent, all the uproar that had nearly overwhelmed the American political scene, would be wrong, cowardly, a betrayal. To abandon Thieu would amount to surrendering America's most fundamental goal in the war, the maintenance in power of an anti-Communist government in Saigon.

But Thieu would not sign the agreement that Nixon regarded as satisfactory. And Le Duc Tho insisted that he would not give another inch. To get Thieu to sign, and to force Tho to give just a bit more, some dramatic action by the United States was necessary. With less than 25,000 American troops in Vietnam, none of them combat personnel, and with the dove strength in the Congress, there was no possibility of escalating on the ground.

The only real option was to expand the bombing campaign against North Vietnam, but there were powerful arguments against that course. Sending B-52s over Hanoi meant risking those expensive weapons and their highly trained crews, because the Russians had been rushing surface-to-air missiles (SAMs) into North Vietnam. For this reason, the lame-duck Secretary of Defense Melvin Laird, his deputy Kenneth Rush, and Chairman of the Joint Chiefs Admiral Thomas Moorer were all opposed.

On the political side, to escalate the bombing after Kissinger's October statement that "peace is at hand" would drive the Nixon-haters in Congress, in the media, on the campuses, and among the general public into a frenzy.

Still, something had to be done to convince Thieu that whatever the formal wording of the agreement said, he could count on Nixon to come to the defense of South Vietnam if (when) the NVA threatened to overrun its cities. And something had to be done to convince Tho that despite the doves in Congress, Nixon could still punish North Vietnam.

Kissinger recommended increasing the bombing south of the 20th parallel in North Vietnam and in Laos, and reseeding the mines in Haiphong Harbor. Haig recommended an all-out bombing campaign by B-52s against Hanoi itself.

Nixon later said that this was "the most difficult decision" he had to make in the entire war. But, he immediately added, "it was also one of the most clear-cut and necessary ones." He issued an order to reseed the mines and to send the B-52s against Hanoi. He told Kissinger he was prepared "for new losses and casualties and POW's," and explained, "We'll take the same heat for big blows as for little blows."[1] Four days later he wrote in his diary, "The North Vietnamese figure that they have us where the hair is short and are going to continue to squeeze us. That is why we had to take our strong action."[2]

To Kissinger, Nixon seemed "sullen" and "withdrawn." He "resented" having to do what he did, because "deep down he was ready to give up by going back to the October draft." His bombing order, according to Kissinger, was "*his* last roll of the dice . . . helpful if it worked; a demonstration to the right wing if it failed that he had done all he could."[3]

Once Nixon set the policy, PR became the obsession. John Scali, White House adviser on foreign affairs information policy, put the problem succinctly to Haldeman in a telephone conversation: "We look incompetent—bombing for no good reason and because we don't know what else to do." On May 8, Nixon had gone on television to explain his reasons for bombing Hanoi and mining Haiphong. That television appearance seemed to Scali to have been unnecessary; the reason for the action was obvious, the NVA Easter offensive. But in December, Nixon absolutely refused to go on television to explain his motives, when his critics and even some of his supporters could not figure them out.[4]

Kissinger badly wanted Nixon to make a broadcast. He had been urging it for weeks. But Nixon, according to Kissinger, "was determined to take himself out of the line of fire."[5] Nixon feared that any attempt to rally the people to support more bombing after "peace is at hand" would fall flat. Instead of announcing the bombing (set to begin on December 18), he decided to just do it.

On the evening of December 14, Nixon told Kissinger to hold a news conference to explain the status of the negotiations. The President followed up with a five-page, single-spaced memo on December 15, and another of two pages on December 16, instructing Kissinger on what to say. He told the National Security Adviser to "hit hard on the point that, while we want peace just as soon as we can get it, that we want a peace that is honorable and a peace that will last." Kissinger should admit that the American goals had been reached "in principle" in the October agreement, but that some "strengthening of the language" was necessary, "so that there will be no doubt on either side in the event that [that agreement] is broken." He should accuse Le Duc Tho of having "backed off" some of the October understandings.

Kissinger should emphasize that with the Christmas season coming on, the President had a "very strong personal desire to get the war settled." But he should also point out that the President "insists that the United States is not going to be pushed around, blackmailed or stampeded into making the wrong kind of a peace agreement." Finally, he should say that "the President will continue to order whatever actions he considers necessary by air and sea," the only reference to the bombing order that had already gone out.[6]

In his memos, Nixon was repetitious to a degree unusual even for him, an indication of the strain he was under, and of the difficulty of his position. Thieu was increasingly being seen in the United States as the sole obstacle to peace, and was thus increasingly unpopular. On his December 15 News Summary, Nixon read that Senator Barry Goldwater (R.-Ariz.), one of the toughest of the hawks, had said that if Thieu "bucks much more," the United States should proceed with its withdrawal and "to hell with him." Nixon circled the comment and scribbled in the margin: "Haig—be sure Thieu sees this."[7]

Kissinger held his briefing on December 16, and said what he had been told to say. He stressed the President's consistency, unflappability, firmness, patience, and farsightedness. He mentioned Nixon fourteen times (he had been criticized by Haldeman for mentioning the President only three times in his October news conference).[8] The net effect was to leave people more confused than ever about what was going on.

On December 17, when the reseeding of the mines began and on the eve of the bombing campaign, Nixon wrote to Thieu. He instructed Haig to fly to Saigon to hand the letter to Thieu, and ordered Haig to tell Thieu that "I had dictated the letter personally and that no one else in our government had seen it."[9] Kissinger claimed that in accord with Nixon's instructions, he had written the letter, but admitted that "contrary to his habit of signing my drafts without change, Nixon toughened it nearly to the point of brutality."[10]

(The endemic tension in the Nixon-Kissinger relationship was threatening to lead to an open break. Kissinger was unhappy with his boss because of his interference, and his back-and-forthing, on the negotiations. Nixon was furious with Kissinger for having put him into his dilemma with the "peace is at hand" statement, for the Fallaci interview, and for his constant leaks to reporters. Further, earlier in December *Time* magazine had named Nixon and Kissinger the "Men of the Year," with their pictures on the cover; Kissinger correctly feared that Nixon resented having to share the spotlight.)[11]

In the letter to Thieu, Nixon repeated a threat that he had been making since October: "General Haig's mission now represents my final effort to point out to you the necessity for joint action and to convey my irrevocable intention to proceed, preferably with your cooperation but, if necessary, alone." Nixon said they had reached the either/or point: "Let me emphasize in conclusion that General Haig is not coming to Saigon for the purpose of negotiating with you. . . . You must decide now whether you desire to continue our alliance or whether you want me to seek a settlement with the enemy which serves U.S. interests alone."[12]

Although Nixon himself would do anything possible to avoid a break, the threat was not meaningless, because as Goldwater's statement indicated, the Congress might carry it out regardless of the President's wishes. Thieu knew that, and he also knew how to read between the lines of Nixon's letter. After reading it, Thieu looked up and told Haig that it was obvious he was not being asked to sign a peace agreement but rather an agreement for continued American support.[13]

On December 18, the Air Force launched its B-52s and fighter bombers against Hanoi. There was an immediate worldwide uproar. The stock market plummeted, suffering its biggest decline in a year and a half, as the Dow Jones industrial index fell 14 points, to 1,013. The moral revulsion exceeded even that reaction. There had been no presidential explanation or announcement of any kind. People everywhere had taken Kissinger at his word, that only a few T's needed to be crossed and a few I's dotted and the negotiations would be wrapped up. The shock was severe, as great as that following the Cambodian incursion of 1970.

Congressional and editorial reaction was extreme, indeed unprecedented. Senator William Saxbe (R.-Ohio) said that Nixon "appears to have left his senses." Democratic Senate leader Mike Mansfield of Montana called it a "stone-age tactic." Senator Edmund Muskie (D.-Maine) called the bombing "disastrous." Senator Jacob Javits (R.-N.Y.) threatened a cut-off of funds. Senator Edward Kennedy (D.-Mass.) said it was an "outrage." In an editorial, *The Washington Post* charged that the bombing caused millions of Americans "to cringe in shame and to wonder at their President's very sanity." In *The New York Times,* James Reston called it "war by tantrum," while Anthony Lewis charged that Nixon was acting "like a maddened tyrant."[14]

There were supporters, including Governors Nelson Rockefeller and

Ronald Reagan and Republican Senators James Buckley (N.Y.), Howard Baker (Tenn.), and Chuck Percy III (Ill.). Connally called Nixon daily to encourage him and assure him that whatever the politicians and media said, the people were behind him.[15]

Nixon's critics charged that he had ordered the most intensive bombing campaign in the history of warfare. That was nonsense. In comparison to what the American Army Air Forces had done to Dresden, Hamburg, Berlin, Tokyo, and other enemy cities in World War II, not to mention Hiroshima and Nagasaki, the bombing of Hanoi during the Christmas season of 1972 was a minor operation. It was conducted under severe restrictions. Everything possible was done to avoid civilian casualties, which amounted to only slightly more than one thousand. This was not terror bombing, as the world had come to know it in the twentieth century.

It was not Nixon who imposed the restrictions; in fact, they frustrated him. The day after the bombing began, he read a report that indicated certain targets had been avoided for fear of civilian casualties. He called Admiral Moorer: "I don't want any more of this crap about the fact that we couldn't hit this target or that one," the President said. "This is your chance to use military power effectively to win this war, and if you don't, I'll consider you responsible."[16] Still the Air Force held back, for example, by refusing to bomb a missile assembly plant in Hanoi because it was next to a housing district.

Nixon's explanation of the cause of the extraordinarily adverse reaction was typical; he personalized it and assigned to his critics the lowest possible motives. In his diary, he wrote that they "simply cannot bear the thought of this administration under my leadership bringing off the peace on an honorable basis which they have so long predicted would be impossible.

"The election was a terrible blow to them and this is their first opportunity to recover from the election and to strike back."[17]

That was by no means the whole truth. The most basic cause for the moral revulsion was the nature of the war itself. Almost no one in the United States had protested the fire-bomb raids of World War II, which set out deliberately to kill civilians. Why the difference three decades later, especially when the Air Force was doing its utmost to avoid killing civilians? Because in 1942–45, the United States was fighting for its life against a foe who was not only pure evil but also powerful enough to threaten the entire world. In World War II there had been no ongoing negotiations with the Germans and Japanese, only a demand for their unconditional surrender. In 1942–45, the Americans were bombing in order to hasten that surrender.

But in 1972, few believed that the United States was fighting for its life, or that the NVA could conquer the world, or that there could be no end to the war until Hanoi surrendered, or that more bombing would bring a quicker end to the war.

The bombing brought Nixon problems that went beyond the continuing storm of protest. If Hanoi was far from being the most heavily bombed city in history, it certainly was the best defended. The SAMs shot down six of the ninety B-52s that flew missions on December 20; the following day, two of thirty were destroyed (the final tally was fifteen B-52s lost). The Air Force could not long sustain such losses. Still, Nixon complained in his diary that there was "too much caution on the military side. We simply have to take losses if we are going to accomplish our objectives."[18]

The bombing was dominating the news to the virtual exclusion of anything else. For example, on December 19 the command module "America" safely returned to earth after a three-man mission to the moon. The event went all but unnoticed.[19]

Hanoi, meanwhile, was accusing the Americans of a double-cross. The Communists charged that Nixon had broken his word. Nixon, furious, wrote on his News Summary, "K-C-Z*—should hit this hard—*Hanoi broke faith.*"[20] Saigon, meanwhile, still refused to sign.

Another problem was Henry Kissinger's duplicity. He broke under the pressure of the protest and began leaking to reporters, most especially Reston, the word that he had opposed the bombing. This infuriated Nixon. He instructed Colson to monitor all Kissinger's phone calls and contacts with the press. The President, according to Colson, "was raving and ranting about Henry double-talking." Colson did as he was told and discovered that Kissinger was calling Reston and others, "planting self-serving stories at the same time he was recommending Nixon be tough on Vietnam."

When Haldeman confronted Kissinger, the National Security Adviser simply denied the facts. "I have never given a personal opinion different from the President's," he claimed, and said he had *not* given an interview to Reston. Haldeman got him to admit that he had called Reston on the phone, just before Reston wrote a column in which he said Kissinger had opposed the bombing and implied that Kissinger was the one moderate, sensible man among Nixon's advisers. Kissinger concluded his conversation with Haldeman by suggesting that it was time for the President to give him a vote of confidence; he wanted a letter from Nixon giving Kissinger his backing and credit for the progress in the negotiations.[21]

DESPITE the adverse reaction from so many commentators, Connally was right in saying that the President had many supporters. In the week before

---

*That is, Kissinger-Colson-Ziegler. See volume two, page 410, for an explanation of Nixon's habits re memos.

Christmas, the Nixons held a series of receptions in their home. Colson, the man who had pushed hardest for Nixon to make a direct appeal to the hard-hats and the ethnics to build his "New Majority," was overjoyed at the guest lists. In a column for King Features Syndicate, he wrote that the lists did not contain the names of "the Morgans, the Mellons or the Rockefellers, but rather the Mazewskis, the Broccolinos, the O'Haras and the Fernandezes." To Colson, this symbolized "the passing of the old establishment and a glimpse of the new."

Colson said it was gall and wormwood to the social reporters, who were accustomed to reporting the "elegance, charm and grace" of the Kennedy guests. Now "the ordinary folks from the heartland—the shop steward, the electrician, the farmer—were the honored guests of an American President for the first time in generations." In fact, Colson had to go back to Andrew Jackson's inaugural to find a comparison. It was "altogether fitting," Colson said, because "these were the people who stood firm in time of national crisis." They were Nixon's people.[22]

The Nixons went to Key Biscayne for Christmas. The President ordered a twenty-four-hour halt in the bombing for the day. In his diary, he characterized himself and Pat as "more and more lonely individuals. . . . It is a question not of too many friends but really too few—one of the inevitable consequences of this position." The loneliness was compounded by the absence of his daughters, who were both with their husbands in Europe.

Five years later, Nixon told an interviewer that he received very few Christmas salutations, even from his Republican allies on Capitol Hill and members of his Cabinet. As a result, "it was the loneliest and saddest Christmas I can ever remember, much sadder and much more lonely than the one in the Pacific during the war."[23]

Nixon did make some telephone calls, including one to Ronald Reagan, who complained about CBS News coverage of the bombing and said that under World War II circumstances, the network would have been charged with treason.

The day after Christmas, Harry Truman died. The Nixons flew to Independence, Missouri, to pay their respects to Bess Truman, and the President proclaimed a national day of mourning. In a statement, Nixon praised Truman as "one of the most courageous Presidents in our history," and a man of "exceptional vision and determination."[24]

It was a handsome tribute, and probably heartfelt. From 1946 through 1952, Nixon had been Truman's severest critic, especially about Truman's conduct of the Korean War. But the view from the White House is 180 degrees different from the view from Capitol Hill, and by 1972 Nixon had a new perspective on Harry Truman's trials and tribulations.

That same day, despite urgings from some of his aides and much of the media that he extend the Christmas Day truce, Nixon personally ordered the biggest bombing raid yet: 111 B-52s over Hanoi. That afternoon, he received a message from Hanoi, proposing that the Kissinger–Le Duc Tho talks resume on January 8. Nixon replied that he wanted technical talks resumed on January 2 (the day before the 93d Congress would convene), and offered to stop the bombing of Hanoi if the Communists agreed. Kissinger also sent a cable. He said he was willing to make one final effort "to conclude the October negotiation," so that the United States and North Vietnam could "move from a period of hostility to one of normalization."

Hanoi agreed, and on December 29, Nixon announced that the bombing north of the 20th parallel was suspended. The next morning, he announced that the Paris negotiations would be resumed.

With the new policy set, Nixon turned to his PR problems. He talked with Scali and Colson, who warned him that the media would ask, Why was the bombing necessary?, and would assert that Nixon was forced back to negotiations because of the world outcry. Others would charge that Nixon suspended the bombing because the Air Force was losing the battle.

On the other side, Haig urged Nixon to keep on bombing. He thought Hanoi was all but on its knees. He was furious to discover that "every single adviser of the President except [me], all of them were calling the President daily, hourly, and telling him to terminate the bombing." But even Haig realized that Nixon's options had run out, because if he continued the bombing after the congressional session began, "there would have been legislative restrictions which would have been national suicide from the standpoint of ever negotiating a settlement."[25]

So the last American action in the Vietnam War was characteristic of all those that had come earlier, cursed by half-measures. From 1964 to 1969 Lyndon Johnson's actions, as described by Nixon, were always "too little, too late." That had also been true of Nixon's ultimatum in November 1969, of his Cambodian incursion of 1970, of his Laotian operation in 1971, of his May 8, 1972, air offensive, and now of his Christmas bombing. He had taken the heat for an all-out offensive without delivering one. It was not that he did not want to, but rather that it was overwhelmingly obvious that the American political system would not allow him to do so.

That simple fact points up once again the wisdom of a comment Dwight Eisenhower often made, that no one should ever lead a democracy into a war without the assured full support of the people. Of course, Nixon had not led the country into the war, but he had been an enthusiastic and significant cheerleader. Once he became the leader, his options were severely limited. He might have been a determined leader under the conditions of World War II; in the war he actually fought, he was a fumbler, even in this last act.

What the bombing had cost America was clear: fifteen B-52s; ninety-three American airmen listed as missing, thirty-one of them POWs; and a revulsion against Nixon such as even he had never before imagined possible. He had made many new enemies but no new friends.

What the country had gained was unclear. Nixon called Hanoi's willingness to resume the talks a "stunning capitulation," one presumably brought about by the bombing.[26] But it had been Saigon, not Hanoi, that had created the stalemate in the talks. In his message to Hanoi, Kissinger had referred to the October agreements; going back to them represented an American, not a North Vietnamese, concession. Kissinger's reference to "normalization" of relations continued the hints he had been secretly making to Le Duc Tho that when peace came, the United States would aid in the reconstruction of North Vietnam, just as it had helped Germany and Japan after World War II.

On December 30, Senator Henry Jackson (D.-Wash.) called Nixon to ask the President to go on television and explain that "we bombed to get them back to the table." Nixon passed the message along to Kissinger with a note: "He is right—*but* my saying it publicly would seriously jeopardize our negotiations."[27]

Nixon had another reason for hesitating to make the claim Jackson wanted. It would have been extremely difficult to get informed observers to believe that Nixon bombed Hanoi to get the North Vietnamese to agree to an agreement that they had already agreed to. It was much easier to believe that Nixon's real target was not Hanoi, but rather Saigon. And, as 1972 came to an end, there was no indication that Thieu was prepared to sign.

NIXON spent New Year's Eve with Pat at Camp David. On New Year's Day she flew out to California for the Rose Bowl parade, while he returned to Washington. It was an unscheduled move, and when he arrived at the Oval Office at 7:30 A.M. he found the door locked. After futile wrestling with the doorknob, he found a guard to let him in. He had written in his diary the previous day that "1973 will be a better year [than 1972]," but it got off to an inauspicious start.[28]

On January 2, the House Democratic Caucus voted 154 to 75 to cut off all funds for Vietnam as soon as arrangements were complete for the withdrawal of all American armed forces and the return of the POWs. On January 4, the Senate Democratic Caucus passed a similar resolution, 36 to 12.

Nixon passed the pressure on to Thieu. Initially he tried to do so through Mrs. Anna Chennault, widow of General Claire Chennault and head of Flying Tiger Airline. He asked her friend John Mitchell to have her use her influence with Thieu, but the "Dragon Lady," as she was called, refused. There was irony here; back in 1968 Mitchell had persuaded Mrs. Chennault to intervene with Thieu to refuse to help Johnson in his election eve bid for peace; now Nixon wanted her to persuade Thieu to cooperate with the President.[29] But she would not.

Nixon then wrote directly to Thieu. The letter, dated January 5, was less threatening than previous ones, and contained a more explicit promise: "Should you decide, as I trust you will, to go with us, you have my assurance of continued assistance in the post-settlement period and that we will respond with full force should the settlement be violated by North Vietnam."[30]

Nixon was not in a position to give such a promise. Without congressional appropriations, he could not come to Saigon's aid.

That same day, he had a meeting with the leaders of both parties. The atmosphere was cold. Nixon announced that he was putting through some of his reorganization plans without waiting for congressional authorization, an announcement that went down badly. Then he spoke briefly on Vietnam. He said he knew many of the men in the room disagreed with his policies, but added that he was determined to persist.

Nixon concluded: "In any event, you have indicated your own positions—some of you—which is in direct opposition. I understand that. I have the responsibility. I take the responsibility and if I fail, you can blame me, and if I succeed, we will all succeed."[31]

On January 6, Nixon returned to Camp David, where he met with Kissinger, who was flying to Paris the next day. The President said that if Kissinger could get Le Duc Tho to go back to the October 8 agreement, "we should take it." Kissinger demurred. Nixon insisted. He did want Kissinger to get some wording changes so that "we can claim some improvement," but the point was that the war had to end, on whatever terms, in this round of negotiations, or the 93d Congress would end it for him.

The President did agree that Kissinger could threaten the North Vietnamese with a resumption of the bombing of Hanoi if they did not cooperate, but then warned him that "as far as our internal planning is concerned we cannot consider this to be a viable option." As to Thieu, Nixon referred to Haig's report: Thieu was saying that "it is not a peace agreement that he is going to get, but a commitment from the United States to protect South Vietnam in the event such an agreement is broken." Nixon said that was exactly right.

As Nixon said goodbye to Kissinger at the door of Birch Lodge, he concluded the evening: "Well, one way or another, this is it!"[32]

FROM the time of the election in November 1972 to the beginning of January 1973, Nixon had been relatively free of Watergate problems. But as the politicians gathered in Washington, and as the date for the trial of Liddy and Hunt and their cohorts approached (jury selection was set to began on January 8), the pressure began to build.

Nixon had anticipated it. On December 11, he had warned Haldeman that Watergate "just won't go away." The President thought "we need something said" before the New Year, and told Haldeman to try "a brief statement" that would "at least get *something* out of the way. Go for the tiniest statement we can make."[33] No one could think of what to say in such a statement, and none was made.

Instead, Nixon's courtiers pointed at each other. On January 3, Haldeman told Nixon that "Colson may have been aware of the Watergate business." Nixon could not believe it. Three days later, Colson met alone with the President. He said that he was concerned, because "this could stretch into the White House."

Nixon looked startled. "You mean Bob and John?" he asked.

"Yes," Colson replied.

Colson explained that money was being paid to Hunt and the other defendants, which could be construed as an obstruction of justice. When he had expressed his fears to Haldeman, however, Haldeman replied, "What's the matter with raising money for defendants? They did it for Angela Davis. Why can't we?"[34]

Hunt, meanwhile, was demanding more money. Colson had stalled by hinting about a pardon to Hunt's lawyer, William Bittman. Colson told Bittman, "You know, a year is a long time. And clemency is something that's generally considered around Christmas time here at the White House." When he passed this along to Dean and Ehrlichman, Colson said that Bittman "was reading me."[35]

In the afternoon of January 8, in Nixon's Executive Office Building (EOB) office, Colson discussed the situation with the President. Nixon said he had heard from Haldeman that Hunt had agreed to plead guilty, and added, "It's the right thing for him to do, Chuck."

"Uh, he's doing it on my urging," Colson replied.

They talked about the failed attempt to bug McGovern's office, which led Nixon to a more general complaint: "That's the thing about all of this. We didn't get a God-damn thing from any of it that I can see."

"Well," Colson said, "apparently we did, of course, at Watergate, mainly [on] Hughes."

There was a pause. Nixon broke it: "Well, don't let it get you down."

"Oh hell no," Colson responded.

"I know it's tough for, uh, for all of you," Nixon went on. "Bob, John and the rest. We're just not gonna let it get us down. This is a battle, it's a fight, it's war and we just fight with a little, uh, you know, uh remember, uh, we'll cut them down one of these days. Don't you agree?"

Colson did agree.

Even as they talked, jury selection for the Watergate burglary trial was under way. "As long as this trial is going on," Nixon declared, "the Congress will keep its God-damn cotton-pickin hands off."

Nixon asked if he was right in thinking that none of the burglars was going to testify, that they would all plead guilty and otherwise keep their mouths shut.

Well, Colson replied, James McCord, head of the burglary team, was going to plead not guilty and might be testifying. It appeared to depend upon McCord and his men getting the same clemency promise Hunt had received.

Nixon was startled. "But you know, Chuck," he said, "it's something they all undertook knowing the risks. Right?"

Colson pointed out that they thought they were working for John Mitchell and that Mitchell would intervene on their behalf.

"Mitchell would take care of them?" Nixon asked. "How could he?" The President added, "No way."

As to Hunt, however, Nixon went on: "Hunt's is a simple case. I mean, uh, after all, the man's wife is dead, was killed; he's got one child that has . . ."

Colson finished the sentence: "Brain damage from an automobile accident."

Nixon brightened up. "We'll build, we'll build, we'll build that son-of-a-bitch up like nobody's business. We'll have [William F.] Buckley write a column and say, you know, that he, that he should have clemency." After all, Hunt had given eighteen years of service to the government.

"That's, that's it," Nixon concluded. "It's on the merits."

As to Liddy, McCord, and the rest of the defendants, Nixon said, "I would have difficulty with some of the others."

Colson assured him that the vulnerabilities of McCord and the Cubans were not as great as Hunt's, meaning they were less likely to get long sentences. He added: "I don't give a damn if they spend five years in jail," and pointed out that they did not have any "direct information," so "They can't hurt us." But Hunt and Liddy had "direct (unintelligible), meetings, discussions are very incriminating to us."

Nixon consoled himself: "Liddy is pretty tough."

Colson said he was a masochist who "enjoys punishing himself." He characterized Hunt and Liddy as "both good healthy right-wing exuberants."

Nixon concluded the conversation: "Well, this is the last damn fifty miles."[36]

JANUARY 9 was Nixon's sixtieth birthday. In an interview, he gave his formula for living: "Never slow down." He admitted that he had many problems, "but boredom is the least of them."[37]

He also wrote by hand a piece of self-analysis: "RN approaches his second inauguration with true peace of mind—because he knows that by his actions, often in the face of the most intense sort of criticism, what he is bringing to the world is a 'peace of mind'—that is, a peace formed by the exercise of hard reason and calm deliberation, and durable because its foundation has been carefully laid." Nixon instructed Haldeman to pass the piece along to the staff and called it "an excellent line for them to take."[38]

That afternoon, Nixon got what he described as "the best birthday present I have had in sixty years." Kissinger cabled from Paris that there had been "a major breakthrough in the negotiations. In sum, we settled all the outstanding questions in the text of the agreement."[39]

Le Duc Tho had accepted Kissinger's revised wording on the DMZ. It made no practical difference. The Accord that had been reached was basically the same as it had been back in October. John Negroponte, Kissinger's aide, was disappointed. He told friends, "We bombed the North Vietnamese into accepting our concession."[40]

Nixon was in a gay mood that evening, as Julie and Tricia, back from Europe, held a surprise birthday party for him. Bebe Rebozo was there, and Bob Abplanalp, and a few other friends. There was some spirited toasting, joking, and lots of laughter. Nixon offered a toast to the men of the U.S. armed forces.[41]

On January 11, the Senate Democratic Caucus voted unanimously to establish a special committee to investigate the Watergate break-in and other Republican activities against the Democrats in the 1972 presidential election. Senate leader Mike Mansfield selected Senator Sam Ervin (D.-N.C.) to chair the committee.

Nixon's initial reaction was to charge foul. If the Senate was going to investigate political campaigns, it should in all fairness include the 1968 campaign. If it did, it would discover that President Johnson had bugged Nixon's airplane, which would establish a precedent for the bugging of the DNC.

Exposing Johnson was a temptation Nixon had felt strongly but so far successfully resisted. To have given in to it during the campaign would have risked losing Johnson's support on his Vietnam policy, invited an active Johnson support for George McGovern, and compromised John Connally's "Democrats for Nixon" operation. With the election safely behind him, Nixon felt the temptation return, but he knew it was dangerous territory, and proceeded cautiously. He told Haldeman to talk to Connally "re the LBJ bug (keep Cols[on] out of it) re judgment as to how to handle it." Nixon thought the threat could be used to "scare Hubert [Humphrey]," but then expressed a major worry: "LBJ—problem of how he'd react."[42]

Put more directly, the threat of revealing Johnson's bugging operation against Nixon might persuade Senator Humphrey to use his influence to limit the scope of the Ervin Committee investigation, but then again it might lead Johnson to encourage the Senate to go even harder against Nixon. That afternoon, Nixon met with Haldeman, whose notes read: "Disc[ussion] re LBJ, Conn[ally] etc. re '68 bug—turn off Hill."[43] The end result was paralysis.

That same day, the trial in Judge Sirica's courtroom began. Hunt pled guilty and said that to the best of his knowledge, no "higher-ups" in the government were involved. The five Cuban defendants also pled guilty, but not McCord or Liddy. Also on January 11, the Justice Department charged CREEP with eight criminal violations of the election-financing law that had taken effect on April 7, 1972.

On January 13, Dean called Haldeman to warn him that "McCord is off the reservation." He used the word "blackmail."[44]

These were ominous developments, obviously, but Nixon did not have time to attend to them. His inauguration was a week away, and he naturally wanted peace in hand by that day.

First it was necessary to get the settlement sealed and delivered, and then to convince the American people that it was the Christmas bombing that had made it possible. Nixon set out to deal with both matters.

On January 13, Kissinger returned from Paris. He flew down to Key Biscayne to brief the President. They talked until 2 A.M. Nixon walked out to the car with Kissinger to say good night and to tell him that the country was indebted to him for what he had done. Nixon later wrote that "it is not really a comfortable feeling for me to praise people so openly," but "Henry expects it, and it was good that I did so." Kissinger replied that it was only Nixon's courage that had made a settlement possible. In his memoirs, Kissinger wrote that he felt "an odd tenderness" that night toward Nixon.[45]

The next morning they turned their attention to Thieu. Nixon wrote him another letter and told Haig to fly to Saigon to deliver it. The letter was full of threats—"I have therefore irrevocably decided to proceed to initial the Agreement on January 23, 1973, and to sign it on January 27, 1973, in Paris. I will do so, if necessary alone"—and promises. If Thieu would sign, Nixon would make it "emphatically clear that the United States recognizes your government as the only legal government of South Vietnam; that we do not recognize the right of any foreign troops to be present on South Vietnamese territory; that we will react strongly in the event the agreement is violated." Nixon concluded, "It is my firm intention to continue full economic and military aid."[46]

Nixon feared that his words would not be enough, but he was determined to prevail. "Brutality is nothing," he told Kissinger. "You have never seen it if this son-of-a-bitch doesn't go along, believe me."[47]

To add to the pressure on Thieu, Nixon had Senators John Stennis (D.-Miss.) and Goldwater warn publicly that if Thieu blocked the agreement, he would imperil his government's chances of receiving any further aid from the Congress.[48] Still Thieu would not yield. He sent a letter to Nixon, raising the same complaints he had made in October—naturally enough, since it was the same agreement. Nixon replied on January 20 with a final ultimatum.

On the PR front, meanwhile, Nixon was also busy. On January 19, he told Haldeman, "We need to get across the point that the reason for the success of the negotiations *was* the bombing and the converse point that we did not halt the bombing until we had the negotiations back on track." He instructed Kissinger to brief the staff on the settlement: "The key to this briefing will be to get a lot of people out selling our line." Nixon wanted "an all out effort with inspired leaks, etc."[49]

ON January 20, 1973, Nixon was inaugurated for his second term. He had hoped to be able to announce that peace had been achieved, but Thieu's intransigence made that impossible. Under the circumstances, the hoopla that ordinarily occurs at inaugurals was distinctly absent, and Nixon's Inaugural Address was short and somber. Ray Price, who wrote it, got in some paragraphs on government reorganization, some on a peace that could last for generations, and some on other Nixonian themes. He also stole some material from John F. Kennedy's Inaugural Address; Nixon's speech urged the American people to be more responsible, to do more for themselves. Nixon said, "In the challenges we face together, let each of us ask—not just how can government help, but how can I help?"

The conclusion was appropriately uplifting: "Let us pledge together to make these next 4 years the best years in America's history, so that on its 200th birthday America will be as young, as vital as when it began, and as bright a beacon of hope for all the world."[50]

The parade following the ceremonies was marred by small groups of demonstrators chanting obscenities and throwing eggs and debris, but it was nowhere near so bad as four years earlier. If Nixon had not yet healed the wounds that divided the American people, if he had not quite yet brought peace, he had gone a long way toward achieving those objectives. The madness and hatred that had been so prominent in 1969 had abated by 1973. Sadly, in part it had been replaced by a bitterness because of the Christmas bombing, and a suspicion because of Watergate. If Nixon deserved credit for gains, he deserved some of the blame for the bitterness and suspicion.

ON January 22 Lyndon Johnson, the man who had been so closely associated with the madness and hatred, died.

Nixon's relationship with Johnson had been almost as tumultuous as his relationship with Truman, nearly as negative, and longer-lasting. He had tilted against Johnson through the 1950s, when he was the presiding officer in the Senate and Johnson was the majority leader; he had been eager to run against Johnson in 1964; from 1965 through 1968 he had been a critic of Johnson's conduct of the war. The two men had said many unkind things about each other in private, and some in public. Johnson's 1966 characterization of Nixon as a "chronic campaigner" had stung Nixon almost as much as Helen Douglas's 1950 description of him as "Tricky Dick."

But war and politics lead to strange alliances. From 1969 to 1973, Nixon and Johnson had been all but partners. As the Democratic Party grew increasingly dovish, Johnson increasingly gave Nixon all the help he could. His key supporters in 1964 became Nixon's key supporters in 1972. Johnson himself did not endorse Nixon in 1972—he explained to Nixon that he had "been sucking at the tit of the Democratic Party for years and can't let go now, even though the milk may have turned a bit sour because of what the poor cow is eating"—but neither did he campaign for McGovern.[51]

It saddened Nixon that Johnson died before peace had been achieved. It gladdened him to know that the achievement of peace with honor would establish Johnson's rightful place in history.[52]

ON January 22 word arrived that Thieu had finally consented to the agreement. The following evening, Nixon went on television to announce that on January 27 the formal signing ceremonies would be held in Paris. A Vietnam cease-fire would begin at midnight that day.

After this announcement, Nixon called Kissinger on the telephone. The President was alone, in the Lincoln Sitting Room. Nixon said he did not want to have any hatred or anything of that sort toward "our enemies," by which he meant the American doves, not the Vietnamese Communists. "On the other hand," he continued, they had to recognize that his foes "are disturbed, distressed, and really discouraged because we succeeded."

Nixon wondered whether commentators would appreciate what he and Kissinger had accomplished, and decided "probably not." He told Kissinger that every success was followed by a "terrific letdown," and urged Kissinger "not let it get to him. There were many battles left to fight; he should not be discouraged."

For his part, Nixon wrote later that he had expected to feel relief and satisfaction when the war ended, but instead was surprised to find himself with feelings of "sadness, apprehension, and impatience." Kissinger was struck by Nixon's being "so lonely in his hour of triumph."[53]

Beyond the letdown he always felt after a crisis, Nixon had reasons for his negative feelings. In the weeks that followed, he often and vehemently maintained that he had achieved peace with honor, but that was a claim difficult to sustain. Seven years earlier, when pressed by reporters to explain what kind of settlement he would accept in Vietnam, he had held up the Korean Armistice of 1953 as his model. What he finally accepted was far short of that goal.

The Korean settlement had left 60,000 American troops in South Korea; the Vietnam settlement left no American troops in South Vietnam. The Korean settlement left no Communist troops in South Korea; the Vietnam settlement left 160,000 Communist troops in South Vietnam. The Korean settlement had established the 38th parallel as a dividing line. It was so heavily fortified on both sides that twenty years later almost no living thing had crossed it. The Vietnam settlement called the 17th parallel a border, but the NVA controlled both sides of it and moved back and forth without any interference. The Korean settlement had left President Rhee firmly in control of his country, to the point that the Communist Party was banned. The Vietnam settlement forced President Thieu to accept Communist membership on the National Council of Reconciliation.

Small wonder that Thieu regarded the settlement as little short of a surrender, or feared that the cease-fire would last only until the Americans got the POWs back and brought their armed forces home. Small wonder, too, that he worried about his future, as his army, the ARVN, was woefully inferior to Rhee's army, the ROK forces (not to mention the NVA).

Thieu did have one asset to match Rhee's of twenty years earlier, a promise from the American President that if the Communists broke the agreement, the United States would come to his aid. But in South Vietnam, in the spring of 1975, that promise would prove to be worthless.

Nixon's defenders assert that had it not been for Watergate, the North Vietnamese would not have dared to launch their offensive in 1975. Or, if they had, that Nixon would have responded with the fury he showed in the spring of 1972, and the American bombing support would have made it possible for the ARVN to once again turn back the invaders.

Nixon's detractors call this scenario nonsense. They assert that all he ever wanted or expected from the cease-fire was a "decent interval" before the NVA overran Saigon. That "decent interval" was until Nixon had successfully completed his second term. They argue further that the Congress was *never* going to give Nixon the funds to resume bombing in Vietnam, and that he knew it, even as he made his promises to Thieu.

No one can ever know what might have been. Everyone knows what did happen.

"DO NOT GLOAT," Nixon had instructed Haldeman when word came through from Kissinger that Le Duc Tho was ready to sign. That was good advice, given Democratic control of Congress, hostility toward Nixon by the media because of the Christmas bombing, the creation of the Ervin

Committee, and the Liddy-McCord trial. Nixon needed to appease his enemies, not antagonize them.

But Nixon ignored his own advice. On January 12, he had told Haldeman that when a settlement was reached, "Every commentator, columnist, college professor, etc., that has hit us, should be badgered all out—in the Congressional Record, with letters—a total attack basis. We should hit those who sabotaged and jeopardized the peace all the way."[54]

Immediately after announcing the cease-fire, Nixon set out after his enemies. In a January 25 memo to Haldeman, he gave his instructions on the line that "Kissinger, Colson, et al" should follow: "At all costs give no quarter whatever to the doves." At every opportunity, they should point out that the antiwar resolutions from the Congress "prolonged the war." The President anticipated that the doves would charge that the January settlement was no different from the October agreements and that therefore the Christmas bombing was unnecessary; that the cease-fire was but a temporary truce to allow the American armed forces and POWs to come home, after which the war would resume; and even that the United States could have had the same deal—the POWs for an American withdrawal—in 1969. He wanted his spokesmen to hit hard on each of these points by emphasizing that what had really been achieved was peace with honor.[55]

Governor Reagan put the theme more succinctly and colorfully in a telephone message to a White House aide, who passed it on to Nixon: "He said to tell you that he was envious of us being in Washington and having the chance to look those 'bastards' in the Congress in the eye now that a solution has been reached."[56]

On January 27, Nixon met with Kissinger, Haldeman, and Colson. Haldeman's notes record Nixon's instructions to Kissinger: "The way to show you & P[resident] don't differ is for *you* to sell what the P did. Esp. sell the hell out of bombing. You appear not to be keen for it." Then Haldeman complained that in his last briefing, Kissinger had mentioned the President only three times, although when things were going badly he had mentioned Nixon fourteen times. "You kept saying we'd kill the critics" when the settlement was in place, Haldeman added, but "you haven't done this at all."[57]

Nixon followed up with further PR instructions for Haldeman. He wanted the emphasis on "the man, not the process," highlighting "the basic color story regarding the courage of the President." The line according to Nixon was "the character of the lonely man in the White House, who, with very little support from the government, active opposition from the Senate, and some in the House, and overwhelming opposition from the media and the opinion leaders . . . alone held on and pulled it out. The missing link now is the profile in courage idea and it's not coming through."[58]

On a News Summary item, Nixon commented more directly on the doves: "Hitler would have Britain and the world if they had been in Churchill's place."[59]

On another News Summary, Nixon read that "the President was deeply hurt that the cease-fire was not acclaimed like V-J Day." He scribbled in the margin, "Z—This is baloney. I didn't expect it. What the Cease Fire *did* deserve was at least a grudging silence from the critics for a few days."[60]

Barry Goldwater complained that the "peace movement" had become a "pick-the-peace-apart movement." Nixon agreed. When one reporter wrote that "it looks more and more like Nixon adopted the strategy of the doves" when he made a "hard-eyed swap," POWs for American withdrawal, Nixon told Kissinger he had to stop beating around the bush, hinting that he had opposed the bombing, and "knock this down."[61]

Nixon's popularity had soared after the January 24 announcement, to its highest point ever, a 68 percent approval rating, but it began slipping soon thereafter, down to the low 60s (with all the criticism, Nixon commented, it was a wonder he had not slipped to 40 percent). Among college students, he rated only 45 percent approval a month after the cease-fire. Nixon figured the reason was "their Profs have had a chance to work them over!"[62]

Peace, even peace with honor, was not victory. And a cease-fire was not even peace. These plain facts became more obvious in the initial post-settlement weeks, as reports from Vietnam indicated that the fighting was resuming. The pick-the-peace-apart sniping increased. It made Nixon seethe with anger. He exploded in a news conference. Asked if he had any plans to "help heal the wounds in this country," such as a general amnesty for those who had dodged the draft, he said, "it takes two to heal wounds, and . . . when I see that the most vigorous criticism or, shall we say, the least pleasure out of the peace agreement comes from those that were the most outspoken advocates of peace at any price, it makes one realize whether [sic] some want the wounds healed."

As Nixon went on, his anger mounted. He said he had ended a long and difficult war, "which was not begun while we were here." Catching himself, he said he did not wish to cast any aspersions on "those Presidents who were in office who can no longer be here to speak for themselves, for the causes of the war." But he did want to say that "we have done the very best that we can against very great obstacles, and we finally have achieved a peace with honor."

Clenching his fists, he declared, "I know it gags some of you to write that phrase, but it is true."

Returning to the subject of amnesty, he said he had "sympathy for any individual who has made a mistake. We have all made mistakes. But also, it is a rule of life, we all have to pay for our mistakes." Amnesty meant forgiveness, and "we cannot provide forgiveness for . . . those who deserted." They would have to play a price, and "the price is a criminal penalty for disobeying the laws of the United States."[63]

The reporters were shocked at the President's display of temper. Walter Cronkite said that what made him gag was Nixon's "very low, uncalled for, gratuitous blow."[64]

Despite Nixon's words, *Time* magazine said that peace with honor was "a dubious and troubling phrase." Nixon circled the remark on his News Summary and commented, "H—K *must* begin to use this term," i.e., peace with honor.[65]

Still the sniping continued. The media reported increasing violations of the cease-fire. "K—this must stop," Nixon thundered.[66] By mid-February, critics were charging that Nixon had accepted a settlement far short of his real wishes because of the world protest about the bombing and because of the B-52 losses. Nixon told "Z and K" that the charge was "ridiculous!"[67]

But no matter how strong the President's words, they could not change the facts. Except for Thieu clinging to power in Saigon, an important point for Nixon, little had been achieved in January 1973 that the Communists had not been offering in January 1969; the bombing had not improved the October terms; the cease-fire was not holding. What Nixon had achieved was impressive, but it was something he never talked about: the withdrawal of American troops from Vietnam without a right-wing revolt in the United States. What he did talk about, peace with honor, he had not achieved.

Nixon desperately wanted the cease-fire to hold, both for itself and to bolster his own claim to having achieved peace. To that end, he urged the South Vietnamese to refrain from attacking the NVA and Viet Cong in South Vietnam.[68] In his own comments, he made a 180-degree turnaround. For six years, he had criticized the North Vietnamese for the infiltration of men and supplies into the South; after the end of January 1973, he downplayed the continuing infiltration, even dismissed it as inconsequential. Asked for a comment on the reports about infiltration in a mid-March news conference, Nixon would say only that he had noted them.[69]

Far from verbally attacking the Communists, much less taking military action against them for the violations, Nixon was promoting reconstruction aid for North Vietnam. His reason was simple: he wanted to give Hanoi a vested interest in the peace. So, while he told Kissinger and others to go after the doves, he simultaneously urged them to help build public opinion for reconstruction aid. As he explained in a March 4 memo to Kissinger, "This is the most effective way to avoid hostilities breaking out again."[70] Six days later, he told Kissinger, Rogers, and Richardson to organize a lobbying effort to persuade Congress to support an aid program for North Vietnam.[71] He wanted them to cite the post-World War II Marshall Plan as a model.

There were dangers in such an approach. The Baltimore *Sun*, among others, supported Nixon, but for reasons he did not appreciate. The *Sun* felt such aid was "a terribly bitter pill to swallow," but necessary for America to recover its self-respect. Nixon commented, "K—My God! Tell Congress we must provide aid to atone for our sin?!"[72] Still, he was determined to keep after it.

Nixon often told his aides to build him up, in this way or that, but when they began promoting the idea of his receiving the Nobel Peace Prize, he drew the line. He told Haldeman he wanted a letter sent to the prize committee withdrawing his name from consideration. Nixon said he should not be honored for simply doing his duty.[73]

Nixon's reaction was realistic. He had not achieved peace, or even the appearance of peace. He had not even gotten America out of the war, because the price he paid to Thieu to accept the agreement was a secret promise to resume the bombing if Hanoi launched an invasion, along with a public promise to resupply ARVN.

What he had done was to give Thieu and the ARVN a chance to survive. Thieu's resignation had been a central Communist demand in 1969; Nixon had effectively won on that point. He had also won Hanoi's promise to release the POWs. And he had managed to extract the American armed forces from Vietnam without setting off a right-wing backlash of epic proportions in the United States. That was a major achievement, one that had eluded Presidents Kennedy and Johnson.

Had Nixon been content to make those points while extending a hand of forgiveness and friendship to the doves and the deserters, rather than insisting that he had won peace with honor while damning the doves and denouncing the deserters, he would have established a firmer base for himself from which to deal with the problems he faced.

But Nixon, who could forgive and even embrace his enemies abroad, whether in Peking or Moscow or Hanoi, could not find it in himself to forgive his enemies at home.

So the active American involvement in the Vietnam War ended, not on a sweet note, but a sour one.

CHAPTER THREE

WAR BETWEEN
NIXON AND CONGRESS
February 1–March 20, 1973

IN THE IMMEDIATE aftermath of the Vietnam cease-fire, Nixon apparently was in a position to overwhelm Congress, not just in the polls, where he had a 60 percent approval rating while respect for Congress had fallen to an all-time low of 26 percent, but in the structure and role of the American government. It appeared to be an ideal time to begin his New American Revolution.

Nixon had an ability to speak bluntly and to express accurately the feelings of millions of his fellow citizens. He did so with regard to Congress, which he characterized as "cumbersome, undisciplined, isolationist, fiscally irresponsible, overly vulnerable to pressures from organized minorities, and too dominated by the media."[1]

But the Democrats in Congress had some assets of their own, assets that went beyond their constitutional power to investigate the activities of the executive branch. One was Nixon's personality. For all his popularity, he had through his actions and words infuriated his opponents. They shook with a rage that was not a helpless rage, because their victory in the November congressional election had given them the power to act on their feelings. The chief causes of their rage were: a quarter century of hating Nixon; the Watergate break-in; the dirty tricks in the last campaign; "peace is at hand" followed by the Christmas bombing; the conditions of the cease-fire coupled with Nixon's assertion that he had achieved peace with honor; Nixon's aggressive insistence on rubbing the doves' noses in the dirt; Nixon's rejection of major parts of one of the Democrats' proudest achievements, the Great Society; and his evident power grab for the White House through the New American Revolution.

As the 93d Congress began its work, John Connally warned Nixon that the mood on Capitol Hill was "the most vicious thing I have ever seen. They are mean and testy."[2]

Some of the more obvious ways the new Congress was expressing its anger were: an all-out investigation of Watergate and of other Republican campaign activities; an all-out determination to limit the President's warmaking power; a continuing attack on the terms of the cease-fire, including a resolve to refuse continuing military aid to Saigon and to reject proposed reconstruction aid to North Vietnam; a readiness for a winner-take-all struggle with Nixon over his New American Revolution.

The Democrats in Congress, and their allies in the intellectual and media communities, had their own catch phrase to rally behind in the struggle; it was the "Imperial Presidency." Nixon complained, correctly, that his enemies had idolized a strong Presidency when FDR, Harry Truman, and John F. Kennedy occupied the White House, but viciously turned against it when the strong President was Dick Nixon. The most visible of these double-standard spokesmen was Arthur Schlesinger, Jr. Other American historians who were prominent in the assault on the "Imperial Presidency" were Henry Steele Commager and Thomas E. Cronin.

The charges they made seemed to Nixon to be the worst sort of hypocrisy. When John Herbers did a major series on the subject of the "Imperial Presidency" for *The New York Times,* Nixon took it apart, detail by detail. In a memo to Ehrlichman, Nixon said that Kennedy had impounded more funds than the Nixon Administration, that Kennedy had instigated more wiretaps, that Kennedy had done far more illegal surveillance, that Truman had stretched the doctrine of executive privilege far beyond anything Nixon ever attempted, and so on. With regard to Truman, Nixon recalled the Hiss case: "We ran into a total stone wall [from the Truman Administration] in a case in which what was involved was not espionage by one political party against another but espionage against the nation itself." In contrast, "We never withhold information" from the Congress.[3]

Nixon, who so often felt sorry for himself, had cause to feel sorry for himself in this case. He surely was a target, and potentially a victim, of congressional anger. Part of the reason was, as noted, his own words and acts and personality, but there was a more powerful force at work here. The Congress wanted to cut the power of the President not just because of Dick Nixon, but for reasons that included the points he had made to Ehrlichman, and even more fundamentally, to reassert its own power, most especially in foreign affairs.

This determination was expressed most directly in the proposed War Powers Act. If passed, it would put a sixty-day limit on presidential commitment of troops to hostilities abroad, or into situations where hostilities appeared imminent, unless the Congress authorized continued action. The intent was to make certain there would be "no more Vietnams," and in that sense the target was more Johnson than Nixon. The bill was not unlike the neutrality acts of the 1930s, which had been designed to keep America out of World War I, and which in the event proved to be a major embarrassment to the government at the beginning of World War II.

The War Powers Act, important in itself, was but part of a larger struggle between the Congress and the President for control of American foreign policy. Not since the neutrality acts had the Congress attempted to interfere significantly in foreign policy. Beginning with American entry into World War II, and continuing through the first quarter century of the Cold War, the Congress could hardly move fast enough to give the power and the decisions to the President. Two classic examples were the Eisenhower Doctrine, which gave Ike the unilateral power to decide when, in what force, and under what circumstances to send troops into the Middle East, and the Gulf of Tonkin resolution, which did the same for Johnson in Vietnam.

The War Powers Act, unthinkable in the forties and fifties and sixties, looked to be unstoppable in 1973.

On the domestic front, meanwhile, Nixon's proposed New American Revolution provided for changes in the American system of government that also were unthinkable in the forties, fifties, and sixties, changes the Democrats and their allies were determined to stop.

Thus did Nixon begin his second term, and the 93d Congress its work, set on a collision course.

Years later, looking back on the period 1973–74, the national memory concentrated almost exclusively on Watergate and its consequences. Most Americans recalled the epic battle between Nixon and the Congress as one that revolved solely around Watergate. But in fact both sides had drawn their troops up in a battle line, established their strategy, and geared themselves for war *before* almost anything was known about Watergate beyond the bare fact of the break-in.

Had there never been a Watergate, there still would have been a war between Nixon and Congress. Of course, not even the most partisan Democrat could have imagined in his most delightful fantasies that Nixon was going to give his enemies so much ammunition to fight with; at the end of January 1973, they feared they were going into the war badly outmanned and outgunned. The precise figures were 68 to 26 in the Gallup approval poll. Even so, Nixon's enemies were resolved to fight to the finish.

THE opening skirmish was over the budget. The federal budget for fiscal 1972 had been set at $260 billion; Nixon had impounded about $10 billion of that amount, which still left a deficit of $25 billion. For fiscal 1973,

Nixon proposed spending $268 billion. His budget called for the elimination of the Job Corps and the Model Cities program, a virtual dismantling of the Office of Economic Opportunity, and drastic cuts in the funding of health, housing, education, and other social programs, with a slight increase in defense spending. It included no tax increase.

In presenting his program, Nixon pointed out that the federal budget had doubled between 1952 and 1962, then doubled again in the past decade. He warned, "If the budget continues to double every 10 years, it will be over a trillion dollars by the nineteen-nineties."[4]

The Democrats, predictably, wanted to cut defense spending and increase social spending. Nixon felt that even though every politician in America gave lip service to holding down spending, the Democrats held the more popular position. "Government spending is a lousy issue," he told his Cabinet. "People are *for* spending. Opposition to raising taxes is a good issue, but being for a balanced budget is impossible." As one example, he said that the federal government was now providing free breakfasts in the schools. "Why not dinners," he asked scornfully.

His own troops, meanwhile, were breaking ranks. Republicans were upset because Nixon's budget included a $12 billion deficit. He argued that his budget would be in balance if there were full employment; as he told the Cabinet, "a 'full employment budget' is our mirror game to explain the deficit."

It was a skirmish Nixon did not want to fight. He confessed to the Cabinet, "I have sat through so many of these budget meetings. They are the most boring, depressing exercise in the world."[5]

In his opening shot, Nixon claimed an inherent authority to refuse to spend funds appropriated by Congress whenever he felt it was harmful to the national well-being. Senator Ervin replied with a proposal for an outright ban on impoundment. A member of Ervin's staff charged that Nixon had "presented a blueprint for Presidential rule of the Government."[6]

The Democrats' opening shot was a bill they pushed through the Senate requiring confirmation of the director of the Office of Management and Budget, previously a presidential appointee not subject to congressional scrutiny. They followed up by introducing the War Powers Act.

Nixon broadened his attack. He went after one of the Democrats' most sacred symbols, farm subsidies. In a February 13 message to Congress, he proposed the elimination of federal payments to farmers to subsidize their crops and an end to government limits on the farmers' acreage planted (the attack failed; subsidies turned out to be invulnerable).

Nixon continued his assault on the Great Society. In a memo to Ehrlichman, he asked for a list of "10 or 15 horrible examples of how money has been wasted in model cities, community action, etc."[7]

Ehrlichman was able to provide plenty of ammunition. He found that Office of Economic Opportunity officials had loaned government money to themselves, and channeled OEO funds to the American Indian Movement (AIM) and the National Welfare Rights Organization, both anti-Nixon political and lobbying groups.[8]

Environmental legislation passed by the Democrats was another target. In some cases, Nixon refused to enforce it; in others, he strove to soften it. For example, when the Big Three automakers requested an extension to meet deadlines for the Environmental Protection Agency's (EPA) emission control standards, Nixon ordered "sympathetic consideration of this request."[9]

With regard to criminals and drug dealers, on the other hand, Nixon wanted tougher laws and more stringent enforcement. He castigated "soft-headed judges" and the "permissive philosophy" that said social injustice breeds crime. He asked Congress to restore the death penalty, and to impose mandatory life imprisonment with no right to parole for drug dealers convicted of a second felony.[10]

There was little new in any of this; most of these skirmishes had deep roots in American politics. The difference was that Nixon fought more tenaciously than his only Republican postwar predecessor, Dwight Eisenhower. Paradoxically, at the same time he also failed to shore up his own position, as he took less care than Eisenhower had done to flatter, cajole, and appease the Republicans in Congress. He reacted to continuing charges that he had ignored Republican candidates in the campaign by denying them. When the Baltimore *Sun* wrote that "Nixon wouldn't be in as much hot water if he used the phone a little more frequently—or maybe the oil can," Nixon claimed he spent more time on the phone with congressmen than any of his predecessors.[11] That could not be proved, one way or the other; what was clear was that Nixon's practice was to rely more on the support of the Silent Majority than on hard-core Capitol Hill politics to promote his policies. He believed that it was the battle for public opinion that mattered.

In place of the oil can, Nixon used a bludgeon. In early March, he told Haldeman he wanted some sympathetic congressman to call on the IRS to initiate full field audits on all members of the Congress, White House staff, and Cabinet. He explained, "these people are in a public position and their returns should be fully checked every year."[12] When Haldeman did not act, Nixon pressed the point. He sent a follow-up memo to Haldeman asking what had happened to his suggestion. He admitted that "it may be that this is not a good idea because it may stir up a lot of our friends as well as others," but he still wanted it done. Again, nothing happened.[13]

At the end of February, the National Governors' Conference convened in Washington. Nixon sent out instructions on how he wanted his staff to handle it: "What matters most to us is not the *substance* of what they decide—but what gets on TV. Get our *best* spokesman on the tube and *where possible* a Democratic governor who supports us on issues."[14]

Vice President Spiro Agnew was scheduled to speak to the governors. He wanted to promote himself to head Nixon's newly created Domestic Council, which Nixon had said would provide for a direct role for state governments in the formulation of domestic policies. Nixon vetoed Agnew's idea. He decided that Agnew should be vice chairman, and told Agnew this would give him "the best of both worlds." As vice chairman, Agnew could have a "direct input on policy questions without the day-to-day responsibilities of dealing with a myriad of questions." Besides, being chairman would "unnecessarily limit the Vice President's ability to travel and require that he greatly increase his staff."[15]

Like all Presidents, Nixon wished he could deal with the Congress as easily as he did with the Vice President, but he could not. The Vice President had no power base of his own; the congressmen did. So Nixon girded himself for battle. It was not unwelcome. The thrust and parry of American politics was his lifelong work. He thought he was the best in the country at it; he had the election results to prove that point; he knew it was going to be a tough battle, but he expected to win.

AT A January 31 news conference, Nixon had been asked if he planned to fly to Travis Air Force Base to meet the first POWs when they returned. He did not, he said, because "this is a time that we should not grandstand it; we should not exploit it. . . . They have a right to have privacy, they have a right to be home with their families just as quickly as they possibly can. And I am going to respect that right." On the other hand, if any of the POWs or their families wanted to visit the White House, Nixon said he was eager to have them.[16]

On February 12, the first of the 591 POWs were released in Hanoi and flown directly to Clark Air Force Base in the Philippines. The press and TV cameras were there to meet them. Nixon was apprehensive. Some of these men had been prisoners for seven years. It was possible that they were scarred, bitter, disillusioned, or broken. They might say or do almost anything.

Nixon's anxieties disappeared immediately. The POWs came down the ramp, walking or hobbling on crutches, saluting the flag. Navy Captain Jeremiah P. Denton, the first man to step to the microphones, said, "We are honored to have had the opportunity to serve our country. . . . We are profoundly grateful to our Commander in Chief. . . . God bless America."[17] Denton set the theme for nearly everything the POWs said in public over the next few weeks; Nixon was delighted and grateful, naturally enough.

That first morning, Colonel Robinson Risner, senior officer in the initial group of POWs, called Nixon in Washington. Nixon was in a meeting with Ehrlichman and Governor Reagan. Told who was calling, he picked up the phone and said hello.

"This is Colonel Risner, sir, reporting for duty."

They talked for a few minutes. Before hanging up, Risner said this was the proudest moment of his life. Nixon was deeply moved. So was Reagan, who pointed out that Risner was a Korean War ace.

"Compare these fine men with those sniveling Ivy Leaguers," Nixon said. He added that Risner had told him it would mean a great deal to the POWs to "meet with me personally, shake my hand, express thanks for bringing the war to an end on an honorable basis and get them out."

His voice shaking, Nixon reported that Risner had told him, "you will have our support unanimously as long as we live."[18]

Over the next ten days, Nixon received many letters and wires from returning POWs and their families. He sent out a handwritten order on how to handle the messages: "H—I think it would mean a great deal to Cabinet and top staff if they could have copies of these—*Don't* put out to press however. Let them leak out. I don't want to exploit them."[19]

Nixon need not have feared. There was no necessity to leak; the former POWs were anxious to tell the country how much they admired Nixon and appreciated what he had done. So much so that reporters began expressing some skepticism, even charging that the ex-POWs had been told what to say. "Ridiculous," responded a Pentagon spokesman, who added that "it insults the POWs' intelligence to say that they could have been brainwashed during a 3-hour lay-over in Clark Field when the North Vietnamese couldn't do it in seven years."

Nixon heartily agreed. He called it "a superb line," and instructed Ziegler to put it out for others to use.[20]

The charges of brainwashing made Nixon furious. He complained to Haldeman that there was a "poison in the upper classes—loss of faith in the country—hate the country—corrupt, prejudiced—McGovern arguments—now seeing just the beginning—as press tries to make POW's a phony deal."

He consoled himself that questioning the spontaneity or truthfulness of the POWs by the press would fail, " 'cause of TV."[21]

Don't exploit the POWs, Nixon had ordered. And it was quite true that he had made no effort to coach them or otherwise tell them what to say. But the temptation to exploit their words proved to be too much for him. He instructed Patrick Buchanan to "compile the best one liners on support of Country, Flag, President by the POW's" and put it out to the media.[22]

Do not gloat, Nixon had instructed Haldeman, but he would have had to have been made of steel not to gloat over the POWs' remarks to the press. As Buchanan pointed out in a memo, they were saying that the antiwar movement prolonged the war, and that the Christmas bombing shortened it while winning the peace. Nixon circled the words and wrote in the margin: "H & K, Let's not miss this opportunity." Buchanan wanted to "regurgitate the pro-amnesty statements of the doves in the past"; Nixon wrote, "H—yes, follow up."[23]

Petty politicking aside, Nixon was profoundly moved by the return of the POWs. Just bringing them home would have been enough, but as one after another said exactly what Nixon most hoped he would say, expressing sentiments that were closest to Nixon's heart, he was all but overwhelmed. He hand-wrote a letter for the top eighteen men in his Administration who were involved in the war, whether at State, DOD, the CIA, or the NSC.

"As I saw our P.O.W.'s come off the plane at Clark Field, I have never been as proud to be an American," he began. Then he thanked the men for helping him achieve peace with honor.[24]

Nixon also seized on a suggestion from singer Sammy Davis, Jr., to hold a gala entertainment on the White House lawn honoring the POWs. The President was so enthusiastic that he sent a five-page, single-spaced memo on the subject to Haldeman, with detailed instructions on how to set it up and carry it out. It was scheduled for May 24.[25]

AT the end of his January 31 news conference, Nixon had been asked to explain his position on the doctrine of executive privilege, with specific reference to a cost analyst in the Pentagon who had been fired after criticizing the Secretary of the Air Force. Nixon admitted that he had been critical of executive privilege back in 1948, when Truman used it in the Hiss case, but he had since become a defender of the doctrine. Still he pledged that he would be "as liberal as possible" in allowing White House aides to testify before the Congress. "We are not going to use executive privilege as a shield for conversations that might be just embarrassing to us, but that really don't deserve executive privilege." He promised a precise statement later that would give the details of his position.[26]

The Air Force whistle-blower case was a minor affair, but the principle involved—Nixon's right to refuse to allow any member of the executive branch to testify before Congress—was of major importance, with the potential of provoking a constitutional crisis. Developments through February brought that crisis closer.

The trial in Judge Sirica's courtroom came to an end in late January. Liddy and McCord were found guilty. In the course of their trial, the former treasurer of the Finance Committee of CREEP, Hugh W. Sloan, Jr., had revealed that $199,000 had been paid to Liddy in 1972, with the approval of John Mitchell and former Commerce Secretary Maurice H. Stans. Sloan said he had "no idea" what Liddy had done with the money.

On February 2, Sirica said it would take Congress "to get to the bottom of what happened in this case." On February 7, the Senate voted 70 to 0 to establish a seven-member select committee to probe all aspects of the Watergate bugging case and other acts of political espionage against the Democrats in the 1972 campaign. Republican efforts to gain equal membership on the committee and to extend the probe's coverage to the 1964 and 1968 campaigns were turned back.

That same day, *New York Times* reporter Seymour Hersh named Haldeman's assistant Gordon Strachan as the White House contact with Donald Segretti of CREEP and the author of the dirty tricks campaign in 1972. Hersh added that Strachan was also the White House contact with Liddy and Hunt. Another contact was Nixon appointments secretary Dwight Chapin (who had left the White House on January 30 to take a job with United Airlines).

On February 8, the federal prosecutor in the Watergate case, Earl Silbert, said he was going to bring all seven defendants before a grand jury in an attempt to "explore every conceivable avenue" of possible higher-level involvement.

On February 10, Nixon met with Haldeman and Ehrlichman to plan a strategy for the Ervin Committee hearings. They decided to do whatever they could to "discredit hearings—cooperate publicly but quietly obstruct."[27]

On February 14, Nixon met with the acting director of the FBI, L. Patrick Gray. The President said he intended to nominate Gray for the post of permanent director. Such a nomination carried with it a great danger, because it would force Gray to testify in confirmation hearings before the Senate. There had been some criticism of the FBI's investigation of the Watergate break-in, but Nixon assured Gray that he was not worried: "I'm not concerned about the substance, about the facts coming out."

Gray was equally confident. He said the FBI had gone after the case vigorously and he was proud of what had been done. He did not tell Nixon that, acting on his own, he had destroyed evidence in the case, in the form of documents John Dean had taken from Howard Hunt's safe in the White House and given to Gray. Nor did he remind Nixon that he had allowed Dean to sit in on FBI sessions with White House personnel. Nixon wrote in his diary, "It is the cover-up, not the deed, that is really bad here," but complained that he was finding it difficult to convince others of that basic fact.

Nixon himself was ambivalent, however. He wrote, "We are going to have to take our lumps and get the thing over as quickly as we can," then immediately added that it might be better to "delay as long as we can and let it drag on and on."[28]

Nixon met with Gray on the morning of February 16, to brief him on what he wanted from an FBI director. Among other things, he wanted

Gray to know that his Administration had done some wiretapping, but not a lot, nothing to compare to Kennedy and Johnson. Besides, "I don't believe we should be defensive. . . . It's extremely necessary. We must not be denied the right to use the weapon. The idea that we're wiretapping a lot of political groups is bullshit."

Gray said he understood.

Nixon turned to the FBI bugging of his 1968 campaign plane. He wanted the man responsible to confess. "Did you follow through on the directive . . . that everybody in the Bureau was to take a lie detector test as to what part they played?" he demanded.

"No, that directive was not given out," Gray replied.

"Well, it's given now."

"Yes sir."

Nixon turned to a recent leak from the FBI reported in *Time* magazine: "This stuff never leaked when Hoover was there. . . . Hoover'd lie detect those guys. . . . You've got to play it exactly that way, you've got to be brutal. . . . The whole damn place ought to be fired. Really, it should, until, just move them all out to the field. I think you've got to do it like they did in the war, you remember in World War II the Germans, if they went through these towns and then a sniper hit one of them, they'd line up the whole goddamned town and say until you talk you're all getting shot. I really think that's what has to be done. I mean I don't think you can be Mr. Nice Guy over there." Gray assured him that "these guys know they can't lie to me like they used to lie to Hoover."

Nixon said he was not referring to "that kind of stuff. Frankly, I am referring to discipline of the highest sensitivity involving what may be political matters."

Nixon had fought many a battle with J. Edgar Hoover over their long careers, beginning in 1948 with the Hiss case, when Hoover had refused to help Nixon, and continuing through Hoover's refusal to investigate Ellsberg. But with Hoover dead, Nixon invented an entirely new relationship between them. He all but overwhelmed Gray with his references to the "deep personal friendship" he and Hoover enjoyed. "Lyndon Johnson told me this," Nixon went on, that "I would find the only person in this goddamned government who was standing with me was Edgar Hoover."

Nixon assured Gray he would never ask him to do anything wrong, but there were "treasonable people" out there in the bureaucracy, and "the way to get them is through you. See?"

"I agree," Gray replied.

"We have got to get them, break them," Nixon said.

"Right, I know that. I agree."

On the other hand, "You don't want to crack any whips that are gonna force some bastard to go out and testify against your nomination. You've gotta be careful. But the moment you're confirmed then I think we've got to have the kind of relationship we had with Hoover."

Gray again agreed. As he left, he assured the President "I'm a Nixon loyalist. You're goddamn right I am."[29]

On February 17, Nixon announced the Gray nomination. By the 28th, Gray had revealed in his confirmation hearings some, but not all, of what he had done for the White House in the Watergate investigation. At 9:12 A.M. on the 28th, Nixon met with John Dean in the Oval Office to discuss the Gray testimony and to deal with the problem of how to handle the Senate's demand that Dean come testify about his relations with Gray.

Nixon opened the discussion as he did nearly every one he held from February through April, by urging Dean to go back and read his own *Six Crises*. He said the FBI would not cooperate with Congress in the Hiss case, even though "that was espionage against the nation, not against the party." So Nixon's subcommittee had gone to work. "We got it done. We got the evidence, we got the typewriter, we got the Pumpkin Papers. We got all of that ourselves. The FBI did not cooperate. The Justice Department did not cooperate."

Nixon went on to admit that he had thought executive privilege wrong in the Hiss case, but "now this [the demand for Dean's testimony] is another matter."

Dean thought that if they could stall, the problem would disappear. "The public is bored with this thing already," he said. Nixon agreed.

Nixon gave Dean an order: "You'd better go over [to the Justice Department] and get in touch with Dick [Kleindienst] and say: 'You keep it at your level.' Don't say the President told you to say so."

As to Congress, Nixon was not worried. "Congress is, of course, on its, its, I guess they are so enormously frustrated that they're irrelevant. Isn't that the point? That's their problem. . . . They become irrelevant because they're so damned irresponsible."[30]

Dean regretted that J. Edgar Hoover was not there to handle the Senate. "He knew how to handle that Bureau."

"He would have fought," Nixon said. "He would have defied a few people. He would have scared them to death. He had a file on everybody. But as for Pat Gray . . ." He did not finish the sentence.

They turned to the Ervin Committee. Nixon feared it would be partisan. He ridiculed Ervin's claim to be a great constitutional lawyer, but admitted that "Ervin works harder than most of our Southern gentlemen. They are great politicians. They are just more clever than the minority. Just more clever!"

Dean had gotten some dirt from Gray and others at the FBI on the

Kennedy and Johnson administrations, which he shared with Nixon. The President had some of his own: "Did your friends tell you what Bobby did?" he asked Dean.

"I haven't heard but I wouldn't be . . ."

"Johnson believed that Bobby bugged him."

Dean said he was not surprised.

They exchanged other horror stories. Then Nixon wondered, who is going to step forward and say in public that the FBI had done this or that? No one, he sadly concluded, because people treated informers like a pariah. "Look what it did to [Whittaker] Chambers."

Nixon changed the subject. He wanted to know when the Watergate burglars would be sentenced. Next week, Dean replied. Nixon wondered if Sirica "is trying to work on them to see who will break down?" Dean thought so.

"You know when they talk about a 35-year sentence," Nixon said, referring to fears that had been expressed that "Hanging John" Sirica would do just that, "here is something to think about. There were no weapons! Right? There were no injuries! Right? There was no success! It is just ridiculous!"

Dean thought that whatever Sirica did, the burglars would keep quiet.

"What the hell do they expect, though?" Nixon asked. "Do they expect clemency in a reasonable time?"

Dean thought it was something that would have to be watched closely.

"You couldn't do it, say, in six months," Nixon interjected.

Dean agreed. He suggested that to protect Liddy and Hunt, "we can give them [the prosecutors] Segretti."

"He was such a dumb figure," Nixon exploded. "I don't see how our boys could have gone for him. But nevertheless, they did. It was really juvenile! But, nevertheless, what the hell did he do? What in the name of Christ did he do? Shouldn't we be trying to get intelligence? Weren't they trying to get intelligence from us?"

They returned to the Ervin Committee. "No hearsay," Nixon insisted. "No innuendo!"

The big thing, he continued, was to stress "the isolation of the President."

"Absolutely!" Dean all but shouted. "Totally true!"

"Because that, fortunately, is totally true," Nixon echoed.

"I know that, sir!"

"Of course," Nixon added, "I am not dumb and I will never forget when I heard about this forced entry and bugging. I thought, what the hell is this? What is the matter with these people? Are they crazy? I thought they were nuts! A prank! I think our Democratic friends know that, too . . . [although] they think I have people capable of it. And they are correct, in that Colson would do anything."

After a pause, Nixon concluded, "But let's remember this was not done by the White House. This was done by the Committee to Re-Elect, and Mitchell was the Chairman. . . . [Attorney General Richard] Kleindienst owes Mitchell everything. . . . Mitchell won't allow himself to be ruined. He will put on his big stone face."

Nixon thought the Ervin Committee wanted big fish—Haldeman, Colson, Ehrlichman, Mitchell. "Or possibly Dean," Dean interjected.

Nixon said Dean was a lawyer with no involvement in the campaign, so he had nothing to fear. The meeting ended. Nothing was settled.[31]

THE recently re-elected President found little to please him, and much to annoy him, in the first two months of his second term. He was unhappy, for example, at the coverage his wife was getting in the press. In a three-page memo to Ziegler, Nixon complained that "despite an unprecedented effort on the part of Mrs. Nixon to handle all sorts of visiting delegations, foreign diplomats, etc., over the past four years we have been unable to break through in terms of getting some kind of coverage in the press." He wanted Ziegler to start counting, how many receptions, how many honorary chairmanships of volunteer organizations, how many and what types of groups, and so on, Pat had met or served or hosted. He told Ziegler that "ten times as many women read the society pages than read the news pages," and he wanted Pat featured in those pages. He admitted it was a tough assignment, "because of the basic antagonism of most of the women's press to anything that we do in the White House."[32]

Ziegler did get some items into the papers. One recorded that Pat spent four to five hours per day on her correspondence, that she received three thousand letters per week and read and personally answered every one of them.[33] But at times Nixon must have wished the press would leave Pat alone. In early February, *The Washington Post* reported in its "Style" section that Pat had resigned as honorary chairman of the Day Care Council of America when the Council criticized the President for his veto of a day-care bill. A Council spokesperson said that "after her initial two days of visiting day care centers and being photographed she never did anything else."[34]

One of Nixon's resolutions going into the new year had been to let the public see more of the human side of President and Mrs. Nixon. He got off to a good start. On February 7, the couple paid a surprise visit to Alice Roosevelt Longworth, Teddy Roosevelt's daughter. She had been unable to attend the inaugural, the first she had missed since 1900, so the Nixons came to her to spend ninety minutes sipping tea and munching cookies, and to provide the press with some lovely photo opportunities.[35]

On the day before Valentine's day, at Julie and David's suggestion

(David was home on leave), the Nixon family took a rare stroll outside the White House, walking across Lafayette Park for a spur-of-the-moment dinner at Trader Vic's in the Statler Hilton Hotel. Even more unusual, after dinner Pat lit a cigarette; she usually made it a rule to never smoke in public, but David was a chain smoker and on this occasion she joined him. When they finished, the party just walked out of the restaurant. The manager said later that the bill, at about $10 a head, would be sent to the White House.[36]

A couple of weeks later, Nixon dictated a memo to Haldeman to be passed on to Julie. It opened: "The President has asked that you get back on the subject of making the White House Staff serve the dinners faster." The problem, Nixon explained, was that the waiters took so long between courses, apparently because they were trained to wait until everyone had finished eating a course before they began to clear. "The President, at the Governors' Dinner, finally signaled them to start clearing himself, which he, of course, should not have to do."

Nixon wanted Julie to get the staff to start clearing as soon as they had put a course on the table, beginning with those first served. "By the time they get back around to you, you've had a pretty good chance to finish if you keep working at it." Nixon wanted the formal dinners finished within one hour.[37]

In mid-February, the National Women's Political Caucus met in Washington. Nixon sent his good wishes. Bella Abzug read it and then called Nixon "the nation's chief resident male chauvinist," while the crowd hissed the President. Nixon commented, "E—is it wise to throw pearls before swine?"[38]

The organization was critical of Nixon's failure to appoint women to high policy positions in his Administration. Nixon worked to mute the criticism. He appointed Anne Armstrong, who had been active on the RNC and was a promoter of feminism in the party, to the post of counselor to the President. Some women's groups called the appointment tokenism. Armstrong denied it, but when asked what her duties were, she replied, "I have a rather generalist role, with diffuse responsibilities."[39]

In mid-February, Nixon appointed marine biologist Dixy Lee Ray to serve as chairperson of the Atomic Energy Commission (AEC). "If it hadn't been for women's liberation movement I doubt the President would have appointed me," she said.[40] Whether that was true or not, Nixon did want maximum publicity out of the appointment. He told Haldeman to get after Armstrong to "broker this hard with the press."[41]

ON February 28, while Nixon and Dean talked, Pat Gray was also talking, to the Senate Judiciary Committee in his confirmation hearings. Gray admitted that he had kept Dean fully informed at every step of the FBI's investigation into Watergate, provided him with documents, and allowed him to be present when FBI agents asked questions of White House personnel.[42]

On March 2, at an impromptu news conference, Nixon said that Dean had informed him "that no one on the White House Staff, at the time he conducted the investigation—that was last July and August— was involved or had knowledge of the Watergate matter." Would the President be willing to allow Dean to testify at the Gray confirmation hearing? Well, Nixon replied, Dean would supply information, but he would not appear personally. The President promised a statement on executive privilege in the near future.[43]

Ten days later, he issued the statement. He swore that "executive privilege will not be used as a shield to prevent embarrassing information from being made available but will be exercised only in those particular instances in which disclosure would harm the public interest." But he then asserted, "The manner in which the President personally exercises his assigned executive powers is not subject to questioning by another branch of Government." Nixon argued that "this tradition rests on more than constitutional doctrine: It is also a practical necessity."

In fact, many argue that there is no such "constitutional doctrine" as "executive privilege" because those words do not appear in the Constitution. Nor was it much of a "tradition," as the claim that the President could refuse to send his White House aides to testify before congressional committees dated back only to Eisenhower (who had made it in the Army-McCarthy hearings of 1954).

Nixon's orders were that no member or former member of the White House staff would appear before Congress, in accord with "well-established precedent." They would provide written answers to written questions.[44]

The following day, Senator Ervin said he could not conceive of Nixon refusing to assist his committee in its Watergate investigation. Ziegler told the White House press corps that was nevertheless Nixon's position. The President then upbraided Ziegler: "Don't you understand that [assistance] is not the issue? We *agree to assist!* We only refuse to testify. Slam this hard today!"[45]

That same day, March 13, the Senate Judiciary Committee voted unanimously to "invite" John Dean to testify before it in the Gray hearings. That afternoon, Dean met with Nixon in the Oval Office. They agreed that Dean would decline the invitation, and that Nixon would then hold a news conference to explain the decision.

Nixon did not want to be stuck in a defensive position, however: he asked Dean, "Have you been able to do anything on my project of getting on the offensive? . . . Have you kicked a few butts around?"

Dean said it was difficult to get hard information. Nixon told him to go after McGovern's contributors.

They turned to the upcoming news conference. Dean asked Nixon practice questions. Did Haldeman know about Segretti's dirty tricks?

"I don't know."

Yes he did, Dean said.

"Well, I don't know anything about that," Nixon declared.

Dean tried another: why didn't the President release the "Dean Report?" (In August 1972, Nixon had said at a news conference that John Dean had investigated and reported to him that no one in the White House had been involved in Watergate. Dean had made no such report.)

The President was stumped. "What do we say to that?" he asked.

There was a long pause. Dean finally prompted Nixon: "We have cooperated with the FBI. We will cooperate with a proper investigation by the Senate."

Nixon made his contribution: "We will make statements."

"And indeed we have nothing to hide," Dean prompted.

"We have nothing to hide," the President repeated.

Nixon liked that idea. He said he had to talk about the issue "because it is not going to get better. It is going to get worse." Therefore, he had about decided to "let it all hang out."

But he immediately saw a flaw in that plan: "They are not going to believe the truth! That is the incredible thing!"

Dean agreed. Their enemies would not be satisfied with sending the seven Watergate burglars to jail; they would attempt to get the burglars to point to men higher up.

"They hope one will say one day, 'Haldeman did it,' " Nixon lamented. "And one day, that one will say I did it." Well, he consoled himself, people might believe that Haldeman was dumb enough to be involved, but no one would think such a thing about the President.

Nixon turned the conversation back to his proposed counterattack. Dean ran through his list of FBI horrors committed under JFK and LBJ. Nixon liked the stories but wondered if it would be wise to "go after the Bureau?" For one thing, the FBI might fight back. For another, revelations of illegal wiretapping and so forth would tarnish the FBI's reputation. "How bad would it hurt the country, John, to have the FBI so terribly damaged?" Nixon asked.

Dean wanted time to think about it.

Nixon was ready to abandon Pat Gray. After the hearings, Nixon felt that even if confirmed, Gray would not make a good director. Dean agreed, but pointed out that Gray was being cooperative with the White House. "He is calling me. He has given me his hot line. We talk at night, how do you want me to handle this, et cetera?" Dean wondered about the attitude of Attorney General Kleindienst. "Nobody is a friend of ours," Nixon reminded him. "Let's face it!"

They took up other problems. Dean warned that Judge Sirica "is a strange man. He's tough. He is tough." He might give a long sentence to force the burglars to talk.

Nixon said he thought the Ervin Committee hearings would be "a big show," but he hoped that after about three weeks, "it will begin to peter out."

Dean did not agree.

Neither did Buchanan, Nixon admitted. "I noticed in the news summary Buchanan was viewing with alarm the grave crisis in the confidency of the Presidency, etc." He asked Dean, "How much of a crisis?" and answered his own questions. "Everything is a crisis, it is a terrible lousy thing . . . among the upper intellectual types, the soft heads, [but] the average people won't think it is much of a crisis."

The Ervin Committee would produce new revelations, Dean warned.

"Is there a higher up?" Nixon asked Dean.

"Is there a higher up?" Dean asked Nixon. Neither man gave an answer.

Nixon said the Democrats wanted Haldeman. Dean said it was Haldeman and Mitchell. Nixon said Colson was not big enough for the Senate to bother with. Dean said Haldeman's problem was "circumstantial." Nixon said that Colson knew "those people like the Hunts and all that bunch, but Bob didn't."

How much did Chapin know, Nixon asked. Nothing, Dean replied. What about Strachan?

"Yes."

"He knew?"

"Yes."

"About the Watergate?"

"Yes."

The President grew alarmed. Strachan worked for Haldeman in the White House; here was the direct tie-in the Democrats were looking for.

"I will be damned!" Nixon exploded. "Well that is the problem . . . not Chapin then, but Strachan."

Dean was encouraging: "They will have one hell of a time proving that Strachan had knowledge of it, though."

Another problem area: if Sirica handed down a stiff sentence, would Liddy break?

"He's a strange man, Mr. President."

"Strange or strong?"

Both, Dean replied. But loyal, too.

"He hates the other side, doesn't he?" Nixon asked.

"Oh, absolutely!"

Nixon changed the subject. "Is it too late to go the hang-out road?" he asked.

"Yes," Dean replied, it was too late.

Nixon said Ehrlichman had always favored hang-out. Dean pointed out that "there are reasons for not everyone going up and testifying." Nixon assured him he had not meant *that* much of a hang-out.

Wrapping up, Nixon told Dean, "This is the last gasp of our hardest opponents. They've just got to have something to squeal about." He continued, "They are going to lie around and squeal. They are having a hard time now. They got the hell kicked out of them in the election. . . . The basic thing is the establishment. The establishment is dying, and so they've got to show that despite the successes we have had in foreign policy and in the election, they've got to show that [we are] wrong just because of this. They are trying to use this [Watergate thing] as the whole thing."

Dean might have tried to ease the President's frustration and anger by assuring him that there was something more to the Watergate investigation than a personal vendetta against Nixon. Instead, he promised the President some hot new material on Teddy Kennedy and Chappaquiddick: "If Kennedy knew the bear trap he was walking into . . ." (On March 1, Nixon had ordered Dean to "write me a memorandum and only for my eyes only, with regard to everything you know about Johnson's use of the FBI for espionage and then go back . . . and get what Kennedy did.")

Nixon interrupted: "Why don't we get it out?" Dean said he was saving it.

As Dean got up to leave, Nixon remarked, "It is never dull, is it?" "Never," Dean replied.[46]

The next day, March 14, Dean declined the Senate Committee's invitation to testify. On March 15, Nixon held his news conference. He explained that Dean was unavailable for testimony because "he has, in effect, what I would call a double privilege," the lawyer-client relationship, as well as "the Presidential privilege." He said he considered it his "constitutional responsibility to defend the principle of separation of powers." He expressed confidence that Senator Ervin, "a great constitutional lawyer," would conduct his hearings fairly, with no hearsay, no innuendo, no guilt by association, but that if Ervin insisted on using a subpoena to force testimony from White House aides, he would refuse and then welcome a court test. "Perhaps this is the time to have the highest Court of this land make a definitive decision with regard to this matter."[47]

Nixon met with Dean again on March 16. He urged Dean to go to Camp David to prepare a full report on Watergate, the hang-out route. Dean was reluctant.[48] The next day, the two men met in the Oval Office. They discussed yet another problem, the Hunt-Liddy break-in at the office of Daniel Ellsberg's psychiatrist. Dean warned that the Ervin Committee might find out about it in CIA files, because "these fellows [Hunt and Liddy] had to be some idiots." He explained that they had borrowed cameras and burglary equipment from the CIA, and Hunt took Liddy's picture "standing proud as punch outside this doctor's office with his name on it," and that they had turned the camera back in to the CIA "and left the film in the camera."

"What in the world," Nixon exclaimed. "What in the name of God?" He asked what they were doing in the doctor's office anyway.

Dean said he did not know, except that they wanted Ellsberg's psychiatric records.

"This is the first I ever heard of this," Nixon declared.

In fact, Ehrlichman had told him about it in the summer of 1972.[49] The purpose was to discredit Ellsberg. Nixon's denial to Dean in March of 1973 brings up an aspect of his conversations about Watergate and related matters that must always be kept in mind when reading the transcripts or listening to the tapes: only Nixon knew that a tape recorder was running. This necessarily makes all his self-serving statements ("This is the first I ever heard of this," "It would be wrong," etc.) suspect. It is simply impossible to tell when Nixon is speaking the truth and when he is establishing a record that would exonerate him.

For example, Nixon wanted Dean to write in his report that "no one on the White House staff is involved, so forth and so on." Dean demurred. He did not think anyone had ever "taken you [Nixon] through this. But the last involvement to my knowledge of the White House was when I came back from a meeting . . ."

Nixon cut him off. "I know nothing about Watergate."

"Right," Dean said. "Well, ah . . ."

"I stayed miles away from it so I didn't know even if there was a White House involvement."

Dean said there was "a preliminary discussion of setting up an intelligence operation," by which he meant the Huston Plan, for gathering intelligence through wiretapping, illegal entry, and other means, under the control of White House aide Tom Huston. Four days earlier, Dean had told Nixon that the problem was that J. Edgar Hoover had "lost his guts" and would not do the black-bag operations for Nixon that he had done for LBJ. So, Dean had gone on, "Tom Huston had your instructions to go out and do it." Now, on March 17, Nixon professed to be astonished to hear about an intelligence operation that involved White House personnel. Dean informed him of a meeting with Mitchell, CREEP Deputy Director Jeb Stuart Magruder, and Liddy where the operation had been set up.

"You heard discussion of that," Nixon conceded, "but you didn't hear any discussion of bugging, did you?"

"Yeah, I did," Dean had to admit. He said it had "distressed" him.

"Well," Nixon pointed out, "you won't need to say in your statement [anything about] the bugging. You could say that they were gonna engage in intelligence operations [but they] must be totally legal. . . . You know what I mean?"

Dean said he did.

"Then, you see," Nixon went on, "that basically clears the President, frankly." Nixon wanted to know who pushed for the break-in to the DNC. Was it Magruder, Colson, Haldeman?

Strachan, Dean said. He added that he could not understand why they decided to go into the DNC. "That absolutely mystifies me as to what—anybody's whose been around a National Committee knows there's nothing there."

Nixon began to explain—"Well, the point is they were trying to see what the (unintelligible) developed in terms of the . . ." but broke off. In the author's opinion, Nixon was about to explain the O'Brien-Howard Hughes connection to Dean, but thought better of it. (O'Brien had been on a handsome retainer from Hughes for years; Nixon feared O'Brien knew about Hughes's contributions to Nixon. In January, Colson had told Nixon that the Watergate bug had produced information on Hughes.)

Nixon went on, "Now Magruder puts the heat on somebody else, you know, the way you see things, 'cause I understand it, is a, that, possibly a friend of mine, that, ah—Sloan. Sloan starts pissing on Magruder and then Magruder starts pissing on, on, who—Haldeman?"

Dean did not think so. He said Magruder should take the heat. Nixon said, "Can't do that." Instead, Nixon instructed Dean, "I think what you've got to do, to the extent that you can, John, is cut her off at the pass. Liddy and his bunch just did this as part of their job." In other words, keep the blame with those who got caught, and protect White House personnel.

As to Segretti and the dirty tricks, Nixon said, "No matter how bad it is, it isn't nearly as bad as people think it was. Espionage, sabotage, shit."

Dean agreed. The intent when Segretti was hired "was nothing evil, nothing vicious, nothing bad, nothing. Not espionage. Not sabotage. It was pranksterism that got out of hand."[50]

On Tuesday evening, March 20, Nixon met with Haldeman to discuss what would happen when Sirica handed down his sentences on Friday. The President noted that McCord did not want to go to jail. What would happen if he decided to talk? "He would have a lot on Mitchell," said Haldeman. Strachan, Magruder, Colson, and others were also vulnerable. Nixon said the worst thing would be to give the impression of a White House cover-up.

Haldeman thought that the worst thing would be "John Mitchell going to jail."

Nixon said he thought that Mitchell would "take cover-up 'til hell freezes over." He added, "You can't figure Magruder did it by himself."

Haldeman pointed out that "Mitchell was clearly aware and fully aware of the Liddy intelligence operation. No question about that."

"But maybe not of the specific," Nixon interjected hopefully.

"But maybe not of the specific act," Haldeman agreed.

"Magruder was aware of the act," Nixon said.

"Well," Haldeman noted, "he says that he wasn't, in court."

Nixon waved that off. "Our real concern is Mitchell." He added sadly, "Maybe they're going to get him anyway."

Haldeman tried some optimism: "John Dean's basic approach to this is one of containment—keep it in this box and he thinks he can. And that box—goes on the theory that Liddy did it without authority from above. . . . Liddy was the responsible guy. . . . He's the highest guy."

The trouble with that, Nixon interjected, was "the judge [Sirica] blasted the hell out of that (unintelligible) didn't get cooperation and so forth."

Haldeman was still hopeful: "Liddy apparently is a little bit nuts and a masochist and apparently he wants to, looks to the martyrdom of doing this. He kind of likes it. . . . That's Dean's hope."

What about Ehrlichman's vulnerabilities?

Haldeman said that "John knows a hell of a lot."

"He does know a hell of a lot," Nixon agreed, "but not about this case."

Haldeman brought up the hang-out possibility. Why not release a statement? Nixon said it would "open too many doors." Haldeman said they would open anyway.

Nixon said he had told Dean to prepare a statement, "any kind of a statement. Of course, I said make it as general as possible but just so somebody can say that the President" had said something. As things stood, "it looks like I am just doing a thumb your nose, screw-off."

Haldeman pointed out that "everybody seems to accept the fact that there is a Dean report to the President," but the trouble was there was no such report. He brightened up: "We can [say] that it was an oral report, not a written report." On that basis, they could make a statement. Nixon warned that they should not claim it was complete, lest something come up later and undermine it.

Haldeman brought up another problem: some $350,000 had been transferred out of CREEP funds in 1972 and brought to the White House, where it was never used. Haldeman said he had sent it back to CREEP after the election.

So what, Nixon asked. Haldeman explained that if the "yellow journals" got ahold of that fact, they could say it was a secret fund controlled by the President's chief of staff.

Nixon said there were secret boxes in every campaign.

"Not that it worries me," Haldeman said, "not that it's ever worried me." But he added, "Maybe there's more to it than . . . I've found."[51]

When Haldeman left, Nixon called Dean on the telephone. Dean said he wanted to give the President a full report, because "I don't think—we have never really done that. It has been sort of bits and pieces. Just paint the whole picture for you, the soft spots, the potential problem areas."

They agreed to meet the following morning, alone, at 10 A.M.

Nixon wondered if Dean could make a report, even if just an oral report, to the Cabinet. Dean was hesitant. Nixon asked if he thought they should just continue to stonewall. Dean said yes. Couldn't Dean make "even a general statement that I could put out," Nixon persisted. Dean wanted to talk to him first. Nixon suggested that he make "a complete statement, but make it very incomplete." Dean wanted to talk first.[52]

Before going to bed, Nixon made a diary entry. He concluded with a succinct summary of dozens of hours of conversations over the past three weeks with Haldeman and Dean: "We are really caught here without really knowing how to handle it."[53]

CHAPTER FOUR

A CANCER
CLOSE TO
THE PRESIDENCY
March 21–April 14, 1973

WHEN ONE STUDIES the transcripts of the conversations between Nixon and Haldeman, Dean, Ehrlichman, Colson, and Mitchell in March and April 1973, one of the things that stands out is the amount of dissembling that went on. Nixon would ask questions to which he already knew the answers, pretend to a surprise that was pure acting, or display outrage or incredulity that covered guilt. When John Dean reported to Nixon at 10 A.M. on March 21, for example, he thought he was giving him new information. Only gradually did he realize that Nixon knew more than he did.

Nixon asked Dean for his judgment "as to where it stands, and where we go now."

Dean said the problem was serious. "We have a cancer—within, close to the Presidency, that's growing. It's growing daily. It's compounding, it grows geometrically now because it compounds itself."

That was a colorful opening, and an apt metaphor. Dean plunged on. The first problem was "we're being blackmailed," and the second was "people are going to start perjuring themselves very quickly." He added "there is no assurance . . ."

"That it won't bust," Nixon supplied.

"That, that [it] won't bust," Dean repeated.

Dean went on to give Nixon a history of the Liddy intelligence operation, starting in 1971 and covering Liddy, Mitchell, Magruder, Colson, Hunt, and Strachan. He said they had been getting information from the DNC bug that was given to Haldeman. Nixon asked if Haldeman had known where it was coming from. Dean professed not to know, but said that "at one point Bob even gave instructions to change their capabilities from Muskie to McGovern, and had passed this back through Strachan to Magruder . . . to Liddy."

Nixon supplied a piece of information on his own: "They had never bugged Muskie, though, did they?" No, Dean said, but they had infiltrated a secretary and a chauffeur into his camp.

Dean then gave Nixon some information that he assumed would be news to the President: "There was a plan to bug Larry O'Brien's suite down in Florida."

"Where'd you learn there was such a plan—from whom?" Nixon demanded hotly.

"Beg your pardon."

"Where did you learn of the plans to bug Larry O'Brien's suite?"

"From Magruder," Dean replied. "Long after the fact," he added.

"Oh," said the President, nonplussed. "Magruder. He knows?"

"Yeah, Magruder is totally knowledgeable on the whole thing."

That news startled the President and caused his concentration to wander. He lost track of where they were. Dean brought him back by confessing that he had known before the fact that Magruder intended to perjure himself before the grand jury.

What did Magruder tell the grand jury, Nixon asked. Dean replied that Magruder had said he did not know what Liddy was doing for CREEP, and that "we had no knowledge that he was going to bug the DNC."

"Well," the President said, "the point is, that's untrue."

"That's right," Dean agreed.

"Magruder did know," Nixon said.

Magruder did know, said Dean. In fact, he gave the order.

Dean plunged on with his history of the case. After the break-in, "I was under pretty clear instructions (laughs) not to really investigate this . . . and I worked on a theory of containment." With the help of Henry Petersen (head of the Criminal Division of the Justice Department), Dean continued, "I was totally aware of what the Bureau was doing at all times. I was totally aware of what the Grand Jury was doing."

Nixon was afraid that Petersen's cooperation with Dean might create some vulnerabilities; Petersen could be charged with not doing an adequate job. For example, why had he not called Haldeman or Colson before the grand jury?

Because, Dean explained, Magruder's perjured testimony gave Petersen no basis to pursue the White House aides. But there was another problem. Liddy and Hunt and the others had demanded money, and it had been paid.

"They put that under the cover of a Cuban Committee," Nixon pointed out. Dean was startled; he had no idea Nixon knew anything about the Cuban Committee (in fact, it was Nixon himself who had originally suggested that conduit, back in June of 1972). Nixon went on, "I would certainly keep that (laughs), that cover for whatever it's worth. Keep the [Cuban] Committee."

Dean was troubled by that order. "That's the most troublesome post-thing," he said, "because (1) Bob is involved in that; John is involved in that; I'm involved in that; Mitchell is involved in that. And that's an obstruction of justice."

How was Haldeman involved, Nixon asked.

Dean explained that the money that went to Hunt and Liddy came from the $350,000 that Haldeman had kept in a safe in the White House—the money that Haldeman had told Nixon the previous afternoon he had returned intact to CREEP. Dean said he had explained to Haldeman what he needed the money for, and Ehrlichman had been involved, and that they all had felt "that there was no price too high to pay to let this thing blow up in front of the election."

More troubles: "This is going to be a continual blackmail operation by Hunt and Liddy and the Cubans." Further, McCord wanted com-mutation, and Colson had talked to Hunt about commutation, and these "are promises, they are commitments. They are the very sort of thing that the Senate is going to be looking most for." Dean hoped the Ervin Committee would not find out. Nixon said that it would be "pretty hard" to uncover because it was all in cash.

More troubles: Dean said that Hunt wanted another $120,000, and he wanted it "by the close of business yesterday." He threatened if he did not get the money, he would bring John Ehrlichman "down to his knees and put him in jail."

The President supposed that threat related to Ellsberg's doctor.

"Ellsberg, and apparently some other things," Dean said.

"I don't know about anything else," Nixon declared.

"I don't either," Dean said, "and I (laughs) hate to learn some of these things."

Nixon pointed out that commutation for Hunt could be based on compassion, because of his wife's death. He admitted that he had dis-cussed commutation on that basis, "and that is the only discussion I ever had in that light" (which was not true—he had discussed clemency for Hunt with Colson and with Ehrlichman in the summer of 1972, and with Colson in January 1973).

Back to the money. Dean said Mitchell was raising funds, because "he's one of the ones with the most to lose."

Nixon cut him off. "How much money do you need?" he asked bluntly.

Dean thought it would cost a million dollars over the next two years.

"We could get that," Nixon stated flatly.

Dean muttered something unintelligible.

"What I mean is," Nixon went on, "you could get a million dollars.

And you could get it in cash. I, I know where it could be gotten." The real problem, he said, was "who the hell would handle it?" He wondered if Dean had any ideas on that.

Mitchell could do it, said Dean.

Nixon thought it should be put through the Cuban Committee: "That would give a little bit of a cover."

Dean said almost anyone could blow at almost any moment. Nixon thought the immediate problem was Hunt, and he wanted it handled "damn soon. . . . You've got to keep the cap on the bottle that much—" Dean agreed.

Nixon was caught in a classic dilemma. His close and continuing involvement in the payment of hush money was making him increasingly vulnerable to charges of obstruction of justice; but the alternative, telling Hunt to go to hell, was too dangerous. The blackmail had to be paid, and Nixon had to stay involved, to guide his aides, to give them orders, to tell them where and how to raise the money.

Because of the Ellsberg and DNC break-ins, because of the attempt to use the CIA to divert the FBI from the investigation, because of the payment of hush money, Nixon and his closest aides all had vulnerabilities that were causing each of them to start looking out for himself. Dean put it bluntly: "Everybody is now starting to watch out for their own behind. . . . They're getting their own counsel. . . . 'How do I protect my ass?' They're scared and that's bad."

Or, as Nixon put it in his diary entry that night, "It will be each man for himself, and one will not be afraid to rat on the other."

The "every man for himself" atmosphere created another problem; in their conversations with each other, the participants lied, dissembled, pretended. They had a vested interest in hiding what they knew while trying to ferret out what the other guy knew. Thus Dean told Nixon he wanted to meet with Mitchell, Haldeman, and Ehrlichman "to figure out how this can be carved away from you, so it does not damage you or the Presidency. 'Cause it just can't. It's . . . not something you are involved in."

"That is true," Nixon said untruthfully.

"I know, sir, it is," Dean went on. "Well, I can just tell from our conversations that, you know, these are things that you have no knowledge of." In fact, as Dean later made clear in his memoirs, the opposite was the case; throughout this March 21 conversation he was startled to find that on detail after detail, Nixon knew more than he did.

Nixon returned to his idea of issuing a statement, going the hangout route. Dean remained hesitant, but he did have an idea. It was to persuade Judge Sirica to delay sentencing for a couple of weeks, meanwhile convening a new grand jury, and sending Magruder and others to testify before it after they had been granted immunity. They could then tell the truth. Of course, the problem with that route was, as Dean said, "some people are going to have to go to jail."

"Who?"

Me, for one, said Dean.

Nixon could not see that. Dean explained that he was vulnerable to an obstruction of justice charge. Why? Nixon asked. Because of the payment of blackmail, Dean said.

"Well," the President went on, "I wonder if that part of it can't be—" After a pause, he plunged: "I wonder if that doesn't— let me put it frankly, I wonder if that doesn't have to be continued?"

Dean cleared his throat but did not speak.

"Let me put it this way," Nixon continued, "let us suppose that you get, you get the million bucks and you get the proper way to handle it, and you could hold that side. It would seem to me that would be worthwhile."

Dean cleared his throat again. Nixon admitted there was another problem, Hunt and his demand for clemency. Dean said the others would be demanding clemency, too, so Nixon was just in an untenable position, because "politically it'd be impossible for, you know, you to do it. . . . I'm not sure that you will ever be able to deliver on the clemency."

Nixon said he could not do it until after the 1974 elections, "that's for sure. But even then your point is that even then you couldn't do it."

"That's right," Dean replied. "It may further involve you in a way you shouldn't be involved in this."

"No it's wrong," Nixon agreed, "that's for sure." Whether he meant it was morally wrong, politically wrong, illegal, wrong because of the time, or just not doable, is unclear.

Back to the question of who was in danger of going to jail. Dean said Ehrlichman was another, because of the Ellsberg break-in. Nixon cut him short to return to the blackmail: "Don't you agree that you'd better get the Hunt thing? I mean, that's worth it, at the moment."

Dean did agree. He brought the conversation back to vulnerabilities. Haldeman could go to jail, he warned.

Nixon shook that off and returned to Hunt. He said that if Hunt did not get his hush money, he would blow, and Haldeman and Ehrlichman and Dean and others would be indicted for sure. In Nixon's judgment, "it's better to fight it out instead." No testimony, no cooperation, no nothing. Then he had second thoughts: "On the other hand, we realize that we have these weaknesses—that, uh, (pause) we've got this weakness in terms of (pause) blackmail."

Dean repeated the obvious; one alternative was to "cut the losses" via the hang-out route, and "the other is to go (cough) down the road, just hunker down, fight it at every corner, every turn, uh, don't let people testify, cover it up is what we're really talking about."

"And just take the heat," Nixon said. A moment later, Nixon told Dean to make some kind of general statement. He wanted Dean to say that Haldeman was not involved, Ehrlichman was not involved, Mitchell was not involved.

Dean said he could do that, but then what about clemency for Hunt and his team?

At that moment, Haldeman came into the Oval Office, in response to Nixon's buzz. Nixon summarized the conversation for him, then got down to the immediate time bomb, Hunt's demand for $120,000 by the close of business yesterday. Nixon told Haldeman getting the money was no problem: "I mean, it's not easy to deliver, but it is easy to get." But paying blackmail meant that "in the end, we are going to be bled to death, and it's all going to come out anyway, and then you get the worst of both worlds. We are going to lose and we're going to look like we covered up."

So paying more blackmail was out of the question, Nixon said. The alternative was to face up to the cost of telling the truth: men would have to go to jail. Nixon said that by all means Haldeman, Dean, Ehrlichman, Mitchell, Chapin, and Strachan had to be protected.

"And Magruder," Haldeman said, "if you can. But that's the one you pretty much have to give up."

But, Nixon pointed out, "if Magruder goes down, he'll pull everybody with him." Haldeman acknowledged that was probable. "I don't think he wants to," Haldeman added, "but I don't think he is able not to."

So it was back to blackmail. Nixon said it would take a million dollars "to take care of the jackasses that are in jail. That could be, that could be arranged."

Dean thought continuing to pay blackmail was "our greatest jeopardy." Haldeman agreed. Nixon brushed them off: "No problem, we could, we could get the money. . . . Mitchell could provide the way to deliver it." The problem was the clemency Colson had promised Hunt.

Haldeman said that paying out the blackmail was a problem, that Mitchell did not want to be involved, that no one in the White House could be involved. But Dean made it clear that they already were involved, that the $350,000 Haldeman had given to Fred LaRue at Dean's insistence had been paid out to Hunt and the others.

Well, Nixon said, "our cover there is just going to be the Cuban Committee did this for them up through the election."

"Well, yeah," Dean said, "we can put that together. That isn't, of course, quite the way it happened."

"I know," Nixon said, "but it's the way it's going to have to happen." That might be called a revisionist approach to history.

They discussed the idea of a new grand jury, with immunity for White House staffers. As so often happened in these conversations about the options, Nixon grew enthusiastic. He convinced himself he had found a way out of the maze. Then he suddenly realized it would not work at all. In this case, a grand jury down the road would do nothing to meet Hunt's demand "as of the close of business yesterday."

The "immediate thing," Nixon concluded, "you've got no choice with Hunt but the hundred and twenty or whatever it is. Right?"

Dean agreed.

Nixon went on, "You better damn well get that done, but fast."

"We've got to act," the President continued. Indeed, they had to. But where and how? Neither Dean nor Haldeman wanted anything to do with paying more blackmail.

The grand jury idea, Nixon finally recognized, was no good. A new grand jury would call Mitchell. "God we can't risk that," Nixon said, "I mean, uh, all sorts of shit'll break loose there." (Nixon was speaking on the assumption that John Mitchell was the guilty man. On February 14, he had asked Ehrlichman, "Who the hell else perjured himself? Did Mitchell?" Ehrlichman replied, "I assume so." That same day he had heard Colson say, "I am sure he [Mitchell] knew about it," and had replied, "He had to know about it." Colson had tried to reassure the President: "John [Mitchell] has the most marvelous and convenient memory." Nixon explained to Kleindienst on February 23 his stance on what happened. Mitchell, Nixon said, "had a horrible domestic problem. Martha was very sick. And John wasn't paying any attention and these kids ran away with it. Now that's the line I've taken and that's the one I want you to take. John Mitchell is a pure, bright guy who would never done such a thing, that the kids ran away with it. And if John did lie, it was simply because he'd forgotten.")

They could not just "hunker down and fight it," Nixon realized, because for sure something would break soon, and as Nixon put it, "when it breaks it'll look like the President—"

"Is covering up," Dean supplied.

Nixon turned to Dean. "John," he said, "you had the right plan . . . before the election. And you handled it just right. You contained it. Now after the election we've got to have another plan, because we can't have, for four years, we can't have this thing."[1]

So, after a two-hour discussion in which not one of the options considered could withstand scrutiny, Nixon concluded by telling Dean to come up with a plan.

The fact was, they were helpless. It was the damnedest thing. This conversation took place in the Oval Office. On Nixon's desk there was a red telephone that dramatically signified his awesome power. But he could not manage to wriggle out of the consequences of a simple break-in in which no weapons were used, no one got hurt, nothing was stolen.

It is a wonderful thing to see the American system of justice at work here. The President appointed and could fire the Attorney General and all other high officials in the Justice Department, but he could not control them. He could not control a grand jury. He could not control or even influence a judge, Sirica, appointed by Eisenhower. He could not get the CIA to lie for him, or the FBI to drop its investigation. He could not control the Congress, and once the Ervin Committee got its hearings under way, he knew it would reveal more dirty tricks, more espionage, more break-ins, more criminal acts—and he could do nothing at all to stop it.

Helpless. The President of the United States and his closest advisers were helpless. Nixon, Dean, and Haldeman conjure up the image of three men in a lifeboat, in the middle of the Atlantic, without sails, paddles, or a motor, no food, no water, no ship in sight, with a storm on the horizon headed toward them, discussing their options.

THAT afternoon, Nixon called his secretary, Rose Mary Woods, to ask if they had any unused campaign funds in hand. Woods said there was $100,000 available (the source of that money is a mystery; it may have come in cash from Howard Hughes, via Nixon's friend Bebe Rebozo). Nixon then buzzed for Haldeman and said the money was available. Haldeman, however, rejected the idea of handing it over to Hunt. "You should stay out of this," he told Nixon. [2]

At 5:20 P.M., March 21, Nixon met with Ehrlichman, Haldeman, and Dean. They were still drifting; as Ehrlichman put it to open the meeting, "Well, you go round and round and you come up with all questions and no answers. Backed up where you were at when you started."

Or as Nixon put it, "Does anybody really think, really think that really we should do nothing? That's the other, I mean, that's the option, period."

Then Nixon trotted out the idea of appointing a "Presidential Panel" to look into the whole Watergate mess. That idea quickly sank of its own weight.

Resignedly, Nixon sighed, "we can't do a damned thing about the participants, who would get it eventually, (unintelligible) why not now?"

Then he caught himself: "We can't, we can't harm the, these young people, I mean I'm damned concerned about all these people that were all working in the White House. . . . Whatever they considered to be the best interests of the country, and so forth."

Haldeman chipped in with a comment that this wasn't a case of "some guy stashing money in his pocket."

Nixon pointed out, "It isn't something, it isn't, it isn't something like Hiss, for example, God-damned treason."

"Or like Sherman Adams," Haldeman added, "or Albert Fall [of Teapot Dome], doing it for his own enrichment."

"That's right," Nixon heartily agreed. "That's the point. That's why I say I'm, I'm going to take a lot of the heat." He coughed, thought about what he had just said, and went on, "Well, we have to realize that, uh, the attrition is going to be rather considerable."

Nixon then returned to his idea about a statement from Dean. "I don't want to get all that God-damned specific," he said, but he did want Dean to report to him that "your investigation indicates that this man did not do it, this man did not do it, this man did not do that."

Then who did? That question brought them right back to whom to sacrifice among all those fine young men who had done what they did for the good of the country.

The problem was, Dean said, none of those present knew criminal law well enough to know who was liable for what. He suggested bringing in Henry Petersen to find out. They could keep it hypothetical. Haldeman suggested that Dean tell Petersen, "you've got, you've got this brother-in-law who has this problem in school," or, "my friend is writing a play."

The obvious trouble with telling Petersen everything they had done, from the Segretti dirty tricks through the Ellsberg break-in to the payment of hush money, was that Petersen would walk out of there and indict every one of them. That option, too, sunk of its own weight.[3]

After the meeting broke up, having reached no conclusions, much less a solution, Nixon called Colson on the telephone to ask if he had any ideas on what to do next. Colson did not.[4] Or, as Nixon put it in his memoirs, "Our strategy sessions were just frustrating and inefficient minuets around the problem."

Dean called Mitchell in New York. He had to talk in code because he heard another receiver being picked up and assumed that Martha Mitchell was listening in. "Did you talk to the Greek?" Dean asked Mitchell, referring to a businessman and contributor of Greek origin.

"Yes I have," Mitchell replied.

"Is the Greek bearing gifts?" Dean asked.

"Well, I'm gonna call you tomorrow on that," Mitchell replied.[5]

And thus ended the first day of spring 1973.

AT 9:11 A.M. on March 22, Haldeman met with Nixon to lay out the whole convoluted story of the payment of the $350,000 to the burglars. Nixon pretended to be unaware of what had happened with the money, although John Dean had just gone through the same story with him the day before. Haldeman's version was that Mitchell told him to use the $350,000, but that he, Haldeman, instead offered to return it to CREEP (he had earlier told Nixon that he *had* returned the money to CREEP).

But Mitchell would not take it back. So Dean told Strachan to give the money to LaRue, who gave it to Hunt.

Nixon and Haldeman agreed that this posed no problem for the White House, as the money was not campaign funds and anyway belonged to CREEP. Besides, as Nixon said, "God damn it, the people are in jail, it's only right to raise the money for them. . . . There's got to be funds. I'm not being, I don't mean to be blackmailed by Hunt, that goes too far, but we're taking care of these people that are in jail.

"My God, they did this for [us]—we're sorry for them."

Nixon could see no obstruction of justice in that. Neither could Haldeman. "When a guy goes and pleads guilty," Haldeman pointed out, "are you obstructing justice?"

That problem apparently settled, they turned to the Ellsberg affair. Ehrlichman had warned the previous day that the break-in to Dr. Lewis Fielding's office in Los Angeles by Liddy and Hunt was an "illegal search and seizure" which, if disclosed, would be "sufficient at least [to declare] a mistrial" in Ellsberg's trial, then going on in Los Angeles. (Ellsberg was being tried for the theft of the so-called Pentagon Papers in 1971.)

Haldeman again explained to Nixon the origins of the Fielding break-in. Nixon, in an innocent voice, asked, "What was the purpose of it though?" To discredit Ellsberg, Haldeman answered.

Why not use the FBI or the CIA, Nixon asked.

"Because things were leaking from all over," Haldeman explained.

Nixon picked up on that line, saying, "It had to be done independently [i.e., by Liddy and Hunt] because of the possibility of leakage." So the cover was national security. Haldeman expressed a doubt "whether that'll hold up. (Unintelligible) that doesn't make it legal."

They went on to other problems. Haldeman said that Dean was now recommending that they "circle the wagons" around the White House, meaning protecting the White House staff at the expense of CREEP people, first of all Magruder and Mitchell. Nixon indicated that needed some thought, and Haldeman left the office.[6]

Mitchell, meanwhile, had arrived from New York. He went straight to Haldeman's office, where the two men were joined by Dean and Ehrlichman. Mitchell said that Hunt's demand for money had been met, although not the entire $120,000; Fred LaRue had put $75,000 into a plain envelope and given it to a courier who had delivered it to Hunt's lawyer.[7]

At 1:57 P.M., the four men went over to the EOB to meet with Nixon in his small office there.

"Well, John, how are you?" Nixon greeted Mitchell.

"Mr. President, I am just great."

"You're a big Wall Street lawyer," Nixon said cheerfully. "You do have to admit you're rich."

"Not in front of all these people who help collect taxes," Mitchell responded. "But I can report that the firm is doing quite well."

Ehrlichman relayed some news; at the Gray confirmation hearings that morning, Gray had testified that Dean had lied to him when asked if Hunt had an office in the White House. Haldeman warned that the next day's headline would be GRAY SAYS DEAN LIES. (He got it right. It is one of the features of these Watergate conversations that the participants so often could predict the next day's headline, or even the headlines that were weeks away. They knew what was coming down on them, but they could not stop the process.)

Nixon kept clinging to a possible statement in the form of a report to him by Dean. He thought it might be sufficient to satisfy the Ervin Committee, but it was also clear that he wanted a document in hand that cleared the President of any wrongdoing, a document that would allow him to say later, after the Ervin Committee made its discoveries, that all he had ever known was what was in the Dean Report.

For such obvious reasons as his own involvement in the cover-up through the payment of hush money, the destruction of materials from Hunt's White House safe, and so on, Dean did not want to write a report. But Nixon ordered him to go up to Camp David on Saturday and do it. Then he turned to what he wanted in the report, starting a general discussion of how much could be admitted and to whom. Mitchell liked the idea of going before a grand jury, with immunity, or going before the Ervin Committee if it agreed to hear testimony from White House personnel in secret, executive sessions.

Well, Nixon asked no one in particular, "You think we want to go this route now, the—let it hang out, so to speak?"

Dean said, "It isn't really that—"

Haldeman cut in: "It's a limited hang out."

Dean repeated that line.

Someone else said, "It's a modified limited hang out."

Nixon said, "Well, it's only the question of the thing hanging out publicly or privately."

Dean said it would get the President "up above and away from it, and that's the most important thing."

"Oh, I know," Nixon quickly agreed. "But I suggested that the other day and we all came down on . . . the negative on it. Now what's changed our mind?"

"The lack of alternatives, or a body," Dean said, laughing.

There were guffaws all around. "We went down every alley," Ehrlichman said, peering over his glasses at the others in a mock search for a volunteer. There was more laughter.

Nixon said that "at the very minimum we've got to have the statement . . . whatever the hell it is. If it opens up doors, it opens up doors, you know."

Ehrlichman tried another joke: "John [Mitchell] says he's sorry he sent those burglars in there, and that helps a lot."

"That's right," Nixon said.

Mitchell took his pipe from his mouth and bowed graciously: "You are very welcome, sir." More laughter.

"Just glad the others didn't get caught," Haldeman contributed.

"Yeah," Nixon added, "the ones we sent to Muskie and all the rest; Jackson, and Hubert, and, uh (unintelligible)."[8]

As the meeting broke up, Nixon asked Mitchell to stay behind. When they were alone, the President recalled Eisenhower's handling of the Sherman Adams case. He said it was a "very cruel thing," Ike's forcing Adams to resign. "And, uh, for that reason, I am perfectly willing to—I don't give a shit what happens. I want you all to stonewall it, let them plead the Fifth Amendment, cover-up or anything else, if it'll save it— save the plan. That's the whole point."

That emotional outburst over, the President had second thoughts. Perhaps he realized he did not have a plan to save. Perhaps he recalled that the tape recorder was running. Whatever his motive, he went on: "On the other hand, I would prefer, as I said to you, that you do it the other way"—meaning, presumably, the modified, limited hang-out route.

He returned to his feelings of sympathy and pain for the predicament Mitchell, Haldeman, Ehrlichman, and the others were in. "It's unfair," Nixon said. He again recalled Eisenhower and Adams. He said that all Ike cared about was "Christ, be sure he was clean. Both in fund thing [Nixon's 1952 "secret fund" that led to the Checkers speech] and the Adams thing. But I don't look at it that way. . . . We're going to protect our people, if we can."[9]

Thus ended the second day of spring 1973.

OVER the weekend, Nixon went down to Key Biscayne, accompanied by Haldeman, while Dean went up to Camp David. At Nixon's direction, Haldeman spent Saturday on the telephone, checking around the country. He talked to Dean, who said he was "concerned re his own ass." (Dean later wrote in his memoirs that it was while he was at Camp David that he decided he had to cooperate with the prosecutors. He therefore retained a criminal lawyer for himself.)

Haldeman checked with Colson; the President wanted to know exactly what Colson had promised Hunt. He also wanted to know if Colson had said, when pressing Hunt to get more information on O'Brien, that the pressure was coming from the President or from Haldeman. Colson assured Haldeman he had not been specific in promising clemency; he had only pointed out that Christmas was the customary time for presidential mercy. On the question of pressing Hunt for more information (which was what led to the break-in in the DNC), Colson claimed that there, too, he had not been specific.

Nixon made two calls of his own that day, to Dean. They were not taped, but ten weeks later Nixon discussed the conversations with Haldeman. By that time, June 4, Nixon was worried about what he might have said. "Suppose I said," he asked Haldeman, 'Well, listen, I understand Bittman's [Hunt's lawyer] taken care of.' "

Haldeman thought that unlikely.

"I might have mentioned that," Nixon persisted, "because I was concerned about it, you know. About whether, uh, Bittman had, uh . . ."

"Yeah," Haldeman said knowingly.

" . . . was gonna blow," Nixon went on. "Not because of Watergate, because he was going to blow on, uh . . ."

"On the other project," Haldeman supplied.

"Yes, that's right."

The "other project" was probably Nixon's call to Dean in reference to the Ellsberg break-in. But Nixon's main point was to check on whether or not Hunt had received his money; Dean had evidently told the President that he had.[10]

Reassured on those vulnerabilities, on March 24 Nixon made some decisions. One was to abandon Gray (although that same day his press spokesman Gerald Warren told the reporters that Nixon had "no intention" of withdrawing Gray's nomination). Haldeman's notes for the day conclude: "Need statement from Dean to cover Cab and Ldrs [in Congress] must assure them P and WH not involved and doing all we can to cooperate. Have to say P. not involved. WH staff and we are vigorously [investigating]."[11]

Back in Washington, there were dramatic developments. Judge Sirica had handed down his sentences the day before, and they were even worse than Nixon had feared they might be. Hunt got thirty-five years, the Cubans got forty years each, and Liddy got twenty years. Sirica recommended that the guilty men cooperate with the federal grand jury, and added that "should you decide to speak freely I would have to weigh that factor in appraising what sentence will be finally imposed in each case." Worse, McCord already had handed Sirica a letter, which was the headline event, because in it McCord said that he and his team had been under "political pressure to plead guilty and remain silent." He said he feared for his life.[12]

Nixon had then called Dean on the telephone for information. How much did McCord know? How badly could he hurt them?

Not much, Dean assured him.[13]

Nixon had Haldeman call Bill Rogers. It was Rogers to whom Nixon had turned back in 1952, at the time of the fund crisis; it was Rogers to whom Nixon had turned back in 1956, at the time of Eisenhower's heart attack. Now he turned to him again.

Rogers's advice was to let it hang out, "whatever the consequences." The Secretary of State knew it would "really be rough," especially if Mitchell was involved, but it had to be done. No executive privilege. No more cover-up. "The best thing is to go ahead, get it out and in the open, let whoever has to, take the lumps."[14]

Over the next few days, Haldeman continued his research into the recent past, trying to figure out who knew what, who had said what to whom, where the vulnerabilities were. Meanwhile McCord testified before Sam Dash, chief counsel for the Ervin Committee, where he named names, while Hunt testified before the federal grand jury. Liddy took the Fifth Amendment before the grand jury. Nixon announced his "absolute and total confidence" in John Dean. Senator Lowell Weicker (R.-Conn.), one of the Republican minority on the Ervin Committee, said he had "always been convinced" that higher-ups in the White House had known about the Watergate break-in, although he had "complete faith" in Nixon's innocence.[15]

WHILE all this bad news was being broadcast, Nixon got an unexpected but very welcome boost from a column by the dean of American newspaper commentators, Walter Lippmann, in—of all places—*The Washington Post*. Lippmann took a long view. He gave Nixon high marks for carrying out the historically necessary, albeit disagreeable, role of having to "liquidate, defuse, deflate the exaggerations of the romantic period of U.S. imperialism and inflation." He contrasted Nixon's realism in foreign affairs and in domestic policy with George McGovern, whom Lippmann saw as the "representative of the unsound Jacobin or Rousseauistic philosophy that man is by nature good and can be made perfect by making the environment perfect."

Nixon commented: "Buchanan—a wise observation."[16]

Three days later, on March 29, Nixon spoke to the nation on television and over the radio from the Oval Office. It was the twelfth time he had spoken on the situation in Vietnam from that room, and it was the most satisfactory one, because he could report that "for the first time in 12 years, no American military forces are in Vietnam. All our American POW's are on their way home. The 17 million people of South Vietnam have the right to choose their own government without outside interference, and because of our program of Vietnamization, they have the strength to defend that right. We have prevented the imposition of a Communist government by force on South Vietnam."

He gave generous thanks to the men of the American armed forces who had made this outcome possible: "Never have men served with greater devotion abroad with less apparent support at home." He called on the nation to provide the veterans with benefits and job opportunities. "Let us honor them with the respect they deserve." As to those who left the country to avoid the draft, Nixon was uncompromising: "Let us not dishonor those who served their country by granting amnesty to those who deserted America."

He recalled all the tough decisions he had had to make, including the April 1970 incursion into Cambodia, the May 1972 bombing of Hanoi, and the hardest of all, the December 18, 1972, decision to order more air strikes against Hanoi. On each occasion, Nixon reminded his audience, the voices of opposition were so loud "they seemed at times to be the majority." But the true majority "stood firm against those who advocated peace at any price." Nixon said that because the people stood firm, former POW Air Force Lieutenant Colonel George McKnight had been able to say to him, "Thank you for bringing us home on our feet instead of on our knees."

Turning to the more general themes of his record in foreign affairs, Nixon spoke of the new relationship with China, of SALT I, and other gains. Then he took up the question, "In view of all this progress toward peace, why not cut our defense budget?" Because, he explained, he intended in 1973 to move forward on SALT II and on mutual reduction of conventional forces in Europe, and "if we cut our defenses before negotiations begin, any incentive for other nations to cut theirs will go right out the window."

A strong America was necessary to world peace. Nixon warned that "the pages of history are strewn with the wreckage of nations which fell by the wayside at the height of their strength and wealth because their people became weak, soft, and self-indulgent and lost the character and the spirit which had led to their greatness." He said he was determined that would not happen to America.

On the domestic front, meanwhile, Nixon said that his wage and price controls had cut the rate of inflation in half, but there were dangers it might start to soar again. Meat prices, for example, had shot up recently. To help housewives meet their budget, Nixon said he was lifting import controls on meat and imposing price ceilings on beef, pork, and lamb.

Nixon balanced that very un-Republican action with a strong defense of a traditional Republican position, holding down the overall federal budget. He said that despite the increases he had already approved in social programs, some congressmen wanted to spend even more. If they had their way, the tax bill to the American people would go up 15 percent. He urged his listeners to write their congressmen to protest. "This is not a battle between Congress and the President," he said. "It is your battle. It is your money, your prices, your taxes I am trying to save."

He concluded with a personal story. A few days ago, he said, he had talked to Air Force Colonel Robinson Risner, who had been a POW for almost eight years and spent four of those years in solitary confinement. Nixon said he had asked Risner how he was able to survive it and come home, standing tall and proud, saluting the American flag. Risner had paused before speaking: " 'It is difficult for me to answer. I am not very good at words. All I can say is that it was faith—faith in God and faith in my country.' "

If the people would met the great challenges of peace with this kind of faith, Nixon predicted, "then one day it will be written: This was America's finest hour."[17]

IT was a strong, effective, boastful speech. Nixon's pride was pardonable; he had accomplished goals that had eluded his predecessors. But the following morning, his address had to compete for the headlines with James McCord, who had told Senate investigators under oath that Hunt and Liddy had assured him the break-in had been cleared with Mitchell, Dean, Haldeman, Colson, and other higher-ups.[18]

Nixon spent most of his time that week on Watergate. In a two-and-a-half-hour conversation with Haldeman, Ehrlichman, and Ziegler, Nixon went round and round on the same questions, exploring the same non-existent options. Who knew about the bugging in advance? Haldeman said Dean believed that Mitchell had ordered it. Nixon could not believe that. He was suspicious of Colson. How badly had Magruder perjured himself? Badly. What about a new grand jury? What about a Presidential Panel, one that could drag out its investigation past the 1974 elections? What about a hang-out? What about a pardon? Or clemency? How dangerous was McCord?

Nixon provided an analogy to put it in perspective: "Let me tell you something. I have been wanting to tell you this for some time. . . . Chambers told the truth, but he was an informer. . . . Hiss was destroyed because he lied—perjury. Chambers was destroyed because he was an informer." Nixon did not explain how that got them anywhere with their problem.

Who to sacrifice? Magruder was the obvious offering, but what if he brought Mitchell down with him? Why not sacrifice Mitchell? For the obvious reason that he was hardly likely to go to prison alone, and he could bring those in the room along with him. What about firing Kleindienst? Nixon thought it better to wait a while before doing that. Instead, he wanted Ehrlichman to put pressure on Kleindienst to let the White House know what Hunt was telling the grand jury.

What about the President going to see Sirica? Too dangerous. Still Nixon was drawn to the idea. "I think the damn thing is going to come out anyway," he said, "and I think you better cut the losses now and just better get it over much sooner and frankly sharper. Let's just say, 'Well, Judge, let's go.' "

Haldeman was unhappy: "How come all the rush now?" He warned that Sirica would want a special prosecutor.

Perhaps that was best, Nixon thought, since Kleindienst would make the appointment. He ordered Ehrlichman to go to work on the Attorney General, both to report on what was being said to the grand jury and to get going on a special prosecutor.[19]

At noon on March 30, Nixon met with Ziegler and Ehrlichman. By now, it was obvious there never was going to be a Dean statement; far from working to protect the President, Dean was working to protect himself. He was recommending that Nixon and his top aides do as he had done and retain criminal lawyers, and had told Haldeman that his own lawyer, Charles Shaffer, had advised him not to write anything down.[20] So Nixon told Ziegler to prepare a Ziegler statement. It should say that "every member of the White House staff has submitted a sworn affidavit to me denying any involvement."

No, Ehrlichman said, we can't do that.

Nixon then decided to waive executive privilege for his staff to appear before the grand jury. In announcing this decision, Ziegler should add, "It is not the objective of the White House to cover up this matter." Nixon went on: "This is totally true—uh—er—untrue."

Then Nixon repeated once more his standing orders that his aides go back to *Six Crises* and read about the Hiss case. He specifically wanted them to go over Nixon's own interrogation of Hiss and Chambers.[21]

This suggestion distressed the aides. Nixon seemed not to recognize that in the Hiss case he had been the prosecutor/investigator, while in the Watergate matter he was the one on the defense, nor that the plain lesson of the Hiss case was that when the opposition controls the Congress, even the President cannot cover up. It gave the aides a sinking feeling in the pit of their stomachs to realize that Nixon would have loved to have been on the prosecuting/investigating side of Watergate. They knew that someone with his skills, armed with the power of subpoena, would have destroyed their woefully disorganized and badly managed defense without difficulty. They also knew that there were Democrats on the Ervin Committee who were almost as ruthless, skilled, and eager to attack as Nixon had been back in 1948.

Ziegler marched out to the press room, where he declared that "no one in the White House had any involvement or prior knowledge of the Watergate event." He then announced that to "dispel the myth . . . that we seek to cover up," the President had directed members of his staff to testify before the grand jury. He claimed this was a "re-statement of a policy which has been in effect." Finally, he announced that the White House was prepared to negotiate with the Senate Select Committee to find some procedure whereby White House staffers could provide testimony "other than in writing" about Watergate.[22]

That afternoon, Nixon flew to San Clemente, where he was scheduled to meet with President Thieu early the next week. Aboard *Air Force One*, Nixon called Haldeman and Ehrlichman forward to his cabin. The President said he had lost confidence in Dean and wanted Ehrlichman to take responsibility for finding out what had happened and to make a damage assessment. In effect, Nixon now wanted an Ehrlichman report.

Ehrlichman feared that doing so would create a document that could be subject to subpoena and thereby put him in legal jeopardy. He therefore asked Nixon to sign a memo ordering him to conduct a fact-finding investigation, so as to create an attorney-client relationship that would protect him. Nixon signed.[23]

NIXON'S flight to San Clemente allowed him to escape the atmosphere in Washington. The meeting with Thieu should have helped divert attention from Watergate, but things did not work out that way. In the first place, continuing leaks from McCord's secret testimony to Sam Dash dominated the headlines. And the Republican senators were growing restive. Senator Robert Packwood (R.-Ore.) had said that Watergate was a "dagger in the heart" of the Republican Party and had called on Nixon to tell the truth. Senator Jacob Javits (R.-N.Y.) echoed that call.[24] And the Thieu meeting failed to produce any real news.

In February, when the POWs had begun coming home, Vietnam was the one bright spot in Nixon's life. By the end of March, even Vietnam was a source of bad news. Fighting had continued in Laos and Cambodia, where the trucks were lined up bumper-to-bumper headed south on the Ho Chi Minh Trail. Kissinger, who had persuaded the press that he had opposed the Christmas bombing, urged Nixon to resume bombing. On March 6, Nixon had given an order for a one-day strike against the Communist infiltration route. He then changed his mind and canceled it the next day, explaining that he did not want to give Hanoi an excuse to delay or stop the return of the remaining prisoners.[25] Such back-and-forthing continued through March.

Peace with honor was endangered. The most dramatic evidence of this was Nixon's decision against meeting Thieu at the White House. The President feared demonstrations but also the distinct possibility that he could not round up enough dignitaries to attend a state dinner. He had opted instead for a small, informal gathering at San Clemente.

In a private meeting, Thieu gave Nixon some details of Communist violations of the agreement. Nixon assured him that the United States would resist blatant violations by force, but Thieu thought the President seemed "preoccupied and absent-minded." They discussed American economic aid for South Vietnam, but as Kissinger noted, the talk had a "slightly unreal quality" because it was obvious that congressional support for such aid "was eroding fast." Nixon did assure Thieu, "You can count on us." But he put his main emphasis on the need for Thieu to lean over backward to carry out his obligations under the provisions of the cease-fire agreement.[26]

Thieu left as he had arrived, without fanfare. He flew to Washington, where Vice President Agnew met him, accompanied by only one Cabinet member, the Secretary of Labor. All the others had found an excuse to skip the arrival ceremony. Kissinger observed that this "was a shaming experience."[27]

Peace with honor had been replaced by embarrassment. Nixon could not make good on his promises of continued aid to South Vietnam, or on a return to bombing if Hanoi undertook another offensive, or on reconstruction aid for North Vietnam. Thieu and his supporters in Saigon were on their own. They no longer mattered to the Americans.

BACK in San Clemente, Thieu's departure brought Watergate to the forefront again. Senator Lowell Weicker (R.-Conn.) helped propel it there, with a demand for Haldeman's resignation. Senator Ervin rejected Nixon's overture for informal testimony by White House aides with some colorful words. He said that "divine right went out with the American Revolution and doesn't belong to White House aides." They were not "royalty or nobility," and if they refused to abide by subpoenas, he intended to have them arrested and cited for contempt.[28]

Haldeman was beginning to bend with the pressure. He suggested to Nixon that he should make a clean breast of his own role in Watergate.

Nixon almost winced. "What do you mean?" he demanded.

"I want to step forward publicly and admit responsibility for Segretti, and my part in raising money for the defendants," Haldeman replied. He said he had already drawn up a statement and thought the best way to release it was to give it to Dan Rather at CBS News.

Nixon put up his hand. "No, Bob," he ordered. "Put *that* out of your mind."[29]

Nixon called Ehrlichman in to discuss Weicker's demand. The President told his two aides that they had to understand Haldeman could never resign. Nixon said Haldeman "is more important to me than Adams was to Eisenhower."[30]

Kissinger backed that up. He told Nixon he had to stick by Haldeman. Nixon wondered, "Suppose there is appearance of guilt?" Kissinger replied, "Even if he is guilty in part they are after him because they know he is the strong man in the administration. He is the most selfless, able person you've got, and you have got to have him."

Colson called to tell Nixon that he had evidence "that Mitchell may be trying to set up Haldeman as a scapegoat." John Connally told Nixon over the telephone that "somebody had to walk the plank." Connally warned Nixon that there were too many people isolating him from what was really going on—meaning, presumably, Haldeman and Mitchell.

Nixon swore to himself that he would have none of this. In his diary, he wrote: "I am not going to allow any of this division business to hurt any of our people. Everyone is going into business for himself for understandable reasons, but we're not going to let it go to the point that one destroys another."[31]

Nixon's resolve to stick by his men did not include Pat Gray. As Ehrlichman told Dean over the telephone, although Gray was still the nominee in name, in fact he was "twisting slowly, slowly in the wind," because the President had decided irrevocably to nominate someone else.[32] On April 5, Nixon had Haldeman call Gray to tell him to request to have his nomination withdrawn. Gray called back immediately and said he would. Nixon told him, "Nobody could feel worse about it than I do."[33]

At that moment, however, Ehrlichman was on the lawn outside La Casa Pacifica, talking to Federal District Judge Matthew Byrne of Los Angeles. Kleindienst had recommended Byrne for the FBI post. Ehrlichman told Byrne that the Gray nomination was being withdrawn, and that Nixon was thinking of nominating Byrne in his place. There was a certain delicacy to the conversation, because Byrne was the judge conducting the Ellsberg trial. Suspicious people might accuse Nixon of trying to influence the judge in a case in which the President had a passionate interest. Nevertheless, Byrne said he would like to be considered.[34]

At that point, Nixon walked out of the house, greeted Byrne, and shook his hand. The President was impressed by "his real steel-like handshake" and his "good tough, cold eyes." No promises were made; it was agreed that nothing could be done until the Ellsberg trial was over, and that could take another month.[35]

The following day, April 6, Gray announced he was withdrawing his name. Nixon called him on the telephone. The President expressed his sympathy, telling Gray, "You're an innocent victim, as we're all aware."

When he hung up, Nixon told Ehrlichman, "He's a broken man. But he wasn't a POW for seven years, was he? It's all relative, isn't it?"

Judge Byrne called Ehrlichman. Now that Gray had actually withdrawn, he wanted Ehrlichman to know of his *very* strong interest in the FBI post. They agreed that nothing could be done until the trial was concluded; Ehrlichman made the point that "a lot depended on what the verdict was." Byrne promised to keep him informed.[36]

ON April 7, Nixon flew back to Washington. In his diary, he chided himself for becoming "too depressed" and "obsessed" with Watergate. But he consoled himself with the thought that compared to the Vietnam War, "these problems do not appear all that difficult."[37] Yet although two and a half weeks had passed since Dean had warned him about the cancer on the Presidency, and although he had since then spent more than one hundred hours exploring options with his aides, aside from ordering Dean to make sure Hunt got his hush money, he had done nothing to deal with those problems.

On board *Air Force One*, he tried to act. He called Haldeman and Ehrlichman forward and instructed them to see Dean as soon as they landed and tell him he was free to testify before the grand jury but not before the Ervin Committee. Before anyone went to that committee, Nixon said, he wanted to strike a deal with Senator Ervin on the conditions under which they would testify.[38]

Unknown to Nixon, on the advice of his lawyer Dean was making arrangements to meet with the federal prosecutors. He intended to trade his information for immunity.

On April 11, Nixon met with Ziegler and Ehrlichman to discuss the prospect that the Ervin Committee would televise its hearings. That bothered Nixon deeply. He knew that without the rules of evidence that applied in a courtroom, the Democrats could use hearsay and innuendo to convict the White House before the television audience. He wanted Ehrlichman to meet with Senator Ervin and the senior Republican on the Committee, Howard Baker of Tennessee, to cut a deal. Nixon would allow his aides to testify if Ervin agreed "not to investigate the Presidency" and if he banned television cameras. Further, the Committee should ask its questions in an informal meeting at the Blair House. In addition, Nixon said that Haldeman should put out a statement, and that Dean should invoke executive privilege before the grand jury.

Ziegler pointed out that "if we cave in," it would make "the Senate look strong, the President weak." That always aroused Nixon, but neither he nor Ziegler could answer Ehrlichman's question: "How can we appear 'strong'?"

Ziegler returned to the old faithful solution: they should put out a statement, then stand on executive privilege, unless Ervin agreed to no television. The press secretary came up with a happy phrase: such a compromise would not be a cave-in, but would represent "peace with honor."

Nixon wondered who would make a statement, and got no answer. He remarked that John Connally had told him, "Do something!" What? No one knew, except that "a statement is a *must*."[39]

The following day, Nixon again talked to Connally. On April 13, he summarized the conversation for Ehrlichman: "Haldeman should take on the Ervin Committee, with no statement in advance. Don't do a Sherman Adams. Get a lawyer. [Remember], Ervin is the enemy. Fight them. Make them look bad. Haldeman be outraged."[40]

Ehrlichman met with Ervin and Baker. Ervin would not make a deal.[41] The TV cameras were going to cover his hearings.

Pressure was coming from another direction. On April 11, Senator Goldwater had said that Watergate was "beginning to smell like Teapot

Dome. I mean, there's smell to it. Let's get rid of the smell." He had added that he was getting calls from Republican friends around the country and they were saying, "No more money to the Republicans until this [is] cleared up." Anne Armstrong commented that Goldwater was "absolutely right." RNC Chairman George Bush called it a "grubby affair" that had to be cleaned up.[42]

Magruder, meanwhile, confessed to perjury, and told the prosecutors that Liddy, Dean, and Mitchell had prior knowledge of the break-in and had participated in the cover-up. Dean was telling them much the same.

So, three weeks after Dean described the cancer, it had indeed grown and compounded. As Nixon noted in his memoirs, in treating the disease, he and his aides had done "nothing more than stew and worry. . . ."[43] His one act, buying Hunt's silence, had done no good at all.

On April 14, at their early morning meeting, Nixon, Haldeman, and Ehrlichman discussed Magruder's testimony. They did not know exactly what he had said, but leaks made them fear the worst. Among other problems, they talked about Dean and the hush money. Their line was that the money was for legal fees and family support. Nixon admitted that "I heard something about that," but claimed it was "at a much later time. And, frankly, not knowing much about obstruction of justice, I thought it was perfectly proper."

The left-wingers always provided support for their people when they got into trouble, Ehrlichman pointed out.

Nixon enthusiastically agreed: "They take care of themselves. They raise—you remember the Scottsboro case? Christ. The Communist front raised a million dollars for the Scottsboro people. Nine hundred thousand went into the pockets of the Communists."

Haldeman laughed, and Nixon concluded, "so it's common practice."

Still Nixon worried. Later in the two-and-a-half-hour conversation he came back to the money that had gone to Hunt. He told his aides, "Dean, Dean, uh, Dean asked, told me about the problem of Hunt— this was a few weeks ago—needed, uh, needed sixty thousand or forty thousand dollars or something like that. You remember? He asked me about it and I said I, I don't know where you can get it. I said I would, uh, I mean, I frankly felt he might try to get it but I didn't know where."

Hardly a word in that paragraph was true, but when Nixon asked, "Am I correct?" Haldeman and Ehrlichman said he was. Of course, they had not been present at the Nixon-Dean March 21 conversation, but they did know that the next morning Mitchell had sent LaRue with the money for Hunt.

ONE of the challenges of reading the Watergate transcripts is trying to keep up with the daily reconstruction of history. These guys could move the pea under the walnut far faster than the human eye could follow. They invented motives for themselves, or presented the most self-serving rationalizations for what they had done and could not escape, or when they could get away with it simply lied. They were not writing a revisionist history, they were writing a Stalinist history.

On April 19, Nixon informed one of his lawyers, special counsel Richard Moore, of his March 21 meeting with Dean. According to Nixon, when Dean had said it would cost a million dollars to keep Hunt quiet, Nixon had replied, "You can't do that." He explained to Moore, "I wasn't prepared to pay any damn blackmail."

Once he got rolling, Nixon was unstoppable. In a rush of words, he gave Moore his version of what happened. "Matter of fact, it was that particular thing that really triggered me. I said, 'Jesus Christ, I mean, these guys are in something here that we gotta knock off,' because I knew—I said, 'Christ, you can't be paying blackmail for years for this sort of thing. It's ridiculous.' Ridiculous. I said 'John, John—how much is it gonna cost to keep on paying this money?' One million dollars? Outrageous, out of the question."

With each other, the Watergate conspirators could not tell such tall tales, because of prior knowledge. So they danced delicate minuets around each other. The day after Nixon talked with Moore, he discussed March 21 with Haldeman.

President: "The only thing that troubles me about this is my own recollection of that conversation, where you were here with him when he said that Bittman had stated that he needed money for Dean's attorney's fees at $40,000."

Haldeman: "I think—I can't figure out when that was and I can't find any notes on it." Then it came to him: "Well, you, you may have said something about, you know, well, you know when he said they had to have the money. You, you may have said something about, well, that we ought to be able to get."

Nixon cut him off: "We didn't, uh, you, uh, Dean, and uh, what . . . How did it eventually get back to Mitchell so that he did that?" Meaning, who called Mitchell and told him to get the money down to Washington in the morning?

"I don't know," Haldeman said.

"Well, Bob," Nixon pointed out, "you were in the room and Mitchell was there." Meaning the following morning, when Mitchell said the thing had been handled, Haldeman was present.

Haldemen insisted that nothing specific had been said. He reported that "Mitchell said to Dean, I'm not sure of the words, but in effect, what he'd done about the Hunt thing. And, uh, Mitchell says, 'Oh, I guess it's taken care of' and we just—nobody asked any more questions or, or gave any more answers. That was the extent of it and we assumed from that thing that Mitchell had it under control."

Nixon was bothered by the money raising part. "I guess we didn't know he [Mitchell] was doing that," Nixon said. He thought a second, then admitted, "Yes, I guess we did know it."

They needed each other. They drew together by agreeing to lie together. The question was, who triggered the pay-off by calling Mitchell? Was that call made after a meeting with the President? Was the pay-off then a result of Nixon's orders?

Nixon knew that was his great vulnerability. He told Haldeman, "March 21st, that is Dean's trump card, that's his trump card."

"No," Haldeman replied.

"You don't think that's his trump card?" Nixon asked incredulously. "What the hell do you think his trump card is?"

Returning to the problem area in March 21, Nixon guided Haldeman into a new version of what happened.

President: "Well, there's no action taken as far as we're concerned. That's the one thing. Right?"

Haldeman: "None."

President: "I don't know, either. Did he call Mitchell then or who did call him, John Ehrlichman?" [Moore had told Nixon the previous day that Dean had called Mitchell; Haldeman had just quoted what was said.]

Haldeman: "I don't know. I don't have any idea. I don't know that anybody did."

Throughout Watergate, Nixon complained that no one ever told him the truth. Throughout Watergate, Nixon coached his associates on the lies they would agree upon. As more information got out, these often changed. Keeping the eye on the pea as the walnuts flashed around was a challenge.[44]

THE discussion at the April 14 meeting turned to the fact that an investigator for the Senate Watergate committee named Harold Lipset had once pled guilty to a reduced charge in a wiretapping case and had received a suspended sentence. To Nixon, that was typical Democratic double standard. Mispronouncing the name, the President said, "You call my attention to the Lipschitz thing only I don't give a damn about the part of this with Hunt, Liddy, and the Cubans [unintelligible] are in this thing. It would be my [unintelligible] a reasonable time had expired after the thing [unintelligible] and before I leave office and they'll get off.

"You get them full pardons. That's what they have to have, John."

"Right," Ehrlichman replied.

"Do you agree?" asked the President.

"Yep, I sure do," said Ehrlichman.

More talk produced the conclusion that Mitchell had to be sacrificed. Who was going to tell him? They ran through a list of possibilities, and settled temporarily on Bill Rogers (although Nixon had doubts because "Mitchell hates Rogers"). They began making up speeches for Rogers to deliver to Mitchell.

Ehrlichman gave it a try. Rogers should say to Mitchell, "The jig is up. And the President strongly feels that the only way that this thing can end up being even a little net plus for the Administration and for the Presidency and preserve some thread is for you to go in and, and, uh, voluntarily, uh make a statement."

"No," Haldeman cut in, "he's got to go beyond that."

Ehrlichman nodded. Rogers should tell Mitchell to say, "I am both morally and legally responsible."

Rogers would not do, they reluctantly decided, because as Nixon put it, "I know Rogers like the back of my hand and Rogers does not like real, mean tough problems and will not do it." Why not Nixon himself as the messenger to Mitchell? Nixon admitted that "I can verse myself in it enough to know the thing, but I am not sure that I want to know . . . I am not trying to duck it." Then he reconsidered and ducked it: "The thing, John, is that there's nobody really that can do it except you." Another half hour of discussion produced the conclusion that Mitchell was never going to confess.

Perhaps Mitchell really was innocent? Ehrlichman thought not. He said he had a taped telephone conversation between Colson and Magruder that proved Mitchell was guilty. Could they use it to blackmail Mitchell? Certainly not, because the tape itself was illegal.

Ehrlichman worried about his own vulnerability. He said he had listened to the tape and thought, "My God! I'm a United States citizen. I'm standing here listening to this, what is my duty?"

Nixon worried about his own vulnerability: "Well the point is you've now told me. That's the problem." Previously, Nixon had said, "my position has been, quite frankly, nobody ever told me a God-damn thing." But now Ehrlichman had told him that Mitchell was guilty.

Haldeman said the evidence was hearsay and not conclusive and that "we still don't know."

"For your information," Nixon said, "here's what he [Mitchell] told Rebozo. He knows very well."

"Boy!" Haldeman exclaimed.

So they trotted out other names of possible men to go tell John Mitchell he had to go to jail, and composed speeches for them to make, and in each case concluded it would not work.

They clutched at straws. Ehrlichman suggested that the President go before the grand jury to say he had new evidence on Mitchell. He could call the Justice Department and say, "I, the President of the United States of America and leader of the free world want to go before the grand jury on Monday."

"I won't even comment on that," Nixon responded.

Intermixed with the Mitchell problem was the Dean problem. Nixon thought that Ehrlichman, in his report to the President, should say, " 'Well, Christ, in fact Dean' and so forth—in other words cut your losses and get rid of him. I mean, give 'em an hors d'oeuvre and maybe they won't come back for the main course. Go out, John Dean."

Nixon thought about that for a moment, shook his head, sighed, and went on softly, "On the other hand, uh, it is true others did know, they did know."

Nixon wanted to "get the other things out of the way. I don't want to be hammered." Ervin had rejected the no-television proposal. What would they tell the Committee when it pressed for witnesses? "Tell 'em we'll resume the bombing," Haldeman quipped. That brought a laugh, but no solution.

Nixon said he was convinced no one wanted to hurt "the President," an attitude he welcomed, "because it isn't the man, it's the Goddamn office" that had to be protected. Back to Mitchell. Nixon thought Ehrlichman was the only one to tell him face to face. He composed a speech: "You've got to say that this is the toughest decision he [the President] has made. It's tougher than Cambodia, May 8th and December 18th put together. And that he, uh, just can't bring himself to talk to you about it. Just can't do it. And he's directed that I talk to you."

Nixon said that he was putting Ehrlichman in the same position vis-á-vis Mitchell that Eisenhower had put Nixon in vis-á-vis Adams (in fact, Ike himself had told Adams he had to resign). Resignedly, he went on, "But John Mitchell, let me say, will never go to prison . . . I think what will happen is that he will put on the Goddamnedest defense that—" and trailed off.

After more round-and-round discussion, Nixon grew decisive: "The boil has to be pricked. That's what December 18th was about. We have to prick the Goddamn boil and take the heat. Now that's what we are doing here. We're going to prick this boil and take the heat." No one knew, however, where to find the needle, or could suggest who should stick it in. They concluded on that note.[45]

At lunchtime, Ehrlichman met with Mitchell. At 2:24 P.M. he joined Haldeman in Nixon's office to report. Ehrlichman said that Mitchell "is an innocent man in his heart, and in his mind, and he does not intend to move off that position." In short, his mission to persuade Mitchell to confess had failed. He ran through the details. In Mitchell's reconstruction of the events prior to the break-in, and after, he had done nothing wrong. It was Haldeman, Dean, Colson, et al., who were guilty.

Nixon summed up: "The fault is the White House's rather than his." He shook his head, then bravely announced that he would not be intimidated by Mitchell's threats. "Throwing it off on the White House isn't going to help him one damn bit," he said. He shook his head again and admitted that if Mitchell did carry out his threat, it would be "a hell of a problem for us."

Haldeman thought Mitchell would never be able to prove White House involvement, but Nixon pointed out, "it's bad if he gets up there and says that. It's a hell of a problem for us."

Haldeman repeated he could not prove anything, but added, "He has a very, very bad tremor." Nixon said he had always had that. "Shakes," he eludicated. Ehrlichman said he had never noticed it before, but at lunchtime "it is as bad as this," and demonstrated.

Because of Nixon's indecision this conversation, like all those that had preceded it, was getting them nowhere. At one point Nixon said, "Well, let me explain my analysis. The—in my opinion, Bob, the forthcoming thing which I think. I tilted against—I think. I am now tilting for."

The President expressed his concern about "dragging the damn thing out. Dragging it out and having it be the only issue in town. Now the thing to do now, have done. Indict Mitchell and all the rest and there'll be a horrible two weeks—a horrible, terrible scandal, worse than Teapot Dome and so forth."

He brightened up: "There is no venality involved in the damn thing, no thievery or anything of that sort." Plus, the only vulnerability the White House staff had was on the blackmail money, and that was not an obstruction, it was simply trying to help the defendants. His aides agreed.

Ehrlichman said that Mitchell had charged that it was John Dean who had talked Magruder into perjuring himself.

"My God," Nixon exclaimed. "Mitchell was there?"

Assured that Mitchell had indeed been present, Nixon asked, "What does Dean say about it?"

Dean's line was that it was Mitchell and Magruder who had agreed on the perjury. Ehrlichman commented: "It must have been the quietest meeting in history because everybody's version is that the other two guys talked."

Summing up, Nixon said, "I guess we're not surprised at Mitchell [stonewalling], are we?"

"No," Haldeman agreed. Because, he added, "What he's saying is partly true. I don't think he did put it [the break-in] together."

But, Nixon pointed out, "He let it all happen himself."

There was a long pause, as Nixon tapped his fingers on his desk. The President sighed. "You know he'll never—he'll never go to prison." Another twenty-second pause. "What do you think about that as a possible thing—does a trial of the former Attorney General of the United States bug you? This God damn case."[46]

Ehrlichman left the meeting to talk to Magruder. An hour later, at 5:15 P.M., he returned to report. Magruder's story was that he had met with Mitchell and LaRue in Florida in the spring of 1972 to present Liddy's plan to bug O'Brien's offices in the Watergate and in Florida, and McGovern headquarters. "Mitchell orally approved it."[47]

The aides lamented how useless the telephone tap in the DNC had been. Haldeman changed the subject. He told Nixon, "You've got a really crunchy decision, which is whether you, whether you want me to resign or whether you don't." He warned that if he went, Dean would have to go too, something the President had already said he did not want, because Dean off the reservation was too dangerous.

Nixon did not want any resignations. As he put it in his diary, that would be "a massive admission of guilt."

That same day, Agnew told Nixon he was "concerned" about a grand jury investigation in Maryland into the awarding of state contracts to construction firms when he had been governor. Apparently there had been some bribe money passed around. Nixon noted that this was a common practice in state government; he jokingly told Haldeman, "Thank God I was never elected governor of California."[48]

Kissinger was also being difficult. He wanted to be Secretary of State. Nixon told Haldeman to tell Kissinger he would have to wait, that Rogers was not going to resign until June. "Henry won't like it," Nixon noted, but he would have to accept it. "It is essential Rogers' [resignation] be delayed until this is over. Now, the hell with Henry on this. Now you gotta talk to Hen—you just say 'and Henry it's not appealable.' You just gotta say that, 'Henry, there are bigger things here.' "[49]

April 14 had already been a terrible day for the President. Adding to his woes, he had to attend the White House Correspondents' Dinner that evening and sit there while *The Washington Post* won most of the awards. His one bright spot was the Gallup Poll. It showed he had a 60–33 approval rating, but he knew that would go down as more Watergate news broke.[50]

Upon returning to his quarters, Nixon called Haldeman. He said Rebozo was with him and that he had just told him about Mitchell's determination to stonewall. Naturally, he added, "Bebe can't believe it."

"Well, I can," Haldeman said.

The important thing, the President went on, was for everybody to stick to the line that the money that was raised and given to Hunt was not to obstruct justice, but to provide legal support.[51] Then he called Ehrlichman to make the same point.

They got around to Dean and the possibility of his blowing.

"Look," said Nixon, "he's gotta look down the road to, to one point, that, uh, there's only one man that could restore him to the ability to practice law in the case things still go wrong." He did not have to say who that one man was.

Nixon went on: "Now he's got to have that in the back of his mind."

After Ehrlichman agreed, Nixon continued: "And he's got to know that'll happen. You know, I don't, you don't tell him, but you know and I know that with him and Mitchell, there isn't gonna be a God damn question. Because we got a bum rap."

What they had done, Nixon said, was perfectly legal, providing support. Ehrlichman agreed.

Nixon wondered again if Ehrlichman could issue an Ehrlichman report, or at least announce that he had conducted an investigation at the President's order. Ehrlichman hesitated.

"You could say," Nixon prompted, "The President wants this matter cleaned up, once and for all.

"After all," he went on, "it's my job and I don't want the Presidency tarnished, but also I don't, I, I, I'm a law enforcement man."

Turning back to resignations, Nixon said he would have none of that. "Whatever we say about Harry Truman," Nixon went on, "while it hurt him, a lot of people admired the old bastard for standing by people who were guilty as hell, and, damn it, I am that kind of person." The President ordered Ehrlichman to reach all those involved and give them the "straight damn line" that "we raised money . . . but, uh, we raised money for a purpose that we thought was perfectly proper." (When he released his own edited version of this tape a year later, Nixon wrote at this point, "RN is referring to E, H, not to himself.") "We didn't want to shut 'em up. These men were guilty."

Nixon went on, with reference to Hunt and his friends: "We weren't trying to shut them up, we just didn't, we didn't want 'em to talk to the press." That was "perfectly legitimate, isn't it? Or is it? Legitimate not to want them to talk to the press?"

"I think it is," Ehrlichman replied, but he was not sure.

It was midnight. Nixon ended his day with a pledge to Ehrlichman: "I am not one who is going to say, look, while this guy is under attack, I drop him."[52]

CHAPTER FIVE

THE FIRING OF HALDEMAN, EHRLICHMAN, AND DEAN
April 15–30, 1973

APRIL 15 WAS a Sunday. Nixon began it with a meeting with Ehrlichman. They discussed possible grand jury action. Nixon was hopeful that the grand jury would indict only Magruder and Mitchell. "Well, Christ Almighty," he reasoned, "that's the fish. The big fish."

Ehrlichman agreed.

"God damn it, what more do they want?"

A special prosecutor, Ehrlichman said. The trouble with that, Nixon pointed out, was "it just puts another loose cannon right there rolling around the deck."

They talked about saving themselves with an Ehrlichman report, but that string had long since run out, and no other options occurred to them. "The whole thing is just monumentally tragic," Ehrlichman sighed.

"It is," Nixon agreed. But "we're not going to let it get us down." With that, he left to attend the White House worship services.[1]

After the services and lunch, Nixon met at 1:12 P.M. with Kleindienst in his EOB office. The Attorney General said he had been up from 1 to 5 A.M. talking with Henry Petersen and Earl Silbert, respectively the Chief Assistant U.S. Attorney and the prosecutor in the Watergate trial. They had told him what Magruder and Dean had been saying; the upshot was that Haldeman and Ehrlichman were in deep trouble. Nixon expressed surprise. He said they had assured him they were clean.

There was an obstruction of justice, Kleindienst said, and he explained carefully to the President that the law did not allow giving money to someone who pled guilty for the purpose of not talking.

"Well, who the hell would" do a thing like that, Nixon wondered.

110

Did Dean say that? That "they gave money for that purpose?" He appeared surprised and outraged.

Kleindienst walked him through the obstruction statutes again. "I can see that, sure," Nixon finally admitted. They got to the point; this story was going to break in the newspapers on Monday or Tuesday. Nixon wanted Kleindienst's recommendation.

A special prosecutor.

Nixon wriggled. It would not look good, he said. It would be embarrassing. "We don't run to the hills." It would reflect badly on "our whole system of justice." Wouldn't it be better to put Henry Petersen in charge?

Kleindienst thought not. He also thought Nixon ought to consider asking Haldeman and Ehrlichman to take leaves of absence.

Nixon resisted that too: "I mean, the point is, if a guy isn't guilty, you shouldn't let him go." Kleindienst agreed. Nixon said his style was to "stand up for people even though they are under attack . . . I can't— I can't let an innocent man down. That's my point."

After fifteen minutes more the Attorney General said, "As the President of the United States, your job is to enforce the law."

The President replied, "A special prosecutor immediately casts a doubt frankly, Dick, on the whole Justice Department. I don't like that." Kleindienst understood, but nevertheless concluded, "That is my recommendation."

Nixon changed the subject to how to deal with the Ervin Committee. After some fruitless talk on that one, Nixon said that it was all CREEP's fault: "If Haldeman had been running it [the campaign] it wouldn't have happened. But look what he was doing, we were on our way to China and then we were on our way to Russia. We weren't in the campaign— they were. We couldn't and that's why we had no control." Having made that excuse, Nixon added, "Well, anyway, I'm not making excuses."

Kleindienst told him Chief Justice Warren Burger recommended the appointment of a special prosecutor. Nixon was set back, but he recovered: "I want to get some other judgments [because] I think it's too much of a reflection on our system of justice and everything else." He said he would think about it—and the tape ran out.[2]

After Kleindienst left, Nixon called Haldeman on the telephone. As usual, the telephone tape recorder was loaded and working. They talked about a special prosecutor, and didn't like that idea; they talked about testifying before the Ervin Committee, and didn't like that either. What they did like was the idea of sacrificing John Mitchell.

"Look," said the President, "if they get a hell of a big fish, that is going to take a lot of fire out of this thing on the cover up and all that sort." Haldeman agreed. Nixon went on: "Explain that they [CREEP] did it, and then of course the cover up comes in and they did that too."

"And it all makes sense," Haldeman said, "it is logical, believable, because it's true."

"Right."

Nixon said Kleindienst had urged him to make a Checkers speech at 9 P.M. that evening, but "I'm not going to do that."

"Oh, I think that would be crazy," Haldeman exclaimed. "I sure do."[3]

Nixon next called Kleindienst and asked him to come back for another meeting, and to bring Petersen with him. When they arrived, Petersen told the President he thought Haldeman and Ehrlichman should resign. He admitted that the evidence against them was not conclusive, but "what you have to realize is that these two men have not served you well. They already have, and in the future will, cause you embarrassment, and embarrassment to the presidency."

"I can't fire men simply because of the appearance of guilt," Nixon responded. "I have to have proof of their guilt."

"What you have just said, Mr. President," Petersen replied, "speaks very well of you as a man. It does not speak well of you as a President." (In an interview years later, Petersen said he was surprised at "the calm with which he [Nixon] accepted what I thought was shattering information." He chastised himself for not being skeptical enough: "Maybe people in power have different rules, but they certainly are not straightforward, certainly not honest. . . . I credited this guy with more character than he obviously had.")[4]

It was after 5 P.M. Nixon decided to go for a sail on the presidential yacht *Sequoia* with Bebe Rebozo. Out on the Potomac River, he told Rebozo that Haldeman and Ehrlichman were in trouble, and asked how much money he, Nixon, had in his bank account. Nixon explained that the two men had served him loyally and he wanted to help them out with their legal expenses. Rebozo would not hear of letting Nixon use his own money; he said he and Nixon's friend Bob Abplanalp would raise $200,000 or $300,000 to give to Haldeman and Ehrlichman in cash, and privately.[5]

The *Sequoia* docked, and Nixon returned to the White House, dreading his upcoming meeting with Haldeman and Ehrlichman.

When they had gathered at the EOB, Nixon told his aides of Petersen's recommendation and his response. Haldeman offered to resign.

"Well, now, hold it," Ehrlichman said. "What about brother Dean?"

What about him? "He's staying right here on the job," Ehrlichman protested, "grabbing every document in sight by day, and talking to the prosecutors by night. The first thing to do is to get him out of here—not us."

"I can't fire Dean," Nixon protested. "I can't risk his going after the President."

Ehrlichman persisted. Perhaps Dean could be persuaded to resign. "Why don't I try my hand at a little resignation note and see whether he'll apply a pen to it."[6]

The President called Henry Petersen on the telephone. Petersen warned him that Liddy was going to say he kept silent on orders from higher-ups. Nixon protested; he said that order came from Mitchell, not the President. The tape machine recorded Nixon's words over the telephone: "Everybody in this case is to talk and to tell the truth. You are to tell everybody, and you don't even have to call me on that with anybody. You just say those are your orders."[7]

That order given, it was back to Haldeman and Ehrlichman. They covered familiar territory, until Nixon asked what Dean had done with the material from Hunt's safe. Ehrlichman said Dean gave it to Pat Gray.

"What did Gray do with it?"

Ehrlichman said he did not know, but he would call Gray and ask. He went to his office, made the call, and returned white-faced.

"What did he say?" Haldeman asked.

"Gray told me not to tell anyone we had turned over the Hunt papers to him," Ehrlichman replied.

"Why not?"

"He burned them. In his backyard."[8]

The material, Ehrlichman explained, contained papers relating to projects Colson had set up, including the bogus cables Hunt had composed to implicate Kennedy in the 1963 assassination of Diem. Ehrlichman would claim in his memoirs that he was "dumbfounded" by this news (although there is no evidence of this in his handwritten notes made at the time), "but Nixon was immeasurably relieved when he heard the evidence had been burned."[9]

Nixon called John Dean on the telephone and asked him to come over for a talk. Dean appeared about 9:15 P.M. Ehrlichman and Haldeman were gone. Dean found Nixon sitting in his easy chair with both feet up on the ottoman, wearing a smoking jacket. He noticed a smell of liquor on his breath. Nixon appeared exhausted. His trousers were in wrinkles and his necktie was stained. Nixon offered a drink, which Dean refused.

Nixon asked Dean to run through the money trail again, which Dean did. Then Nixon wanted to know how much Henry Petersen knew. Dean said Petersen had kept him posted right along. Nixon said Petersen had suggested that Liddy be told to tell the truth. Dean thought that was a good idea.

Nixon placed another call to Petersen. Winking at Dean, Nixon told Petersen that Dean had just left the room, and then repeated, "You tell him [Liddy] I have called you directly tonight and that you have it direct from the President . . . that he is to tell everything he knows." Why not? Liddy could only implicate Mitchell. Dean had the impression Nixon was protecting himself with Petersen, and wondered if the conversation had been recorded. That raised another suspicion in Dean's mind: "Was he recording me?"[10]

Hanging up, Nixon asked Dean what he thought about a Haldeman and Ehrlichman resignation. Dean thought it could not be avoided.

"What about you, John?" Nixon asked. "Are you prepared to resign?" Dean said he was.

Nixon remarked that it wasn't fair, it wasn't right, "but what can you say?" He looked off helplessly.

Dean said, "I want you to know I understand the important thing is the Presidency."

Nixon agreed. Then he turned to another tough one. Had Dean told the prosecutors about his conversations with the President? Dean said he considered them privileged and had not.

"That's right" Nixon said, nodding vigorously. "And I don't want you talking about national-security matters, or, uh, executive-privilege things. Uh, those newsmen's wiretaps [back in 1969] and things like that—those are privileged, John. Those are privileged. Not that there's anything wrong with them, understand. But they're national security. There's no doubt about that."

Dean agreed.

Nixon pulled his feet off the ottoman and sat up. He asked if Dean remembered the cancer close to the Presidency meeting. Dean did. "When *was* that?" Nixon asked.

Dean said he could not remember but would look it up. Good, said Nixon, do that. "That's when you brought the facts in to me for the first time, isn't it? And gave me the whole picture?"

Dean thought the President was posturing, that he knew what he had said was a lie. Nixon leaned toward him. With a mischievous look on his face, he said, "You know, that mention I made to you about a million dollars and so forth as no problem. . . ." He laughed: "I was just joking, of course, when I said that."

At one point in the conversation, Nixon got up out of his chair, went to a corner, and said in a barely audible tone, "It was probably foolish to have discussed Hunt's clemency with Colson." What he said, the way he said it, and his leading questions combined to make Dean "think that the conversation was being taped." As he left, Dean said he "would hate to have anything I have started here by talking to the prosecutors and getting these facts out—uh, I would hate to have any of that ever result in the impeachment of the President."

Nixon shook his head. "Oh, no, John, don't worry about that. We're going to handle everything right."[11]

Before going to bed, Nixon talked over the telephone with Haldeman, then Ehrlichman, then Petersen. Nothing was settled. They would get back on it in the morning.

THE Monday morning papers were full of leaks and rumors, and demands for a special prosecutor. A number of Republican congressmen expressed their unhappiness with the continuing stonewall tactics by the White House. Most ominous was Minority Leader Ford's comment to a GOP gathering that "prominent Administration figures" linked to Watergate by leaks should "go before the Senate [Ervin] committee, take an oath, and deny it publicly."[12]

Washington was consumed with Watergate. The nation's capital had always had a tendency to be a one-issue town, but not since Pearl Harbor had it been so completely concentrated on one event—not even the Army-McCarthy hearings of 1954 could rival Watergate. Nixon consoled himself with the thought that "in the country it is not that big . . . at the moment." But he knew it would expand soon, and recognized that "we are going to have one hell of a time."[13]

To contain the situation, Nixon and Ehrlichman got to work over breakfast on the morning of April 16 going over the drafts of resignation letters Ehrlichman had prepared for Dean to sign. Then they went to the Oval Office, where Haldeman joined them.

The immediate problem was what Dean was telling the prosecutors. Nixon was deathly afraid that Dean was informing them about the wiretaps of 1969, taps placed by the FBI on members of Kissinger's NSC staff, and by men working for the White House on the telephones of news reporters. Ehrlichman assured him it was all national security related, covered by executive privilege, nothing to worry about—unless Dean talked.

He introduced the next problem: people would want to know why the President had not acted when he received the Dean Report. Ziegler was recommending that Nixon say that Dean had "disserved" him, that the Dean Report was "inadequate," and that the President had therefore ordered another report.

From Ehrlichman, Nixon said.

Ehrlichman was unhappy with that prospect.

"Yeah," said Nixon, "well, somebody's got to do it."

"Well," responded Ehrlichman, "you can downplay who did it."

Haldeman had an idea: "You [Nixon] can say you did it yourself by talking to all the people concerned."

Nixon thought it would be better if he said, "I made my own investigation of the matter."

Ehrlichman liked that.

They continued their effort to rewrite the history of the past few weeks, making up stories about who did what. Ehrlichman said that when Hunt threatened to blackmail him, he told Hunt to forget it.

"Wait," interjected the President, "wait. Hunt sent a message to you? I didn't know about that."

Ehrlichman said Hunt had sent the message via Dean.

"I didn't know that," said Nixon. In fact, on March 21 Dean had made that threat perfectly clear to Nixon.

They made up more stories, about how the President, when he finally realized the full implications of Watergate, stepped forward and took control and got to the bottom of it all. Then Nixon concluded, "I can say that the Watergate case has been broken."[14]

Haldeman and Ehrlichman left the room, laughing, and Dean came in. After some beating around the bush, Nixon asked Dean what he thought about resigning. "Well," Dean replied, "I think it ought to be Dean, Ehrlichman and Haldeman."

"Well," Nixon responded, "I thought Dean at this moment." With a jerky motion, he slid two letters across his desk for Dean to read. In the first, Dean said he was resigning immediately "as a result of my involvement in the Watergate matter." In the second, he requested an immediate leave of absence, for the same reason.

Dean read them over, lost his composure, regained it, and said, "What I would like to do is draft an alternative letter putting in both options, and you can just put them in the file." His gesture of defiance worked; Nixon retreated from his request for a signature and agreed.

Then Nixon suggested that Dean prepare a letter of resignation for Haldeman and Ehrlichman. He added that they were ready to step down.

"They stand ready?" Dean asked, surprised.

"With head erect, they said, 'Look, we will leave in a minute. We will leave today, do whatever you want,'" Nixon said. That was not true; Ehrlichman had said the opposite.

There followed yet another review of what Dean had said on March 21. Nixon made some additional remarks for the record: "I guess I should have assumed somebody was helping them [Hunt, Liddy, et al.]. I must have assumed it." In fact, he had ordered it.

There was a further review of the March 21 conversation, with Nixon interjecting, "I didn't know that," or, "This is the first time I heard that." He made up more stories about what he had done to get to the bottom of the matter.

"One other thing," Nixon said toward the end of the meeting. "On this privilege thing." He was referring to his order to Dean not to talk about the 1969 telephone taps. "Nothing is privileged that involves wrong-doing.

"On your part or wrongdoing on the part of anybody else." (Earlier that morning, Haldeman had advised the President to "make sure the tape machine is working" before he talked to Dean.) "I am telling you that now I want you when you testify, if you do, to say that the President told you that. Would you do that? Would you agree to that?"

Dean would.

But it turned out the President did not mean to tell the truth about everything: "Let me say with regard to what we call the electronic stuff they heard . . . in the leak area of the national security area—that I consider privileged."

Dean understood.

Not that it is any big deal, Nixon said, "but I do think it is privileged."

Changing the subject, Nixon asked, "What got Magruder to talk?" He added hopefully, "I would like to take the credit."

So would Dean, who told the President that Magruder talked when he learned that John Dean was incapable of telling a lie and would therefore expose Magruder's perjury.

Nixon liked that "incapable of telling a lie" line. "Thank God," he exclaimed. Then he gave Dean some words to live by: "Don't ever do it [tell a lie], John. Tell the truth. That is the thing I have told everybody around here. God damn it, the truth."

"That's right," Dean said enthusiastically.

"That son-of-a-bitch Hiss would be free today if he hadn't lied about his espionage," Nixon said. In fact, Hiss was free, had been for years.

Nixon went on: "But the son-of-a-bitch lied and he goes to jail for the lie rather than the crime. So believe me, don't ever lie with these bastards."

Then he had a nice afterthought: "Also there is a question of right and wrong, too."

And then another afterthought: "There are gray areas."

Nixon went on to make up a story for Dean to tell the grand jury. He should say that when he told Nixon that there was a cancer on the Presidency, "the President went out and investigated on his own . . . and as a result of the President's actions this thing has been broken."

Still, Dean should not lie. But "if you feel I have done the right thing, the country is entitled to know it. Because we are talking about the Presidency here."

Dean said Nixon had "done nothing but try to get to the bottom of this thing."

Nixon agreed.[15]

When Dean left, Haldeman and Ehrlichman returned. The President was pleased. He said Dean was "quite the operator," that he had agreed to everything the President asked, and that he swore he had never mentioned the wiretaps to anyone.

That problem settled, they returned to the PR aspects of the case. The story they would tell was this: when Dean returned from Camp David without a report, Nixon went to work because he realized there was more to the case than he had imagined.

Nixon critiqued the scenario: "How do I get credit for getting Magruder to the stand?"

That was easy, Ehrlichman said. "You took Dean off of the case right then."

How could that be explained, Nixon wondered.

Because Dean had failed to produce a report, Haldeman supplied.

"You began to move," Ehrlichman offered.

What did I do next? Nixon asked.

You called in the Attorney General and Petersen, Ehrlichman supplied.

"This is very good," Nixon said. "Now, how does that happen?" What he meant was, how could he explain not giving an Ehrlichman report to Kleindienst? And how could he explain doing nothing before Magruder started talking?

No answer. Nixon then asked if it wouldn't be wise to put out the Ehrlichman report. It would not be wise was Ehrlichman's conclusion. It consisted of only a few handwritten notes. On that unhappy note, the meeting broke up. [16]

Haldeman came back into the Oval Office. He said that Len Garment, who was slated to replace Dean as the President's legal counsel, had been studying Watergate. Garment wanted to see Nixon, "and what he will say to you is that it is clear to him that you are in possession of knowledge that you cannot be in possession of without action on. And that your action has to include cutting cleanly and that you've got to remove me and probably Ehrlichman."

Haldeman said he would issue a statement, admitting that he had sent the $350,000 that was used for blackmail back to CREEP, but claiming that "I acted at all times at the instigation of and through John Dean. In other words I didn't do any of this."

Nixon was alarmed. He feared throwing off everything on Dean because Dean might get into "other things. See what I mean? I don't want him—he is in possession of knowledge about things that happened before this [the taps]." Another option sunk.

Haldeman said Garment was advising that Nixon do something "bold, new, you know, really some kind of a dramatic move." He added that Kissinger thought so too. Kissinger wanted Nixon to make a nationwide television address, that night. Of course, he added, that was Kissinger's solution to any problem.

Nixon did not like that idea, either. [17]

When Haldeman left, Petersen came in for what turned out to be a two-hour meeting. Petersen told Nixon what the grand jury had heard about Haldeman and Ehrlichman. It included the hush money, that Ehrlichman had told Hunt to get out of the country, turning the contents of Hunt's safe over to Pat Gray (who had lied to Petersen about it), and other things as well.

The question arose, was it Colson who put the pressure on Magruder to have Liddy break into the DNC?

"I don't know," Nixon said. "We don't know that. If we learn that, that's going to be a very damaging piece of information because our information is that O'Brien was a specific target of the Liddy operation."

"I don't know that," Petersen said.

The President wanted to know who was the corroborating witness for Magruder. Was it Liddy?

"Basically," Petersen answered, but he pointed out, "This man is crazy, Mr. President. He's burning his arms. He showed the prosecutor and said, 'I will stand up to anything. I've made myself endure this to prove to myself that I can take anything. Jail will not break me' and what have you. You've got to be a crazy man to sit there and burn yourself to see if you can withstand the pain."

Petersen then warned that there was "a lot of movement" among the participants and potential witnesses. "Nobody wants to be the last one in. They're all trying to get in first to talk and get the best deal they can. Those who have not been contacted are nervous and waiting." They all wanted immunity.

"I'm so sick of this thing," Nixon moaned. "I want to get it done and over, and I don't want to hear about it again." He reflected, then went on: "Well I'll hear about it a lot, but I've got to run the country too."

Petersen returned to the need for resignations. Nixon still resisted. On that inconclusive note, the meeting ended.[18]

As Petersen left, Ehrlichman and Ziegler came in. Nixon summarized his conversation with Petersen. He complained about that "damned dumb Gray, Director of the FBI," lying to the man in charge of the Criminal Division of the Justice Department. "Oh," Nixon lamented, "he's dumb."

They turned to the PR problem. Ziegler wanted a presidential statement saying White House aides would testify before the Ervin Committee. Ehrlichman liked the idea, as that would put them on the "high ground. And then let them pull us off."

Ehrlichman said it would be a full court press. Ziegler started to explain what that was. Nixon cut him off. "I know what the hell a full court press is," he snapped. The meeting ended with nothing settled.[19]

Dean returned, with a copy of his proposed letter of resignation. It incorporated a statement that Haldeman and Ehrlichman had requested immediate leaves of absence.

"You don't want to go if they stay?" Nixon asked. Dean did not. They discussed Haldeman's and Ehrlichman's involvement, but ended the meeting without resolving the issue of resignation.[20]

That evening, Nixon telephoned Petersen to find out what Fred LaRue had told the grand jury in the afternoon. He promised Petersen he would not reveal anything he heard. Petersen then gave the bad news: LaRue had admitted to participation in a cover-up and an obstruction of justice, and implicated Mitchell. Even worse: Dean had told Silbert that in return for immunity, he would testify that Haldeman and Ehrlichman were involved. That shook the President considerably; he had to ask Petersen to repeat it three times. In view of this development, Petersen added, the prosecuting team would probably have to indict the President's aides.

Another difficulty: there had been leaks about possible resignations. A reporter had called Petersen to ask him if it were true that "two or three people in the White House were going to be thrown to the wolves." On that unhappy note, Nixon's day finally ended.[21]

NIXON began the morning of April 17 with his regular Oval Office meeting with Haldeman. The President was saying they should consult with John Connally on what to do next when Rose Woods walked in. Nixon apologized—he had hit the wrong button, something he often did—and Woods left.

Haldeman said the pressure to act was intense, that they had to do something, soon. "We have to get out in front some way." Nixon advised him to sit down with Ehrlichman "and do some hard thinking about what kind of strategy you are going to have with the money. You know what I mean?" Haldeman knew.

Nixon complained that Dean "tells me one thing and the other guy something else. That is when I get mad. Dean is trying to tell enough to get immunity and that is frankly what it is, Bob."[22]

Haldeman left. Nixon went through a series of ceremonial meetings with visiting dignitaries. At lunchtime, Haldeman, Ehrlichman, and Ziegler joined the President in the Oval Office. Ehrlichman said he had just spent an hour with Colson, who wanted to see Nixon badly.

"I don't want Colson to come in here," Nixon snapped.

Ehrlichman then offered an action plan, which consisted of firing Dean.

Nixon did not like that. Dean knew too much. For example, Dean knew about the $120,000 for Hunt.

"Is he holding that over your head?" Ehrlichman asked, alarmed.

"No, no, no," Nixon exclaimed. "I don't think Dean would go so far as to get into any conversation he had with the President—even Dean I don't think."

But he wasn't sure. Dean was not like Haldeman and Ehrlichman. Nixon paid them a heartfelt tribute: "I know that you'll go out and throw yourselves on a damned sword. I'm aware of that. I'm trying to think the thing through with that in mind because, damn it, you're the two most valuable members on the staff. I know that. The problem is, you're the two most loyal and the two most honest. You know how I feel about that. It's not bull—it's the truth."

But Dean—"what the hell does Dean know? What kind of blackmail does he have?"

The President answered himself—it was the hush money. And he explained to Ehrlichman why he could not fire Dean: "He'd go out and say, 'Well the President's covering up for Ehrlichman and Haldeman.' Alright. There you are. Because he knows what I know."

They went back to March 21. Haldeman said he was present when Dean reported to Nixon (he was not, although he did come in at the end of the meeting). "Good!" Nixon exclaimed. "What did we say?" He supplied his own answer: "Remember he said how much it was going to cost . . . I just shook my head."

Did Haldeman remember? Haldeman did. "I didn't tell him to go get the money, did I?" asked the man who had told Dean to get the money.

"Absolutely not!" Haldeman assured him.

The President sighed. "We've got a pretty good record on that one, John, at least." This was at least the fourth time these two had gone through March 21, changing the story each time.

How to deal with Dean, if he could not be fired? Haldeman suggested a suspension. That got nowhere. Ehrlichman suggested passing the word to "everybody in the place that he's a piranha." Nixon had another idea, to cut off Dean by eliminating the possibility of his obtaining immunity. The President could do that by making a blanket statement that no one on the White House staff should have immunity.

Ehrlichman liked that: "This has been a law and order administration," he pointed out.[23]

As his aides left, Nixon went to work on the statement he intended to issue later that afternoon.

He called for Henry Petersen, who came in at 2:39 P.M. Nixon told him what he intended to say and Petersen expressed alarm. If Nixon denied Dean immunity, and Dean then refused to talk, Haldeman and Ehrlichman would walk away free. Nixon replied, "Let me handle Haldeman and Ehrlichman."

Petersen wanted the President to fire Haldeman and Ehrlichman. "I don't want to belabor the point," he said, but "I have made it clear that in my view that I think they have made you very very vulnerable. I think they have made you wittingly or unwittingly very very vulnerable. . . . They eroded confidence in the office of the Presidency by their actions."

The two men went back and forth on the question of resignations, and on immunity for Dean. Petersen warned that Dean's lawyers were saying that if Dean went to trial, they would put the whole Nixon Administration on trial. Nixon groaned. Petersen said he was "just shocked" by John Mitchell. Nixon agreed. He said the whole trouble was people trying to protect Mitchell.

Petersen told him that "LaRue broke down and cried like a baby yesterday. . . . It is a terrible thing."

Nixon assured Petersen that "I am just trying to do the right thing in a way that is—"

"Mr. President," Petersen cut in, "if I didn't have confidence in you—I wouldn't be here."

Nixon told Petersen his philosophy: "In this thing—in these things— you've got them, you handle them and go on to something else—that's what we are going to do."

"Damn," Petersen said, "I admire your strength, I tell you."

"Well," Nixon modestly responded, "that's what we are here for."

They turned to Gray and the burning of Hunt's papers. Petersen said Gray claimed he never read the material. Did Dean? Nixon asked. Dean said not. Nixon was relieved.

Back to Mitchell. Nixon predicted that Mitchell "will never plead guilty, never. Fight it all the way down the line. What would you do if you were Mitchell?"

"I think I would probably go to Saudi Arabia to tell you the truth," Petersen answered.

"Poison," was Nixon's suggested solution.

"When I think about the former Attorney General of the United States being subject to criminal trial—" Petersen responded.

"For obstruction of justice," Nixon cut in. "Not the bugging—the obstruction of justice." And he ushered Petersen out of the office.[24]

After another meeting with Ziegler to go over his statement, at 4:42 P.M. Nixon took the stage at the White House press room and read a three-page statement. He said he was directing his aides to testify voluntarily before the Ervin Committee, reserving the right to exercise executive privilege when appropriate. He said there had been a great fuss over whether the hearings would be televised, but claimed that had never been a central issue to him, and indicated he had no objection.

Then he announced that on March 21, "as a result of serious charges which came to my attention, some of which were publicly reported, I began intensive new inquiries into this whole matter." He said he had reviewed the facts with Kleindienst and Petersen and could now report "that there have been major developments in the case concerning which it would be improper to be more specific now, except to say that real progress has been made in finding the truth." He pledged that if any member of his staff were indicted, he would immediately suspend that man.

Next, he announced what amounted to his solution to the Dean problem: "I have expressed to the appropriate authorities my view that no individual holding, in the past or at present, a position of major importance in the Administration should be given immunity from prosecution."

He concluded, "I condemn any attempts to cover up in this case, no matter who is involved." He thanked the reporters, and walked out of the room.[25]

Ziegler stepped to the podium, to announce that the President's previous statements denying Watergate involvement by White House staff members were now "inoperative."

Nixon went over to his EOB office for a postmortem with Bill Rogers. The President told Rogers, "I'm thinking of Haldeman and his kids, Ehrlichman and Dean and his. You know what I mean. I'm thinking of the possibility of their mocking a great career. Their service has been efficient—marvelously [unintelligible]."

They discussed the President's announcement. The immediate result, Nixon lamented, will be "terrible."

"No doubt about that," Rogers said.

Nixon consoled himself: "I'll be here, all along, Bill. The jury indicts, moves. We're going to get on with this country. A lot of people in the country, we may find, they feel the President is doing the best he can in the damn thing. If I had wanted to cover up—they probably think the President can cover up. If I wanted to, I sure haven't done it very well, have I?"

The press, Rogers said, "will persecute people."

One thing, Nixon said, was "it sure shows the system works, though, doesn't it?"

Rogers thought Haldeman and Ehrlichman should resign.

"That isn't fair," Nixon protested. "I've got to live with myself. I don't want to do it in that [unintelligible]." The trouble was, he said, he did not know the facts.

Haldeman and Ehrlichman came in. Rogers assured them that an indictment was not a conviction, that they had rights, that they would get their day in court. They went through the "tough parts." One was Gray's destruction of evidence. Rogers pointed out that Gray claimed he had been told to do that.

Nixon exploded: "He was *not* told to do that."

Another tough part was the $350,000. Nixon told them about LaRue's breaking down and crying before the grand jury.

"That's a-right," Ehrlichman quipped, in a poor attempt at imitating an Italian accent. "Are you going to have spaghetti tonight?" he asked Rogers.

"Spaghetti and singing Toscanini," Rogers replied, laughing.

Nixon proposed a counterattack. He wanted Ehrlichman and Haldeman to get lawyers and file libel suits against Dean. "Use the most vicious libel lawyer there is." Not just against Dean, but Weicker too, and McCord and others.

"John," Nixon said to Ehrlichman, "You may as well get at the libel thing and have yourself a little fun." Ehrlichman commented, "Might make expenses." Nixon offered to help pay the legal fees. Ehrlichman declined.

"Let me ask you this," Nixon said, then paused. Finally he plunged on: "Legal fees will be substantial [unintelligible]. But there is a way we can get it to you, and, uh—two or three hundred thousand dollars—"

"Let's, let's wait and see if it's necessary," Ehrlichman said.

Nixon explained that there was a fund used by "Bebe for getting things out." There was "no strain," he added. The money "doesn't come outta me." He said he had told Rebozo to "be sure that people like, uh— who have contributed money over the contributing years are, uh, favored and so forth, in general."

Nixon then promised that if his aides had to resign, he would offer them a place with the Nixon Foundation (which was set up to create a Nixon Library). "The Foundation is going to be a hell of a big thing," he assured them, "it's bound to be."

Haldeman said, "I hope to get funding for the ability to clear my name and spend the rest of my life destroying what some people like Dean and Magruder have done to the President."[26]

THE next morning, April 18, there was pandemonium. Garment sent word to Nixon that Dean was "charging around the White House like a wild animal." Ziegler, at his morning press briefing, infuriated the reporters. Clark Mollenhoff of the Des Moines *Register,* a former Nixon aide and a great bear of a man who expressed indignation with a roar, exploded. "Do you feel free to stand up there," he asked Ziegler, "and lie and put out misinformation and then come around later and say it's 'inoperative'? That's what you're doing." With disgust in his voice, he concluded, "You're not entitled to any credibility at all."

The American Newspaper Guild president sent a telegram to the White House demanding an apology from the President to the press "on behalf of yourself and all those in your Administration who have so willingly and freely heaped calumny" on the news media for its coverage of Watergate.[27]

Dean threatened Ziegler. He said, "I can't take this rap. I'll have to call on some friendly reporters." The President told Haldeman he was deeply concerned about how to handle Dean. He did not want to appear to be hitting him. He told Ziegler to tell Dean that he was *not* being thrown to the wolves. Ziegler went out to make the call. Nixon explained to Haldeman that "Dean has a gun to our head" because of the Ellsberg break-in and the Hunt blackmail threat. Ziegler returned to say that Dean had told him "the important thing now is that we get the President out in front."[28]

But the following morning, April 19, Dean issued a public statement in which he asserted that "I will not become a scapegoat in the Watergate case."[29]

Nixon met with Haldeman and Ehrlichman that afternoon. "Don't know what the son-of-a-bitch is going to say [next]," Nixon complained. "That goddamn Dean." He thought one way for him to head Dean off would be to go to Petersen himself and confess to the Ellsberg break-in. He would explain it had to be done for national security reasons, and J. Edgar Hoover had refused to do it because Ellsberg's father-in-law was a friend of Hoover's.

(The previous day, according to Ehrlichman, Nixon had telephoned explicit instructions to Petersen that there was to be no investigation of the Fielding break-in. "It is so involved with national security that I don't want it opened up," Nixon had said. "Keep the hell out of it!" He had hung up and turned to Ehrlichman: "That should keep them out of it. There is no reason for them to get into it. What those fellows did was no crime; they ought to get a medal for going after Ellsberg." On April 19, Nixon told Petersen in an Oval Office meeting that "Hunt was involved in the Ellsberg thing as part of the plumbing operation.")

Now, he said that another way to head Dean off would be for Haldeman and Ehrlichman to take leaves of absence. They were reluctant. So was Nixon, who remarked that their leaving would create another problem—who would replace them? "There ain't anybody around here to do this son-of-a-bitching thing. It's hard to find anybody that wasn't involved."[30]

That evening, Nixon flew down to Key Biscayne. He took Ziegler with him, and Pat Buchanan, but not Haldeman or Ehrlichman. The weekend papers were full of leaks and rumors about what Dean knew, what Dean had told the prosecutors, what evidence Dean had, what Mitchell had told the grand jury, and so on. Nearly every story pointed to a Haldeman/Ehrlichman involvement.

Nixon spent much of the weekend talking about whether or not to fire his aides. In giving advice, Ziegler played it both ways. So did Buchanan. He told Nixon no one who was innocent should be fired, but any aide who could not maintain his viability should step forward and resign.

On Easter Sunday morning, Nixon got on the phone. He called Haldeman to remind him "how much tougher it was last Easter." He called Ehrlichman to urge him to "stay steady." He called Dean and wished him well, urged him to stop by the Oval Office anytime, and reminded him he was still the President's counsel.[31]

On Monday morning, Nixon conferred with Buchanan and Ziegler. They agreed that Haldeman and Ehrlichman had to resign. Nixon asked Buchanan to call and tell them. Buchanan said he thought Ziegler should do it. Ziegler stared out the window.

"I will face this on my own," Nixon finally vowed. He said he would make the case to his aides. "I must separate the Presidency from them." With tears running down his face, he again told Ziegler to call Haldeman.

Ziegler made the call. He reported to Nixon that Haldeman had accepted the decision like a man.

Then Haldeman called back. He had talked to his lawyers, and to Ehrlichman, and had changed his mind. Ehrlichman wanted to be detached from Haldeman; Haldeman was digging in. He knew how to arouse Nixon's emotions. "In all the other important decisions the President has operated from strength," he told Ziegler. "This would be the first real victory of the establishment against Nixon. This is what the media wants . . ." Nixon backed down.[32]

Instinctively, he decided to do a political canvass. He called friends and associates around the country for advice. Bill Rogers told him Haldeman had to go, but Ehrlichman might be able to hold on. John Connally seconded Buchanan's either-way advice: if they were guilty, out; if they could not refute the allegations, out. "Someone has to walk the plank," said Connally. Bryce Harlow and Henry Kissinger said about the same.[33]

That same day another politician, then serving as Ambassador to India, wrote Nixon. Pat Moynihan had no advice on what to do about the aides; he did want to make an observation. It was this: "It has not really been evil that has brought on the present shame, but innocence. What struck me most, and alarmed me most, about the almost always decent men who came to Washington with you was how little they knew of government, and especially of standards of personal behavior required of men in power." Moynihan thought the responsibility for this situation lay with the academic world, which had failed to teach morality and ethics. Nixon wrote on the letter, "A very thoughtful note."[34]

On April 22 Liddy announced that no matter what the President told him to do, he would not talk to the prosecutors or the grand jury or Sirica or anyone else. A month earlier that would have been wonderful news for Nixon, but by now it scarcely mattered. Hunt had not talked, either, something that a month earlier Nixon was ready to pay $1 million to obtain, and for which he had ordered blackmail paid; yet by late April it hardly mattered what Hunt did. Magruder had talked. LaRue had talked. Mitchell was in danger of turning on the White House. Worst of all,

Dean—who knew damn near everything—was threatening to talk, even beyond what he had already revealed.

On Wednesday morning, April 25, Nixon met with Haldeman and Ehrlichman, to discuss yet again their possible resignations. Ehrlichman, who had been told by Haldeman that the President had a tape recording of the March 21 ("cancer close to the Presidency") conversation with Dean, told Nixon that firing his two top aides would not help him, because "it's entirely conceivable that if Dean is totally out of control and if matters are not handled adroitly, that you could get a resolution of impeachment . . . on the ground that you committed a crime and that there is no other legal process, available to the United States people, other than impeachment. Otherwise, you have immunity from prosecution."[35]

Nixon looked stunned. Haldeman wrote later that the President "never recovered from this statement."[36]

Ehrlichman predicted that it would become a case of Dean's word against Nixon's word. He therefore recommended that Nixon listen to the March 21 tape, or have Haldeman do it, to hear "what actually was said then . . . and then analyze how big a threat it is."

For Nixon, that was simultaneously no solution at all and a possible salvation. He knew what he had said on March 21. He also knew that he had lied about what he had said—lied to Haldeman, to Ehrlichman, to Petersen, to Kleindienst, and even to Dean (when he claimed he was just joking about knowing where to get the hush money).

But Nixon also knew that there were sentences of his on that tape that would exonerate him.

He tried a partial confession: he admitted he had said to Dean, "Well, I guess we can get a million dollars," but said he had meant it as a joke. "Now, I don't know, how does that one sound to you?"

"That sounds tough," Ehrlichman said, "yet it's manageable."

Nixon thought they could "point out that was triggered."[37]

Still the President worried. "What would you fellows answer," he asked anxiously, "if Dean testifies that there was a discussion in which I said Hunt's lawyer had to get paid off?" What indeed? The only answer Ehrlichman could give was to listen to the tapes and hope that they were not that bad.

Nixon tried a fuller confession: he admitted he had said to Dean, "Well look, for Christ sake, take care of him [Hunt]. Be sure the son-of-a-bitch won't talk."

That was extremely serious, but Ehrlichman thought they should listen to the tape before anyone went into a panic.

Back to resignations. Ehrlichman suggested that Nixon fire Dean, let Haldeman take a leave of absence, and keep Ehrlichman. Nixon made an offer to his aides: "Let me ask you this, to be quite candid. Is there any way you can use *cash?*"

"Ehrlichman and I looked at each other," Haldeman later wrote. "Here we were being drummed out of office for supposed hanky-panky concerning cash paid to defendants and now the President was offering *us* cash." Each aide said no. Nixon persisted: "There's a few, not much. As much I think as 200 [thousand dollars] available in '74 campaign funds already." Haldeman said taking that money would only compound the problem. He left to listen to the March 21 tape and make a damage assessment.[38]

At 4:40 P.M., Haldeman returned to Nixon's EOB office. "Well, that is hard work," he began. "Good God! It's amazing, it works awfully well." (So far as this author can tell, this was the first time Haldeman had listened to one of the tapes; Nixon had not yet listened to any of them.)

Haldeman launched into a word-by-word report on the March 21 conversation. Haldeman was a loyal aide. He did not complain that Nixon had lied to him; he did try to put the best possible face on Nixon's incriminating statements, and to dig up sentences that Nixon could use to exonerate himself.

The one he emphasized was Nixon's statement that "It would be . . . wrong." Nixon latched onto that one hard: "That's not bad," he said enthusiastically.

Nixon turned to the harder part. He knew he had said "we can get the money," and he knew he was not joking when he said it. How would they wriggle out of that one?

Haldeman suggested that Nixon could claim he was just feeling Dean out, trying alternatives, exploring options: "You ask people questions on the basis of—, to try and see what direction they're going."

Nixon brightened up: "It's his, his word against the President's."

Then he grew worried: "I hope to God he didn't have a tape recorder in his pocket."

Back to "it would be wrong." Haldeman wrote later that "Nixon clung to that word 'wrong' like a drowning man in a hurricane." Still Nixon worried. Perhaps he had said "wrong" about the timing of clemency, not about the million dollars in hush money. Haldeman, who had just listened to the tape, inexplicably replied, "No, you said getting the money was wrong."

Then Nixon said, incorrectly, "We didn't furnish any money, thank God." Haldeman did not correct him, although Haldeman had been present the morning of March 22 when John Mitchell assured Dean, Haldeman, and Ehrlichman that the money Hunt demanded had been paid, and had just so reported to Nixon.

No matter how much Nixon and Haldeman reassured each other, the President knew that Dean could report the truth of what was said, which raised the danger of the dreaded prospect of impeachment. He grew gloomy. Haldeman tried to encourage him: "Agnew for President? Even your worst enemies don't want to do that."

"I have got to put the wagons up around the President on this particular conversation," Nixon moaned, referring to March 21. "I just wonder if the son-of-a-bitch had a recorder on him. I didn't notice any but I wasn't looking." Haldeman said it was all but inconceivable that Dean had a recorder. Dean had come in to warn the President about the compounding cancer, not to trap him. He said Nixon must have surprised Dean by saying "we could get the money. I think that's the last thing he expected you to say."

Nixon disagreed. He said angrily, "What did he expect me to say, we can't do it?"[39]

Nixon left to go to the Oval Office for a meeting with Henry Petersen, only to be hit by another blow. The Justice Department had decided it would have to inform Judge Matthew Byrne, presiding over the Ellsberg trial, of the break-in at Ellsberg's psychiatrist's office. Nixon had no choice but to agree.

He had much bigger problems than Ellsberg, anyway. That evening, he called Haldeman at his home. "Is there any way," he asked, "even surreptitiously or discreetly or otherwise I mean, that, ah, way you could determine whether uh, this matter of whether Dean might have walked in there with a recorder on him?"

No way, Haldeman replied, but he assured the President the possibility was remote.

But if he did, said Nixon, "the point is that's a real bomb, isn't it?"

Nixon expressed his ultimate nightmare: that Dean would walk into Henry Petersen's office in the morning and plunk down a recording of March 21.

"Virtually impossible," said Haldeman.

But what if, asked the President. He knew that the claim Haldeman had made in the afternoon, that March 21 could be explained away as the President exploring options, would never hold up if Dean had a tape.

"God damn," said Nixon, "where do you carry them, in your hip pocket or your breast pocket?"

Under your arm, like a pistol holster, said Haldeman. If Dean had a tape, it was going to be rough. "All right," Nixon said, if so, "bring it out and fight it out and it'll be a bloody god damn thing, you know in a strange kind of way that's life, isn't it [unintelligible] probably be understood and be rough as a cob, and we'll survive." The President thought that "you'll even find a half a dozen people that will be for the President," down in Mississippi if nowhere else.

Haldeman thought there would be "a lot more than that."

Nixon thought so too. "There's still a hell of a lot of people out there, you know, they, they want to believe, that's the point, isn't it?"

"Sure," said Haldeman. "Want to, and do."

"All right," said Nixon, before returning to the question of a Dean tape. Could Haldeman check on that for him?

There was no way, Haldeman said.

Well, mused the President, "if worse comes to worst, and he has one, well, we've got one," and he laughed.[40]

In a second call, Nixon went through the whole discussion again. This time he concluded, "I'm damn glad we have it [the March 21 tape], aren't you?" Haldeman said he was, because there were some helpful passages on it. Nixon observed that there were things on that tape he wished he had not said, but there were some good things to balance it out. In other words, if Dean had a tape it would be a disaster, but so long as Nixon had sole possession of a tape and could use it selectively, a tape would be a great asset.

In his memoirs, Nixon wrote of the March 21 tape: "I had not finally ordered any payments be made to defendants, and I had ruled out clemency."[41] In fact, he had twelve times ordered Dean to get the blackmail money to Hunt, which was done the next morning.

THE next morning, April 26, Nixon met with Haldeman in the Oval Office. The President got straight to the point: "I don't think it should ever get out that we taped this office, Bob. If it does, the answer is, we only taped the National Security information. All other information is scrapped, never transcribed. Get the point? That's what I want you to remember. You never want to be in a position to say the President taped somebody." Then he ordered Haldeman never to disclose the contents of the March 21 tape to anyone, including Ehrlichman.

Nixon then took up Ehrlichman's mention of impeachment. "I slept a little on that," he said. "My God, what the hell have we done to be impeached?" He insisted on his innocence.

Nixon turned to Ehrlichman's recommendation that he fire Dean. He asked Haldeman, "does that unnecessarily give Dean a motive where he'll go wild against not only Ehrlichman and Haldeman, but *the President?* We can't let that happen."

The telephone rang. It was Kleindienst. Judge Byrne had hit the roof over the Ellsberg break-in. Flushed with anger, the judge had sent the jury home and it looked like he was going to declare a mistrial. Nixon was ashen-faced as he hung up the phone.

It rang again. The President listened aghast as he was informed that *The New York Times* had gotten onto the story that Pat Gray had burned the documents from Hunt's safe, and intended to publish it in the morning.

Nixon hung up, then asked his operator to get Kleindienst. "Don't you think Gray ought to resign?" the President asked. "How do we handle it? What can we do? I know this is, uh, an awful thing . . . or, sure, sure, it's going to come out in the paper. But Dick, Dick, for crying out loud, Goddamnit, these damn things happen."

Kleindienst resisted the idea of Gray resigning, so Nixon rang off, then called Petersen to enlist his aid. "Would you mind discussing it with Kleindienst?" he asked. "I think, uh, let's not put it in a context where I, uh, I love him too, I love *all* of you, but you know what I mean, I want him to be out of the way so that he doesn't look like an ass."

Petersen, too, put up some resistance. The President pressed: "I just can't, uh, believe, I just can't believe that anybody's *gonna* believe that the Director of the FBI was handed some documents and told to destroy 'em. Ha! You wanna see? My god, yes, and that he did it, I mean destroyed them!"

Nixon hung up, and turned back to Haldeman. He wanted his chief of staff to take a leave of absence. Ehrlichman too: "The shit has hit the fan with this one [the Gray revelation]."

The President said he would not give the press the satisfaction of making a Checkers speech. He suggested that Haldeman go back and read *Six Crises* (according to Haldeman, that was the 1,091st time he had made that suggestion). He brought up the Sherman Adams case again.

Then the President let go a tirade. "We've got to get out the Goddamn story, Bob," he declared. (There are at least a thousand memos from Nixon to Haldeman in the Nixon archives that begin with some version of that line.) "People have forgotten the violent years involved. They have forgotten . . . I mean, 'Fuck you, Mr. President. Fuck you, Tricia' and all that shit, but just words, but what violence, the destruction, the teargassing, the commotion." Almost never did Nixon use such language, even when quoting others. Seldom had he expressed his resentment and anger so vehemently.

"And the fucking Secret Service can do one thing," he went on. "I want those threats collected. I told you that before. I mean, we don't have any *investigators*, that's our *problem*, see?" The self-pity, always close to the surface with Nixon, boiled over. The Secret Service and the FBI would not do for him what they had done for LBJ and JFK. Haldeman would not carry out his orders. He did not have any investigators. He felt so sorry for himself.

That afternoon Nixon had a five-hour meeting with Haldeman, all of it on Watergate. They went round and round. At one point Haldeman said, "I'm afraid that's one thing I've lost under this is trust in anybody. Just try to figure who you can trust and who you can't."

"Except me," Nixon interrupted. "You've got to trust me."

"Oh, I do," Haldeman assured him. "I'm talking about any of the others."

They danced around the possibility of Haldeman's resignation.

Haldeman said he was better off inside than outside. "I'd have a hell of a time if I resigned, because I'd lose all of the facilities in one way or another and you lose that fear, [unintelligible] you see, which should be, which is an extremely important fear to have in the mind of the prosecutors and other people."

Besides, Haldeman added, his resignation would not satisfy the wolves, but encourage them to go for more. "I know who the target is, Bob," Nixon reassured him. "I know they hate my guts and they're always gonna hate my guts." But, he added, the Republicans who were screaming for some kind of action would be satisfied with Haldeman's and Ehrlichman's resignations.

Haldeman raised other objections to his resignation, pointing out how it would hurt, not help, Nixon. The President agreed in general, but he said that if Haldeman stayed on he would be concentrating on Watergate matters and "it impairs your operation. It impairs John's operation and I've got this God-damned Congress to deal with. I've got a hell of a lot of battles to fight. And I've got to clear the God-damned air."

They returned to March 21, and invented their fourth story about how to explain the money part. Haldeman pointed out that Hunt's threat related to the Ellsberg break-in, not the cover-up. Nixon liked that. "You, you've hit upon a very important point there, that in terms of the conversation we had with him, had nothing to do with Hunt blowing on the Watergate."

"That's right," Haldeman enthused. Or on the cover-up, Nixon added. "That's right," Haldeman repeated.

"Hunt was gonna blow on the national security matters," Nixon said.

"That's right," Haldeman nodded.

"And therefore I was deeply concerned," Nixon went on. Haldeman agreed.

"And that's what got us into the whole thing," Nixon concluded.

Thus they had moved from (1) knowing nothing about a money discussion on March 21 through (2) refusing to pay blackmail onto (3) raising money but only for legal fees which was perfectly proper to (4) raising money for Hunt in order to guard national security.

After more round and round, Nixon sighed and said, "Well, I've got to live with it." He brightened and added, "Let's face it, I can do this job better than anybody else."

"That's right," said Haldeman. [42]

NIXON went up to Camp David for the weekend. On Saturday morning, April 28, he walked into the living room at Aspen Lodge and was startled to see Tricia sitting on a couch in front of a blazing fire. She said she had been up all night talking with Julie and David about Watergate; the three of them had also conferred with Pat. Tricia wanted her father to know that the family was agreed that he had no choice but to fire Haldeman and Ehrlichman.

Tricia confessed that she had never been an admirer of either man, but swore that "I made my decision carefully and objectively." She said she was speaking for David, Julie, and Pat.

She left, and Bill Rogers arrived. He said the leave of absence option was gone, that it had to be resignation. Nixon asked him to convey this decision to Haldeman and Ehrlichman, but Rogers would have none of that. Nixon would have to do it himself.[43]

In the evening, Ehrlichman called on the telephone. He said Nixon should face up to the reality of his own responsibility, that all the illegal acts ultimately derived from the President. Nixon thought that Ehrlichman wanted him to resign. Ehrlichman said he had evidence that Nixon knew about the forged cables Hunt had created about the Diem assassination.[44]

Early Sunday morning, Nixon called Haldeman and asked him to come up to Camp David, and to bring Ehrlichman with him. Haldeman requested separate meetings when they arrived; Nixon agreed.

Ziegler met them at the helicopter pad. He said the President had told him that "he [Nixon] intends to resign." Nixon had said that was a "firm decision."

Haldeman went over to Aspen Lodge. Nixon was waiting for him. They went out on the terrace to look at the tulips. Nixon told Haldeman, "I may not be alive much longer."

In a melodramatic voice, he went on: "You know, Bob, there's something I've never told anybody before, not even you. Every night since I've been President, every single night before I've gone to bed, I've knelt down on my knees beside my bed and prayed to God for guidance and help in this job.

"Last night before I went to bed, I knelt down and this time I prayed that I wouldn't wake up in the morning. I just couldn't face going on."

Nixon said he knew it wasn't fair, that he felt enormous guilt, that he knew the responsibility was his—but he still wanted Haldeman's resignation.[45]

Then it was Ehrlichman's turn. Nixon repeated his line about wishing he would not wake up in the morning. Ehrlichman was deeply moved. (Years later, when he discovered that Nixon had used the same language with Haldeman and gone through the same performance, he was furious.) "It is like cutting off my arm," Nixon said of the decision to let Ehrlichman go. He began crying uncontrollably. Ehrlichman put an arm on his shoulder to comfort him.

"Don't talk that way," Ehrlichman said. "Don't *think* that way."

"You'll have to resign," Nixon said. Ehrlichman nodded.

"You've been my conscience all through this mess," Nixon went on.

"You were right about a lot of things—you were right about Colson and you were right about Mitchell." But he still had to go.

"You'll need money," Nixon said. "I have some—Bebe has it—and you can have it." According to Ehrlichman, Nixon offered "a huge sum." Ehrlichman refused, pointing out the obvious: "That would just make things worse." He did ask Nixon to do one thing for him: "Just explain all this to my kids, will you? Tell them why you had to do this?"[46]

After Ehrlichman left, Nixon called Kissinger on the telephone. The President, "nearly incoherent with grief," according to Kissinger, said he needed him "more than ever." Kissinger characterized the call as "at once a plea and a form of blackmail." Nixon went on, "I hope you will help me protect the national security matters now that Ehrlichman is leaving."

Kissinger claimed, in his memoirs, that "I had no idea what he was talking about." This from the man who goaded Nixon into going after Ellsberg, and who set Nixon to ordering the 1969 wiretaps on his own aides![47]

Later that afternoon, Nixon had Kleindienst come up to see him. He, too, had to resign. Nixon said he would persuade Elliot Richardson to leave the Defense Department to replace Kleindienst.

The President summoned Richardson to Camp David and told him there that he had just gotten through "the toughest thing I have ever done in my life." Then he told Richardson he was needed more at Justice than at Defense. He promised Richardson full control of the Watergate investigation; it would be his "specific responsibility to get to the bottom of this. Anybody who is guilty must be prosecuted, no matter who it hurts." It would be up to Richardson whether he appointed a special prosecutor.

Nixon leaned forward. He looked Richardson straight in the eye. He said he must believe that the President had not known anything about White House involvement in Watergate before he had begun his own investigation in March. "Above all," he concluded, "protect the presidency—not the President if he's done anything wrong."

Richardson was the very epitome of the East Coast Establishment (which was one reason Nixon wanted him). He could be as pompous as the President. He told Nixon, "I hope you will respond to the crisis of confidence that Watergate has created by opening your administration and reaching out to people in a more magnanimous spirit."

But Richardson was also a D-Day veteran. He was one of those junior officers at Utah Beach who had led the way up and over. No man who had been through that experience ever again had anything to fear.

"Mr. President," Richardson concluded, "I believe your real problem is that you have somehow been unable to realize that you have *won*—not only won, but been re-elected by a tremendous margin. You are the

President of *all* the people of the United States. There is no 'they' out there—nobody trying to destroy you."

Nixon made no reply, nor did his expression change. But it was obvious that Richardson had a lot to learn.[48]

THE following evening, April 30, at 9 P.M., Nixon went on national radio and television to explain the changes in his Administration. Haldeman, watching at home, kept notes; to him, Nixon appeared "shaken, not exhibiting the normal confidence we associate with the Pres. Obviously in heavy weather."[49]

Nixon spoke from the Oval Office. He opened with a claim that when he first learned of the break-in, he had been "appalled" and "shocked." He had "repeatedly" asked those conducting the investigation whether there was any involvement by any members of his Administration, always to be assured there was not.

Then, on March 21, "new information came to me." At that point, he "personally assumed the responsibility" for the investigation, because "I was determined that we should get to the bottom of the matter, and that the truth should be fully brought out—no matter who was involved."

But he wanted to be fair. He would not take precipitate action that could harm an innocent person. Still, he knew that "in the final analysis, the integrity of this office—public faith in the integrity of this office— would have to take priority over all personal considerations."

Therefore, that day he had accepted resignations from "two of my closest associates in the White House—Bob Haldeman, John Ehrlich- man—two of the finest public servants it has been my privilege to know."

Kleindienst had also resigned, Nixon went on, as had the counsel to the President, John Dean.

(Ehrlichman had urged Nixon to say he was firing Dean, but Nixon did not want to goad Dean further; this was the first Dean knew of his resignation.)

Nixon did not want to blame any of the men who had resigned for his troubles. He did explain that in 1972 he had been so busy running the country that he had allowed others to run his re-election campaign. "Alleged improper actions" took place within CREEP, Nixon said, and "the easiest course would be for me to blame those to whom I delegated the responsibility to run the campaign." But it was never Nixon's style to take the easy way. "That would be a cowardly thing to do," he said, and rejected it.

Nor would he blame subordinates "whose zeal exceeded their judg- ment and who may have done wrong in a cause they deeply believed to be right."

The man at the top had to bear the responsibility. "That responsi- bility, therefore, belongs here, in this office. I accept it."

He had not said what "it" was, beyond the "alleged improper actions." There followed a non sequitur: "I pledge to you tonight, from this office, that I will do everything in my power to ensure that the guilty are brought to justice." So much for his assumption of the responsibility.

The President grew philosophical. He said some people were saying Watergate showed that the American political system was bankrupt. The opposite was the case, Nixon said. Watergate proved that the system worked—"a system that in this case has included a determined grand jury, honest prosecutors, a courageous judge, John Sirica, and a vigorous free press."

Nixon gave a discourse on the challenges facing the nation in foreign and domestic affairs. He said he was glad to be done with Watergate, which had been taking too much of his time, and getting back to work. He concluded by saying that he had 1,361 days remaining in his term. "I want these to be the best days in America's history, because I love America."[50]

As the cameras blinked off, Nixon sighed. He felt that with this speech he had "at last and once and for all put Watergate behind me as a nagging national issue."[51]

Nixon's attempt to talk his way out of Watergate was based on his philosophy that if he successfully handled the PR aspects of a problem, he had solved the problem. It was a philosophy he never abandoned. In an article in January 1989, in *TV Guide*, Nixon wrote: "In short, the media don't have to be convinced. They have to be outfoxed, outflanked and outperformed."[52] The thought arises that he did not mean the media, but rather the American people. His April 30 speech was designed to outfox and outflank them.

In fact, the speech made everything worse. Partly this was due to its self-pitying tone, and partly because Nixon took responsibility for nothing specific, admitted nothing, and revealed nothing; but mainly it was because the speech contained so many full lies and half-truths that it could not withstand scrutiny. It made Nixon more vulnerable than ever. He had fed Haldeman, Ehrlichman, Dean, and Kleindienst to the wolves, but that only aroused appetites rather than satisfying them.

The speech was of a piece with the cynicism that had prevailed in every Watergate discussion in the Oval Office from March 21 to April 30; in that sense at least it was an accurate reflection of the inner workings of the Nixon White House.

CHAPTER SIX

GROWING
VULNERABILITIES
May 1–June 15, 1973

THE DEPARTURE of Haldeman, Ehrlichman, and Dean brought major changes in Nixon's daily routine, and in his conversations and meetings. He had been accustomed to starting his days with Haldeman in the Oval Office, where he would give out his instructions as Haldeman scribbled away on his yellow legal pads, taking down the action orders. Since January, these two had spent large parts of the remainder of the day in meetings with Ehrlichman and Dean, discussing their problems. As noted, there was a lot of lying and dissembling going on, but Nixon could be relatively open and relaxed with his three aides (although after March 21 he was guarded with Dean). From May 1 on, there was no one left with whom Nixon could relate as he had with Haldeman, Ehrlichman, Dean, Colson, and John Mitchell. Always somewhat isolated, he now became all but completely so. There was no one he could talk to openly and honestly—not even his family.

As the storm hit him full force, Nixon had thrown the others out of the lifeboat to save himself. This meant he also had to face the storm by himself.

To be sure, John Connally was there. On May 2, Connally announced his conversion to the Republican Party, and his intention to stand by Nixon. And Bebe Rebozo and Robert Abplanalp were unquestionably loyal. So was Alexander Haig. But Nixon was not about to confess to any of them. Haldeman, Ehrlichman, and Dean had brought him up short, on occasion, by reminding him that they knew, and he knew that they knew, that he was guilty of cover-up and obstruction of justice. After April 30, there was no one around Nixon who could do that, so he retreated into a fantasy world in which he evidently came to believe his own vehement denials of involvement and became ever more reckless in the lies that he told the public.

There was another major change. From March 21 to the end of April, Nixon had tried, however hopelessly and ineffectively, to take the initiative. During those six weeks, he had been ahead of events, thanks to his inside information about who was saying what to the grand jury, and he had attempted to anticipate and control developments through manipulation of Henry Petersen, through payoffs to Hunt, through the "Dean Reports," the "Ehrlichman Report," and the "Ziegler Report," and finally by firing Haldeman, Ehrlichman, Dean, and Kleindienst.

But in May, Nixon was forced on the defensive. He had to react to public disclosures. The disclosures ranged from the revelations of witnesses before the Ervin Committee to grand jury indictments. On a daily basis Nixon was buffeted by new information reaching the public about his Administration's actions over the previous four years, in effect a history of the questionable, illegal, and seamy acts of his first term.

Worst of all, the media, after eight years of ignoring the wiretapping and other illegal acts of the JFK and LBJ administrations, and after four years of virtual silence about those of the Nixon Administration, now began to report every unverified accusation. The press and the TV news programs became mirror images of the Nixon Administration. They printed or broadcast rumors and gross exaggerations of the nature and extent of the criminal acts of the Nixon White House. The Democrats, justifiably outraged by the actions of Richard Nixon and his friends, made unjustified comparisons of Nixon with Hitler, talked darkly about the coming of fascism to America, and denounced the Imperial Presidency they had done so much to create.

The net effect was to make Nixon, who had in most areas of his criminal acts only followed where his Democratic predecessors had led, appear to be unique. He underwent a pounding from a torrent of criticism such as had never before descended upon an American President, not even Andrew Johnson, not even Herbert Hoover.

To his detractors, he deserved it all and had no one to blame but himself; to his supporters, whose numbers were dwindling but still large, he was the victim of a media run amok, aided by a Democratic Congress that had lost all sense of proportion and fair play. Somehow Richard Nixon stood up to all this, and fought back.

THE immediate reaction to the firing of Haldeman and Ehrlichman was a hugh sigh of relief. According to John Chancellor of NBC TV, the "Germans" were "by far" the most unpopular of the 2.5 million federal employees. He quoted congressional "sources" who said that there was "dancing in the halls" at the news. According to ABC TV, the reaction on Capitol Hill "couldn't have been happier."[1]

There was a sense that the boil had been lanced. Senator George McGovern praised Nixon: "It is not an easy thing for a President to admit a mistake, but it is perhaps essential to the nation that he can." McGovern was critical of Nixon on one point: "The Watergate scandal is not, as the President implied, typical of the political process. Our politics is better than that. And Watergate is worse than the tactics of any national campaign in my memory or modern times."[2]

But many Democrats, and a few Republicans, demanded more. Unwilling to believe that the resignation of Haldeman and Ehrlichman had restored health to the body politic, they wanted Nixon to resign too. Representative John E. Moss (D.-Calif.) urged House leaders to open a formal inquiry into the possible impeachment of the President. House Democratic leader Thomas P. O'Neill (D.-Mass.) said that was "premature," but added that he and many other Democrats were taking the suggestion seriously. Representative Bella S. Abzug (D.-N.Y.) demanded an immediate investigation to determine whether grounds for impeachment existed.

On the Republican side, Senator Barry Goldwater of Arizona said that impeachment was not something to be done "willy-nilly," but added that if it were shown that Nixon had in any way been "dishonest about this, then I think impeachment would certainly come."[3] And Senator Charles Percy introduced a resolution calling on Nixon to appoint a special Watergate prosecutor from outside the executive branch. The resolution requested that the name of the appointee be submitted to the Senate for confirmation. The resolution passed. In the House, eighteen Republicans introduced a similar resolution.[4]

One Republican who stood by the President was the governor of California. Ronald Reagan said that while the Watergate bugging was "illegal," the word "criminal" was too harsh to apply to it. He said the convicted conspirators should not be considered criminals because they "are not criminals at heart."[5]

Early on the morning of May 1, Haldeman went to his office. He wanted to consult his files in preparation for his upcoming appearances before the grand jury and the Ervin Committee. He discovered an FBI agent posted outside his office, placed there by acting Attorney General Richardson. Haldeman asked if he could go in. "Yes," the agent replied, "but you'll have to leave your briefcase outside because you can't remove anything."

Nixon came down the hall, on the way to the Oval Office. He saw the FBI agent and lost his temper. In an act quite untypical of him, he shoved the guard roughly against the wall. A little later, Nixon went to a Cabinet meeting. There he expressed his outrage at the posting of the guards. He also lashed out at Percy, who was thought to have presidential ambitions; Nixon swore that he would never make it "as long as I have anything to say about it." After the meeting, Nixon apologized to the agent he had shoved.[6]

The incident provided evidence of how little Nixon had accomplished with his April 30 speech. There were guards in the White House, literally right next to the Oval Office. They were not there by order of the President—to the contrary—nor was their function to keep protesters and demonstrators out. Rather, it was to keep Nixon's closest associate over the past four and a half years from removing any part of his own files. Nixon was still President. That red telephone still stood on his desk. But his power was eroding.

The next morning, May 2, a *New York Times* feature story by Seymour Hersh charged that Haldeman, Ehrlichman, Mitchell, Magruder, LaRue, and Dean had all been involved in a conspiracy to cover up the truth about the DNC break-in by obstructing the FBI investigation, and that the conspiracy had begun immediately after the burglars' arrest. Hersh wrote that "everyone involved in the operation repeatedly lied to Federal investigators, prosecutors, other White House officials, and finally, to President Nixon." In a related story, the *Times* reported that Colson had admitted that Hunt had written a fake cable implicating President Kennedy in the assassination of Diem.[7]

That afternoon, Nixon had a meeting with Ehrlichman. The President said that Agnew had a potential problem with federal prosecutors in Maryland, who were investigating a kickback scheme. Then he turned to a more pressing problem, what to do about his Undersecretary of Transportation, Egil "Bud" Krogh, former head of the Plumbers. Henry Petersen was pressing Krogh for an affidavit setting forth the facts concerning the break-in to Dr. Fielding's office. Krogh wanted to know whether or not he should resign.

Nixon put some leading questions to Ehrlichman about the facts in the case, arousing Ehrlichman's suspicions. Ehrlichman wondered if "he might be recording our conversation."

"In March [1973] I learned some things [from Dean]," Nixon said. When Kleindienst had confirmed the Fielding break-in, he went on, "I acted instantly. I said to Kleindienst and Petersen: 'By all means, get it to the prosecutor or Dean will hold it over your head.' As soon as it came to my attention—that's the important point—it was relayed to California."

Ehrlichman knew that was not true. "What about that phone call to Henry Petersen on April 18 when you told him to stay out of it—that it was a national security matter?" he asked. "You obviously knew a lot about it then."

Nixon changed the subject. He said Krogh should resign. "You know," Ehrlichman said, "it would be terribly unjust if Krogh were punished for this Fielding thing. Please promise me you won't let him go to jail for it—after all, he was just doing what you wanted him to."

"You mean a pardon?" Nixon asked.

"Yes."

"All right."

Then Nixon asked Ehrlichman a question: "Did I know about it sooner?" Ehrlichman nodded. "Well, if I did, it evidently didn't make an impression on me," Nixon said. "I didn't remember it."[8]

As Ehrlichman left, after what turned out to be his last ever face-to-face talk with Nixon, Haldeman came in for what turned out to be his last Oval Office meeting with Nixon. Haldeman opened with a recommendation, that Nixon appoint Haig as his chief of staff. Nixon demurred; he said he did not want another chief of staff, that he intended to handle the details himself. Haldeman said that was obviously impossible; Nixon needed help now more than ever, and Haig was the logical man for the job.

Haig was no longer on Kissinger's staff. In January, Nixon had appointed him Vice Chief of Staff of the Army, with a promotion to four-star rank, breathtaking progress for a man who had been a colonel four years earlier when he joined Kissinger's staff, and had held no field command since. Nixon did accept Haldeman's recommendation, but before making the appointment he checked with Kissinger. (Haldeman had made the point that Haig's main qualification was being "diplomatic enough to have served under Henry Kissinger and survived," but by this stage Kissinger was jealous and suspicious of Haig and fearful of Haig's ambition.)

Kissinger was hesitant to agree. According to one account, he made his standard threat—he would resign if Haig got the appointment. Rose Woods reportedly told Kissinger, "For once, Henry, behave like a man." Nixon, in what Kissinger called his "infinitely ingenious" way, came up with an argument to convince Kissinger; it was that Haig's appointment was designed to keep Agnew from "trying to step into things. Well, Agnew can't—we just can't allow that to happen." The President told Kissinger, "You and I are going to handle [foreign policy]. I've just got to get somebody that can—it's a curious thing—that can handle [Haldeman's job] so that you and I can do the other, see." Then, according to Bill Gulley, director of the White House Military Office, Kissinger agreed, "but only on the condition that he'd never have to go through his former deputy to see the President."[9]

So it was settled. The appointment set off some petty power struggles between Kissinger and Haig, as the courtiers maneuvered over proximity to the President. Gulley recalled "their infantile squabbles over who was going to get the number two room, next to the President, when they traveled abroad."[10] But it also gave Nixon, in Haig, a man he admired for his toughness, his intelligence, his stamina, and his ability to drive and inspire people. It did not, however, give the President a chief of staff who was familiar with the details of Watergate, the Plumbers, Nixon's private finances, and so forth. Haig would be of little help to the President in making up stories about what had happened in the preceding four years.

The barrage from the press continued. On May 3, Hersh had the lead story in *The New York Times*. It concerned Republican "sabotage and espionage efforts" in the 1972 campaign. The following day, the front page was taken up with Watergate: the destruction of campaign finance records by CREEP; an order by Judge Byrne that Hunt's grand jury testimony about the Fielding break-in be given to him immediately; a Martha Mitchell story about attempts to make her husband a scapegoat; a Gallup Poll that showed 50 percent of those queried thought Nixon was involved in the cover-up; leaks from Haldeman's and Ehrlichman's testimony the day before to the grand jury; and more.[11]

The barrage went on all week—Segretti was indicted; Krogh resigned; details from Hunt's testimony about the Fielding break-in; a plea by Martha Mitchell that Nixon resign ("ridiculous," her husband commented); CIA assistance to Hunt and Liddy for the Fielding break-in; the revelation that Nixon had offered the FBI directorship to Judge Byrne while the Ellsberg trial was going on; and more.[12]

Even more troublesome for Nixon were reports that Dean had taken documents from the White House and placed them in a safe deposit box, then given the key to Judge Sirica. These documents, Nixon knew, were part of the Huston Plan. Richardson announced at a news conference that he would appoint a special prosecutor to conduct the Watergate investigation, and give him "all the independence, authority, and staff support needed to carry out the tasks entrusted to him."[13] Nixon's erstwhile supporter from the campaign, George Meany of the AFL-CIO, turned on him. On May 8, Meany said that the Nixon Administration was "steeped in scandal and twisted by privilege." He called for a "vigorous and impartial investigation of this sickening chapter in the history of dirty politics."[14]

Nixon did get a bit of support from an unlikely source. Senator William Proxmire (D.-Wis.) charged that the press was being "grossly unfair" to Nixon. He said the reporters were conducting a campaign of "McCarthyistic destruction." But, Proxmire added, he believed that Nixon was "involved in Watergate up to his ears." Agnew echoed Proxmire's criticism of the press when he charged that the techniques being used were "a very short jump from McCarthyism."[15]

The reporters, meanwhile, were furious with Ron Ziegler. His brash manner and his many contradictory statements had destroyed his credibility. Haig and Connally advised Nixon to get rid of Ziegler, but when Nixon asked Haig to find a replacement, Haig discovered there were no volunteers. Gerald Warren, Ziegler's deputy, did agree to conduct the daily press briefings.[16]

On May 7, Warren issued a statement on Watergate: "Any suggestion that the President was aware of the Watergate operation is untrue; any suggestion that the President participated in any cover-up activity or activities is untrue; any suggestion that the President ever authorized the offering of clemency to anyone in this case is also false."[17]

Besides putting Warren up front to face the wolves, Nixon made personnel changes designed to rebuild his Administration. He moved James Schlesinger from the CIA to the Pentagon, to replace Richardson as Secretary of Defense. He appointed Schlesinger's deputy William Colby to become director of the CIA, and Clarence Kelley, the chief of the Kansas City police, as director of the FBI. At the urging of Republican congressmen, he persuaded Mel Laird and Bryce Harlow to join the White House staff as counselors to the President, while John Connally agreed to join that staff as an adviser without pay. Fred Buzhardt, a West Point graduate and general counsel of the Defense Department, who was a friend of Haig's, joined Len Garment (acting legal counsel to the President). In effect, Buzhardt became Nixon's defense lawyer for Watergate; this followed a Richardson announcement that Nixon could not rely on the Attorney General for legal advice but would have to hire his own lawyer. Nixon was "deeply disturbed" by Richardson's statement, but he made no public protest.[18]

On another reorganization front, however, Nixon retreated. Ziegler issued a statement announcing that the super-Cabinet that Nixon had set up in January as part of his plan for highly centralized control of the bureaucracy was now defunct. It had collapsed, Ziegler explained, with the resignations of Haldeman and Ehrlichman; Nixon would return to the traditional system of direct contacts with the regular Cabinet members.[19]

One of those Cabinet members was becoming a major problem for the President. Richardson had said at his confirmation hearings before the Senate that he felt "betrayed by the shoddy standards of morals" in the Nixon White House. Richardson had said that although he would appoint a special prosecutor, he intended to retain "ultimate responsibility" for the Watergate investigation. Several senators challenged that position; Richardson bent with the pressure and began to hint that he would give the special prosecutor complete independence.[20]

Richardson's independence was threatening Nixon. The President told Bill Gulley, "When the Attorney General gets a memo from the President . . . he shits in his pants."[21] Richardson, however, appeared to be a man in complete control of his sphincter muscles.

Nixon's New American Revolution, which he had announced with fanfare and to which he had intended to devote his energies, had been forgotten.

•

ON May 9, Nixon spoke at a Republican fund-raising dinner in Washington. It was a $1,000-a-plate affair, with fifteen hundred persons in the audience. Those were impressive figures, but Nixon was embarrassed when the press reported that five hundred diners were admitted free, and even more embarrassed when Goldwater refused to attend.

Nevertheless, Nixon counterattacked vigorously. Clenching his fist, jabbing with his finger, he took on his critics. Three times he promised that "we will get to the bottom of this very deplorable incident." He pledged that the guilty would be prosecuted and punished, and swore that he would not allow Watergate to deter him from going forward with his program of peace in the world and reform at home.

He concluded on a personal note: "I have had, as you know, some political ups and downs during my 27 years in politics, and I have known times when I wondered if I had very many friends. . . . When you win, they are all your friends, and when you lose, it is pretty hard to find them. . . . Let me say, I don't stand here tonight as a loser. . . . I shall always remember this group tonight, remember that when the going was tough, you hung in there. . . . Let me remind you that the finest steel has to go through the hottest fire, and I can assure you, my friends, this room is full of fine steel tonight."[22]

Nixon's riposte did not slow the offensive. On May 11, *The New York Times* reported that in 1969 Nixon had ordered wiretaps placed on the telephones of reporters and NSC staff members. That same day, Judge Byrne dismissed the charges of espionage, theft, and conspiracy against Ellsberg. "Bizarre events have incurably infected the prosecution of this case," Byrne said, referring to the Fielding break-in and wiretaps on Ellsberg's telephone.[23]

Three days later Senator Stuart Symington (D.-Mo.) revealed that at a closed hearing before the Senate Armed Services Committee, Deputy Director Vernon Walters of the CIA had admitted that Haldeman, Ehrlichman, and Dean were involved in the attempt in June 1972, right after the break-in to the DNC, to compromise the CIA through a cover-up. A simultaneous leak from the Ervin Committee staff quoted former acting FBI Director Pat Gray as saying that he had warned the President that he was being "wounded" by men around him "using the FBI and CIA."[24]

The Ervin Committee hearings were scheduled to open, on national television and radio, on May 17. Nixon tried to seize the initiative and divert attention with a major policy proposal and a startling admission. On May 15, the President recommended to congressional leaders that they create a bipartisan commission to study the possibility of limiting the Presidency to a single six-year term and doubling the term of House members to four years. He thought the commission could also examine possible campaign reforms. Under ordinary conditions, such a proposal from the President would have been the lead story of the day; in May of 1973 it went all but unnoticed. The new DNC chairman, Robert Strauss, dismissed it as "another delaying tactic and whitewash effort."[25]

Nixon tried again the next day as the White House acknowledged that the President had "personally authorized the use of 17 wiretaps against 13 members of his own Administration and four newsmen." The statement explained that the reason was national security: Nixon had given the authorization in order to plug leaks about the American bombing of Cambodia.[26]

This admission failed to keep the opening session of the Ervin Committee from the front pages, or to diminish the size of its audience. It was larger than the audience for the Army-McCarthy hearings of 1954, larger than the audience for Nixon's Checkers speech in 1952. The cameras concentrated on Senator Ervin, as he banged down his gavel and opened: "We are beginning these hearings today in an atmosphere of utmost gravity." Then they swung around to the rear of Room 318 of the Old Senate Office Building, to capture the reaction of a young man in a paint-spattered T-shirt, Dr. Daniel Ellsberg.[27]

Ervin got off to a deliberate start. The Committee questioned secretaries and minor staff people, who revealed nothing that was not common knowledge through leaks. Nixon, however, continued to receive blows from outside the hearing room. Martha Mitchell, ever quotable, told an impromptu news conference outside her Fifth Avenue apartment that Nixon "might be impeached if he did not resign." She said her husband had been protecting the President, but the President's men "tried to make my husband the fall guy. But he's the good guy. John Mitchell was the honest one in the whole lousy bunch," she asserted.

Now Richardson announced that he had chosen Archibald Cox, a professor of law at Harvard, as Special Prosecutor. Cox was not only a Harvard man, he had been Solicitor General in the Kennedy and Johnson administrations. He invited Ethel Kennedy to his swearing in. There was consternation in the White House; Haig and other aides to the President warned him that Cox was a "Kennedy stooge" out to "get the President."[28]

Nixon did not need the warning. He later wrote: "If Richardson had searched specifically for the man whom I would have least trusted to conduct so politically sensitive an investigation in an unbiased way, he could hardly have done better than choose Archibald Cox." Cox's former colleague at Harvard, Henry Kissinger, told Nixon, "Cox will be a disaster. He has been fanatically anti-Nixon all the years I've known him."[29]

Richardson had approved a charter for Cox that amounted to a fishing license. The Special Prosecutor not only had full powers to investigate the break-in, but "all offenses arising out of the 1972 Presidential Election . . . and any other matters which he consents to have assigned to him by the Attorney General." Cox had authority to conduct grand jury proceedings, to grant immunity, to initiate prosecutions, and to frame indictments. He had virtually unlimited funds. No time limit was put on his activities. He could be removed only if he committed "extraordinary improprieties." Cox quickly gathered a staff of eighty investigators. Seven of the eight senior staff people had been in the Kennedy or Johnson Administration; more than half the lawyers were Harvard Law School graduates. As a generalization, it is fair to say that they may have assumed Nixon was guilty. From the White House perspective, the Special Prosecutor's Office appeared a vanguard for Senator Edward Kennedy's march to the White House.

To defend him, Nixon had only Garment, Buzhardt, and part-time assistance from Charles Alan Wright. Nixon had once tried to get Wright fired by the University of Minnesota because Wright had written an article favorable to Alger Hiss; by 1973, Wright was at the University of Texas and Nixon had characterized him as "a distinguished constitutional scholar." Garment, Buzhardt, and Wright had a half dozen young lawyers working for them.[30]

The Cox appointment was an illustration of how much power had slipped from the President's hands. He had to have Richardson; the Congress would not confirm Richardson without the Cox appointment; Nixon could not prevent Cox from taking up his duties and proceeding with his independent investigation. The Congress, which had been overwhelmed by the executive branch since FDR's days, was reasserting itself.

As the lesser figures before the Ervin Committee revealed more of the inner workings of the Nixon White House, rumors were abroad about what John Dean was going to say. Nixon still worried that Dean would report the March 21 conversation. Nixon and Haig phoned Haldeman to ask him to help devise a strategy to deal with Dean. Haldeman said he would testify that the thrust of the March 21 meeting was to "probe" Dean. He would swear that Nixon had said that paying blackmail would be wrong. He would not admit that he had listened to the March 21 tape; he would claim that his testimony was based on notes he had made during the meeting itself.

Nixon decided to pre-empt Dean by issuing a statement that would vitiate the thrust of Dean's testimony. He asked Haldeman to help him prepare it. Nixon told Haldeman he was going to admit "everything."

"I'll say I ordered the Plumbers," Nixon declared. "I had the Huston Plan. I told Haldeman and Ehrlichman to meet with the CIA." He would explain that it had all been done for national security reasons: "I'm going to put an NSC cover on the whole thing."

Haldeman's cooperation was crucial to carry off Nixon's plans, but Haldeman had problems of his own. Money, for one; his legal fees were mounting. Nixon had to withdraw the offer of a job for Haldeman on the

Nixon Foundation because of "the problem that you may be indicted."
(A few days later the Nixon Foundation president, Leonard K. Firestone,
announced that plans to build a library and museum as a monument to
the President had been put aside; the Foundation went into limbo.)

Haldeman had an idea. He wrote Nixon to suggest that Nixon get
his friend, Hobe Lewis, editor of the *Reader's Digest*, to pay a $50,000
advance to Haldeman and Ehrlichman for exclusive rights to anything
they might write regarding Nixon's first term. Nixon called Haldeman
the following day; he thought the idea was excellent and he had a twist
on the deal. Instead of writing their own memoirs, they should work on
Nixon's memoirs. "Talk to Hobe on a confidential basis," Nixon said, "and
tell him that the President intends to write his memoirs, and I want you
two to begin the job of preparing the basic documents. . . ."

The next day, Nixon called again, with another angle. "I've decided
today that I will give you all of the White House tapes," Nixon told
Haldeman, "from the time we installed the system until April 30 of this
year. You can tell Hobe Lewis, on a strictly confidential basis, that you
own them. They ought to interest him in retaining you to do the Nixon
research."[31]

Haldeman did not follow up on this extraordinary offer, but he did
help Nixon prepare his statement anticipating Dean's testimony and he
did speak out in defense of the President in response to Symington's
continuing charges that Nixon had told Walters to have the CIA tell the
FBI to stay out of the Watergate investigation. "I can flatly say that the
President was not involved in any cover-up of anything at any time,"
Haldeman told reporters on May 21.[32]

The next day, Nixon issued his own statement. It was as brazen as
Haldeman's, more explicit, and far more extensive. Nixon stated that
"grossly misleading impressions . . . as to my own role" in Watergate had
to be corrected.

He then went on to "state categorically":

1. I had no prior knowledge of the Watergate operation.
2. I took no part in, nor was I aware of, any subsequent efforts
that may have been made to cover up Watergate.
3. At no time did I authorize any offer of executive clemency
for the Watergate defendants, nor did I know of any such offer.
4. I did not know, until the time of my own investigation, of
any effort to provide the Watergate defendants with funds.
5. At no time did I attempt, or did I authorize others to attempt,
to implicate the CIA in the Watergate matter.
6. It was not until the time of my own investigation that I learned
of the break-in at the office of Mr. Ellsberg's psychiatrist, and
I specifically authorized the furnishing of this information to
Judge Byrne.

7. I neither authorized nor encouraged subordinates to engage in illegal or improper campaign tactics.

That was high-risk politics. Men Nixon had fired, or cut loose, who were under indictment or who were going to be indicted, could prove that Nixon was lying on every point except number one. Haldeman and Ehrlichman knew that points two through seven were untrue; Colson knew that points three, five, and seven were untrue; Mitchell knew that points four and seven were untrue; Segretti, Magruder, and others knew that point seven was untrue; Walters knew that point five was untrue. And Dean knew that every point except the first was untrue. All the President's men had strong motives to rescue themselves at Nixon's expense.

Nixon obviously counted on the loyalty of Haldeman, Ehrlichman, Mitchell, and Colson. The others were not highly enough placed, nor creditable enough, to refute him—except possibly Dean. And if Dean called Nixon a liar, it would be his word against the President's. Unless the existence of the tapes became known.

Those tapes would provide evidence that Nixon had lied on points two through seven. And although the only men who had participated in the conversations in the Oval Office and the EOB who knew the rooms were bugged were Nixon and Haldeman, there were others who knew of the existence of the system. Haldeman's aides Larry Higby and Alexander Butterfield knew. Rose Mary Woods knew. Some half dozen Secret Servicemen knew. And there were now in existence a grand jury, the Ervin Committee, five or six other committees of Congress, all asking questions of men under oath, about the inner workings of the White House.

Nixon had made himself vulnerable to a long list of people. But then what choice did he have? His options were: to keep quiet, but to do that in the face of the accusations being made would have led to an assumption of guilt and possibly a move to impeach; to admit everything, which would have assured impeachment; or to resign. So of necessity he made himself vulnerable, and hoped the people he had deserted would remain loyal.

In his May 22 statement, Nixon went on to admit to, explain, and justify the 1969 wiretaps, the preparation of the Huston Plan, and the creation of the Plumbers. These were all legal and necessary national security operations, he claimed, and they had nothing to do with Watergate. With regard to the Fielding break-in, Nixon admitted that because of the seriousness of the Pentagon Papers theft, he had told the Plumbers unit "as a matter of first priority [to] find out all it could about Mr. Ellsberg's associates and his motives," but "I did not authorize and had no knowledge of any illegal means to be used to achieve this goal." Had he known that Liddy and Hunt intended to break in to Dr. Fielding's office, "I would have disapproved. Consequently, as President, I must and do assume responsibility for such actions despite the fact that I at no time approved or had knowledge of them." He admitted also, "With hindsight, it is apparent that I should have given more heed to the warning signals I received along the way about a Watergate cover-up and less to the reassurances [that no one on the White House staff was involved]."[33]

Those who commented on the President's statement did not know that six of the seven opening points were untrue. But they noticed the President's retreat. R. W. Apple wrote in *The New York Times* that in August 1972 Nixon had claimed that no one on the White House staff was involved. Then on April 17, 1973, he had said that any White House employee who was involved would be discharged. Then on April 30 he had fired Dean and accepted resignations from Kleindienst, Haldeman, and Ehrlichman. "Throughout these and other statements," Apple noted, "the President offered no apologies for his own conduct, no suggestion that he might have erred." Now that too was changing.[34] Despite the risks he had taken in issuing it, Nixon's May 22 statement had not settled anything. It had only asked: Where would it end?

NIXON needed a break from the battering. On May 24 he got the best possible one short of the destruction of the Ervin Committee and the grand jury. The President hosted what he called "the largest and most spectacular White House gala in history." His guests were the returned POWs, and they gave him what he needed, enthusiastic proof that there were people out there who believed in him.

The idea for the gala had come from Sammy Davis, Jr. The entertainers included Republican stalwarts John Wayne and Bob Hope. But the driving force was Dick Nixon. He oversaw the details, he arranged the choreography. Mrs. Nixon pitched in. The White House staff had protested that thirteen hundred guests (the POWs and their wives and mothers) were too many, and had urged that the dinner be held at a hotel ballroom. Instead, Pat had arranged for the construction of a canopy on the South Lawn. She found and rented enough china and crystal elegant enough for the occasion. She supervised the arrangements, from individual place cards to flower centerpieces on each of the 126 tables.[35]

The purpose was to honor the man who had brought the POWs home.

The festivities began in the early afternoon. Pat had a tea for the wives and mothers, while Nixon gave a briefing to the POWs in the West Auditorium of the State Department. When he arrived, at 2:30 P.M., the men gave him a standing ovation. A broad smile spread over Nixon's face. He raised his right thumb high into the air. That brought more cheers from the audience.

Nixon opened by pointing out that he had addressed many distinguished audiences, but "this is the most distinguished group I have ever addressed, and I have never never been prouder than I am at this moment to address this group."

He outlined the upcoming events of the afternoon and evening, then apologized for not having a receiving line. He explained that he and Pat had timed it out, and discovered it would take three hours and twenty minutes to shake hands with all the guests, "assuming we didn't chat as you went through the line." That would last so long "it would be after dinner" before they finished, and "you missed enough meals in Hanoi without missing one in the White House tonight," so he had regretfully abandoned the reception line.

After three more paragraphs of apology, he said he hoped to meet each man in the room after his speech, but "just remember we must get through in time for dinner which begins around 6:30 as far as you are concerned."

Then he briefed them. He said that when he had entered the White House, "the American people seemed to have lost their way. There was a desire to move away from responsibilities in the world. There was a lack of national pride, a lack of patriotism." That had all been turned around. America was once again the nation that all others looked to as a force for peace in the world.

He explained that he had achieved this success by keeping America's defenses strong, and through secret negotiations. "I want to be quite blunt," he went on. "Had we not had secrecy . . . let me say quite bluntly, there would have been no China initiative, there would have been no limitation of arms for the Soviet Union and no summit, and had we not had that kind of security and that kind of secrecy that allowed for the kind of exchange that is essential, you men would still be in Hanoi rather than Washington today."

In case anyone failed to connect the need for secrecy with the current revelations, the President added: "And let me say, I think it is time in this country to quit making national heroes out of those who steal secrets and publish them in the newspapers."

The men leaped up to applaud, shout, cheer, whistle, stamp their feet, shake their fists at reporters, and generally register their contempt for Daniel Ellsberg, *The Washington Post,* and *The New York Times,* and their total support for their Commander in Chief.

When the cheering stopped, Nixon continued: "We must have confidentiality, we must have secret communication. . . . I can assure you that in my terms of office as President I am going to meet my responsibility to protect the national security of the United States insofar as secrecy is concerned."

The President said his first term had not been easy, "but looking toward the balance of the second four years, let me say I feel better, because out in this room, I think I have some allies, and I will appreciate your help."

The men rose for another long ovation. Nixon then stood on the stage for over an hour as the men filed past. He shook the hand of each; each assured the Commander in Chief that he could count on the POWs.[36]

The dinner was magnificent. Nixon and his wife moved from table to table, posing for photographs and signing autographs. When Nixon got to the table where Senator John Stennis (D.-Miss.) was seated, Stennis remarked to the men, "You fellows wouldn't be here if it weren't for the guts of this man."

After dinner, Nixon began the toasts. He said, "The most difficult decision that I have made since being President was on December 18 of last year." There was a thunderous burst of applause. "And there were many occasions in that ten-day period after the decision was made when I wondered whether anyone in this country really supported it. But I can tell you this: after having met each one of our honored guests this evening, after having talked to them, I think that all of us would like to join in a round of applause for the brave men that took those B-52s in and did the job, because as all of you know, if they hadn't done it, you wouldn't be here tonight."

The toast brought on cheers, whistles, shouts, and applause that went on for almost five minutes.

Brigadier General John Flynn, USAF, the ranking POW, rose to respond. He said that everyone present knew that the December 18 decision had put the President "in a very lonely position. The decision was contested, but I would like to also report to you that when we heard heavy bombs impacting in Hanoi, we started to go and pack our bags, because we knew we were going home, and we were going home with honor.

"Now, sir, in recognition of your fortitude, and your perseverance under fire, the returnees would like to present to you a token of our esteem to you, sir."

Flynn handed Nixon a plaque inscribed to "Our leader—our comrade, Richard the Lion-Hearted."

The serious part of the evening having concluded, the entertainers took over. Bob Hope cracked jokes, Sammy Davis sang and danced. There were pop and country singers, Hollywood actors, other celebrities. John Wayne got the biggest hand when he said to the POWs, "I'll ride into the sunset with you anytime." The climax came when Irving Berlin led the party in singing "God bless America, my home sweet home."[37]

Nixon said that it was "one of the greatest nights in my life." After midnight, he went into the Lincoln Sitting Room where he sat before the fire. There he read a note one of the POWs had handed him. It was a message of support that concluded, "Don't let the bastards get you down, Mr. President."

The contrast between the splendid evening and the debilitating effects of the Watergate investigation struck him "with an almost physical force." His moment of triumph was a fleeting moment. (In the morning newspapers, the reception did not even make the lead story, which was that Jeb Magruder had agreed to plead guilty and serve as a prosecution witness of the dozen or so men expected to be indicted.)

Julie and Tricia came into the Lincoln Sitting Room. Tricia recorded in her diary what happened. They entered, she said, expecting to talk about the gala. But "when we saw his face, we realized that his spirit was troubled." Nixon always had a letdown after a triumph, but this one went beyond anything his daughters had seen. Their father complained about the "rather negative reception of all the POW ceremonies" by the press. "He correctly stated the reason for this apathy: in giving a good play to the ceremonies they feared they would build him up.

"Very simply, he said to Julie and me, 'Do you think I should resign?'

"It was not what he said but the way he said it that produced an internal earthquake in us."

"Don't you dare!" and "Don't even think of it!" the girls responded.

He wanted them to give him reasons for not resigning. They had lots of them—he had done nothing wrong, the country needed him, and so on. "He smiled at us and tried to say something to cheer us up, but it was almost more than I could bear to stay there and see his sadness. . . ."[38]

NIXON's all but exclusive concentration on Watergate matters, and Haldeman's departure, meant there was considerable slippage in the Executive Department. As one consequence, Nixon was losing his grip on operations in Indochina, as Congress asserted its authority in appropriations to hamper his ability to enforce the armistice.

In the aftermath of the January cease-fire and the return of the POWs, there were scattered but significant firefights in South Vietnam. In Cambodia, where the cease-fire did not apply, the Khmer Rouge were on the offensive. Nixon wanted to carry out bombing missions in both countries, but the opposition within the Congress was strong and growing. In mid-April, Bill Timmons, the White House liaison with Congress, reported that Senator Stennis would support the bombing in Cambodia, but he could not support any renewed bombing of North Vietnam. "K—note," Nixon wrote on Timmons's memo: "Enlist his support for the strike in South Vietnam."[39]

The fact that even Stennis was drawing a line indicated how nervous the Congress had become over Indochina operations. That became even more apparent in May, when Timmons reported that the House had attached an amendment to a Supplemental Appropriations bill that prohibited the use of any funds in the Supplemental to support bombing in Cambodia. The Administration had to have the Supplemental; Nixon could not afford to veto it. He now had to face squarely a situation he had dreaded for four and a half years, a complete cut-off of funds.

Timmons included an analysis of the reasons for the Administration's defeat. They included a poor presentation by the State and Defense Departments, Republican jitters (a recent poll showed that fifty GOP seats were in jeopardy as a result of Watergate), worry that the Communists would capture more POWs, and concern over the constitutional authority to continue the bombing.

Timmons concluded, "It was a terrible mistake to join this issue with Congress at this particular time. . . . The publicity and psychological stakes were too high to gamble for so little return." Only $25 million was involved, as there were but two months left in the fiscal year. "In the future," Timmons wrote, "I must take responsibility for reviewing every legislative proposal, even the usually routine supplementals." Nixon scribbled on the memo, "Haig—I totally agree. Both State and Defense should have done a better job. N.S.C. should flag such items for RN more carefully in the future."[40] It was the kind of detail Haldeman would have seen to automatically.

ON May 14, the Santa Ana *Register* charged that Nixon had used $1 million in campaign funds to purchase his San Clemente home. Ziegler furiously denied the story, but it would not die. On May 25, the White House released a written statement. It said that Nixon had purchased the property in 1969 for $1.5 million. He had borrowed $450,000 from his friend Robert Abplanalp for the down payment. In December 1969, he sold 21 of the 26 acres on the estate to an unnamed investment company headed by Abplanalp for $1,249,000. Ziegler said the statement "spoke for itself," but reporters noted that "Orange County, Calif. property records show no evidence that the property has been legally divided. A wall, paid for by the Federal Government, has been built around the entire 26 acres, and the Nixons are the only ones residing there."[41]

The reporters hounded the White House for more details. Gerald Warren supplied a few. He disclosed that the government had spent $39,525 on improvements at San Clemente, mostly for security measures. The statement gave reporters a target to shoot at. The General Services Administration (GSA) became involved; on June 14, the GSA said $703,365 had been spent on Nixon's homes in California and Florida. A week later, the figure had escalated; a House subcommittee concluded that Nixon's homes had cost the taxpayers $17.1 million—$10 million for fixed improvements and $7.1 million in personnel costs.[42]

Most of that money had gone for office space, or legitimate security measures, and would be recovered when Nixon left office and the government removed the equipment. But some of it at least provided permanent improvements that greatly enhanced the value of Nixon's properties.

To many Americans, the idea of the President getting rich at their expense was more offensive than ordering bugs put on snoopy reporters, or covering up Watergate. In his first national campaign, in 1952, Nixon had had to defend himself against charges of financial improprieties; now, in his last national campaign, to save his second term, he had to do so again.

Reporters began investigating his tax status. It turned out that as President, Nixon had paid no state or local income taxes. When he sold his New York apartment, he had avoided paying a capital-gains tax by saying that he was applying the profit to the purchase of his new "principal residence" in San Clemente. But in California, he argued that he occupied La Casa Pacifica "for brief periods of time" and that his principal residence was the White House (federal officials do not pay income tax to the District of Columbia), even though he was a registered voter in California.[43]

There was a potential embarrassment that was even greater. By May of 1973, Nixon's net worth was almost $1 million, a threefold increase since he had moved into the White House. The President had an annual salary of $200,000, plus a $91,000 expense allowance. Yet he had paid virtually no federal income taxes since 1969, primarily thanks to huge deductions he claimed for the gift of his Vice Presidential papers to the National Archives.

Nixon's vulnerabilities were compounding, extending far beyond the confines of Watergate and the cover-up. The bombing campaign in Cambodia, using government funds on his private homes, fudging if not cheating on his taxes, accepting huge unsecured loans from millionaire buddies—all threw Nixon more than ever on the defensive, where he hated to be, and made it that much more difficult for him to mount a counterattack, as he so badly wanted to do.

Nixon's critics hurled accusations at him, then when he tried to deal with the charges, the critics said he was so overwhelmed by Watergate that he was neglecting his duties as President. But when he tried to deal with his duties, the critics charged that he was trying to divert attention from Watergate.

It was true that Nixon was spending three quarters or more of his working time on Watergate and related matters. His neglect of other areas was costing him support. On May 15, Lou Harris passed on some poll results to the President. They showed that Nixon had positive ratings on his handling of foreign affairs, but on the domestic side the results were dramatically different. On handling the economy, the President got a 25 percent positive, 70 percent negative poll; on controlling the cost of living, the result was 17 percent positive, 79 percent negative.

The most obvious cause of the distressing figures was inflation. The inflation rate had fallen to 3.4 percent at the end of 1972, but by May 1973 it was back to 9 percent because in January, Nixon had abolished Phase II price controls and Phase III had not worked. The problem with Phase III was that it was a voluntary program for wage and price controls, based on informal pressure, or "jawboning." The "guidelines" for increases called for a ceiling of 5.5 percent, but with no enforcement machinery, the inevitable happened. Food prices were rising at an alarming rate, nearly doubling in one year in some cases. The chief cause was the massive grain sale to the Soviet Union. Harris told Nixon that "some bold steps must be taken in the whole economic area."

Nixon scribbled a note on Harris's memo for his Treasury Secretary, George Shultz: "I would like for you to give me a reaction. Sometimes political (i.e., confidence considerations) must override economics."[44]

Pressure on Nixon came from another direction; his old backer and millionaire friend, Elmer Bobst, called Rose Woods. She passed his message on to Nixon: although Bobst "likes George Shultz personally he is a scholar and not a practical person." Bobst "practically begs that you talk with John Connally and Arthur Burns and see that some stronger moves are taken." Bobst said that Phase III "is less than nothing."[45]

Nixon did confer with Connally, Burns, and others. They all urged tighter controls. In the Senate, meanwhile, a bill was moving forward that would impose a ninety-day freeze on prices, wages, and dividends.

Nixon had to act, and he did. On June 13, he went on nationwide radio and television to announce his decisions. His calm, matter-of-fact presentation, his confident speaking voice, constituted a response to those critics who were saying that Watergate had paralyzed Nixon.

Nixon opened with a brief account of the economic record of the past two years, then announced that "effective immediately I am ordering a freeze on prices . . . It will cover all prices paid by consumers. The only prices not covered will be those of unprocessed agricultural products at the farm levels, and rents." The freeze would last for sixty days. The reason prices on the farm were not frozen was to increase supplies; Nixon called on the farmers to plant more, harvest more, as he also called on Congress to give him authority to impose export controls on food products.

Nixon was equally bold in other areas. He wanted new authority to reduce tariffs. He wanted quick congressional action to get on with the Alaskan pipeline, in order to combat a shortage of oil that was threatening to become serious, and that had already led to sharp increases in gasoline prices at the pump.

The President said his sixty-day freeze would be followed by Phase IV, which would be designed to put into place a new and more effective system of controls, tougher than Phase II. But he also promised that Phase IV "will not be designed to get us permanently into a controlled economy. On the contrary, it will be designed as a better way to get us out of a controlled economy, to return as quickly as possible to the free market system."[46]

The following morning, for the first time in weeks, Nixon got the headlines for something he did the night before, rather than something the White House had done months or years before, and for something that was a positive step rather than a denial.

NOTHING short of war, however, would push Watergate out of the spotlight. Certainly Nixon's May 22 statement of denial did not. Prominent Republicans were among the doubters. Senator Percy, for example, called the statement a step in the right direction but added that it was not enough "to accept 'responsibility' in the broadest, most imprecise sense of that word." He called Watergate the "darkest scandal in American political history," indicated that he could hardly believe that Nixon was not involved in the cover-up, and asked the President to reveal the facts rather than letting them be "dragged out piece-meal by investigatory bodies or the press."[47]

Nixon, incensed by what he characterized as the "sanctimony" of his critics, wanted to reveal the wiretap activities of his precedessors. He knew that Robert Kennedy had bugged Martin Luther King, Jr., as well as reporters. He had heard that Jack Kennedy bugged Bobby's office, and the home of eighty-one-year-old Bernard Baruch and his wife. Johnson had tapped the Mississippi Freedom Democratic Party, Bobby Kennedy, and others. Franklin Roosevelt had used the FBI for political purposes. Nixon wanted "everything out on the Democrats"; but his staff resisted. The aides argued that if he did make such charges, it would look as if he was trying to divert attention from himself by smearing others. Nixon countered that he was being made to look unique, which was true— if he could have convinced the public that what he had done was standard operating procedure, he might have lessened the shock and reduced the sense of outrage that greeted each new revelation. But the aides prevailed, and nothing was done.[48]

On May 29 Kissinger, for the first time, tried to help. He had previously denied (on May 14) that he had authorized any wiretaps, but now he admitted that "his office" had supplied the names of NSC staff members to the FBI for the 1969 taps. Kissinger called taps "a distasteful thing in general," but stoutly defended them as necessary to safeguard national security.[49]

The reporters covering the story were not above using illegal methods. On May 29, *The Washington Post* carried a story by Bob Woodward and Carl Bernstein stating that the Watergate prosecutors had told the

Justice Department that there was justification for calling Nixon to answer questions before the grand jury. Ziegler issued a statement carried by the *Post* alongside the story; he said it reflected "a shocking and irresponsible abuse of authority on the part of the federal prosecutors, if in fact, they made the statements attributed to them." He pointed out that communicating information relating to grand jury proceedings was a violation of law. Special Prosecutor Cox agreed; he issued his own statement saying he had made no such decision (about Nixon's appearance), and added that he had instructed the prosecutors to refrain from leaks and rumors.[50]

They continued anyway, from every direction. Ehrlichman was reported to have told the Chairman of the Senate Subcommittee on Intelligence Operations, John McClellan (D.-Ariz.), that Nixon had ordered him and Haldeman to tell the CIA to tell the FBI to go slow on its Watergate investigation. The following day, May 31, Haldeman was reported to have denied "categorically" before the McClellan subcommittee that there had been any attempt to cover up. That same day Senator Ervin did some leaking of his own; he said that if the documents John Dean had given to Judge Sirica about the Huston Plan were made public, they would come as "a great shock to the American people." The documents, according to Ervin, revealed a "Gestapo mentality" in the White House.[51]

Vernon Walters got involved. He told the McClellan subcommittee that the White House had not been worried about national security when it ordered the CIA to tell the FBI to go slow, but rather about the political implications. He released a series of memos from June 1972 to prove his point, and said that he and Pat Gray "did not see why he or I should jeopardize the integrity of our organizations to protect some mid-level White House figures who had acted imprudently . . . He [Gray] felt it important that the President should be protected from his would-be protectors."[52]

On June 3, *The Washington Post* and *The New York Times* reported that John Dean had told investigators that he had met alone and in small groups with Nixon on forty occasions from late January to early April of 1973 to discuss the cover-up. Dean was quoted as saying that Nixon had shown a "great interest" in ascertaining "things were handled right— taken care of." Dean reportedly charged that Nixon had a "substantial knowledge" of the cover-up, and had testified that Nixon had told him that raising a million dollars to buy the silence of Hunt and his friends would be easy. The White House issued strong denials.[53]

When Nixon caught the words "million dollars," he later confessed, he "felt a sudden sense of dread." When he read the details, he felt "discouraged, drained, and pressured." He asked Haig if he should resign. Haig said no. Instead, Haig urged him to listen to the tapes "and to construct an unassailable defense based on them." Nixon agreed to do that. Haig produced a list of Nixon-Dean meetings between February 27 and April 1973. There were thirty-four in all. As Nixon looked at the list, he later wrote, "an uneasy feeling came over me as I wondered what we might have talked about in all those conversations."[54]

Nixon called Haldeman. "I'm up at Camp David and I'm trying to straighten out the facts here," the President said. He complained about Dean. In a second call, he said, "We're trying to work out a game plan for the week when Dean testifies." Dean was scheduled to go before the Ervin Committee on June 18.[55]

The following morning, June 4, aide Steve Bull set up a tape machine in Nixon's EOB office and showed the President how to work it. Nixon put on the earphones and started listening. He put in the entire day on that task.

Late that afternoon, Nixon called Haldeman. "I listened to every damn thing," the President said, "and Bob, this son of a bitch [Dean] is bluffing." It was an extraordinary statement, but Nixon went on to explain what he meant: "We sent Buzhardt over—and this is just for your private information—he went through the files and not a God-damn memo in the files!"

"Really?"

"None. Period. He didn't make any."

In other words, Dean had no documentary evidence to back up his charges. Nixon went on to mention his fears about what he might have said to Dean in his telephone conversation on March 22 (when he asked Dean if Hunt had received the hush money). Had Dean mentioned this to Haldeman?

"No," Haldeman assured Nixon. "Not at all."

Nixon was relieved. He said he was glad he had kept the tapes; they would prove his innocence.

One minute after hanging up, Nixon called Haldeman back. "Sorry to bother you again," the President said, "but the one thing which, of course, is a sticky point, is with regard to the 21st and if you'd give some thought with regard to how you could pre-empt that sometimes, uh, I think it would be very good."

Haldeman mumbled, and Nixon went on: "I don't know how the hell you can, but, uh . . ."

"I think we can somehow, and I think . . ."

"Somehow just put it out, you know?" the President concluded.[56]

Nixon called Haig and Ziegler into his office. Haig was hopeful. "Nobody in Congress likes him [Dean]," he assured the President. "We can take the son of a bitch on."

"That's right," Nixon said. Then he grew worried. "We have one problem: it's that damn conversation of March 21st due to the fact that, uh, for the reasons (unintelligible). But I think we can handle that."

So did Haig (who had not listened to the tape, by his own account).

"Bob [Haldeman] can handle it," Nixon explained. "He'll get up there and say that—Bob will say, 'I was there: the President said—' "

"That's exactly right," Haig nodded. He added that if the questions got too sticky, "You just can't recall."

Nixon sighed. "As you know," he said, "we're up against ruthless people." Then he recalled that on March 21 he had told Dean that clemency could not be considered until after the 1974 election, and cheered up. Then he wondered how many people knew about the tapes—as well he might have, as he had just added Haig and Ziegler to the already long list—and reassured himself that "not even Buzhardt knows," and Buzhardt was his own lawyer.

Well, Haig interrupted, Buzhardt knows, "but he's the only one that knows."

"All right," Nixon said. "No further. He shouldn't tell anyone. Uh, I don't want it put out."

Nixon had just put in eight hours on the tapes. He sighed. "This is hard work. But I've got to do it. Got to do it. And it's best for me to do it, too."

"Only you," Haig said. "Only you."

"Thanks a lot, Al," the President said sarcastically.

For over an hour, Nixon, Haig, and Ziegler discussed the meaning of the tapes. Ziegler, who apparently had listened to parts of them, continually insisted that Nixon had done nothing wrong and had nothing to worry about; in this, like most sycophants, he was doing his prince a disservice. For example, Nixon said he had asked about the possibility of going the hang-out route, only to reject that option.

"You see," Ziegler interjected as he explained to Nixon what Nixon had said, "Mr. President, what you were talking about, what you had in mind, was not, at least in my impression . . ."

"Cover-up," Nixon offered.

" . . . awareness of payments to people," Ziegler went on.

"Huh?"

"Er, awareness of payments to people. What you had in mind was . . . relaying the hang-out in terms of Segretti . . ."

"Segretti planned the God, God damn Watergate," Nixon said.

"That's right," Ziegler agreed.

Steve Bull joined them. He pitched in to help Ziegler remind the President that Dean had said no one in the White House was involved. Nixon said he never knew about the Ellsberg break-in until April 17, when Dean told him Ehrlichman had a problem. Nixon went on: "I didn't know about a God damned thing." His aides agreed. "You were talking about political problems," Ziegler offered, "not illegal problems. Political problems as they relate to the Ervin Committee hearings and what could come out in the course of those hearings."

Nixon, in a tone of voice expressing confusion and doubt, said, "I mean, God, maybe we were talking most about a cover-up—Watergate. I really didn't . . . I didn't know what the hell—I honestly didn't know."

What did Ziegler think about how to handle "the whole Dean problem?"

"Let Dean run his string a little bit," Ziegler suggested.

"Not until the twenty-first of March did he come in and talk about a cover-up," Nixon declared.

"And he did not in any way suggest that he was involved directly," Ziegler offered.

Nixon shook his head. "On the twenty-first he did," the President corrected Ziegler.

"Did he?"

"He said, 'Even Dean.' "

There was a pause. Nixon mumbled, "I didn't want to burn Mitchell."

"That's right," Ziegler agreed.

"The key to this thing, Ron, is Mitchell. Always been the key. You haven't had a cover-up, Dean did it—shit, he didn't do it for Haldeman and Ehrlichman. . . . He did it for John Mitchell. So did Magruder do it for Mitchell. Magruder lied for Mitchell. You know that."

"Sure."

"That's the tragedy of the whole thing. Mitchell would never step up to this. Well, would you? Former Attorney General step up and say you bugged? Shit, I wouldn't."

Back to Dean. Nixon said, "He might well have drawn the conclusion, Ron, that the President wanted him to keep the lid on."

"Yeah, the political lid in the Ervin Committee hearings, not the legal lid in terms of the trial [of Hunt, Liddy, et al.]."

"That's the difference. I see," said Nixon.

"That's the difference," Ziegler repeated.

"We were talking about the Ervin Committee," Nixon reassured himself. "We weren't talking about the trial."

"We were concerned about the Ervin Committee," Ziegler agreed. "And what they would press for in terms not of illegality, but in terms of political embarrassment."

Nixon was satisfied that he was innocent. "Don't you think it's interesting, though, to run through this?" he asked. "Really, the goddamn record is not bad, is it?"

"Makes me feel very good," Ziegler answered.

But worries returned. Nixon recalled Dean's statement that "I was over this like a blanket." Nixon then asked: "How does that strike you? Was he telling me that there was a cover-up?"

"Not at all," Ziegler chipped in.

Still Nixon worried. "Who the hell is going to answer Dean?" he asked. "He saw me alone, Ron. How do we handle that?"

Before Ziegler could reply, Nixon supplied a partial answer: "Haldeman can handle him on the 21st, which is the tough one, but he can handle him." He complained that Dean had promised him not to be a traitor, but "God damn it, the son of a bitch defects."

So what about the $350,000 that Haldeman moved from the White House back to CREEP, where it was used to buy the burglars' silence? Nixon asked if there had been any talk about that money on March 21.

"Not at all," Ziegler said. "I don't think there was any talk about the three-fifty until into April."

"Oh, yes there was," Nixon corrected him. "March 21st. We had a talk about it."

"You sure?"

"I'm sure. Dean told me. Dean talked about the three-fifty that Haldeman had (unintelligible), Hell yes, I said."

Ziegler tried a different tack to reassure Nixon. He said he could just say that before March 21, the President had not known a thing.

"I should have reacted before the twenty-first of March," Nixon confessed. "Dean shouldn't have had to come in to me with the 'cancer in the heart of the presidency,' which, to his credit, he did." Nixon said that Haldeman had not done that, Ehrlichman had not done that.

This threw Ziegler into confusion. He hemmed and hawed, until the meeting ended with a presidential sigh. "God, I'm worn out," said Nixon.[57]

One reason for the President's weariness was that after a long, tough day, he had engaged in an aimless conversation that had produced nothing more than a hope that Haldeman would somehow find a way to explain away March 21, and reassurances from his aides that there was nothing to worry about. Nixon knew they were dead wrong.

DEAN's statement about having had forty meetings with Nixon led to questions about the documentary record of those meetings. Warren replied on June 4: he said the logs recording the time and place of the meetings would not be released either to the federal prosecutors or the Ervin Committee. "That would be Constitutionally inappropriate," Warren said, because it would violate "the basic doctrine of separation of powers. The President's logs are not subject to subpoena."

In printing the statement, the newspapers immediately noted that the proscription conflicted with statements from Richardson and Cox, who insisted that they did have the power of subpoena over those logs.[58]

Thus did the battle enter a new stage. Nixon had started out by insisting that no one on his staff would testify before a grand jury or any congressional committee. Then he had said his aides could supply written answers. Then it was testimony in executive sessions, with immunity. Then it was without immunity. Finally it was in open session, but the investigators could not have any White House documents.

In the struggle for evidence, Nixon had strengths and weaknesses. He had physical control of much of the material, but not all—John Dean had already given to the authorities the Huston Plan, for example. Nixon had the doctrine of executive privilege working for him, a doctrine that has no basis in the Constitution but is well established by precedent, albeit only in general terms. As against this, Nixon had promised Richardson that he would not interfere with the work of the Special Prosecutor. And in their demand for the logs of the Dean-Nixon meetings, Richardson and Cox had not only that promise to support them, but congressional outrage (if Nixon ignored a subpoena) and the power of public opinion.

In this opening skirmish, Nixon did badly. The day after Warren put out the statement of defiance, the White House retreated. Warren made a "speech of contrition." He said the documents might be made available voluntarily even though Nixon considered them presidential documents and therefore not subject to subpoena. Immediately after that, however, Sam Dash, chief counsel for the Ervin Committee, said he would subpoena the logs.[59]

On June 5, leaks from an Ehrlichman deposition revealed the motive for the original break-in at the DNC: Ehrlichman was quoted as saying that Magruder had been told by Colson that Nixon wanted information on O'Brien.[60]

The following day, Nixon announced that Mel Laird had taken Ehrlichman's place on the White House staff, and that Al Haig was retiring from the Army in order to serve full time as White House chief of staff. The Laird appointment was greeted with enthusiasm in the Congress, the Haig appointment with silence. Nixon also announced that the logs of his meetings with Dean would be given to the Ervin Committee.[61]

On June 5, Nixon took the sudden decision to make a public appearance. He asked his aides to find a suitable venue; they came up with a two-year-old invitation from Florida Technological University in Orlando. On June 8, Nixon flew down to give the commencement address.

He talked about soaring prices. He explained that one cause was that "all over the world today people are living better. Oh, there are many terribly poor people in the world, including some in the United States, but they live better. As a result, the demand for meat . . . has gone up." He was reassuring: "This is a problem but we have the means to deal with it."

His conclusion was appropriate to the mood of graduation day: "In the whole history of the world, there has never been a time I would rather be a graduate than in the year 1973 in the United States of America." What the reporters commented on, however, was that he did not mention Watergate. No matter what he did, or did not do, Watergate would not go away.[62]

ON June 9, Chuck Colson, who had resigned in March, stepped forward. He told *The New York Times* that he would stake his life on Nixon's disclaimer of any knowledge of a cover-up. Colson said the whole thing was Mitchell's fault. Haldeman, meanwhile, said that Nixon had urged his aides, both before and after the election, to clear up the Watergate case "so that it won't be hanging over into the second term."[63]

On June 14, Magruder appeared before the Ervin Committee. He admitted that he had lied to the grand jury, but insisted that he was now telling the truth. And the truth was that Colson "called me one evening and asked me in a sense would we get off the stick and get the budget approved for Mr. Liddy's plans, that we needed information, particularly on Mr. O'Brien."[64]

In short, day after day the pounding went on. Never before had the American people learned so much, so soon, about the inner workings of an Administration; and there had been so much to learn. The option of escape via resignation increasingly came into Nixon's mind, but whenever he mentioned it to his family or his chief of staff, he was told not even to think about such a thing. There was the matter of his pride, and of meeting his responsibilities, and of doing what the millions of Americans who had voted for him and believed in him expected him to do. There was also the stark fact that if he resigned, Spiro Agnew would become President.

Agnew had political problems, but recently his problems with the law were looming even larger. Investigators in Maryland were beginning to bring indictments in a payoff scheme that apparently would reach to the governor's office at a time when Agnew was the governor.

On June 14, Nixon met with Agnew in the Oval Office. He gave the Vice President thirty minutes, and marching orders. Agnew had been pestering the White House staff for an expanded role in domestic affairs, and reminding the aides that Nixon had promised to give him more responsibilities. Agnew's specific demand was that he be made the "energy czar."

What Nixon wanted from Agnew was a more spirited defense of the President. He refused to make a commitment to a new role for Agnew; instead, he urged the Vice President to "speak out in support of the Administration," and to answer Watergate charges. Then he dismissed him.[65]

Soviet leader Leonid Brezhnev was coming to town in two days, for his second summit meeting with Nixon. Five months earlier, Nixon had anticipated that the meeting would be one of the capstone events of his eight-year Presidency. Now the press, the TV commentators, and many in the Congress were treating it as an unwanted interruption and intrusion into the real business of the nation, Watergate. Nixon, meanwhile, had little more to defend himself with than the words of two men, Haldeman and Agnew, who themselves were likely to be indicted for criminal acts in the near future.

CHAPTER SEVEN

FOREIGN AFFAIRS
February–June 1973

As Watergate compounded, taking Nixon's time and draining his energy, Henry Kissinger stepped forward to "hold foreign policy together."[1] It was inevitable. He was the only major figure from the first term untouched by Watergate, and the Secretary of State was weak. In fact, Secretary Rogers was in an unhappy position. Nixon ignored him. He found out about major policy initiatives by reading the newspapers. Kissinger, not content with the reality of power, wanted the symbols as well—he was pressing Nixon to appoint him Secretary of State. It was common knowledge in Washington that Nixon had promised to do that, when the time was right, making Rogers a lame duck.

Kissinger was insisting on being both National Security Adviser and Secretary of State, even though the idea of one man holding both jobs badly confused the roles of the Adviser and the Secretary. The Adviser's job was to coordinate the work and recommendations of the various departments and agencies that had a foreign-policy concern, including State, Defense, Treasury, CIA, and NSC. The Secretary's job was to run the State Department and implement policy decisions by the President. Kissinger insisted that he have both jobs, or he would resign, and so badly did Nixon need him—or at least need his reputation to bolster the Administration—that the President agreed. Nixon did stand up to Kissinger on the question of timing. He told Kissinger he would have to wait.

As he waited, Kissinger worked at reaching a cease-fire in Cambodia and enforcing the cease-fire in Vietnam, at preparing for Brezhnev's mid-June visit to the United States, at preparing a new policy initiative toward Europe, and on the endemic Middle East crisis. The Middle East had been the one area where Nixon had allowed Rogers some freedom of movement, but Rogers's attempts to reach a compromise in the wake of the Israeli victories in the 1967 war had gotten nowhere. Although Israel had not annexed the territories it had seized from Egypt (the Gaza Strip and Sinai), from Syria (the Golan Heights), and Jordan (the West Bank and parts of Jerusalem), the Israeli military occupied the conquered territory and the Israeli government simply refused to consider any of the peace plans Rogers put forward.

Since 1956, when Eisenhower had put America into the Middle East as an honest broker, the area had produced many headaches and few rewards for American Presidents. The stresses and strains were obvious, above all the need for Arab oil, which had grown to the point that by 1973 about 40 percent of America's oil came from the Middle East, as against the strength of the American Jewish community in American politics. Jewish political strength came about because the Jews were well organized, were almost of a single mind with regard to Israel, were active in politics, and were major financial contributors. In addition, Israel had strong moral support from Americans of all faiths, and was widely respected.

To maintain an even-handed position between Arabs and Israelis, an American President had to carry water on both shoulders. He also had to do what he could to keep the Soviets from meddling in the area. For Nixon, there was a further complication; the American Jewish community and its political advocates held his policy of détente hostage to the question of Jewish emigration from the Soviet Union.

Kissinger wrote in his memoirs that Nixon "was convinced that he owed nothing to Jewish votes and that he could not increase his Jewish support regardless of what he did."[2] The statement ignored this fact: many of Nixon's biggest contributors were Jewish. It ignored another fact: Nixon had a deep and genuine admiration for Israel, in part because he appreciated Israel's strong anti-Soviet foreign policy. He also liked Israel because of its underdog status and "screw you" attitude toward the rest of the world. Nixon could and did indulge in crude anti-Semitic jokes, he could and did make Kissinger and the other Jews among his aides squirm in discomfort or embarrassment; but he would never let Soviet arms prevail over American arms in the Middle East, and he would never let Israel be overrun by the Arabs.

The complexities and contradictions that are always present in the Middle East were compounded during the Nixon Administration by the complexities and contradictions of Richard Nixon. This showed clearly in a series of handwritten Nixon remarks on memos from Kissinger.

In October 1972, Kissinger had sent to Nixon a memo from Defense Secretary Laird urging secret contacts with Egypt to take advantage of Egyptian President Anwar el-Sadat's expulsion of the Soviets. Nixon commented, "K—I lean to Laird's view. The conduct of the American Jewish community on the Soviet visa problem—clearly indicates they put Jewish interests above US concerns. This we *cannot* do."[3]

In February 1973, a month into Nixon's second term, Egyptian National Security Adviser Hafiz Ismail came to Washington for meetings. His purpose was to pressure the United States to get Israel to return the conquered territory. Kissinger gave Nixon a memo with the usual three options: do nothing, do something, or go all-out to force an agreement, using secret talks. Nixon noted in the margin beside option one: "K— Absolutely not. . . . I have delayed through two elections and this year I am determined to move off dead center—I totally disagree. This thing is getting ready to blow."

Beside option three, Nixon wrote: "The preferred track for action. At the same time keep the public track going for external appearances— but keep it from interfering with the private track."

In a general comment at the end of Kissinger's memo, Nixon wrote that it was time to move toward a settlement. "We are now Israel's *only* major friend in the world. I have yet to see *one iota* of give on their part. . . . This is the time to get moving—and they must be told that *firmly*. . . . The time has come to quit pandering to Israel's intransigent position. Our actions over the past have led them to think we will stand with them *regardless* of how unreasonable they are."[4]

Nixon's comment showed a firmer grasp on the situation than Kissinger was displaying. Nixon was aware of the seriousness of the problem and the need to move soon, before Egypt in desperation at the Israeli refusal to give an inch launched an attack. For his part, Kissinger confessed that "we knew astonishingly little of Egypt's real thinking."[5]

All through 1971 Sadat had threatened war. When the year ended with no action, Egypt looked pathetic. Egyptian desperation increased. In 1972 Sadat kicked out the Russians; there was no Israeli response, nor any American help or reward for Egypt. By early 1973, Sadat was so openly proclaiming he would have to go to war that people assumed he couldn't possibly mean it.

Kissinger, especially, could not believe it. He later wrote that in his talks with Ismail in February and March 1973, "I played with him. . . . Ismail told me several times that the present situation could not continue. He asked me whether the United States did not understand that if there weren't some agreement then there would be war. . . . There wasn't even a slight smile on my face, but in my heart I laughed and laughed. A war? Egypt? I regarded it as empty talk, a boast empty of content."[6]

Kissinger was not alone. On March 1, Israeli Prime Minister Golda Meir came to Washington. She told Nixon that the Arabs had no military option. "We never had it so good," she proclaimed, indicating that she was ready to accept the status quo indefinitely. Then she asked Nixon's approval of a new package of military aid. Despite his tough words on the

Kissinger memos only a week earlier, he gave it. A few days later he announced that the United States was supplying Israel with forty-eight Phantom jets. As Nixon had just promised Ismail that the United States would use its influence with Israel to work toward a settlement, the Egyptians felt more alone than ever.[7]

Despite his realistic analysis of the problems in the Middle East, Nixon did not have the time or energy to devote himself to dealing with those problems, nor the wisdom to resolve his ambivalences about Israel. He could not or would not work through his Secretary of State and the State Department. Kissinger was preoccupied with Southeast Asia, the Soviet Union, and Europe. America had no real policy in the Middle East.

WHEN Nixon launched the December 1972 bombing of Hanoi, the press in Western Europe was highly critical. So were most of the politicians; the notable exception was British Prime Minister Edward Heath. Nixon was furious with the others. On February 1, 1973, he told Heath, "What you did, did not go unnoticed and what others did, did not go unnoticed either. It is hard to understand when allies turn on you."[8]

But Nixon had been one of NATO's earliest, and remained one of its strongest, supporters. He did not allow his anger to influence his policy. Instead, he decided to reach out to the Europeans with a new initiative. His idea was to reassure them that they were still first in his heart and mind, despite the opening to China and détente with the Soviets.

The idea had merit, but the execution was poorly done. Nixon did not pay sufficient attention to detail, nor did he think through his actions. He announced the new policy in a picture-taking session on February 15 with the Supreme Allied Commander in Europe, General Andrew Goodpaster. He said that 1973 would be the "Year of Europe."[9]

The forum and the nature of the announcement were all wrong. Nixon's remark seemed offhand, and it received little attention. Nor was there any follow-up until April 23, by which time Watergate commanded the front pages of European as well as American newspapers, and then it came from Kissinger, not the President.

In a major public address, Kissinger announced plans to develop "a new Atlantic Charter" and declared that 1973 would be the "Year of Europe." What this meant, he did not explain; reporters took the meaning to be an attempt to distract attention from Watergate. Europeans were suspicious, if not hostile; they thought the Americans were treating them as another geopolitical piece on the chessboard rather than as allies. The State Department was surprised. Secretary Rogers had not been informed that Kissinger would be making this major address.

What little effect the "Year of Europe" had was counterproductive.

Europeans had not been consulted, and they were unimpressed at being awarded a particular, limited time in the sun by the United States.[10]

The only real attempt to provide some substance to the initiative came on May 31–June 1, when Nixon met in Reykjavik, Iceland, with French President Georges Pompidou. Nixon delivered a carefully crafted speech. He said the "Year of Europe" initiative had nothing to do with the upcoming Brezhnev summit, or with his own domestic problems. He denied that his Russian and Chinese policy "downgrades the importance and concern we have for our real friends." He said he had "no more illusions than you do about what they [the Soviets] want." It was important for NATO to remain strong, he asserted: "Otherwise, those shrewd and determined men in the Kremlin will eat us one by one. They cannot digest us all together but they can pick at us one by one."[11]

The generalizations were valid; the specifics wanting. The "Year of Europe" faded away, forgotten and unwanted. Nixon's attempt to link his Administration with such dramatic breakthroughs as the Roosevelt-Churchill Atlantic Charter and the Truman Administration's unveiling of the Marshall Plan sank without a trace.

IN Indochina, the fighting continued. In violation of the cease-fire agreement, the North Vietnamese were sending truckloads of supplies down the Ho Chi Minh Trail. They made a tempting target. On March 6, Nixon had ordered a bombing strike, only to cancel the order the following day. Kissinger was unhappy. He blamed Watergate, reasoning that Nixon feared stirring up even more criticism.[12]

That March, and again in April, Kissinger recommended a resumption of the bombing in South Vietnam, but Nixon would not act. On April 15, he discussed Vietnam with Nixon. It was a Sunday. Nixon spent more than twelve hours that day on Watergate problems. He found it difficult to focus on Kissinger, who accused Hanoi of stalling on a meeting in Paris to discuss cease-fire violations. He urged Nixon to bomb in Laos and in Vietnam on both sides of the DMZ. Still Nixon would not act—in Kissinger's view, because of his preoccupation with Watergate. "But for Watergate we would surely have acted in April," Kissinger later noted.[13]

Of course, the United States already was acting in Cambodia, where B-52s were carrying out extensive bombing raids against the Khmer Rouge, who were conducting an offensive against the Lon Nol government. Lon Nol had overthrown Prince Norodom Sihanouk in 1970; Nixon's Cambodian incursion of that year had been designed, in part, to support Lon Nol; by 1973, such are the vagaries of international politics, the Soviet Union was supporting Lon Nol, the Chinese were supporting Sihanouk, and the North Vietnamese were supporting the Khmer Rouge (a decade later, in 1983, the United States and China were supporting

Sihanouk *and* the Khmer Rouge against a Vietnamese puppet regime).

Congress, in 1973, wanted no part of a policy propping up Lon Nol. Majority Leader Tip O'Neill remarked that Cambodia was not worth the life of one American flier.[14] On June 4, the Senate would approve an amendment to cut off all funds for military operations in Indochina.

MORE conscious of its own strength than at any time since Reconstruction, the 93d Congress set out to prevail on policy toward the Soviet Union. Its method was linkage, a Nixon-Kissinger term that they hated when it was turned against them; its goal was to trade American grain for Jewish emigration.

In February, Brezhnev wrote Nixon about the agenda for the summit they had agreed to hold in June. Brezhnev said he looked forward to the signing of a treaty on the non-use of nuclear weapons and to the completion of SALT II, as well as agreements on trade and economic arrangements, cooperation in science, technology, health, and the peaceful use of nuclear energy. Further, Brezhnev wanted to talk about the Middle East, about European security, about mutual and balanced force reductions in Europe, and the relations between the two Germanies.[15]

That was a full enough agenda for a year's worth of talk, but Senator Henry Jackson (D.-Wash.) added to it. On March 15, he introduced in the East-West Trade Relations Bill his amendment tying the grant of most-favored-nation (MFN) status for the Soviet Union to Jewish emigration. He had seventy-three co-sponsors in the Senate. Jackson and his co-sponsors had rejected Administration pleas that they wait until they learned the results of meetings then going on in Moscow, between Treasury Secretary Shultz and Brezhnev, on the subject of MFN status and Jewish emigration.[16]

At those talks, Brezhnev told Shultz that the exit tax charged to emigrants (in theory to pay for their education) was not being collected. He also indicated that the Soviets would ease their restrictions on Jewish emigration in practice, although they would not change their laws or otherwise bow to American pressure on this internal matter.

The Nixon Administration moved quickly to solidify détente and give it economic meaning, beyond the sale of grain to the Soviets. On March 20, the Export-Import Bank granted a loan of $202 million for Soviet purchase of American industrial equipment. Eight days later the U.S.-USSR Trade Council opened in Moscow; there were nearly three-hundred American firms in its membership. On April 12, Armand Hammer of Occidental Oil signed a multi-billion-dollar chemical-fertilizer barter arrangement.[17]

On April 10, Nixon submitted the Trade Reform Act of 1973 to Congress. It included MFN status for the Soviet Union. Jackson and his many friends immediately protested in the strongest terms. Nixon commented in his memoirs on the rare convergence: "On the one side the liberals and the American Zionists had decided that now was the time to challenge the Soviet Union's highly restrictive emigration policies, particularly with respect to Soviet Jews. On the other side were the conservatives, who had traditionally opposed detente because it challenged their ideological opposition to contacts with Communist countries."[18] Kissinger wrote that "it was galling that the issue chosen by our critics was a subject in which we had every reason to take pride: Jewish emigration from the Soviet Union."[19]

By this time, mid-April, Nixon was spending almost every waking moment on Watergate. The Jackson Amendment was one of the few other subjects for which he would take time. He met with American Jewish leaders. He was frank, straightforward, realistic, honest. He told them the obvious, that it was "utterly unrealistic to think that a fundamental change in the Soviet system could be brought about because we refused to extend MFN status." He gave them a vivid image to contemplate. "The walls of the Kremlin are very thick. If you are inside, there is a chance that they will listen to you; if you are outside you are not even going to be heard." He cited statistics; in the first three years of his first term, before détente, Soviet Jews were allowed to emigrate at an average rate of 5,000 a year. In 1972, the year of détente, they came out at a rate of 31,400. In 1973, even that pace was being exceeded.[20]

Brezhnev told Kissinger that he was free to inform Congress that the exit tax had been suspended. Nixon was elated. Expecting to celebrate a great achievement, just when he needed one so badly, on April 18 he called congressional leaders, including Senator Jackson, to the White House. In the Roosevelt Room, he told them the Soviets had removed the major obstacle to the granting of MFN and had proved the advantage of quiet diplomacy on human rights.

The politicians listened politely enough, in what Kissinger called a "grumbling silence at another of Nixon's coups."

Then Jackson spoke up. What the Soviets had done was not enough, he declared. They would have to give assurances not only on the exit tax, but also guarantees on a minimum number of exit visas, and they had to ease emigration not only for Jews but for all nationalities.[21]

The reaction of the Nixon Administration is nicely summed up in John Ehrlichman's handwritten notes of a meeting between Nixon, Federal Reserve Board chairman Arthur Burns, and Shultz. It took place in the Oval Office immediately after the congressmen left the Roosevelt Room.

> Jackson irresponsible. Would sacrifice disarmament unless USSR *publicly* disavows Jewish policy.
> PRESIDENT: This could lead to anti-Semitism.

SHULTZ: I was stunned. Two hours on plane with him [Jackson] and thought he was ok.

PRESIDENT: I'll lay it out on TV! No summit on account of this.

Jackson outflanked [Senator Jacob] Javits [R.-N.Y.]. Javits position, let's think this over.

Burns to see Javits.

SHULTZ: Jackson says, Soviets need our grain.

PRESIDENT: He is risking five great initiatives. A storm will hit American Jews if they are intransigent.[22]

Two days later, Nixon held a Cabinet meeting. There he complained about "professional Jews," and said, "I'm not a professional Quaker and they hate me for it." Then he spoke to the problems the Jackson Amendment created for Brezhnev, warned that Jackson was jeopardizing SALT II, and pointed out that the right approach was to work quietly and behind the scenes with Brezhnev rather than to confront him directly.[23]

In May, Kissinger flew to Moscow to prepare for the summit. He discussed Jewish emigration and got Brezhnev to agree to look at a list of 1,000 hardship cases of aspiring Jewish emigrants compiled by American Jewish leaders, and to keep up an annual level of Jewish emigration of 36,000 to 40,000.[24] But his major concern was SALT II.

The U.S. position on arms control was to set an overall equal aggregate of 2,350 ICBMs (Intercontinental Ballistic Missiles), SLBMs (Submarine Launched Missiles), and heavy bombers, with a freeze on MIRV (multiple independently targetable re-entry vehicles) testing and deployment. The proposal was a one-sided ploy. The United States had fully tested, developed, and deployed its MIRVs, while the Soviets had not even tested a MIRV. Kissinger admitted that the American proposal "neatly shut the Soviets out of MIRVing their ICBM force, which comprised 85 percent of their total throwweight, without significantly curtailing any program of our own."[25] Brezhnev told Kissinger the obvious, that the American proposal was unacceptable. The Soviets, for their part, proposed a freeze on testing and deployment of all new strategic systems, which Kissinger and others saw as aimed at the American Trident system, and thus unacceptable. So SALT remained in a stalemate on the eve of the summit.[26]

Kissinger did get agreement on the wording of the Prevention of Nuclear War (PNW) agreement, which was important to the Soviets but a throwaway for Nixon. On many occasions in the 1960s the Soviets had proposed a pledge on "no first use of nuclear weapons," something the Americans resisted because it would deny to NATO the use of its nuclear deterrent in the event of a conventional Red Army offensive in Central Europe. The wording Kissinger agreed to pledged both sides to use their best efforts to prevent nuclear war; in Raymond Garthoff's words, the agreement "can be regarded either as profoundly important, or as frosting on the detente cake."[27]

On the eve of the summit, then, SALT was in trouble, MFN status for the Soviet Union was in trouble, and PNW had been rendered innocuous. Nixon's political base, meanwhile, was eroding, indeed was in danger of disappearing, because John Dean was scheduled to begin his testimony before the Ervin Committee on the day Brezhnev arrived. With great difficulty, Nixon's aides were able to persuade a reluctant Senator Ervin to postpone Dean's appearance while Brezhnev was in the United States; they were not, however, able to keep Watergate stories from dominating the front pages of the newspapers.

BREZHNEV arrived on June 16. Nixon had arranged for him to spend his first two days at Camp David, overcoming jet lag. On the morning of June 18, the two leaders had their first meeting in the Oval Office. Only Soviet translator Viktor Sukhodrev was with them. Kissinger complained in his memoirs that he asked Sukhodrev for the record, but Sukhodrev "never got around to providing it." Thus, Kissinger wrote, "the full record of what was discussed will have to await the relevant Nixon tapes. The President did not tell me what had transpired."[28]

In his memoirs, Nixon provided an outline of what was discussed, along with two direct quotations that may have come from the tapes. The conversation began with each man assuring the other that he spoke for his people, a questionable assertion in each case. They discussed the agenda for the next few days. Then Brezhnev, squeezing Nixon's arm to emphasize his seriousness, said, "We know that as far as power and influence are concerned, the only two nations in the world that really matter are the Soviet Union and the United States. Anything that we decide between us, other nations in the world will have to follow our lead, even though they may disagree with it."

Nixon injected a touch of realism. He said that he recognized the reality of superpower pre-eminence, nevertheless both sides had allies. "They are all proud people, and we must never act in such a way that appears to ignore their interests."

After an hour or so, the two men invited their advisers to join them. Brezhnev quoted a Russian proverb: "We say, 'Life is always the best teacher.' Life has led us to the conclusion that we must build a new relationship between our countries." He announced that he had invited Nixon to visit the Soviet Union in 1974 and that Nixon had accepted the invitation.

Nixon was struck by the contrast between Brezhnev in 1973 and Khrushchev in 1959 (when Khrushchev had met in the Oval Office with Eisenhower). Because Khrushchev was speaking from a position of relative weakness, Nixon noted, he "had felt that it was therefore necessary to take a very aggressive and boastful line." But Brezhnev was speaking from a position of equality, at least in nuclear capability, so he "could laugh and clown and vary his stern moods with warmth, based on the confidence that comes from holding very good cards."[29]

Nixon failed to note that among those good cards was Brezhnev's knowledge that Watergate had given the Soviets an advantage, insofar as Nixon badly needed a success.

The main business of the summit was SALT II, but it remained in a stalemate. The Americans proposed a freeze on testing and deploying MIRVs on land-based missiles, which the Soviets rejected out of hand, for reasons already noted. Nixon had never been much interested in the details of arms negotiations, and in June 1973, he was badly distracted. He made no effort to bridge the gap, or to make more realistic, even-handed proposals. He may have calculated (he would have been right to do so) that his political position precluded his making any concessions; the conservatives in the Senate on whom he had to depend for his own survival in office would have turned on him quickly and viciously had he cut a deal with Brezhnev on strategic arms.

What Nixon did do was persuade Brezhnev to agree to set a date to achieve a "permanent agreement" on strategic offensive limitations—the end of 1974. Brezhnev was reluctant because he could see no way to bridge the wide differences in approach between the two sides, but he agreed because the final statement on "Basic Principles of Negotiations on Strategic Arms Limitations" was so vague and general as to be meaningless.[30]

In return, Brezhnev got the PNW agreement, although not in the wording he wanted. Rather than a treaty renouncing nuclear weapons in the event of war, PNW committed both sides to a renunciation of the threat of or use of force not only between the USA and the USSR but between them and third countries. It further committed the superpowers to consult on an urgent basis if the risk of war appeared high.[31]

Nixon was pleased with this outcome. He felt Brezhnev's motive for PNW was to prevent the formation of an American-Chinese anti-Soviet military alliance, and that Brezhnev had figured the Americans would be much less valuable to the Chinese if they signed a treaty that prevented them from bringing their nuclear weapons into play. Nixon had escaped that trap.[32]

On June 22, Nixon and Brezhnev signed the PNW treaty in a formal ceremony in the East Room of the White House. That afternoon the two parties flew in *Air Force One* to California. The Soviet delegation stayed at La Casa Pacifica. Brezhnev stayed in Tricia's small bedroom, while Foreign Minister Andrei Gromyko stayed in Julie's. Nixon and Kissinger got a chuckle out of the thought of those two surrounded by ruffles and lace and floral designs, and a bit of satisfaction from the thought that the political leaders of the capitalist power had accommodations that were so relatively simple, especially in comparison to the lavish quarters of the political leaders of the Communist world.[33]

At noon on Sunday, June 23, Nixon, Kissinger, and Brezhnev met, with only interpreter Sukhodrev present. Their subject was China. Brezhnev was agitated. In describing the Chinese, he used words like "sly," "perfidious," and "moral degenerates." He implied that Mao suffered from a mental disorder, and said that whether sane or not he had a "treacherous character."[34]

Nixon did not reply directly, but he did say that Brezhnev was exaggerating the Chinese threat. In Nixon's view, it would be at least twenty years before China had a military capacity to threaten the Soviet Union or the United States.

Brezhnev disagreed.

"How long do you think it will be until China becomes a major nuclear country?" Nixon asked.

Brezhnev held up his two hands with fingers spread. He said, "Ten, in ten years, they will have weapons equal to what we have now. We will be further advanced by then, but we must bring home to them that this cannot go on. In 1963, during our Party Congress, I remember how Mao said: 'Let 400 million Chinese die; 300 million will be left.' Such is the psychology of this man."[35]

Brezhnev evidently did not propose a joint U.S.-Soviet strike against Chinese nuclear facilities (or if he did, Nixon and Kissinger chose not to mention it in their memoirs, the only sources available on this conversation). Twelve years earlier, the Kennedy Administration had considered such a strike and discussed it with Khrushchev, but the option had been rejected.[36]

Nixon changed the subject to Cambodia. It was very much on his mind; on June 21, the day before he flew to California, Nixon had called Speaker of the House Carl Albert to ask his help in defeating an amendment to cut-off funds for bombing in Cambodia. In handwritten notes summarizing his comments to Albert, Nixon wrote: "I told him: 1, We had a chance for a settlement. 2, It would be betrayal if Congress took the Senate line. 3, I would have to put blame on Congress for consequences. 4, I would veto. 5, If this sentiment had prevailed in the House in November, December, and January, our POWs would still be in Hanoi." Albert, according to Nixon, "said he would do his best but didn't seem overly enthusiastic."[37]

In San Clemente, Nixon put the pressure on Brezhnev. He declared that if the Communists continued their offensive in Cambodia, "the reaction of many people in this country will be that Soviet arms made it possible." The implication was that such action would endanger détente. Brezhnev, highly agitated, strongly denied that he was sending new Soviet military equipment to Cambodia. He insisted that he was 100 percent for peace in Indochina. Predictably, he said the problem was the Chinese, and returned to the original subject, saying with some emotion that the United States should not enter into a military alliance with China.[38]

In the evening, Nixon was host for a reception attended by a few Hollywood stars, then for a small dinner party. To get over his jet lag, Brezhnev retired early. So did Nixon, who by 10:30 P.M. was in bed in his pajamas, reading.

There was a knock on his door. A Secret Service agent had a message from Kissinger; Brezhnev wanted to talk. Nixon had his valet Manolo Sanchez light a fire, and dressed. Kissinger came into the room.

"What is this all about?" Nixon asked.

"He says he wants to talk," Kissinger replied.

"Is he restless or is this a ploy of some kind?" Nixon asked.

"Who ever knows with them?"

They went to Nixon's study, where Brezhnev, Anatoly Dobrynin, and Gromyko joined them.

"I could not sleep, Mr. President," said the smiling Brezhnev. He then began talking about the Middle East, with great intensity. The conversation lasted three hours. It was not a subject Nixon wanted to discuss. He wanted to stall on the Middle East until after Kissinger had replaced Rogers as Secretary of State, and until after Israel's elections in late October. As noted, Kissinger had treated with scorn the Egyptian threat that unless Israel's occupation of the territory taken in 1967 ended, there would be a new war.

But Brezhnev insisted something had to be done, soon. He proposed that the United States and the Soviet Union enter into an agreement, then and there, that would force Israel to withdraw to the 1967 borders in return for an end to the state of belligerency. Negotiations with the Palestinians would then lead to a real peace, guaranteed by the super-powers.

Whatever the merits of Brezhnev's proposal, he must have known, as Kissinger noted, that he was asking the impossible. The beleaguered Nixon could not abandon the Jews; even had there been no Watergate, Nixon would not have done so. Still Brezhnev persisted. He indulged himself in an hour-and-a-half monologue. "If there is no clarity about the principles," he said, "we will have difficulty keeping the military situation from flaring up. . . . I am categorically opposed to a resumption of the war." But if the superpowers did not act, Egypt would have to attack.

The warning was clear, and accurate, but it was not believed. Nixon listened calmly. He finally brought the midnight session to an end by pointing out that the situation was not as simple as Brezhnev had presented it, and promised to look over the record in the morning. "I hope you won't go back empty-handed," Nixon said. "But we have to break up now. It would be very easy for me to say that Israel should withdraw from all the occupied territories and call it an agreed principle. But that's what the argument is about." He agreed that the Middle East is "a most urgent place," and said it "will be our project this year."[39]

The following day, June 24, marked the end of the summit. Nixon and Brezhnev flew together on the short helicopter ride to El Toro Marine Corps Air Station. Brezhnev used the opportunity to suggest that the talks on mutual force reductions in Europe might get started with a simultaneous reduction of U.S. Army and Red Army troop strength in Europe—perhaps ten thousand men. But, as with most other subjects discussed at the summit, nothing came of the idea.[40]

At El Toro, in final remarks at the airfield before Brezhnev boarded the airplane for his return to Moscow, Nixon put the best summary he could muster on the accomplishments of the summit. He characterized the PNW agreement as not only important in the process of détente, but also "a landmark agreement for the whole world." Noting that it depended on the will to carry forward its spirit, he stressed that PNW took on "added meaning because of the personal relationship" that had developed between himself and Brezhnev. That was a nice touch, given Nixon's growing political vulnerability. He could not resist a trace of hyperbole: PNW "means that we are dedicating ourselves to build a new era not only of peace between our two great countries but of building an era in which there can be peace for all the people of the world."[41]

The summit had produced a number of new agreements covering specific areas: transportation, agriculture, oceanic studies, taxation, commercial aviation, the peaceful uses of atomic energy, and trade. The agreements, important in themselves, continued the détente process. But the summit had not produced any breakthroughs of the magnitude of SALT I or the ABM Treaty that had been achieved in Moscow a year earlier. Although PNW was a major prestige item for Brezhnev, it was an agreement without substance. No progress was made on SALT II, beyond Brezhnev's reluctant assent to achieve meaningful arms reductions by the end of 1974. The Soviets did not come away with MFN status. Still, the process of détente was intact, solidified by the Soviet invitation to Nixon to return to Moscow in 1974. The summit had neither raised nor dashed hopes for an end to the Cold War. And it had brought only the most temporary easing of Nixon's Watergate problems.

FOR a few days, thanks to his friend Brezhnev, Nixon had been free of contact with his foes in Congress. But when Brezhnev left, Congress was still there.

On June 25, John Dean began his testimony and the House voted to cut off funds for bombing in Cambodia, through an amendment added to a bill raising the national debt ceiling. On June 27, Nixon vetoed the bill because of the "Cambodian rider." In his veto statement, he said, "After more than ten years of suffering and sacrifice . . . it would be nothing short of tragic if this great accomplishment, bought with the blood of so many Asians and Americans, were to be undone now by congressional action." He warned that stopping the bombing would "effectively reverse the momentum towards lasting peace in Indochina set in motion last January," that it would lead to a Communist victory in Cambodia, which in turn would jeopardize the overall peace in Southeast Asia, and would call into question the national commitment to the Vietnam settlement.[42]

The House sustained Nixon's veto, but it was a hollow victory for the President because the vote was 241 to reject, 173 to uphold. That was 35 votes short of the two-thirds majority needed to override, but it was the largest antiwar vote in the House to date. It signaled the end of American military involvement in Indochina.

Nixon's aides, led by adviser Mel Laird and opposed only by Kissinger and Haig, urged the President to accept a compromise offered by the House leadership; he could have funds for more bombing that summer only if he agreed to an August 15 cut-off date. Kissinger, bitter and furious, said, "This is one of the most vindictive, cheap actions that I've seen the Congress take," but neither he nor Nixon could stem the tide. On June 30, Nixon agreed to compromise, and Congress extended funds to August 15. After that, all military activity throughout Indochina was banned. Kissinger later wrote that Nixon's "surrender would have been inconceivable had not the John Dean testimony drained all his inner resources."[43]

The war in Indochina was not over. There were just bad feelings, recriminations, accusations, and more bloodshed, and little hope for the people of Indochina. Nixon had not ended the war, as he had promised to do, nor won the peace. But the American military involvement was ended, although very much against his will and his better judgment. Congress, which had struggled so long with Johnson and Nixon for control of policy in Indochina, had at last prevailed. Kissinger is undoubtedly right; it never could have done so if Watergate had not intruded.

CHAPTER EIGHT

DEAN'S TESTIMONY
AND BUTTERFIELD'S
REVELATION
June 25–July 31, 1973

ON JUNE 20, Barry Goldwater wrote Nixon a note. He typed it on his little portable typewriter because he did not want anyone else to see it. He knew Nixon would be "angry with me for saying these things, but I have never been one to hold back when I think words are needed."

He complained that Nixon was isolating himself. "You have not started to get acquainted with the Congress," he wrote. Republican leaders were complaining "that they had seen more of Brezhnev than they had seen of their own President." He offered advice: "You have to stop living alone. You have to tear down that wall you have built around you. You have to emerge from the cocoon that you have been in all the years I have known you." And then a remarkable statement from the former Republican presidential nominee, a man who was admired by Republicans around the country, a man who knew the party regulars: "No one whom I know feels close to you."[1]

Nixon apparently did not reply. Certainly he did not act on Goldwater's suggestions. The day John Dean began his testimony, June 25, Nixon must have realized that it was critical for him to act. He might have returned to Washington to meet privately with Goldwater and other senior Republican congressmen. He could have asked for advice and support.

Instead, the President hunkered down in San Clemente. He saw only Haig, Ziegler, and one or two other aides. He left the spotlight to shine exclusively on Dean, who was making the most sensational charges ever made against a sitting President to a fascinated audience of millions of Americans.

Dean sat alone before the Senate Committee, his blond wife and his lawyers seated behind him. He read a prepared statement that was 245 pages long. He read in a monotone. It took him a whole day to complete the statement.

Dean acknowledged that he had participated in the cover-up, but insisted that he had known nothing in advance about the break-in. He depicted himself as a restraining influence with regard to the Huston Plan, and as a virtual double agent in the White House since early April, attending meetings with Nixon and his principal aides while cooperating with federal prosecutors.

Dean described Nixon as having some knowledge of the cover-up from the time of the break-in. He said that the President had permitted the cover-up to continue through early April of 1973, even after being warned about the dangers. He said Nixon had discussed with him the possibility of executive clemency for the Watergate burglars and the payment of hush money.

According to Dean, Haldeman and Ehrlichman were the prime orchestrators of the cover-up, and it was when he had come to believe they were setting him up that he had decided to cooperate with the prosecutors. He charged that Mitchell was deeply involved, and had been the man who made the cover-up payments to Hunt. He also told the Committee that Nixon had tried to set up Mitchell as the fall guy.

Dean said that in his April 15, 1973, meeting with Nixon, which took place after he had started talking to the prosecutors, the President had asked him a number of "leading questions" in an evident effort to create a record that would "protect himself." He thought the President might have tape-recorded that conversation.[2]

THERE was more. Dean gave dates and details along with quotations and speculations. For example, on the "Dean Report" that Nixon cited in his August 29, 1972, statement on Watergate, Dean said that when he heard the President mention that so-called report, he began to think for the first time that "I might be being set up in case the whole thing crumbled at a later time." He quoted himself from the March 21 meeting: "I began by telling the President that there was a cancer growing on the Presidency and that if the cancer was not removed that the President himself would be killed by it. I also told him that it was important that this cancer be removed immediately because it was growing more deadly every day."

Dean made one stab at protecting his old boss. He said he still clung to a belief that Nixon "did not realize or appreciate at any time the implications of his involvement," and he followed up that feeble gesture with a blanket indictment of Haldeman, Ehrlichman, Colson, and associates: "The Watergate matter was an inevitable outgrowth of a climate of excessive concern over the political impact of demonstrators, excessive concern over leaks, an insatiable appetite for political intelligence, all coupled with a do-it-yourself White House staff, regardless of the law."[3]

Nixon was one of the minority of Americans who did not watch Dean testify on television. Ziegler told reporters at the Western White House that Nixon had spent the day working on routine business. Ziegler said that staff members watched the proceedings and prepared summaries of Dean's testimony, which they gave to Haig, who in turn took them to the President.[4]

The reports, Nixon wrote in his memoirs, "filled me with frustration and anger." He accused Dean of "re-creating history," and charged that Dean not only made self-serving statements but told outright lies.[5] After two and a half pages of closely argued legalistic rebuttal of Dean's statement, Nixon provided a summary that was direct and insightful: Nixon wrote that Dean's testimony was "an artful blend of truth and untruth, of possible sincere misunderstandings and clearly conscious distortions." But, he noted, "the real issue had already changed. It no longer made any difference that not all of Dean's testimony was accurate. It only mattered if *any* of his testimony was accurate."[6]

Nixon was exactly right on that point. Even before Dean spoke one word, Watergate was the political story of the decade. At the end of the day on June 25, it had been elevated to a new level. For the first time, the President had been directly accused of participation in the cover-up, and the accusation came not from a reporter, or from an unnamed "high-level source," or from a political opponent, but rather from the President's own legal counsel. This shocked and stunned an already stupefied American public.

Dean provided no direct evidence to sustain his charges. He brought no tape recordings with him, nor any documents signed "RN" directing a cover-up or the payment of hush money. His case rested on the accuracy of his memory. If the President chose to deny what Dean had said, it would be Dean's word against Nixon's word.

Dean's strength was that for the most part he had told the truth. Nixon realized that; in his memoirs, he confessed that "Dean's account of the crucial March 21 meeting was more accurate than my own had been."

Nixon's strength was that he had the tapes, and could use them selectively to refute Dean. But even with that asset, Nixon had a weakness that he described with clarity and insight: "In the end it would make less difference that I was not as involved as Dean had alleged than that I was not as uninvolved as I had claimed."[7]

That admission came years later. At the time, Nixon followed his instinct, which was to deny and prepare a counterattack. On June 26, Warren told reporters that the President stood behind his May 22 statement on Watergate. In that statement, Nixon had insisted that he knew nothing about the cover-up before March 21, that he had not known about paying money to the Watergate burglars for their silence, and that he had not authorized any offer of clemency.[8]

Even as Warren was talking to the reporters, Dean was telling the senators cross-examining him that Nixon's May 22 statement was "less than accurate." Dean also disputed each of a series of presidential explanations, describing them as misleading, unfounded, or overly broad.

Senator Herman Talmadge (D.-Ga.) noted that Dean had made "very strong" charges against the President, charges "that involve him in criminal offenses." Then he bluntly asked Dean: "What makes you think that your credibility is greater than that of the President, who denies what you have said?"

"I have told it exactly the way I know it," Dean responded. "I am telling you just as I know it."[9]

Out in San Clemente, Warren reported that Nixon spent June 26 working in his office with Haig and other aides. The President did not watch television or listen to Dean on the radio, but he was receiving summary reports from aides.

That day, the House voted again to cut off funds for bombing in Cambodia, and the General Services Administration announced that the federal government had spent more than $703,000 on the President's San Clemente property. The GSA added that although the Secret Service justified certain improvements on security grounds, there were such items as a $132,852 landscaping bill.[10] The next day Fred LaRue pleaded guilty to one count of conspiracy to obstruct justice. He admitted to taking part in a scheme to destroy incriminating documents and to misleading the FBI and the Watergate grand jury with false testimony. He also acknowledged funneling more than $300,000 to the burglars in order to buy their silence.[11]

The GSA report and LaRue's confession hurt Nixon's credibility just when he most needed to have it boosted. Still, he was the President, while Dean was a young, cold-hearted, cold-blooded lawyer who had confessed to a felony (participation in the cover-up), double-crossed his old boss, turned informer, had an unsympathetic manner, and no documents to prove his charges.

That last point was critical. When pressed during the cross-examination to explain why he could not recall the precise words used during his September 15, 1972, meeting with the President, Dean said he had made no notes on Nixon's words because "I thought they were very incriminating to the President of the United States."[12]

On the second day of cross-examination, June 27, Senator Daniel Inouye (D.-Hawaii) read a letter he had just received from J. Fred Buzhardt at the White House. It constituted Nixon's initial counterattack against Dean, although how much of a role Nixon played in the preparation of the letter and attached statement is unclear. Warren told reporters that the Buzhardt letter "is not the President's position, it is not the White House position. We are not commenting on the testimony or the evidence." In Washington, the White House press office released a statement on Buzhardt's behalf which attempted to dissociate Nixon from the letter.[13]

The implication is that Buzhardt proceeded on his own. Whether or not that is true, it is impossible to say, because through 1990 Nixon had managed to keep the relevant documents under seal. If it is true, it was so uncharacteristic of both Nixon and Haig as to be unique. It is much easier to believe that Nixon, ensconced in La Casa Pacifica, stage-managed the whole affair, working through Haig, telling Buzhardt exactly what to put in the letter and the statement, than it is to believe the opposite, which is that Richard Nixon's lawyer acted without his client's knowledge or consent.

Senator Inouye assumed Nixon was behind it. He announced that he would test Dean's credibility by using the Buzhardt statement as the basis for his cross-examination, "as a substitute, admittedly not the very best, but a substitute for cross-examination of Dean by the President of the United States."

The Buzhardt document, however, was not a series of questions, but a series of assertions and charges. Some highlights: "John Dean knew of and participated in the planning that went into the break-in . . . John Dean was the principal actor in the Watergate cover-up . . . It must have been clear to Dean as a lawyer when he heard on June 17 of Watergate that he was in personal difficulty . . . He must have immediately realized that his patron, Mitchell, would also be involved . . . [Dean is] the principal author of the political and constitutional crisis that Watergate now epitomizes."

In a final paragraph, Buzhardt, or whoever wrote the document, provided what was and has remained a basic Nixon defense: "It would have been embarrassing for the President if the true facts had become known shortly after June 17th, but it is the kind of embarrassment that an immensely popular president could easily have weathered. The political problem has been magnified one thousand-fold . . . because the White House was led to say things about Watergate that have since been found untrue. These added consequences were John Dean's doing."[14]

Dean responded, point by point. But it remained his word against Nixon's. He did release some documents on June 27, and they caused an uproar almost as great as his first day of testimony. The documents constituted the White House "enemies list," which had been prepared by Dean, Colson, and others, for various purposes over the past two years; those purposes ranged from starting IRS audits to banning the enemies from White House social functions.

Along with politicians and political pundits, there were numerous print and television journalists on the list, which guaranteed it a big play in the media. Commentators expressed shock, dismay, outrage. It immediately became a prestige item to have one's name on the list. The spirit of the whole thing was well stated by Dean in an August 16, 1971, memo accompanying the master list: "We can use the available federal machinery to screw our political enemies."[15]

Little noticed in the explosion of emotion over the revelation that the Nixon White House kept an enemies' list was that nothing connected Nixon with it. Nor was it noticed that the IRS in fact had *not* gone after the people on the list; indeed, for four years Nixon had been complaining on a regular basis to his aides that he could not get the IRS to go after his foes (especially galling to Nixon as Robert Kennedy had been able to get the IRS to do an extensive audit on Nixon in 1963 and had gone after many others as well).

Dean's presentation of shocking documents, even though they had nothing to do with Watergate, bolstered his credibility. Meanwhile Buzhardt's statement lost credibility, because on June 28 he insisted that it "does not represent a White House position" and had not been reviewed by the President. To which Senator Ervin replied that the "only reliable way" to test the credibility of a principal in a criminal case was to examine him under oath. He said he "would leave it up to" the President whether he wanted to appear, and did not directly call for Nixon's appearance as a witness, but he told a reporter that he could "draw any deduction you want." The Committee vice chairman, Senator Howard Baker, Jr. (R.-Tenn.), said that Dean's testimony had been "mind boggling." Baker added that the Committee would have to determine some way to "gain access to the President's knowledge." Warren immediately replied from San Clemente that Nixon was opposed to answering a committee subpoena on the ground that it would be "constitutionally inappropriate."[16]

The Ervin/Baker statements immediately created a constitutional clash. Nowhere does it say in the Constitution that the President must, or must not, respond to a subpoena from Congress, either to produce documents or appear himself. Precedent was unclear. Thomas Jefferson had produced some documentation in the Aaron Burr affair; Abraham Lincoln had given written replies to congressional committees, and appeared before one on a single occasion. Harry Truman, as Nixon so well knew, had refused to cooperate in any way at all with the House committee on which Nixon sat when it was investigating the Hiss affair. As Nixon also knew, Dwight Eisenhower had refused to cooperate with Senator Joseph R. McCarthy's subcommittee investigating the Army.

But constitutional precedents aside, the Ervin/Baker point was simple common sense. Nixon and Dean had called each other liars. Neither had produced any solid documentary evidence to prove his accusation. Since Dean took no notes in his private meetings with Nixon, and since

Nixon took no notes, evidently there was no documentary evidence. It was thus one man's word against the other's word. The only way to settle that was a direct confrontation.

Or, for Nixon to use the tapes to refute Dean. Nixon had in his possession tape recordings on which Dean had enthusiastically agreed with Nixon's assertion that the President had known nothing about the whole Watergate mess, and other statements that exonerated Nixon. He had tapes on which he said that to provide clemency before the 1974 elections would be wrong, tapes on which he said it would be wrong to pay blackmail money, tapes on which he told Henry Petersen to tell Howard Hunt to tell the truth, tapes on which he instructed Dean never to tell a lie, tapes on which he told Dean that when he said raising a million dollars in hush money would be easy, he was only joking.

Nixon must have been terribly tempted to bring those tapes out, but he must also have been deathly afraid that the existence of the tapes would be revealed. If the American public and the American politicians ever learned that Nixon was secretly taping the conversations in his offices and over his telephones, Nixon could anticipate an uproar.

Another danger is simply stated—he was guilty. If he was not quite as guilty as Dean alleged, he was a lot more guilty than he ever would admit. And the full extent of his guilt was on those tapes. He knew he had not been joking when he said he could raise the million dollars, he knew he had ordered the payment of hush money, he knew he had ordered a cover-up back in June 1972 and kept it in operation for the past year. He knew the truth.

By building his tape library, he had constructed both scaffold and noose, and his ultimate defense.

To release or not release the tapes? What if he released selected portions of them, and then lost control? But he was the President. The doctrine of executive privilege protected him. The tapes were no different from memos, letters, and other written documents. They were not subject to subpoena from either of the other two branches of government. But obviously if Nixon tried to use parts of the tapes and withheld the rest, there would be a clamor for full release, a clamor led by Special Prosecutor Cox, Judge Sirica, Senators Ervin and Baker, and the media. Nixon could well win the technical battle and keep his control of the tapes, but at great cost in public support.

The convolutions and complexities compounded each other. By the end of June 1973, the number of people who knew about the tapes had grown significantly. Beyond the original list, now Buzhardt knew, Haig knew, Steve Bull knew. Haldeman had told Haig that if he was asked by the Ervin Committee (he was scheduled to appear in July) about a White House taping capability, he intended to tell the truth.[17] Better for Nixon to anticipate the inevitable and reveal the tapes himself than wait for the

Ervin Committee to drag the information out of a witness. Or was it better to use the tapes selectively and secretly and hope that no one on the Ervin Committee would think to ask the right question?

Nixon was in an agony of indecision, and he was isolated. He could not or would not turn to others for advice; there is no evidence that at this critical juncture he asked anyone for an opinion. He could have asked those who knew about the tapes. They were all current or former members of his White House staff. But there was not among them—Haldeman, Ehrlichman, Haig, Ziegler, Bull, Buzhardt—one man who had ever stood for public office. Their sensitivity to public opinion and political realities was minimal. Besides, Nixon hardly trusted them.

He could not turn to the senior Republicans in Washington, because had he done so he would have had to reveal to Goldwater, Ford, et al., that since 1970 he had been tape-recording *their* conversations in the EOB and the Oval Office, and on the telephone. Besides, he hardly trusted any of the Republican politicians.

He could not turn to his family for advice. It would have been too painful to reveal to Pat, Tricia, Julie, Ed Cox, and David Eisenhower that they, too, had been secretly recorded.

Because he trusted no one except himself, because what he had done in setting up and operating the taping system was too embarrassing and too incriminating to reveal to those who might have given him advice, Nixon had to make his decision on how to most effectively use the asset of the tapes in isolation.

At the critical moment in his career, he was alone.

He made his decision. It was to use information from the tapes in a selective manner, by providing edited transcripts to the Republican staff members of the Ervin Committee. The transcripts would include the material that could be used to embarrass or refute Dean, or to prove the President's non-involvement. If all worked well, Nixon could have the benefit of the tapes without the embarrassment of revealing them, not to mention the disaster of having to surrender them to the courts or to the Congress.

The implementation was carried out in this way: Buzhardt secretly dictated to Republican Chief Counsel Fred Thompson over the telephone a listing of Nixon's meetings with Dean and a summary of Nixon's account of those meetings. The summary drew heavily on the tapes; it contained some verbatim and near-verbatim quotes. It was skillfully done, in that in most cases the summaries were in agreement with Dean's testimony, but they usually added a remark or two that gave an interpretation more favorable to Nixon, and of course "that would be wrong" and similar statements.[18]

Thus did Nixon make available for the first time to people outside the White House some of the fruits of his tape-recording system. Thus did he make himself more vulnerable while increasing his risks.

DEAN's testimony ended on June 30. The Ervin Committee then went into recess for the Fourth of July holiday week. Nixon seized the opportunity to start a counterattack. It began on the night of June 29, when David and Julie Eisenhower appeared on ABC TV's "Jack Paar Tonight" show. "You don't always know what those men are doing," Julie said, referring to unnamed White House aides. She added, "I don't think you can judge the entire Administration through this one matter."

David referred specifically to Haldeman, Dean, and Ehrlichman. "These men made an error in judgment, and they're going to pay for it," he said. "The men who are charged with poor judgment—criminal acts in some cases—are, in fairness to them, the men who brought about an era of tranquillity and will ultimately prove to have played a role which will reflect to Richard Nixon's great credit." He asserted that the purpose of the cover-up was to keep the President in ignorance. "Julie and I are both convinced that when this is resolved, the President's involvement will be found to have been nil."[19]

On July 1, from San Clemente, Nixon gave a nationwide radio address on the economy. He announced tough action against inflation. For example, the Administration was running a check on the 3,100 largest corporations, and "any whose price increases since January cannot be justified by cost increases will be required to roll back their prices." The Cost of Living Council had already identified more than one thousand gas stations that had raised their prices above permitted levels, and those prices had been rolled back.

Still there were gasoline shortages. Nixon announced the appointment of a new high-level White House energy office, and he asked Congress to create a new Cabinet department devoted to energy and natural resources. He called on Congress to deregulate natural gas, to license new deepwater ports, to streamline the process of getting nuclear reactors on line, and to ease off on the environmental restrictions on surface mining of coal.

On agriculture, Nixon said he was taking steps to increase supplies, including freeing up 40 million additional acres for planting. He was also imposing export controls on some crops, including soybeans, in order to bring down prices.

These were all temporary measures, the President promised. He warned that "in the long run, dependence on controls would destroy the economy and demolish our prosperity."[20]

Under ordinary circumstances, such an announcement would have dominated the newspapers and weekend talk shows on television, but in

July 1973, it was scarcely noticed. The same fate befell another Nixon announcement, on July 2—that Huang Chen, China's senior diplomat in Washington, would be visiting the Western White House that week for talks with Kissinger and Nixon. Even the news that the Air Force was intensifying the bombing in Cambodia failed to override Watergate.[21]

On July 4, Nixon attended a party for the Western White House staff at the San Clemente Inn. He joined the crowd in singing "Happy Birthday" to Julie, who would be twenty-five years of age on July 5. Julie gave an interview to two wire-service reporters. She revealed that two months earlier, on May 4, her father had considered resigning over Watergate, but that the family had talked him out of it because resignation would be an "admission of wrongdoing" and because the country needed him.

"He was playing the devil's advocate," Julie explained. "See, the thing is, he really loves the country, and he'd do anything that was best for the country. He would say, 'Should I resign? Would it be better for the country? Would the wounds heal faster?' We said no . . . that he was the man for the job, and he had started things and needed to finish them."

Julie said the enemies' list had nothing to do with her father. She complained that the press made a hero out of Daniel Ellsberg, who stole documents and broke the law and endangered national security. "This could have had greater consequences than bugging the Democratic headquarters. The bugging was ludicrous. I don't know what they thought they were going to find out. The whole stupidity of it is just unreal."[22]

Nixon's holiday week counterattack included an attempt on his part to anticipate his enemies' next move. It took no great intelligence apparatus to figure out what it would be—when the Ervin Committee reconvened, it would certainly issue a subpoena for White House documents and might demand a personal appearance for Nixon to testify under oath. The Special Prosecutor would also be demanding documents, as would the Watergate grand jury. There was no other way to determine who was telling the truth, Dean or Nixon.

Thus was set in motion would what turn out to be a thirteen-month struggle. In anticipating his enemies, and in answering their demands even before they were made, Nixon took a position that he was to hold to through his Presidency, through the 1970s, and through the 1980s. Although he had to retreat a little bit here, a little bit there, for the most part he was able to hold his ground even into the 1990s.

His position was simply stated in a July 7 letter to Ervin: "I shall not testify before the Committee or permit access to Presidential papers."

His reasons were manifold. First, his refusal to cooperate was "based on my Constitutional obligation to preserve intact the powers and prerogatives of the Presidency." He argued that "no President could function if the private papers of his office, prepared by his personal staff, were open to public scrutiny." It was essential that his aides be free to consult "in complete candor," confident that "their tentative judgments, their exploration of alternatives, and their frank comments on issues and personalities at home and abroad remain confidential."

As to his own situation, "I have concluded that if I were to testify before the Committee irreparable damage would be done to the Constitutional principle of separation of powers."

He noted that he was already cooperating with the Committee, by not invoking the doctrine of executive privilege with regard to testimony by his aides concerning possible criminal conduct. In addition, he had waived the attorney-client privilege with regard to Dean's testimony. And he promised a public statement "at an appropriate time" on "the subjects you are considering."[23]

Nixon's defiance caused a storm. Senator Inouye said Nixon's testimony was "vital to his future." While "silence does not necessarily indicate guilt," he said, "unfortunately many people do interpret silence in that manner." Senator Talmadge thought that "public records belong to the American people" and that the Committee had "a right to see those records and to subpoena them if necessary." He urged Nixon to make a voluntary testimony: "If he has nothing to hide, why does he refuse to appear?" Senator Baker expressed the hope that "some other means can be worked out" to obtain Nixon's account of events, while Senator Ervin commented, "If a President wants to withhold information from the Committee and the American people, I would just let him take the consequences of that."[24]

On July 7, the day he wrote Ervin, Nixon broadened his counterattack with a memo to Haig on marching orders for the PR front. Nixon opened with a complaint: "We have tried to get a point across using only one bullet [while] our opponents have been enormously effective in getting three or four rides out of the same story." Nixon wanted more Cabinet officers and Republican politicians to speak out in defense of his aides; he wanted Haig to leak stories on the use of the FBI and the military by the Kennedy and Johnson administrations for wiretapping and surveillance activities, and of the IRS for political purposes; he wanted Richardson to rein in Cox and take him to task for conducting "a partisan political vendetta rather than [doing] the job he was appointed to do— bring the Watergate defendants to trial at the earliest possible time."

That sounded brave and bold, but the trouble was all those lines of attack had already been tried and failed, as Nixon knew perfectly well. He ended his memo with a recognition of its futility; he said he feared Richardson would "be a relatively weak reed in this respect."[25]

When Nixon returned to Washington at the end of the week, however, his most pressing problem was not a probable subpoena for documents, but how to answer a question Senator Baker had asked John Dean: "What did the President know and when did he know it?" The question, in its original formulation, referred specifically to Dean's assertion that on September 15, 1972, it was his impression that Nixon was well aware of the various cover-up activities. This contradicted directly Nixon's claim that he knew nothing about the cover-up until March 21, 1973.

To deal with the question, Nixon turned to Haldeman, who had just flown to Washington from California to prepare for his own appearance before the Ervin Committee. Nixon asked Haldeman to review the September 15 tape, which Haldeman began doing on July 10.

That same day the Committee reconvened. John Mitchell was the witness. Mitchell stood four-square behind his President and friend. He flatly contradicted much of Dean's and Magruder's testimony. For example, he said he had not approved the wiretapping of the DNC and he denied receiving information based on the transcripts of intercepted telephone calls. He said he never approved the destruction of wiretap memorandums, nor had he played any role in collecting and distributing hush money to Hunt, Liddy, and the burglars. At one point he accused Magruder of "a palpable, damnable lie."

Senator Talmadge wondered "why on earth" Mitchell had not walked into Nixon's office and told him the truth about the crimes and conspiracies and cover-ups.

"It wasn't a question of telling him the truth," Mitchell replied. "It was a question of not involving him at all so that he could go through his campaign without being involved in this type of activity, and I am talking about the White House horrors particularly.

". . . I was sure that, knowing Richard Nixon, the President, as I do, he would just lower the boom on all of this matter and it would come back to hurt him and it would affect him in his re-election."[26]

Altogether, the first eleven days of July were relatively good ones for Nixon. Whatever Dean, Magruder, and LaRue said or confessed to, they were small fry; the big enchiladas—Mitchell and Haldeman—had stuck by him. Julie and David Eisenhower had been forceful and persuasive in their defense of the President. In his letter to Ervin, Nixon had taken a position that was apparently unassailable. And the Mitchell testimony meant that it was no longer Richard Nixon's word against John Dean's word; Nixon now had the support of the former Attorney General.

His Presidency, although battered, appeared to be safe. The Dean testimony did not provide a compelling reason for impeachment. Mitchell had stood behind the President, and the only two major witnesses left, Haldeman and Ehrlichman, were going to do so. Unless the Ervin Committee, the Special Prosecutor, and Judge Sirica could get their hands on incriminating White House documents, they had run out of options.

•

ON the morning of July 12, the Committee met to consider issuing a subpoena for documents. Senator Baker was able to convince his fellow members that they should make one more attempt to obtain Nixon's voluntary cooperation. Baker drafted a letter to Nixon that Ervin signed. "The committee feels that your position . . . measured against the committee's responsibility to ascertain the facts . . . presents the very grave possibility of a fundamental constitutional confrontation between the Congress and the Presidency. We wish to avoid that, if possible."

At 5:30 A.M., Nixon had awoken with a sharp pain in his chest. He lay in bed with a pain that reminded him of a cracked rib he had suffered while playing football at Whittier College. Doctors examined him; White House physician Dr. Walter Tkach said it was pneumonia.

The President was lying restlessly in bed about midday when Haig came in and said Senator Ervin was on the telephone and wanted to talk. Nixon took the call, even though every breath caused a sharp pain.

Ervin opened by saying his committee had sent the President "a little note."

"I read about your letter," Nixon answered. "Your committee leaks, you know."

Ervin said he did not know how the letter had already made the newspapers. He assured the President that the Committee did not want a constitutional confrontation, but the members took the view that executive privilege did not cover criminal or political acts.

"You want your staff to go through presidential files," Nixon said. "The answer is no." He asked what papers Ervin specifically wanted, but warned, "I am not going to have anyone going through all my files."

Ervin said he wanted all relevant papers.

"Your attitude in the hearings was clear," Nixon said, raising his voice despite the pain it caused. "There's no question who you're out to get."

"We are not out to get anything, Mr. President," Ervin replied, "except the truth."

Nixon softened a bit. He said he was willing to consider a meeting, but just between the two of them. "A man-to-man talk." Ervin said he would consult with his committee.[27]

Despite a 102-degree temperature, Nixon dressed and kept his afternoon appointments. Toward evening, chest X-rays showed Tkach's diagnosis was correct, and Nixon was driven to Bethesda Naval Hospital, where he was given inhalation therapy.

On July 13, Richard Moore, a special counsel to the President working under Leonard Garment, appeared before the Ervin Committee. Garment had requested that Moore be heard. Moore described himself as a "source of white-haired advice and experience" to the President and his young aides. He said he had attended some of the March meetings in the Oval Office where Watergate was discussed, and he was certain the President knew nothing of the cover-up. He also quoted Nixon as saying to him on May 8, 1973, "I have racked my brain, I have searched my mind. Were there any clues I should have seen that should have tipped me off?"

Moore further quoted Nixon as telling him about the hush money demand by Hunt, "That isn't the point. Money isn't the point. You could raise money, money is not the point. It's wrong, we could not, shouldn't consider it and it's stupid because the truth comes out anyway."[28]

No senator asked Moore how he happened to remember so exactly the President's words.

Nor was Moore the only one to provide direct quotes. Buzhardt had done so in the summary he had given to the minority staff of the Committee. Further, Haldeman was listening to the September 15 tape, with the intent of using selected parts of it when he testified.

Nixon and his defense team were not just playing with fire, they were all but shoving their hands into it. Sooner or later some Committee staff member, or some senator, was going to ask how these men had developed such fabulous memories. If the quotations were coming from documents, the Committee would demand to see all of them rather than relying on selected parts from Nixon loyalists. If the quotations were coming from another source, the Committee would want to know what that source was.

Nixon, meanwhile, was slowly improving in the hospital, though it was all but impossible for him to sleep. He spent hours on the telephone, conferring with aides. By Sunday, July 15, his temperature had dropped below 100 degrees and for the first time in three days he was able to eat a full meal. Dr. Tkach told reporters that he had been giving Nixon lectures for four years about getting more relaxation. The President always listened very attentively, Tkach added, "and then goes about his business exactly as before." On Monday morning, July 16, Nixon was able to get out of bed for about twenty minutes, and was performing breathing exercises. Tkach said that he had started to cough, a good sign, showing that the viral pneumonia was receding.[29]

THAT same Monday morning, Alexander Butterfield went before the Ervin Committee.

Butterfield had come to the White House in 1969 after a distinguished career in the Air Force, where he was a much-decorated pilot. He had known Haldeman at USC, where they had been classmates; Haldeman had chosen Butterfield to be his chief administrative aide. In March 1973, Butterfield had left the White House to become chief of the Federal Aviation Administration.

On July 13, as Moore was testifying, members of the Ervin Committee staff had met with Butterfield to ask him questions about White House routine. Donald Sanders, of the minority staff, had been curious about Dean's statement that he had suspected during one of his conversations that he and Nixon were being recorded.[30] Scott Armstrong, of the majority staff, was curious about some of the direct quotations from the President on the Buzhardt summary. (Armstrong was a classmate of reporter Bob Woodward in Wheaton, Illinois.)

Armstrong showed Butterfield a section of the Buzhardt summary. Butterfield read it. He expressed surprise at the amount of detail and at a direct quotation.

"Where did you get this?" Butterfield asked.

From the Buzhardt summary, Armstrong replied. He asked if it could have come from someone's notes of a meeting.

"No, it seems too detailed," Butterfield answered.

"Was the President's recollection of meetings good?"

"Yes, when I came I was impressed. He is a great and fast learner. He does recall things very well. He tends to over explain things."

"Was he as precise as the summary?" Armstrong asked.

"Well, no, but he would sometimes dictate his thoughts after a meeting."

"Were his memos this detailed?" Armstrong asked.

"I don't think so," Butterfield answered.

"Where else could this have come from?" Armstrong persisted.

"I don't know," Butterfield answered. "Well, let me think about this awhile."[31]

In an interview in 1989, Butterfield said, "I made a conscious decision before going into that session not to reveal the taping system's existence unless, I want to repeat that, unless I were asked a very direct question pertaining to such a system."[32]

Armstrong did not press the point. But then Donald Sanders took up the questioning. From 1959 to 1969 he had been an FBI agent; from 1969 until he joined the Ervin Committee staff as part of the Republican minority team, he had been chief counsel for the House Internal Security Committee (successor to the House Committee on Un-American Activities). He was friendly to the President, and his background suggested that he would do all he could to protect Nixon.

In a 1989 interview, Sanders said that as he sat through Armstrong's questions, "I felt a growing certainty that the summaries had to have been made from a verbatim recording." He wondered if Butterfield would answer truthfully if asked about a hidden recording system. He reasoned that if such a system existed, "the President would never have said anything incriminating on record. . . . Remarks on it would be self-serving [and] . . . would prove the President's innocence." But, he wondered, "if there were exculpatory recordings, why hadn't the President revealed the system and used it to his advantage? I was mystified that Ervin's staff hadn't asked Butterfield about tape recordings."

Nixon had supplied the material that gave Sanders the suspicion that there were tapes, but by withholding so much and by not revealing the source, the President had badly confused even the minority counsel.

"My heart was pounding and my breath was shortened as I began questioning," Sanders said. He asked Butterfield if he knew of any reason why the President would take Dean to a corner of a room and speak to him in a quiet voice, as Dean had testified.

"I was hoping you fellows wouldn't ask me that," Butterfield replied. "I've wondered what I would say. I'm concerned about the effect my answer will have on national security and international affairs. But I suppose I have to assume that this is a formal, official interview in the same vein as if I were being questioned by the committee under oath."

"That's right," Sanders replied.

"Well, yes," Butterfield said, "there's a recording system in the White House."[33]

Butterfield went on to explain the system, in detail. The staff members were thunderstruck. Immediately after the session they went to their superiors. There was a flurry of activity, which culminated in arrangements for Butterfield to appear before the full Ervin Committee, and the television cameras, on Monday morning, July 16. For once the Committee did not leak. When Butterfield told his story to the nation, to all but a handful of insiders it came with the force and surprise of an earthquake.

To Nixon, Butterfield's relevation was as unwelcome as an earthquake. He had thought his secret was safe, because he assumed that any member of his staff who knew about the taping system would raise the doctrine of executive privilege before revealing it.[34]

To Dean, Butterfield's revelation was as welcome as an all-day soaking rain after months of drought. He called the news "absolutely fantastic!" and described himself as "ecstatic."[35]

To most Americans, the distinctly different reactions of Nixon and Dean answered the question, Who was telling the truth? Dean wanted the tapes played, in full, in public. Nixon wanted the tapes kept sealed within the White House, where he could continue to make selective use of them.

Depending on their own political positions, Americans were outraged or deeply depressed by the news. George Meany, president of the AFL-CIO, who had refused to support McGovern in the 1972 campaign, said the news was "so fantastic as to be almost beyond belief." Nixon's former Interior Secretary, Walter Hickel, said, "America will be sick at heart." Carl Albert called it "an outrage, almost beyond belief."[36]

Nixon and Haig spent several hours in the President's hospital room discussing the possible effects. Nixon raised the idea of destroying the tapes. Haig thought Nixon ought to talk to his lawyers before acting.

Nixon did order the removal of the taping system. Not because it was wrong, but because it had become such an embarrassment.

IT was wrong, in that the telephone company requires a beeping device on tape-recorded telephone conversations, but was it wrong morally and politically? Ray Price, one of those who was recorded without his knowledge, thought not. He pointed out that "from the standpoint of privacy, the only real question was what was done with the tapes." As Nixon was present when the words were said, obviously nothing on the tapes was a secret to him. Speaking for himself, Price declared, "I took no offense at it."[37]

In some part, the taping system was a defensive system that was all but forced on the President by the existing technology. Nixon's panic over the thought that John Dean might have had a hidden tape recorder on him while in the Oval Office makes the point. Lyndon Johnson feared that his first Attorney General, Robert Kennedy, used a hidden tape recorder in Oval Office meetings. Short of having the Secret Service conduct a hands-on search of all visitors to the Oval Office, the President could never be sure *he* was not being secretly recorded.

The system was defensive in another sense. Back in 1954, at a Cabinet meeting with Nixon in attendance, Eisenhower had said, "You know, boys, it's a good thing when you're talking to someone you don't trust to get a record made of it. There are some guys I just don't trust in Washington, and I want to have myself protected so that they can't later report that I said something else."[38] As Nixon trusted almost no one, he needed more records than Ike.

There were other precedents. President Roosevelt had made secret recordings. So had Presidents Kennedy and Johnson.

It was Nixon's bad luck that he was the one who got caught. The full weight of the moral opprobrium came down on him. He tried to deflect it. The afternoon of July 16, following Butterfield's testimony, he had Buzhardt send a letter to Ervin. It confirmed the existence of the taping system, but pointed out that it was similar to the ones used by Kennedy and Johnson. But rather than confess or acknowledge the truth of what Nixon charged, aides to Nixon's predecessors protested. Joseph Califano, Jr., one of Johnson's top aides, called the Buzhardt statement "a damned outrageous smear, a total smear on a dead President. There was absolutely no secret wiring in the place" when Johnson was President. Arthur Schlesinger, Jr., a Kennedy aide, said it was "inconceivable" that JFK would have approved such a taping system.[39]

But he had. And Johnson had recommended to Nixon that he retain the system that he, Johnson, had installed in the White House. Despite recommendations from two former Presidents, Eisenhower and Johnson, and despite the Kennedy precedent, Nixon had removed the system in 1969, only to replace it with a more extensive one in 1970.

On July 17, 1973, Buzhardt produced sworn affidavits from Army Signal Corps technicians who had installed the Johnson system; the following day, the Kennedy Library admitted that there were 125 tapes and 68 Dictabelt recordings of Kennedy conversations.[40] But the damage to Nixon had already been done, and the admissions helped him not at all.

In the hospital, meanwhile, Nixon met with Haig, Ziegler, Buzhardt, Garment, and Charles Alan Wright of the White House legal team. The lawyers wanted Nixon's permission to review the tapes.

"No. Never." Nixon cut off the discussion. "No, no, no," he said.[41]

Well, then, what about destroying the tapes? John Connally had sent a message urging that course: "Please, Bob," he had told Haldeman, "use your influence to convince the President to burn the tapes. Tell him to do it right. Have Ziegler assemble the White House press corps in the Rose Garden, pile up all the tapes, set a match to them, and let them film the bonfire. Say they must be destroyed now that their existence has been made public."[42]

There was a perfect cover. Nixon could say that the conversations dealt with national security affairs and matters highly embarrassing to politicians from both parties. Since that was true, and since every politician who had been in the Oval Office since 1971 was at that moment racking his brain to remember what he had said there, a bonfire would have elicited protests and criticisms, but it would not have destroyed the President. Nor would it have been illegal; Nixon regarded the tapes as his personal property, a position upheld by the precedent that any President's papers are his personal property. As the tapes had not been subpoenaed, burning them would not be destroying evidence in a criminal case.

Still, a bonfire would have raised another storm. Garment warned that it would forever seal an impression of guilt in the public mind. Vice President Agnew visited Nixon in the hospital and said he agreed with Garment.

More important, so did Haldeman, and his point had nothing to do with public opinion, but rather got straight to the heart of the matter. As Nixon put it in his memoirs, "Haldeman said that the tapes were still our best defense, and he recommended that they not be destroyed."[43]

There were two basic factors at work. First, the tapes *were* Nixon's best defense, just as Haldeman said, for the obvious reason that they contained so many exculpatory statements by Nixon, statements that he had made in his own transparent way whenever he remembered that the recorder was running. Nixon had already drawn on that asset in the preparation of the Buzhardt summary for the minority staff of the Ervin Committee. Second, as Haldeman put it, Nixon "just never dreamed it was possible that the tapes would ever be heard by anyone other than himself."[44] They were his property. They were protected by executive privilege. Everything Nixon had said in his July 7 letter to Ervin ("I shall not . . . permit access to Presidential papers") applied equally to the tapes.

Nixon did not destroy the tapes because they constituted his best defense, if used selectively, and because he was certain he could command complete control of them. What Nixon did not anticipate was the persistence with which Ervin, Cox, and Sirica would demand access to the tapes, or the power of public opinion they would muster behind that demand, or the independence of the Supreme Court. These were fatal misjudgments on his part.

On Saturday, July 21, Nixon wrote a private note on the subject: "If I had discussed illegal action, I would not have taped. If I had discussed illegal action and had taped [it] I would have destroyed the tapes once the investigation began."

Whether this was self-deception or pure cynicism, or something in between, is impossible to say. He certainly had discussed illegal action on March 21, indeed had ordered it (the payment to Hunt), and it had been carried out. The attempt to use the CIA to turn off the FBI back in June 1972, the break-in to Dr. Fielding's office, and other Nixon Administration actions had some cover of national security; but the Hunt payment was in direct response to blackmail.

With regard to Nixon's second sentence, he explained/confessed in his memoirs that he decided the tapes were "my best insurance." If other aides turned against him, as Dean had done, "the tapes would give me at least some protection."[45]

As to releasing those parts of the tapes that were exculpatory, Nixon realized that was no longer an option. He explained in a scribbled comment on his bedside note pad in the hospital: "Tapes—once start, no stopping."[46]

On July 17, Ervin wrote Nixon to inform him that the Senate Select Committee had voted unanimously to request that the President provide it with "all relevant documents and tapes under control of the White House" that related to Watergate and associated activities. He requested a response "at your earliest convenience," and signed off with an expression of regret at Nixon's illness and a hope for a speedy recovery.[47]

Nixon took a week to reply. When he did, he said no, citing executive privilege. He also assured Ervin that the tapes would not settle anything. "I personally listened to a number of them," Nixon wrote. "The tapes are entirely consistent with what I know to be the truth and what I have stated to be the truth." He admitted that people with different perspectives might interpret the material in different ways, but warned that there were "a great many very frank and very private comments" on subjects that had nothing to do with Watergate but which would cause great embarrassment and harm.

"Accordingly, the tapes, which have been under my sole personal control, will remain so. None has been transcribed or made public and none will be." He stood "categorically" behind his May 22 statement.[48]

Thus was joined the battle of the tapes. It looked like it was going to be a long-drawn-out battle, possibly lasting into the fall, perhaps even to the end of the year. And Nixon went into the battle at less than full strength. On the same day that Ervin made his request, Seymour Hersh revealed in *The New York Times* that American B-52 bombers had made at least 3,500 secret raids over Cambodia in 1969 and 1970, and that the Pentagon had falsified reports on those raids with the full knowledge of Defense Secretary Laird and President Nixon.[49]

The following day, July 18, the White House announced that the President was putting Phase IV into effect. It ended the freeze on prices for health care and food; that meant an immediate jump in prices in the grocery stores. It also forced the Administration to admit that the freeze instituted in June had been a mistake. Nixon's statement was unusual in other ways; he conceded that "confidence in our management of our fiscal affairs is low, at home and abroad," while the closest he could come to being upbeat was to say, "we should not despair of our plight."[50]

BATTERED though he was, Nixon was determined to fight. On July 20, he left the hospital. That morning, he spoke in the Rose Garden to the White House staff. He thanked the members for carrying on in his absence. He went on: "As you can imagine, while I was there, I had a lot of chance to think, to sleep, to rest. It is a little difficult, I must say, to do some of those things when you are not used to it." Catching himself, he explained, "I mean I am used to thinking but not to—not sleeping and resting."

Nixon said that Rose Woods had sent him selected portions of the incoming mail while he was in the hospital, and much of it had been encouraging. But, he continued, some of the well-intentioned advice he received, "I am not going to take." Well-wishers had wondered if the burdens of his office might have caused his illness and urged him to consider "either slowing down or even, some suggested, resigning."

He gave a ringing response: "Any suggestion that this President is ever going to slow down . . . or leave his office until he . . . finishes the job he was elected to do, anyone who suggests that, that is just plain poppycock. We are going to stay on this job until we get the job done."

The President concluded, "And what we were elected to do, we are going to do, and let others wallow in Watergate, we are going to do our job."[51]

Nixon's counterattack was weakened by his own Cabinet and staff. Agriculture Secretary Earl Butz said that consumers were suffering from the effects of the June freeze; Labor Secretary Peter Brennan said Nixon had erred when he taped telephone calls; counselor Laird said the President "will dislike me more as time goes on"; Kissinger denied that he knew anything about the falsification of reports on the Cambodian bombing and called it "deplorable."

White House aide Bruce Herschensohn called Nixon's attention to these statements and commented that they "constituted a breach of loyalty like nothing I've seen before. It is terribly destructive at this time, and I would hope you could tell them to knock it off or ask them to go home. If I'm wrong, ask me to go home." Nixon scribbled on the memo, "Bruce— You are exactly right."[52]

Nixon's News Summary that day, July 23, reported that John Osborne had written in the *New Republic* that Nixon had used the tapes in preparing his May 22 statement. Osborne wrote that he had learned that the tapes gave a mixed and confusing picture, with parts supporting Nixon's contentions and other parts contradicting him. Nixon commented, "Al— could this be one of our own people talking to Osborne?" Insofar as Osborne had it exactly right, the question answered itself.

The same News Summary reported that Nixon's approval rating had fallen to 40 percent; the 28 percent drop in six months was the sharpest in the history of the Gallup Poll. Nixon commented, "Al—this includes Dean week—it does not include Hospital or Tapes—We can expect this to discourage our Congressional and Party types."

The Summary quoted a Chicago *Tribune* headline: "Facts Batter Sense of Trust." Nixon commented, "Al and Z—This is the basic problem."[53]

Indeed. And it was that day that Nixon told Ervin his committee could not have access to any of the tapes. Ervin spoke for many when he remarked, "John Dean has said he told the President about the Watergate cover-up, and an unaltered tape of that conversation would offer the best contemporary evidence that Dean was telling the truth. I can think of no rational reason for the President not turning over the tapes unless the evidence found in them would be against him."[54]

Nixon made no reply, but he did move aggressively in other areas. Ervin had said that J. Edgar Hoover never permitted burglaries by the FBI; the White House found a 1961 Hoover memo to the Attorney General, Robert Kennedy, that said: "In the interests of national safety microphone surveillances are sometimes used even though trespass is necessary." Nixon instructed Ziegler, "a good point for all hands to hit."[55]

On July 25, the Shah of Iran came for a visit. Walter Cronkite observed that this was Nixon's first state meeting in the Oval Office without a secret tape recording. Nixon reacted: "Z—point out there was *no* taping until June, 1970."[56]

Nixon's pursuers were also active. Special Prosecutor Cox demanded access to the tapes. Nixon's lawyer, Charles Alan Wright, said no. The Ervin Committee issued a subpoena on Nixon for the tapes of his meetings with John Dean. Nixon refused to comply. Judge Sirica issued a subpoena on Nixon to produce documents and tapes for the grand jury. Nixon replied that it would be inconsistent with the public interest and with the constitutional position of the Presidency to comply, so "I must respectfully decline to do so."[57]

The Ervin Committee action marked the first time a congressional committee issued a subpoena to a President, and the first time since the Aaron Burr treason trial in 1807 that a subpoena had been served on a President.

Nixon's refusal to comply with the subpoenas created what John Chancellor on NBC TV called "one of the most serious and significant constitutional disputes in our history." The Ervin Committee, Cox, and Sirica all indicated they were going to press their demands; Ervin said he wanted a declaratory judgment in court. White House spokesman Warren said Nixon would abide by a "definitive" decision from the Supreme Court.[58]

Archibald Cox, on television, said that Nixon's position, while "presented in good faith," was "quite wrong," because the precedents cited by Nixon in support of his refusal applied to supplying documents to Congress and not to a presidential refusal to supply courts and grand juries with information pertaining to possible charges of obstruction of justice and perjury. Cox turned Nixon's use of the Jefferson precedent against him, pointing out that while Jefferson had refused to respond to a subpoena calling on him to appear in the Richmond, Virginia, court in the Burr trial, Jefferson had supplied the court with documents relevant to the case.

Evidently Nixon had not known the details of the Jefferson-Burr case. He scribbled on a News Summary that quoted Cox, "Al—I would like a brief memo from Wright on this issue—Is Cox on sound ground?"[59] He was.

The Select Committee, meanwhile, said it was ready to compromise. It proposed that Nixon allow a private audition of the tapes by Senators Ervin and Baker, along with Cox. They would screen out statements unrelated to their investigations before making the information public. Ervin explained that on reflection he did not want to go to the Supreme Court with a lawsuit because "it is quite possible the Supreme Court would hold adversely to the committee."[60]

Nixon made no immediate reply.

Two of Nixon's former associates rallied to his cause. John Ehrlichman told the Ervin Committee that neither he nor the President had authorized the break-in to Dr. Fielding's office, then insisted that the break-in was entirely within the President's legal authority to protect national security. Brash and combative, Ehrlichman battled with his questioners, called Dean a liar, stood 100 percent behind the President, and explained that his own theory was that the cover-up was intended to mask the involvement of John Mitchell in the Watergate burglary. He quoted Haldeman as having asked him if it was possible "we are taking all this anguish just to protect John Mitchell."[61]

On July 30, Bob Haldeman replaced Ehrlichman on the witness stand. He was brazen in his lies: "President Nixon had no knowledge of or involvement in either the Watergate affair or the subsequent efforts of a 'cover-up.' " Haldeman said he was certain of his facts, because he had taken to California with him the March 21 tape, listened to it, and could swear that Dean had lied. Haldeman said that the President had not indicated that he had discussed clemency for the burglars, nor had he given any indication that he was aware of payments to silence the conspirators.

Crew-cut, sharply dressed, straight-faced, exuding sincerity, Haldeman made a strong impression. Like Ehrlichman, Haldeman put the blame on Mitchell and CREEP. "At the White House, at least," he said, "John Dean was the only one who knew that the funds were for 'hush money' if, in fact, that is what they were for."[62]

How believable he was depended on the listener. What outraged the senators was that he had listened to the tapes they wanted so badly to hear. "The United States Senate can't have those tapes but you, a private citizen, can?" Senator Ervin spluttered.[63] The struggle for the tapes was intensifying.

CHAPTER NINE

THE STRUGGLE
FOR THE TAPES
August–September 1973

JUDGE SIRICA wanted to hear the tapes; Senator Ervin wanted to hear the tapes; Special Prosecutor Cox wanted to hear the tapes; the media wanted to hear the tapes; the public wanted to hear the tapes. It was a commonplace of Washington political gossip that Nixon would have to give up either the tapes or his office.

All through August the President's situation seemed desperate, only to get worse. Every time he counterattacked, he lost ground. Each time it appeared that his luck had finally turned, there was another disaster.

Yet not only at the end of August, but to the end of September—another month of unmitigated woe—he retained possession of the tapes and of his job. In a lifetime of playing it tough, Nixon had never played it tougher.

He met the incessant demands for the tapes with a flat no. Through Gerald Warren, he declared that he and he alone would decide who would be given access to the tapes, based on his judgment "of who could best assist him in determining the facts of the Watergate matter without jeopardizing the confidentiality of the tapes."[1]

Haldeman, testifying before the Ervin Committee, continued to assert that the tapes he had listened to proved that Nixon was telling the truth. Senator Ervin charged that Haldeman's testimony was part of a "planned action" by the White House to "leak" a favorable version of the taped conversations.[2] Ervin should have said "Nixon" instead of "the White House." Within the Oval Office, Nixon was very much in charge, despite—or perhaps because of—a sharp split among his aides. His lawyers were urging him to be conciliatory, as Haig and Ziegler urged him

202

to stick it to the opposition. Haig, Buchanan, and others wanted to relieve Watergate pressure by demonstrating that the Democrats had done similar things. George Bush, chairman of the Republican National Convention (RNC), agreed with them. He released an affidavit that linked the Ervin Committee's chief investigator, Carmine Bellino, to a 1960 wiretapping. Bush said this was "just a first step in showing that that Ervin bunch is not so holier-than-thou."[3]

On August 1, Nixon fired a shot at a black-tie state dinner for Japanese Premier Kakuei Tanaka. He opened an impromptu toast by saying that the audience must be wondering what he and Tanaka had talked about in their afternoon meeting. "It would make very lively chitchat to say that, like a couple of desert rug merchants, we haggled over what is the textile quota going to be," but that had not been the subject. Instead, they had discussed what their legacy would be. "Do we leave the memory only of the battles we fought, of the opponents we did in, of the viciousness that we created, or do we leave possibly not only the dream but the reality of a new world?"

Then he interrupted his flow. Growling, shaking his head from side to side as he did when he was angry, he said, "Let others spend their time dealing with the murky, small, unimportant, vicious little things. We have spent our time and will spend our time in building a better world."

He raised his head and brightened up a bit, and spoke in praise of President Eisenhower, who had recognized the importance of Asia. He wandered into a disjointed passage about how the 200 million people in America had their faults, but were totally dedicated to "building a better world." Then his anger returned, and he growled even as he made a request that this generation of Americans "not let ourselves be remembered only for the petty, little, indecent things that seem to obsess us at a time when the world is going by."[4]

The petty, little, indecent things would not go away. In the week that followed, they dominated the news. There were revelations about government spending on Nixon's California and Florida homes, more than $10 million, according to the GSA. A Colson memo made public by the Ervin Committee linked the ITT contribution to the Republican National Convention and the settlement of an antitrust action against ITT. It implicated Agnew, Mitchell, Kleindienst, Ehrlichman, Connally, and others. Pat Gray told the Ervin Committee that he had warned Nixon in June 1972 that his aides were trying to "mortally wound" the President, but for reasons Gray could not understand, Nixon had ignored him. Gulf Oil, Goodyear Tire and Rubber, Braniff Airways, Phillips Petroleum, Minnesota Mining and Manufacturing, Ashland Oil, American Airlines, and other corporations admitted to the Justice Department they had made illegal campaign contributions to CREEP, and in nearly every case explained that they had done so in response to pressure from the White House and/or CREEP. Chrysler Corporation disclosed that Nixon's personal attorney, Herb Kalmbach, had asked for a major gift, at a time when Chrysler was preparing to seek a delay in implementation of federal standards for auto emission controls.[5]

A Gallup Poll, conducted on August 3–6, reported that Nixon's approval rating had fallen to 31 percent, the lowest popularity rating for a President since Harry Truman's last month in office (January 1953) and 4 percentage points lower than Lyndon Johnson's worst month (August 1968).

As his popularity sank, so did Nixon's ability to govern recede, and his anger mount. He tried to persuade Congress to reconsider its cut-off of funds for bombing in Cambodia, but failed. On August 3, Nixon released a letter he had written to the Speaker of the House and the Majority Leader of the Senate. In it he said he recognized that Congress had required an end to the bombing by August 15 and pledged that he would obey the law. "I cannot do so, however," he went on, "without stating my grave personal reservations concerning the dangerous potential consequences of this measure."

Nixon wrote that the Congress had undermined any incentive the Communists had to negotiate a settlement in Cambodia, and warned that "this abandonment of a friend will have a profound impact in other countries, such as Thailand, which have relied on the constancy and determination of the United States, and I want the Congress to be fully aware of the consequences of its action."[6]

Political commentators interpreted the letter as an attempt on Nixon's part to shift onto Congress the blame and the responsibility if Cambodia should fall to the Communists. In that sense, Nixon had made a mistake—it certainly did him no good to point a finger of blame at the institution that was taking the lead in investigating his actions. He would have been wiser to have made the point that the Cambodian rider marked the first time in American history that Congress had used its power over the purse strings to force a President to end a military operation. That would have been a reminder that more was involved here than just Dick Nixon and his foes.

Instead, what Nixon did was to step up the bombing. He pounded the Communist troops around Phnom Penh with B-52 bombers and F-111 fighter bombers, increasing the tonnage of explosives right up to the cut-off date of August 15. Altogether, from the time of the armistice in Vietnam (January 1973) to August 15, the U.S. Air Force dropped more than 240,000 tons of bombs on Cambodia, which was 50 percent more than the total of conventional explosives dropped on Japan in World War II.[7]

•

IN the first week in August a new problem emerged that was all but unbelievable. It concerned Vice President Agnew and some petty graft that he had been involved in as governor of Maryland back in the sixties. It could hardly have come on at a worse time, or been more perplexing, or put Nixon into more of a quandary. No matter what he did, he was going to make new enemies, raise new doubts and questions about his own motives, and thus weaken his own position.

In April, Haldeman had informed Nixon that Agnew was under investigation by the Justice Department, specifically by the U.S. Attorney in Baltimore, George Beall, the younger brother of Senator J. Glenn Beall, a Republican. In June, Richardson told Haig that the allegations were serious; at the end of July, Richardson told Haig that he had never seen such a cut-and-dried case. He said Agnew was potentially indictable on more than forty counts. Haig passed this information on to Nixon.[8]

From what Richardson said, Beall's case against Agnew was so strong that the investigation could not be derailed, or turned off, or ignored. Nixon wanted an independent evaluation; he sent his own lawyers, Buzhardt and Garment, to meet with Richardson to go over the evidence. They reported back that this was one of the most solid cases they had ever seen. Their recommendation was that Agnew resign.[9]

Nixon did not want to move that fast. There were too many factors coming to bear for hasty action. Nixon's mind raced through some of them. In the first place Agnew, untouched by Watergate, was popular with conservative Republicans, whose support Nixon had to have if he were to survive in office. But Agnew might be used to take the glare of Watergate publicity off the President. And if Agnew had to leave office in disgrace, that might satisfy the press and the public's lust for blood, allowing Nixon to survive on the basis of "enough is enough." Barry Goldwater thought that making Agnew a sacrificial lamb was Nixon's major motivation in dealing with the situation.[10]

Tempting though that solution was, Nixon was aware of the trap it contained. As Haldeman had put it months ago, Agnew was Nixon's insurance policy. Not even Nixon's worst enemy would want to impeach if it meant that Agnew would become President. Viewed from that perspective, an Agnew resignation would hurt Nixon far more than it would help him.

And yet, Nixon felt that if he sacrificed Agnew, he could follow it up with his own quid pro quo and get rid of Archibald Cox. The Special Prosecutor continued to demand documents and tapes and to make himself obnoxious and dangerous to Nixon. In July, Nixon had been furious when he had read a Los Angeles *Times* story that Cox was looking into his real estate transactions. The President was extremely vulnerable here—he had made large profits, he had not paid large taxes on these profits, he had accepted "loans" from Rebozo and Abplanalp to make the investment, he had used creative accounting methods. Nixon had ordered Haig to tell Richardson to order Cox to back off. Cox had drafted a statement in which he denied that he was investigating Nixon's finances. Richardson had read it over the telephone to Haig. Haig called it "inadequate" and handed the phone to Nixon, who heatedly demanded stronger wording.[11]

By mid-August, Cox was arguing that Nixon had already waived executive privilege on the tapes through his selective disclosures of some of the material. "Not even a President," Cox argued in a brief to the U.S. District Court, "can be allowed to select" certain accounts for public release and then "frustrate further inquiries by withholding the best evidence of what actually took place."[12] So Agnew for Cox made a nice trade-off for Nixon, especially as Agnew was no real friend or confidant.

For four years Nixon had used Agnew to attack his enemies in the press, in television, in the Establishment. He had not consulted with Agnew. The Vice President has reported that he never, ever, had a chance to participate in any decision. "Every time I went to see him and raised a subject for discussion," Agnew said later, "he would begin a rambling, time-consuming monologue. Then finally the phone would ring or Haldeman would come in, and there would be no time left for what I really had come to talk about. . . . He preferred keeping his decision-making within a very small group. I was not of the inner circle."[13]

In the Watergate crisis, Agnew had been useful to Nixon. He had spoken frequently and forcefully in Nixon's defense. He could expect, or at least hope, that Nixon would feel sufficient gratitude to come to his defense. But personal loyalty was not one of Nixon's virtues. The President always put his own interests, or his perception of the best interests of the nation, ahead of the interests of his friends and associates.

Agnew became quite bitter about his treatment. Richard Nixon, he later wrote, "played me as a pawn in the desperate game for his survival."[14]

Actually, he did not. This was the one crisis in Nixon's political life in which he refrained from behind-the-scenes manipulation. He did not nudge, or push, or pull, or otherwise interfere. He neither sacrificed nor tried to save Agnew. He stood aside and allowed events to run their course.

He removed himself from the action for the obvious reason that he had no choice, or rather that all his choices were bad ones. By far the best outcome for Nixon personally would have been to keep Agnew in office for as long as possible, first under indictment, then in a criminal trial. With some imagination, some manipulation of the legal system, and great good luck, the whole thing might have been dragged out to 1976. Had that happened, how many Democrats would have been willing to impeach Nixon? But standing up and fighting for Agnew was not an option open to Nixon, not after his Attorney General told him it was an open-and-shut case and his own lawyers reported that they agreed.

Agnew's problem was the same as Nixon's. He was guilty.

Nixon could not stand up for Agnew, but neither could he denounce the Vice President and demand his resignation. Barry Goldwater, among others, warned him that if he did so he would infuriate conservative Republicans and split the party.[15]

On Monday morning, August 6, Nixon met with Richardson to discuss Agnew. "His reaction was remarkably objective and deliberate," Richardson reported in an interview. "He was disturbed and concerned with the correctness of any action or anything he did or did not do." The President felt "that he ought not to try to be fully informed about the state of the evidence, and that his position ought to be more insulated." Richardson did manage to tell Nixon that he had irrefutable documents that proved Agnew's guilt. Nixon asked for an independent assessment by Henry Petersen; Richardson agreed.[16]

Nixon made no attempt to hear Agnew's side of the story. Instead, he flew up to Camp David, where he conferred with Haig and Harlow. Those two then flew back to Washington, met with Agnew, and told him to resign. They said that they were speaking for the President. Agnew demanded a face-to-face meeting with Nixon.[17]

The following morning, August 7, *The Wall Street Journal* reported that Agnew was suspected of extortion, bribery, and tax evasion, and that he was one of the targets of a Baltimore grand jury that had been meeting for several months, investigating kickbacks paid by contractors, architects, and engineers to officials of Baltimore County and the state of Maryland.[18]

At midday, Nixon returned from Camp David. That afternoon, he met for an hour and a half with Agnew in his EOB office. According to Agnew, Nixon indulged in a monologue. He related what Richardson had told him. He seemed sympathetic and solicitous; he said he understood the pressures on a governor to raise campaign funds, and that he knew where and how that money had to be raised. (Nixon had remarked to Haldeman back in April, when he first heard of Agnew's troubles, "Thank God I was never elected governor of California.")

When Agnew finally got a chance to reply, he protested that he was innocent, the victim of a conspiracy. He said Richardson was out to get him, and requested an independent review of the case.

Nixon responded that he too was having problems with Richardson, and then, as if the thought had just occurred to him, he said he would appoint Henry Petersen to "take this thing over and do an independent review of everything that has been done and report back to me."

Nixon did not ask for Agnew's resignation, nor did Agnew bring up the subject. Agnew did say he intended to hold a news conference to deny the charges and damn the allegations made against him. Nixon cautioned him to be careful about what he said.[19]

In the news conference, Agnew was his usual aggressive self. "I have no intention to be skewered in this fashion," he began. He called the "defamatory statements" being made about him "false and scurrilous and malicious." The first question was, Did he receive $1,000 a week in continuing kickbacks? "Damned lies," Agnew replied.[20]

Telephone calls and telegrams poured into Agnew's office, overwhelmingly favorable. Haig and Buzhardt reported to Nixon that Agnew had won a short-term political victory. But Buzhardt reminded him that in view of the evidence the Justice Department had on Agnew, the blanket denials simply would not hold up. He anticipated a long-term disaster. Nixon decided neither to defend Agnew nor to ask for his resignation. That was sensible, even if inevitable.[21]

THAT same day, August 7, the Watergate phase of the Ervin Committee hearings came to an end. For some weeks, Nixon had been promising that when the hearings were completed he would make a statement on the charges and allegations. Columnists and commentators gave that promise a big buildup. ABC TV reported that Nixon was planning a two-part statement and that his aides said he was approaching the matter with "strength and conciliation." When he read the report on his News Summary, Nixon wrote in the margin, "Al—Tell *all* staffers to quit speculating with Press re what RN is going to do."[22] Then he went off to Camp David, to spend almost a week working on his response. With him were Ray Price and Pat Buchanan, Rose Woods, Al Haig, Ron Ziegler, Pat and Tricia. This heavy concentration on the statement raised expectations. Some members of his staff, ignoring his orders, put out the word that this would be his definitive response.[23]

It was not. On August 15, Nixon went on national television and radio, looking drawn and a little sad. He repeated what he had been saying all along, that he was innocent of any wrongdoing, and asserted that "the time has come to turn Watergate over to the courts," so that "the rest of us [can] get on with the urgent business of our nation."

As he had done back in May, Nixon accepted "full responsibility" for any abuses and expressed "regret that these events took place," without specifying what the abuses and events were. Then he contradicted himself, in the key paragraph: "I had no prior knowledge of the Watergate break-in; I neither took part in nor knew about any of the subsequent coverup activities; I never authorized nor encouraged subordinates to engage in illegal or improper campaign tactics.

"That was and that is the simple truth."

Insofar as the tapes, if made public, would prove the opposite, Nixon's assertion indicates how confident he was that he would never lose control of the tapes. He recognized, however, that he needed to justify his refusal to turn over the evidence, and he devoted most of his speech to defending the principle of executive privilege. He pointed out that the law protected the confidentiality of certain conversations, such as those between lawyer and client, a priest and a penitent, or a husband and a wife, then declared that "it is even more important that the confidentiality of conversations between a President and his advisers be protected." For him to turn over the tapes to the courts or Congress would "set a precedent that would cripple all future Presidents." Even though the tapes would prove his innocence, he would never release them.

Turning to the lesson of Watergate, the President said that some of his aides had acted on an assumption that "their cause placed them beyond the reach of those rules that apply to other persons and that hold a free society together." This was certainly wrong, but whose fault was it? Nixon answered his question: The attitude became "fashionable in the 1960's as individuals and groups increasingly asserted the right to take the law into their own hands, insisting that their purposes represented a higher morality." So it was not surprising, "even though it is deplorable, that some persons in 1972 adopted the morality that they themselves had rightly condemned and committed acts that have no place in our political system."

He concluded by asking those who had supported him in 1972 "for your help to ensure that those who would exploit Watergate in order to keep us from doing what we were elected to do will not succeed."[24]

Nixon claimed in his memoirs that the speech "hit a responsive chord. The numbers of telegrams and phone calls to the White House immediately after it was over were the biggest since the days of my Vietnam speeches. People were tired of Watergate."[25]

Many of those calls and telegrams were manufactured by his own aides, as they always did after a major speech. It gave the boss a boost to see the telegrams stacked on his desk.

Pat Nixon was pleased. She let it be known that she had "the feeling that Watergate is behind all of us now." The President, she said, "spoke from the heart and it went to the hearts of the American people."[26]

In fact, the speech fell flat. James Reston dismissed it: "He introduced not a single new fact and answered none of the major ambiguities or contradictions." Senator Edward Brooke (R.-Mass.) charged that "he did not tell the American people what he knows." Democratic politicians were predictably scathing; what hurt more was Barry Goldwater's reaction: "In my opinion the President did not add anything to his other speeches that would tend to divert suspicion from him."[27]

Nixon did have defenders. Teamsters president Frank Fitzsimmons called the speech "wonderful." And Governor Ronald Reagan described it as "the voice of reason."[28]

As to Nixon's central point, Senator Ervin dismissed it out of hand. If the President turned over the tapes, Ervin said, "the Constitution would not collapse, the President would not be destroyed and the heavens would not fall."[29]

Nixon was more interested in the public's perception than the pronouncements of politicians. He could not have been happy with the findings of the Gallup Poll, taken the following day. Gallup found that 77 percent of those questioned had watched or heard the speech, an astonishingly high percentage. Half said they did not believe his assertion of innocence, 58 percent rejected his charge that antiwar protests and civil rights groups helped create the atmosphere that led to the Watergate crimes, and only 27 percent thought Nixon was convincing.[30]

Pollster Albert E. Sindlinger got better results by asking different questions. He asked whether those questioned agreed or disagreed with Nixon's call to turn Watergate over to the courts while "the rest of us get back to the urgent business of our nation." Some 69 percent agreed; only 27 percent disagreed. Asked who they would vote for if the presidential election of 1972 was "held tomorrow," 59 percent said Nixon, only 30 percent McGovern. The President was pleased. He told Haig to "get these figures out."[31]

That was done, with appropriate trumpeting. So were the results of another Sindlinger national poll, one that asked which was the more morally reprehensible, the drowning of Mary Jo Kopechne or the bugging of the DNC. By 44 percent to 34 percent, the respondents judged Senator Kennedy's role in the Chappaquiddick incident as more blameworthy than the break-in.[32]

Three days after his speech, Nixon went to New Orleans to address the national convention of the Veterans of Foreign Wars and got several rousing ovations from an enthusiastic audience of several thousand delegates. His subject was the secret bombing of Cambodia in 1969; he insisted it was "absolutely necessary," that it had saved American lives, and that it had forced the Communists to the negotiating table. His face flushed with excitement as the veterans cheered.

Nixon showed some signs of strain, however. Three or four times he stumbled over a word in the speech, something that seldom happened. Also unusual was a public display of anger. When the presidential party had arrived at the Rivergate Convention Center and Nixon moved through the crowd to the entrance, Ziegler—accompanied by reporters and cameramen—sought to follow him. Nixon grabbed Ziegler by the shoulders, spun him around, and pushed him away, toward the reporters. The President growled, "I don't want any press with me and you take care of it."[33]

The television evening news highlighted the shove and the growl, while downplaying the speech and its reception. There was press speculation that Nixon was either "on the sauce" or "off his rocker." In Washington, rumors went around that he had gone to the hospital in July not for viral pneumonia but because he had suffered a stroke.[34]

The reporters were hunting, aroused by Nixon's bleeding from his multiple wounds. He tried to turn on them. From New Orleans, he flew to San Clemente, where he held an unscheduled news conference, outside, on the bluffs overlooking the Pacific. It was carried live on television and radio, his first televised news conference in fourteen months. The questions were hostile; so were Nixon's answers.

Nixon was clearly nervous. He slurred and mispronounced several words and his voice quavered noticeably. The press emphasized this in its reporting.

Tom Jarriel of ABC News asked the President how he could justify allowing Haldeman to listen to tapes when he knew Haldeman was likely to be indicted on criminal charges. Nixon replied that Haldeman had listened to only one tape that had been made September 15, 1972, and that Haldeman had been a participant in the conversation. "He did not listen to any tapes in which only Mr. Dean and I participated," Nixon said.

It was not true; Haldeman had listened to the March 21, 1973, tape as well, when Dean warned Nixon about the cancer on the Presidency. Haldeman had been present for only the last third of that meeting.

Nixon answered the next question with a long, complex justification of the principle of confidentiality.

Peter Lisagor noted that Nixon claimed he tried to get all the facts, but pointed out that John Mitchell had said that if the President had "ever asked him at any time about the Watergate matter, he would have told you the whole story, chapter and verse." Why hadn't Nixon asked?

Because, Nixon explained, he expected Mitchell "to tell me in the event that he was involved or that anybody else was. He did not tell me. I don't blame him for not telling me. . . . I regret that he did not, because he is exactly right, had he told me, I would have blown my stack."

Dan Rather of CBS News was recognized. "Mr. President," he began, "I want to state this question with due respect to your office, but also as directly as possible."

"That would be unusual," Nixon quipped.

"I would like to think not, sir," Rather responded.

"You are always respectful, Mr. Rather," Nixon said. "You know that."

"Thank you, Mr. President," Rather replied. Then he asked if Nixon had tried to bribe Judge Byrne in the Ellsberg trial with his offer of the directorship of the FBI. Certainly not, Nixon answered. He gave a long explanation. He said he had only shaken hands with Byrne, after Ehrlichman informed Byrne of the FBI job. He never mentioned the FBI to Byrne. He concluded, "That is what happened and obviously, you, in your commentary tonight, can attach anything you want to it.

"I hope you will be just as fair and objective as I try to be in giving you the answer. And I know you will be, sir."

The next question let Nixon express his confidence in the integrity of Vice President Agnew. Then he was asked if he ever considered resigning.

Absolutely not.

Nixon urged that people end their obsession with Watergate and get on with the business of the nation. A reporter interrupted him; Nixon snapped, "Just a moment. We have had 30 minutes of this press conference. I have yet to have, for example, one question on the business of the people, which shows you how we are consumed with this. I am not criticizing the members of the press . . . but let me tell you, years from now people are going to perhaps be interested in the efforts of this Administration to have a kind of prosperity that we have not had since 1955— that is, prosperity without war and without inflation."

He added quickly that he did not mean to be critical of Kennedy and Johnson. Then he criticized Kennedy and Johnson for placing many more wiretaps than he ever had.

Did he still consider Ehrlichman and Haldeman to be "two of the finest public servants you have ever known?" he was asked.

"I certainly do." They had served with great distinction, at great personal sacrifice. There had been scandalous conduct, but "Thank God there has been no personal gain involved. That would be going much too far, I suppose." He predicted that "they will be exonerated."

When Nixon said in his August 15 statement that there were those who would exploit Watergate to keep him from doing his job, who were "those," he was asked.

"Where the shoe fits, people should wear it," Nixon replied. "I would think that some political figures, some members of the press, perhaps, some members of the television, perhaps would exploit it. I don't impute, interestingly enough, motives, however, that are improper."

Then he imputed improper motives. The President said there were a great number of people who did not accept the results of the 1972 election: "After all, I know that most of the members of the press corps were not enthusiastic—and I understand that—about my election. . . . What I am saying is this: People who did not accept the mandate of '72, who do not want the strong America that I want to build, who do not want the foreign policy leadership that I want to give, who do not want to cut down the size of the government bureaucracy that burdens us so greatly and to give more of our government back to the people, people who do not want these things, naturally, would exploit any issue if it weren't Watergate, anything else—in order to keep the President from doing his job.

"And so I say I impute no improper motives to them; I think they would prefer that I fail."[35]

Nixon's performance got rave reviews from his lawyers. Buzhardt, Garment, and Charles Alan Wright sent him a joint telegram: "Congratulations from all your lawyers on a superb press conference which we believe will go far to put Watergate to bed. Not only was the press conference a full answer to public demands but it also should provide the frosting on the cake for our legal case."

Nixon scribbled a reply: "Many thanks for a splendid argument in court."[36] He was referring to Wright's appearance before Judge Sirica that day; Wright had maintained that the President was the sole judge of what records should be made available. He said that Nixon had told him that one of the tapes contained "national security information so highly sensitive" that even Wright could not be told its nature; he did not add that none of the lawyers had had access to any of the tapes.[37] He was deceiving his lawyers by not leveling with them. What were they so pleased with? That he got through it? Nixon was deceiving everybody, first and foremost himself.

When Nixon complained that the reporters had asked him about nothing but Watergate, he was making an obvious observation. But he did not draw the obvious conclusion: that they were not going to stop and he had to deal with Watergate.

NIXON would have welcomed any chance to get off the subject of Watergate and onto foreign policy. According to Kissinger, he had toyed with the idea of making a plea in his August 15 statement to end the Watergate inquiries so as not to increase the foreign-policy perils. Kissinger had appealed to Haig, Garment, and Wright not to link foreign policy and Watergate; they had agreed with him; Nixon had dropped the idea. Perhaps it was a good thing he did so because, again according to Kissinger, Nixon's attention span for foreign policy had been declining. Kissinger claims that "he would sign memoranda or accept my recommendations almost absent-mindedly now."[38]

But the paper Kissinger had most wanted Nixon to sign was one dismissing Rogers, and the President still resisted doing it. Kissinger wrote in his memoirs that Nixon had always distrusted the State Department, because it was "fuzzy-minded and a nest of holdover liberal Democrats." He got back at it by keeping Rogers on as Secretary of State. In addition, Kissinger went on, "I remain convinced that he wished to establish, for once, a relationship of primacy over his old friend and mentor Bill Rogers," because he had been forced to come to Rogers for help in moments of weakness or danger, such as the Checkers speech and Ike's

1955 heart attack.[39] Stories circulating in Washington said that Kissinger was slandering Rogers.

Whatever Nixon's motives were, whether they were as devious as Kissinger judged them, what is clear is that Kissinger was trying to force Nixon's hand. Kissinger's immense popularity with the press stood in sharp contrast to Nixon's unpopularity and Rogers's near invisibility. The press could not praise Kissinger highly enough, nor stress more strongly that he was untainted by Watergate or any other domestic scandal. And Kissinger had repeatedly told Nixon that either Rogers went or he would resign.

On August 8, Nixon had told Haig to suggest to Rogers that he resign. Rogers said that if the President wanted his resignation, he would have to ask for it himself. On August 16, Nixon called Rogers to his office; Rogers made it easy for his old friend by handing over a letter of resignation free of recrimination or argument.

Four days later, before Nixon announced the resignation, Rogers held a news conference. He condemned the Ellsberg break-in and said that the government must not become "so obsessed with security matters that laws are freely violated." He added that security for the United States depended on "the fact that we are a law-abiding nation."[40]

On August 21, in San Clemente, Nixon—floating on his back in his swimming pool—casually told Kissinger that he would open his news conference the following day with the announcement that Rogers was leaving and Kissinger would become Secretary of State.

"I hope to be worthy of your trust," Kissinger said.[41]

Kissinger's confirmation hearings extended over a two-week period, and included some embarrassing questions. This was, in part, Rogers's revenge. On August 25, Rogers criticized the White House–sanctioned wiretapping of three high-ranking foreign service officers under a 1969–71 program that Nixon had called "necessary to find and stop serious national security leaks." Rogers said he had never been informed that top officials in his department were being spied upon and stated that had he been asked, he "would not have approved the wiretaps."[42] Kissinger had approved them; indeed, he had told the FBI what officials he wanted wiretapped. Because Rogers made a public issue out of it, the Senate Foreign Relations Committee had to ask Kissinger about the taps. But no senator pressed hard, on the taps or on the coup that toppled Salvador Allende in Chile, or on the secret bombing of Cambodia, or on much of anything else. The general attitude was, Thank God we have Henry, let's confirm him so he can run foreign policy while we get after Nixon for Watergate.

On September 21, the Senate confirmed Kissinger by a vote of 78 to 7. The next day Chief Justice Burger administered the oath of office in the East Room of the White House. Nixon, Kissinger wrote, "seemed driven by his own demons. He did not join in the family gathering in the Red Room with the Chief Justice just before I was sworn in. His remarks at the swearing-in ranged from the perfunctory to the bizarre."[43]

That is accurate. Nixon began by pointing out that Kissinger had overcome intense congressional opposition to win confirmation, which was not true. He said the appointment represented a series of historic firsts: Kissinger was the first naturalized citizen to become Secretary of State; Kissinger was the first Secretary to have visited Peking and Moscow before his appointment; Kissinger was the first Secretary of State since World War II who did not part his hair.[44]

In his response, Kissinger pointed out that "there is no country in the world where it is conceivable that a man of my origin could be standing here next to the President of the United States."

To Kissinger's dismay, Pat Nixon refused to join the receiving line after his swearing in, and Dick Nixon disappeared immediately afterward, not even making an appearance at the traditional reception in the State Dining Room.[45]

THE Kissinger appointment was Nixon's only action that summer that got general approval from the reporters. Everything else he did was scrutinized, criticized, picked apart, as the press called his motives as well as his actions into question. The media went after Nixon with extra zeal on his income tax and his real estate transactions, as these were issues with which the average American could identify much more readily than he could with arguments over executive privilege or wiretapping for national security purposes.

On August 27, in an attempt to stem the tide of comment on Nixon's San Clemente purchases, the White House issued a detailed analysis of where the money came from, and what happened to the profits. The statement declared: "The President has instructed that this be done so that once and for all the entire transaction is spelled out." It identified Rebozo and Abplanalp as the men who put up the money, as a loan.

The analysis, designed to confuse, did so. The details were overwhelming. What appeared to have happened was this: Rebozo and Abplanalp put up the money; Nixon made the purchase; he then sold some of the property back to Abplanalp at a handsome profit; he evidently paid no tax on that profit.[46] Given that impression, and given the news-making character of the two millionaires who served as Nixon's angels, it was hardly surprising that the media jumped on the story, or that the reporters filled their accounts with hints and innuendoes.

ON August 29, Nixon's lawyers rejected the Ervin Committee's demands for tapes; they charged that Ervin and his associates had conducted a "criminal investigation and trial" that exceeded the authority granted to

Congress by the Constitution, and that the senators were illegally attempting to determine "whether or not criminal acts have been committed and the guilt or innocence of individuals." They concluded that the President "owes no duty" to either the Congress or the courts to provide tapes or documents.[47]

That same day, Judge Sirica ordered Nixon to make seven tapes subpoenaed by Cox available to him so that he could decide whether or not they should be presented to the Watergate grand jury.

So now there was a court order to turn over the tapes. In saying no to the Ervin Committee's demand, Nixon was entering into a political struggle. If he refused Sirica, it would put him into a legal struggle that would invite a constitutional crisis. Recognizing this, Sirica gave Nixon five days to appeal his decision.

Nixon's initial reaction was defiance. From San Clemente, he issued a statement. Noting that Sirica's order was "inconsistent with the President's position relating to the question of separation of powers," the statement declared: "The President consequently will not comply with this order." It left open the possibility of a compromise, however, with a follow-on sentence: "White House counsel are now considering the possibility of obtaining appellate review or how otherwise to sustain the President's position."[48]

Nixon wanted to tough it out, but Wright and the other lawyers were urging him to accept Sirica's offer to appeal. The implication was clear: if Nixon lost in the U.S. Court of Appeals, he could then take the case to the Supreme Court. He had already said he would accept a "definitive" decision from the Supreme Court, although he had refused to define what he meant by "definitive." To take the appeal route was to leave the ultimate decision in the hands of the Supreme Court.

There were both possibilities and pitfalls in that course. Nixon had appointed four of the nine justices, including the Chief Justice (Warren Burger, Harry Blackmun, Lewis Powell, and William Rehnquist). A unanimous opinion against Nixon seemed unlikely; anything less than unanimous Nixon might claim was not definitive and he could continue to defy. If that happened, the Court commanded the U.S. Marshals, but the President commanded the U.S. armed forces. It might come down to the classic confrontation between Chief Justice John Marshall and President Andrew Jackson: "John Marshall has made his decision, now let him enforce it."

But if it came to such open defiance, Nixon would certainly be impeached by the House and tried before the Senate. That would take his fate out of the hands of the Supreme Court and put it in the hands of the Senate; to prevail in the Senate, he would have to have the support of conservative Republicans and Southern Democrats, who were precisely the politicians most likely to be unsympathetic toward him if he defied the Supreme Court.

There was also public opinion to think about. Nixon believed that in the end public opinion would decide, and he sensed that he would have a difficult time persuading the public that he had a duty or a right to defy an order from the Supreme Court.

On August 30, Nixon met with Wright and Buzhardt. At the conclusion of the meeting, the White House announced that Nixon would appeal Sirica's ruling.[49] That decision had the immediate benefit of putting off the crisis and buying time.

It did not give Nixon a chance to rest, relax, reflect, and regroup, because he had problems that would not wait. One was Agnew. The Vice President had asked for a meeting. On September 1, Nixon flew back to Washington for a get-together. Agnew was blunt. He told Nixon he could not get a fair trial in Baltimore, that "zealous prosecutors determined to ruin me" would play on the ignorance and innocence of a jury to get a conviction. He was also bold. He said rather than face a trial, he wanted to be impeached. And he wanted the impeachment proceedings on national television. That way, he said, he could take his case to the people as a whole; more to the point, judgment would be passed by congressmen "all of whom had experienced the problems of raising campaign funds [and] would understand the situation much better than a Baltimore jury."[50]

Nixon expressed sympathy. He said he knew state government salaries were meager and that three quarters of the governors accepted campaign contributions from state contractors. But the President had no comment on going the impeachment route.[51]

Agnew's idea in demanding impeachment was that it would stave off the all but certain indictment from the Baltimore grand jury. His argument was that a sitting Vice President could not be subject to a federal or state criminal indictment. But Richardson had already gotten an opinion on that point, which was that while the President probably could not be indicted, because he would then be directing his own prosecution and/or could pardon himself, the Vice President could do neither and hence could be indicted.[52] Nixon, meanwhile, stayed as aloof from Agnew and his problems as he could.

What Nixon did do was attempt to get the public, the politicians, and the press to focus on something other than Administration scandals. To that end, he had his aides write a new "State of the Union" address calling attention to all the problems the Congress was ignoring because of its obsession with Watergate. Then he called a news conference for September 5, to talk about those problems.

They were real enough. One was inflation. Another was national defense. A third was energy (Nixon was proposing the Alaska pipeline, deregulation of domestic gas, a greater use of coal, and so forth, and warned that "if the Congress does not act upon these proposals, it means that we will have an energy crisis. . . . It means that we will be at the mercy of the producers of oil in the Mideast"). Other problem areas in which he had asked for legislation included better schools, better communities, and new housing. Nixon wanted action in all these areas.

Nixon's problem was that none of the issues could command the public's attention, certainly not in competition with Watergate. Since Kennedy's inauguration twelve years earlier, when the bland fifties gave way to the turbulent sixties, the public had got hooked on the nightly news. What was happening in Washington was not necessarily entertaining, but it certainly was fascinating. And it was reported in ever-increasing detail, as the television networks went from fifteen to thirty minutes of national news per night, as the staffs of the network news programs doubled and then doubled again, as the numbers of investigative reporters covering the White House and Washington increased geometrically.

People's appetites were vastly increased, as was the media's ability to satisfy them. What was needed was real events of dramatic impact. Through the sixties, the civil rights movement, the riots in the ghettos, the rise of the New Left, and most of all the war in Vietnam had provided the subject matter.

Nixon, coming to office in 1969, had promised to calm things down, and to some extent he had succeeded. The irony was that he now was paying the price for his own successes. There was relative peace in the cities, the civil rights movement had lost its steam, the New Left had had its last hurrah with George McGovern, and most important of all, no American boys were dying in Vietnam.

By shutting down American participation in the war in Vietnam, Nixon had released the flood of Watergate. Once the dam broke, he could not stop the flow, not even when competing events, such as war in the Mideast or the energy crisis, became dramatic, serious, and fundamental.

CERTAINLY neither inflation nor Nixon's housing program were going to divert the reporters' attention from Watergate and related scandals. At Nixon's September 5 news conference, the subjects the media wished to discuss were Nixon's problems, not the nation's problems. One of the first questions concerned Nixon's houses. How much had the government spent on them? Why had it been necessary for him to release so many conflicting reports on the real estate deals? Had he paid any taxes on the profits?

Nixon began his response by saying he did not resent questions of that sort. Then he explained that the value of his property at San Clemente had been reduced by the Secret Service expenditures for security equipment and fences and the like, because they blocked out the view of the mountains. He said he had borrowed the money to buy the houses, and he still owed it. He claimed that the IRS had done a full audit on his income tax returns for 1971 and 1972 and had not ordered any change. He did not say whether he had paid a capital-gains tax.

Tom Jarriel of ABC News asked what Nixon meant when he said he would accept a "definitive ruling" from the Supreme Court on the tapes. Nixon said it would be inappropriate for him to respond. Dan Rather reminded Nixon that Lincoln had declared, "No man is above the law," and asserted that for most Americans, a Supreme Court decision was final. "Would you explain to us why you feel that you are in a different category, why, as it applies to you, that you will abide only by what you call a definitive decision and that you won't even define 'definitive'?"

Nixon reminded Rather that Lincoln had suspended the writ of habeas corpus. He explained the importance of the principle of confidentiality in the Oval Office. He concluded, "Now, when we come to the Supreme Court, the question there is what kind of an order is the Supreme Court going to issue, if any. I will simply say that as far as I am concerned, we are going to fight the tape issue. We believe that we will prevail in the appellate courts. And so, consequently, I will not respond to your question. . . ."

Richard Valeriani of NBC News wanted to know how Nixon proposed to restore confidence in his leadership. The President agreed that it was a problem. He confessed that "it is rather difficult to have the President of the United States on prime time television . . . by innuendo, by leak, by, frankly, leers and sneers of commentators, which is their perfect right, attacked in every way without having some of that confidence being worn away." So what did Nixon intend to do to restore confidence? "Well, not allowing my own confidence to be destroyed; that is to begin. And second, it is restored by doing something."

That brought him back to the theme he had hoped would prevail in the news conference. He called again for action in the problem areas, and said that as the nation began to move to solve them, "that will restore the confidence. What the President says will not restore it, and what you ladies and gentlemen say will certainly not restore it."

Would he give his personal assurance that there was nothing on the tapes that would reflect unfavorably on him?

"There is nothing whatever," Nixon replied.

Well, then, suppose he won before the Supreme Court, and established the right of confidentiality for future Presidents, would he then be willing voluntarily to produce the tapes to dispel doubt about their content?

"It would not be appropriate to comment," Nixon responded, so long as the case was in the appeal process.[53]

On that negative note, the news conference ended. If Nixon was going to get the media to pay attention to something other than Watergate, he was going to have to come up with something better than the Alaska pipeline, or more schools.

As one indication of how much importance the media attached to Watergate, William Shawn, editor of *The New Yorker*, put Elizabeth Drew to work keeping a journal of what was going on in Washington (meaning Watergate). She began by covering the September 5 news conference. She noted that "the President's demeanor changed when he dealt with the questions about Watergate and about his property. He became tense, and he breathed hard. If one stood far enough to his right, one could see that, behind the lectern, his hips swiveled in a circular motion, as if within an invisible Hula Hoop."[54]

When a journalist as adroit as Drew watched for and wrote such things, it was obvious that Nixon was living under a microscope. Nearly every reporter in Washington was scrutinizing him for signs of a crack-up.

On September 5, *The Washington Post* reported that Nixon had tapped the telephone of his brother Donald. The newspaper said the reason for the tap was concern about Donald's "involvement with the financial empire of billionaire Howard Hughes." The White House responded that "if" the Secret Service wiretapped Donald's phone, it was as a part of the "protective function of the Secret Service." But a spokesman for the agency, asked to comment, said that the Secret Service did not provide security services for the President's brother.[55]

That embarrassment was followed almost at once by another: *The New York Times* reported that Nixon had evidently paid no income tax in 1970 or 1971, giving him membership in the "zero taxpayer's list" of people with income in excess of $200,000 who paid no federal income tax. He had managed the feat, it appeared, by taking a more than $500,000 deduction for his gift of his vice presidential papers to the National Archives. But questions were being raised by a public interest law group, on the grounds that a 1969 law abolished the deduction for gifts of their papers by public officials. Nixon, apparently, had backdated his gift of his papers to beat the July 25, 1969, deadline. There was also a question about the nature of the "gift." It was not free and clear; Nixon had retained controls over the use of his papers and had retained from the collection his correspondence with his VIP associates and friends (Eisenhower, de Gaulle, Macmillan, Kennedy, etc.), which greatly diminished the value of the collection.[56]

It was hard to defend a President who placed a wiretap on his brother and cheated on his income tax, but Nixon had his defenders. One of the few was the Vice President. Speaking at a Republican fund-raiser in St. Charles, Illinois, on September 8, Agnew picked up on Nixon's current theme. He said that "morbid preoccupation" with Watergate "obstructs" the will of the people because it distracted the government from its necessary work. Referring to recent stories, Agnew said, "It's very easy to go around accusing people of anything and sometimes the motives of the accusers should be closely examined before any dignity is given to such charges." He was interrupted by applause almost two dozen times by an audience of almost five thousand. He did not mention his own problems.[57]

Two days later, RNC Chairman George Bush told state delegates at the annual meeting that the Republican Party had survived the Watergate scandal. He also charged that the Democratic Party was "too far left for the American people." Nixon told the delegates during a White House reception that he planned to campaign for Republican candidates for Congress in 1974, and for the party presidential nominee in 1976.[58]

John Connally weighed in. After meeting with the RNC, Connally talked with reporters. Asked if Nixon could be justified in ignoring a Supreme Court decision to release the tapes, Connally said, "We're leading ourselves into believing the Supreme Court is the ultimate arbiter of all disputes, and I don't believe it. I think there are times when the President would be right in not obeying a decision of the Supreme Court." Connally's words, and the fact that he had met privately for forty-five minutes with Nixon that morning, encouraged speculation that the President was thinking about appointing Connally Vice President should Agnew resign or be indicted and found guilty.[59]

Nixon was involved in a flurry of activity that week. Besides the RNC meetings, he had one with his Cabinet on energy policy. When it ended, he gave a personal briefing to the White House press corps. "We do not face a crisis" with regard to energy, he said, but "we face a problem." He outlined the solutions he was proposing—the Alaska pipeline, deregulation of gas, legislation permitting strip mining of coal, relaxation of emission standards, as well as a long-term solution, the development of nuclear power plants.[60]

Nixon also had a series of meetings with congressional leaders. He opened a White House conference on drugs. He met with his economic advisers. That one led to some controversy. Both Mel Laird, counselor to the President, and Arthur Burns, chairman of the Federal Reserve Board, predicted that Nixon would raise taxes in order to balance the budget and reduce interest rates. That led Caspar Weinberger, Secretary of HEW, to send a memo to Nixon indicating his "strong opposition" to a tax increase. Nixon scribbled on the bottom of the memo: "I agree—there will be no tax increase. However Arthur Burns will continue to talk about it despite my position." Still, Nixon was not worried. He noted,

"The Congress is our safeguard—They will *never* pass a tax bill this year."[61]

Nixon also worked closely with Buzhardt, Garment, and Wright on the brief they were going to file in the Court of Appeals, explaining why the President should not and could not give the tapes to Judge Sirica. Nixon made numerous marginal comments, some of them of major import. Where the brief suggested that impeachment by Congress, rather than legal action by the judiciary, was the proper course, Nixon wrote, "The impeachment section is too long. It will be used out of context by the press against the President." He suggested that on page 28 they do some direct quoting of Senator Ervin, who had upheld the principle of confidentiality back in Harry Truman's day.[62]

As the lawyers presented the revised brief to the U.S. Court of Appeals, they were hopeful. But rather than a ruling in Nixon's favor, the Court made an unusual proposal. The seven judges unanimously urged the President to seek compromise. They suggested that he submit the tapes to Cox and Wright, who would examine them and decide what parts could properly go to the grand jury. Nixon wanted no part of such a deal, and the idea collapsed.[63]

ANOTHER idea that was collapsing was Agnew's proposal to go the impeachment route. Leaks and rumors were headline news; they suggested that the White House was trying to persuade Agnew to resign, that Richardson was ready to present the evidence against Agnew to a grand jury, and/or that Agnew was getting ready to plea-bargain. It was all true. On September 19, Haig told Agnew that after he was indicted and the evidence made public, Nixon would call for his resignation. Agnew demanded a meeting with the President. Haig arranged one for the next day.

"I have not misused the public trust," Agnew opened.

"I believe you," Nixon replied.

Agnew said Richardson was being "totally unreasonable," that he was demanding Agnew's admission to multiple crimes, that he wanted Agnew to "grovel" before he would agree to a plea bargain.

"Will you support me?" Agnew asked Nixon. "It is impossible to do anything else but fight."

"You must do what is best for you and your family," Nixon replied.

Agnew said he would be willing to resign and plead *nolo contendere* to a tax misdemeanor charge, but his price was high. He wanted an absolute guarantee that he would not be prosecuted on any felony charges, such as bribery or extortion. He would not accede to Richardson's demand that he admit the government's case against him was valid. He would take his chances on a trial in court rather than crawl.[64]

When Agnew left, Nixon called in Buzhardt and Haig. He told them to tell Richardson that he must not force the country "into the nightmare of a trial" by insisting on unreasonably tough terms. The next day, Buzhardt reported back that a deal had been struck. Agnew would admit to knowledge that some people were alleging that he had taken money for preferential treatment, but not to having actually done so. Richardson could live with that. Buzhardt told the President, "I think it is just about over."[65] But the next morning, September 22, *The Washington Post* carried a front-page story about Agnew's plea bargaining, and CBS reported that Henry Petersen had told his associates, "We've got the evidence. We've got it cold."[66]

Agnew was furious. He broke off the bargaining sessions with Richardson and prepared to fight. On September 25, he met with Nixon. He informed the President that he intended to take his case to the House of Representatives, to insist on an impeachment hearing. He would meet with Speaker of the House Albert that afternoon.

Before he could do so, Richardson issued a statement. The Attorney General said that he, Petersen, and Beall had been meeting with Agnew's attorneys since September 12 in an attempt to reach an agreement, but "no satisfactory resolution" had been found. Therefore, the Justice Department was going to present the evidence against Agnew to the grand jury.

One half hour after the Richardson statement was made public, Agnew met with Albert and other House leaders. Citing what he believed to be his constitutional immunity to ordinary court proceedings, Agnew handed over a letter that said he "cannot acquiesce in any criminal proceeding being lodged against me in Maryland or elsewhere," and asked for the House to "discharge its constitutional obligation" and begin an impeachment inquiry.

If Agnew thought that the Democrats were going to solve his immediate problem for him, that they would save him from the grubby business of a trial over bribery and throw him into the spotlight of an impeachment trial, he was seriously mistaken. Albert heard him out and then issued a statement. It said in its entirety: "The vice president's letter relates to matters before the courts. In view of that fact, I, as Speaker, will not take any action on the letter at this time."[67]

Nixon issued his own statement. He noted that Agnew denied the charges against him and urged that the Vice President be accorded "the same presumption of innocence which is the right of any citizen." He noted that Agnew "during these past four and a half years, has served his country with dedication and distinction," which nicely avoided comment on Agnew's activities as governor of Maryland.[68]

Deputy Press Secretary Warren told the White House press corps that Nixon had taken a neutral position on Agnew. The President had neither approved nor disapproved of Richardson's move to send the evidence to the grand jury.[69] In the midst of these unhappy developments, there was one bright spot. On the same day, September 26, Pat Buchanan appeared before the Ervin Committee. The Committee had been suffering some postpartum depression ever since Butterfield revealed the tapes, because the action had moved to other arenas. Cox, Sirica, Agnew, Richardson were the headline makers. The Committee's investigations were concentrating on small people and small matters, such as Hunt and the ITT scandal. Buchanan offered an opportunity to take the investigation back into the Oval Office and to break some new ground.

Committee counsel Sam Dash opened with some aggressive questioning about campaign tactics. "What tactics would I be willing to use?" Buchanan answered Dash. "Anything that was not immoral, unethical, illegal or unprecedented in previous Democratic campaigns." He produced facts and figures to show that the Democrats had written the book on dirty tricks in American politics. His bold, dogmatic style, his indignation that the Democrats dared accuse anyone of unfair or unethical practices, his good looks and strong voice, quite overwhelmed the Committee. Dash got him off the stand as quickly as possible.[70]

Nixon watched the hearing and was elated. He called Buchanan and invited him over to the White House for a little celebration. At 6:30 A.M., Buchanan came into the West Hall, where the Nixons were waiting for him. Pat gave him a hug and whirled him around in a little dance.[71]

Nixon's joy was short-lived. On September 29, Agnew went on a rampage. Speaking to a cheering, sympathetic audience at the convention of the National Federation of Republican Women, he took as his theme the need for secrecy in grand jury proceedings. Without naming Petersen or citing his words, Agnew said that his actions were "unprofessional and malicious and outrageous." In analyzing Petersen's motives, Agnew charged that his "ineptness in the prosecution of the Watergate case" had made it necessary to appoint a special prosecutor. Petersen and Richardson "are trying to recoup their reputation at my expense," Agnew said. "I'm a big trophy."

Again without naming Petersen, Agnew charged that he had not only "failed to get any of the information out about the true dimensions of the Watergate matter," but had through "ineptness and blunder" hampered the "prosecution of high crime figures."

He concluded with a roar: "I will not resign if indicted! I will not resign if indicted!" The crowd shouted its approval.[72]

Nixon was in dismay. Agnew's charges against Petersen were uncomfortably close to the truth; Agnew's defiance—while exciting the right wing—was only adding to Richardson's stature with the rest of the public and making it more difficult for Nixon to contemplate firing Cox. Further, while Agnew's display provided a temporary distraction from Nixon's problems with the courts over the tapes, in the long run it could only add to the President's problems by presenting an image of an executive branch involved in a total war with the legislative and judicial branches of the government.

THE great opportunity the Agnew situation offered was that sacrificing the Vice President would give Nixon an excuse to get rid of Cox; the great danger the Agnew situation represented was that it was making the dread word "impeachment" respectable. As Nixon saw his own situation, the "danger of being impeached would come precisely from the public's being conditioned to the idea that I was going to be impeached. In the end, therefore, it would come down to a race for public support: in other words, a campaign."[73]

For a man sometimes described as the smartest politician in Washington, and for a lawyer with a deserved reputation for brilliance, this was a profound misjudgment. The public plays no direct role in an impeachment. Only once every four years does the public choose the President; to remove a President from office requires one half of the House and two thirds of the Senate. Thus the ultimate power in the American system resides with the legislative branch. Congress can remove the President from office, but the President cannot remove the Congress or individual congressmen. In that stark sense, the American system is a parliamentary one, except that it takes two thirds of the Senate (although only one half of the House) to execute a vote of no confidence.

Nixon's fate rested not with the public, but with his fellow politicians. They would, of course, be strongly influenced by the ebb and flow of public opinion, but Nixon could not campaign with them the way he could with the public. In a real campaign, Nixon could attack; in defending himself against impeachment charges, his "so's your old man" offensive— accusing the Democrats of being the originators of dirty tricks, wiretapping, and so forth, as Buchanan had done—was not working, could not work. Historians would pass judgments on FDR, JFK, and LBJ, but the politicians could not. To say that the Democrats started it was true but irrelevant. Nixon would have to defend himself, not denigrate his past opponents. Under the best of circumstances, Nixon was not very good at defending himself, and Watergate put him in the worst of circumstances.

Republicans in the House constituted Nixon's first line of defense, Republican senators his last. If he could hold onto a majority of the congressmen of his own party, he would probably not be impeached and certainly not found guilty (there were 239 Democrats in the House in the 93d Congress, 192 Republicans, but Nixon could hope for solid support from most of the Southern Democrats. In the Senate, 44 members were Republicans, and he only needed 34 votes to survive an impeachment trial).

Nixon's strongest argument against an attempt to impeach him was a telling one—that the Democrats were trying to overturn the results of the 1972 election. He hoped/planned/worked to persuade the public that such was their aim. But that defense brought him right back to the starting point, what had actually happened, because if the Democrats could convince the public (and themselves, and some of their Republican colleagues) that Nixon had won in 1972 by manipulating the Democratic nomination process, by covering up the Watergate break-in, by dirty tricks and chicanery, why then, the results of the '72 election ought to be overturned. Not in the sense of putting McGovern in, but in the sense of getting Nixon out.

To save himself, Nixon had to defend what he had done. And he could not do that with mirrors, or press releases, or public assertions of innocence; he could only do so by producing the record, and thanks to Butterfield, everyone in the country knew that the record was available.

So it all came down to the tapes. Nixon's attempt to take the high ground, to argue that he could not release the tapes because it would violate the principle of confidentiality and thus weaken future Presidents, had not worked, could not work. The principle of confidentiality did not cover criminal conspiracies. For Nixon to say that national security would be damaged if the tapes were made public impressed almost no one, for the simple reason that no one was asking for all the tapes, just those that covered Watergate conversations. Nixon's assertions that the tapes proved he was innocent, take my word for it, flew in the face of common sense, because if they did, he would certainly release them.

Of course, he had tried selective disclosure, when he made the self-serving portions of his tapes available to the Republicans on the Ervin Committee staff. But that had led to the Butterfield revelation and thus made his problem immeasurably worse.

A Gallup Poll showed that by a 61–32 percent margin people felt Nixon should release the tapes; a Louis Harris survey showed that by a 54–34 percent margin people felt that Congress would be justified in beginning impeachment proceedings against Nixon if he refused to obey a court order directing him to turn over the tapes.[74]

So Nixon went to work on his own compromise proposal. He would have Rose Mary Woods type up "summaries" of the subpoenaed tapes and then submit those to Cox and Sirica.

That ought to work, he figured, that ought to satisfy them. Full of confidence in his idea, he held a news conference on October 3. R. W. Apple of *The New York Times* was reminded of an old Nixon, "the Nixon whose voice didn't quaver, the Nixon who dealt confidently with a wide range of questions, the Nixon who clearly felt on top of his job, the Nixon who could even manage a bit of humor." The President was not as stiff as he had been recently. He leaned casually on the lectern and engaged in some banter with reporters.

Asked about the tapes, he calmly replied that "it would be inappropriate for me to talk about what should be done with regard to compromise," and would say no more.

The volatile issue was Agnew. Nixon was circumspect in his answers. He noted that the Vice President "is elected by all the people. He holds that office in his own right, and the decision as to whether he should resign is for him to make." He had not advised Agnew on what to do—"this matter is one for him to decide." He said Agnew, like anyone else, should have the presumption of innocence, and pointedly noted that "the charges that have been made against him do not relate in any way to his activities as Vice President." He agreed that the charges were serious.

Nixon made his own opportunity to defend Henry Petersen. He denied that Petersen was the source of the leaks that so bedeviled Agnew and praised Petersen for years of distinguished service in the Justice Department.

Only once did he get a bit sarcastic. Reminded that he had claimed at his last news conference that the government work on his home in San Clemente had diminished the value of the property, he was asked how extensive work by a landscape architect could have done so.

"I really think anything I would say in answer to your question," Nixon replied, "in view of the way you have already presented it as a statement, would not convince you or anybody else." He would say no more.[75]

BEAUTIFUL fall weather had come to Washington. Nixon, meeting in the Oval Office with a group of senior citizens from Whittier, who were on a bus tour of the United States, was in excellent spirits. He said he envied them, being able to see the country. He was reminded of his mother, who had missed the fall colors after she moved from the Midwest to California. He said he had taken a car ride with General Haig the previous day, down into Virginia, and had noticed the leaves. He promised the old folks they would find "the colors are very beautiful, and something we don't have in California." Catching himself, he quickly added, "We have almost everything else, though."[76]

That surely was the old Nixon. He was back on track, taking charge, campaigning. On October 3 he flew down to Florida for the weekend; when he arrived, he got some good news—Agnew's lawyers were ready to resume discussions about a plea bargain. Evidently the Vice President had decided against trying to fight it out.

The only disturbing note was a message from Rose Mary Woods. She reported that there was a 18½-minute gap on the tape of Nixon's

June 20, 1972, conversation with Haldeman. But since the subpoenaed tape for that date was for a meeting with Haldeman *and* Ehrlichman, that hardly mattered. Compared to the Agnew problem, Nixon felt, "a few minutes missing from a non-subpoenaed tape hardly seemed worth a second thought." He got to work on his summaries of the subpoenaed tapes.[77]

CHAPTER TEN

THAT
INCREDIBLE MONTH
October 1973

RICHARD NIXON took pride in his ability to stay calm in a crisis. Indeed, he thrived on crises; it was the inevitable letdown that he feared. In October, as he put it in a nice piece of alliteration, "all the crises reached a concerted crescendo."[1] He survived them, though not unscathed.

Going into October, Nixon's most immediate problem was the upcoming expected ruling from the Court of Appeals on the Cox subpoena for seven Watergate-related tapes. He anticipated the worst, an order to comply. To turn them over would invite calls for either resignation or impeachment; to refuse such a court order was out of the question.[2] He had decided to deal with the dilemma by releasing edited "summaries" of the subpoenaed tapes. Secluding himself at Camp David, together with Rose Mary Woods and aide Steve Bull, he began to prepare the summaries. After his October 3 news conference, he moved his base of operations to Key Biscayne.[3]

So, when the next crisis came, Nixon was down in Florida. It took him by surprise. On Saturday morning, October 6, Syria and Egypt attacked Israel. Although the United States maintained the most extensive and expensive intelligence-gathering operation in the free world, neither the CIA nor the armed services had warned the President of this possibility. In fact, the previous day the CIA had reported that war in the Middle East was unlikely. The Agency had dismissed the recent troop movements in Egypt as annual maneuvers.[4]

Israel was also surprised, in part because the attack began on the religious holy day of Yom Kippur. Egypt and Syria crossed into the territories occupied by Israel since 1967 with tanks, missiles, planes, and infantry. The Syrians drove the Israelis off the Golan Heights, the Egyptians destroyed the much-vaunted Bar-Lev defense line, then drove several miles deep inside the Sinai and entrenched.

These were stunning victories, as shocking to Israel as the attack itself. Israel had badly underestimated its enemies, the Arabs' willingness and ability to fight, as well as the equipment available to them. Assuming a quick victory in any outbreak of hostilities, the Israelis had stocked military "consumables" on the basis of a three- or four-day war. But as early as October 8 it was obvious that this war was going to last for weeks, not days, and that it would consume matériel at a horrendous rate. The scale of the Arab offensive was far beyond anything previously seen in the Middle East; aircraft were being shot down by the dozen, ammunition expended at a ruinous rate, tanks destroyed in almost unbelievable numbers (the amounts of tanks involved, and the losses, rivaled the 1944 Battle of the Bulge).

This was war by proxy, in a way—American arms versus Soviet arms. From the first, Nixon assumed that the Soviets were behind the Arab offensive, and from the first he was determined that Soviet arms would not prevail. But he had other objectives that pulled him in different directions. He wanted to preserve détente as much as he wanted to prevent an Arab victory. He wanted to keep the Soviets out of the Middle East as much as he wanted to preserve détente. He wanted to avoid a superpower confrontation. And he wanted to use the opportunity presented by the initial Arab victories to begin the process of creating a genuine peace in the Middle East. These were ambitious goals, and on the face of it seemed mutually exclusive.

Complicating everything, Watergate and Agnew made it all but impossible for Nixon to concentrate on diplomacy; meanwhile, his Secretary of State was all too ready to take up the burden. Kissinger was willing, even eager, to take advantage of Nixon's preoccupations to ignore the President as he dealt with the crisis. It was two and a half hours after he had the news that Kissinger called Al Haig in Key Biscayne to inform him that war had broken out. He did not ask to talk to the President. He had already contacted the Israelis, the Soviets, the Syrians, the United Nations, the Egyptians, and Jordan. This set a pattern that persisted, justified by Kissinger on the grounds that "it was not clear that Nixon retained enough authority to manage the manifold pressures about to descend on him." He had no doubt about his own authority. "From the outset," he later wrote, "I was determined to use the war to start a peace process." He told Haig, "After we get the fighting stopped we should use this as a vehicle to get the diplomacy started."

Nixon flew back to Washington, to confer with Kissinger. The President told the Secretary that after Israel won the war—"and they'll win it, thank God, they should—[we must not allow Israel to] get away with just having this thing hang over for another four years and have us at odds with the Arab world. We're not going to do it anymore."[5] In other words, Nixon was going to give the Israelis the arms they had to have to win the war in order to force them to accept a peace settlement they did not want.

At 10:15 A.M., October 8, Nixon gave a briefing to White House reporters. To show that he was in command, he reported that he had met with Kissinger shortly before midnight, and again at 7:30 A.M. that morning. He said that the United States would move in the United Nations to stop the fighting.[6]

Actually, he had told Kissinger that since the Arabs were winning, the first move was to stall until the tide turned. "I had absolutely no doubt or hesitation about what we must do," Nixon later explained. He told Kissinger to "let the Israelis know that we would replace all their losses," and asked him to work out the logistics for doing so.[7]

ON the afternoon of October 9, Nixon met with Agnew. The Vice President had come to announce his intention to resign. He had struck a simple and straightforward deal with the Justice Department. In return for his resignation and a plea of *nolo contendere* to one count of having knowingly failed to report income for tax purposes, he would get a sentence of three years probation and a $10,000 fine, but no further prosecution.

Nixon shook Agnew's hand. He motioned to the chairs in front of the fireplace; they sat down. Nixon thanked Agnew for his campaign help and the way he had handled assignments. He asked about Mrs. Agnew and the family. He said he knew the "tragedy" must be painful for them.

"I know you have made this decision for the good of the country," Nixon went on, in the face of the obvious fact that Agnew had made the decision for his own good (but then Agnew, in his resignation letter, stressed that "it is in the best interests of the nation that I relinquish the Vice-Presidency").

More realistically, Nixon went on, "And also I believe that you are doing the best thing for yourself and your family."

Nixon's face was "gaunt and sorrowful," Agnew reported. "It was hard to believe he was not genuinely sorry about the course of events." Agnew attempted to take advantage of what he perceived to be the President's emotion. He said he would like to have some foreign assignment; if that was not possible, he would appreciate anything Nixon could do to get some corporation to put him on a retainer as a consultant. The President replied that Agnew could always count on him as a friend.

Agnew got up to leave, his eyes brimming at Nixon's words. Nixon rose, put his arm around Agnew's shoulders, shook his head, and said again how awful it all was. Agnew got the feeling that Nixon couldn't wait for him to get out of there. They shook hands and Agnew walked out.[8] They never spoke again.

Now there was no Vice President, at a time when Nixon's chances of serving out his second term ranged from poor to nonexistent. This was a startling development, full of complexities.

Speaker of the House Carl Albert was the next in line. This created an impossible situation, for both political and personal reasons. With Nixon's survivability in doubt, it was all but out of the question that the Democrats would force him from office to replace him with a Democrat. Further, Albert did not want the job, as he did not feel qualified and did not want to expose his personal life style to the glare of presidential publicity. (He had just driven his car through a plate-glass saloon window.)

With Agnew's resignation, the Twenty-fifth Amendment came into effect. It had been written to deal with presidential disability (Ike's 1955 heart attack had been the proximate cause), but included a section dealing with a vacancy in the Vice Presidency (there had been no Vice President from April 1945 to January 1949 under Truman, and again from November 1963 to January 1965 under Johnson). The amendment required the President to select a new Vice President, subject to confirmation by a simple majority of both houses of Congress.

The terms of the amendment gave Nixon an invaluable asset: in the event of his resignation, impeachment, or death, it was nothing less than the ultimate prize in American politics. He was sure to spend that asset in such a way as to do himself the most good. But because of the Albert situation, and because the wording of the amendment made the selection mandatory, he had to spend it quickly. Nor could he spend it freely, as his selection was subject to congressional confirmation.

Under ordinary circumstances, Nixon would have given his full attention to this momentous decision, but October 10 was not an ordinary occasion. Nixon's biggest personal problem was not selecting a replacement for Agnew, but finding some way to avoid the demands of the Special Prosecutor for the Watergate tapes. The Court of Appeals would be handing down its ruling in a day or two. Nixon's biggest presidential problem was the war in the Middle East. He had many other worries; that day, for example, *The New York Times* reported that Bebe Rebozo had admitted to Ervin Committee investigators that he had accepted $100,000 in cash from Howard Hughes as a campaign contribution.

Who can say what went through Nixon's mind? As an aide to Congressman Gerald Ford, Robert Hartmann, has commented: "No man living can outguess Richard Nixon when it comes to figuring things out to the third, fourth, and fifth degree of indirection."[9]

In this case, Agnew's resignation did not set Nixon to thinking about his replacement. Instead, it got him to thinking about the Special Prosecutor and his subpoenas. After Agnew left the Oval Office, Richardson came in. Nixon's first words to him were, "Now that we have disposed of that matter [Agnew's resignation], we can go ahead and get rid of Cox."[10]

Cox was becoming an obsession. That same day, Rose Mary Woods passed on to Nixon some words from his very first political adviser, Murray Chotiner. "This guy Cox will use anything and everybody," Chotiner had said. His advice was that this Watergate thing "has to be taken away from him."[11]

If one keeps Hartmann's comment in mind, Nixon's line of reasoning appears to this author to have been as follows: firing Cox, the quid pro quo for Agnew's resignation (although only Nixon saw the connection between an Agnew resignation and a dismissal of Cox), would free him from further subpoenas for Watergate-related tapes. He could expect to continue to defy the Ervin Committee and the Watergate grand jury successfully, on the basis of separation of powers, confidentiality, and executive privilege. If he got rid of Cox, the prosecution of Watergate crimes would be done by the Justice Department. If the Attorney General, or Henry Petersen, or anyone else in the Department tried to issue a subpoena for additional tapes, Nixon could fire him. Meanwhile, the summaries he was preparing to satisfy the original Cox subpoenas (assuming the Court of Appeals ordered him to comply) would satisfy the public, and the politicians, that he was not placing himself above the law.

With Cox gone, in short, the only way Nixon could be forced to produce more tapes, or complete transcripts as opposed to his own edited summaries, was through the impeachment process. He was certainly vulnerable there. No one could argue against the right of the House to impeach—Section 2 of Article I of the Constitution states that the House of Representatives "shall have the sole Power of Impeachment." Nor could anyone argue against the right of the House to demand whatever evidence it felt it needed to meet that constitutional obligation.

In short, if Nixon could get rid of Cox and get away with the presentation of summaries of the subpoenaed tapes, his fate would rest with the House of Representatives, more particularly with the Republicans and Southern Democrats in that body. If he could hold them against an impeachment inquiry, he could protect the tapes. If he could protect the tapes, he could survive. If he had to give up the tapes, he was doomed.

Back to the Twenty-fifth Amendment. What Nixon most needed to buy with the asset that Agnew's resignation and the terms of the amendment gave him was support in the House. He would select the man who would be most pleasing to his supporters in the House.

As Agnew was entering his *nolo contendere* plea in a federal courtroom in Baltimore, Nixon was meeting with the congressional leaders to discuss the war in the Middle East. The President said he was maintaining an even-handed policy, hoping to continue good relations with both sides while avoiding a confrontation with the Soviets.

The congressmen, as always, had conflicting goals. "Mr. President," Senator Mansfield said forcefully, "we want no more Vietnams."

But another congressman asked apprehensively, "Is Israel going to lose?"

"No," Nixon reassured him. "We will not let Israel go down the tubes."

It looked like he was being too optimistic. The Soviets had that day begun to resupply the Arabs with badly needed arms and munitions. The Americans had not sent anything to the all but desperate Israelis. Nixon was checking almost hourly with Kissinger; he wanted to know why an American airlift was not under way, as he had ordered.

According to Kissinger, it was because of obstacles put up by Secretary of Defense James Schlesinger. He did not want to offend the Arabs, so he had refused to allow El Al transport planes to land at American military bases to pick up the equipment.

Kissinger's critics say that it was he who was holding up the operation. In this version, Kissinger secretly instructed Schlesinger to hold back. His motive was to make it plain to the Israelis that they could not exist without the United States, so that they would be more willing to accept his dictates when hostilities ended. In other words, Kissinger wanted to teach the Israelis a lesson and use the prospect of increasing supplies to force them to accept his advice. Kissinger vehemently denies the charge.

Admiral Elmo Zumwalt, Chief of Naval Operations, strongly supports it. Zumwalt testified that Kissinger "ordered Jim Schlesinger, in the name of the President, to stall in responding to Israeli requests for arms. At the same time, he told the Israeli ambassador that he was exerting every effort to get Schlesinger moving. . . . He did not scruple to deceive his allies or besmirch the reputation of his colleagues."[12]

There were additional complications to this unseemly squabble. It is also charged that Kissinger attempted to link Israel's needs with the problems of détente. The Secretary supposedly tried to use the delays in the airlift to bargain with American Jews to get them to curtail their support for Senator Jackson's amendment to the trade bill that required the Soviet Union to allow free Jewish emigration in return for MFN status.[13] Admiral Zumwalt tried to undercut the Secretary of State by privately telling Senator Jackson that it was Kissinger, not Schlesinger, who was holding up the flow of supplies to Israel.[14]

Who was in charge? Who was responsible? The available record makes it impossible to tell; our only sources are the self-serving memoirs of the participants. But what was happening was clear: Israel was losing, the Soviets were resupplying their clients, the Americans were not. Nixon gave a direct order: "Tell Schlesinger to speed it up," he said to Kissinger.[15] Still nothing happened. One obvious reason was that Nixon did not attend a single formal meeting on the war that week. The only official he talked to was Kissinger, which left Kissinger free to do whatever he wished and claim he was speaking for the President.[16]

WASHINGTON was all in a tizzy, not with events in the Middle East, which were scarcely noticed, nor with developments in the State Department and the Department of Defense, which were not noticed at all, but with the selection of Agnew's replacement. The atmosphere has been likened to a political convention. Scores of names were reportedly under consideration. Those most often mentioned were Governors Nelson Rockefeller and Ronald Reagan, John Connally, Elliot Richardson, Barry Goldwater, Melvin Laird, George Bush, Hugh Scott, and Howard Baker. Warren Burger's name started popping up. The President spent much of the afternoon of October 10 conferring with congressional leaders, Cabinet members, and his aides. Rumor and speculation swept the city. It was being said that the man picked would have to promise that he would be a "caretaker," that is, that he would not be a candidate for the Presidency in 1976. This quickly became common wisdom, something taken for granted, although no one explained how such a promise could be enforced in the event. Politicians tried the impossible, to outguess Nixon. Some said he would choose a figure of national stature, to provide stability for his Administration. Others predicted that he would never pick a man who attracted wide support, for fear that a figure who inspired national unity would tempt Congress to drive Nixon from office. There were numerous other guesses.

John Connally was Nixon's first choice. He admired Connally more than any other man in American politics. He had frequently engaged in fantasies in which he dumped Agnew for Connally. He turned often to Connally for advice on major problems. He wanted Connally to head the Republican ticket in 1976.

But Connally, a turncoat Democrat, had enemies on both sides of the aisles. As a Lyndon Johnson protégé, as a Texas wheeler-dealer businessman and politician, he had a past that might turn his confirmation hearings into a circus. Mike Mansfield, among many other Democrats and almost as many Republicans, told Nixon that a Connally nomination would stir strong opposition. Certainly Connally would not help Nixon win any support from Republicans or Southern Democrats in the House. Reluctantly, Nixon gave up on Connally.[17]

Among those Nixon conferred with were the Minority Leaders, Congressman Gerald Ford and Senator Hugh Scott. The President told Scott his mind was completely open. He met with Ford in his EOB office for an hour and a half. Nixon and Ford went back to 1948, when Ford had become a congressman and joined the Chowder and Marching Club, a group of junior Republican members of the House that Nixon had helped to organize two years earlier. They had worked together on various political tasks over the following quarter century. In 1960 and again in 1968, Nixon had hinted to Ford that he was under consideration for the second spot on the ticket. As President, Nixon had used, abused, and manipulated Ford on a regular basis. The most important case was getting Ford to begin an impeachment inquiry against Justice William O. Douglas in retaliation for the Senate's rejection of two Nixon nominees for the Supreme Court. The attempt failed badly and made Ford look excessively partisan, somewhat foolish, and weak.

Ford nevertheless remained loyal. During the 1972 campaign, at Nixon's behest, he played a hidden role in preventing the House Banking Committee from investigating the money trial in the Watergate break-in case, which helped immeasurably in keeping Watergate out of the news during the campaign.

Despite all that Ford had done for Nixon, the two men were hardly friends. Indeed, Nixon was somewhat contemptuous of Ford. Alexander Butterfield summed up the attitude in the White House toward Ford when he commented, "Nixon had Ford totally under his thumb. He was the tool of the Nixon Administration—like a puppy dog. They used him when they had to—wind him up and he'd go 'Arf, Arf.' "[18]

At their October 10 meeting, Ford found Nixon sitting in his leather chair, in a corner, his feet up on an ottoman. Ford remembered that Nixon "was about as relaxed as I'd ever seen him." The President was casually dressed, in a sports jacket and a pair of slacks, and was puffing on a pipe.

"Mr. President," Ford said, "I've never seen you smoke a pipe."

"Well, I do it when I'm alone," Nixon replied, "or when I'm with an old friend like you."

Ford had never before seen Nixon so relaxed, casually dressed, or smoking. That all this was new to Ford tells a great deal about how close their quarter-century-old relationship was.[19]

Nixon told Ford that he wanted help in making his selection for Agnew's replacement. He said there were three criteria he would go by: first, the choice must be a strong man capable of taking over the Presidency; second, he should share Nixon's views on foreign policy; third, he should be someone who could be quickly confirmed by the Congress. Nixon asked Ford, as he had Scott, to have the Republican members of Congress make written recommendations, listing their choices. He indicated he was also having RNC Chairman Bush poll the national Republican leadership, while he polled the Cabinet and White House staff. He wanted the votes in his hands, in sealed envelopes, by 6 P.M. the following day.

After Ford left, presidential advisers Bryce Harlow and Mel Laird came in. Between them, they knew the House as well as any two men in the country. They told the President he had but one choice, Jerry Ford.

Speaker of the House Albert came next. He told the President that Ford was the only Republican who could be quickly confirmed.[20]

At Nixon's request, late that evening Laird called Ford on the telephone. "Jerry," Laird said after some small talk, "if you were asked, would you accept the Vice Presidential nomination?"[21]

Curiously, Laird never asked Ford if he had any skeletons in his closet that would embarrass him during confirmation hearings. Nixon had confessed to Ford that afternoon, "If I'd known about this [Agnew's problem with kickbacks in Maryland] I wouldn't have had him on the ticket."[22] Ford thought Nixon had been derelict for not checking. And, of course, there was Nixon's secret fund in 1952 that had caused him such agony, and Eisenhower so much difficulty, not to mention the Tom Eagleton affair of 1972. Nevertheless Nixon did not check on Ford.

The truth is that Nixon had made up his mind before he saw the results of his poll of Republicans in Washington and around the nation, indeed before Agnew resigned. The poll itself showed how popular Ford was in the House, as well as how little support he had outside that body. The RNC responses were 56 for Reagan, 51 for Rockefeller, 47 for Connally, 47 for Goldwater, a scattering for others, with only 9 for Ford. From the Cabinet and White House staff, there were 4 votes for Rockefeller, 3 for William Rogers, 2 for Reagan, 1 for a number of others, and 2 for Ford (presumably from Laird and Harlow). From the Senate, there were 6 for Rockefeller, 5 for Goldwater, 4 for Connally and Reagan, 1 or 2 for a few others, and only 1 for Ford.

But from the House, there were 80 votes for Ford, 35 for Rockefeller, 23 for Reagan, and 16 for Connally. Ford's own ballot, incidentally, put John Connally first, Mel Laird second, and Rockefeller or Reagan third.[23]

Nixon could hardly have been surprised by the results of his poll. He was one of the best when it came to counting votes in the Congress, almost as good as Laird and Harlow. That was why he had picked Ford even before he opened a single ballot. Ford would help him most with the Republicans in the House, and on the afternoon of October 10 these were the men whose support was critical to his own problem. It is unlikely that anything Nixon heard in his extensive consultations on the afternoon of October 10 was new to him. Nixon's polling brings to mind Ford's comment about how Nixon consulted with his fellow politicians: "Making up his mind and then pretending that his options were still open—that was a Nixon trait."[24]

Figuring out Richard Nixon's motives for doing anything is a popular parlor game. In this case, although his motives seem to this author to have been simple and straightforward, people close to Nixon have offered alternative interpretations. Haldeman told this author that Nixon picked Ford because he reasoned that as the members of the House knew Ford so intimately, they would never impeach Nixon if it meant Ford would become President.[25]

Colson claimed that Nixon told him Ford was his "insurance policy" against impeachment.[26]

In Kissinger's view, Nixon figured that Ford's "selection would dampen desires to impeach him [Nixon] because the Congress would not want to run the risk of placing a supposedly inexperienced man in charge of foreign affairs."[27]

If all this was true, Nixon made a misjudgment. "Jerry is popular because he is not a leader," a Republican congressman commented. "If he were a leader, he would not be popular."[28] That made him as acceptable to the Democrats as he was to the Republicans in the House. William Dixon, one of the senior Democratic investigators for the House Judiciary Committee that conducted the confirmation hearings on Ford's nomination, noted that the Committee's real agenda in the fall of 1973 was to gear up for a full-scale impeachment inquiry. He felt that inquiry would get started as soon as Ford was confirmed and sworn into office. "All of the Democrats understood what we were doing,' " Dixon said. "We needed to put [Ford] in so we could remove Nixon. We couldn't get Nixon out until we got Ford in. We weren't just making Ford President—we were saving the presidency."[29]

Nixon's concern was saving the President. He did not select Ford in order to make it easier for the Democrats to impeach him. Nor did he expect to be impeached, or forced to resign. He made no attempt to get Ford to agree that in return for the Vice Presidency he would grant Nixon a pardon if worse came to worst. What he did ask of Ford the morning of October 11 was that he promise he would not be a candidate for the Presidency in 1976. Ford said he intended to retire in January 1977.

"Well, that's good," Nixon replied, "because John Connally is my choice for 1976. He'd be excellent."

"That's no problem as far as I'm concerned," Ford said.[30]

The following evening, October 12, Nixon gathered the Cabinet, some congressmen, Kissinger, Haig, and others to announce his choice. The TV cameras and radio microphones were present. *The New York Times* reported that Washington was "nearly apoplectic with speculation, suspense and surmise."

To Hartmann, the President appeared to be "visibly wallowing in his stellar role." For nearly ten minutes, Nixon recounted the triumphs of his first term. Then he again asked the American people to free themselves "from the obsessions of the past and turn to the great challenges of the future." It was time for a new beginning.

"As the audience wriggled in their wretched seats," Hartmann recorded, "he tossed off his first clue." Nixon said he had chosen a man with twenty-five years of experience in the House. Every eye in the room turned to Jerry Ford. People jumped to their feet and began to applaud. Many clustered around Ford to pump his hand and slap him on the back.

"Ladies and gentlemen," Nixon said laughing, "please don't be premature. There are several here who have been in the House twenty-five years."

He rambled on, trying to prolong a suspense that was gone. Finally, he said he would submit the name of Gerald R. Ford for confirmation as Vice President.

The East Room resounded with whoops, whistles, and Rebel yells. Ford leaped to the platform, where he linked arms with a beaming Nixon.

"They like you," Nixon said in a stage whisper to the beaming Ford.[31]

THAT was the one bright spot in a miserable day. That afternoon, the House had given its final approval to the War Powers Act. Egil "Bud" Krogh was indicted for his role in the break-in at the office of Ellsberg's psychiatrist. (Nixon sent Krogh, one of the Plumbers, a note: "The situation is really topsy-turvy when a man who stole hundreds of top secret documents [Ellsberg] goes free on a technicality and those who were trying to expose him are prosecuted. Your courage—under great stress—inspires us all.")[32] And three hours before Nixon made his announcement about Ford in the East Room, the U.S. Circuit Court of Appeals had handed down a 400-page-long decision. By a vote of 5 to 2, the judges ruled that Nixon had to turn over the seven tapes subpoenaed by Cox to Sirica, and that Sirica was free to turn them over to the grand jury after he had reviewed them and pulled personal or national security material. "Though the President is elected by nationwide ballot," the judges in the majority declared, "and is often said to represent all the people, he does not embody the nation's sovereignty. He is not above the law's commands."[33]

THE court ruling, although unwelcome, was not unanticipated. Nixon was prepared to deal with it. The Middle East crisis, by contrast, required quick decisions and improvisation. After the ceremony in the East Room, Nixon retired to the West Hall for a late dinner. Pat, David, and Julie joined him. As he was finishing his steak, Haig walked in with a message from the Soviets. It was a complaint that the Americans had been oversupplying Israel. Kissinger characterized it as "pure insolence," because the Soviets had been flying hardware into Egypt and Syria for three days, while no American planes had yet flown to Israel.[34] (This failure to act, of course, contradicted Nixon's direct orders.)

The President dealt with the situation the next morning. Nixon, according to Kissinger, "was in good form, still exuberant over achieving surprise in naming Ford." Further, "Nixon was buoyed by crisis, as always." Kissinger explained that Schlesinger was still stalling, that the Defense Department did not want to use American planes to supply Israel, even though the Portuguese government had agreed to allow the transports to use the Azores for refueling. The most Kissinger could get Defense to agree to do was send three C-5As to Israel. More than that, Schlesinger feared, would alarm the Arabs and the Soviets.

"We are going to get blamed just as much for three planes as for 300," Nixon snapped. He called Schlesinger on the telephone. The President said he would take the heat if the Arabs cut oil supplies. "Get them in the air, *now*," he ordered.

A bit later, he learned that there was disagreement in the Pentagon about which kind of planes to use. Exasperated, Nixon told Kissinger, "Goddamn it, use every one we have. Tell them to send everything that can fly." By 3:30 P.M. that day, October 13, thirty C-130 transports were on their way to Israel.[35]

Kissinger later characterized the period from October 13 to 20 as "the week of the airlift."[36] Soviet and American planes flew into the Middle East in a steady stream (there were 550 American missions). In the end American deliveries to Israel substantially exceeded those of Moscow to the Arabs, proving that America's military capacity in time of crisis was superior. Within a couple of days the Israelis had crossed Suez at two points, nearly encircled the Egyptian Army in the Sinai, driven the Syrians back from the Golan Heights, and pushed forward to the outskirts of Damascus.

These were momentous events in world history. Had Nixon not acted so decisively who can say what would have happened? The Arabs probably would have recovered at least some of the territory they had lost in 1967, perhaps all of it. They might even have destroyed Israel. But whatever the might-have-beens, there is no doubt that Nixon played a central role in a courageous action. He made it possible for Israel to win, at some risk to his own reputation and at great risk to the American economy. He showed that despite the buffeting he was taking over Watergate, he was still in command.

Whether he was right is another question. Because Israel won, the Israelis emerged from the Yom Kippur War more intransigent and more self-confident than ever. The Arabs, meanwhile, used their losses as an excuse to raise the price of oil drastically, thereby causing a worldwide inflation that adversely affected the economies of everyone, everywhere. These were unhappy developments, obviously. But there was something else.

American politicians, pundits, and newspaper publishers frequently refer to Israel as America's ally. Israel is not America's ally. There is no alliance between the United States and Israel. But there is an American moral commitment to Israel, one that is so strong as to be unbreakable, in part precisely because nowhere is it spelled out in a treaty. In October 1973, Nixon met that commitment. He put it best in his own crude way: "We will not let Israel go down the tubes." He knew that his enemies, who included some of Israel's best friends, would never give him credit for saving Israel. He did it anyway.

AFTER he started the airlift in motion, Nixon turned to the Court of Appeals. He had already decided not to move the case on to the Supreme Court, but instead to offer summaries of the subpoenaed tapes as a compromise. But he realized that Cox would not be satisfied with just seven tapes, that he would be back for more. Nixon concluded, in his own words, that "firing [Cox] seemed the only way to rid the administration of the partisan viper we had planted in our bosom." [37]

Actually, it was the one sure way to ensure an impeachment inquiry. It was quite remarkable that Nixon, who could see so clearly what Israel needed and what had to be done to meet those needs, could so misread his own domestic situation. In notes he made for himself that morning for later discussion with Haig and Ziegler, he began: "We must not kid ourselves, we must face these facts." He then went into a survey of his slippage in the polls since mid-August.

Nixon had so isolated himself that Haig and Ziegler were now almost the only advisers he talked to about his Watergate-related problems. They had replaced Haldeman and Ehrlichman. Haldeman and Ehrlichman were not exactly experts on American politics, but they were sophisticated practitioners of the arts of wheeling and dealing when compared to the Army officer and the former Disneyland barker. Haig and Ziegler were much too inexperienced to be good choices for the men to help Nixon face the facts. He would have been far better off talking to Harlow and Laird.

Nixon was in fact shrinking from the facts. In his own way, he recognized that such was the case. He wrote in his notes, "Are we facing the fact that the public attitudes may have hardened to the point that we can't change them?"[38] Then he set out to change them, in an inept, poorly conceived, and badly executed performance that all but doomed his Presidency. It came about because of his failure to see what was obvious to the most casual and innocent observer, that the public trust in him was essential to his survival, and that public trust in him depended on the continued independent operation of the Special Prosecutor.

Of course, his dilemma was that if he allowed Cox to continue to operate independently, it would almost certainly cost him control of the tapes.

If Nixon had faced the facts in October 1973, he would have resigned.

But if he had resigned when there was any hope left, he would not have been Nixon. And to those who said that he had lost his political base, could no longer govern, and should therefore resign for the good of the country, he could reply that what he had just done that morning for Israel proved the contrary.

So Nixon, Haig, and Ziegler decided to go forward with their proposed compromise, an offer to Sirica to supply typed summaries of the conversations in lieu of the tapes. They realized they had to offer some kind of verification of the accuracy of the summaries. Nixon's lawyer, Fred Buzhardt, suggested Senator John Stennis (D.-Miss.) as the ideal person to listen and verify.

Stennis was one of the oldest members of the Senate (he was seventy-two years old and had entered the Senate in 1947). Although he was a staunch supporter of segregation and states' rights, he was widely respected. He had been a circuit judge. He had been a leading hawk who had kept the secret of the Cambodian bombing. He was close to Nixon, but he had also been a co-sponsor, along with Senator Jacob Javits, of the War Powers Act. And he was partially deaf.

On Sunday morning, October 14, Nixon invited Stennis to a White House worship service. Afterwards, Nixon stopped him to ask if he would be willing to verify the accuracy of the summaries. Stennis, according to Nixon, said that he would.[39] Haig then called Richardson, who had earlier that morning rejected the proposed compromise, to inform the Attorney General that Stennis would authenticate the summaries.

Nixon makes it clear in his memoirs, without ever saying so directly, that the whole thing was a shell game. He anticipated a Cox rejection of the Stennis compromise which would either force Cox to resign or force the Justice Department to fire him. Haig spelled out the details for Richardson. He said that "this was it" as far as access to presidential materials was involved, that Cox would have to agree to stop using the subpoena power to demand more tapes, and that the President expected Richardson's support when the inevitable showdown came with Cox.[40]

Richardson wrote that it was not until months later that he realized, "The name of the game had been: get rid of Cox."[41] At the time, after a series of talks with Haig on the telephone, Richardson agreed to present the proposal to Cox.

In the United Nations that week, the United States and the Soviet Union alternated between urging a prompt cease-fire and using delaying tactics to postpone one, depending on which side was winning. By the 17th, the Israelis were applying newly arrived American matériel with good effect. That morning a delegation of foreign ministers from Saudi Arabia, Morocco, Algeria, and Kuwait called on Nixon to press the Arab cause. They pointed out the obvious, "Israel is not being threatened by the Arabs with annihilation," and they were moderate in their demands—a return to 1967 borders and respect for the rights of refugees.

"I will work for a cease-fire," Nixon promised the Arab ministers, "as a basis to go on from there for a settlement on the basis of Resolution 242." (Security Council Resolution 242, adopted November 22, 1967, called for recognition of Israel by the Arabs, secure boundaries, free navigation of regional waterways, Israeli evacuation of conquered territories, and a national homeland for Palestinians.) The President urged the Arabs to exercise restraint and told them, "I know how people feel, I understand. . . . You have my pledge."

Growing exuberant, Nixon promised that Kissinger would act as a negotiator and implied that this ensured success. The Arabs were pleased. Afterward the Saudi foreign minister told reporters, "The man who could solve the Vietnam war, the man who could have settled the peace all over the world, can easily play a good role in settling and having peace in our area of the Middle East." Nixon was naturally delighted by this endorsement, although it was not clear whether "the man" cited was Nixon or Kissinger.[42]

That same day the Organization of Arab Petroleum Exporting Countries (OPEC) voted to reduce crude oil production. On October 19, Nixon sent Congress a request for $2.2 billion in emergency aid for Israel.

THROUGH October 18 and 19, Richardson met with and talked by telephone to Haig, Wright, Garment, and Buzhardt. There is confusion and contention over who agreed to what. As Nixon understood it, Richardson had accepted the Stennis comprise and was willing to tell Cox that he was forbidden to sue for any further presidential documents. According to Haig, if Cox did not accept the deal, he would have to resign in protest against it. He would not have to be fired.[43] Either way, Nixon would not have to relinquish any additional tapes, not even in summary form.

Nixon then met with Senators Ervin and Baker. He outlined the Stennis compromise. There is heated controversy over what the President said. Both Ervin and Baker changed their accounts on a number of occasions. Nixon said they agreed to the compromise; they claimed that they said they would present it to the Committee for consideration. Nixon either did or did not make it clear that part of the deal was no more tapes, whatsoever. He promised that the Senate Select Committee could have the Stennis-authenticated summaries. Baker said he thought Nixon had promised a verbatim transcript of the seven tapes. "I would not accept anybody's interpretation of what the tapes contain," he insisted.[44] Nixon asked the senators not to talk to the press. When they left, he felt he had won—he ordered Haig to telephone the Cabinet, the White House staff, and Jerry Ford to notify them that Baker and Ervin had agreed to the Stennis compromise. "Everyone was elated by the news," Nixon claimed.[45]

Certainly Nixon was elated. He had finally taken the offensive, just when it appeared he was in rout. The previous day, spokesman Warren had conducted a tumultuous briefing in which he had tried to explain to skeptical reporters, who were shouting their questions, that there was nothing wrong with Rebozo's having accepted cash contributions from Hughes. The papers were carrying more stories on Nixon's financing of his California and Florida homes. That morning, October 19, George Meany had opened the biennial AFL-CIO convention by saying, "Never in history has a great nation been governed so corruptly." Most ominous, that day John Dean pleaded guilty to a single count of conspiracy to conceal the truth about the Watergate break-in, in exchange for a grant of immunity from prosecution on any other charges. This freed him to testify as a major prosecution witness in the upcoming Watergate trials.[46]

But with the Stennis compromise and his perception that Ervin and Baker had agreed to it, Nixon was ready to strike back. At 8:15 P.M., on Friday, October 19, he issued a statement complaining that "the Watergate issue has taken on overtones of a partisan political contest," which was hampering his ability to carry out foreign policy at a time of great tension. He had therefore concluded it was necessary "to take decisive actions" to avoid a constitutional crisis. Without mentioning that this was the last day on which he could either comply with the Court of Appeals ruling that he had to deliver up the subpoenaed tapes or be held in contempt, he said he was going to present to Sirica summaries "prepared by me personally from the subpoenaed tapes." They would contain a "full disclosure of everything that has any bearing on Watergate." Stennis would authenticate them. Ervin and Baker had agreed to the procedure.

Nixon noted that Cox had not agreed, but said he was going ahead anyway, and added that he had ordered Cox, "an employee of the executive branch, to make no further attempts by judicial process to obtain tapes, notes, or memoranda of Presidential conversations." This would spare the nation "the anguish of further indecision and litigation" about tapes.[47]

Initial reaction was mixed. Some congressmen praised Stennis. David Broder wrote a column saying he was the logical man for the job. But law school professors surveyed by The New York Times said that far from avoiding a constitutional crisis, Nixon was creating one. And Cox, in a brief statement, challenged Nixon's "exaggerated claims." He added that he would not accept Nixon's order that he cease his attempts to obtain additional White House tapes.[48]

•

As Nixon was working out the details and the PR of the Stennis compromise, he received an urgent message from Brezhnev. The Soviet leader had persuaded Sadat to accept a cease-fire in place. Now he wanted Kissinger to come to Moscow for consultation on implementation.

Nixon and Kissinger delayed through the day of October 19, Nixon because he had Cox and Stennis on his mind, Kissinger because he was in no hurry to achieve a cease-fire. Having delayed the flow of equipment to Israel long enough to make certain the Israelis knew how utterly dependent they were on the United States, Kissinger now wanted to delay long enough to allow the resupplied Israeli Army to win significant victories so that the Arabs understood that American arms would always prevail over Russian arms in the Middle East.

Just before midnight, October 19, Nixon was free to turn his mind to the Middle East problem. He called Kissinger shortly before the Secretary departed for Moscow. Kissinger does not mention this call in his memoirs, and Nixon does not report what he said, but the evidence indicates that there was a sharp split between the President and the Secretary of State. Kissinger wanted a simple cease-fire, nothing more. Nixon wanted to take advantage of the opportunity to go for something more significant, a genuine peace between Israel and its neighbors.

After Kissinger left, Nixon sent a letter to Brezhnev, through the Soviet Embassy in Washington. He said he was granting Kissinger "full authority" and that "the commitments that he may make in the course of your discussions have my complete support." He appealed to Brezhnev for "a firm commitment from both of us to devote our personal efforts to achieve that goal [a final peace] and to provide the strong leadership which our respective friends in the area will find persuasive."

Nixon added a handwritten postscript to his letter: "Mrs. Nixon joins me in sending our best personal regards to Mrs. Brezhnev and to you." This made it impossible for Kissinger to rewrite the letter before delivering it to Brezhnev, and is a good indication of how well Nixon knew and mistrusted his Secretary of State.[49]

Kissinger very much wanted to change the content and meaning of the letter. In his memoirs, he claims "I was horrified" by the grant of "full authority" as it deprived him of his capacity to stall on the cease-fire.[50] But there was something much more fundamental involved. Kissinger's real objection was that he only wanted to work for a cease-fire, not for a full-scale final peace agreement. So, as Soviet specialist Raymond Garthoff notes, "Kissinger decided, not for the first time while on a mission in Moscow, to ignore the president's instructions."[51]

This even though Nixon had followed up his oral orders with a two-part cable that Kissinger received shortly after arrival in Moscow. It was a remarkable document, one that showed Nixon at his best, and all the more remarkable as he dictated it on the morning of October 20, a day on which he had a great deal on his mind.

In the cable, Nixon demonstrated that he saw the picture whole and that he was ready to take big risks to achieve big gains. The fluctuations of the war, the way in which first one side and then the other had won battlefield victories, the clear lesson of how dependent the two sides were on the superpowers, the sheer scale of the conflict, all combined to create an opportunity that Nixon was smart enough to see and bold enough to seize.

Nixon told Kissinger that he was convinced the Soviet Union and the United States should jointly use the war to impose a comprehensive peace in the Middle East. Nixon argued that he would best serve Israel's interests if he used "whatever pressures may be required in order to gain acceptance of a settlement which is reasonable and which we can ask the Soviets to press on the Arabs."

The President listed the obstacles that had previously made a solution impossible. Israel's intransigence, the Arab refusal to bargain realistically, and America's own "preoccupation with other initiatives." None should be allowed to stand in the way of a permanent settlement at this time. "U.S. political considerations," Nixon wrote—meaning the Jewish vote in America—"will have absolutely no, repeat no, influence on our decisions in this regard. I want you to know that I am prepared to pressure the Israelis to the extent required, regardless of the domestic political consequences."

Nixon ordered Kissinger to pass along an oral message to Brezhnev; he should point out that unlike the situation with regard to MFN status for the Soviets, which depended on congressional approval, Nixon in the Middle East could act without consulting Congress.

In conclusion, Nixon wrote that he now understood how right Brezhnev had been, back at San Clemente in June, when he insisted that the superpowers could impose a peace on the Middle East. Nixon went on: "The Israelis and Arabs will never be able to approach this subject by themselves in a rational manner. That is why Nixon and Brezhnev, looking at the problem more dispassionately, must step in, determine the proper course of action to a just settlement, and then bring the necessary pressure on our respective friends for a settlement which will at last bring peace to this troubled area."[52]

Kissinger was aghast. In a cabled reply, he said that it would be "tough enough" to get Israel to accept a cease-fire, and "impossible" to get "a global deal." Furious, he also telephoned Washington to tell Al Haig, in vivid terms, of his extreme displeasure at Nixon's orders.

"Will you get off my back?" Haig snapped back. "I have troubles of my own."

"What troubles can you possibly have in Washington on a Saturday night?" Kissinger asked.[53]

Haig told him. Kissinger then realized that Nixon's preoccupations with events in Washington would be so total that he could safely ignore the President's orders.

For a fleeting moment, there had been a real possibility of the two superpowers banding together to attempt to enforce a general peace on the Middle East. In Kissinger's judgment, it could not work, so he scuttled the prospect without even informing Nixon. The opportunity was lost. We cannot know if Nixon and Brezhnev could have made peace between Israel on the one hand, Egypt and Syria on the other. We do know that because of Kissinger the attempt was not made.

For nine months, Nixon had been complaining that Watergate was preventing him from concentrating on the real problems of the world. Through that period, Kissinger had complained that preoccupation with Watergate was weakening the United States in the world arena. But when Nixon tried to break out, to show what a master he was of the international scene and how capable he was of recognizing and seizing an opportunity, and thus show how badly his country needed him and would profit from his talents, Kissinger used Nixon's preoccupation with Watergate to frustrate his boss.

AT 1 P.M. in Washington, Saturday, October 20, at the National Press Club, Cox held a press conference. "I'm certainly not out to get the President of the United States," he said at the outset, but he was out to get the President's tapes and he would not accept a summary of them, whether verified by Stennis or not. Nixon had presented Stennis to the nation as a reasonable alternative, a compromise. Cox had to undercut that perception. He was wise enough to avoid any question of Stennis's integrity; what he did was stress the dangerous precedent of bypassing established institutions and procedures for evaluating evidence. He explained that Stennis would see only documents prepared by Nixon's aides, and that such documents could not be presented as evidence in the trials resulting from grand jury indictments. The courts would insist on the full tape. Finally, Cox asserted that Nixon's demand that he cease submitting subpoenas for further tapes would irreparably damage his ability to carry out his mandate and that it violated the guidelines set forth by Richardson to the Senate in May.[54]

In short, Cox rejected the Stennis compromise and defied the President. He surely knew that he left Nixon with no alternative but to fire him, although he claimed that only Richardson could do that.

Nixon, furious, spoke to Haig. On the President's order, Haig telephoned Richardson. Haig said the President was ordering the Attorney General to fire the Special Prosecutor.

Richardson said he wanted to see the President.

Haig said that if Richardson would do as he was told, the Administration could do him "a lot of good." He specifically "dangled the prospect of White House support" for the 1976 Republican presidential nomination before Richardson.[55]

Richardson said he wanted to see the President. Haig set up a meeting for 4:30 that afternoon.

Nixon, so often described by Kissinger and others as "beside himself with anger," had cause to be beside himself with anger. In Moscow, his Secretary of State was ignoring his orders. In Washington, the Special Prosecutor had just told him to stuff it. Within the Administration, his Attorney General was defying his orders. He was at risk of being cited for contempt by the federal district court, as Sirica's order to produce the tapes had run out at midnight, October 19/20.

Somehow Nixon got a grip on himself. His meeting with Richardson was tense, but there was no table-pounding, no shouting, no uncontrolled outburst.

Nixon's first words were, "Brezhnev would never understand if I let Cox defy my instructions." Richardson brushed that aside. He said he could not fire Cox, because he had promised the Senate during his confirmation hearings that as Attorney General he would "not countermand or interfere with the Special Prosecutor's decisions or actions." He had also said that the Special Prosecutor's "ultimate accountability is to the American people." Therefore, rather than fire Cox, he would resign.

Nixon appealed to Richardson to delay his resignation for a few days because of the critical situation in the Middle East. When Richardson refused, Nixon said bitterly, "I'm sorry that you insist on putting your personal commitments ahead of the public interest."

"Mr. President," Richardson replied, "I can only say that I believe my resignation *is* in the public interest."

Nixon said their perceptions of the public interest differed.[56]

Richardson handed in his resignation. That made William Ruckelshaus, his deputy, the acting Attorney General. Nixon immediately had Haig give Ruckelshaus an order to fire Cox. Ruckelshaus refused.

"Well," Haig said, "you know what it means when an order comes down from the commander in chief, and a member of the team can't execute it."[57]

Ruckelshaus sent in his resignation. Nixon refused to accept it. After all, Ruckelshaus had made no promises to the Senate. Instead, Nixon instructed Haig to fire him.[58]

That made the Solicitor General, Robert Bork, the acting Attorney General. Bork went to the White House, where he received his commission and had a talk with Nixon. The President told Bork he was putting the Special Prosecutor's Office under the jurisdiction of Henry Petersen's

Criminal Division, and he wanted the Justice Department to carry out a "prosecution and not a persecution." Bork believed that the President had the right to fire Cox and had no personal compunctions about doing it. So it was done.

There was later much heated argument about whether or not the President had the right to fire the Special Prosecutor. The case seems to make itself. Nowhere in the Constitution do the words "special prosecutor" occur. He was appointed by the Attorney General; he and his staff drew their salaries from the Department of Justice; they were a part of the executive branch; there can be only one chief executive at a time. Unquestionably Nixon had the right to fire Cox.

But to be right is not necessarily to be wise. Government is built on trust, and over the past nine months public trust in Nixon and the government had been badly eroded. The firing of Cox shattered it. Nixon had broken no law in firing Cox, but he had badly hurt himself. One of the most politically astute of men, he had made a major political misjudgment. He thought that the public would stand with him in support of the Stennis compromise and the firing of Cox; instead it turned on him.

But he had no choice except to fire Cox. It had nothing to do with Brezhnev, or the crisis in the Middle East, or the Constitution. The Cox rejection of the Stennis compromise was bad enough; the Cox rejection of the prohibition on access to any additional tapes was disastrous. Nixon did not fire Cox to protect the principle of executive privilege and confidentiality, but to protect himself from his own words.

At 8:22 P.M. that Saturday night, Ziegler went to the White House briefing room to announce that Cox had been fired, that Richardson had resigned, that Ruckelshaus had been fired, and that the office of the Watergate Special Prosecutor had been abolished. The Justice Department was taking over the prosecution of Watergate.[59]

Within the hour, teams of FBI agents descended on the offices of Cox, Richardson, and Ruckelshaus to seal off the premises. They barred access by members of Cox's staff. Richardson later wrote that by this act, "Presidential power was asserted more blatantly than at any other stage in the whole sordid history of Watergate. A government of laws was on the verge of becoming a government of one man."[60]

The "Saturday Night Massacre," as it came to be called, produced an extraordinary outburst. *The New York Times* declared, "The President's dramatic action edged the nation closer to the constitutional confrontation he said he was trying to avoid." The newspaper quoted scores of politicians from both parties who called for impeachment proceedings.[61]

John Chancellor, in a special report on NBC TV, opened by saying, "The country tonight is in the midst of what may be the most serious constitutional crisis in its history." That statement, keeping in mind the secession of the Southern states in 1861, justified Nixon in later calling much of the reaction "almost hysterical."[62]

But Chancellor was by no means alone.

Senator Kennedy said that Cox's firing was "a reckless act of desperation by a President who is afraid of the Supreme Court, who has no respect for law and no regard for a man of conscience."

Senator Muskie said Nixon's action "threatens to destroy our system of laws. It smacks of dictatorship."[63]

Columnist Carl Rowan asked: "Has President Nixon gone crazy?"

Ralph Nader said Nixon was "acting like a madman, a tyrant, or both."

Senator Robert Byrd said that the Cox firing was a "Brownshirt operation" using "Gestapo tactics."[64]

Representative John Anderson commented: "Obviously, impeachment resolutions are going to be raining down like hailstones."[65]

Archibald Cox said: "Whether ours shall continue to be a government of laws and not of men is now for Congress and ultimately the American people" to decide.[66]

Henry Ruth, of Cox's staff, declared: "I'm going home to read about the Reichstag fire."[67]

The public too was furious. On Sunday Oliver Quayle conducted a national telephone poll for NBC. He reported that fully three-fourths of the nation sided with Cox. Western Union reported the "heaviest concentrated volume [of telegrams to Washington] on record." A Gallup Poll showed that Nixon's approval rating was down to an astonishing 17 percent.[68]

Nixon confessed that "I was taken by surprise by the ferocious intensity of the reaction. For the first time I recognized the depth of the impact Watergate had been having on America. I suddenly realized how deeply its acid had eaten into the nation's grain." Nevertheless, he insisted, "I had no other option than to act as I did" in firing Cox.[69]

Of course, it was not the "acid" of Watergate that had caused the reaction; it was the President's defiance of the court order to produce the tapes and his firing of Cox. These events dominated public consciousness so completely that people forgot or ignored almost everything else, even events of truly world-shaking significance. At the conclusion of her 5,000-word journal entry on the events of October 20, Elizabeth Drew noted, "It is announced on the radio that Saudi Arabia has cut off its oil supplies to the United States," and commented, "Can't think about that now."[70]

THE Saudi action added to the urgency of getting a cease-fire in the Middle East. Kissinger understood this, but he also knew that the Israelis wanted more time to complete their offensive movements and, possibly, capture the Egyptian Army in the Sinai. He was therefore prepared to stall in his talks with Brezhnev. But the Soviets were as intent on saving the Egyptian Army as the Israelis were on destroying it. To Kissinger's consternation, Brezhnev proposed an immediate cease-fire in place, and he wanted the United States to join the Soviet Union in introducing a cease-fire resolution in the Security Council immediately.

Kissinger asked for time to consult with Israel. He flew off to Tel Aviv, where he pressed the Israelis to accept a cease-fire in place. They wanted to destroy the Egyptian Army first. He wanted them to win, but not win so big that they would be immune to pressure for compromise. So he indicated to them that he would "understand if there was a few hours 'slippage' in the cease-fire deadline while I was flying home." He pointed out that "in Vietnam the cease-fire didn't go into effect at the exact time that was agreed on," and said he would scotch efforts to provide U.N. supervision for the cease-fire. On that basis, the Israelis reluctantly accepted a cease-fire.[71]

At 12:52 A.M. on October 22 the Security Council adopted Resolution 338, jointly sponsored by the United States and the Soviet Union, mandating a cease-fire in the Middle East. Kissinger had successfully ignored Nixon's instructions that he work with Brezhnev on a comprehensive peace settlement. Because he had achieved a cease-fire, and because Nixon was totally immersed in his own problems, the President made no complaint, then or later.

NIXON spent Sunday, October 21, in the White House, meeting with Haig, Ziegler, Garment, and others, seeking ways to repair the latest damage to the Administration. *The New York Times* described the atmosphere at the White House as "somewhat grim. But there was no discernible feeling of what was felt by many outside—that the Government was on the verge of unraveling." Nixon was described as "enduring with equanimity another difficult episode in the Watergate troubles."[72]

Ziegler released a written statement that would be delivered to Judge Sirica on Monday morning; it contended that Nixon's plan to give the court a "summary" of the contents of the Watergate tapes "satisfies" the order to turn over the tapes themselves.[73]

The Washington Post reported that aides were predicting Nixon would ride out the storm; even better, that he would "achieve a political vindication comparable to the one that Truman eventually won for his firing of MacArthur." The *Post* quoted Buchanan as saying, "You don't go after a President for making an unpopular decision, especially in a period of international crisis like this."[74]

Melvin Laird joined the counterattack in an appearance on "Meet the Press." Although he had said the previous week that he had warned

Nixon he would face impeachment should he defy the order on the tapes, now he claimed that the summaries Nixon was offering would be satisfactory and that there would be no impeachment proceeding.[75]

Bork announced that the Justice Department would continue its investigation into Watergate. Petersen would be in charge. Bork quoted Nixon's instructions: "It is my expectation that the Department of Justice will continue with full vigor the investigations and prosecutions that had been entrusted to the Watergate Special Prosecution Force."[76] Bork also said he would support Cox's proposal to extend the Watergate grand jury for another six months.

ON Monday, October 22, the Middle East cease-fire went into effect. Within hours, it was broken. Each side accused the other of violations. Insofar as it was Israel on the offensive, few could believe the Egyptians were to blame. The Israelis completed their encirclement of the Egyptian Army on the east bank of Suez.

In the Monday morning newspapers, editors were scathing in their denunciations of Nixon. The Chicago *Tribune*, for decades a staunch supporter of Nixon, called his attempted compromise on the tapes "possibly the worst blunder in presidential history." The New Orleans *States Item* called Nixon a "dictator." The Charlotte *Observer* found his actions "ruthless and dictatorial."[77]

That afternoon, Nixon flew by helicopter to Camp David to spend the night. Critics in Washington said he was escaping the constant sound of car horns around the White House, where pickets carried signs reading "Honk for Impeachment."[78]

He was beleaguered, and embattled as he had never been before. There were those who worried that he was not in control. George Meany referred to "the dangerous emotional instability" of the President. Buchanan called this "one of the most incredible, inexcusable, irresponsible statements ever made."[79] Nevertheless, rumors persisted. Warren was asked if Nixon was using drugs, or seeing a psychiatrist. Stories about his drinking spread. Julie Eisenhower admitted that "he was drinking a little more than he ever had before, but at dinnertime, when he was trying to unwind." She insisted that he did not drink during the day.[80]

(Was drinking a problem for Nixon? There is much conflicting evidence on both sides of the question, enough to make any final judgment impossible. It is this author's opinion that his drinking was not a problem for Nixon. That he sometimes drank to excess is clear, but never to the point that he was out of control. Indeed, it is remarkable how little he relied on drugs or booze to get through such great physical and emotional stress, how much he drew on his own strength.)

At noon Tuesday morning, October 23, Congress reconvened. In the House, twenty-one resolutions for Nixon's impeachment were introduced.

Carl Albert, who would become President if Nixon were impeached and found guilty before Ford was confirmed, held a meeting of Democratic leaders in his office. They emerged to tell reporters they wanted a "responsible inquiry" on the charges and to assure the nation that they would head off "any sudden demand" for an immediate impeachment vote.[81] Newspapers around the country called on Nixon to spare the nation by resigning. Senate Republican leaders passed a resolution recommending the appointment of a new special prosecutor.

Kissinger, meanwhile, had returned to Washington. Shortly after he arrived, Nixon received an urgent message from Brezhnev. The Soviet leader accused the Israelis of breaking the cease-fire and urged Nixon to stop them. He implied that the United States might have colluded in Israel's offensive. Nixon replied that he had told Israel to stop the fighting and asked Brezhnev to do the same with the Egyptians. For his part Kissinger admitted that the Israeli case was not credible and confessed that he had the "sinking feeling" that "this new fighting was continuing far beyond the brief additional margin I had implied."[82]

Far more important to Nixon personally was the scheduled appearance of his lawyer, Charles Alan Wright, before Judge Sirica that afternoon. Nixon had announced that he was going through with his plan to offer the summaries in place of the tapes themselves (although the Stennis verification was no longer a part of the compromise), but the uproar over the Saturday Night Massacre forced him to reconsider. He met with Haig, Garment, Buzhardt, and Wright to discuss his problem. They wanted him to yield on the tapes, and warned that if he did not, an impeachment resolution could well race through the House. He knew the implications, he said, "both for the principle of executive privilege and for my personal situation." (Garment and Wright did not know what the implications for Nixon's personal situation were, as they had not heard the tapes.)

Nixon raised the possibility of stalling by appealing to the Supreme Court the Court of Appeals ruling that he must turn over the subpoenaed tapes. But he realized that this could lead to an "even more binding decision" that would cause "even greater damage."

That option rejected, there was unanimous agreement that Nixon should yield. For him, "it was a wrenching decision."[83] That afternoon, Wright stood on the steps outside Sirica's courtroom to announce, "This President does not defy the law." Nixon would turn over the subpoenaed tapes.

On Wednesday, October 24, Nixon received a detailed memo from the chairman of the Council of Economic Advisers, Herbert Stein, outlining various problems in the economy. Even before the Arabs began their oil boycott the United States faced a fuel shortage. Little had been done to deal with it, beyond a presidential exhortation to the public to turn the turn the thermostats down to 68 degrees and to join car pools. In the past, Nixon had read such memos carefully and made numerous observations in the margins; this time, he simply scribbled "excellent—lucid and convincing" on the cover sheet and let it go at that.[84]

He had often said the country did not need a President for domestic affairs. Now he seemed to be proving it. As to his claim of meeting his responsibilities to pass on a fully functioning Presidency, it could be charged that he was doing the opposite. His intransigence and defiance made it all but inevitable that the Congress would go after his office as well as his person. Congress had done so in the most dramatic fashion by passing the War Powers Act, which severely limited the freedom of manouver on the part of the President in a crisis situation. If Nixon had not been embattled by Watergate, it is possible the Congress would not have passed the bill. When it did so, it challenged Nixon.

On October 24, he took up the challenge. He issued a ringing veto. He called the bill "both unconstitutional and dangerous," and charged that it would "seriously undermine this Nation's ability to act decisively and convincingly in times of international crisis."[85] His message was not convincing; two weeks later the House and Senate voted to override and the War Powers Act became law. It was so poorly thought out, and so badly written, that it barely affected the powers of future Presidents; still it could hardly be said that Nixon had managed to preserve and pass on all the inherent powers of the office.

In the Middle East, Israel ignored a second Security Council cease-fire resolution. Sadat sent a message to Nixon, pleading with him "to intervene, even on the ground, to force Israel to comply with the cease-fire." And the Soviets were publicly warning Israel that if it did not stop its advance there would be "gravest consequences."[86] Israel ignored the warning, so on October 24 Sadat publicly called on both the United States and the Soviet Union to send forces to Egypt to ensure the cease-fire. Nixon replied that it would not be possible, and warned that if "the two great nuclear powers" did send troops, "it would introduce an extremely dangerous potential for direct great-power rivalry in the area."[87] Ambassador Dobrynin, meanwhile, called Kissinger to say that the Soviets would support a resolution in the Security Council calling for the dispatch of Soviet and American troops. Kissinger told Dobrynin that the United States would veto any such resolution.

At 9:35 P.M. another message from Brezhnev arrived at the White House. He proposed to "urgently dispatch to Egypt Soviet and American military contingents, to insure the implementation" of the cease-fire. He added what Kissinger regarded as an ultimatum: "I will say it straight that if you find it impossible to act jointly with us in this matter, we should be faced with the necessity urgently to consider the question of taking appropriate steps unilaterally." There was some evidence that the Soviets were mobilizing airborne troops for that purpose.[88]

Brezhnev's message prompted an American response that escalated an American-Soviet divergence over how to achieve a common objective—the cease-fire—into a dramatic military confrontation. Whether or not the President was involved in the critical decision and actions cannot be said. Nixon claims in his memoirs that "Haig informed me about this message," and that he ordered Haig to hold a meeting with Kissinger and others. He says he told Haig, "we needed action, even the shock of a military alert."[89]

But Kissinger reports, "I asked Haig whether I should wake up the President. He replied curtly: ' no.' " Kissinger adds, "I knew what that meant," and explains he understood that "the President [was] too distraught to participate in the preliminary discussion." Modestly, he adds, "It was a daunting responsibility to assume," but he assumed it anyway, because "from my own conversation with Nixon earlier in the evening, I was convinced Haig was right."[90]

Kissinger aides asserted, later, that Nixon had been drinking.[91]

Kissinger called a meeting in the White House. The Chairman of the Joint Chiefs of Staff, the director of the CIA, the Secretary of Defense, Haig, and some others attended. The participants decided on action. At 12:25 A.M., October 25, a message went around the world. American forces everywhere were put on DEFCON III (Defense Condition 3, short of full readiness, higher than a normal alert status). It included the Strategic Air Command (SAC) and the North American Air Defense Command, thus involving strategic nuclear forces. The 82d Airborne Division went on high alert. Sixty B-52s in Guam were returned to the United States to join the SAC alert. The aircraft carrier *Franklin Delano Roosevelt* and its squadron moved from the western to the eastern Mediterranean; the carrier *John F. Kennedy* and its escorts moved to the Mediterranean.

At 2 A.M. Kissinger met with the Joint Chiefs. Admiral Zumwalt kept notes. Nowhere in them does Nixon's name occur. Zumwalt got the impression that "the President had nothing at all to do with it." Defense Secretary Schlesinger told an aide that Nixon was not involved.[92]

Nixon awakened on Thursday morning, October 25, to discover that the armed forces he commanded were on a nuclear alert.

At 8 A.M., the President met with Haig and Kissinger. They told him what had happened. At nine, together with Kissinger, Nixon briefed the bipartisan leadership, whose members were scared almost to death, as was the rest of the world. Representative O'Neill reported that "Kissinger had barely opened his mouth when the president interrupted him and started talking to us about the history of communism in the Soviet Union. He rambled on for almost half an hour. . . . Nobody could understand what, if anything, this had to do with the Middle East war."[93]

The more conservative congressmen were in an "I told you so" mood; always critical of détente, they felt this crisis showed how wrong Nixon had been to trust Brezhnev.

"I have never said that the Soviets are 'good guys,'" Nixon responded. "What I have always said is that we should not enter into unnecessary confrontations with them."[94]

But of course, his Administration had just done so. Kissinger's maneuver had grossly exaggerated the supposed threat. In his critical October 24 message, Brezhnev had not challenged Nixon; he had appealed to the President to act together in defense and support of a jointly sponsored cease-fire. And threatening the Soviet Union with a nuclear exchange was an inappropriate response to the problem. That problem was not Soviet adventurism, but Israel's refusal to abide by the cease-fire.

Brezhnev ignored the American nuclear alert, but he also made no further reference to unilateral Soviet troop movements. The Security Council passed a third cease-fire resolution, "demanding" (no longer "urging") that the parties return to the positions of October 22. Sadat dropped his request for American and Soviet troops, asking instead for an international force to implement the cease-fire. And, the really critical development, the United States compelled Israel to accept the cease-fire and allow resupply of the cut-off Egyptian Army. This was done by Kissinger, who admits that he does not recall whether he checked with Nixon before making it clear to Israel that it had to comply, or else. Kissinger does say he acted "in Nixon's name."[95]

THE President's lack of involvement in what he called the most serious crisis in Soviet-American relations since the Cuban missile crisis of 1962 was not known in October 1973. Had it been, many would have sighed with relief ("Trust Henry" was the watchword of the day). But as it was, people suspected that Nixon had called the alert, and that he had done so not for any legitimate reason, but to defuse his Watergate-related problems.

"A crisis a day keeps impeachment away" was the quip running around Washington. Kissinger held a news conference on the morning of October 25; reporters were hostile and skeptical. Furious, the Secretary told the reporters, "It is a symptom of what is happening to our country that it could even be suggested that the United States would alert its forces for domestic reasons." He promised to make the record available when the crisis ended (seventeen years later we still await that record), and assured the reporters, "I am absolutely confident that it will be seen that the President had no other choice as a responsible national leader."[96]

Nixon called Kissinger from Camp David to congratulate him, and to ask for more. He wanted the Secretary to summon the heads of the

Richard Nixon at his most typical, working the telephone, January 17, 1974.
Despite his Watergate woes, he had cause to smile: that day Egypt and Israel
had reached an accord on the separation of their armies in Sinai.

ALL PHOTOS NIXON PRESIDENTIAL MATERIAL PROJECT
UNLESS OTHERWISE SPECIFIED

Nixon and his friend Bebe Rebozo on the beach at Key Biscayne, Florida, early in 1974. With Rebozo, as with no one else, he could relax and escape, momentarily, the intense pressure he was under because of the various investigations into Watergate.

The Nixons in *Air Force One*. As always, he is working and she is giving him her support.

OPPOSITE: President Nixon meets his National Security Adviser, Henry Kissinger, January 14, 1973, at the Key Biscayne airstrip. Kissinger had flown from Paris, where he had completed the cease-fire agreement with the North Vietnamese, for which Kissinger received the Nobel Peace Prize and Nixon, in his own view, no credit at all.

Chief Justice Warren Burger swears Nixon in for his second term, January 20, 1973.

John Ehrlichman and H. R. "Bob" Haldeman on *Air Force One*, April 27, 1973. Two days later Nixon told them they would have to resign.

Israeli Prime Minister Golda Meir, Nixon, and Kissinger, May 1, 1973. They worked well together. In October, Nixon would supply the weapons that made it possible for Israel to prevail in the Yom Kippur War.

John Dean poses for a formal photograph, May 7, 1973, ten days after losing his job as Counsel to the President. On June 25 he told a Senate committee that Nixon had known about the Watergate cover-up for as long as eight months.

OPPOSITE:
Vice President Spiro Agnew defends himself against "false and scurrilous and malicious" charges that he accepted bribes as Governor of Maryland. It was August 8, 1973.

Nixon, Pat, and Rebozo share a happy moment in a golf cart at La Casa Pacifica, August 20, 1973.

Nixon and Leonid Brezhnev at Camp David, July 20, 1973. Nixon had given Brezhnev the windbreaker with the Presidential Seal on it. Later he gave the Soviet leader a Lincoln Continental, which was donated by the Ford Motor Company.

Dan Rather of CBS-TV asks Nixon a hostile question, September 5, 1973. They often clashed at these news conferences, each playing to his own audience.

Press Secretary Ron Ziegler assures doubting reporters that all is well on October 10, 1973, the day Vice President Agnew resigned.

Kissinger, Nixon, Congressman Gerald Ford, and White House Chief of Staff Alexander Haig, on October 13, 1973, the day after Nixon nominated Ford to the vice presidency.

Senator Sam Ervin (second from left), Chairman of the Senate Select Committee investigating Watergate, Nixon, Senator Howard Baker, ranking Republican on the Committee, and Haig on October 19, 1973. In July, the Committee hearings had revealed the White House taping system; Ervin and Baker were pressing the President for the tapes of conversations about Watergate.

On December 6, 1973, in the House Chamber, Ford is sworn in as Vice President. The happiest man in America was Speaker of the House Carl Albert (far left) who until this moment had stood one heartbeat away from the Presidency.

Nixon and Haig, May 23, 1974. White House aide Jeb Magruder had just been given a ten-month prison sentence for the Watergate break-in and cover-up; the House Judiciary Committee had warned Nixon that failure to turn over the Watergate tapes it had subpoenaed "might constitute a ground for impeachment"; he had cause to look worried.

Nixon with Anwar el Sadat in Egypt, June 12, 1974. They were greeted by one of the largest crowds in history, and it was overwhelmingly friendly toward Nixon.

Nixon and Brezhnev on the Black Sea in the Crimea, June 30, 1974. Their summit had failed to achieve any breakthroughs, but they did have a philosophical discussion in which they agreed that the younger generation was soft and selfish.

Nixon in Moscow, working the crowds, July 1, 1974. Nixon's critics wondered if he was going to ask for political asylum.

Senate Republican Leader Hugh Scott, Senator Barry Goldwater, and House Republican Leader John Rhodes emerge from an Oval Office meeting, August 7, 1974. Goldwater had just informed Nixon that he had lost almost all support in the Senate, including his. It was the effective end of the Nixon Presidency.

OPPOSITE BOTTOM:
August 7, 1974. Nixon informed his family that he would announce his resignation the following day. Over Pat's protest, he insisted on recording the moment "for history" and called in the White House photographer, Ollie Atkins.

ABOVE:
Atkins also took a less formal shot.

The next morning he took a photograph of Nixon with his secretary of more than twenty years, Rose Mary Woods.

August 9, 1974. Nixon says farewell to the Cabinet and White House staff, and to the nation. Pat and Tricia Cox had objected to the presence of television cameras, but Nixon insisted, saying he owed it to his supporters. Opposite: Pat Nixon kisses Betty Ford as the Nixons prepare to leave the White House by helicopter for the last time. A couple of hours later Nixon's resignation took effect and Ford became President.

AP/WORLD WIDE PHOTO

Nixon at the Oxford Union Debating Society, November 30, 1978. He wowed the young British students and television audiences in France during the same trip. He was on his way back.

For the first time, four Presidents in the Oval Office at once (with Rosalynn Carter in the background). Ford, Carter and Nixon were about to depart for Anwar el Sadat's funeral, October 8, 1981. The dominant personality in the room is obvious.

AP/CHARLES TASNADI

Nixon on NBC-TV's "Meet the Press," April 10, 1988, kicking off his author's tour for his book *1999: Victory Without War*. He became a prolific and highly successful author in his retirement.

David and Julie Eisenhower and the Nixons arriving for the dedication ceremonies at the Richard Nixon Library and Birthplace, July 19, 1990. He had managed what had seemed impossible sixteen years earlier—he had his own Presidential library. Even better, he—not the National Archives—got to decide what documents and tapes would be available to scholars. His was the last laugh.

"They are leaders who have made a difference. Not because they wished it, but because they willed it."

RN

Four Presidents circulate among the life-size bronze statues of some of Nixon's favorite world leaders in the Nixon Library (above) and pose with their First Ladies in front of the reflecting pool. Ford, Reagan, and Carter had kept a careful distance from Nixon for years; in the Republican conventions from 1976 through 1988 Nixon's name had never been mentioned; but by 1990 the party leaders embraced and praised him without stint. It was the ultimate triumph of his unbelievable comeback.

networks to the White House for a briefing on the alert. He told Kissinger to stress his (RN's) indispensability, to ask the television bosses how they would have liked it if Carl Albert had been in command. A few minutes after he'd hung up, Nixon had another idea. He called Kissinger back to ask him to call Jewish leaders to the White House for a similar briefing. "Get that whole bunch in a room and say you are American first. . . . Who is going to save Israel and who will save it in the future?"

Kissinger described these pleas as "pathetic" and urged Haig to persuade Nixon to drop the idea. That was done.[97]

A PRESIDENT, any President, expects—can count on—the people to rally behind him in the midst of a crisis. Yet what Nixon got in the October crisis was not support, but sneers, suspicions, and skepticism. Nixon was right to say the President needed support in a crisis, but for him it was too late. All his actions and statements had become suspect.

In this atmosphere, the first step in the impeachment process began, with the referral of impeachment resolutions to the House Judiciary Committee. As Nixon was dealing with the Middle East crisis, Committee Chairman Peter Rodino (D.-N.J.) was telling the press that he would "proceed full steam ahead" on the impeachment inquiry.[98]

Nixon had twice postponed a news conference to explain the Cox firing. He was roused by charges that he was afraid to face the reporters. Julie, who was so like her father in so many ways, expressed his mood in her diary entry that day: "Fight, fight, fight."[99] On October 26, at 7 P.M., Nixon held a news conference in the East Room of the White House. It was carried live on radio and television.

Considering what he had just been through, his appearance showed how much strength he still could draw upon, how he could mask fatigue and hide his anger. James Reston described him as looking "healthy and vigorous . . . remarkably calm and lucid."[100]

The President opened with a statement on the Middle East situation. He defended the nuclear alert with serenity and skill. He seemed in complete command of himself and of a wide range of complicated problems he faced. He was ready to meet his opposition halfway; he stated he would be appointing a new special prosecutor and would cooperate with him.

But the reporters wanted more. "Mr. President," Dan Rather asked, "I wonder if you could share your thoughts, tell us what goes through your mind when you hear people, people who love this country and people who believe in you, say reluctantly that perhaps you should resign or be impeached."

Nixon half-smiled, half-grimaced. He gave an awkward little shrug, sighed, and replied, "Well, I am glad we don't take the vote of this room, let me say." He reminded Rather that in the past four years, and especially during the Christmas bombing, he had been called "tyrant, dictator, and so forth." People had said, "He has lost his senses, he should resign, he should be impeached." But he had stuck it out, and been proven right.

He pointed out that he had not defied the Court of Appeals ruling, instead had complied with it. As to what was going through his mind, he said he intended to meet his responsibilities. "The events of this past week," he said, then interrupted himself: "I know, for example, in your head office [CBS TV] in New York, some thought that it was simply a blown-up exercise; there wasn't a real crisis. I wish it had been that. It was a real crisis."

He continued, "I had a basis of communication with Mr. Brezhnev [that] we not only avoided a confrontation but we moved a great step forward toward real peace in the Mideast." So long as he could make that kind of contribution, he would stay in office.

Nixon had avoided Rather's trap, fairly gracefully and certainly effectively. He turned to the next question. Did he think Cox had been out to get him?

Nixon would not question Cox's motives.

Did he think the country had been put through too many shocks lately?

Nixon began to answer with some calming words about the great strength of the American people, but his emotions finally took over. He said the biggest difference he had seen in the past quarter century in politics was the rise of the electronic media. The thought of television reporting in the past week set him off.

"I have never heard or seen such outrageous, vicious, distorted reporting," he charged. His fists were clenched. He thrust his jaw forward. His eyes blazed. "I am not blaming anybody for that," he declared, looking directly at Rather. "Perhaps what happened is that what we did brought it about, and therefore, the media decided that they would have to take that particular line." He said that when people are "pounded, night after night, with that kind of frantic, hysterical reporting, it naturally shakes their confidence."

Visibly recovering his composure, he pointed out that "even in this week, when many thought that the President was shell-shocked, unable to act, the President acted decisively in the interests of peace." He repeated that he would continue to do so.

Nixon handled a series of questions on the oil shortage, on the relationship between Rebozo and Hughes, and on his recent exchanges with Brezhnev briefly and ably.

Jerry terHorst of the Detroit *News* wanted to know how the President was bearing up emotionally under the stress of recent events. Nixon said those who had seen him in action the past week thought he had borne up rather well. "I have a quality which is—I guess I must have inherited it from my Midwestern mother and father—which is that the tougher it gets, the cooler I get." Terrible things had been said about him, he realized that, and they did tend to get under the skin. But, "I have learned to expect it. It has been my lot throughout my political life, and I suppose because I have been through so much, that may be one of the reasons that when I have to face an international crisis, I have what it takes."

Robert Pierpoint, also of CBS TV, referred to Nixon's answer to Rather's earlier question. Pierpoint asked what it was about television coverage "that has so aroused your anger."

"Don't get the impression that you arouse my anger," Nixon snapped back. A nervous laugh ran through the room.

"I'm afraid, sir, that I have that impression." More laughter.

Nixon stared at Pierpoint. With a tight grin, his hands clenched behind his back, he growled, "You see, one can only be angry with those he respects."[101] Reporters gasped audibly, while up in family rooms, watching on television, Pat and Julie winced.[102]

He had let the reporters get to him, and aroused their wolfpack instincts. At issue now was not Cox, nor Sirica, nor foreign policy; at issue was Nixon's judgment, his sudden mood switches, his stability, his anger, perhaps his capacity to govern. He loved talking directly to the people on television, he always claimed. On October 26 he did so, and did himself much harm.

THE press conference was not a success, but Nixon went on to press his points as if it had been. Nixon pushed the three-pronged strategy he had attempted to launch with the reporters: dramatizing himself as a peace-maker; depicting himself as the victim of a vindictive media; and demonstrating his willingness to cooperate with the Watergate investigation by appointing a new special prosecutor.

Bush met with Jewish leaders, who had been contacting New York Democrats to "point out that they ought to deescalate their criticism of the President, that they ought to knock off this talk of impeachment, and ought to shut up when it comes to criticizing the President." Bush reported back that "They make no bones about the fact that they are extremely grateful for what you have done in the Middle East." He was encouraging the leaders to take out full-page ads praising the President for his handling of the crisis. Bush assured him the telephone campaign was working: "Some of the people they have called have guaranteed they would pull back from previously stated positions on impeachment." Nixon scribbled on Bush's memo, "Good!"[103]

Pat Buchanan, on the CBS morning news program on October 29, went after the networks. He charged that the atmosphere at Nixon's conference was that of a bullring. In his opinion the Administration ought to make a legislative effort "to break the power of the networks."[104] David

Eisenhower, out of the Navy and in his first year of law school at George Washington University, tried to make the point on NBC TV the following day that there was too much "reporting without applying any perspective to it at all." In his view, the "irresponsibility" of the media had been "matched by the irresponsibility of people they quote."[105]

Julie Eisenhower spent the week traveling across the country, appearing before Chambers of Commerce, Little Leaguers, Republican groups, college and high school students, and local television shows. She defended her father and denounced the networks.[106]

None of this activity had much effect. What concerned the nation in the last week of October was a new special prosecutor. Nixon had promised there would be one, but he had also said in his news conference that he had no intention of providing any more presidential documents or tapes. Haig backed the President, but acting Attorney General Bork did not. Bork let it be known that he felt that whoever took the job "ought not to have any strings on him from anybody." He added that "no reputable man with a reputation to maintain" would accept the post without assurances of his right to subpoena the White House.[107]

Bork's statement put Nixon back where he had been before he fired Cox, vulnerable to a special prosecutor's demand for more tapes. Nixon realized that the reaction to the firing of Cox left him with no choice, however, and he entered into a deal with the Justice Department. The first part was the appointment of a new Attorney General. The political reality was that Nixon had to appoint someone whose independence was above question; no man close to him could be confirmed. So he chose Senator William Saxbe of Ohio, who although a Republican had been often at odds with Nixon as a critic of Nixon's Vietnam policy, and of Watergate.

The second part of the deal was the selection of the new special prosecutor and the laying down of the conditions of his appointment. Haig suggested Leon Jaworski, a Houston lawyer, for the post. Jaworski was an old friend of Lyndon Johnson and of John Connally and a former president of the American Bar Association, so there could be no question about his credentials. He insisted, just as Bork had predicted, on total independence. Nixon could not resist. The President agreed that in the event of an impasse, Jaworski could sue him in the courts for evidence. Nixon also agreed that before Jaworski could be fired, there would have to be a supportive consensus of the Majority and Minority Leaders of the House and Senate and the ranking majority and minority members of the House and Senate Judiciary Committees.[108]

Nixon had made his situation worse, at least according to Jack Porter of Houston, a former national committeeman who had played a key role in getting Ike the nomination in 1952. Porter called Rose Woods and asked her to pass along a message. "He feels you will live to regret the appointment of Leon Jaworski as Special Prosecutor because he is an extreme liberal and will cause you all the trouble he can."[109]

The House Judiciary Committee met on October 30 to take the first official step toward possible impeachment of a President in 105 years and only the second in American history. By a straight party vote of 21 to 17, the Committee approved a grant of broad subpoena power to Chairman Peter Rodino.

OCTOBER 1973, a month of shocks and storms and surprises, ended with another sensational disclosure. On the last day of the month, Buzhardt told Sirica that two of the subpoenaed tapes Nixon had promised to turn over to the court did not exist. Nixon claimed he had just discovered the tapes did not exist. He did not explain how that could be, since he had been working on the summaries for Stennis since early October. Nor did he say how he had intended to explain the non-existing tapes to Stennis.

Judge Sirica was astonished. He complained that the original subpoena had been issued in July, yet "here it was the end of October, and the White House was making the first public admission that the two critical tapes didn't exist."[110]

Buzhardt explained that the first nonexistent tape involved a telephone conversation between Nixon and John Mitchell on June 20, 1972. There was no tape because Nixon had made the call from the residential part of the White House on a phone that was not plugged into the taping system. The second nonexistent tape involved a conversation between Nixon and John Dean on April 15, 1973; there was no recording for the simple reason that the machine had run out of tape.

Almost no one believed a word of it. People spoke of "missing tapes" rather than "nonexistent tapes," implying that something sinister had happened. It seemed obvious Tricky Dick was back, doing business at his old stand.

Actually, Nixon was telling the truth. The irony is that it was on April 15, with Dean in the office, that Nixon had told Petersen over the telephone to order Liddy to tell the truth; it was during that conversation, also, that Nixon had said in his own transparent way that he had only been joking when he said he could raise $1 million for hush money. Nixon would have loved to have had that tape. Double irony—it was on April 15 that Nixon had gone into a corner and lowered his voice, to say that it had probably been foolish of him to talk about clemency for Hunt. Nixon's whispered admission first aroused Dean's suspicion that he was being taped; Dean's suspicion led to the direct question to Butterfield that led to the revelation of the taping system.

Nixon's luck that day was not just bad, it was disastrous.

The reaction to the news of the nonexistent tapes was almost as severe as that following the firing of Cox. Barry Goldwater said Nixon's credibility "has reached an all-time low from which he may not be able to recover." Senator James Buckley of New York said that the burden of proof had "dramatically shifted. As of this moment, President Nixon has the clear burden of satisfying the American people that he has been speaking the truth." Senator Ervin, shaking his head, commented that "everything about this has been curious from the first day."[111] Newspapers across the land and the political spectrum called for Nixon's resignation or his impeachment. This included the Atlanta *Constitution,* the Salt Lake *Tribune,* the Boston *Globe,* the Honolulu *Star-Bulletin,* and the Detroit *News.*

ON November 1, Nixon had an Oval Office meeting with Israeli Prime Minister Golda Meir. She thanked him for his support during the critical days earlier that month, when he had ordered the airlift that saved Israel.

"I never believe in little plays when big issues are at stake," Nixon responded.[112]

After saying goodbye to Meir on the White House lawn, Nixon scribbled a note on his briefing paper:

There were no missing tapes.
There never were any.
The conversations in question were not taped.
Why couldn't we get that across to people?[113]

Then he made a sudden decision to get out of Washington. He ordered a helicopter; it took him to Andrews Air Force Base, where he got on *Air Force One* and flew off to Florida. He had a minimum support staff of Secret Service agents with him. No one else.

It was unprecedented. Ordinarily when he traveled he was accompanied by senior aides, members of his family, and the White House press corps. Haig, Ziegler, Rose Mary Woods, and the press corps were caught by surprise; two hours later they got a commercial chartered jet to carry them down to Florida.[114]

Nixon alone, fleeing Washington, fleeing the reporters, fleeing his aides, fleeing his family. It was the end of an incredible month.

CHAPTER ELEVEN

"I AM NOT A CROOK"
November–December 1973

NIXON'S SUDDEN, solitary flight to Florida significantly strengthened the sentiment that "the President has got to go." In the wake of the firing of Cox, the nuclear alert, and the revelation that two subpoenaed tapes were nonexistent, his retreat shook his friends and emboldened his enemies. A prominent Texas businessman, a strong supporter of Nixon, told Elizabeth Drew, "No corporate executive would survive this. . . . Why does this guy go off every weekend during crises? A businessman would stay there if he discovered he had a massive problem. This guy goes off alone."[1]

Senator Buckley said he thought the President would resign. *The New York Times* said, in an editorial, that he should resign. Joseph Alsop told CBS that Nixon should resign, not for moral reasons but "because he can't work." Edward Brooke of Massachusetts became the first Republican senator to call for his resignation; two Democratic senators had already done so.[2] *Time* magazine, in its first editorial in fifty years, said that Nixon "and the nation had passed a tragic point of no return" and called on him to resign.[3]

"The Congress is like a school of fish," one politician remarked. "They [the members] . . . dart one way, and then another. You don't know which fish will dart out and make the next move that they will all follow."[4] In this case, the school of fish did not follow Brooke; instead, the inherent conservatism of the congressmen held them back, along with the frightening consequence of a resignation before Ford was confirmed—Carl Albert would become President. Senator Kennedy called for the prompt confirmation of Ford, to clear the way; *Time*, in its editorial, had described Ford as an "unmistakable improvement over the grievously wounded Nixon."

Through the first week of November, Nixon continued to bleed. He was at a 27 percent approval rating. Steve Bull revealed in Sirica's courtroom that Nixon had known five weeks earlier that the two subpoenaed tapes did not exist, and that in September he had taken a dozen tapes to Camp David, but returned only four or five to a safe in the White House. When Bull further revealed that still other tapes had gone down to Key Biscayne, the newspapers were full of the various adventures of the White House tapes.

Worry over Nixon's isolation mounted. John Herbers wrote in *The New York Times*, "The narrowness of Mr. Nixon's day-to-day contacts has become a matter of growing concern." Herbers charged that Nixon's circle had contracted to Haig and Ziegler.[5]

Nixon's own lawyers were urging him to resign. Buzhardt and Garment had made a discovery. Back in May, Nixon had told Cox that he could prove that he was not involved in the cover-up. The "proof" was a conversation he had held with John Dean on April 15. "I have Dean on tape," Nixon had said to Cox (this was well before Cox knew of the White House taping system). On June 11, Cox sent a letter to the White House asking for that "tape." Buzhardt had taken the letter to Nixon, who said there was no tape, but "there is a Dictabelt, that is what I was talking about." Nixon explained that it was his normal practice to dictate his recollections at the end of each day. The President added that he would not turn over the Dictabelt to Cox, because it was covered by executive privilege. Buzhardt passed the word to Cox.

After Butterfield revealed the taping system, Cox put in a subpoena for the April 15 Nixon-Dean conversation. That turned out to be one of the nonexistent tapes. Buzhardt then began a search for the Dictabelt. If he could find and produce it, the Dictabelt would allay at least some of the suspicions that Nixon had destroyed the "missing" tapes. But he could not find it; the Dictabelt was also nonexistent.

Angry, chagrined, embarrassed, and potentially in some personal legal danger—Buzhardt had told Cox that there was a Dictabelt—Buzhardt and Garment flew down to Florida to confront Nixon. They got to see only Haig and Ziegler. When Haig told the President that the Dictabelt was nonexistent, Nixon's suggestion was a simple one. "Why can't we make a new Dictabelt?" He had some handwritten notes of the meeting he could use to dictate a recording that could be submitted to the court as the original.

When Haig took this idea back to the lawyers, they were shocked. Garment pointed out that Nixon's words put them all in jeopardy of being cited for obstruction of justice. He wanted Nixon to get another lawyer, and he joined Buzhardt in recommending that Nixon resign.

Haig protested that was impossible. Carl Albert for President? The lawyers said the resignation could wait until Ford was confirmed. Haig resisted, making it clear he did not want to carry such a recommendation to Nixon. The lawyers said they would do it; Haig would have none of that. He went to see Nixon, and Nixon sent back word to his lawyers that he did not want to see them.[6]

Nor would he resign. Ever. "We will take some desperate, strong measure," he told Ziegler, "and this time there is no margin for error."[7]

He began by having Warren announce at his daily news briefing, "The President has no intention of resigning."[8] Next, Julie spoke for him, in an interview from the White House published on November 4. She vehemently denied the allegations against her father. He had done nothing wrong, his health was excellent, there was nothing irregular about his finances, he would not resign.

"I think that any man who didn't know in his heart that he had nothing to hide, that he had done everything humanly possible to clear things up" would continue his fight. If he were guilty, "how could he really go through all these months?" she asked. "It wouldn't be possible, would it, if you really think about it?"

Was the family discussing resignation?

"No, of course not. You know, there are a lot of times when I feel anger and frustration, but copping out isn't the answer, ever."

Asked how her father dealt with the pressure, she said he often sat at the piano alone, playing soft, melodic tunes. "Sometimes all alone at night, you'll hear this music in the hallways." He also liked to watch movies with his family. Julie confessed that "lots of times he'll choose a horrible lemon, and we'll be all there making catcalls and saying, 'oh this is terrible.' My father will say, 'Keep quiet. Give this show a chance.' And he will sit through. Everyone will have snuck out."

But her father got his best relaxation in Key Biscayne or San Clemente, because "this [the White House] is just a pressure-box atmosphere. If we could live anywhere else, it would be just great. I guess it's because the phones are always ringing. People are always around. It's not really a home."[9]

In *The New York Times*, Rabbi Baruch Korff, chairman of the National Citizens' Committee for Fairness to the Presidency, took out a full-page advertisement, supporting Nixon and charging that the media had "scandalized him, brutalized him, savaged him day after day, night after night, and now they have come to bury him, draped in infamy, with the White House for a coffin." For all their "pious rhetoric," the ad read, history would judge the reporters "for what they are—ASSASSINS."[10]

ON November 7, the anniversary of his stunning triumph in the 1972 presidential election, Nixon spent the day conferring with labor leaders, industry leaders, governors, mayors, and congressional leaders on the energy crisis. His enemies were mounting their own offensive. That same

day, the Congress overrode his veto of the War Powers Act. Several
Republicans, for the first time, voted to override a Nixon veto, as did
numerous Southern Democrats. There was no doubt that Senator John
Tower (R.-Tex.) was correct in his analysis, that the Congress was swept
up "in the hysteria of Watergate and desire to punish this President."[11]

STILL, the energy crisis afforded him an opportunity to speak to the nation
as its leader on a subject that had everyone worried, many frightened,
the kind of crisis that the cumbersome Congress was helpless to solve.
That evening, Nixon went on nationwide television and radio looking and
sounding fit and confident, appropriately worried, but in command. He
began with a description of the problem: an energy shortage had loomed
even before the war in the Middle East, which with the OPEC embargo
had become a crisis. America was 2 billion barrels of oil per day short of
its expected imports, or a full 10 percent short of demand. He pointed
out that for two years he had been urging Congress to take action, but
without success. "I realize that the Congress has been distracted in this
period by other matters," he said, but the time to act had come.

The American people would also have to act. "The fuel crisis need
not mean genuine suffering for any American," Nixon said, "but it will
require some sacrifice by all Americans." He used the stimulus words all
Presidents use when they feel it necessary to summon the people to solve
a problem, words like "unity" and "challenge" and "battle" and "service."

One, two, three, four, Nixon ticked off the things that had to be
done. More coal. Fewer commercial airplane flights. A 50-mile-per-hour
national speed limit. The Alaska pipeline. More nuclear plants. Car pool-
ing. A relaxation of environmental regulations. Thermostats turned down
to between 65 and 68 degrees.

"We have an energy crisis," Nixon said, "but there is no crisis of the
American spirit." He recalled the Manhattan Project, and the Apollo
project. He announced "Project Independence." "Let us pledge that by
1980, under Project Independence, we shall be able to meet America's
energy needs from America's own resources."

It was Nixon doing what he had been elected to do, providing statesmanlike leadership, facing a problem rather than covering it up or trying
to duck it, asking the people to join him in a national effort. But he spoiled
the effect. Rather than signing off with a "God bless you," he turned to
some handwritten notes he had scribbled down at the last minute.

He noted that this was the anniversary of his election, and praised
himself for his accomplishments since then (America out of Vietnam, the
POWs returned, no more conscription, a reduced unemployment rate,
lower inflation). But, he went on, he realized that "the deplorable Watergate matter" had raised doubts as to the integrity of the President.
Some publications had even called for his resignation.

"Tonight I would like to give my answer to those who have suggested that I resign.

"I have no intention whatever of walking away from the job I was elected to do." He pledged that so long as he was physically capable of working sixteen to eighteen hours per day for peace abroad and prosperity at home, he would do so. He pledged to do all that he could do to remove the doubts about his integrity, and to be worthy of the trust the people had placed in him.[12]

Naturally, the television commentators after the speech, and the newspapers the following morning, featured the "no intention" of resigning segment of the speech rather than the energy crisis. *The Washington Post* dismissed the President's energy proposals as too little, too late. The Dow Jones average dropped 24 points, the biggest decline in eleven years.[13] Even worse for Nixon, the November 8 newspapers carried yet another story about the subpoenaed tapes that had been delivered to Sirica. It appeared there was something missing in one of the tapes.[14]

Despite these developments, Nixon continued his counterattack. Between November 9 and 15, he held a series of meetings with all the Republicans and some of the Southern Democrats in Congress. The theme was candor. Nixon told the Republicans that he planned to make public the subpoenaed tapes after they were submitted to the federal grand jury. He issued a lengthy statement explaining why the tapes of two conversations did not exist.[15] He tried jokes: he said if he gave a speech and said, "I didn't do it," the Democrats would say, "The son of a bitch is lying," while the Republicans would say, "Well, he's lying, but he's our son of a bitch." He made promises: Jaworski "should have everything, and when he asks for it, he will get it." He fought back: he had not abandoned antitrust action against ITT or raised milk price supports in exchange for campaign contributions, nor had he used campaign funds to improve his homes in California and Florida. "If I wanted to make money," he pointed out, "I would not be in this business. If I wanted to cheat, I wouldn't do it here."

Nixon tried sympathetic understanding: he knew what a burden Watergate was for the Republicans, he knew that "your careers are involved, you are worried about the polls and about whether the money is going to come in for your campaigns." He urged a sense of perspective: "In the history books twenty-five years from now what will matter is the fact that the President of the United States in the period from 1969 to 1976 changed the world." He tried threats: "If you cut the legs off the President, America is going to lose," and, "If you continue to diminish the authority of the Presidency, our allies will consider leaning toward the Soviet Union."[16]

He issued warnings: the Republican congressmen should be careful about their own finances and campaign contributions to "be sure to keep the jackasses from taking over." He asked for sympathy: describing his personal plight, he said, "It's been seven months of pure hell over Watergate."

The effect of his week-long blitz was mixed. Representative Dan Kuykendall (R.-Tenn.) said afterwards, "No fair-minded person could fail to believe the President was telling the truth." Senators Stennis and James Eastland (D.-Miss.) were 100 percent behind Nixon. But Representative Paul McCloskey (R.-Calif.) complained about "an air of unreality" in the sessions because Nixon was "adopting the posture that the opposition to him is politically and partisanly motivated rather than motivated by a search for truth." And Senator Charles Mathias (R.-Md.) spoke for many Republicans when he said they were sort of "get-acquainted" sessions "after we've been doing business for five years."[17]

Other Republicans shared Mathias's irritation. Nixon had ignored them for years, had refused to campaign for them, had sucked up campaign funds from their districts and left nothing for them, had asked their support while giving them nothing—and now he wanted them to save him. Their feeling was they had been and were being used by someone who had never done anything for them, and never would. "When it's a question of me and thee in politics," one Republican commented, "it's usually thee who has to go."[18]

Tip O'Neill, Democratic leader in the House, spoke for the Democrats when he charged that Nixon was trying to "curry favor with his prospective grand jurors" through the sessions. He characterized them as "unbecoming, if not improper."[19]

Nixon ignored O'Neill's carping. That same day, at one of the briefing sessions, the President was asked, "Is there another shoe to drop?"

"As far as I'm concerned," a seemingly confident Nixon replied, "as to the guilt of the President, no." He added, "If the shoes fall, I will be there ready to catch them."

Later that afternoon, Haig told Nixon there was another potential problem, the "gap" in the June 20 tape of the Haldeman-Nixon conversation. It was longer than the five minutes Woods had estimated, Haig reported (Nixon already knew that; he had listened to the tape). But Nixon was not worried—Buzhardt was going to look into it, see if he could find an explanation, and attempt to recover the lost conversation through electronic means.[20]

Nixon drove over to the Sheraton-Park Hotel, to speak to the National Association of Realtors. He appeared before a gigantic replica of the American flag, made of colored lights. Beaming and waving his arms over his head to loud cheers from a most appreciative audience, he looked terrific. He praised the realtors for their Americanism and their salesmanship. He said his only investments were in real estate. He praised his Administration for its manifold accomplishments. He urged the realtors to get behind Project Independence.

In conclusion, he turned to "the problem of the campaign of 1972 and the issues that arose out of it." He admitted that mistakes had been made by overzealous aides, "mistakes that I never approved of, mistakes that I would not have tolerated, but mistakes for which I will have to take responsibility.

"But let me say this: Mistakes are one thing; as far as the President of the United States is concerned, he has not violated his trust, and he isn't going to violate his trust now. . . . I can assure you that no matter what some of my good-intentioned friends and, certainly, I would say, honest opponents, may suggest to the contrary, I am not going to walk away until I get the job done."

That was what the realtors wanted to hear. As one, the members rose to applaud and cheer, and shake their fists at the television cameras.[21]

THE applause ringing in his ears, Nixon set out for the Deep South, where he still had many friends and admirers. He had speeches scheduled in Florida, Georgia, and Tennessee. His first stop was Walt Disney World in Orlando, where he faced the Associated Press Managing Editors Association and took questions in a forum that, if not as friendly as the realtors, was less hostile than the working reporters. There was a big media buildup for the appearance, which was broadcast live on nationwide television and radio. The questions were tough; Nixon's answers gave the appearance of candor; in the highlight of the evening, he described himself in words that no one had ever thought he or she would hear an American President use. But then he was asked questions no one could have imagined would ever be asked of an American President.

The opening question, from John Quinn of Gannett Newspapers, was: "Can we keep [our] republic, sir, and how?"

Nixon assured Quinn that the republic would survive Watergate, and added that he was going to stay at his post, working for the cause of peace and the cause of prosperity without war.

He was asked to explain, again, how it happened that there were no tapes of his telephone conversation with John Mitchell on June 20, 1972, or his Oval Office talk with John Dean on April 15, 1973. Nixon gave a detailed but convoluted answer that said little that was new. Except that, possibly anticipating the certain uproar that would come when it was revealed to the public that there was a gap on one of the subpoenaed tapes, he talked about the technological shortcomings of his taping system.

It was a cheapy, he said, costing only $2,500. President Johnson had "much better equipment, but I found—and I am not saying that critically—but I found that in this instance it was a Sony, a little Sony that they had and that what they had are these little lapel mikes in my desks." At this point, he rubbed the American flag pin in his lapel. As a result, "the reason that you have heard that there are difficulties in hearing them [the tapes] is that the system itself was not a sophisticated one." He did not mean to suggest that a listener could not get the facts, because he was certain that when the facts came out, they would prove his innocence. He had listened to them, and he knew.

What then was his reaction when he learned that certain tapes did not exist? "Very great disappointment," Nixon replied, "because I wanted the evidence out." Running on, he got hopelessly tangled in his own words, finally wrapping up: "I should point out the tape of September 15, when, as you recall, has been testified that I was first informed there was a cover-up—that, of course, is there."

Shaking his head, he gave a bit of a grin and said, "I just wish we had had a better system—I frankly wish we hadn't had a system at all, then I wouldn't have to answer this question."

Did he tell Cox to stay out of the Ellsberg case? No, he had never spoken to Cox. He did tell Petersen to stay away from national security matters.

Did he still believe Ehrlichman and Haldeman were two of the finest public servants he had ever known, and were guiltless?

"First, I hold that both men and others who have been charged are guilty until I have evidence that they are not guilty." Later in the session, his error was pointed out to him, and he corrected himself. He meant to say they were innocent until proven guilty.

Was it true that he paid only $792 in federal income tax in 1970, and $878 in 1971? Nixon replied that an audit of his personal finances would be made available at the end of the meeting, which would answer all questions. He said there were lots of gimmicks for tax deductions "which most of you know about, I am sure—if you don't, your publishers do." He explained that he had taken a half-million-dollar deduction for his donation of his vice presidential papers to the National Archives, that he had done so on Lyndon Johnson's advice, and said that now he was sorry he had done it, because "I will be glad to have the papers back, and I will pay the tax because I think they are worth more than that." The law, meanwhile, had been changed; since 1969 it was not possible to take a deduction for the donation of private papers. "So I am stuck with a lot of papers now that I have got to find a way to give away or otherwise my heirs will have a terrible time trying to pay the taxes on things that people aren't going to want to buy."

In another wonderfully Nixonian paragraph, the President urged "all new politicians" to "run your own campaigns." He said he used to run his and was widely criticized for it, but when he did, there was no hanky-panky. In 1972, however, he was too busy, because "when you are President, you don't watch as closely as you might. And on that, I say if mistakes are made, however, I am not blaming the people down below. The man at the top has got to take the heat for all of them."

That got him going. As the next questioner began to speak, Nixon interrupted him to say he wanted to add a few words on his tax payments. All that he owned in this world, he claimed, was a couple of pieces of property. "I am the first President since Harry Truman who hasn't owned any stock since ever I have been President. I am the first one who has not had a blind trust since Harry Truman." Not that he meant to imply that other Presidents had done anything wrong.

It was reminiscent of his 1952 Checkers speech, when he had stressed the smallness of his total holdings, then "laid bare" his financial record. As he had done in 1952, he asked his own question (because "some of you might be too polite to ask such an embarrassing question"), which was, "Now, Mr. President, you earned $800,000 when you were President. . . . How could you possibly have had the money [to buy the property in California and Florida]? Where did you get it?" And what about stories that he had used campaign funds to make the purchases?

"Well, I should point out I wasn't a pauper when I became President." He caught himself and immediately added, "I wasn't very rich as Presidents go." When he left office, in January of 1961, after four years as a congressman, two years as a senator, and eight years as Vice President, "you know what my net worth was? Forty-seven thousand dollars total, and a 1958 Oldsmobile that needed an overhaul."

"Now, I have no complaints," he assured the audience and the nation. And he explained that he had made big money between 1961 and 1968, from his writing and from his law practice. And that was where the money came from to buy the real estate. "Let me just say this," he went on. "I made my mistakes, but in all of my years of public life, I have never profited, never profited from public service—I have earned every cent."

Scowling fiercely, his body tense, his hands clasped behind his back, he leaned forward. Beads of sweat popped up on his brow.

"I welcome this kind of examination," he declared, "because people have got to know whether or not their President is a crook. Well, I am not a crook. I have earned everything I have got."

Having settled that point, he turned to the next question, which was, Did you order your brother Don's telephone tapped? Nixon admitted that he had, for security reasons.

How did he feel about criticisms that he wasted fuel by flying *Air Force One* around the country, along with a backup airplane? Well, he had to use the big plane; for example, he had wanted to fly to Orlando on a JetStar but was told he could not because of inadequate communications. But he did save some fuel by ordering that the backup plane stay home. "I don't need a backup plane. If this one goes down, it goes down—and then they don't have to impeach."

The audience tried to laugh. After some short questions and long answers on the energy crisis, the session finally, mercifully, came to an end.[22]

It had been an ordeal, for Nixon, for the editors, for the viewing and listening audience. Elizabeth Drew commented that "It is humiliating to see a President subjected to humiliation . . . difficult to watch a President running and maneuvering like a hunted man."[23] Others were not so much humiliated as embarrassed by Nixon's assurance that the nation's leader was not a crook.

THAT Nixon had felt the need to assert that he was not a crook compounded his problems. And it had not been a spur-of-the-moment statement, but one he had planned to make because he thought it essential. He quickly realized that he had made a big mistake, as variations on the line were used by stand-up comedians across the country, in and out of Congress.[24] Nixon had made himself into an object of ridicule.

He said what he said because he was who he was. Charges of political corruption he could handle with relative calm, because he could always reply that the Democrats did it first and anyway he was not involved, although he manfully took the responsibility for "mistakes." Charges of financial corruption were another case altogether. They stung. They left him feeling abused, assaulted, violated, misunderstood, mistreated. They aroused his combative instinct as nothing else.

Partly this was because the charges involved people close to him. Bebe Rebozo for one, John Connally for another, Pat and Tricia and Julie most of all. That Rebozo was pilloried for his handling of the $100,000 cash contribution from Howard Hughes and other money made him furious. Charges that Pat had accepted illegal gifts aroused his protective instincts and his fury.

He was full of self-pity. It was so unfair, and he was so helpless. He knew that Eisenhower had accepted free services from his millionaire pals. He knew that Ike had kept expensive presents from foreign governments (forbidden by law only after 1961). Yet gossip columnists in Washington accused Pat of unethically keeping jewels given to her as state gifts, when Pat had listed the jewels in a gift register so that they could go to the Nixon Library when he left office. That one hurt, the more so when she came to him to ask in despair, "What more can they possibly want us to do?"[25]

Back in 1952, it was Pat who had suffered the most from charges that her husband had kept campaign contributions and used them to live a life far beyond his means. It was Pat who suffered most when he made the Checkers speech and spelled out some of the details of his financial position. He had done it anyway, and he celebrated the anniversary of the speech each year thereafter; Pat refused ever to talk about it.

In 1973, as in 1952, Nixon saw himself as the victim of a double standard. In each case, he had done nothing that other politicians did not do regularly. Yet the media went after him while it left the others alone. He was neither the first nor the only President to profit while in office. His immediate predecessor had made big money during his incumbency; where were the critics?

Nixon's anger was compounded by another long-harbored resentment. Some of his predecessors had not been touched by financial scandal while in office because they were so filthy rich when they entered they did not have to add to their fortunes. The most obvious of these was Jack Kennedy. Where Nixon had to beg money from contributors to finance a campaign, Kennedy could just sign another personal check. Nixon would have had to have been a saint not to feel resentment at that situation.

There was much truth to feed Nixon's outrage. Johnson had used the office to further enrich himself, just as he had wiretapped his opponents. The Kennedy fortune was large, much of it made by Joe Kennedy in questionable ways. Ike was a millionaire before he entered office (thanks to *Crusade in Europe*), and he did accept and keep expensive gifts and services.

There was also truth in Nixon's defense. In his memoirs, he devoted ten pages to rebutting the charges of financial impropriety. If not as fully convincing as his reply to the fund charges in 1952, he did have a case. Nevertheless, when he said, "I am not a crook," millions of his fellow citizens assumed that once again Nixon was saying the opposite of what he meant.

It was sad that he felt the need to say it, and a mistake for him to do so. But he had to do it, to reassure the people he loved and respected above all others, those whose approval meant the most to him. He began his defense of his financial dealings in his memoirs with these words: "I grew up in a home where politics was frequently discussed, and where the greatest contempt was reserved for politicians on the take."[26]

He remembered, as if it were yesterday, when the Teapot Dome scandal broke in 1924. He was eleven years old. Frank Nixon had denounced the corrupt politicians and the high-priced lawyers who defended them. Dick read the newspapers for more details. "When I get big," he announced one day after reading the paper, "I'll be a lawyer they can't bribe."[27]

Hannah Nixon, delighted by her son's sincerity and honesty, had quoted that line on numerous occasions both before and after he became famous. Richard, delighted by his mother and father's approval, retained a vivid memory of the occasion. So, when he declared that he was not a crook, he was speaking to his parents up in heaven as much as to his audience on earth.

•

GOING into the holiday season, Nixon's situation looked to be desperate. His lawyers had advised him to resign. The press had demanded that he resign. Prominent Republicans had urged him to resign. Democrats from outside the South appeared determined to impeach him. His approval rating was disastrously low. Could he stay in office through Thanksgiving? Christmas? Many thought not.

Actually, although he was politically wounded, as the override of his veto of the War Powers Act showed, he was by no means finished. This was less because his case was a good one, or that he was presenting it effectively, more because of his own insistence that he would never, ever resign, coupled with the extreme reluctance of many politicians to go through with impeachment.

It was his own party that wanted him to resign, supported by the major media outlets and many big businessmen. In 1974 all Republican representatives, and about one third of the senators, would have to face the voters. It was clear that they would have a better chance of raising money and winning votes if Richard Nixon were gone from the White House. Few of the politicians or the businessmen were courageous enough to make a public call for his resignation, but nearly all of them wished he would do it.

He would not. There were his mother's dying words to him. "Richard, don't you give up," she had said. "Don't let anybody tell you you are through."[28]

There was his family. Pat remained quiet, as always, Tricia grimly determined, as always, Julie outspokenly in favor of fighting, as always. And there were his own instincts.

The chances for impeachment seemed to be even less than for Nixon's resignation. There was first of all the sheer improbability of the thing, impeaching and driving from office a man who had just one year earlier won 60 percent of the vote. There was fear of the precedent it would set. There was public opposition. Even though Nixon had fallen to below 30 percent in his approval rating, well over half the people opposed impeachment, while only 37 percent supported it.[29] There was the muddle over the Vice Presidency. And there was, as always with American politicians, the next election to think about.

Was there a case for impeachment? Nixon was certainly guilty of many serious blunders, of telling many lies, but was he guilty of crimes? Perhaps his financial dealings, coupled with such items as impoundment of funds, the secret bombing of Cambodia, the actions of the Plumbers, and the wiretapping of officials and reporters, would be sufficient to allow the Democrats to use their majority in the House to impeach; but the odds were overwhelming that such charges would not be persuasive enough to lead two thirds of the Senators to vote guilty.

Nixon had made mistakes. He had acted in a high-handed fashion. He had made many enemies. But so had all his predecessors, and none of them had been impeached and found guilty.

It came back to crimes, or what was called the "smoking gun." Without it, Nixon might be impeached, but never found guilty. So had he committed crimes? Provable crimes?

He had ordered break-ins and wiretaps that were clearly illegal, but his cover for them was all but unbreakable. National security had become a fetish since Pearl Harbor; every President since 1941 had used it as an excuse/reason to break the law. Perhaps Nixon had gone further, perhaps he was more guilty—but then his provocation was greater. Daniel Ellsberg had taken classified documents from the Pentagon, he had passed them around, he had violated the law—and he had been lionized by the same media that wanted to persecute Richard Nixon. Whatever Nixon's enemies said, Republican and Southern Democratic senators were not going to find him guilty of a crime because he tried to discredit Ellsberg, no matter what methods he had used.

It all came down to Watergate; indeed, without Watergate, almost none of the multitude of charges being made against Nixon would have seen the light of day. And with regard to Watergate, there was no proof of any kind that he had advance knowledge of the break-in at the DNC, or that he had ordered it. But there had been a cover-up, and he had been deeply involved in it, and that was a crime. If his actions could be proven, not many Republican and almost no Southern Democratic senators were going to stick with him.

Could his involvement in the cover-up be proven? Easily. It was right there on the tapes. Irrefutable. He had told Haldeman and Ehrlichman to tell the CIA to tell the FBI to back off. He had told John Dean to get the hush money and pay it.

Could the tapes—the full, unedited tapes, not a summary—be made available to the House Judiciary Committee? Probably not. Nixon had by no means run out of stalling tactics. He still had options. His greatest asset was his continued physical control of the tapes. The ones that had been subpoenaed, the ones he had promised to turn over to Sirica, were ambiguous, or could be made to appear so. The argument could be made that when Nixon said such and such, or so and so, he was only exploring alternative possibilities in his mind.

Nixon claimed that he was involved in a battle for public opinion. In his own mind, he said, "the main danger of being impeached would come precisely from the public's being conditioned to the idea that I was going to be impeached. In the end, therefore, it would come down to a race for public support."[30]

That may have been true of impeachment, but it was not true with regard to his staying in office. To stay in office, he did not need the public, he did not need the House, he did not need the media; to stay in office, he needed one third of the Senate, period. And so long as he could hold onto the tapes of June 23, 1972, and March 21, 1973, he would have that one third, and more.

Which is not to say that public opinion did not matter, or that Nixon was wrong in saying the conditioning of the public to the idea of impeachment was critical to him as well as to his enemies. And with regard to the public, he still had strengths. Not personal ones, perhaps—millions who voted for him did so because they did not like George McGovern, not because they liked Dick Nixon, and almost everything Nixon had done in the last year made them like him even less—but institutional ones. People wanted to believe in the President, people wanted to rally behind the President, people realized that Nixon was the only President they had. If he had abused their trust, he had not yet completely lost it. He could count on the way the American people made the Presidency into almost a religion as a sustaining force.

He could, that is, so long as there were no more bombshells.

NIXON'S swing through the South after the disaster in Orlando was a success. From Orlando, he flew to Macon, Georgia, to give an address at the Walter George School of Law at Mercer University. A crowd of twenty thousand friendly and cheering people met him at the airport, carrying signs saying, "We Love and Support President Nixon" and "Keep Up the Good Work." In Memphis, a similar warm welcome was punctuated by a sign: "I believe in Nixon and America."[31]

Nixon was in Memphis to meet with the Republican governors at their annual conference. The governors were depressed; recent polls indicated that less than one quarter of the American people identified themselves as Republicans. As in his meetings the previous week with Republican congressmen, Nixon was upbeat and candid; the governors were nonetheless worried.

"Are we going to be blindsided by any more bombshells?" one asked.[32]

Nixon immediately thought of the gap on the tape of his June 20, 1972, conversation with Haldeman. He rationalized that he had not yet heard from Buzhardt on whether or not the conversation could be "recovered," and if not, could be explained. So he replied, "If there are, I'm not aware of them." Headlines the next morning read: "NO MORE BOMBSHELLS."

On the plane ride back to Washington, however, Haig told Nixon that Buzhardt had not been able to recover the conversation, nor could he explain the gap.[33] So even as the newspapers hit the streets, Buzhardt appeared in Sirica's court to inform the judge that there was an 18½-

minute gap in the subpoenaed tape, and he could not explain why it was there.

Sirica responded by asking to have custody of the tapes turned over to the court. "This is just another instance that convinces the court that it has to take some steps, not because the court doesn't trust the White House or the President [but because] the court is interested in seeing that nothing else happens."[34]

The nation responded to the news with shock, followed by massive disbelief. Even before the discovery of the gap, three out of every five Americans polled suspected that the tapes, when handed over to Sirica, would already have been altered to protect Nixon. After the announcement, people polled suspected Nixon by a three to one majority (half those identifying themselves as Republicans shared the suspicion).[35]

Damage control by the Nixon Administration was pathetic. The "gap," Buzhardt had to confess, was the result of an erasure. He thought it might have been caused "by the depression of a record button during the process of reviewing the tape."[36] Rose Mary Woods then testified that she had been transcribing tapes on October 1 when the telephone rang. In reaching for the phone, she said, "through some error on my part," she pressed the "record" button rather than the "stop" button. But she insisted that she had talked for only five minutes over the telephone, and could not explain why the gap was 18½ minutes long. [37]

Sirica then called Haig in to testify. Haig related that Nixon had told him that Woods had been "somewhat imprecise" when she informed him of the gap. He developed his own theory, that Woods was "tired and couldn't remember how long she had been on the phone." He added that "I've known women that think they've talked for five minutes and then have talked for an hour."[38] Overall, Haig thought it possible some "sinister force of energy" had erased the tape.[39]

The court appointed a team of six experts to study and explain the gap. The experts concluded that the erasures were deliberate. Nixon and his supporters challenged that finding.[40]

The 18½-minute gap remains one of the many unsolved mysteries of Watergate. Haldeman's notes for the conversation do exist; they constitute the first documentary evidence of Nixon's initial reaction to the arrest of the burglars in the DNC (the conversation took place three days afterwards). The notes are relatively innocent; Nixon ordered Haldeman to make certain his EOB office was thoroughly checked for electronic bugs at all times, and to start a counterattack ("for diversion") by pointing out that "libertarians" had created public callousness through their praise of Ellsberg.

There are no marching orders to cover up, or to do anything illegal.

Much worse, far more damaging things were said by Nixon on other tapes. Why destroy those 18½ minutes and leave so much else?

Haldeman speculates that after Butterfield revealed the existence of the taping system, Nixon set out to destroy the evidence. He began by listening to the first recorded conversation he had on Watergate and erasing 18½ minutes. But, Haldeman speculates further, he botched the job, due to his ineptness with anything mechanical, and he realized that it would take years of effort to erase everything, so he gave it up.[41] Wood's testimony before Sirica partly reinforced Haldeman. She said that Nixon at Camp David had listened to the tape on a Sony machine: "The President listened to different parts of the tape, pushing the button back and forth."[42]

The Haldeman theory sounds reasonable, but it is inconclusive. No one will ever be able to prove that Nixon did the erasing, or even that the erasure was deliberate. The gap (which is unique; there are no others on the tapes) created no new legal problems for Nixon.

On the public relations front, however, it was a disaster. The "Rose Mary stretch" to the telephone became a national joke. So did Haig's "sinister force." Once again, Nixon and his people were the objects of ridicule. The suspicion and scorn that surrounded the Administration grew.

NIXON had rejected out of hand Len Garment's advice that he resign; but on November 24, Garment was back with another recommendation. The energy crisis was sweeping the nation. Americans, accustomed to cheap, unlimited energy, were facing a future full of doubt. Confusion and despair abounded. The situation created a heaven-sent opportunity for Nixon to show more leadership. Garment told Nixon people were desperate for "a sense of direction," wanted to be shown that "someone is in control, taking care of people's basic needs in a bewildering, even frightening time. . . . It's up to you to give the people the feeling that someone's in charge."

Garment urged Nixon to be "exceptionally tough," and to establish national priorities, even if it meant banning Sunday driving. If he did not act, Garment warned, his critics would "say you were brooding over Watergate, paralyzed, unable to control your advisors, when you should have been thinking of the people's needs, planning ahead, acting."[43]

On November 25, the President responded in a special televised address to the nation. He spoke on the crisis and what he was doing about it. He wanted to arouse the people, but not alarm them. Although shortages could run as high as 17 percent, America was still far better off than Europe, where a three-day work week had been decreed and seven nations had banned Sunday driving. Things were not going to get that bad at home. Already the nation was moving to meet the crisis; the previous week, Nixon said, he had signed the Alaska pipeline bill, and

Congress had passed a fuel allocation bill. He had appointed an Energy Emergency Action Group, under former Governor of Colorado John Love. Now Nixon had a series of additional actions to announce.

First, he was reducing the flow of gasoline supplies from refiners to retailers by 15 percent, so as to continue a near-normal production of heating oil. Second, he was asking all gasoline filling stations to close down their pumps between 9 P.M. Saturday night and midnight Sunday on a voluntary basis beginning immediately, and asking Congress for legislation to make such closing mandatory. Third, he was asking Congress to impose a national speed limit of 50 miles per hour (55 for trucks and buses that used diesel fuel). Fourth, he was ordering a 25 percent reduction in jet fuel for passenger flights. Fifth, he wanted Congress to give him the authority to order the curtailment of ornamental outdoor lighting for homes and nearly all commercial lighting. He would set the example by cutting back on the lighting on the national Christmas tree. Sixth, he was instituting a program of allocations for heating oil, which would include a reduction of 15 percent for homes, 25 percent for commercial use.[44]

Except for the Christmas tree lights, these were all serious steps that met Garment's recommendations for tough action. As always, there were those in Washington who did not think they were tough enough. Governor Love, for example, had wanted to make the closing of filling stations on Sundays mandatory immediately; he counseled that it could be imposed under the Economic Stabilization Act. But Nixon wanted a fresh legislative mandate to make certain that Congress explicitly shared in the responsibility for such an unpopular measure. Further, Love was rumored to want rationing, which Nixon opposed, as did Treasury Secretary Shultz. Within a week, Love resigned. Nixon appointed William Simon, a conservative investment banker and Deputy Secretary of the Treasury, to replace Love. Simon told reporters his solution for gasoline shortages was to let prices rise.

Love's resignation illustrated a point Garment had made in his November 24 memo. No matter how tough Nixon was on energy, Garment had written, he had to be realistic; Watergate would still be there. In a statement following his resignation, Love did not cite policy differences with Nixon. Instead, he said, "It's been difficult to try to do anything meaningful and even to get the attention of the President."[45]

That judgment undercut Nixon's closing section of his energy address. The President had promised to give the crisis his full attention.[46]

In the first week of December, as Nixon's energy measures went into effect, there were noticeable changes on the American highways. There were fewer cars on the road, especially on Sundays, and they drove slower than they had since World War II (when, to save rubber, the national speed limit was 35 miles per hour). Businesses dependent on traffic—motels, drive-ins, tourist attractions—experienced a sharp drop-off in trade. Truckers, protesting the lowered speed limits, blocked some highways. In a few states the national guard had to be called out. All this distracted attention from Nixon's problems, but not in a way that was of much help to him.

ON December 6, after pro forma confirmation hearings, Congress approved Ford's appointment as Vice President (92–3 in the Senate, 387–35 in the House). If Nixon believed that putting Ford into the number-two spot ensured that he would not be impeached, as Haldeman has asserted, the thunderous cheers and applause that greeted the vote proved how wrong he was. Many Republicans in private, and some in public, expressed the hope that Ford would quickly become the nation's thirty-eighth President. Democrats who wanted no part of a Carl Albert Presidency said openly that they were now ready to impeach. Albert himself was visibly relieved, indeed overjoyed. [47]

Ford met with Nixon. Nixon wanted Ford's swearing-in ceremony in the White House, but Ford wanted it to take place in the Capitol, where he had served for twenty-five years and where he had been confirmed. Haig was opposed; he wanted it in the East Room of the White House, where he could control the audience. He feared the reception Nixon might receive in the House Chambers. But Ford told Nixon that "the place to have it is in the Capitol. That would be a much better place for my relations with the Congress and for yours as well," and Nixon agreed. [48]

At 5:30 P.M. the two men entered the House Chamber, to rising applause. Nixon was beaming, as if the applause was for him. For all that he had endured from these politicians, after all the damage that he had suffered, he assumed a posture of full command, carrying out the ceremony with total aplomb.

"I am a Ford, not a Lincoln," the new Vice President said, in an opening that captured the nation's heart. "My addresses will never be as eloquent as Mr. Lincoln's. But I will do my very best to equal his brevity and his plain speaking." His confirmation, he said, "demonstrated to the world that our great Republic stands solid, stands strong upon the bedrock of the Constitution." For his part, Ford hit exactly the right note. Nixon, however, must have had at least a touch of trepidation, as it was obvious that most of those in the chamber could hardly wait to drop the word "Vice" from Ford's title.

Following the ceremony, Nixon and Ford drove to the White House, where they met alone. "Congratulations," Nixon said. "It's good to have a teammate at last." He then assured Ford that he was innocent of all Watergate complicity. Nixon said the charges against him were just partisan attacks that would soon go away, as people grew tired of them. [49]

•

NIXON was right in saying that people were growing tired of Watergate, but wrong in thinking that for that reason it would go away. There were continued truck blockades on the interstate highways. In the first week of December, fighting in Vietnam reached pre-armistice levels. In the Middle East, the cease-fire was barely holding and there was no disengagement in sight. The inflation rate was rising and threatening to get much worse as fuel costs escalated. The Japanese and Europeans were desperate for fuel. Ford's confirmation and inaugural ceremony were historic events.

Yet the top of the news, on television and in the papers, was Nixon's financial situation. Rumors, innuendos, charges filled the press and the networks.

It was obvious that Nixon needed to do something to answer the charges. He had a precedent in the Checkers speech, but it was not relevant, because Nixon had given the Checkers speech, which was brilliant or maudlin depending on one's point of view, within days of the accusation. In 1973, the accusations had started in January and were increasing in number and seriousness eleven months later, but still Nixon had done little to refute them.

At the end of the first week of December Nixon issued a statement on his finances. Ziegler explained that the delay had been caused by three factors: it took time to gather the data; Nixon had not initially seen the peril in which the accusations placed him; the President clung stubbornly to the idea that his finances were private. His critics suggested a fourth reason: Nixon was fearful of new disclosures and wanted the attacks to run their course before making his defense.[50]

The delay hurt him in another way, by reinforcing the impression that he would not answer charges until absolutely forced to do so. He had waited too long to force the resignations of Haldeman and Ehrlichman in the spring, too long to respond to the clamor for a news conference, too long to release the tapes. The result was that he seemed to make gestures to public indignation at precisely the point when those gestures had lost their power to soothe. Another price had to be paid. By releasing his financial record, he was setting yet another precedent that could only weaken the office and its holders.

In his covering statement, released on December 8, Nixon said that the tax and financial records he was making public would "lay to rest . . . false rumors" and answer "questions outstanding in the public mind" about his affairs. He added that he was making the records public "because the confidentiality of my private finances is far less important to me than the confidence of the American people in the integrity of the President."

He dealt head on with the charges that $10 million or more of government money had been spent on his residences in Florida and California. The figure was grossly exaggerated, he said, and in any case most of the money had been spent on office complexes near his private homes, not on the homes themselves. What was spent on the homes was for security purposes, and did not increase their value; indeed, if anything, the devices lowered the value.

Nixon said that the Western White House complex would continue to be "a valuable asset" for the nation, as a conference center. In order to make it a greater asset, he wished to add La Casa Pacifica to the complex. "Accordingly, at the time of my death or that of my wife, whichever is later, we intend to make a gift to the people of the United States of my home at San Clemente."[51] (Six years later, he sold La Casa Pacifica at a hefty profit to a consortium of Orange County businessmen.[52])

The detailed report showed that Nixon had made $328,000 in 1969, and paid $72,700 in taxes. In 1970, he made $263,000 and paid $793. In 1971, he made $262,000 and paid $878. In 1972, the figures were $269,000 and $4,300.

Those were the figures that looked awful and hurt the most. Especially damaging was the relevation that Nixon had escaped taxes thanks to his more than half-million-dollar deduction on his gift of his vice presidential papers to the National Archives (that deduction alone was worth more than $300,000 to him), and that he had backdated the deed of gift in order to evade a change in the law made by Congress in 1969.

There were other problem areas. Some of the money had come from salary, some from interest, some from book royalties. But the bulk of it came from his real estate investments. In 1967, Nixon had borrowed money from two Miami banks to purchase 199,891 shares of stock in Bebe Rebozo's company, Fisher's Island, Inc., for $1 per share. After becoming President, Nixon sold the stock back to Rebozo and other investors in the closed corporation for $2 per share.

Nixon wasn't the only one to benefit. Rose Mary Woods had purchased 10,000 shares at $1 each, which the Fisher's Island corporation had bought back at $2 per share. Manolo Sanchez, Nixon's valet, turned over 1,000 shares at identical prices. Pat Buchanan held 3,000 shares.

Nixon had another deal going in Key Biscayne. In 1967, he had purchased two vacant lots on the island from the Cape Florida Development Company, for $38,080. He brought Tricia in as his partner. In late 1972, the partners sold the lots for a profit of $111,000, with Tricia getting $45,000 and the President the rest.

The record Nixon released said, in summary, that in addition to his real estate holdings (which he had just told the National Association of Realtors were his only investment), he had $149,000 in a checking account at the Rebozo Bank in Miami, $27,000 in a savings account there, and $250,000 in certificates of deposit.[53]

To the average voter, these were stupendous figures. Even to Nixon's big money friends, men like Rebozo, Abplanalp, Elmer Bobst (who had given Julie a $25,000 trust fund in 1958), or Don Kendall, chief executive officer of Pepsi-Cola, these were not paltry sums. Still, except for the questionable deduction for backdating the vice presidential papers, Nixon had done nothing illegal. It is not against the law to make a profit on real estate transactions. It is not against the law to borrow money from your friends. It is not against the law to help out your secretary, your valet, your speechwriter, or your children with their financial situations.

Nor was Nixon the first President to profit from his association with millionaires. Lyndon Johnson had hardly set a good example in this regard, and come to that neither had Dwight Eisenhower. Eisenhower had gotten a highly favorable ruling from the Truman Administration Treasury Department on his earnings from *Crusade in Europe*—he paid at a capital-gains rather than ordinary income rate, which was worth $250,000 or more to him (to Truman's fury, the Eisenhower Treasury Department ruled that Truman had to pay at the income tax rate on his memoirs!).

But Nixon was the one who got caught. It infuriated him, especially because his attempt to rescue himself through the unprecedented release of his records only made matters worse. On the day he released his statement, he declared that he would let the Joint Congressional Committee on Internal Revenue Taxation review his deductions and the profits from his San Clemente transaction. He promised that if the Committee decided his deductions were not allowable, he would pay whatever tax might be due. Four months later the Committee ruled that he owed nearly half a million dollars and he had to pay up. That probably did not hurt as much as the public's reaction at the time of the release of his records: only 26 percent thought he had been honest, while 56 percent though he had been dishonest.[54]

He had lost the battle for public opinion on this issue. Although the Congress was never going to impeach him over his finances—he was surely right in asserting that few politicians in Washington could survive intact the kind of searching examination of their tax returns that he had undergone—he had lost where it counted most. He saw himself as an honest man unfairly pilloried; the public saw him as Tricky Dick.

ON December 17, the Senate voted 75–10 to confirm William Saxbe as Attorney General, but only after Saxbe assured his colleagues that he would "vigorously support" the Special Prosecutor in his investigations. "I'll fight for his right to proceed as he sees fit," Saxbe said of Jaworski. "It's a covenant I made with myself that the chips were going to have to fall as they may."[55]

Mel Laird announced, on December 19, his resignation as presidential counselor, effective February 1, 1974, and said he believed a vote on impeaching Nixon "would be a healthy thing."[56] The same day, Chairman Rodino of the House Judiciary Committee said that he hoped to report to the House on the impeachment inquiry in April. He also announced the selection of John M. Doar, fifty-two, a Republican who had been a member of the Johnson and Kennedy administrations in the Justice Department, as special counsel to the committee to head the impeachment probe.

Billy Graham, in *Christianity Today*, expressed his confidence in Nixon's integrity, but added that "some of his judgments have been wrong and I just don't agree with them." Nixon, he said, "has made mistakes, and this is one of them: you cannot, as President, isolate yourself."[57]

Graham's criticism, mild as it was, hurt a lot, because it was so unusual for him. Barry Goldwater, always outspoken, cut to the quick with his criticism. "I've never known a man to be so much a loner in any field," he said in an interview in the *Christian Science Monitor* printed on December 19. "The President, I think, thinks of himself as the supreme politician in this country. And being a loner, I think he sits by himself and tells himself what he's going to do. Now he went through this gesture period of having congressmen and senators down to see him—but it seems to have ended. . . . He's not getting advice . . . and when he gets it, he doesn't listen to it."[58]

If it came to impeachment, Graham would not have a vote, but Goldwater would. Hours after his interview appeared in the *Monitor*, Goldwater received an invitation to have dinner that very evening in the White House. Other guests included Bryce Harlow and his wife, Pat Buchanan and his wife, Ray Price, Julie and David Eisenhower, Rose Woods, and Mary Brooks, director of the U.S. Mint.

When the guests had assembled in the Yellow Oval Sitting Room, before a crackling Christmas fire, Pat Nixon greeted them. They sipped at their sherry and exchanged small talk. The President entered, quite amiable, even garrulous. He moved around the room, shaking hands. As usual, his conversation in such a situation was stilted. He jumped from topic to topic. Goldwater recorded: "His mind seemed to halt abruptly and wander aimlessly away. Each time, after several such lapses, he would snap back to a new subject. I became concerned. I had never seen Nixon talk so much, yet so erratically—as if he were a tape with unexpected blank sections."

Pat moved the party into the private family dining room. Nixon, at the head of the table, rambled on about the wines. Then he wanted advice on whether or not he should take a train to Florida, in view of the energy crisis. He struck Goldwater as talking "gibberish." The senator snapped out, "Act like a President."

There was a cold, embarrassed silence. Then Nixon got going on the train again. He was hunching over his plate and dropping his shoulders, continuing his "ceaseless, chippy chatter . . . incessantly sputtering something, constantly switching subjects." Goldwater wondered, "Is the President coming apart because of Watergate?"

Unexpectedly, Nixon turned to Goldwater, at the other end of the table, to ask, "How do I stand, Barry?"

There was another silence. Everyone turned to the senator with frozen smiles. Goldwater said people were divided, that some wanted him to go and others wished him to stay.

Julie looked at her plate. Price and Buchanan stared off into the distance. Woods toyed with her salad. Nixon peered into the bottom of his wineglass.

Finally, Nixon spoke. He returned to the subject of the train to Florida, then got going on the energy crisis. Harlow offered his views. Nixon cut him off, to launch an attack on the liberals in the media. Once again Goldwater wondered about the President's mental balance.

Nixon took up foreign policy. Pat jumped in to criticize Kissinger for taking too much credit. David and Julie supported her vigorously. Nixon observed that all the initiatives, to China and the Soviet Union and the rest, had been his.

This went on through the dinner. Goldwater recorded that Nixon "jabbered incessantly, often incoherently, to the end." Deeply worried, even distressed, Goldwater phoned Harlow the following day; Harlow told him that Nixon had been drunk before and during dinner, which explained his behavior.[59]

On December 22, Nixon attended the annual meeting between the President and the Joint Chiefs. Admiral Zumwalt, who was upset over cuts in the Navy's budget, wanted to tell Nixon his feelings. Secretary of Defense Schlesinger warned him not to do so. According to Schlesinger, "to give a briefing like that in the White House these days would be just like shooting yourself in the foot. The President is paranoid."

Zumwalt tried to make his case anyway, but was able to deliver only a small part of his briefing because "the President used the ostensible budget meeting to engage in a long, rambling monologue, which at times almost seemed to be a stream of consciousness, about the virtues of his domestic and foreign policy. He repeatedly expressed the thought that the eastern liberal establishment was out to do us all in and that we should beware." Nixon saw the various attacks on him "as part of a vast plot by intellectual snobs to destroy a president who was representative of the man in the street." To Zumwalt, "it was clear he perceived himself as a fighter for all that was right in the United States, involved in mortal battle with the forces of evil."

Zumwalt felt that while Nixon certainly was not "the haggard, palsied, drunken wreck" portrayed in the Washington rumor mill, "he did present the very disturbing spectacle of a man who had pumped his adrenalin up to such high pressure that he was on an emotional binge. He appeared to me to be incapable of carrying on a rational conversation."[60]

Nixon retreated to Camp David, where on December 23 he scribbled across the top of one of his yellow pads, "Last Christmas here?"

On Christmas Day, he was back in the White House, with his family and Rose Mary Woods. Over the turkey dinner in the Red Room, Pat tried to cheer up her downcast husband, but he remained subdued. Finally he grew nostalgic and began to talk about his first Christmas away from home, at Duke University Law School. He was one of only two students who could not afford the trip home for the holidays, he recalled, and a kindly professor had invited the two young men to his home for Christmas dinner. Nixon said he had never forgotten that kindness.

He switched to more current events. He mentioned some of his triumphs—the trip to China, the meeting with Brezhnev in Moscow, his conversations with Golda Meir in October. He announced a decision to fly to San Clemente for New Year's Eve on a commercial airline, in order to save fuel.[61]

During Christmas week, he did have occasions to act presidential. He got in a blast at Congress for failing to act on his energy proposals. On December 24, he had signed the District of Columbia Self-Government Act. On the 28th, he signed the bill creating the Lyndon Johnson Memorial Grove on the Potomac, and the Endangered Species Act. None of this roused him out of his depression. The flight on United Airlines to California turned out to be a big mistake; Tricia reported that it was the "most strained" she ever experienced. For the five-and-a-half-hour flight, the eyes of his fellow first-class passengers were glued on him—even during the movie. When he got to San Clemente, there was an unusual cold snap, and La Casa Pacifica was not heated.

On New Year's Eve, Nixon asked Rebozo if he should resign. Rebozo's answer was predictable: "No, you can't. You have to fight."[62]

After toasting in the New Year, with who could guess what emotions, Nixon went to bed. He picked up a tortoise-shell-bound note pad Pat had given him, which he kept at his bedside table, and jotted down the time—1:15 A.M. He wrote, "The basic question is: Do I fight all out or do I now begin the long process to prepare for a change, meaning, in effect, resignation?"

His answer was as predictable as Rebozo's to the same question. The idea of resignation was "anathema," not so much because of his personal desire, more because of the good of the country. If he resigned, it "would change our whole form of government." The precedent would give future opponents of future Presidents "a formidable new leverage." In addition, if he resigned, "the press will become a much too dominant force in the nation." Finally, his resignation "could lead to a collapse of our foreign policy initiatives."

So, "the *answer—fight.*"

When he woke later that morning, he picked up the pad and added further reasons to resist resignation, such as to do so "admits guilt." He made a resolve: "Only substance, not politics, must affect this decision." Then he listed the priorities of his tactics. Number one was to hold a press conference.[63]

THE obvious conflict between his resolve to emphasize substance and his priority, to start his next counterattack with a public relations thrust, was typical of the man. Despite the tremendous strain he was under, the ever-increasing pressure, the nightmarish quality of his problems, the sense of falling and falling and falling further into a void, he remained true to his instincts. He would fight back as he had from the lowest point in the Hiss case, and from the lowest point in the 1952 fund crisis, by making his case to the public.

The difference was that in 1974, the substance was not there. In taking his case to the public, he was shooting blanks. Worse than blanks, really, because the ammunition he had in his arsenal would, if used, backfire on him, as his arsenal was the tapes.

What was at stake was not the future of the Presidency, but rather the future of Richard Nixon. Although his argument that his resignation would weaken his successors had merit, indeed was all but irrefutable, his difficulty was that by remaining in office he was inevitably weakening his successors, as the War Powers Act showed. This simple truth made it impossible for him to decide on a clear objective, the first requirement of a successful counterattack. Should he go after public opinion? Or the media? Or the Congress? Or the courts?

Nor could he choose a clear tactical concept. Should he use arguments about the future of the Presidency? Or about the importance of his foreign-policy initiatives? Or about the unfairness of the Democrats in attacking him for actions for which their Presidents had set the precedent? Or about the dangers to the Republic if the Democrats got away with reversing the results of the 1972 election?

Or should he emphasize his innocence? Only a convincing case that he was innocent would save him now. He knew that, because he knew that his fellow politicians lived in the here and now. Their idea of a long-term future was the next election. They believed that future Presidents would have to take care of themselves. Their concentration was on Nixon and what he had done, not future Presidents and what they might do.

All Republican representatives, and some senators, were most concerned with the effect of a continued Nixon Presidency on their own re-election chances in November. Democrats had to wonder if they might not be better off with a beleaguered and defiant Nixon rather than a reassuring and confidence-inspiring Ford in the White House. But they also had to recognize that their strongest supporters, the ones who put up the money or did the volunteer campaign work, lusted to see the hated Nixon brought down. Every even-numbered year in American political life, beginning in January, the politicians cast their votes on the basis of what effect those votes would have in November. Those were the rules of the game Nixon had played by all his life, and he had no reason to think they would be any different in 1974.

It all came back to this: he was guilty of covering up, and his own words provided the irrefutable truth of his guilt. His fate resided in his tapes, the tapes he had once counted on for his salvation. If he could hold onto them, he might survive. If he lost control, he was doomed.

CHAPTER TWELVE

PEACE, PROSPERITY, AND PUBLIC RELATIONS
January–March 1974

NIXON SPENT the first two weeks of 1974 at La Casa Pacifica, in seclusion. Except for Haig and Ziegler, he saw none of his aides. Except for Secretary of State Kissinger, he saw no one from the Cabinet. Roy Ash, director of OMB, flew out to go over the budget with Nixon, but he never got to see the President. Bebe Rebozo flew out to be with his friend; the two men went for some roving freeway drives together. Sometimes Ed and Tricia Cox, and Pat, joined them. Once they drove to Palm Springs, to spend the night as guests at the magnificent estate of Walter Annenberg, U.S. Ambassador to Britain. On the way, they stopped at a McDonald's restaurant in Banning; Nixon stayed in the car to eat his hamburger and fries.

It was a dreary time. It rained almost constantly, there was a minor earthquake, and the tide in front of Nixon's home was the highest in three hundred years. Nixon dealt with bouts of insomnia by playing the piano in the early hours. Only twice did he get to play golf.[1]

The New Year got off to a terrible start, as Nixon embarrassed his wife and his friends and his brother. Nixon had appointed Pat chairman of the new twenty-five-member National Voluntary Service Advisory Council, for a regular government consultant fee of $138.48 for each day she worked at council duties. On January 1, Warren had to admit that it was illegal for the President to name his wife to any governmental position and that Mrs. Nixon's name had accordingly been withdrawn. The same day, reporters interviewed Mrs. Edward Nixon, the President's sister-in-law. They wanted to know what Nixon's youngest brother, Ed, did to earn his $21,000 annual consultant's fee from a tax-exempt foundation

289

created by Leonard Firestone and others to build the Nixon Presidential Library.

"I don't want any publicity," Mrs. Nixon told the reporters. "While he's off being paid to do nothing, I'm here alone. I'm trying to teach school and I've got two kids and let me tell you, it's tough."[2] Meanwhile, as the 1973 income tax forms began to arrive at American households, the papers were full of critical stories about Nixon's tax returns.

There were some changes in the President's legal team. Charles Alan Wright, upset that he had not been told about the nonexistent tapes, unhappy because he had not been allowed to listen to the tapes that did exist, returned to the University of Texas Law School, although he remained available for counsel. Buzhardt was named as a presidential counsel, technically a promotion but widely seen as a reflection of presidential dissatisfaction with his work. Garment also got a technical promotion, to the post of assistant to the President for domestic affairs. Both Garment and Buzhardt continued to work on Watergate legal matters, but on Chuck Colson's suggestion Nixon named Boston lawyer James St. Clair to head his legal defense team.

St. Clair had been an assistant to Joseph Welch as Army counsel during the McCarthy-Army hearings in 1954. Many who had watched the dramatic confrontation between Welch and Senator Joseph R. McCarthy felt that Welch had destroyed McCarthy with his seemingly naïve courtroom manner. Nixon, Colson, and Haig may have hoped that St. Clair had learned from the master, Welch, and could similarly destroy John Dean on national television.

Nixon still had supporters. On January 7, Bob Stripling sent Woods a handwritten letter from Texas. He commended her for her "poise and indulgence" in her recent appearance in Sirica's courtroom, and asked her to "remind your boss that the people of this country outside the environs of Washington and New York" were behind the President. Woods showed the letter to Nixon, who scribbled on the bottom a reply: "Dear Strip, many thanks. We shall eventually win as we did with your superb help in the Hiss case."[3]

On January 6, Nixon made his first public appearance in two weeks, when he attended services at the San Clemente Presbyterian Church. Sad to relate, he couldn't even go to church without being heckled. Demonstrators surrounded the church, waving hostile banners, chanting for impeachment, and booing Nixon when he emerged.[4]

His friends tried to cheer him up. John Wayne came for dinner. On January 9, his staff had a surprise birthday party for him. He offered a lick of a huge cake to his dog, King Timahoe, explaining that he had acquired King on his birthday five years earlier. Nixon leaned against the desk on which the cake was sitting, slipped, and got his hand and jacket covered with icing. He glanced around in confusion, hoping someone would think of some way to deal with the situation.

"Let King lick it off," one of his aides suggested. Nixon sat in his chair, stuck out his arm, and King happily licked him clean.[5]

John Connally called, to wish him a happy birthday, but the sentiment was marred by the gossip Connally passed along. He had just been in Washington, he said, where he learned of a group of Republicans from the West (he called them the "Arizona Mafia") that was plotting to force Nixon to resign. "Some of them are men you think are your very good friends," Connally warned. Their plan was to delay the impeachment vote until the summer, to visit Nixon after he returned from the scheduled summit conference in Moscow in June, and to tell him so many Republicans in the House were going to lose their seats if he stayed in the White House that he had to resign. Although Haig said this was just the Washington rumor mill at work, Connally told Nixon it was serious.[6]

There was more unwelcome news. On January 6, Gallup released poll figures that showed Nixon had fallen 39 points in his approval rating in the past year. He was down to 29 percent. It was the steepest decline since Gallup first started the poll back in the 1930s.

Nixon was getting some work done in California. On January 2, he signed a bill to reduce speed limits nationwide to 55 miles per hour. The next day, he signed a bill raising Social Security benefits. Later that week he issued a statement admitting that he had taken "traditional political considerations" into account in ordering an increase in milk price supports in 1971, but asserted that charges that he had granted favors to milk producers and to ITT in return for campaign contributions were "utterly false." He had HEW Secretary Caspar Weinberger leak a proposal for federally supported private medical insurance for all Americans.[7]

But what captured the headlines was his defiance of a subpoena from the Senate Select Committee for some 492 Watergate-related tapes and documents. In a January 4 letter to Senator Ervin, Nixon said that "to produce the material you now seek would unquestionably destroy any vestige of confidentiality of Presidential communications." He accused Ervin and his colleagues of wanting to "rummage" through his files in a fishing expedition that would "serve no legislative purpose which I can discern." Nixon admitted that in "the current environment" there would be "some" who would "distort my position as only an effort to withhold information," but said he would take that risk anyway, because he had to "protect the Office of the President against incursion."[8]

On January 13, after three rounds of golf with Rebozo on Annenberg's private course, Nixon flew from the Palm Springs airport back to Washington. He used a small government aircraft, a JetStar, rather than *Air Force One*, to save fuel.

•

As always the turning of the calendar into an even-numbered year concentrated the minds of the politicians on the first Tuesday in November. With gas lines, truckers' strikes, and double-digit inflation, the voters were unhappy, which made incumbents fearful. The most worried incumbent was the man at the top, even though he was not up for re-election.

Still, Nixon was far from despairing. He believed that "the same two issues that had swayed off-year elections for as long as I had been in public life, would ultimately tip the balance in this one, too." Those issues were peace and prosperity.[9] Those issues were his. He had brought peace to the world, and despite inflation and the energy crisis, the country was prosperous. For that reason, he thought Goldwater and other Republicans were wrong in their gloomy predictions. He expected his party at least to hold its own in the 1974 elections.

Nixon's anticipation showed just how skewed his thinking had become. No matter how prosperous and peaceful the country was in 1974, the issue that dominated all others was Richard Nixon and his role in the Watergate cover-up. All he had to do to realize that was to glance at the newspapers or the evening television newscasts. On December 23, 1973, OPEC had raised the price of oil again; the hike meant that oil had gone up 387 percent in two months. Kissinger correctly called this jump "one of the pivotal events in the history of this century . . . a colossal blow to [European, American, and Japanese] balance of payments, economic growth, employment, price stability, and social cohesion."[10] Even leaving aside the economic impact, the political effects of the price rise were staggering, more so than Watergate and its aftermath. Yet the news in America remained dominated by the person of Richard Nixon and his past actions.

To some extent, Nixon was aware of this problem. On January 5, he had written a note to himself: "Above all else: Dignity, command, faith, head high, no fear, build a new spirit, drive, act like a President, act like a winner." That was good advice, certainly, but he spoiled much of the effect of it by going incessantly on the counterattack. His note continued, "Opponents are savage destroyers, haters. Time to use full power of the President to fight overwhelming forces arrayed against us."[11]

Nixon carried that urge to confrontation with him back to Washington. As he worked on his State of the Union address, and all the positive and leadershiplike points he wished to make, his mind returned over and over again to his central problem. So he was tempted to destroy the tapes. He entertained the idea of using the State of the Union address to announce that "Enough is enough," and that therefore he was destroying the tapes. Haig and Ziegler talked him out of it. They argued that it was not the time to draw lines and force confrontations.[12] Besides, to destroy the tapes now would surely lead to a national uproar that would make even the reaction to the firing of Cox look mild.

Nixon went back to revise the State of the Union speech. As he did so, he put Buchanan to work on a speech for Ford. On January 15, Ford delivered it to the American Farm Bureau Federation in Atlantic City. In a style typical of Buchanan but untypical of Ford, the Vice President lashed out at Nixon's foes, calling them "a few extreme partisans." He charged that "their aim is total victory for themselves and the total defeat not only of President Nixon but of the policies for which he stands." If they were successful, Ford said, "the super-welfare staters" would take control. "We can expect an avalanche of fresh government intervention in our economy, massive new government spending, higher taxes and a more rampant inflation."[13]

That same evening Barry Goldwater spoke at a Republican fund-raiser in Baltimore. He said he did not think Nixon "will ever resign and I don't believe the liberal Democrats have what it takes, either in evidence or guts, to push through an impeachment." Asked about rumors that he was slated to be the bearer of the Republican Party's message to Nixon that he had to resign, Goldwater denied it. Indeed, he said, in his opinion Nixon had "started a recovery" and was "better off now" than two months earlier. He concluded, "Let's get off his back."[14]

A week later, Congress reconvened. After talking in the halls with his colleagues, Goldwater sounded less sure of Nixon's future. He said that unless some "magic" redeemed the President, "it's going to be god-damned tough for any Republican to get re-elected." He feared Watergate would cost Republicans a "disastrous" 10 percent of the total vote, and admitted that "many Republican members of Congress would like to run this year without Mr. Nixon." He added: "We have a good man in the vice president and there would be no transition problem at all." Ford, he said, was "Mr. Clean, an All-American boy. Everybody likes him."[15]

That same day, January 22, Nixon met with eighteen Republicans from the House. He authorized Representative Peter Frelinghuysen (N.J.) to quote his remarks to the press. "There is a time to be timid," the President had said. "There is a time to be conciliatory. There is a time, even, to fly and there is a time to fight. And I'm going to fight like hell."[16]

Positive developments in foreign affairs reinforced Nixon's truculent mood. They were not of his making, but he took the credit for them. There was a nice piece of irony here. Henry Kissinger had been awarded the Nobel Peace Prize for his role in achieving a cease-fire in Vietnam, but the man who deserved the credit for the settlement, or the blame for the flawed agreement, was Nixon. The President made the policy in Vietnam; the National Security Adviser carried the messages. In the Middle East in 1974, however, it would be Kissinger who supplied the energy and the skill that led to a cease-fire and then a disengagement, Kissinger who deserved the credit.

Kissinger was aware of the irony. When he had learned that he, along with Le Duc Tho, was being given the Nobel Prize, back in October of 1973, Kissinger had gone to see Nixon. He acknowledged that "there was no recognition for which he [Nixon] yearned more than that of peace-maker," and that "only those who knew Nixon well could perceive beneath the gallant congratulations the strain and hurt that I was being given all the credit for actions that had cost him so much."[17]

At the beginning of January 1974, Kissinger flew to San Clemente for a series of meetings with the President. Nixon's preoccupation with Watergate and his own future was such that he could give his attention to foreign policy only in fits and starts. Kissinger covered for him. At a January 3 news conference, he had stressed that Nixon was functioning effectively in foreign affairs. Asked about rumors that he, the Secretary of State, and not Nixon, the President, was actually in control of American foreign policy, Kissinger dismissed them as "totally incorrect."[18]

A week later, Kissinger had inaugurated what he described as "shuttle diplomacy." Moving back and forth between Egypt and Israel, displaying indefatigable energy and an impressive sensitivity to nuance and to each side's needs, as well as to the personalities of Golda Meir and Anwar Sadat and to the conflicting demands of the Egyptian and Israeli armed forces, Kissinger managed to achieve a disengagement. It was a great accomplishment, and Kissinger fully deserved the tribute Nixon paid him for his "enormous stamina, his incisive intellect, and, not least, his great personal charm."[19]

On January 17, the disengagement of Egyptian and Israeli troops had been achieved. On January 21, Kissinger returned to Washington, where he briefed Nixon. He found the President "elated" and "extraordinarily proud" of the role the United States had played.[20] But the disengagement was only a first step in bringing about a normalization of relations, and from the perspective of American voters not the most decisive step. The OPEC embargo of oil remained in place. Nixon wanted Sadat's help in bringing it to an end, as a quid pro quo for Kissinger's having saved his army from the Israelis. But although Sadat was the leader of the most populous Arab nation, of all the Arab leaders he controlled the least amount of oil. Saudi Arabia controlled the most, and King Faisal would not lift the embargo until a Syrian-Israeli disengagement took place. Nixon appealed to Sadat to go to Faisal to get him to lift the embargo; Sadat sent an envoy; Faisal stalled. The embargo continued.

So did the gas lines, and sky-rocketing inflation, and truckers' strikes. Congress, meanwhile, had failed to act on most of Nixon's energy proposals. The United States, as a consequence, was having an energy crisis in the midst of its Watergate crisis. Worse for Nixon, as he tried to lead the country, was the climate of disbelief which led otherwise sensible people to doubt that there really was an energy crisis. People said it was all a put-up job by the oil companies to increase their already gross profits.

So widespread were the rumors that Nixon decided to attack them head on in a nationwide radio address. Speaking on January 19, he assured his audience that the energy shortage was "genuine," and praised the American people for the conservation measures they had already taken.

Nixon wanted people to take the situation seriously, but he did not want to frighten them. He declared, "Scare stories that the American people will soon be paying a dollar for a gallon of gas are just as ridiculous as the stories that say that we will be paying a dollar for a loaf of bread. The American people cannot afford to pay such prices, and I can assure you that we will not have to pay them."[21]

Democratic leaders in the Senate responded with a call for gas rationing. Nixon refused even to consider it. That left him stuck with a Congress that would not pass his proposals, with an escalating inflation rate, with a Dow Jones average that had fallen from 1,000 a year earlier to the 800s, with gas lines, with sharply rising food prices and possible wheat shortages, all in the midst of his personal crisis. The newspapers and television news programs continued to headline Nixon's taxes, the money spent on his homes, the tapes, and other past actions, rather than his leadership in the energy crisis.

Washington was obsessed with the question of Nixon's credibility. James Kilpatrick, a Nixon supporter, said in his column that Republicans had to confront the "monstrous idea" that their leader was a liar. Kilpatrick did not want to believe it, "but only Richard Nixon himself can dispel the idea now."[22]

Nixon moved to do that. On the morning after his radio address on energy, he had Haig brief Senator Hugh Scott (R.-Pa.) on the Nixon-Dean meeting of March 21, 1973. Haig showed Scott the edited transcript of the conversation, the one originally done for Senator Stennis. Scott later told reporters that having seen the evidence, he was confident "the President would be exculpated entirely."[23]

The following morning, January 21, Nixon summoned Ford to the Oval Office for a one-hour and forty-five-minute meeting. Nixon did 90 percent of the talking. He insisted that he had material in hand that would prove his innocence, and offered to show it to Ford, who responded that he thought it would be better if he did not look at it. Nixon assured Ford he had "absolutely nothing" to do with the 18½-minute gap.

"Then," Ford recorded, "he began to ramble about the political history of our time and the things we'd done together in Congress years before." Ford found it "embarrassing." He kept looking at his watch, but Nixon failed to take the hint and continued to talk "irrelevancies." He struck Ford as "a prisoner in the Oval Office."[24]

When Ford finally got away, reporters pounced on him. He assured them that the President was in good health, "mentally and physically." On the subject of the March 21 tape, Ford said that he took Scott and Nixon's word for it that the tape contained no evidence that Nixon had done anything impeachable.[25]

Leon Jaworski, meanwhile, had been listening to the tape, rather than reading a White House-prepared and Nixon-approved summary of it. He was "stunned" to hear Nixon urging his aides to commit perjury and moving people around as "chessmen" to "cover this thing up."

Jaworski told Haig that he thought Nixon was guilty, a remark that left Haig "surprised" and "visibly shaken." Haig tried to talk him out of the evidence of his own ears, but could not. Jaworski let St. Clair know that he expected the grand jury to request an opportunity to meet with and question the President. St. Clair rejected the possibility of presidential testimony, but Jaworski said he was going to pursue it.[26]

On January 22, Jaworski met with St. Clair again. The lawyers in the Special Prosecutor's Office (who outnumbered Nixon's lawyers 25 to 1) had listened to the tapes that had been turned over to Sirica in late November. The tapes had convinced them that not only was the President guilty, but it was likely that other tapes would add to the evidence against him. Accordingly, Jaworski was requesting twenty-five more taped conversations from the White House. St. Clair said he would pass on the request to Nixon.[27]

Others wanted evidence only Nixon could give. Out in California, Ehrlichman's trial for the break-in at Daniel Ellsberg's psychiatrist's office was about to begin. Ehrlichman was seeking a subpoena to force Nixon to testify personally in the trial. Ehrlichman's point was that he had acted in good faith to carry out Nixon's orders to find and then plug the source of leaks. Warren, speaking for St. Clair, announced that the President's attorneys would "recommend that he respectfully decline to appear."[28]

More ominous was a January announcement from the leaders of the House Judiciary Committee that they would seek broad subpoena powers from the full House for the impeachment inquiry. Nixon might be able to stall and otherwise frustrate the California court and the Special Prosecutor, but the House had an absolute, constitutional right to impeachment, and thus had a clear claim on any documentation of any type it might subpoena.

That morning, Nixon presided over a National Security Council meeting. Admiral Zumwalt, who was acting Chairman of the JCS that day, recorded in his notes that Nixon "castigates every ethnic group in the U.S. as being against him—the Jews, the blacks, the Catholics, the Wasps etc." Zumwalt was also concerned about Haig, who was putting in long hours at Nixon's side, seven days a week, frequently until midnight or 1 A.M., "yet Nixon has an almost paranoid resentment of anytime Haig is not available." But "Nixon is so paranoid and so emotional that no one can bear to spend the long hours with him he demands."

At the NSC meeting, Nixon did most of the talking. Some of what he said, so Zumwalt recorded, "made perfect sense. At other times he rambled, or even indulged in non sequiturs. . . . He said that it was his theory that in a second term a President ought to be sort of like an extinct volcano—the first term was the time for erupting." That was a complete switch from what Nixon had said a year earlier, to his Cabinet, when he swore he would not be an extinct volcano in his second term.

"The President discussed strategic doctrine. It was clear he didn't know anything about the new strategic doctrine that he approved." Nixon talked about the need for a new foreign policy toward Latin America; Zumwalt noted that he had said the same thing at every meeting for the past three and a half years "and not a damn thing has ever come out of [it] and nobody has ever followed up on it." Summing up, Zumwalt said Nixon's performance was not alarming, but "neither was it a reassuring one."[29]

NIXON was scheduled to give his State of the Union address on the evening of January 30. On the morning of that day Murray Chotiner, who had been in an auto accident a week earlier, died as a result of his injuries. Nixon, in a short statement, praised Chotiner as "an ally in political battles, a valued counselor, and a trusted colleague." But above all, Nixon went on, Chotiner had been his friend, and that friendship "never wavered; in periods of adversity it grew strong." It was Chotiner who had stood beside Nixon in the 1952 fund crisis, who had advised him to lash back at his accusers. It was Chotiner who had advised him always to attack, never defend. As Nixon put the last-minute touches on his State of the Union address, he had his friend very much on his mind.

During the drive from the White House to the Capitol, Nixon and Pat sat silently in the car. No President had ever approached a State of the Union address in circumstances less auspicious, not even Johnson in 1968. Nixon was down to a 26 percent approval rating. So tense was the situation that Nixon had discussed with his wife and daughters the possibility that the President might be subjected to hostile demonstrations from the congressmen.[30]

Nixon entered the House Chamber in a fighting mood. The applause and cheers from a small but vocal group of Republican loyalists reinforced his determination. His manner and his bearing, as well as speech, affirmed his eagerness to strike out and to defend his stewardship.

He launched into a portrait of the state of the nation he had inherited five years earlier. "Cities burning and besieged . . . spiraling rise in drug addiction . . . America's youth under the shadow of the military draft . . . air getting dirtier, our water getting more foul."

But after five years of his leadership, "We find a record of progress to confound the professional criers of doom and prophets of despair." There was peace with honor in Vietnam, peace in the cities, peace on the campuses. The rise in crime had been stopped, a massive campaign against drug abuse organized, the draft eliminated, the air getting cleaner and the water purer. There was prosperity, and a program to hold down inflation.

Good as his record was, he wanted to make it better. He wanted an energy-independent America, and a lasting peace, and an end to inflation, and high-quality health care for all, and better transportation, and better education, and sweeping welfare reform, and power sharing and revenue sharing with the states. He wanted new laws to protect the basic rights of privacy of individuals.

"I can understand that others may have different priorities," he said toward the end, but his own "one overriding aim" was to establish a new structure of peace. "This has been and this will remain my first priority and the chief legacy I hope to leave from the 8 years of my Presidency."

The reference to eight years brought cheers from Republicans, many of whom rose to their feet to applaud. Nixon looked up to his family in the gallery; they were beaming.

He concluded by saying that he hoped the 93d Congress would mark the era "when America ended its longest war and began its longest peace." There was more applause, and the first shuffling to leave the chamber and find the TV cameras began, but before anyone got out Nixon folded over his speech, looked up, and announced he wished to end on an extemporaneous and personal note.

He turned to "the so-called Watergate affair." He said he had voluntarily provided to the Special Prosecutor "all the material that he needs to conclude his investigations and to proceed to prosecute the guilty and to clear the innocent. I believe the time has come to bring that investigation and the other investigations of this matter to an end. One year of Watergate is enough."

Hisses and boos could be heard from the Democratic side of the chamber at what amounted to Nixon's announcement that Jaworski was not going to get his hands on any more tapes. Nixon plunged on. He said he recognized that the House Judiciary Committee had "a special responsibility" because of the impeachment hearing, and promised that he would "cooperate" with it in its investigation. But there was "one limitation." He would never do "anything that weakens the Office of the President or impairs the ability of the Presidents of the future to make the great decisions. . . ."

Again hisses and boos could be heard. Nixon ignored them. Scowling, perspiring heavily, chin jutting forward, clinching and thrusting his fist, he said he had been elected to do a job. "And I want you to know that

I have no intention whatever of ever walking away from the job that the people elected me to do for the people of the United States." In the gallery, Haig, Woods, David and Julie Eisenhower, Ed and Tricia Cox, and Pat Nixon all leaped to their feet, vigorously applauding, smiling, nodding their heads in agreement. Some Republicans and Southern Democrats joined them. Most Democrats stayed in their seats.[31]

The waves of approval, and the groans of dismay, that swept through the House Chamber were fittingly symbolic. For a quarter of a century, Nixon had practiced the politics of divisiveness. Here, in a setting and a forum that were designed, more than any other in American politics, to promote national unity, he was still practicing the politics of divisiveness, confronting and attacking his enemies, just as Murray Chotiner had taught him to do from the beginning.

IN early February, Nixon received a memo from Leonard Garment, passing along a copy of a memo from Democratic strategist Sol Linowitz that Linowitz had distributed to his party's leadership. Garment thought Nixon ought to read it.

Linowitz had written that it was the conventional wisdom that Nixon, as a "crippled" President, would *have* to cooperate with Congress, but he asserted that such was "a wrong view. A 'crippled' Nixon is far more apt to seek to assert his authority to prove that, in fact, he has not been defeated. He is apt to make moves which will use all of his executive power forcefully and to prove that he is still the President." Linowitz thought the "right way" for Democrats to deal with Nixon was to approach him in a spirit of compromise, to put aside the abuses of Watergate and focus on cooperation.

Nixon scribbled on the side of the Linowitz memo: "Al—note the portions I marked. Some of our liberal friends may *fear* the President *will* resist *strongly*. When we react *weakly* we get nothing but contempt from them. *Strong* action is the only correct posture at this time."[32]

He got started the morning after his State of the Union address, when he joined three thousand prominent Washington residents for a National Prayer breakfast at the Washington Hilton Hotel. In his remarks, he recalled that the first time he addressed a prayer breakfast as President, he had said that every American President had been a religious man and belonged to a church. He went on, "You know, the difficulty with a President when he makes a statement is that everybody checks it to see whether it is true." In his case, people had pointed out that Lincoln had not belonged to a church. Nixon acknowledged the fact, but gave detailed evidence that Lincoln prayed, that he referred to the Almighty, to the Universal Being, sometimes to God.

Nixon concluded on a nice Lincolnian note: "Too often I think we are a little too arrogant. We try to talk to God and tell him what we want, and what all of us need to do and what this Nation needs to do is to pray in silence and listen to God and find out what He wants for us, and then we will all do the right thing."[33]

On February 6, Nixon released a letter to Judge Gerhard Gesell of the U.S. District Court for Washington, saying that he would not supply the Senate Select Committee with five specified taped conversations. His reason was that the Committee would make the conversations public, which would "seriously infringe upon the principle of confidentiality."[34]

Jaworski, meanwhile, told the press that the White House had refused to turn over tapes and other evidence he had requested.[35] That morning, Nixon attended a breakfast meeting of the Congressional Chowder and Marching Society. In informal remarks that were leaked to the press, he was upbeat. The Republicans would do much better than predicted in the 1974 elections, he asserted, and he named four Republicans he considered to be in good position to succeed him in 1976: Ford, Reagan, Rockefeller, and Connally.[36]

David Eisenhower lent a hand to Nixon's attempt to build some momentum. He held a news conference. David's appearance, in the EOB, was part of Nixon's campaign to build public confidence by making his family members available to the news media. David told reporters, "I don't think there is the faintest possibility of him resigning under any circumstances, and impeachment is just not going to happen." He described Nixon as a "brilliant man with a mind of steel." He said the President's spirits were "fine," because Nixon believed he had turned the corner in his State of the Union address. Referring to Mitchell, Colson, Haldeman, and others who were in trouble for Watergate-related crimes, David said Nixon might have a "slight sense of remorse over the tragedy that has befallen individuals, but it's not something he lets obsess him or drive him."

Asked about how his own wife was holding up, David said that Julie "is tough—tough as hell—and honestly caught up in the emotional defense of her father. That's her character." Asked what he called his father-in-law when they were alone together, David replied, "Mr. President." He added that Nixon was "a strange man. He can get to the heart of things."[37]

Others wanted to get to the heart of things. That same day, the House voted 410–4 to give subpoena power to its Judiciary Committee for its investigation. The vote was a crushing blow to Nixon.

But that was a problem for the future. For the present, Nixon was living day by day. He repeated his calls for congressional action on energy, on comprehensive health insurance for all employees and paid in part by the federal and state governments for the poor, on education, and on privacy protection. He ordered a month-long freeze on diesel fuel prices in an effort to end a strike by independent truckers; within a few days, they were back on the road. The President then proposed (February 9) a $16 billion program for mass transit.

On February 12, Lincoln's birthday, Nixon paid a surprise visit to the Lincoln Memorial, where he delivered an impromptu speech to the tourists who happened to be there in which he compared himself to the Civil War President. Lincoln had also been vilified, Nixon said, but he had the character to "stand tall and strong and firm no matter how harsh or unfair the criticism might be." He noted that Lincoln had been deeply hurt by what was said about him, but he had "the great strength of character never to display it." Reporters were reminded of Lyndon Johnson's visit to the Memorial on Lincoln's birthday six years earlier; Johnson had also drawn a comparison between his ordeal and Lincoln's. A few weeks later, Johnson had announced that he would not seek re-election.[38]

That evening, the President attended Alice Roosevelt Longworth's ninetieth birthday party. He told reporters he was going to the Bethesda Naval Medical Center the next day for his twice-postponed annual physical examination. "I don't know why I have to have one," he remarked, "but they make me do it."[39] Following the exam, the doctors reported that he was in "excellent" condition and showed "no evidence whatsoever of any emotional strains." The doctors said they wished he would "get more sunshine," and more sleep. Shortly after the exam, Nixon flew to Key Biscayne.[40]

On St. Valentine's Day, February 14, Nixon drove up to Miami to speak at the dedication of the Cedars of Lebanon Hospital Center. The ceremony was held on the lawn of the center; it was Nixon's first appearance outdoors since the 1972 campaign. He agreed to speak in order to promote his proposal for national health insurance, which was the subject of his remarks, but his presence provoked his critics while providing his supporters with an opportunity to show their feelings. A battle of hand-painted signs ensued; on one side, the slogans included "Exorcise Nixon" and "Impeach and Imprison," while on the other there were signs calling for "Three More Years" and "Keep Nixon."

Hecklers tried to drown out the President with chants of "Impeach Nixon Now," but he was a master at handling such situations. Turning his back on the hostile elements of the crowd, who were cordoned off, and using the mike effectively, he managed to make himself heard. Still there were embarrassing moments. When he said his plan would mean that "no American will ever be denied health care because of lack of ability to pay," a male voice from the side interrupted, "Pay your taxes!" When he referred to his Quaker background, there was another shout, "You're no Quaker, you're a faker!"[41]

Four days later, speaking at an "Honor America Day" rally before twenty thousand people in Huntsville, Alabama, with Governor George Wallace beside him on the stage, Nixon got a much friendlier reception for his theme speech: "What's Right with America." As the audience waved American flags, Nixon called out, "I thank you for reminding all of America that here in the heart of Dixie we find that the heart of America is good, the character of America is strong and we are going to continue to be a great nation."[42]

The public appearances helped rouse Nixon's spirits. For the past year, he had seldom made marginal notations on the flow of memos that crossed his desk, but in February 1974, he had a revival. When he received a long memo from Bryce Harlow entitled "Areas of Presidential Concern" in the middle of the month, he reacted like the old Nixon. Harlow pointed out that a change in statistical methods for reporting unemployment was likely to raise the national unemployment figure by over 1 percent. Nixon noted: "Bryce—this is *bad* news for our candidates. Be sure Bush et al are warned. The B.L.S. [Bureau of Labor Statistics] is not known for its objectivity in election years where Reps are concerned."

Beside a paragraph reporting on antibusing amendments in the House, Nixon scribbled, "Bryce—Lean all *our* people to a *strong* antibusing position. Weinberger & Saxbe should be so informed." Nixon handed down other marching orders beside Harlow's paragraphs, and noted at the end of the memo, "Bryce—Good!"[43]

On February 21, Nixon presided over a Cabinet meeting, the first in months. Although the Republicans had just lost a special election for Gerry Ford's seat in the House, the President was optimistic about the prospects for November. Encouraging pessimistic Republicans for congressional elections was a familiar role for him, and he showed that he still had the touch. "The worst time to have a let-down is when things seem to be going against you," he told his Cabinet. "I think the Democrats are going to get some rude shocks. Their worst handicap will be overconfidence." He said he got lots of mail and talked to lots of people. "I want to assure you that we have a lot of supporters in this country," so when they went out to make speeches, "don't back down—let our people know we still have some spunk." He reminded the Cabinet of all the accomplishments of the Administration. "If people want the good old days of wars, riots, mass civil disobedience, the burning of draft cards, racial confrontations, higher taxes, and all the rest, then that is their prerogative." But he was sure the people wanted what the Nixon Administration had given them. He concluded, "we aren't crippled, we have brought peace, and we aren't going to quit."[44]

At a news conference on February 25, he continued to project a positive image. Although he appeared nervous at the start, and soon was perspiring profusely under the hot television lights in the White House East Room, he spoke in slow, measured tones and was subdued. He did not have any particularly good news to announce, but he did manage to reach a statesmanlike level on a number of occasions.

He opened with prepared remarks on gas lines, the oil embargo, rising gasoline prices, and the Middle East. He reported that Kissinger was continuing his shuttle diplomacy in an attempt to disengage the Syrian and Israeli forces, that success was imminent, and that it would lead to a lifting of the embargo, followed by plentiful gasoline supplies and a halt in the rise in prices. But he warned that the United States would not allow itself to be "blackmailed" by the Arabs, implying that if OPEC continued the embargo it would be difficult for Kissinger to bring off a disengagement. He criticized Congress for not acting on his energy proposals, such as deregulation of natural gas, and warned that if the Democrats passed a bill that forced a rollback in the price of gasoline, he would veto it, because a rollback would lead to shortages that would require rationing. The right way to deal with the energy problem was to increase supplies.

In the question period, he was asked to comment on the Soviet expulsion of author Alexander Solzhenitsyn. Did he think it would undermine détente?

He did not. If he thought that breaking relations with the Soviets could help men like Solzhenitsyn, he would break relations. But obviously that would only make things worse. He also pointed out that in earlier times, instead of being expelled to Paris, Solzhenitsyn would have been sent to Siberia.

"Do we want to go back to a period when the United States and the Soviet Union stood in a confrontation against each other and risk a runaway nuclear arms race . . . or do we want to continue on a path in which we recognize our differences but try to recognize also the fact that we must either live together or we will all die together?"

Nixon managed to get through the Watergate questions without losing his temper. Helen Thomas of UPI asked if he would be willing to waive executive privilege to give the Judiciary Committee whatever documents and tapes it requested. Nixon replied that he was prepared to cooperate with the Committee "in any way consistent with my constitutional responsibility to defend the Office of the Presidency against any action which would weaken that office."

Would he resign if the polls indicated that the Republicans were going to take a trouncing in November? He would not, but then he did not expect such an outcome. "What will affect the election in 1974 is what always affects elections—peace and prosperity." He had brought peace, and once the oil embargo was lifted he expected prosperity, so he anticipated a good year for Republican candidates.

Not even Dan Rather could shake him. Rather wanted to know if

Nixon, as "an experienced student of the Constitution," considered it necessary to prove that the President had committed a crime for him to be impeached, or was simple "dereliction of duty" enough?

"Well, Mr. Rather," Nixon answered, "you don't have to be a constitutional lawyer to know that the Constitution is very precise in defining what is an impeachable offense. . . . A criminal offense on the part of the President is the requirement for impeachment." He added, "I do not expect to be impeached."[45]

Nixon stayed on the offensive. On February 26, he blasted the Democrats in Congress for acting "irresponsibly" on education legislation and health insurance. That afternoon, he signed a proclamation designating March 29, 1974, as "Vietnam Veterans Day." The date marked the first anniversary of the day the last American troops departed from Vietnam. Nixon wrote the proclamation himself. He pointed with pride to his accomplishments, and got in some digs at his opponents. "I know that there are some who quarrel with the phrase I have often used," peace with honor. But it was true. Seventeen million people in South Vietnam "would now be under Communist control" had it not been for his policies. So would the 7 million people of Cambodia. The peoples of Malaysia and Singapore, of Indonesia and Thailand, and others, would "have a much greater danger threatening them of aggression sweeping over the entire peninsula of Southeast Asia." To those who said the domino theory was false, Nixon replied: ask the dominoes. The Americans who fought in Vietnam, the men he was honoring, had given the 250 million people of Southeast Asia "a chance—not a guarantee, but a chance—to choose their own way, a chance to remain free from a takeover by aggression from outside forces."[46]

Given the way the fighting was going in Indochina—badly for the South Vietnamese and the Cambodians—and given the shameful treatment accorded the American veterans home from Vietnam by the American people, Nixon was swimming against a strong tide. His insistence on doing so demonstrated both his courage and his political savvy—what he was saying was what the conservative Republicans wanted to hear.

On the morning of February 28, he went to the Shoreham Hotel to speak to the 1974 Young Republican Leadership Conference. It was an ideal audience for him, strongly conservative and highly partisan. But instead of playing to the young Republicans' prejudices, Nixon gave them some realistic remarks that amounted to a rebuke. He knew they were critical of détente, so he took some care in explaining the policy to them. He pointed out that negotiations with another country did not mean approval of that country's system, that the alternative to negotiation was mutual destruction, and that what he was trying to do was to build a system that would allow different governments to settle their disputes without war. "There are easier ways to demagogue this problem," he admitted; to say that the way to deal with an unfriendly government was "have nothing to do with them, threaten them, deny them this, do this or that or the other thing." If such negativism would work, he said, he would indulge in it—but it would not.

Without saying so directly, Nixon reminded his audience of how indispensable he was. "I know the leaders of the Soviet Union," he pointed out. "I know the leaders of the People's Republic of China. I know the leaders of the other Communist nations. I totally disagree with their systems; they totally disagree with ours." He had made peace in Southeast Asia, he had gone to China, he had achieved détente with the Soviets. He would continue to strengthen the structure of peace "over the next three years."

Nixon was often at his best in speaking to young people. On this occasion he said he had noticed how many youngsters yearned for the fifties, which looked placid, peaceful, and prosperous to them, in contrast to the sixties and seventies. He understood their nostalgia, but he insisted that the seventies were not a bad time to be young. "Let me tell you this is a good time to be your age, it is a good time to be living in America, and it is a good time to be interested in and to participate in politics."

Nixon remarked that George Bush had told him as he came into the hall that there were many potential politicians in the room. He wanted to give them some advice. "First, and this one is going to surprise you, don't assume that the time to run for an office is only when it is a sure thing. Show me a candidate who is not a hungry candidate, show me a candidate who isn't willing to take a risk and risk all, even risk losing, and I will show you a lousy candidate." Nixon wanted Republican candidates who got in there and fought when it was hard and tough.

"Second, in life generally and in politics particularly, you don't win them all. I am an expert on that. And also, you never win even when you win big and just assume, well, now the job is done because the battle always goes on." That was the American system, and "that is the way it should be."

His closing bit of advice brought the youngsters to their feet, cheering and whistling: "You learn from your defeats, and then you go on to fight again—never quit, never quit."[47]

FEBRUARY ended on a high note for Nixon, but on March 1 in Sirica's courtroom, the grand jury handed down indictments of four former White House aides, Ehrlichman, Haldeman, Colson, and Strachan, along with Mitchell, Robert Mardian, and Kenneth Parkinson of CREEP. All seven were charged with conspiracy, together with other persons "known and unknown," for arranging hush money payoffs for the Watergate burglars, for wiretapping, for offering executive clemency, for destroying documents, and for having lied to various investigative bodies. A central figure in the grand jury's narrative of events was John Dean, who had pleaded guilty to one count of conspiracy and who was cooperating with the prosecution. Mitchell and Stans were already on trial in New York for campaign financing violations, and John Connally was under a grand jury investigation for violations in connection with the milk producers.

A year earlier, on March 21, 1973, Dean had warned Nixon that the people closest to him were in danger of being indicted. The President had refused to believe him. Now it had happened.

Nixon decided to deal with the repercussions of the indictments, which were dominating the news during the first week in March, with a news conference, his second in eight days. The first question, from Frank Cormier of the Associated Press, concerned the tapes. Nixon had said he would turn over to the House Judiciary Committee all the materials that had been made available to the Special Prosecutor. Would he turn over other materials requested or subpoenaed by the Committee?

Nixon said the subject was under discussion between St. Clair and John Doar, that he would respond to written interrogatories, and that he was willing to testify under oath before the chairman and the ranking minority member of the Committee. He added that the White House had already supplied Jaworski with nineteen tapes and seven hundred documents, and pointed out that Jaworski had said that the grand jury "had all the information that it needed in order to bring to a conclusion its Watergate investigation."

Helen Thomas reminded Nixon that his former top aide, Bob Haldeman, had been charged with perjury because he had testified that Nixon said, "It would be wrong to pay hush money to silence the Watergate defendants, and last August you said that was accurate. Can you, and will you, provide proof that you did indeed say it would be wrong?"

Nixon went into a long explanation of his March 21, 1973, conversation with Dean and Haldeman. He said that it was then that he had learned, for the first time, that money had gone to the defendants "for the purpose of keeping them quiet, not simply for their defense." Had it been for their defense, it would have been proper, but if it was to keep them quiet, "that, of course, would have been an obstruction of justice." Nixon admitted that he had considered various options with Dean, but "the bottom line" was that although the money could be raised, clemency could not be offered.

"I then said that to pay clemency was wrong. In fact, I think I can quote it directly. I said, 'it is wrong, that's for sure.' Mr. Haldeman was present when I said that. Mr. Dean was present. Both agreed with my conclusion."

(In fact, Haldeman only came into the room later. As to what was said: Dean had made the point that Nixon might not ever be able to deliver on clemency. Nixon had said he could not do it until after the

1974 elections, and perhaps not even then. Dean had agreed. Nixon had said, "No, it's wrong, that's for sure.")

In his news conference, Nixon admitted that "when individuals read the entire transcript of the [March] 21st meeting, or hear the entire tape where we discussed all these options, they may reach different interpretations, but I know what I meant, and I know also what I did."

(He was certainly right about differing interpretations. After listening at least two dozen times to the tape, this author still cannot tell for certain whether the President meant it would be wrong to grant clemency morally, or wrong to do so before the 1974 elections, or wrong for political reasons, or whether he was speaking for the record, knowing that a tape recorder was running. So it is impossible for anyone other than Nixon to say what Nixon meant. What he did is clear: he ordered Dean to get the money to Hunt; he did not grant clemency.)

In his news conference, he claimed, "I never at any time authorized the payment of money to any of the defendants." He added that he had sent Dean to Camp David to make a full report of everything that he knew. "In other words, the policy was one of full disclosure, and that was the decision that was made at the conclusion of the meeting." As the opposite decision was in fact made, Nixon's statement showed how confident he was that he was not going to lose control of those critical tapes.

Would he consider granting clemency to his aides if they were found guilty?

"Under no circumstances," Nixon replied. "That would be improper, and I will not engage in that activity."

Martin Schram of *Newsday* asked for clarification.

"What I am saying," Nixon explained, "[is] that I am not going to grant clemency because they happen to be involved in Watergate—that, I am ruling out."

Back to the House Judiciary Committee and more evidence. Nixon had said he wanted an expeditious conclusion to the impeachment hearings. Would he help speed up the process by supplying whatever materials, tapes, documents, and so forth the Committee demanded?

No, Nixon replied, because that would slow rather than speed the process. "All that is really involved [in the demands for more tapes] is to cart everything that is in the White House down to a committee and to have them paw through it on a fishing expedition," and it would take a year or more to get through it.

Well, then, would he release the tape of March 21 to the public, so that the people could judge whether he was telling the truth or not? Nixon replied that the problem with that proposal was that the tape was evidence in a criminal case, and to release it might prejudice the rights of the defendants. Still, he was considering doing so, because "any individual who is looking at it objectively not only hears it or reads what the transcript is but also sees what was done after that particular conversation took place, will conclude, first, that the President had no knowledge before the 21st; second that the President never authorized clemency, in fact, rejected it on several occasions in that meeting; and third, that the President never authorized the payment of money to the defendants for the purpose of hushing them up."

What had he meant, then, when he said earlier that people might reach a different interpretation when they heard the tape?

"What I say is that I know what I said," Nixon replied. "I know what I meant, I know what I did, and I think that any fair-minded person will reach the same conclusion that I have repeated here several times."

How could that be, he was asked, when it was known that $75,000 was paid to Hunt right after that meeting?

"I have no information as to when a payment was made," Nixon snapped. "All I have information on is as to my own actions and my own directions, and my actions and directions were clear and very precise. I did not authorize payments, and I did not have knowledge of payments to which you have referred."

His hands gripped the lectern. The tenseness of his body revealed his conscious attempt to control his anger. Although he was sweating, his face bespoke sincerity. He was the picture of an honest man whose integrity had been impugned.[48]

On March 21, 1973, Nixon had told Dean that the payment to Hunt should be made through the "Cuban Committee," as "that would give a little bit of a cover." Dean had replied, "We can put that together. That isn't, of course, quite the way it happened."

"I know," Nixon had admitted, "but it's the way it's going to have to happen."

Evidently he had convinced himself that it had happened through the Cuban Committee. It had not, and Nixon's insistence to the contrary, in the most public forum possible, a news conference on national radio and television, was compounding his problem.

The day after the news conference, Nixon sent a memo to Haig, in which he said that so far as the impeachment inquiry was concerned, "the law case will be decided by the PR case." He followed up with another memo: "St. Clair sees it too much as a trial, not a public relations exercise. We must work on him to get him to understand what we are up against."[49]

Despite Nixon's concern about his concentration, St. Clair did him a great favor that week. Following the news conference, the reporters were stirring up another controversy that revolved around the issue of Nixon's admission that Dean had told him money was being used to buy silence from Hunt and the others. As Nixon had complained earlier that year, snoopy reporters were always checking up on his statements. In this case, they pointed out that in an August 15, 1973, statement, Nixon said that Dean had told him the money had been used for attorneys' fees and family support, not to purchase silence. They also pointed out that federal law required that anyone who knew of the commission of a felony—such as obstruction of justice—report it to proper authorities. That Nixon had not so reported was a criminal act, or so it was said.

St. Clair had an answer to that one. In a *New York Times* interview, he dismissed the issue of misprision as one which "doesn't make much sense as a legal question," since Nixon "is the chief law enforcement officer in the country." How could he have reported to himself? His obligation was to see to it that the law was enforced; St. Clair cited as evidence that Nixon had fulfilled his duty the fact that the Watergate conspirators were under indictment.[50]

NIXON's immediate problem, toward the end of that long, cold, unhappy winter, was to discredit the House Judiciary Committee. His strategy was twofold, first to charge it with undertaking a fishing expedition with no clear idea as to what it might catch or even what constituted a legal catch, and second to present himself as an active and indispensable President.

Rodino's committee certainly was casting a wide net. In early March, it issued a report that listed six broad areas under investigation. They were: domestic surveillance, including the Plumbers, the Huston Plan, and wiretapping; intelligence activities and "dirty tricks" in the campaign; Nixon's finances; the use of government agencies for political purposes; bombing Cambodia secretly; and impoundment of funds.

One had only to go back to Lyndon Johnson's Administration to realize the weakness of most of the charges. Any in-depth investigation of Johnson would have revealed that he had set ample precedents for Nixon in every area. That did not make what Nixon had done right or legal, but it did open the Democrats to a charge of hypocrisy for attacking him for things Johnson had done. Johnson had wiretapped and secretly tape-recorded, he had spied on domestic political opponents, he had spent federal money on his ranch and taken a huge tax deduction for his papers, he had played dirty tricks in his campaigns, he had used government agencies for his political gain. So had Jack Kennedy done such things (except using his office to make money), and come to that, so had Franklin Roosevelt.

The idea that Nixon's bombing of Cambodia was an impeachable offense was ridiculous. The House had voted unanimously for the Gulf of Tonkin resolution in 1964; it had voted the funds to carry out the bombings from 1965 to 1973; the President was the Commander in Chief; the congressional vote to end the bombing as of August 15, 1973, in effect sanctioned the bombing until then.

But then the Committee was fishing in uncharted waters. In the only previous impeachment of a President, the President had deliberately violated the law, the Tenure of Office Act. Andrew Johnson had removed Secretary of War Edwin Stanton for the specific purpose of testing the constitutionality of the act. The Supreme Court later ruled the act unconstitutional. The impeachment of Johnson was widely regarded, in the twentieth century, as a partisan and vindictive action that brought shame on the Congress. It set no approved precedents.

Nixon was correct in challenging the House to find a crime if it wanted to impeach him. No crime, no case. And the only crime that he could be charged with was obstruction of justice, that is, a cover-up of the original Watergate break-in. In every other area, if the Democrats persisted, the Nixon forces could counterattack. On February 26, Buchanan sent Nixon a memorandum outlining thirty examples of privacy invasions by Kennedy and Johnson, and concluded, "these are but some of the recorded instances. Lord knows what it would look like if the truth were known."[51]

As it had always been, Nixon's problem was that he was guilty of covering up and his defense was that he alone had the evidence. Without the tapes, Rodino and his colleagues were going to have difficulty catching any fish at all, much less a keeper. To get the evidence, the House Judiciary Committee would have to use its subpoena power, which in the event that Nixon refused to comply, would force a constitutional crisis nearly everyone wanted to avoid.

Aware of all this, Rodino was moving ahead cautiously, letting the red hot Democrats on his committee investigate for the purposes of embarrassing Nixon rather than for the narrower purpose of impeaching him, while bowing to conservative Republicans by not moving too quickly on exercising the subpoena power already granted by the House. Everyone in Washington, meanwhile, and millions around the country, were aware that most Republicans wished with all their hearts that Nixon would just resign and go away, while many Democrats hoped with all their hearts that for the rest of their lives they could have Dick Nixon to run against.

In this complex and confusing situation, Nixon tried to overwhelm Congress with new legislative proposals while trying to convince the country that he was still in charge, still the man who could bring peace and prosperity to the nation for all time. On March 8, the day Colson, Ehrlichman, and Liddy were indicted for the break-in at the office of Ellsberg's psychiatrist, Nixon presented himself rather improbably as the leader of campaign reform. In a radio address, he recommended more detailed financial disclosures, sharp limits on what individual contributors could give (no more than $3,000 for a congressional campaign, $15,000 for a presidential candidate), a severe curb on the flow of cash (any contribution of more than $50 would have to be by check, and disclosed), reform of campaign practices (no more dirty tricks), and shortened presidential campaigns (primaries in the summer, nominating conventions in September).

Nixon's proposals were, for the most part, welcome to the Democrats, while the Republican leaders indicated that they disagreed fundamentally with every one of them, except Nixon's rejection of public financing of campaigns. That was the one the Democrats wanted. Nixon said it was "taxation without representation," because it "would take your money— no matter what your political preference—and distribute it to candidates for whom your voluntary support might be withheld." Finally, Nixon proposed to reduce the number of campaigns by passing a constitutional amendment that would change House of Representative terms from two to four years, and presidential terms from four to six, with a one-term limit.[52]

Campaign reform was a new issue for Nixon. He had done nothing to prepare the politicians or the public for it. He certainly could not have expected much action, not during his term anyway. But to use one of his favorite phrases, it did put him "out in front" on the question of campaign reform, it gave the country something to talk about—however briefly— other than Watergate, and it rallied some support for him from groups that had long since been advocating such changes.

As with détente, one wonders that Nixon had not prepared the way for his proposals. As it was, what should have been important news, and provoked at least a national debate, was buried on the back pages and quickly forgotten.

IN mid-March, Kissinger provided the Nixon Administration with a great victory. On the 18th the Arab oil ministers lifted the oil embargo uncon-ditionally. Two weeks earlier, Egypt and the United States had formally re-established diplomatic relations. Nixon had provided the guidance for Kissinger, which consisted of the common sense approach of not linking the embargo directly to the disengagement of Syrian-Israeli forces but recognizing that such linkage was inevitable. But the President had not been involved in the day-to-day negotiations. Kissinger wrote that al-though he reported to Nixon regularly on progress, "there was an un-characteristic detachment, almost as if he had become an observer of his own Presidency."[53]

These related developments served American interests well. They gave the United States a central role in Middle East diplomacy, and they excluded the Soviet Union from the main arena of diplomatic action. Best of all for Nixon, they opened to him the possibility of a triumphal visit to Egypt while reinforcing his claim as world statesman. The man who had brought peace to Vietnam, opened to China, established détente with the Soviets, had now brought peace to the Middle East. It was an im-pressive list of accomplishments. Unfortunately for Nixon, few in the United States paid much attention, and those who did gave the credit to Kissinger, who would stay in office even if Nixon were driven out.

•

IN Washington, the crocuses were up, the forsythia in bloom. These promises of spring were, as always, welcome, especially to the Nixons, who were not traveling to Florida or California as often as they had in the past, nor going up to Camp David, so as not to subject themselves to criticisms for wasting fuel while people sat in the long, frustrating lines at service stations (and suffered through a form of rationing; people whose license plates ended in an odd number could purchase gas only on odd-numbered days, those with even numbers on even-numbered days).

To relax, the Nixons took to visiting David and Julie Eisenhower at least twice a week. The Eisenhowers lived in a white-brick house in Bethesda, which they were renting from Bebe Rebozo. The house was set on an acre of ground and was secluded. It was only twenty-five minutes by car from the White House. The Nixons would have the White House chefs prepare a meal and bring it along. As soon as they arrived, Nixon would light a fire. The family sat on a glassed-in porch. Conversation was far removed from Watergate; David described the evenings as "dream-like." Pat would try to divert her husband from his worries by pointing out the birds at the feeder, or the flowers coming into bloom.

"Many evenings," Julie recorded, "my father reminisced about the car and train trips he and mother had taken during their courtship and early married years. He wistfully talked about planning a train trip in late spring, or perhaps a summer train ride across America. As he spoke of the past and of the future, ignoring the present, he steadfastly was trying to sustain a lifelong philosophy of not giving in to defeat."[54]

David was in low spirits, as he confessed in a letter to his father-in-law. He said he had "never accepted that life could be so unfair," but urged Nixon to keep his spirits up. "Hope means determination." Nixon replied that David's words gave him "a much needed lift. . . . Julie and you have been a great comfort to us this past year. We only regret that you both had to suffer with us one blow followed by another."[55]

It was a particularly painful time for Pat, who had to endure much, not least reporters eager for a scoop. They pressed her on her husband's condition constantly, often at the most inappropriate moments. When she hosted a reception at the White House for the annual meeting of the Religious Broadcasters of America, reporters ignored the event and asked her if Nixon were sleeping well.

Pat's eyes flashed. "He doesn't sleep long but he sleeps well," she replied, adding that sometimes his sleep was "interrupted by telephone calls."

Was he getting up in the middle of the night to play the piano? He plays "before he goes to bed," she responded. Thrusting her arm up, fist clenched, she added, "He is in great health, and I love him dearly and I have great faith."

In the receiving line, many women remarked that they had faith in Nixon and were praying for him. "Pray for the press," Pat replied. Immediately a reporter asked, "Does the press need prayers?"

"We all do," Pat answered. "Who doesn't?"[56]

The reporters were obnoxious, but they were only asking what their readers wanted to know. Everyone in the country was obsessed with Nixon, his health, his personality, his actions, his intentions. Vicious rumors made the rounds, and not just in Washington. They had the President drinking, or not sleeping, or taking drugs, or the victim of a stroke. After decades of almost daily exposure to him, the American people still were confused about the character of their leader.[57]

To prove that he was not breaking up or on the verge of doing so, and to make his case against the House Judiciary Committee, Nixon took to the road. He badly needed to get out of Washington, where the leaks were hurting him. The *Post* reported them. The most damaging concerned his statement to Dean, "No it's wrong, that's for sure." The *Post* said that "informed sources" who had heard the tape (evidently from the Special Prosecutor's Office) were of the opinion that when Nixon had used the word "wrong," he meant impractical, not immoral.[58] Seymour Hersh reported in *The New York Times* that the hush money payment had been made to Howard Hunt less than twelve hours after Nixon's meeting with Dean.[59] The House Judiciary Committee had requested (not subpoenaed) forty-two additional Nixon tapes.

Wherever Nixon appeared that week, a battle of handmade signs ensued, reminiscent of the 1968 presidential campaign. There were "God loves Nixon" signs in Nashville, and "Support our President" in Chicago, and "Three More Years" in Houston, countered by signs asking, "If It Was Wrong, Why Did You Do it?" and "No More Years."

In Chicago, on March 15, Nixon spoke at a question-and-answer session of the Executives' Club. The friendly audience greeted him with a two-minute standing applause; one questioner identified himself as a Republican state senator and said he wanted to tell Nixon, "you are thought of belovedly by thousands of people." The event was on national television and Nixon used his opportunity effectively. He was calm and smiling as he answered soft questions.

Would he encourage young people to go into politics? Yes. What about energy? The worst was over. Peace? He had "won a peace," and with help would create a structure that would "keep the peace for a generation and longer."

What about Watergate? Nixon pointed out that he had made "an unprecedented turn-over of confidential materials," including "caseloads of documents."

Nixon asked his own question: "Well, why not just give the Judiciary

Committee the right to come in and have all of the tapes of every Presidential conversation, a complete right to go in and go through all of the Presidential files in order to find out whether or not there is a possibility that some action had been taken which might result in an impeachable offense?"

The reason why not was the usual one: he did not want to weaken the Presidency. "It isn't a question that the President has something to hide." Without confidentiality, future Presidents would be "surrounded by eunuchs."

Would he resign? Never. That would be the easy way, but he would not give in to the temptation because "resignation of this President on charges of which he is not guilty, resignation simply because he happened to be low in the polls, would forever change our form of government."[60]

In Nashville, on March 16, Nixon helped to dedicate a new wing for the Grand Ole Opry. Tennessee's two Republican senators were at the airport to greet him, as was the Republican governor. Indeed, the visit had all the appearances of a campaign stop shortly before an election—crowds, banners, bands, advance men, and crowd-pleasing oratory that emphasized what a wonderful place Nashville was, how much Nixon liked country music, his wife's birthday, and so on. In the new hall, Nixon played "Happy Birthday" for his wife, and "My Wild Irish Rose," and "God Bless America" on the piano. He tried to make a yo-yo work. He exchanged jokes with singer Roy Acuff.[61]

There was one embarrassing moment. When the program ended, Pat got up from her chair and crossed the stage, her arms outstretched in delight and thanks. But her husband was already turning away, gesturing to the master of ceremonies that he was finished. "Some of the more cynical correspondents covering the evening," according to Julie, "interpreted the President's action as a sign of odd indifference to his wife." She explained that it was just his way; that he would often hold hands with Pat, but only in private.[62]

On March 19, Nixon flew to Houston to address the National Association of Broadcasters. The day got off to a bad start; Senator James Buckley had called for his resignation. That cut especially deep because the senator's brother, William F. Buckley, was perhaps the most respected and certainly the most widely read conservative spokesman in the nation, and the brothers were known to be close. Senator Buckley said there was a "crisis of the regime," marked by "spreading cynicism" and "frustration and impotence becom[ing] the dominant political mood in the nation." He said a "perception of corruption had effectively destroyed the President's ability to speak from a position of moral leadership." He also feared the "melodrama" of a Senate trial in which "the Chamber would become a twentieth-century Roman Coliseum as the performers are thrown to the electronic lions."

Buckley made another point: if Nixon stayed in office, the Democrats would win big in November, and the nation would face "the risk of a runaway Congress that could commit us to new and dangerous programs." Conservatives would have to face the fact that keeping Nixon in office would hurt their cause. So Buckley called on Nixon to perform "an extraordinary act of statesmanship and courage" and resign.[63]

The first question from the broadcasters was Nixon's reaction to Buckley's statement. Nixon replied that "while it might be an act of courage to run away from a job that you were elected to do, it also takes courage to stand and fight for what you believe is right, and that is what I intend to do." He referred to the December 1972 bombing of Hanoi. Many had called for his resignation then; he had gone down in the polls; his closest advisers told him to call off the bombing. But he had stuck to his guns, and been proven right. "Now, I want future Presidents to be able to make hard decisions, even though they think they may be unpopular, even though they think they may bring them down in the polls, even though they may think they may bring upon them criticism from the Congress which could result in demands that he resign or be impeached."

Following some questions on energy and inflation, Nixon recognized Dan Rather. There was much stirring in the audience, people caught their breath, leaned forward, stood up, anticipated a clash.

"Mr. President—Mr. President," Rather began, trying to be heard.

"Are you running for something?" Nixon asked. The audience laughed, nervously.

"No, sir, Mr. President," Rather responded. "Are you?"

When the laughter died, Rather asked how Nixon could claim he was cooperating with the investigations of Watergate when he had refused to testify before the grand jury and was withholding evidence. Nixon replied that Jaworski had said he had all the information he needed for the full story on Watergate, and that it would not be in the interest of the United States for any President ever to appear before a grand jury.

Rather persisted. "Given the constitutional assignment to the House of Representatives of an impeachment investigation without qualification," he said, "how can the House committee do its job as long as you, the person under investigation, are allowed to limit their access to potential evidence?"

Nixon did not answer directly. He did point out that the Constitution said the President could be impeached only for treason, bribery, or other high crimes or misdemeanors. "It is the Constitution that defines what the House should have access to and the limits of its investigation, and I am suggesting that the House follow the Constitution. If they do, I will."

Tom Brokaw of NBC News followed up on Rather's questions. He pointed out that only one other President had been the subject of an impeachment investigation, and that Andrew Johnson had given the Congress everything it asked for when he was impeached. "Aren't your statements to that matter historically inaccurate or at least misleading?" Brokaw asked.

Nixon replied that the Judiciary Committee was trying to set a precedent that would destroy the American political system. "If all that a Congress under the control of an opposition party had to do in order to get a President out of office was to make an unreasonable demand to go through all of the files of the Presidency, a demand which a President would have to refuse, then it would mean that no President would be strong enough to stay in office to resist that kind of demand." America would become a parliamentary democracy, which was not at all what the framers of the Constitution wanted. Nixon concluded his answer, and the meeting, by vowing: "I will not participate in the destruction of the Office of the President of the United States while I am in his office."[64]

What an extraordinary man. After an ordeal like that, he was out the next morning at the Johnson Space Center in Houston, waving to the crowds, smiling, bouncing, thrusting his hands over his head and giving his familiar V-sign, all pumped up. Handing out citations to Skylab 3 astronauts, he spoke without notes, without missing a beat, even getting in one of his awful jokes (referring to the astronauts' medals, he said, "I hope they will never have to hock them"). He said he would like to volunteer for a space voyage, and gave the crowd his blood pressure (120 over 72). He spoke of the need to cooperate with the Russians in space, and elsewhere. He brought up a favorite theme, that Americans were a "great people," and insisted that a great people had to be an exploring people. He worked in the Boy Scouts.

In conclusion, Nixon wanted to say something about the Apollo 13 crew. They did not make it to the moon, but "they didn't fail, because you are only a failure when you give up, and they didn't give up." He ended by asking the audience to give a big hand to the Clear Lake High School Band for its rendition of "Hail to the Chief."[65]

Here was Nixon back at the old stand, working the crowd with professional aplomb. Whatever the intellectuals back East thought about Dan Rather and his smart-aleck remarks, the heart of America was with him. Unless the Democrats could get the goods on him, solid, unambiguous evidence, they were never going to drive him from office. And no matter what Republicans who were worried about their future and the future of their party might want, as Nixon's response to Buckley showed, they were never going to get him to resign unless they helped to gather that evidence.

•

IF it was up to Nixon, no one was ever going to see any more documentation or hear any additional tapes. Jaworski subpoenaed the White House for further material; Nixon said no. When Senator Scott warned that a continued refusal to turn over evidence to the House Judiciary Committee would in itself be grounds for impeachment, Nixon still said no. He did so in full realization that "we were over a barrel." He knew that if he refused to comply with the Committee demands, he would be cited for contempt of Congress. At 2 A.M. on March 22, he jotted on his note pad, "Lowest day. Contempt equals impeachment."[66] But then, so did compliance.

The damning evidence was leaking anyway. The Los Angeles *Times* reported that the March 21, 1973, tape was "not ambiguous." Nixon had said that the conversation could be subject to different interpretations; the unnamed *Times* source said that was not true: "When you hear the tape, you have a lot more respect for Dean's integrity and what he told the Senate Watergate Committee. It is that explosive."[67]

Ziegler denied the story and accused the House Judiciary Committee of leaking. At Nixon's urging, he used the leak to bolster the case for refusing to turn over any further evidence—the Committee obviously could not be trusted. The President, Ziegler emphasized, was determined "not to irreversibly erode the office of the Presidency."[68] But Senator Baker, interviewed on CBS TV's program "Face the Nation," urged Nixon to turn all relevant tapes and documents over to the Committee. Baker had support from Senator Robert Griffin of Michigan, the Republican whip; Senator Wallace Bennett (Utah), the secretary of the Senate Republican Conference; and Senator Bill Brock (Tenn.), the chairman of the Senate Republican Campaign Committee. Along with Scott, these men were the Republican leaders in the body that would be judging Nixon if it came to an impeachment and trial.

So the tension centering on the House Judiciary Committee and the tapes grew. It mesmerized Washington. And no amount of grandstanding by Nixon out on the hustings was going to make it go away. Only he could do that, by producing the evidence that he was innocent.

BECAUSE the evidence proved the opposite, Nixon decided that instead of producing it, he would concentrate on the job he had been elected to do and hope that forceful leadership would divert the public and the politicians from Watergate. In the first week of spring, he made a series of addresses and appearances designed to show off a confident President.

He got started with a nationwide radio address on American education. He called for action on legislation he had previously proposed to limit forced busing, and for support of an anti-busing amendment, in support of the principle of neighborhood schools. He wanted more federal funding for elementary and high schools, but less federal control. He asked for $1.3 billion in funds to support the Basic Educational Opportunity Grants Program, so that "every qualified student in America has an opportunity for post-secondary education." He wanted to expand the Guaranteed Student Loan program.[69]

Two days later, on March 26, he gave a thoughtful and upbeat speech to members of the American Agricultural Editors' Association in the EOB. His theme was the need to increase production, avoid controls, and provide incentives to America's farmers. He promised that fertilizer prices would go down as the price of oil dropped.[70] The following day, he sent a formal recommendation to the House and Senate for his proposals for campaign reform legislation.

That evening, Nixon went to the Hilton in Washington to speak at a fund-raiser for the Republican Congressional Committee. It was something of an embarrassment that there were empty tables at the rear of the ballroom, and that for the first time in memory no Republican governor was in attendance. But those who did pay $1,000 to be there gave him a warm welcome, and he was relaxed and at ease in one of his most familiar roles—speaking to the faithful, attempting to rouse their spirits at a time when the prospects looked bleak.

He opened by saying he was aware that prices had gone up; he had been in politics long enough to recall when $50 per plate was considered large. He said that paying $1,000 was rather like making a bet at the track, and he wanted to assure the diners that they had made a good bet on a solid horse. That got him going on his favorite campaign themes, peace and prosperity. His Administration had brought about both, and because it had, Republicans could anticipate victories in November. They could point to other accomplishments, such as the end of the draft, the end of the campus riots, and a start on eliminating the plague of drugs in America.

Republicans did not have to stop with self-praise for past accomplishments; they could also talk about the future. His Administration would provide health insurance for all Americans, including insurance for catastrophic illnesses, and it would do so based on private insurance rather than socialized medicine. It would stop busing. It would achieve a welfare reform that would "make it less profitable for a person to go on welfare than to go to work." It would revitalize the railroads, rebuild the merchant marine, improve mass transit, and achieve independence in energy. And it would do all this without raising taxes, or increasing the size of government and the bureaucracy, or imposing controls on the economy. In sum, "candidates who support this Administration will have a strong case to take to the people this fall."[71]

On March 29, he seized an opportunity to remind the public of who he was and what he had accomplished when he spoke on the parade grounds at the National War College at Fort McNair, Washington, D.C. The occasion was the Vietnam Veterans Day ceremonies. With an American flag flying behind him, and another on his lapel, he gave a short but forceful statement. He praised the men who had fought in Vietnam. He said that "this generation of Americans will be remembered because we not only ended a war and ended it honorably, but because we went on from there to build a structure of peace in the world that will last."[72] He followed up two days later with a radio address that promised more help for Vietnam veterans from the Veterans Administration.

Taken altogether it was a bravura performance, showing once again the great inner strength of this man, able to keep his chin up despite body blows that would have felled an ox. Alas, it did little good. Although his specific proposals were progressive and positive and needed, and although in many cases they were programs the liberals only wished they had put forward, they were all but ignored.

Even worse for Nixon, his pep talk to the Republicans, along with his offer to campaign for their candidates, fell flat. Of the eleven Republican senators seeking re-election, only Henry Bellmon (Okla.) said he wanted Nixon to campaign for him. One senator told a reporter that most people would regard close association with Nixon as "the kiss of death."[73] Bob Finch, former Secretary of HEW and a man who had been close to Nixon for decades, said that he "couldn't run for dogcatcher without it turning into a referendum on Watergate."[74] Right-wingers in the party expressed fears that Nixon would enter into an arms control agreement with Brezhnev when he went to the Moscow summit in June, while Senator Jacob Javits charged that Nixon was trying to appease the conservatives in an attempt "to please a given number of senators: 33 plus one." Javits said it was "tragic" that Nixon was playing "impeachment politics."[75]

The leaks continued to erode his defenses. One was that at least ten of the forty-two tapes sought by Jaworski did not exist. Another anticipated Nixon's nomination of Leonard Firestone as Ambassador to Belgium. The press reported that Firestone had contributed $100,000 to the 1972 campaign, and his brothers another $100,000. A third said that the House Government Operations Committee was going to report that $17 million in federal funds had been spent on the President's homes. The columnists were saying that Nixon's struggle over procedures with the House Judiciary Committee only fed the suspicion that he feared a battle over substance.

At a meeting of officers of the building and construction unions, George Meany was cheered by the hard-hats—the same men who had marched in support of Nixon during the Vietnam War—when he said that "the American people have completely lost confidence" in the President and called for his impeachment. Meany shared the fears of conservatives who suspected Nixon was about to enter into an arms control deal. Kissinger was currently in Moscow, preparing for the summit; Meany said, "I pray every night that Henry Kissinger won't give the Russians the Washington Monument—he's given them every goddamn thing else."[76]

Senator Buckley, responding to Nixon's blitz of legislative proposals, pronounced the Administration's obituary. "The Nixon presidency is burned out," Buckley told a college audience. "There may be signs of energy, but there can never again be life. The spirit of the Nixon Administration has been shattered forever, irrevocably."[77]

On March 30, even Nixon's Vice President appeared to turn on him. Speaking to a group of Midwest Republicans, Ford drew cheers when he said that "the political lesson of Watergate is this. Never again must America allow an arrogant, elite guard of political adolescents like CREEP to bypass the regular party organization and dictate the terms of a national election."[78] The effect, Ford aide Bob Hartmann noted, "was electric. The Vice President was instantly hailed as the *de facto* head of the Republican Party."[79] The effect was strengthened when Senator Percy and Governors Reagan and Rockefeller, who were present, endorsed Ford's remarks. It was strengthened a couple of weeks later, when John Osborne of the *New Republic* reported in his weekly article "White House Watch" that Ford had told him in an interview that Kissinger had asked about Ford's intention, and been reassured that he intended to keep him in his Cabinet. Osborne wrote that Ford would get rid of Secretary Schlesinger at DOD, and of Ron Ziegler.

Ford had said that "President Nixon is in great health, mentally and physically." Osborne asked him what prompted him to remark on Nixon's mental condition. As Osborne summarized Ford's response, "The hours he's had to spend with the President, mostly listening to Mr. Nixon talk about this and that, have on a few occasions driven the Vice President close to distraction. This . . . indicates that the President has undergone a change of personality in the past year or so."

Ford later said he thought the interview with Osborne was "off the record," but he did not deny the substance.[80]

Bryce Harlow resigned. George Shultz left Treasury, to be replaced by William Simon. Mel Laird left.

The only man who spoke up for Nixon in that first week of spring was one whose support Nixon could have done without. Bob Haldeman, under indictment in connection with the cover-up, spoke to the Young Presidents' Organization on the subject of "crisis management." Haldeman asserted that Nixon "didn't know a damned thing about Watergate" and "didn't know about a cover-up." Asked about Nixon's greatest weakness, Haldeman said it was Nixon's "softheartedness at the personal level," his inability to dismiss or discipline people.[81]

All in all, Nixon was undergoing a barrage such as no previous President had ever had to face, not even Andrew Johnson. It was no good comparing himself to Lincoln and his ordeal, because even at his lowest moment, when terrible things were being said about him, Lincoln had plenty of creditable defenders. Nixon had Ziegler, Warren, Haig, his own lawyers, and Haldeman.

CHAPTER THIRTEEN

EXPLETIVES DELETED
April–May 1974

ON THE WHITE HOUSE lawn, workers were sawing deadwood from the giant elms and replacing sod where crabgrass and dandelions had intruded. It had been a full year since those tasks were last performed. All around the capital the tulips and the cherry blossoms were about to bloom. As it had been before 1974 and would be again, Washington was about to become one of the most beautiful cities in the world.

Despite these welcome appearances of normalcy, 1974 was not a normal year. There was a great deal of work to be done, because the previous twelve months had been a time of shocks and surprises, topped by the Mideast confrontation and the energy crisis. In addition, since 1941 Washington had been a wartime capital more often than not—the United States had been involved in foreign wars for eighteen of the past thirty-two years. But since the end of January 1973, no American soldier had been in combat anywhere in the world, there was no more draft, and defense expenditures were going down for the first time since 1953. There was promise that such expenditures could go down even further, as a result of arms control agreements that Nixon and Brezhnev had indicated they were eager to enter into at the upcoming Moscow summit. Scheduled for the beginning of summer, normally that event would have commanded Washington's attention.

But in 1974, about the only attention the summit got was warnings from conservatives that Nixon had better not allow himself to be seduced by Brezhnev. The liberals, who should have been ecstatic at the possibility of real arms control for the first time since the Cold War began, and who should therefore have been supporting Nixon, instead chose to warn him that he could not use diplomacy to escape his Watergate problems. Historically, governments that are in trouble at home have manufactured foreign crises, or even gone to war, to divert attention. In 1974, liberals accused Nixon of seeking peace in order to divert attention.

The obsession with the past had gripped the capital for over a year. When last the workmen were cutting out the deadwood, John Dean had started to implicate the President in the cover-up. The summer of 1973 had been consumed with the Ervin Committee hearings. As the first leaves started to fall, it was the "Saturday Night Massacre," not the Mideast and energy crises, that filled the newspapers and evening news broadcasts. Even the first snowstorm, which ordinarily captivates the capital, had yielded pride of place to the public uproar over missing tapes.

About once a month, Nixon had tried counterattacks. Initially they were mostly negative, consisting of denials, or the dismissal of Haldeman and Ehrlichman, or the firing of Cox. More recently, he had been more positive, making proposals to deal with the energy crisis and other problems. Neither approach had worked. In the past couple of months, he had advanced a legislative program, with the emphasis on health insurance for all, more grants and loans to college students, welfare reform, mass transit, and other items that ordinarily would have found strong support from the liberals. But they ignored them, because Nixon had proposed them.

"Never question another man's motives" was one of Ike's favorite maxims. In Nixon's case, over the past year, it had become habitual for the politicians on both sides of the aisle always to question Nixon's motives rather than deal with his proposals. The nation has paid a heavy price for these suspicions; seventeen years after the spring of 1974 all the problems remained, and no one has yet come up with better solutions than Nixon had offered.

The President had been reduced to spending hours in mundane meetings with obscure persons. At the beginning of spring, he invited at least a dozen people from around the country who had taken out newspaper advertisements praising him to the Oval Office for private audiences.

In the news reports, in the first days of April, Nixon was being pilloried for his tax returns from 1969 to 1973. The Joint Committee on Internal Revenue Taxation, and the IRS, ruled that he owed $432,787 in back taxes, plus interest. *The New York Times* put a box of figures on page 1, showing "Undeclared Nixon Income and Impermissible Deductions." By far the biggest item was the gift of his vice presidential papers. He got a double whammy on that; the deduction was disallowed, but the Archives kept the papers. Leaks from the congressional committee charged that the papers were never worth the amount Nixon deducted anyway, as he had culled the papers before turning them over the National Archives, keeping for himself his correspondence with various VIPs as well as sensitive files "respecting J. Edgar Hoover, Jacqueline Kennedy and the Vietnam war." Most of the papers Nixon did turn over, according to leaks, were newspaper clippings, "thank you" notes, and turn-downs of speaking invitations.[1]

This author has worked extensively in Nixon's vice presidential papers in the National Archives. He can affirm that the VIP correspondence has been pulled; he can state, however, that the papers contain thousands of items of great interest and value, including handwritten notes, handwritten speech drafts, memos, and intimate correspondence. There can be no doubt whatsoever that had Nixon chosen to sell the papers to autograph collectors, he could have realized close to a half-million dollars for them.

Nixon had cause to protest either the finding that he owed back taxes or the Archives' position that the papers now belonged to the government, but he did neither. Instead, as he had promised, he got started on paying up.

On April 2, French President Georges Pompidou died. On April 5, Nixon flew to Paris for memorial services. In a statement at Orly Airport, he included a paragraph that seemed to some observers to be more anticipating his own autobiography than describing Pompidou's life: "His last months were a period of true greatness, because despite the adversity, he rose above it and served to the last with all of the courage and all the distinction that had been the mark of his life of service to his country."[2]

Nixon was in Paris for three days. After the mass for Pompidou in Notre Dame Cathedral, he held private meetings with European and Asian leaders. In this international setting, two sides to President Nixon were on view. The first was the world statesman. Le Figaro, the leading conservative paper in Paris, titled its account of his doings "The Sovereign of the Western World." It spoke of his "Operation Charlemagne," and in a cartoon depicted its version of Nixon's relationship to European leaders. A crowned woman, representing Europe, knelt before Nixon, who was seated on a throne. She kissed his extended hand; his feet were on a black-bordered death notice, presumably Pompidou's. By contrast Le Monde, the most respected newspaper in France, said that Nixon had demonstrated spectacularly his continuing ability to dominate international politics.

The other Nixon on view was the working politician. On three occasions he plunged through police lines to shake hands and talk with curbside crowds. He asked a policeman, in English, "How do you like your job?" When he got a blank stare, he told the crowd (again in English), "Forty years ago I majored in French. After four years I could speak it. I could write it. I read all of the classics. And today I just understand a little" (only the last sentence was true). The French people responded with almost universal bafflement to Nixon's American electioneering techniques; a high French official leaked a letter in which he said Nixon had "shamelessly substituted a publicity campaign for the mourning of an entire nation, introducing an atmosphere of loud feverishness, the discourtesy of which is equaled only by its clumsiness." *Le Monde* expressed its indignation in a front-page editorial titled "The Nixon Festival."[3]

BACK in the States, House Judiciary Committee Chairman Peter Rodino held a briefing. He noted that his committee had requested tapes and documents from the White House more than a month ago, that Nixon's lawyers had since stalled on a response, and that the Committee's patience "is now wearing thin." He reminded the White House that his committee had been granted subpoena power and demanded a response to the request by April 9.[4]

On April 9, St. Clair told the House Judiciary Committee that the White House needed more time to decide how to respond. He promised that by April 22 the White House would be ready to furnish materials that "will enable the committee to complete its inquiry promptly." He did not say what that material would consist of, or what form it would take.[5]

When Nixon returned to the States, he signed a bill raising the minimum wage from $1.60 to $2 per hour, with a further increase to $2.30 on January 1, 1976.[6] Then he flew to the Midwest. His first stop was in Ohio, where he inspected tornado damage in Xenia. The next day, he went campaigning in Michigan.

In so doing, he was taking a risk. The occasion was a special election in Michigan's 8th Congressional District, for a seat that had been held by the Republicans since 1932. The Democratic candidate, J. Robert Traxler, was saying that Nixon was the only issue; the Republican, James Sparling, was charging that Traxler was a tool of the labor unions. The national press declared that Nixon's foray into the district made the election a test of his political strength.

If nothing else, Nixon showed his drawing power. More than 7,500 people greeted him at the Saginaw airport, while in the small towns of Bad Axe, Cass City, and Sandusky, none larger than 3,000 inhabitants, he drew crowds of 2,000 or more. His speeches hit on his standard themes of peace and prosperity. As always, he praised the local high school bands, the weather, the Boy Scouts, the Girl Scouts, and the great state of Michigan.[7]

Five days later, Traxler won the election; Sparling ran eleven points behind the Republican candidate of 1972.

That was a minor irritant. Nixon had meanwhile taken an all but lethal blow. On April 11, the House Judiciary Committee voted 33 to 3 to subpoena forty-two tapes. Republicans Edward Hutchinson (Mich.), the ranking minority member of the Committee, Charles Wiggins (Calif.), and Trent Lott (Miss.) voted nay. Lott's district had given Nixon his highest percentage in 1972: 87 percent. The Committee subpoena gave Nixon until April 25 to respond.

There seemed no way Nixon could refuse. Executive privilege, so useful to him in fending off Sirica, Cox, Jaworski, and Ervin, apparently was of no use in his struggle with the Judiciary Committee as it undertook its constitutionally mandated impeachment inquiry.

If Nixon refused to comply, he would almost certainly be impeached because of the refusal. If he had any doubts about that, the Republican leadership in the Senate moved to dispel them. In a meeting with presidential assistant Dean Burch, Senators Hugh Scott (minority leader), Robert Griffin (whip), John Tower (policy chairman), Norris Cotton (N.H.—conference chairman), Wallace Bennett (Utah—conference secretary), and William Brock (Tenn.—campaign chairman) told Burch that if Nixon refused to cooperate, "the first article in the bill of impeachment could well be contempt of Congress."[8]

Five days later, Jaworski appeared before Sirica, seeking an order forcing Nixon to yield sixty-four additional taped conversations. On April 18, Sirica issued the subpoena.

Nixon's instinct was to tell them all to go to hell. St. Clair and Buzhardt told him that was not an option. Reluctantly, he recognized the reality—he had to make some kind of accommodation. He wondered if an abridged transcript or summary would suffice. Haig thought so; the lawyers did not. Nixon said that to comply fully would open him to an unending series of demands for more.

"We have to put out something," Buzhardt pointed out. "We have to take the mystery out of those tapes." He suggested full, verbatim transcripts of relevant material.

Ziegler was opposed. He feared the effect of Nixon's rough language on the President's image. Nixon agreed with Ziegler. Buzhardt suggested they delete the offensive language. On that basis, Nixon then gave his tentative approval.[9]

Rose Woods and a team of fifteen White House secretaries went to work transcribing the subpoenaed tapes. Then St. Clair, Buzhardt, and two of his assistants, Richard Hauser and Jeff Shepard, read the transcripts to compare them to the tapes. Ziegler's aide, Diane Sawyer, checked them again. Finally, Nixon read the typed pages. He eliminated words, phrases, passages. He crossed out curse words, insulting references to various senators, discussions in which he considered options that he later turned down, and other material. He, or his typists, heard things later listeners did not hear, and failed to hear things that they did. For example, in the White House version, Nixon says: "In order to get off the cover-up line," which the House Judiciary Committee's investigators heard as "in order to get on with the cover-up plan." In the White House version, Nixon says that the burglars "are covered on their situation," while the Committee heard "our cover there." Some particularly damaging words or sentences were marked "unintelligible" or "inaudible."*

The White House tape players failed to pick up a passage from Nixon's March 22 conversation with John Mitchell, in which Nixon had said, "I don't give a shit what happens. I want you to stonewall it, let them plead the Fifth Amendment, cover-up, or anything else, if it'll save it—save the plan." The House investigators did hear the passage; when it was revealed, it appeared that Nixon had made a transparent attempt to cover it up. But, as he pointed out in his memoirs, it would have been ridiculous for him to eliminate a passage from his transcripts when it was on one of the tapes that had already been handed over to the Committee. Further, he also failed to include his follow-on sentence to Mitchell: "On the other hand, I would prefer, as I said to you, that you do it the other way."[10]

Still, Nixon's claim that the material he released was accurate, complete, and would tell the whole story was a blatant falsehood. Professor William B. Todd of the University of Texas, one of the world's great scholars in textual criticism and bibliography, subjected the transcripts to the kind of analysis he would ordinarily use for a Shakespeare folio or a 1776 edition of *Wealth of Nations*. He concluded: "Throughout recorded history no author has ever produced, albeit unwittingly, a text so systematically debased and corrupt." Among many other items, Todd pointed out that the electronic bugs in the EOB worked perfectly for hours of conversation in which little of consequence was said, but suddenly were "inaudible" for 367 remarks in a short, single conversation. After giving many such examples, Todd concluded that "much of all this reflects persistent editorial expurgation, not repeatedly convenient electronic breakdown."

---

*In the White House version, when Nixon complains that the bug in the DNC produced nothing, Colson replies, "Well, frankly we did," followed by a pause and then a new subject. In the special prosecutor's version, Colson replies, "apparently we did, of course, at Watergate mainly on Hughes." The special prosecutor's version was not available to scholars until June 1991, when the Nixon Presidential Materials Project released twenty-eight hours of tapes, primarily from the period January through April 1973. There were no great surprises, no smoking guns; there were additional details on how Mitchell got the money for Hunt, how deeply Mitchell was involved, how inventive Nixon was in explaining his motives, how quickly he could convince himself of his own innocence, how realistic he could be about dangers (did Dean have a tape?), how much he loved *Six Crises* and the Hiss case, and other Nixonana, as well as further confirmation that Hughes was the target of the original bug. The tapes are "sanitized." The Archives removed national security–related material, purely personal items, and items that would damage a living person. Nixon had an opportunity to censor material, and did; how much he took out is not clear.

Todd noted, in addition, how many times various damaging passages had gone through various typewriters and secretaries, leading to "countless indications of lacunae in the conversations or inexplicable non sequiturs." He also remarked on "silent deletions," that is, material removed but not noted. His conclusion was that the printed version of the transcripts "submits nothing which can be accepted with any confidence. To the contrary it proceeds in an obscurantic manner where more is taken away than is ever given, where thousands of words disappear without notice and hundreds of other lie hidden in deceptive disguise, where teams of editors and typists labor strenuously to accomplish always less and less, and where then, all this done and undone, the author himself now confidently proclaims that we have enough and more than enough."[11]

How Nixon thought he could get away with all this is a mystery. Perhaps he counted on the public's faith in the Presidency, that people wanted to believe in the President so badly that they would believe, no matter what. Perhaps he felt he would never lose control of the tapes themselves, so no one could ever check up on him. Perhaps he thought that even if textual criticism took place, or even if the tapes became public and could be compared to his version, it would take so long that he would have completed his term. Perhaps he just did not care.

His lawyers were disturbed at Nixon's excisions, but he told them there was a distinction between what he did and what he talked about and considered doing, and that as only he knew when he was innocently exploring options, only he could decide what to leave in and what to take out.

Finally, someone—Nixon says it was Buzhardt—came up with the suggestion that such excisions be characterized as "material unrelated to Presidential action deleted," which was done.

But by far the most famous deletions were of expletives. Whenever Nixon used a curse word, he crossed it out and substituted the phrase "expletive deleted." That turned out to be a big mistake, as it gave an entirely erroneous impression of Nixon's ordinary language. The truth is that Nixon swore less often, and less coarsely, than any of his immediate predecessors. The expletives deleted consisted, overwhelmingly, of "damn," "hell," "Christ," "What in the name of Christ," "Goddamn," "this crap," and so forth. Nixon seldom used "shit" and never, on the tapes this author has listened to, the common slang word for sexual intercourse that almost all American males use when they are angry or want to show in an all-male gathering that they are one of the guys. On occasion he would say "asshole," but never—at least in the sixty hours of tapes available for listening in the National Archives—does he refer to a woman's anatomy in an obscene way. In fact, he was rather circumspect in his word choice, old-fashioned, generally avoiding rough language; when he used words like "Hell" and "damn" he did so in a low-key, almost embarrassed sort of way. Anyone who knew Eisenhower, or Johnson, or Kennedy cannot fail to be struck by the contrast.

Yet the idea that Nixon swore like a muleskinner is now firmly established in American political folklore. In the introduction to *The New York Times* printed version of the White House tapes, the editors expressed the attitude of most Americans when they wrote, "shit was the mildest of the deleted expletives." They did not explain how they knew that; it is certain that they had not heard the tapes when they wrote it.

Had Nixon left the words he used in the transcripts, almost no one would have noticed them; because he took them out, he set off an uproar that matched, and possibly exceeded, the reaction to the Saturday Night Massacre. In a sense, he was ultimately done in, not because of the deeds he had done, but for words he never used.

Of course he had no one to blame but himself. He was the one who eliminated the words and substituted that ridiculous phrase. He was warned about the probable effect; Buzhardt's aide Jeff Shepard told him he was making a mistake. Nixon replied, "If my mother ever heard me use words like that she would turn over in her grave." Initially, his secretaries took out "God" and left "damn," but when Nixon reviewed the transcripts he ordered it all taken out. He repeated his concern about his mother and added that he was worried about the reaction in the Bible Belt.[12]

Working on the transcripts was tedious, time-consuming, frustrating, and enervating. On April 20, at the end of a long day, Nixon scribbled a note: "D-Day. 1. Any more tapes will destroy the office. 2. Leaving the question open will only invite more unreasonable demands. 3. Better to fight and lose defending the office than surrender and win a personal victory at disastrous long-range cost to the office of the Presidency."[13]

The note described the situation; it did not record a decision. The work on the transcriptions went forward. There were over one thousand pages. Nixon hoped that by making the whole thing public before he handed it over to the Committee, he would accomplish two objectives. First, the sheer bulk of the transcripts would bring home dramatically just how much the Committee was asking of the President. Second, the most damaging parts would be submerged in the mass of material. Because of the deletions, and because in verbatim transcripts of conversations one cannot see the facial expressions, the body language, or be privy to prior knowledge that only requires a "you know?" for the speaker to carry on, much of what eventually appeared was incomprehensible. Certainly none of it was conclusive in the sense of producing the "smoking gun" that by this time had become most people's definition of what was an impeachable offense.

Nevertheless, the mood in the White House was one of melancholy and inevitability. Nixon's lawyers were downcast. Haig was worried. Ziegler did as he was told and he told the President what he knew the President wanted to hear. There was a vacuum of advisers, a result of the Nixon method of governing. He had never had a kitchen cabinet, a group he trusted. Instead, there had been small factions and individuals who had independent access to the President, but who did not function as a group. There had been Haldeman and Ehrlichman, who had worked as a team; there had been Colson, who worked on his own; there had been Dean, off by himself; there had been Mitchell; off to the side there had been Garment; there had been Harlow and Laird for political wisdom; then there had been Buchanan and Price, the speechwriters; there had been Abplanalp and Rebozo, the friends. But there was no group of men who could sit down with the President and undertake full-scale, unambiguous, straight-from-the-heart discussions of Nixon's problems and what to do about them.

ON April 24, St. Clair requested and got a five-day extension on the House Judiciary Committee's subpoena for the tapes. St. Clair gave no hint that the White House was going to hand over edited transcripts rather than tapes.

That week, government agencies announced that the gross national product was down by the greatest amount since 1958, and that the rate of inflation in the first three months of 1974 was 14½ percent.

On April 25, Nixon took time off from his editing to fly to Jackson, Mississippi, to address the Mississippi Economic Council. Down in the Magnolia State there were still those who wanted to believe in the President, as Nixon said, and they came out by the thousands. Indeed, he got the largest and most enthusiastic public reception he had received in over a year. More than ten thousand jammed the Mississippi Coliseum, while thousands more gathered outside to listen to Nixon on a loudspeaker. Senators Eastland and Stennis were there, along with the governor and most of the congressional delegation. Mississippi had given Nixon his largest margin of support in 1972, 78 percent, and the popular view there was that Nixon was being persecuted by liberal Democrats and the news media. A poll of newspaper readers in Jackson revealed that 98 percent thought Nixon should "hang in there" and serve out the remainder of his term.[14]

Nixon returned the warm feelings. He told his audience that "no State in the Union is represented by men in the Congress who more vigorously speak up for . . . the Nation than [those from] Mississippi." He praised Eastland specifically, and said of Stennis, "when they write profiles in courage, he will be there." He said that while he had engaged in debates with his good Democratic friends over the decades, "I can assure you that whenever the issue was the honor of America or the strength of America or respect for America, Mississippi spoke as one voice for America and not for any one party."

In the body of his remarks, he assured the Economic Council that 1974 would be a good year, 1975 a better one, and 1976 the best ever.[15] He left immediately after the speech, to fly back to Washington to go back to work on the tapes.

Three days later, he got some good news, almost the first in a year. Mitchell and Stans, on trial for accepting a $200,000 campaign contribution from fugitive financier Robert Vesco, were acquitted by a jury in Washington. The verdict was made even sweeter by the implication drawn from it; John Dean's testimony had been central to the prosecution's case, so as one White House aide put it, "by implication [it] makes John Dean a liar, which makes one wonder how many other lies he's told."

Nixon never got anything for free. In this case, the downside was that the Mitchell/Stans acquittal on lack of solid evidence made the tapes that much more valuable. The acquittal had given the House Judiciary Committee pause; spokesmen indicated that it would drop its inquiry into the Vesco case as a potentially impeachable offense. But it also strengthened Rodino's determination to have the tapes themselves; he told reporters that he would accept nothing less.[16]

Still, Nixon got a boost from the verdict. The people had spoken, through a jury, and they had acquitted his men. He had always trusted the people. He was ready to turn to them for a decision. He would give them a goodly portion of the transcripts of the tapes that the politicians, the judges, the reporters, the newscasters, and the prosecutors had been clamoring for ever since Butterfield revealed their existence. Let the people judge.

NIXON spent Monday, April 29, at Camp David, working on the speech he would deliver that night as he released the transcripts of the subpoenaed tapes. Ray Price was with him. When they finished the text, Nixon invited Price to join him for a drink on the Aspen terrace. Dusk was falling on a pleasant spring evening. As the two men sipped their martinis, they reminisced about the dramatic weekend they had spent at that spot exactly one year earlier. Nixon wondered aloud, as he had done many times, whether he had done the right thing in firing Haldeman and Ehrlichman. They talked about the Watergate struggle over the past year, then turned to other events. They reviewed the Middle East crisis, the economic and energy problems, the battles with Congress over the War Powers Act and over the budget, and relations with the Russians.

Price, growing emotional, turned to Nixon and said that he had never admired him so much as he had for the way Nixon had stood up to the pressures of those twelve months. Then they climbed into the helicopter for the short flight to the White House.[17]

At 9:01 P.M., from the Oval Office, Nixon began speaking to the nation. An American flag hung behind him; he wore another in his lapel. On his desk sat a pile of folders, containing 1,200 pages of transcription from forty-six taped conversations (including eight already in the possession of the House Judiciary Committee). The President looked grave and a bit haggard, but in command of himself. He spoke confidently. He was taking one of the biggest risks in a career full of risk taking, but he had brought himself to a peak for this presentation.

Nixon opened by saying that the actions he was about to take "will at last, once and for all, show that what I knew and what I did with regard to the Watergate break-in and cover-up were just as I have described them to you from the very beginning." Indicating the folders, he said that they contained "all the relevant portions of all of the subpoenaed conversations that were recorded," as well as transcripts of conversations that had not been subpoenaed. He announced that they would all be delivered to the Committee in the morning; unstated but understood was the point that the tapes themselves would not be delivered. Nixon did say that Rodino and Hutchinson (ranking minority member of the Committee) could come to the White House to listen to the actual tapes to determine for themselves that the transcriptions were accurate.

He returned to the theme that the materials he was releasing "will tell it all." Again unstated but understood was a basic point: that with this action, Nixon was drawing a line. No more tapes. Ever.

Nixon confessed that he was violating his own deeply held belief in the principle of executive privilege. He said he was doing so because the public had come to believe that "the tapes must incriminate the President, or otherwise he would not insist on their privacy. . . . I want there to be no question remaining about the fact that the President has nothing to hide in this matter."

He had come to his decision, he explained, because over the past year "the wildest accusations have been given banner headlines and ready credence as well. Rumor, gossip, innuendo, accounts from unnamed sources . . . have filled the morning newspapers, and then are repeated on the evening newscasts day after day."

The distinction between fact and speculation had been blurred. He wanted to return to the basic question, which was "whether the President personally acted improperly in the Watergate matter." Only one man had made that charge, the discredited John Dean. Yet his testimony had sparked an impeachment inquiry, which was putting the nation through a "wrenching ordeal."

Returning to the subject of the transcripts, Nixon said, almost sheepishly, "I realize that these transcripts will provide grist for many sensational stories in the press. Parts will seem to be contradictory with one another, and parts will be in conflict with some of the testimony given in the Senate Watergate committee hearings." Parts "will embarrass me and those with whom I have talked," parts would become "the subject of speculation and even ridicule," and parts "will be seized upon by political and journalistic opponents."

But despite the confusions and contradictions, "what does come through clearly is this," that John Dean lied when he said the President knew about the cover-up in September 1972. "I first learned of it when Mr. Dean himself told me about it in this office on March 21—some 6 months later." His revelations on that date came "as a sharp surprise."

Nixon said he realized that when people saw the transcript of the March 21 conversation, they would find ambiguous words, and discussions that explored many options, but "the record of my actions is totally clear now, and I still believe it was totally correct then." Although the transcript "is one [in] which different meanings could be read in by different people," Nixon insisted that in the end, "I did not intend the further payment to Hunt or anyone else be made."

He quoted himself, from the tapes. To Haldeman and Ehrlichman: "It is ridiculous to talk about clemency. They all knew that," and "we all have to do the right thing. . . . We just cannot have this kind of a business." To Henry Petersen: "I want you to be sure to understand that you know we are going to get to the bottom of this thing." To John Dean: "Tell the truth. That is the thing I have told everybody around here."

Anyone who read the transcripts with an open and fair mind, he said, would have to conclude "that I personally had no knowledge of the break-in before it occurred, that I had no knowledge of the cover-up until . . . March 21, that I never offered clemency for the defendants, and that after March 21, my actions were directed toward finding the facts and seeing that justice was done, fairly and according to the law."

In summing up, Nixon said, "I know in my own heart that through the long, painful, and difficult process revealed in these transcripts, I was trying in that period to discover what was right and to do what was right." He hoped and trusted that his fellow Americans would reach the same conclusion.

In his last paragraph, he quoted yet again another President who had been "subjected to unmerciful attack," Abraham Lincoln. Lincoln had said he did the best he could: "If the end brings me out all right, what is said against me won't amount to anything. If the end brings me out wrong, ten angels swearing I was right would make no difference."[18]

It was an effective performance under the circumstances. Nixon had been smart enough to hit his biggest single problem, the March 21 tape, head on. By putting his own interpretation on it before the public read it, he had stolen a march. His admission that he had considered paying Hunt's hush money was inescapable, given what was on the tape; his insistence that he had never authorized the actual payment was a daring gamble, in view of the fact that $75,000 had been handed over to Hunt's lawyer within hours of the meeting. But the clemency issue bolstered his position. He had said that clemency would be wrong, and clemency had not been given.

The sheer bulk of the material he released precluded instant analysis. Many of the residents of Northwest Washington spent most of April 30 reading the documents, published in book form by the Government Printing Office. It was 1,308 pages long, with a 50-page foreword by St. Clair ("In all of the thousands of words spoken, even though they are unclear and ambiguous, not once does it appear that the President of the United States was engaged in a criminal plot to obstruct justice"), with a pale blue cover that carried the presidential seal. The title was *Submission of Recorded Presidential Conversations to the Committee on the Judiciary of the House of Representatives by Richard Nixon*. It sold for $12.25.

Nixon's boldness in releasing his edited version of March 21 exposed him to counterattack, one that John Doar mounted immediately. Doar called the transcript "not accurate." He said that many of the "unintelligibles" in Nixon's version were perfectly clear to him, and they were damning to Nixon. Doar advised Rodino—and Rodino agreed—that it would not be "prudent" for Rodino and Hutchinson to go to the White House to verify the transcripts. And Rodino's committee, in a partisan vote of 20–18 on May 1, informed Nixon that "you have failed to comply with the Committee's subpoena."[19]

In his speech, Nixon had not mentioned the latest Jaworski subpoena, but on May 1 the White House announced that the President had invoked executive privilege and would refuse to supply the Special Prosecutor with any more material for the trials of Nixon's aides. The statement asserted that disclosure of any more conversations "would be contrary to the public interest" and that "a President is not subject to compulsory process from a court."[20]

In the uproar, that was hardly noticed. By May 2, people around the country were reading the transcripts, large parts of which were being published in the press. They were fascinating, absorbing, dramatic beyond anything the country had ever before seen. The Pentagon Papers had also stirred up the nation, but to nothing like the extent that the transcripts did. Here was the President in the most intimate conversations with his most intimate aides. Some readers were shocked by the material. Nixon's contempt for so many people, his vindictiveness, his apparent vile language, his double-dealing, his cold cynicism, his overwhelming anger, all reinforced the views the Nixon-haters had held for years, while they shook his supporters. Still, in a quick scan no one could find a smoking gun, which led many Republicans to let go with a huge sigh of relief.

IN the turmoil, Nixon stuck to his schedule. On April 30, he spoke to the U.S. Chamber of Commerce in Washington. On May 1, he issued a Law Day proclamation ("every person knows that no man or woman is above the requirements of the law").[21] On May 3, he flew to Phoenix, Arizona, to address a Republican rally. He drew fifteen thousand cheering partisans, along with a few hecklers and some "Out Now" signs. He was combative: "I simply say this tonight: the time has come to get Watergate behind us and get on with the business of America." He vowed that he would stay on and meet America's challenges.[22] At a reception at Barry Goldwater's mountaintop house, both Goldwater and John Rhodes told him how pleased they were that he had complied with the demand for the tapes, and promised their continuing support.[23]

From Phoenix, the President flew to Spokane where he presided at the opening ceremonies for Expo '74. Then it was back to Washington, and on up to Camp David, to assess the reaction to the transcripts.

It was overwhelmingly negative. Partly this was because of what was in the transcripts, which by now people had had a chance to read. The impact came not so much from anything specific, not even the discussion of hush money payments, as from the tone of the conversations. Another reason was the large number of "unintelligibles," especially when the President was speaking—this inevitably raised suspicions. Further, the President who had insisted most strongly on his right to privacy had done more than any other President to destroy his own privacy. Worst of all were those "expletive deleteds," which instantly entered the language and made Nixon the butt of innumerable jokes.

In addition, Nixon paid a price for something he had counted on to sustain him, the people's belief in the sanctity of the office of the President. In his first term, he had participated aggressively in building the image of the President, as Kennedy and Johnson had done before him. The transcripts showed that nowhere is the political game played in a rougher or rawer way than in the Oval Office; they did not show that in this regard Nixon was not much different from his immediate predecessors. He suffered inordinately because he was the man who busted the myth.

By the end of the first week in May the adverse reaction had become a veritable deluge. On the 7th, Senator Scott renounced his support of Nixon because of the "immoral" activities revealed in the transcripts. Scott said they showed "deplorable, disgusting, shabby, immoral performances" by all participants in the conversations.[24] John Rhodes said he could not disagree with Scott, and on May 9 declared that "the content of the transcripts is devastating." Senator Marlow Cook (R.-Ky.) accused

Nixon of "moral turpitude."[25] Many other Republicans said similar things; privately most Democrats said worse things, publicly they wisely kept silent.

Eric Sevareid of CBS labeled the conversations a "moral indictment without known precedent." The newscasters delighted in reading passages to their audiences. William Safire, once Nixon's favorite speechwriter, now a columnist for *The New York Times*, charged that the transcripts revealed a man "guilty of conduct unbecoming a President." They illuminated Nixon's "dark side," his "sleazy" acts, his "fear" of personal confrontations. Safire concluded, "the reaction after reading the poisonous fruit of his eavesdropping tree is (expletive deleted)!"[26]

Editors who had always been supportive turned on Nixon. In his Sunday column William Randolph Hearst, Jr., called the transcripts "damning." They showed Nixon as a man "with a moral blind spot" and made his impeachment inevitable. "The gang talking on the tapes, even the censored version, comes through in just that way—a gang of racketeers talking over strategy. . . . [Nixon] stands convicted by his own words as a man who deliberately and repeatedly tried to keep the truth from the American people."[27]

The Chicago *Tribune* was appalled. "He is humorless to the point of being inhumane," the paper said in an editorial. "He is devious. He is vacillating. He is profane. He is willing to be led. He displays dismaying gaps in his knowledge."[28] The Omaha *World-Herald*, which had three times endorsed Nixon for President, called for his resignation because of "the appallingly low level of political morality in the White House."[29] The Los Angeles *Times* and the Cleveland *Plain Dealer* called for his impeachment.[30]

This extraordinary outburst stunned the people closest to Nixon. "If there is a hell on earth," Rose Woods told Julie Eisenhower, "we are living through it now." Julie herself was all but overwhelmed by a "feeling of helplessness." She has confessed that "the tide engulfing the Administration . . . was almost unbearable."[31]

Nixon had presented the transcripts in a carefully crafted speech in which he made the best possible case for what he had said and how he had said it. The reaction, however, only confirmed his earlier judgment that releasing any portion of the tapes would be disastrous. They showed that Nixon was the opposite of the carefully nurtured public image he had spent so much time and effort building.

There was a sense of betrayal, felt most keenly in precisely that group Nixon most counted on for support, the Silent Majority. The White House line defending Nixon changed from denial of any involvement or knowledge to denial that the President had committed a specific act that justified impeachment. But a Harris Poll indicated that by May 7 the public, by a 2–1 margin, rejected Nixon's version of what the transcripts showed.[32]

A Roper Poll indicated that impeachment sentiment rose from 53 percent to 58 percent after the release of the transcripts. Trends charted by Roper also showed that as understanding of the impeachment process rose, so did the idea that it should occur. Further, as the thought of impeachment became more familiar, it became less frightening.[33]

The American people made a judgment. While many still disagreed over whether or not the President had committed a crime, most decided that the man revealed in the tapes was not the kind of man they wanted for their President. As Professors Gladys and Kurt Lang put it in their scholarly study of the polls and Watergate, "Insofar as the Watergate affair was the battle for public opinion, which Nixon considered it to the very end, it had been effectively lost with the release of the edited tapes."[34]

DESPITE the deluge, Nixon did not flinch in public.

Instead, he fought back. He authorized Ziegler to release a statement: "The city of Washington is full of rumors. All . . . are false, and the one that heads the list is the one that says President Nixon intends to resign. His attitude is one of determination that he will not be driven out of office by rumor, speculation, excessive charges, or hypocrisy. He is up for the battle."[35]

On May 5, Jaworski told Al Haig that Nixon had been named an unindicted co-conspirator by the Watergate grand jury. Jaworski said he doubted that Nixon could be indicted so long as he was President, but the grand jury's action gave Jaworski leverage to propose to Haig a deal: If Nixon would turn over eighteen of the subpoenaed sixty-four tapes, the Special Prosecutor would drop his suit for the remainder and not reveal that Nixon had been named an unindicted co-conspirator. If Nixon did not accept this compromise, Jaworski threatened to announce the grand jury's action in open court.

Jaworski was attempting to blackmail the President, who called the offer a low blow, but nevertheless Nixon was tempted by the thought of finally bringing an end to the ceaseless battles over evidence. Haig was more than tempted; he wanted to accept. "We're at the point that we can see the barbed wire at the end of the street," the chief of staff pointed out. "What we have to do is mobilize everything to cut through it." But St. Clair opposed; he feared a Jaworski double-cross. Haig urged Nixon to at least listen to the tapes Jaworski wanted before rejecting the offer out of hand.

At 8 P.M. on May 5, in his EOB office, Nixon began listening. He stayed at the task until the early hours, and began listening again in the morning. That afternoon, he heard the June 23, 1972, conversation with Haldeman. What he heard decided him. He would not give that tape, or any others, to Jaworski; he also decided he would not allow his lawyers or anyone else to hear them.

"Perhaps this is Armageddon," he told Ziegler, "but I would rather leave fighting for a principle." He had St. Clair call Jaworski and tell him, no more tapes. Period.[36]

The Vice President was unhappy with the stonewalling. In a speech at Eastern Illinois University on May 9, Ford asserted that "truth is the glue that holds government together." He conceded that truth could be "brutal," but he warned: "The time has come for persons in political life to avoid the pragmatic dodge which seeks to obscure the truth."

The next morning, the President summoned the Vice President to the Oval Office. Solicitously, Nixon wondered if Ford should not slow down. He was worried about Ford's health and the effect of all his trips and speechmaking. He wanted Ford to take a good rest. He never mentioned Ford's remarks of the previous day, nor did Ford accept Nixon's advice. He continued his travels, according to his aide Bob Hartmann, "seeking every possible excuse to stay out of Washington, D.C."[37]

After Ford left, Nixon called in the reporters and photographers for a photo opportunity. As he chatted with Housing and Urban Development director James Lynn ("What about your department?" he asked Lynn. "Don't overlook the long term") the cameras clicked away. To Elizabeth Drew, "his face looks fatigued and puffed. His eyes seem sunken in his tired face." But she also noted, "it is a wonder that the President can go through this."[38]

That evening, Nixon went on a cruise on the *Sequoia* with Pat, Julie, and David. He vowed to them that he would fight to the end, that he would go "constitutionally down the wire." He said he would go to the Senate for an impeachment trial so long as just one senator believed in him. He insisted that was the way it would be.

The following afternoon, Julie and David held a press conference in the White House garden. Julie repeated what he had said, and in a reply to the inevitable question of whether he would resign, she said, "Absolutely not, no." Asked who she blamed for her father's "predicament," she replied, "You begin with a break-in, third-or-fourth-rate burglary."[39]

Reporters accused Nixon of using his daughter to shield and protect himself. Julie insisted that the charge was not true. She explained that because Tricia was never happy with a public role, and because her mother refused to comment on Watergate, her outspokenness was exaggerated.

"My father never asked me to be out front," she later wrote. Recalling that period, she remembered her father more than once asking her, with a voice full of concern, "You don't have any trips scheduled this week, do you, Julie?" She thought that he was perhaps anticipating some new disclosure and did not want her to have to face the reporters.

"I did not want Julie to take the brunt of the Watergate questioning," Nixon later declared, "but she could not bear the fact that there did not seem to be anyone else who would speak out for me. Whenever I suggested that she not become so involved, she always replied, 'But, Daddy, we have to fight.' "[40]

Actually, there were some who would speak out for Nixon. Ziegler, of course, and Warren, but others too. Ken Clawson issued a statement that Nixon would not resign "even if Hell freezes over." Bebe Rebozo told CBS TV, "Public opinion sometimes can be distorted."[41] Al Haig, on ABC TV's "Issues and Answers," said that "excesses and distortions" in investigating Watergate might lead to "the cure being worse than the illness."[42] As to the possibility of resignation, Haig told reporters that Nixon would only resign "if he thought that served the best interests of the American people." He was determined to put the public interest ahead of his own personal interest.[43]

In so saying, Haig was preparing Nixon's final defensive position. It was simple but strong—would the country be better off with Nixon out of the White House? It had the advantage of looking to the future instead of constantly defending or explaining or alibiing about the past. Nixon made the point directly, in a private talk with Nelson Rockefeller that was leaked. Nixon allegedly asked, his voice dripping with scorn, "Can you see Gerald Ford sitting in this chair?"

"Of course I never said anything like that," Nixon told Ford when the Vice President confronted him with the quote. "It's just another story that our enemies made up. The press is always exaggerating. Don't pay any attention to it." Ford wanted to believe him, but he was not "completely convinced."[44]

Shortly thereafter, Nixon returned to the theme in an interview with James Kilpatrick. Nixon said that he was "sleeping well," that he had no "tingling nerves" or "churning stomach." He made the case for his indispensability. If America did not seize "this moment," he said, "the world will inevitably move to a conflagration that will destroy everything that we've made—everything that this civilization has produced." Kilpatrick noted that Nixon's "conversation tends to run off on tangents" and was "littered with broken sentences," but he added, "The President plainly is in command."[45]

Meanwhile, on May 9 the House Judiciary Committee opened its long-awaited hearings to determine whether to recommend the impeachment of Richard Nixon. The television cameras were there for an eighteen-minute public ceremony, then banned for closed sessions, as John Doar began to present the evidence.

WHILE Nixon waited for the wave of emotion that had greeted the initial reading of the transcripts to recede, he worked at being presidential. On May 13 he met with Caspar Weinberger to discuss the status of pending health and education legislation. At the conclusion of the meeting, Weinberger urged Nixon not to resign. "Don't worry," the President replied. "There isn't any chance of that whatever."[46]

Then the President made a national radio address in support of his proposed comprehensive health insurance plan. He pointed to the reality and size of the problem—25 million Americans had no health insurance at all, and millions of others had inadequate protection; less than one half the population under sixty-five years of age had protection against catastrophic health costs, and almost none over sixty-five had such protection; preventive services, mental health care, outpatient services, and medication were excluded from most policies. He offered a solution—a plan that provided for extensive, uniform health coverage without raising taxes, without threatening the private health insurance industry, and without establishing a new federal bureaucracy. He would do this through a comprehensive requirement for employers to provide health insurance to employees, through an improved Medicare plan, and through assisted health insurance for low-income and unemployed people, paid for by the federal and state governments. He was making a special provision for children, including preventive care, eye and hearing examinations, and regular dental care up to age thirteen. He urged the Congress to act.[47] Two days later he issued a statement asking for more funding to support the elementary and secondary schools.[48]

HEW submitted to Nixon a draft of regulations in response to Title IX (Outlawing Sex Discrimination in Higher Education) of the Education Act of 1972. The regulations would eliminate all scholarships based on sex, and any sex discrimination in the use of facilities, including athletics. Nixon scribbled on the bottom of a memo on the subject: "The answer is *No!* Tell Weinberger to reassess all this and prepare a bill to go to Congress which I can submit and provide thereby an excuse for not going forward with this monstrosity."[49]

The President was also unhappy with a proposal for a five-year federal financing proposal for the Public Broadcasting Corporation. The stated purpose was to insulate public broadcasting from political considerations; Haig informed Nixon in a memo that Burch, Ken Cole, Garment, Harlow, and Timmons all supported it. Nixon scribbled: "For budgetary reasons and others I favor *ending* it or a *very* limited proposal. *Not* a 5 year proposal."[50]

Nixon also signed bills providing for drug and alcohol abuse prevention, proposed reforms in the state workers' compensation system, and made a nationwide radio address on the economy. He noted that stagflation had set in—the nation had the highest inflation rate in twenty years simultaneously with a slowdown in production and employment—but promised that "the worst is behind us."[51] None of this made the front pages, which continued to be devoted to Watergate-related features.

•

THERE was certainly plenty to write about. On May 14 Nixon took a heavy blow when Richard Mellon Scaife, heir to the Mellon fortune and a $1 million contributor to Nixon's 1972 campaign, published an editorial in his newspaper, the Greensburg (Pa.) *Tribune-Review*. Scaife urged the President to "step aside" under the terms of the Twenty-fifth Amendment until his guilt or innocence was determined in a Senate trial. In a scathing 900-word editorial, Scaife concluded, "He makes us feel, somehow, unclean."[52]

On May 15, U.S. District Court Judge Gerhard Gesell sentenced Dwight Chapin to 10–30 months in prison for lying to a grand jury about his involvement in dirty tricks in the 1972 campaign. That afternoon, Nixon dictated a letter to Chapin: "Words can hardly convey the concern I feel at the special hardships you and your family have endured these past months." He said he realized that Chapin had some "difficult days ahead," but hoped he knew that many would be praying for him, "and that includes all of us in the Nixon family." In a handwritten postscript, Nixon told Chapin, "Your T.V. appearances have been examples of 'Profiles in Courage!' Everyone agrees."[53] So Chapin got Nixon's prayers, and his admiration, but not his pardon.

That same day, the House Judiciary Committee, by a vote of 37–1, issued two new subpoenas on Nixon for more tapes.

The byzantine atmosphere in the White House was haunting the President. John Connally called to pass on a remark his old Texas friend Jaworski had made to him. It was a message to Nixon, and it was ominous: "The President has no friends in the White House."[54]

Not everything broke against Nixon. Inevitably as people got over their shock at the President's transcripts, emotions cooled. They began looking beyond his language, to find that the tapes were as ambiguous as Nixon claimed they were. He had ordered hush money paid, but then he had appeared to back off that route. His greatest embarrassment was that the money was paid; his defense—that he knew nothing about it— was, if not solid, or even substantial, at least something. And as St. Clair told reporters on May 16, "You can't incriminate a man for what he says. It has to be something he does."[55]

In the immediate aftermath of the release of the transcripts, Republicans all across the board had asked/demanded/urged Nixon to resign. By mid-May, his absolute refusal to even consider that course was beginning an have an effect. He was helped by his Vice President, who told a fund-raiser in Dallas that he "very strongly disagreed" with GOP leaders who were calling for Nixon's resignation. Senator Strom Thurmond (R.-S.C.) pointed out that Nixon was "the only President we have," while Senator Carl Curtis (R.-Nebr.) warned against "mob rule."[56]

Democrats, who had a vested interest in prolonging the Republicans' agony, took up the theme. Senator Mansfield declared, "Resignation is not the answer. This nation is going through a purgatory of sorts at present, but out of this turmoil will come a better U.S." Senator Byrd warned that if Nixon terminated the impeachment inquiry by resigning, "a significant portion of our citizens would feel that the President had been driven from office by his political enemies. The question of guilt or innocence would never be fully resolved."[57]

RNC Chairman Bush echoed that theme. "The constitutional process has to be allowed to work," he said on ABC TV's "Issues and Answers." Bush also tried to reduce the partisanship; when asked whether Nixon's troubles were caused by a political "vendetta" against him, Bush replied, "Absolutely not." To the contrary, he claimed that "it is the Republicans" rather than their opponents "that care the most about Watergate. . . . We always thought the Democrats did more of that kind of thing."[58]

Barry Goldwater, who was widely rumored to be the man who had been tapped to go to the Oval Office to speak for the Republican senators and inform Nixon that he had to go, said he would do no such thing. Goldwater did predict that if Nixon became convinced that his remaining in office would hurt the Republican Party, he would resign. Goldwater added that if the Republicans in the House sensed "an overwhelming decision in favor of impeachment then I think we might have to consider going to the White House before the vote."[59]

Nixon had survived the reaction to the transcripts. Democrats and Republicans agreed that there should not be a resignation, at least not yet. But by no means did this solve the President's problems, because the antiresignation sentiment only strengthened the case for more evidence. Unlike the pressure for resignation, that was pressure Nixon would find it difficult if not impossible to resist.

If he doubted that, he got strong reminders from two sources that he could not dismiss as enemies. On May 15, Julie visited with Republican members of the House Judiciary Committee. They told her to tell her father that he must comply with the Committee subpoenas. She passed the message along in a note to the President. Republicans, she said, would have little basis for supporting Nixon "unless they see all the evidence which they feel fits in the category of a legitimate area of inquiry." The issue transcended partisanship: "Even Republicans," Julie noted, "sincerely believe compliance necessary, above and beyond politics."[60]

Ford, stopping off in Washington between his flights around the country, called on Nixon. He told the President he could no longer support his stonewalling Committee requests. Ford warned that if Nixon refused to supply the relevant information, there would be a confrontation between the President and the Congress which the President would almost certainly lose.

"We're handling it this way because we think we're right," Nixon replied. "I know you and others would do it differently, but we think we're right and we're going to continue to do it this way."[61]

What Julie and Ford did not know, but Nixon did, was what was on one of those subpoenaed tapes, that of June 23, 1972. To give it up was to give up.

ON May 20, Judge Sirica ordered Nixon to turn over to the court the sixty-four tapes subpoenaed by Jaworski (and by the defendants in the cover-up trials). In so ruling, Sirica rejected St. Clair's argument that the Special Prosecutor, as an employee of the executive branch, could not compel the President to produce documents. Jaworski, in response, had charged that Nixon's attempt to limit his right to resort to the courts "would make a farce of the special prosecutor's charter."[62]

St. Clair promptly appealed Sirica's ruling, thus beginning what became *United States* v. *Nixon*. St. Clair asked for a decision from the Court of Appeals; if the timing worked out, it would not act before the Supreme Court went into summer recess, thus buying Nixon time until at least the fall. But Jaworski petitioned the Supreme Court to take immediate jurisdiction. St. Clair then urged the Supreme Court not to "rush to judgment" by agreeing to accelerate the process. He declared that Nixon "opposes any attempts to shortcut the usual judicial processes" because of the importance of the issues involved.[63]

ON May 22, the President wrote to Rodino. He said the Committee's demands had become a "never-ending process," and that if he gave in, he would "fatally compromise" the "institution of the Presidency." He insisted that the Committee already had "the full story of Watergate," and charged that the demands for more evidence would "merely prolong the inquiry." Therefore, he "declined to produce the tapes."[64]

It was a decisive, bold, and carefully thought out act. In practice, Nixon was denying that the Judiciary Committee was entitled to see whatever it wanted to see as it carried out its impeachment inquiry. Rodino called Nixon's refusal to honor the subpoena "a very grave matter."[65] A week later, the Committee formally notified Nixon that his refusal "might constitute a ground for impeachment," and by a vote of 37–1 issued a new subpoena.

Judge Gesell, meanwhile, ruled that the Fourth Amendment guarantee against unwarranted breaking and entering could not be suspended in the name of national security. He was commenting on the pre-trial argument made by Ehrlichman and Colson that they could defend themselves in the Ellsberg case on the ground that the break-in at Dr. Fielding's office was a legitimate national security operation. Gesell ruled that Nixon had no power to authorize a break-in without a search warrant, no matter what was involved. Without a warrant, "to enter and search the homes and offices of innocent American citizens" was illegal. Gesell wanted the evidence, in the form of tapes and other documents, as did Ehrlichman and Colson. The judge said he would have to throw out the trial if he did not get it.[66]

The Judiciary Committee's case and Gesell's logic did not convince Nixon. On what was becoming a regular evening cruise on the *Sequoia* with Republicans and Southern Democrats from Congress, the President told Representative William Dickinson (R.-Ala.), "there are some tapes that are so sensitive to national security that [I won't] release them under any circumstances, even if it mean[s that I have] to leave office."[67]

Despite Nixon's defiance, his defenses everywhere were crumbling. In Gesell's courtroom, Colson copped a plea. He pled guilty to a charge of obstructing justice by scheming to defame and destroy Daniel Ellsberg. In exchange, the charges against Colson for the break-in at Dr. Fielding's office and for his role in the Watergate cover-up were dropped; the price he paid was a promise to cooperate in the investigations and trials of his former colleagues.[68]

Even more ominous was a May 31 announcement from the Supreme Court. It granted Jaworski's plea for prompt consideration of Nixon's claim of executive privilege over the sixty-four tapes, rejecting St. Clair's request that it delay. It would rule before taking the summer recess. Nixon had promised to abide by a "definitive" ruling, although he continued to refuse to say what he meant by "definitive."

There was a single piece of good news. Vice President Ford, in his wanderings around the nation, had spoken out in Nixon's behalf. "The preponderance of the evidence," Ford said on June 5 at a Republican dinner in Ohio, "is that [Nixon] is innocent of any involvement in any cover-up." Nixon sent Ford a handwritten thank-you letter, beginning "Dear Gerry" (misspelling Ford's nickname). "This is to tell you how much I have appreciated your superb and courageous support over these past difficult month. . . . History, I am sure, will record you as one of the most capable, courageous and honorable Vice Presidents we have ever had."[69]

On June 7, in a long diary entry, Nixon summed up where he stood. He noted that political analyst Theodore White had told Rose Woods that while two weeks earlier he thought the House would vote to impeach, and that the Senate would sustain Nixon by five or six votes, now he believed that the House would not impeach. According to Nixon, Connally "strongly held the same opinion." The reason was purely political, not legal. As Nixon put it, House members were concerned that if they voted to impeach, "they ran the risk of taking the responsibility for whatever goes wrong in foreign and domestic policy after that." The Democrats had a special reason to vote against impeachment, because if they were successful, "they put in office as an incumbent Ford, who would have a united party and an administration behind him against whoever they ran for President."

There was another plus: Al Haig had told the President that the Senate Watergate Committee had a "pretty devastating report on [Hubert] Humphrey and also one on [Wilbur] Mills." The trouble was that the Republicans would not leak it, according to Nixon, because Republicans, "like conservatives generally, are responsible and play with Marquis of Queensberry rules, whereas the liberals go just the other way." (Actually, the House Judiciary Committee had already leaked that Humphrey and Mills, and before them Lyndon Johnson, had accepted contributions from the Associated Milk Producers, as had at least sixteen members of the Judiciary Committee.)

The unfairness of it all depressed Nixon. He noted in his diary that "what we have done as compared with previous administrations is hardly worth mentioning," but because of the "double standard" of the press, Democratic misdeeds got a one-day play and then were dropped, while anything Nixon did "gets enormous play."

Nixon took heart from "one thing that seems to disturb our opponents in the media," the simple fact that he had "hung on." He reflected: "I don't quite know how I have done it" because there were times of "considerable discouragement." Still, he had persevered and intended to continue to do so.

He wondered about his mistakes—firing Ehrlichman and Haldeman, for instance, or appointing Richardson as Attorney General—and most especially not destroying the tapes after Butterfield revealed their existence. He recalled that Agnew had advised him to burn them. "We should have done it," he wrote. The Agnew resignation was regrettable, but necessary; unfortunately, "all it did was to open the way to put pressure on the President to resign as well." The lesson was that "any accommodation with opponents in this kind of a fight does not satisfy—it only brings on demands for more."

Despite "all the pain and suffering that it caused," the Cox firing was the "right thing to do," because otherwise he would have indicted the President.[70]

Nixon had, of course, already been named as an "unindicted co-conspirator" by the Watergate grand jury, news that was revealed on June 6 by the Los Angeles *Times*. The story said that the grand jury had wanted to indict Nixon but had been told by Jaworski that there was a constitutional question of whether a sitting President could be indicted. It also said that Jaworski was prepared to argue in court that the President, as an unindicted co-conspirator, could not withhold evidence.[71]

As the bad news continued, Nixon's case looked hopeless. It appeared he would have to defy the House Judiciary Committee, the Sirica order, Gesell, and quite possibly a majority on the Supreme Court. The act of defiance would probably lead to impeachment; delivering up the June 23, 1972, tape certainly would lead to impeachment.

In response, Nixon prepared to shore up his last defense, which turned on the question, would it be wise to drive him from office? Not, would it be fair, or just, or deserved, but would it be good for the country? To make that point as forcefully as he possibly could, Nixon prepared to leave the country, to go abroad in order to remind the American people that no matter what the Democrats thought of him, he was deeply respected around the world.

CHAPTER FOURTEEN

HOUNDED AT HOME,
HONORED ABROAD
June 1–July 3, 1974

NIXON WAS building his defense around the theme that it would be unwise to get rid of him. He felt he was on the verge of achieving his first priority as President, the erection of a solid structure of lasting peace. He reviewed his progress in a commencement speech on June 5 at the Naval Academy. In the Mideast, he said, his policies had brought a cease-fire between Israel and the Arabs. Relations with the Soviet Union had never been better, and were still improving. Nixon told the midshipmen that the "great people" of America and Russia, "who worked together in war, are now learning to work together in peace. Ultimately, we hope that the United States and the Soviet Union will share equally high stakes in preserving a stable international environment." He defended détente and lashed out at its critics. He too was for human rights, he said, "but we cannot gear our foreign policy to transformation of other societies. In the nuclear age, our first responsibility must be the prevention of a war that could destroy all societies."[1]

Those were the words of a hardheaded realist. He directed them at Senator Jackson and other foes of détente, men with their own political ambitions who were trying to use his Watergate woes to scuttle his foreign policy. In a typically bold move, Nixon was going abroad to use his foreign-policy achievements, most of all détente, to turn the tables on his Watergate enemies.

His opportunity came because of the successful shuttle diplomacy of Henry Kissinger. For thirty-two days, from late April through May, the Secretary had traveled back and forth between Jerusalem and Damascus in an effort to achieve a disengagement between Syrian and Israeli troops. In mid-May, discouraged, he had sent a message to Nixon saying he was coming home, that his task was impossible. Nixon had sent back a message of encouragement and told Kissinger to make one more try. The President also sent a message to Prime Minister Meir, urging her to make "a supreme effort to seek a compromise." On May 29, the apparently impossible was achieved, and Nixon was able to announce an agreement to disengage the contending forces.[2]

Kissinger's reward was to be lionized by an American press that was tearing down his boss and needed a hero. *The New York Times* called him "the president for foreign affairs." Legislators spoke of him as a "national asset" and a "diplomatic wizard."[3] *Newsweek*'s cover showed him in a Superman suit. Kissinger wrote that he had achieved "the high point of public acclaim ever accorded to a Secretary of State."[4]

Nixon, who had cause to be jealous, was generous in his praise: "Secretary Kissinger deserves enormous credit for the work that he has done in keeping this negotiation going and finally reaching an agreement."[5]

Nixon wanted some of the reflected glory, indeed wanted to put himself into the spotlight, for many obvious reasons. All through May, Haig had sent Kissinger instructions to explore the possibility of a presidential trip to the Middle East when the disengagement was complete; in Kissinger's view, Nixon's desire to make a Middle East visit was the motive that had led the President to insist that he stay on to finish the job.[6]

At the end of May, Nixon announced that in ten days he would be traveling to Egypt, Syria, Saudi Arabia, Jordan, and Israel. His purpose was "to firm up the gains we had made and to lay the groundwork for more progress in the future."[7]

His enemies insisted that his purpose was to distract public attention from Watergate and to prove how highly regarded he was abroad. Perhaps, but if those were his motives, he chose an odd way of achieving his goals. Rather than court publicity and approval from the opinion makers, he scorned them. On June 2, he met with his military aide, Lieutenant Colonel John Brennan, who was responsible for *Air Force One*. Brennan passed Nixon's orders on to Ziegler in a June 3 memo:

The President very emphatically related to me his views regarding press pools. I am instructed to inform you, in very forceful terms, that *never*, under *any* circumstances, on *any* leg of *any* trip, will a representative from the following be allowed on the press pool:

New York Times	Washington Post
Time Magazine	Newsweek
CBS	Richard Lerner from UPI.

Brennan added that Nixon said "this is not appealable," and told Ziegler, "do not bring the subject up to the President and he wants to hear no more about it." That was a "direct command from the President. . . . Being tunnel-visioned, narrow-minded Military people, we in this [Office of the Military Assistant] intend to carry out fully the instructions of our Commander-in-Chief."[8]

THAT Nixon needed a respite from the Watergate stories was certainly true; that he needed to show that he, not Kissinger, was the "president for foreign policy" was obvious, In the week before he left, his legal struggle over the tapes intensified, while a series of minor events seemed to show that he had lost control of his own Administration.

Ehrlichman and his lawyer were demanding access to Ehrlichman's notes of his meetings with Nixon, to use in his trial. St. Clair had indicated that the President would yield those notes, but he had evidently failed to check this out with Nixon. On June 5, Buzhardt informed Judge Gesell that Nixon retained the ultimate authority and control over the Ehrlichman papers, and he would not provide them for the trial. On June 7, Gesell, visibly angry, said that Nixon's decision "borders on obstruction" and threatened to cite the President for contempt.

St. Clair then persuaded Nixon to offer a compromise, which the President did on June 10. He informed Gesell that he would provide those documents from Ehrlichman's file that he, Nixon, "determined to be relevant."[9]

That same day, Nixon responded to a May 30 letter from the House Judiciary Committee, in which the Committee had challenged his refusal to comply with subpoenas of May 15. The subpoenas were for tapes, not Ehrlichman's notes, and included the tape of the June 23, 1972, conversation with Haldeman and Ehrlichman. That one Nixon would never yield, as he made clear in a letter to Rodino. He based his refusal to comply on familiar grounds. "The question at issue," he wrote, "is where the line is to be drawn on an apparently endlessly escalating spiral of demands for confidential Presidential tapes and documents." The Committee said it was the sole judge of the issue; Nixon replied flatly, "I cannot accept such a doctrine." He asserted executive privilege and claimed that "the voluminous body of materials that the Committee already has . . . does give the full story of Watergate, insofar as it relates to Presidential knowledge and Presidential actions."[10]

There was a chorus of criticism from the Democrats and some Republicans, and from the press and editorial writers. Far more important, Nixon's drawing of a line highlighted the crucial nature of the upcoming Supreme Court decision on whether on not he had to turn over more tapes, including June 23, 1972, to Jaworski.

Nixon had problems not only with the legislative and judicial branches of the government, but even within his own Administration. More than any other modern President, Nixon had sought control over the vast federal bureaucracy, but by the late spring of 1974 his once-feared White House staff had become enfeebled and he was presiding over a loose confederacy of departments and agencies that felt free to defy the White House. Donald Santarelli, director of the Law Enforcement Assistance Administration, told a reporter, "There is no White House any more." Another minor official, scheduled for dismissal for failure to display the required loyalty to Nixon, was still in place after fourteen months. "They forgot about me," he explained. "There's no interference at all, and we are accomplishing things we never could before."

The word in the agencies was that with Haldeman and Ehrlichman gone, and Haig consumed with Watergate, authority had been decentralized and departments and agencies were on their own. Agriculture Secretary Butz told reporters, "I now have a great deal more autonomy than I did a year ago." Other Cabinet members said they were now free to make their own appointments, a complete reversal of the situation when Haldeman was Nixon's chief of staff. Under Haldeman, the White House had done the lobbying with Congress on legislation; now Defense Secretary Schlesinger, and other department heads, did their own. Cap Weinberger told a news conference on June 5 that he was holding up recommendations for welfare reform, because Nixon did not want to take on the Congress on an issue that might be beaten.[11]

Nixon could not persuade his Cabinet members to support him in public. On June 9, Rabbi Baruch Korff sponsored a lunch of the National Citizens' Committee for Fairness to the Presidency at the Shoreham Americana Hotel. Korff invited all the Cabinet, plus the Republican senators; only Earl Butz and Senator Carl Curtis (Nebr.) showed up, especially embarrassing since the President himself came and delivered the main speech.

Nixon opened with a vulgar paraphrase of Lincoln: "What we say here will probably be little noted by the media, but what you have done here and throughout the United States will be long remembered, not only by this President but by all future Presidents for whom you are working." (The theme of Korff's group was to reaffirm "our faith in God and country, in constitutional government, in the Presidency and in our beloved President.")

Then Nixon paraphrased Ike: "I want you to know that I realize you come from the heart of America, and you have touched our hearts." When he turned to his upcoming trip, he was more original. He was going to the Middle East, he said, to continue his initiative to build a structure of peace. "The cause you are working for is this office," he noted, and a strong Presidency was "indispensable to what we want to build, we as Americans: a peaceful world for our children and our grandchildren and for those of others who have been our friends, and even those who have been our adversaries and our enemies." He concluded, "a strong American Presidency is essential if we are to have peace in the world."[12]

Hyperbole, cried his opponents. An obvious truth, replied the shrinking number of his defenders. A deeply held personal belief, concludes this biographer. Nixon meant what he said, as he showed in the week that followed. With the Arabs and the Jews, he was at his best—skillful, diplomatic, telling each side things it did not want to hear in such a way that it could not tune him out, displaying a grasp of a complex situation, showing an ability to think on a scale that impressed even Kissinger, all in the face of personal travail at home. He proposed solutions to intractable problems that were simultaneously subtle and just plain common sense. They held great promise. The world would be much better off today had they been adopted.

They were not because, while Nixon had everything going for him in the way of insight, good ideas, and a balanced approach that took the various needs of the various governments into account, he did not have the power of the Presidency to back him up.

He resolved not to allow his perilous position to deter him. On a solitary walk along a muddy path at Camp David shortly before leaving, he reflected that he had less than two months before the Supreme Court would hand down its decision on the tapes. If it went against him, he was finished—assuming that the Court's judgment was "definitive." He decided, as he wrote in his diary, that "the thing to do is to just treat every day as basically the last one." So long as he was President he would do his best.

That thought led to further reflection. Looking back over the period from January 1973, he felt that "the great tragedy" was all that had been lost. He had "had to spend an inordinate amount of time" on Watergate, at the cost of building his structure of peace and instituting his New American Revolution. Still, there had been one good thing: "Perhaps the year has taught us all somewhat more compassion and understanding." Then another thought, that canceled out the positive one; he had learned "how bitter and fanatical the opposition is."[13]

Nevertheless, he stuck to the job at hand. Before departing, he met with the leaders of the American Jewish community. He told them that there were limits to how much military equipment the United States would provide Israel, that Israel's true security lay not in more arms but in compromise with its enemies, and that each new war would be more costly because the Arabs were learning how to fight and there were so many more of them.

After the meeting, he made a diary entry: "As a matter of fact, whether Israel can survive . . . with a hundred million Arabs around them I think is really questionable. The only long-term hope lies in reaching some kind of settlement now while they can operate from a position of strength, and while we are having such apparent success in weaning the Arabs away from the Soviets and into more responsible paths."[14]

On the eve of his departure, following a family dinner, he went to the Lincoln Sitting Room to dictate a note on the problems and opportunities he would face in the Middle East. He resolved to "do everything possible to see that we leave a structure on which future Presidents can build." He realized that the question of his personal future undercut his position: "The press . . . will be more obsessed with what happens with the minuscule problems involved in Watergate than they are with the momentous stakes that are involved in what I will be doing and saying in the Mid-east."[15]

HE was right. He wanted to be the honest broker between the Arabs and the Jews, to force people around the world to concentrate on the peace process in the Middle East, to make a dramatic contribution toward achieving a solution of the world's most intractable problem, but scarcely had he taken off on *Air Force One* on the morning of June 10 when he was beset by yet another Watergate-related problem.

It concerned Kissinger. The morning papers were full of accusations, rumors, and innuendoes about Kissinger's role in the 1969–71 program of wiretapping reporters and NSC staffers and in the formation of the Plumbers in the White House. *The New York Times* and *The Washington Post* led the way. A *Times* editorial accused Kissinger of dissembling in previous testimony before the Senate and hinted at the need for prosecution.[16]

This was the first time Kissinger had been touched by scandal. It came at a point when not only had he become used to being praised for saving the world, but Nixon was taking his place at center-stage. The charges, he confessed, left him "shattered."[17] He was also furious, and determined to defend himself.

On *Air Force One*, Haig came forward to Nixon's cabin office to report that Kissinger was saying he would hold a press conference at the first stop, in Salzburg, Austria (where Nixon intended to rest to overcome jet lag). "A *Times* editorial isn't a charge, Al," Nixon told Haig. "It's nothing more than a *Times* editorial, and that doesn't mean a goddamn thing. If he holds a press conference, he'll only play into their hands by giving them a Watergate lead for their first story from this trip." That was, of course, exactly what Nixon wanted to avoid. Further, lots worse things had been said about Nixon, who was at least as thin-skinned about personal criticism as Kissinger, yet Nixon had shrugged them off. Why couldn't Kissinger?

Haig indicated that Kissinger was going to hold his press conference, whatever the boss said or wanted. Nixon replied that in that case, Kissinger should not be defensive or deny his role, but take the offensive by insisting that the wiretaps were legitimate and necessary to protect national security.[18]

Kissinger would have none of that. Nor could he break his single-minded concentration on his own situation to take into consideration Nixon's situation. Haig told Kissinger that the President wanted him to endure the assault and just wait for the story to spend itself; Kissinger coldly rejected that option.[19]

Instead, on arrival in Salzburg, Kissinger called a press conference. He denied, falsely, all the charges against him. He told the reporters that he would leave to history the judgment of his diplomacy. "What I will not leave to history is a discussion of my public honor."

Sensing his inner fury, a reporter asked if it was fair to assume that if the campaign against him were not stopped, he would resign. "I am not concerned with the campaign," Kissinger replied. "I do not believe that it is possible to conduct the foreign policy of the United States under these circumstances, when the character and credibility of the Secretary of State is at issue. And if it is not cleared up, I will resign."[20]

In the uproar that followed, senators, reporters, editorial writers, and critics all backed down. It was unthinkable that the one senior official in the Nixon Administration who still commanded widespread respect should step down; it was unthinkable that the diplomatic genius who had won the Nobel Peace Prize for the Vietnam cease-fire and had brought about the disengagement of forces in the Middle East step down; it was unthinkable that the United States, and the world, lose Secretary Kissinger even as it replaced the veteran Nixon with the inexperienced Ford. From Washington to Salzburg, politicians, members of the media, and the public rushed to assure Henry that he was loved.

Except for Nixon. His reaction struck Kissinger as "churlish." The President refused to speak to the Secretary. He did issue a statement, saying that Kissinger's honor did not need defending, thus implying that the press conference had been unnecessary. Haig told the press, in background comments, that Kissinger was "overwrought and cranky from the prolonged Mid-east negotiations."[21]

Nixon did make a diary entry: "The mistake [Kissinger] made, of course, was to hypo his case with the threat to resign, which, among other things, is an empty cannon."[22]

As irritating as Kissinger was Nixon's leg. He was suffering from phlebitis, an inflation of a vein. His left leg was swollen to almost twice the size of the right. Dr. William Lukash examined him and warned him the danger of phlebitis was that a blood clot might form and break loose into the bloodstream. If that happened, it could reach Nixon's lungs and cause a fatal embolism. Although the doctor thought Nixon had already passed the crisis, he told his patient to wrap the leg in hot towels at least four times a day and to stay off his feet as much as possible.

Nixon called in Haig, showed him the swollen leg, told him to keep the number of people who knew about it to a minimum and to swear them to "absolute secrecy."[23]

Of course, the President cannot be in a life-threatening situation without word leaking, and in any case Nixon walked with a noticeable limp throughout his Middle East journey. When the full story became known, and people recalled how much time Nixon spent on his feet that week, in defiance of Lukash's orders, inevitably there was speculation that he had a suicidal impulse.

Perhaps he did. Perhaps the psychohistorians, who have had a grand time with this incident, are right in asserting that he thought to himself, "What a way to go!" But the evidence is, at best, inconclusive. It seems equally valid to assign to Nixon the best of motives, rather than the worst. Perhaps he thought he had a job to do and only he could do it, that he was a soldier in the front lines of the battle for peace and that he could not shirk his duty, no matter what the risk. In any case, only he could ever know for sure. What we know is that he stuck to his schedule, that he prepared the ground for Carter/Sadat/Begin Camp David agreements of 1979 that finally brought peace between Egypt and Israel, and that he survived his physical ordeal in good health.

Air Force One landed at Cairo International Airport at midday on June 12. The Nixons were greeted by President and Mrs. Sadat. The two Presidents climbed into an open-top Cadillac for a motorcade to Quabba Palace. This made the Secret Service unhappy; since November 1963, American Presidents rarely rode in open cars. Evidently Sadat gave a guarantee that there would be no assassination attempts in his country. Kissinger was also unhappy, not about the convertible but about his being "relegated to . . . a subsidiary role." He confessed he found it "disconcerting, even painful."[24]

For Nixon, the motorcade provided a badly needed and all but impossible to believe lift. More than a million people lined the streets, to give him what he called "the most tumultuous welcome any American president ever received anywhere in the world."[25] There may have been a touch of Nixonian hyperbole in that statement, considering Woodrow Wilson's welcome in Europe in the winter of 1918–19, or Ike's 1959 trip to India, but he could not have been far off the mark. Kissinger pointed out that trucks were seen picking people up at the tail end of the motorcade and moving them up to the front, but he also noted that "the enthusiasm and friendliness could not have been organized."[26]

That enthusiasm was overwhelming. People chanted "Nik-son, Nik-son, Nik-son" as the Cadillac moved along. They waved signs and banners. They smiled and shouted and sang. Tears rolled down faces. That their joy was spontaneous and genuine there can be no doubt; as Nixon later put it, "you can turn people out but you can't turn them on".[27]

In part, the emotion stemmed from Sadat's popularity. In part, it reflected the hopes of some of the poorest people on earth that the leader of the richest people on earth would bring them economic aid on a massive scale. In part, it showed how fed up the Egyptians were with the Russians, who had been the stingiest allies imaginable. In part, it was a form of thank you to Henry Kissinger for having saved the Egyptian Army and brought about the disengagement.

But at its heart the tribute was to Richard Nixon, peacemaker. To the Egyptian people, the Nixon visit represented the end of war and the beginning of peace.

Nixon stood through the entire motorcade. He was in pain, he was in danger. But he was aware of the symbolic significance of letting the Egyptians—indeed, the whole world—see him standing beside Sadat. So, despite his phlebitis, and despite the plus-100-degree heat, he stood.

Sadat was also in some danger. He had suffered two heart attacks a few years earlier and needed to take care of himself. Knowing this, and recognizing that Sadat was one of the truly great men of the century (a judgment that nearly everyone who ever came into contact with Sadat also made), Nixon noted in his diary, "The thing that I am really concerned about is what would happen if he were to pass from the scene."[28]

The two Presidents were so moved by the experience that at Quabba Palace they discarded their prepared speeches to make impromptu remarks. Sadat, welcoming Nixon, said, "This is a unique moment and a major turning point which should not be lost, but rather, grasped." Nixon said that "We stand here at a time in history which could well prove to be not only a landmark but which could well be remembered centuries from now as one of those great turning points which affects mankind for the better." He said the people who had greeted them made him "realize what we owe to them and what we owe to future generations." He pledged to work for a "peace which is permanent and just and equitable."[29]

At the state dinner that evening, Sadat got a bit more specific and a lot tougher. He said he recognized how complex the conditions in his area were, but insisted that there could be no peace "without a political solution to the Palestinian problem," one that met the "national aspirations of the Palestinians." Nixon, necessarily, stuck with more general themes. He promised that the United States would play "a positive role" in the peace process and pointed out that the American people had "no designs on any nation in this area." Their only interest was in peace and "the right of every nation and every people to achieve its own goals in its own ways by its own choosing," the closest he came to mentioning the Palestinians. He said "I do not come . . . with ready-made solutions for these complex problems," then gave a heartfelt tribute to Sadat.[30]

In private talks, Nixon was struck by Sadat's "subtlety and sophistication." The Egyptian leader was well aware of the limitations Nixon had to work within, and was practical enough to respect them, but he also insisted that Nixon hear his point of view. He did not press Nixon on American ties to Israel, but he did make a strong appeal for the return of the occupied territories, for the rights of the Palestinians, and for the status of Jerusalem. Nixon was sympathetic but noncommittal. Both men found it more enjoyable to indulge in a bit of Russian-bashing. Sadat said that he had kicked them out because "We just gave up on them."[31]

On June 13, the two leaders and their entourages rode in an opulent Victorian railroad car down the Nile Delta to Alexandria. The car had open sides; all along the route the crowds gathered, in even greater numbers than the day before, to see Nixon and Sadat. Estimates ran up to 6 million people, all cheering. It was a celebration more fitting to the founder of the city than two twentieth-century politicians, but again there could be no doubting the genuineness of the emotion it expressed.

The two Presidents held an impromptu press conference on the train. Nixon used it as an occasion to say in public what he had already told Sadat in private, that taking on the big problems immediately could only lead to failure. The Palestinian question, the status of Jerusalem, the occupied territories—they could only be dealt with after Egypt and Israel achieved peace between themselves. "What is needed," Nixon said, "is the step-by-step approach, not because we want to go slow, but because we want to get there."

That led to a question for Sadat: did he foresee direct discussions with Israel?

"No, not at all," he replied. Then, after a pause, he added, "Not yet."[32] Those were the most significant words of the entire occasion.

There were some practical results from the meeting. On June 14, the two Presidents signed the "Principles of Relations and Cooperation Between Egypt and the United States." The document called for consultations at all levels, active cooperation in the pursuit of peace, and so forth. It agreed to establish working groups on such subjects as the reconstruction of the Suez Canal, seeking private investment from the United States in Egypt, cooperation in establishing nuclear power plants in Egypt, in space research, in medicine, and cultural exchanges.[33] In a somewhat poignant gesture, Nixon invited Sadat to visit him in Washington later in the year.

But clearly the real significance of the trip was symbolic. As with Nixon's journey to China two years earlier, what was said and agreed to was much less important than the simple fact of the two leaders getting together. Egypt had broken relations with the United States in the wake of the 1967 Middle East war; the United States had supplied Israel with the military hardware in October 1973 that had frustrated Sadat's attempt to take back the occupied territories; despite this, Nixon and Sadat were now together, arms linked, praising each other in what could only be called a love fest. So close had the two men drawn that when Sadat expressed admiration for the presidential helicopter, Nixon made him a gift of it on the spot.

For Nixon, it was a personal triumph. No doubt he could not have done it without Kissinger; no doubt, either, that Kissinger could not have done what he did without Nixon. Sadly, Nixon was not able to enjoy his triumph. Kissinger noted that Nixon's reception in Egypt "alternately buoyed and depressed him." The meetings with Sadat "illuminated what Nixon's policy had accomplished; they also faced him with the stark truth that he would not be part of the future he had made possible. More and more often as the trip progressed, his face took on the waxen appearance and his eyes the glazed distant look of a man parting from his true— perhaps his only—vocation; it was excruciatingly painful to watch."[34]

No wonder. If June 12–14, 1974, was one of the highest points of Nixon's life, it was simultaneously one of the lowest. His unprecedented reception in Egypt, the symbolic significance of it all, failed to help, much less solve, his personal problems back home. He couldn't drive Watergate off the front pages, not even for one day. Come to that, his trip did not even make the lead. On June 13, the headline story in *The New York Times* covered some leaks from the House Judiciary Committee about what was on the March 21, 1973, tape. Second billing went to a Seymour Hersh report on a ruling from Judge Gesell on the Ehrlichman trial. Third place went to the Secretary of State ("CAPITAL RALLYING ROUND KISSINGER"). Only on the far left of the front page did Nixon's reception in Egypt get a mention; it was accompanied by a silly photo of Kissinger, Nixon, and Sadat being entertained by a belly dancer.

Never had a President, not even Wilson, been so honored abroad, so hounded at home. Seldom had a President done more for world peace.

FROM Egypt, Nixon flew to Jidda, the administrative center of Saudi Arabia, for a meeting with King Faisal. The crowds were respectable but not demonstrative, rather like their king. At a reception at the Royal Guest Palace, Faisal looked "doleful"; Kissinger guessed that the reason was that someone had slipped up and permitted Mrs. Nixon into his presence. He recovered sufficiently to make some formal remarks, beginning, "I extend to you a warm welcome in this land of the heavenly message that illuminated for all humanity the path of righteousness and wisdom." Then he passed along some of that wisdom: there would be no peace without a settlement of the status of Jerusalem, without a return of the occupied territories, and without a homeland for the Palestinians.

Nixon, in response, said that "peace must be built carefully, step by step." In a nice touch, he concluded: "Let me say that while we will treasure most the wisdom that we will take with us after this visit, we, of course, will need the oil to carry us to our next stop."[35]

In private talks, Nixon urged Faisal to get behind an effort to allow Jordan to negotiate with Israel over the Palestinian question, rather than demanding that the Israelis talk directly to the Palestinian Liberation Organization. Faisal was noncommittal. The king did say he would do his best to lower oil prices.

The next stop was Damascus. Nixon was taking a risk in going there. The United States did not have diplomatic relations with Syria. The Syrians had been viciously anti-American and anti-Israel in their propaganda, and were the most pro-Russian of all the Arabs. President Hafez el-Assad had called Nixon an evil man under the control of the Zionists. He had told his people that it was only because of Nixon that Israel had been saved in October 1973. But he knew that Nixon was the key to peace in the Middle East, and he wanted him to come to Syria to demonstrate that he too was a world leader who demanded respect from the American President. Nixon, who had swallowed a lot to go to China, could swallow some more if it brought Assad in on the peace process.

Nixon and Assad got through the important symbolic act quickly and smoothly; on the steps of the Presidential Palace they appeared together to announce the resumption of diplomatic relations. In the private talks, Assad was direct, far more so than Sadat or Faisal. He wanted to know what Syria's role was in the step-by-step approach Nixon kept talking about. Was the United States fully behind U.N. Resolution 242? Had the President cut a deal with Sadat to get the Israelis out of the Sinai? If so, would he encourage Israel to vacate the Golan Heights at the same time? What were his views on the final borders of Israel?

Nixon did not want to be pinned down. Such details awaited discussion and developments. He could not speak for Israel. He refused to be explicit. Without making a commitment, he hinted that he endorsed Assad's position on frontiers. If unsatisfactory to Assad, it was good diplomacy nevertheless.[36]

Nixon's overall impression of Assad was favorable. He found Assad to be a man of "a great deal of mystique, tremendous stamina, and a lot of charm." He laughed easily, even while taking a hard line. He came down strongly against a separate Egyptian-Israeli peace, but still managed to be reasonable.

In his diary, Nixon wrote that "Pat noted that he [Assad] had a flat head in the back which she said was probably because he hadn't been turned when he was a baby." That led Nixon to a curious comparison; he wrote that Assad reminded him of Pat Buchanan, not only because he had a forehead like Buchanan, but because "he has the same kind of brain and drive and single-mindedness that Pat has. The man really has elements of genius, without any question."[37]

From Damascus, Nixon flew to Israel. One might have expected his hosts to make an effort to outdo the Egyptian reception, to show Nixon how much they appreciated his bold and courageous action in October 1973, when he ordered the Pentagon to resupply the Israeli Army, and to remind him that they, not the Egyptians, were America's true friends in the Middle East. Further, this was the first visit of an American President to Israel, another reason to put on a show.

But Israel was in the midst of one of its periodic political crises. Golda Meir had resigned in the spring of 1974; Yitzhak Rabin had taken over as Prime Minister, head of a shaky coalition government. Important elements in that government were distinctly unhappy with Nixon's peace program; where the Arabs wanted him to keep at it, and even speed it up, the Israelis wanted him to slow down. They wanted rifles and ammunition from Nixon, not questions; tanks and airplanes, not pressure to compromise with their foes. They had read his remarks in Cairo, Jidda, and Damascus with growing dismay.

As a result, Nixon's reception in Israel was correct but unenthusiastic (Nixon politely called it "restrained")—under the circumstances, almost an insult.

In addition, many American Jews had immigrated to Israel, and the Israelis generally were more up to date on American politics than any of the Arabs. So, for the first time on his Middle East journey, Nixon saw while driving in from the airport the kind of hostile signs he was accustomed to seeing at home, along with some that were new. "Remove All the Expletives," one read. "You Can't Run from Justice," said another. "Welcome President Ford," and "We Are All Jew Boys," a reference to remarks that were reported to be on the tapes, along with "Out Now," added to the list.[38]

Most Israelis were embarrassed by these crude attempts to meddle in America's domestic affairs, but it was also true, as Kissinger pointed out, that Israel was the only country that Nixon visited in the Middle East "where the peace process seemed to require justification."[39]

Nixon thought Israel was the country that most needed the peace process, and he did not hesitate to say so. The occasion was the state dinner at the Knesset, where he made some extemporaneous remarks. He began with a graceful gesture that was typical of the man. He had twice been a loser himself, and appeared to be on the verge of being driven from power. His heart went out to other politicians who had lost—recall his note to Hubert Humphrey after the 1972 Democratic Convention—and now it went out to Meir. There she sat, in the great hall of the Knesset, with her political enemies who had driven her from power seated all around her.

Nixon said he would exercise the presidential prerogative of breaking precedent to propose the first toast to Meir, even though she was no longer Prime Minister. Also typical of Nixon, he began the toast with a reminder of who he was: "I have had the great privilege over the past 27 years to travel to over 80 countries. . . . I have had a chance as President to meet, talk to, and evaluate most of the leaders on the current scene today and those who have been on it over the past 5 years."

He looked at Meir, who was both flustered and flattered, and went on: "No leader I have met, no president, no king, no prime minister . . . has demonstrated . . . greater courage, greater intelligence, and greater stamina, greater determination, and greater dedication to her country than Prime Minister Meir."

After the toast was drunk, she replied: "As President Nixon says, presidents can do almost anything, and President Nixon has done many things that nobody would have thought of doing. All I can say, Mr. President, as friends and as an Israeli citizen to a great American President, thank you."

Nixon then went on to speak of the need to "create a better world for those thousands of children we saw on the streets here, yes, and the thousands of children I have seen in the streets of Cairo, Leningrad, London, Japan—all over the world." He praised the Israeli Army and the courage of its soldiers. Then he switched into his main theme: "It also takes courage, a different kind of courage, to wage peace." Turning to Rabin, he said that the new Prime Minister and his Cabinet had two courses that were open to them. "The one is an easy one . . . and that is the status quo. Don't move, because any movement has risks in it." Anyone who knew Nixon knew that when he said there were two choices, and began by describing the "easy way," that way would also be the wrong way. So it was in the Knesset. Looking directly at Rabin, Nixon said: "There is another way. The other, I believe, is the right way. It is the way of statesmanship, not the way of the politician alone. It is a way that does not risk your country's security. That must never be done. But it is a way that recognizes that continuous war in this area is not a solution for Israel's survival and, above all, it is not right. . . ."[40]

In private talks the following day with Rabin, Nixon pressed his point. Rabin wanted Nixon to commit the United States to an arms package for Israel; Nixon wanted Rabin to commit Israel to negotiations with the Arabs. For all that Rabin headed a fragile coalition, he was in a stronger position than Nixon, who knew that if he tried to force Rabin to compromise, and Rabin resisted, as he surely would, the only result would be to multiply Nixon's domestic opponents. The Arabs had no strength in the American Congress; the Jews had a great deal.

Nevertheless, Nixon pressed. He told Rabin that he realized most Israelis, and most American Jews, wanted to go back to the good old days of unquestioning American support for Israel: "Just give us the arms and we can lick all of our enemies and all of the rest." Bluntly, Nixon went on: "I don't think that's a policy. I don't think it is viable for the future. Time will run out."[41]

That Nixon's words had no effect is obvious. That he was right is equally obvious.

Of course, generalizations about peace were not a policy either. Nixon had been talking peace for a week without ever getting very specific. Sadat had warned him that there could be no peace without a solution to Jerusalem, without an Israeli withdrawal from the Sinai and from the Golan Heights, and without a homeland for the Palestinians. Nixon knew that Jerusalem was out of the question, that the Golan Heights would be difficult at best, that progress on Sinai was possible only within the context of a peace agreement between Egypt and Israel, and that the Israelis were determined never to talk to the PLO. A comprehensive settlement was pie in the sky; that is why he emphasized step-by-step. But what, the world wanted to know, was the next step?

Nixon's answer was to turn to Jordan. His policy proposal was to give the moderate King Hussein a Jordanian presence on the occupied West Bank and make him the spokesman and negotiator for the Palestinians. The implication was that the Palestinians would find their homeland on the West Bank, under Hussein's leadership.

To further that goal, Nixon flew from Jerusalem to Amman, for meetings with Hussein. The two men talked in generalities, necessarily so as Nixon brought with him no promises from Rabin. But the king promised Nixon "restraint and moderation," which was encouraging. In his toast at the state dinner, Nixon concluded: "I do not tell you where this journey will end. I cannot tell you when it will end. The important thing is that it has begun."[42]

ON June 19, Nixon flew back to Washington. When his helicopter touched down on the South Lawn of the White House, Ford and a small delegation of Cabinet members were there for a welcoming ceremony. "Blessed is the peacemaker," said Ford; Nixon said of the Middle East, "where there was no hope for peace there is now hope."[43] In a briefing for congressional leaders, whose concern was less with peace and more with satisfying Israel, Nixon was as blunt as he had been in Jerusalem. He said the United States would "make Israel strong enough that they would not fear to negotiate, but not so strong that they felt they had no need to negotiate."[44]

It was a nice phrase, even if decades ahead of its time. Nixon was in no position to dominate developments. His return to Washington only reminded him of how tenuous it was. He had hoped to get a lift in the polls from his "Journey for Peace," but he had not. Ziegler told him he had gotten five or six minutes on the network news programs each night while he was in the Middle East; Nixon replied, "Compare that with the eight or ten minutes on Watergate for over a year!"

Still, Nixon reminded himself that "the most important thing, of course, is to keep working to make sure the trip bears the fruits of peace or at least of progress." And, he noted in his diary, the trip did "put the whole Watergate business into perspective—to make us realize that all the terrible battering we have taken is really pygmy-sized when compared to what we have done and what we can do in the future . . . for peace in the world."

What he personally could do was, at best, problematical. What he had done was create a situation that, with luck, his successors could build on. He had shown, as he put it in his diary, that "the Arabs really want to be friends of the Americans, and now it's up to us to be their friends and also to prove that friendship with America is worthwhile."[45]

Nixon's trip was symbolic rather than specific. What he had stressed was a goal rather than a route. His point was simple—that the Israelis and the Arabs would someday have to become good neighbors. He pledged that the United States stood ready to help them figure out how to do so. Unfortunately, it seemed as impossible to them as it did obvious to him. Unfortunately, too, he was in no position to make promises about the future of American policy. But he had tried, at a physical expense and political risk. What he got, from the warring parties, was more hostility. On the day he came home, the PLO launched some terrorist raids on Israeli settlements and Israeli planes struck back with bombs and rockets against refugee villages in southern Lebanon.

THE night he got back, Nixon went for a two-hour dinner cruise aboard the *Sequoia*, with Pat, Julie and Tricia and their husbands, and Rose Mary Woods. He badly needed rest and relaxation. His leg was still swollen and painful, he had jet lag, he needed sleep. The following day, accompanied by his family, he took the helicopter up to Camp David.

The family, too, needed to get away from Washington. Pat was proud of her husband's role in the Middle East, and euphoric over the reception he had received in Egypt, but she was also exhausted—and was going to be off in less than a week for a trip to the Soviet Union. Julie had been traveling, defending her father, and she too was showing signs of wear.

"It hurt me to see Julie daily grow quieter and more inward," Nixon later wrote. But she always bounced back when reporters asked about the President. Her eyes would flash as she assured the press that her father "does not want me out here because he does not want anyone to construe that I am trying to answer questions for him." She held the news conferences anyway, because "I feel as a daughter it is my obligation to come out here. . . . I am not trying to answer questions for him. I am just trying to pray for enough courage to meet his courage."[46]

As Nixon tried to rest his leg and catch his breath between the Middle East and the Moscow trips, the press and politicians hammered away at him. There were more stories about his income taxes. The House Judiciary Committee leaked more details from the tapes he had handed over, details that showed vast differences between the transcripts he had made public and what was actually said. The Committee subpoenaed 49 additional tapes, bringing the total demanded to 147. Subjects covered included ITT, the milk fund, domestic surveillance, and the IRS. Conservative senators, always loyal to Nixon, spoke out against his stonewalling on the tapes; among them were Norris Cotton (R.-N.H.), Stennis, and John McClellan (D.-Ark).

On June 24, on CBS TV, Dan Rather revealed that the President was suffering from phlebitis; the White House later confirmed the story. The speculation that he was suicidal began immediately.

Up at Camp David, even as he was preparing for the summit in Moscow, Nixon worked on his legal problems. The task was made more difficult because Fred Buzhardt had suffered a heart attack and could not work. There were briefs to file and oral arguments to prepare for the Supreme Court hearing on *United States* v. *Nixon.* The legal team also had to respond to demands for documents in the Ellsberg break-in case. Someone had to answer the subpoenas from the House Judiciary Committee. Common Cause was suing for tapes. Sirica and the Ervin Committee were still demanding material.

On June 21, Judge Gesell gave Colson a sentence of from one to three years in prison, plus a $5,000 fine, for obstruction of justice in the Ellsberg case. In a courtroom statement, Colson said, "I can work for the Lord in prison or out of prison." He also said that "President Nixon on numerous occasions urged me to disseminate damaging information about Daniel Ellsberg."[47] That was particularly ominous, because Colson had promised to give evidence and was expected to be one of the star witnesses in the impeachment proceedings before the whole House.

The Judiciary Committee, meanwhile, completed its six weeks of listening to John Doar present the evidentiary material, and was about to go public for its vote on whether or not to recommend impeachment. Nixon was ready for the test, even confident. In all the mass of evidence Doar had put forward, there was no "murder weapon," no "smoking gun" to link the President directly to a crime. On June 22, Nixon telephoned Joe Waggonner (D.-La.), a strong supporter. Waggonner told him that even if the Judiciary Committee recommended impeachment, there were at least seventy anti-impeachment votes among the Southern Democrats. They would never break, Waggonner said, unless Nixon were held in contempt of the Supreme Court. With 70 Democratic votes, Nixon calculated, he would need only 150 Republicans to reach a majority against impeachment. He thought he could get that number.[48]

He could, that is, if he could get a favorable, or at least a split, decision from the Supreme Court in *United States* v. *Nixon*. He reflected in his diary that the justices all read *The Washington Post* daily, which did not bode well for him ("the poison they see in *The Washington Post* must really seep in"), but then he brightened at the thought that the justices would not want to set a "devastating precedent." In either case, he knew he was looking at a "climactic decision" in a month or so. He resolved, again, "to live every one of [the next thirty days] up to the hilt and not be concerned about what happens in between." Considering what had happened in the past year, he felt "it's just miraculous that we are still in the game at all." He confessed that he was depressed, but said he had more sympathy for "people who don't have strong physical or emotional faculties as I have."[49]

HE needed all his strength and faculties to get ready for Moscow. Never had he gone abroad with worse prospects. It was not just Watergate, although obviously developments at home were undercutting his influence abroad. He was going to Moscow to arrange for trade agreements with the Soviets, and to enter into an arms control treaty. But, as Kissinger aptly put it, "conservatives who hated Communists and liberals who hated Nixon [had come] together in a rare convergence, like an eclipse of the sun."[50] The liberals' issue was Jewish immigration; the conservatives' issue was no trade with the enemy; the military and its friends wanted no arms control. Nixon rightly noted that this convergence would have existed regardless of the state of American domestic politics, but it was equally true that Watergate emboldened the foes of détente.[51]

Senator Jackson demanded more Jewish emigration as the price of most-favored-nation trading status for the Soviet Union, despite the hundredfold increase in such emigration quietly won by the Nixon Administration since 1969. What Jackson really wanted was the issue, not the emigration. Secretary of Defense Schlesinger had entered into an alliance with Jackson, as had Admiral Zumwalt and other high-ranking military men. They wanted to scuttle SALT II. Congressmen who had little interest in and no understanding of the arms control process wanted to deny Nixon any overseas victories. Thus, as Kissinger pointed out, "liberal and conservative opponents of Nixon could unite on the proposition that he must not be permitted to save his Presidency by deals in Moscow." This meant that Nixon "had no domestic base for any significant agreement in Moscow regardless of its content."[52]

That was true, but to some extent the fault lay as much with Nixon and Kissinger as with their opponents. The President and the Secretary had done almost nothing over the past year to build a constituency for arms control. This was in accord with their penchant for indulging in secrecy and surprise in foreign policy, but the secrecy and surprise that had worked when they operated from a position of strength only aroused suspicions and resistance when they operated from a position of weakness.

There was a base for building support for détente, had Nixon had the time, energy, and inclination to shape it. A current Gallup Poll showed that while Nixon's approval rating was only 26 percent, approval for his foreign policy was at 54 percent. But it was his foes who were at work, on the radio talk shows, in the newspaper columns, on the college campuses, at the chamber of commerce meetings, chipping away at the structure of détente. Jackson and other Democratic congressmen had joined forces to form the Committee for a Democratic Majority (CDM). It included prominent men from the media, labor, and academia; its cause was a harder line in foreign relations, greater emphasis on defense, and a campaign against détente. A CDM task force headed by Eugene Rostow published a pamphlet, *The Quest for Detente*, the first major all-out attack on Nixon's policy.[53]

Even more damaging to Nixon, his Secretary of Defense was opposing his policies. Schlesinger had made public a letter that dissociated the Defense Department from the Administration's position on the need for a MIRV agreement. Nixon had called Schlesinger into the Oval office, where he was forced to deal with the Secretary, in Kissinger's words, "as if the latter were a sovereign equal."

Nixon made an almost plaintive plea to Schlesinger: "We need your help. Help Kissinger to devise a way around this. I will take on Brezhnev. I made the speech about the U.S. being second to none. The American people in their simplistic way are not on a peace-at-any-price kick, but they want peace. Many of my friends are horrified at our even talking to the Soviet Union. But are we going to leave the world running away with an arms race, or will we get a handle on it?"[54] Schlesinger was unmoved.

On June 20, Nixon met with the NSC. The President opened the meeting by asking Kissinger to outline the situation. The Secretary of State said that without an agreement, the Soviets would soon pass the United States in number of MIRVed missiles. "Our real choice is either to achieve constraints on their programs, or have a build-up of our own. The worst case is to have no constraints on their program and no build-up of our own."

Nixon intervened to say he feared that was exactly what would happen. "If there were no constraints, we could raise hell to try to up Congressional support and that might happen. But I am mainly concerned that it might not happen either."[55]

Schlesinger sharply disagreed. He advocated putting forth a hard-line proposal that would give the United States an overwhelming advantage. It was a proposal the Soviets were certain to reject out of hand—indeed, they already had.

"I think we should try to use this time to frame a more practical approach to the problem," Nixon said. "We have to accept the fact that Secretary Schlesinger's proposal simply has no chance whatever of being accepted by the Soviets, so we should try to work out something consistent with our interests that will."

There was a moment of silence. Then Schlesinger, sitting next to Nixon, said, "But, Mr. President, everyone knows how impressed Khrushchev was with your forensic ability in the kitchen debate. I'm sure that if you applied your skills to it you could get them to accept this proposal."

The Secretary's sneering tone was unprecedented. Nixon commented in his diary that evening that Schlesinger's remark "was really an insult to everybody's intelligence and particularly to mine." It was more—it was an insult to the President himself, and inexcusable.

Vice President Ford broke the long silence that followed with a plea for a huge increase in the defense budget. He argued that a buildup would "give us a bargaining position with the Soviets." Nixon disagreed: "We aren't going to be able to bluff them in this particular case."

Nixon pointed out that his successor would face dangers on all sides, because a future President might be someone who "despite all the white-hot talk that the United States has to be number one and so forth, would cave in to the peacenik views that the establishment press would undoubtedly be expressing once they got one of their own in office."

Then there was the Congress. "If we get into a runaway race," Nixon warned, "it may be that they [the Soviets] will be uninhibited and we will be inhibited." He pointed out that Brezhnev could take a decision and make it stick, while a President "can't ever be absolutely sure that his decision will be carried out." An agreement, any agreement, to limit arms was an advantage to the United States, Nixon argued, because "when we constrain ourselves, it may be that we are constraining ourselves in an area where we wouldn't be doing anything anyway," because of congressional resistance to more spending.[56]

Never stated during the NSC meeting was the fact that the numbers of missiles being talked about were, in Dwight Eisenhower's word, "fantastic." The Joint Chiefs had told Ike when he entered office in 1953 that if they could hit seventy targets in the Soviet Union, they could guarantee that the Red Army could not carry out aggressive war. When he left office in 1961 the number was up to seven hundred. He had commented, "Why don't we go completely crazy and plan on a force of 10,000?"[57] By 1974, the two sides were talking about *limits* of around 2,500 missiles each, many of them MIRVed. The arms race was moving ahead on its own momentum, not in response to any strategic necessity; if the Soviets built 100,000 missiles, the Americans would want as many, not because they were needed to deter, but because the Soviets had that many.

The bureaucratic infighting continued right up to the day of Nixon's departure. On the key issue of MIRV, Schlesinger wanted to put a limit on the number of missiles but not on the MIRVs, which meant that the United States could retain or even increase its large superiority in numbers of warheads. Another important issue was the Threshold Test Ban (TTB). The Soviets were proposing an upper limit on the size of underground nuclear tests. The Defense Department and the Joint Chiefs, along with Senator Jackson and other foes of détente, were opposed. They did not want to limit American testing of nuclear devices, and they advanced the familiar argument that the Soviets would cheat (the Soviet counterargument was that on-site inspections were not necessary as explosions above the threshold could be detected by seismic equipment).

Admiral Zumwalt worked directly and indirectly to undercut TTB. He got a JCS position paper against it, and sent the President a long letter stating his opposition. He leaked information to Jackson ("Bless him," Zumwalt said of Jackson). He conspired with Schlesinger on tactics: Schlesinger warned him, "You should be aware that the President thinks that the JCS are all 'a bunch of shits' and that you are 'the biggest shit of all.' "[58]

While Nixon was in Moscow, Zumwalt retired, on June 30. Hours before his retirement became effective, he gave a provocative "Meet the Press" television interview that he had been virtually ordered not to give. Haig then ordered Schlesinger not to attend Zumwalt's retirement ceremony and not to present him with a medal, as was customary. Schlesinger ignored the order, attended the ceremony, and awarded the medal.[59]

Although one of Nixon's arguments for staying in office was that he was indispensable to a successful American foreign policy, the lack of discipline within the most important department of the government on the most important foreign-policy issue of the day is but one indication of how weak the argument actually was. Going into the Moscow summit, which Nixon had hoped would be the climax of the détente policy, with the capstone being a SALT II that would initiate a whole new era in arms control, the President had no team behind him. The senators who would have to ratify any treaty wanted no part of SALT II, whether because they did not want to allow Nixon to wriggle out of Watergate via a foreign-policy triumph or because they opposed arms control; the military had gone public with its opposition even before Nixon could make his formal proposals to Brezhnev; the media was far more interested in Nixon's phlebitis than in TTB or MIRV; the public could hardly understand the issues, but a majority felt the safest course was never to trust the Russians to the slightest degree.

Still Nixon was closer to realism than his opponents. If he did not have a constituency behind him for détente, neither did his opponents have a consensus for escalation. It was one of his most important responsibilities to prevent a runaway arms race, and he was doing his best to meet it. The problem was that his best, in the circumstances, was almost worthless. With his own Secretary of Defense openly disagreeing with him, with the House on the verge of voting impeachment, with a grand jury naming him an unindicted co-conspirator, with the courts demanding his most secret documents, with the media hounding him, he was all but helpless.

Everyone understood this, which was why conservatives warned him not to attempt to make any deals with Brezhnev, liberals accused him of seeking peace to escape Watergate, and Brezhnev wondered why Nixon was coming and what the Russians would do with the President once he arrived. According to Raymond Garthoff, Brezhnev was suspicious that "the whole Watergate issue was a plot by American opponents of détente."[60] Brezhnev told Walter Stoessel, American Ambassador to Moscow, that he respected Nixon for fighting back, but that he was "amazed" the United States had reached such a point that "the President could be bothered about his taxes."[61]

That was a worldwide attitude. Even Western Europeans, living in democratic states and accustomed to political scandals, were bemused by Watergate. They could not understand what all the hullabaloo was about. To the British, with their Official Secrets Act, nothing that Nixon had done seemed that out of the ordinary, much less illegal. The Italians simply threw up their hands at the crazy Americans. To the French, Watergate confirmed their suspicions about the naïve Americans. In West Germany, the frequent comparison of Nixon to Hitler by his enemies in America showed either how little the Americans understood Hitler, or how little they understood Nixon, or both. Nixon's friends in China, meanwhile, could not understand why he just didn't shoot his critics.

Virtually everywhere, the people of the world watched the Watergate spectacle unfold with amazement. The general attitude was that Nixon was the best President the United States had had since World War II. It was unbelievable that the American people were trying to throw him out of office, simply because he wanted a little inside information about what his political opponents were up to, and had told a fib or two about the break-in.

In the United States, in turn, people were amazed that foreigners could not understand why Nixon had to go. The gap in empathy between the United States and the rest of the world, which ran both ways, had never been greater.

On June 25, as Nixon and his party left for Europe, gallows humor in Washington wondered if he were going to ask for political asylum in Moscow.

THE first stop was Brussels, for what should have been a grand occasion, the twenty-fifth anniversary of NATO. It had a special significance for Nixon, who as a young congressman had represented an isolationist district but who had, at some risk to his career, been a strong supporter of NATO. But the ceremonies were more sour than sweet. Reporters watched closely to see if he limped or not; the European statesmen acted as if the cancer on the Presidency was a cancer on the person. They never brought up Watergate, but it never left their minds. In Kissinger's biting phrase, they treated Nixon with "the solicitude shown to terminally ill patients."[62]

Nixon's leg was still swollen and painful, but he was determined not to let it show. As always, he was sensitive to the political and PR problems his health situation created. He told Ziegler that "We must make sure that people never get the idea that the President is like Eisenhower in his last year or so, or like Roosevelt, or, for that matter, even like Johnson when everybody felt that Johnson was probably ready to crack up, and was drinking too much and so forth. I think we can avoid this by proper handling."[63]

Nixon worked at showing how fit he was. He told the press he was not feeling the pain he had felt in the Middle East. He mingled with crowds on the streets of Brussels, presenting the picture of a superactive President. Walking from the U.S. Embassy to the royal palace for lunch, he broke free from his party—to the consternation of the Secret Service— and strode over to an iron fence surrounding a park in front of the palace, to poke his hand through the bars to shake hands with spectators, campaign style.[64]

Like Nixon's domestic foes, the European leaders worried that Nixon would cut a deal with Brezhnev in order to outmaneuver his Watergate problems and at the expense of the NATO defenses. Nixon knew what they feared, but he also knew what NATO and the West needed, and he was forthright in his toasts and speeches. "In the world in which we live with the nuclear threat that overhangs it," he said, "there is no alternative to peace, there is no alternative to negotiation."[65]

HE arrived in Moscow on June 27, to begin the negotiation. The Russians were on their best behavior. All the big guns were there to meet him at the airport: General Secretary Brezhnev, President Podgorny, Premier Kosygin, Foreign Minister Gromyko, and Ambassador Dobrynin. They turned out a crowd to cheer the American President. Brezhnev then took Nixon to the Kremlin, for a private meeting, where he reported that he had recently met with Senator Kennedy and former Ambassador Averell Harriman, both of whom said they supported détente. Nixon said that was fine, that he wanted both parties to get behind détente: "Let's get them all a little pregnant."[66]

At the state dinner that evening, in Granovit Hall at the Grand Kremlin Palace, Nixon gave a long toast. Referring to the 1972 Moscow Summit, he noted that "we have moved in those 2 years from confrontation to co-existence to cooperation." He listed all the agreements that had been signed, then reminded his hosts—and Congress and the American public—how they had been achieved: "They were possible because of a personal relationship that was established between the General Secretary and the President of the United States."[67] The Soviets, who were more interested in détente than in preserving Nixon in office, omitted that line when reporting Nixon's remarks in *Pravda*.

After the banquet, Nixon called Kissinger and Haig to his car so that they could talk without being bugged. "My personal relations with Nixon were unusually distant at this point," Kissinger later wrote, while Nixon remarked that Kissinger "seemed depressed." Each man indulged in a bit of amateur analysis to explain what was happening. Nixon wrote that Kissinger was down because of the wiretap charges made against him; Kissinger wrote that Nixon found it "hard to bear" that the Secretary of State was sure to stay in office while the President was likely to be driven from office. In addition, Kissinger felt that "the physical effort required to keep functioning seemed to consume more and more of Nixon's energy." The President was "preoccupied and withdrawn."[68]

Actually, there was a policy explanation for the subdued mood. Each man wanted SALT II, no doubt for reasons of ego, and certainly in Nixon's case to improve his chances of surviving, but also because it was the right thing to do. But both men knew they were not going to get a treaty. The Soviets were never going to accept the Americans' final offer, and Nixon could not offer more; in fact it was doubtful that he could hold the Pentagon and its many friends in the Senate to support what he was already offering. Nixon and Kissinger loved surprises and breakthroughs, but they knew they were not going to get any out of this summit.

That was obvious at the first formal session the following day. The Soviets had agreed, in preliminary talks with Kissinger in March and in arms control talks in April, to the TTB. But to Nixon's surprise, as they wrangled over the threshold level, Brezhnev suddenly suggested that they solve the issue by agreeing on a comprehensive test ban (CTB, that is, no testing at all). Nixon, citing the problem of verification, said flatly, "We cannot go to a total test ban." He mentioned his domestic problems, but added that they were not decisive. He would continue to move toward détente "because it is indispensable for the peace of the world." He claimed, "I can handle our so called hawks—but only one step at a time." He said he wanted to reach the goal of a CTB (this was news to Kissinger), but by a different route than immediate agreement. The Soviets dropped the subject.[69]

The next day the principals flew to Yalta, in the Crimea, to continue their talks. Nixon had objected to going to Yalta, but Brezhnev—who had a dacha there and who loved the resort—said everything had been prepared, and insisted. As it was the name rather than the place that Nixon objected to, because of the association of Yalta with the 1945 summit where Roosevelt supposedly "gave away" Eastern Europe (a charge Nixon himself had frequently made), the solution was easy. The formal meetings were in the Oreanda Hotel in Yalta; the Russians simply rechristened it the "town of Oreanda," put up some freshly painted signposts, and it became the "Oreanda Summit."[70]

Brezhnev's dacha was part of a beach complex set into the steep hills that dropped into the Black Sea. He took Nixon for a walk to a building cut into the rock, rather like a grotto. The two men talked alone an hour, something that always made Gromyko and Kissinger anxious, as they worried about what their bosses might cook up in their absence.

Well might they worry, because although Nixon had nothing new to offer Brezhnev, the Soviet leader had another surprise for Nixon. He offered a mutual defense pact, where each country would come to the defense of the other if either it or its allies were attacked. Nixon gave no direct answer, but he did note in his diary, "This smacks of condominium in the most blatant sense." The object was China, although Brezhnev denied it, claiming indifference to Mao and his forces.

Brezhnev brought up the Middle East. He pointed out that the warnings about the explosive situation there he had given the previous year in San Clemente had been proven true. He insisted that the Soviet Union had done everything possible to restrain the Egyptians and Syrians in October 1972, but "we were unable to do so."

Nixon brought up the problem of Jewish emigration and MFN status for the Soviet Union. He urged Brezhnev to make "some sort of a gesture on Jewish emigration if only to pull the rug out from under Jackson." And he gave a prescient warning: "If detente unravels in America, the hawks will take over, not the doves." Brezhnev protested that Jewish emigration was at an all-time high and said he would have Dobrynin get the statistics to Kissinger.[71]

After an hour or so, the leaders allowed Gromyko, Kissinger, and other advisers join them. They took up MIRV. Kissinger said the Soviet proposal was impossible; it would "be represented in the U.S. as our accepting a freeze while permitting the Soviet Union to catch up." He warned that without an agreement, the United States could put MIRVs on five hundred more Minuteman missiles. He then made a counterproposal that the Russians said would freeze them while leaving the United States free to build all it wished. Nixon slipped Kissinger a note: "Use that 'forensic ability' Schlesinger told us would be sufficient to convince them." Kissinger tried, without success. Nixon suggested they go for a boat ride. They had reached an impasse on the issue that had brought them together, the limitation of offensive nuclear weapons.[72]

On the boat, after lunch, Nixon and Brezhnev grew quite chummy. Sitting together in the stern, Brezhnev put his arm around Nixon and said, "We must do something of vast historical importance. We want every Russian and every American to be friends that talk to each other as you and I are talking." Nixon made the point that the danger in advanced nations was "the weakening of character." Brezhnev quickly agreed. He said his sociologists and psychiatrists were studying the problem. The leaders agreed that "as people got more material goods they became less 'hungry,' lost their drive, and become almost totally obsessed with self, selfishness, and every kind of abstract idea."

Nixon said that "our goal must be the reduction of nukes." Brezhnev responded, "We must destroy the evil that we have created." As on CTB, in short, they agreed on the end goal while disagreeing sharply on how to get there.[73]

On the drive to the airport the next morning, the conversation continued. Referring to Jewish emigration, Brezhnev said, "As far as I am concerned, I say let all the Jews go and let God go with them." He said a nuclear war would destroy the civilized countries, that the white races would disappear, and that the yellows and blacks would remain to rule the world. Nixon was a bit more practical. He said it was essential to reach agreement on offensive weapons before the end of the year, because otherwise the Congress would go forward with a greatly expanded defense budget. He suggested an informal "mini-summit" before Christmas some place in between Moscow and Washington. Brezhnev agreed.[74]

There were more ceremonies to go through, more meetings, some agreements, more speeches, but essentially the summit was over. Accords were signed that included economic, industrial, and technical cooperation, as well as agreements in the fields of energy, housing construction, and artificial heart research. The joint Soviet-U.S. space mission was going forward. Each side agreed to limit itself to one ABM site, but that only put into writing what had already been planned in practice. TTB, at 150 kilotons, was agreed to (but not ratified by the Senate). Clearly the summit had failed.

Whose fault was it? American reporters, and later commentators, blamed Watergate and Nixon's weakened position. Nixon would have none of that. He argued in his memoirs that the impeachment hearings "did not play a major part" at the summit. He did blame domestic politics, the failure to produce MFN status for the Soviets and the agitation over Soviet Jews, for making "it difficult for Brezhnev to defend detente to his own conservatives." Beyond the politicians, there were the Pentagon and the Soviet military, each alarmed at the prospect of arms reduction and unwilling to adjust to peace. Nixon concluded, "These problems would have existed regardless of Watergate."[75]

True enough, but obviously Watergate did not help any, either. Brezhnev had come to the meeting determined to make progress. In a speech in June, shortly before the summit began, he had declared that "It is an immeasurably greater risk to continue to accumulate arms without restraint" than to risk an arms control agreement. He criticized the age-old dictum, "If you want peace, be prepared for war." Instead, he said, "In our nuclear age, this formula conceals a special danger. . . . In recent years such a mass of weapons has been accumulated as to make it possible to destroy every living thing on earth several times over."[76]

Nixon too wanted progress, as he agreed with Brezhnev's analysis. But he had no flexibility in his negotiating stance. Schlesinger, Zumwalt, Jackson, and the others had tied his hands, using Watergate as the rope. He was brutally frank about this in his diary: "We went as far as we could go at this point [on arms control] without raising an issue which could have lost us some of our good conservative supporters." He even expressed the thought that "It's probably just as well that we were unable to reach any agreement because to have to take this thing on now would mean that we would have to be opposed to some of our best friends prior to the impeachment vote."[77]

In addition to the constraints imposed by Watergate on Nixon, there was the physical toll imposed on him by the year-and-a-half-long investigation and by his phlebitis. At the public sessions, reporters commented that "his face appeared heavy and mask-like."[78] His attention seemed to wander at times, and he appeared distraught. He did not have command of the statistics and often cited incorrect figures. The drive that had produced the opening to China and SALT I just was not there anymore.

Of course Brezhnev could have yielded more than he did, been more forthcoming, more trusting, more cooperative. But then he had to be leery of Nixon. Although he went out of his way to say on a number of occasions that he expected Nixon to survive in office, he must have doubted it, and he did not want to link détente to Nixon personally. To do so carried with it the risk that if Nixon were driven from office, détente would go with him. So Brezhnev held back.

July 2 was the last day of the summit. Nixon and Brezhnev put the best face they could on the results of their meetings. At a final banquet, hosted by Nixon at Spaso House, the American ambassador's residence, the atmosphere was warm. Brezhnev said he looked forward to their informal summit in the fall. In the toasts, Nixon stressed the "personal relations and the personal friendship" between them, while Brezhnev stressed relations between the Soviet Union and the Congress and the American people. Nixon told Kissinger, within earshot of the Soviet interpreter, to pursue the idea of a U.S.-Soviet mutual defense pact in the back-channel negotiations with Dobrynin for the planned mini-summit. Kissinger, aghast at the idea, indicated that he would rather resign. Later, on his own authority, he told Dobrynin it was not a useful line to pursue. Nixon, busy with his own problems, never brought up the idea again.[79]

So the summit was barren. The failure warrants a question. "What if" history is fruitless, but harmless, and can be illuminating. Thus the question: what if there had not been a Watergate break-in and subsequent cover-up? Nixon still would have won the 1972 election with a big mandate. He could have claimed, with justice, that his three great initiatives— Vietnamization, the opening to China, and détente with the Soviets— had been endorsed. By implication, so had his efforts to achieve peace in the Middle East. In the year and a half following his second inaugural, he might have established formal diplomatic relations with the Chinese, reinforced and reformed the ARVN, and laid the basis for SALT II. In Moscow, he could have signed a comprehensive arms control agreement. Without Watergate, Schlesinger never would have dared insult him in a Cabinet meeting, Zumwalt would not have dared lead a revolt of the Pentagon, Jackson could not have held MFN hostage to Jewish emigration, Israel and the American Jewish community could not have ignored his demands that they seek compromise with the Arabs.

Or so at least it seems to this author. Of course we can never know. But it does appear that Watergate, despite what Nixon wrote in his memoirs, did play a decisive role in the demise of détente.

ON July 3, Nixon and his party flew back to the United States. *Air Force One* landed at Loring Air Force Base at Limestone, Maine, for refueling. Vice President Ford led a welcoming party. At the airfield ceremony, Ford gave Nixon a lavish introduction, saying the world was now "a little safer and a little saner" thanks to Nixon's travels.

The crowd, composed almost exclusively of military personnel, was friendly. Nixon spoke of peace, and the need to stay strong and stick by America's allies, and the achievement of the summit.[80]

Then he flew off to Key Biscayne, to spend the Fourth of July weekend there.

CHAPTER FIFTEEN

JULY 4, 1974

NIXON SPENT the Fourth of July at Key Biscayne, worrying about his problems and wondering about his future.

The rest of the country spent the nation's 198th birthday trying to celebrate, doing the usual things—backyard cookouts, dances, parades, swimming, hiking—but without the usual good spirits. The country was divided as it had not been since the Civil War, and—pray God—never will be again. The division resulted not from a policy issue, but a personal one: what had Richard Nixon done, and when did he do it, and what should be done about it?

I was camping in the Black Hills, with my wife and children. It is not my style to get into political arguments with strangers. On that Fourth of July, however, I got into a half dozen or more arguments over Nixon. At Sylvan Lake, at a bar in Rapid City, in the campgrounds, Nixon supporters squared off against Nixon foes. One man, also middle-aged, also with his family, cautious and conservative in his demeanor, told me, "I think Nixon is the best President we have ever had." I said I thought he was the worst. Another commented that he could not see what Nixon had done that was so terrible. I listed for him the various charges in the articles of impeachment and said I thought Nixon should not only be indicted and found guilty, but punished by being sent to jail. We were drinking; he came close to hitting me. I left the bar. He followed, shouting that I was a Communist swine.

I attracted such attention and castigation because of my appearance as much as my views. At that time I was writing a dual biography of Crazy Horse and Custer; to get the feel of my subjects I was imitating them in some superficial ways, such as living in a tent, riding horses, cooking fresh meat over an open fire, and so forth. As both Crazy Horse and Custer had long flowing hair, I had hair hanging below my shoulders. This automatically branded me as anti-Nixon and brought out the fighting instincts of his supporters. We, the American people, were so divided that even our hairstyles provoked antagonism.

My personal experiences have no place in a biography of Richard Nixon, except that I am convinced that on that day my experiences were typical of those happening around the country. Richard Nixon and his actions obsessed the nation that Fourth of July; on the day above all others that should draw the American people together in peace, harmony, and celebration, we were furious with each other, angry either at the President or at his foes, depressed and in agony.

But although the division within the nation whirled around the person of Richard Nixon, by no means was he solely responsible. Long hair vs. short hair, dirty blue jeans vs. business suits, marijuana vs. liquor, rock music vs. love ballads, no sex outside marriage vs. free love, unquestioning patriotism vs. demonstrations against the government, blind trust that even if you disagreed with the President you assumed he was telling the truth vs. the assumption that if the President said it then it must be a lie—all these divisions, and many others, predated Watergate and the Nixon Presidency. To focus on Nixon is to ignore the Vietnam War, and the baby boom, and worldwide developments. The advice, "Don't trust anyone over thirty," had found a receptive audience before Nixon and Watergate.

The conversation Brezhnev and Nixon had on the boat on the Black Sea about the loss of character[1] speaks to the point. The scene itself is remarkable; there was Brezhnev, the author of the doctrine that the Soviet Union had the right to crush the slightest move toward democracy throughout its empire, the man who buried the Khrushchev attempts at reform and reinstituted a Stalinist system within the Soviet Union and among its satellite nations, along with Nixon, the author of the Watergate cover-up and the man who set out to crush his domestic political opponents at the expense of the law and common decency, bemoaning the loss of character. What a pair they were to be discussing such a subject.

And yet, they were hardly alone. Around the world, men their age agreed with them. The generation that had fought World War II felt that their children had lost the very qualities that they, their parents, had sacrificed to preserve.

Fifteen years earlier, in 1959, when he first met Brezhnev (at the kitchen debate with Khrushchev), Nixon had taken an opposite line. In 1974 he bemoaned the materialism of youth, but back in 1959 he had tried to impress the Russians with American material success. In a television address to the people of the Soviet Union, Nixon had bragged that in the United States, 31 million families owned their own homes, 56 million had automobiles, 50 million possessed television sets, women bought nine dresses per year, and so forth.

There is another difference. In 1959, Nixon had arrived in Moscow "keyed up and ready for battle." In 1974, he had arrived keyed up, but ready to seek cooperation. Rather than brag about the American way of life, he joined with Brezhnev in regretting rampant materialism.

What caused these changes in Nixon's approach and thinking? First of all, the different situations. In 1959, he was a candidate for the 1960 Republican nomination looking to impress American voters; in 1974, he was the President with his last election behind him and keenly aware of his responsibilities for world peace and security.

Second, he had matured. He knew more and thought about it harder in 1974 than in 1959. Third, in 1959 he was forty-six years of age, a relatively young man to hold the second highest position in the nation, while in 1974 he was past sixty years of age, which put a four-decade gap between him and the new voters. Fourth, the generation coming of age *was* very different from his generation.

These differences have been much commented upon and worried about, and many of them are obvious. The baby boomers did not have the sense of consensus, of team, of common sacrifice, of dedication to country that was one of the hallmarks of the generation that went through the Depression and fought World War II. The baby boomers have been described as the "me" generation, full of a sense of self, as opposed to a "we" generation full of a sense of community. Unless public life touched them directly—as in, above all else, conscription into the armed services—they were relatively uninterested in public life. The evidence was everywhere and obvious—they did not read newspapers as regularly as their parents, they did not participate in political activities (above all in exercising the right to vote) as regularly as their parents, they were cynical about politicians and politics, the books they bought were guides to self-improvement rather than to public improvement, they tended to spend rather than save, and to spend on pleasure rather than security, and so forth.

Why these differences between the generations? Again, the reasons have been much commented upon and worried about, and many of them are obvious. Vietnam was not World War II. As a cause, preserving the Thieu government in Saigon could not be compared to the need to destroy Hitler and the Nazis. Had the baby boomers been asked to make sacrifices that made sense to them, they might have done so. The parents themselves bore some of the responsibility; many middle-class Americans had vowed that their children would never go through what they had endured in the Depression and the war, so they had moved to the suburbs and given their children, the baby boomers, a life of affluence and security the likes of which the world had never before seen.

Further, the baby boomers had been shortchanged on their education. As they filled the grade schools, then the high schools, and finally the colleges and universities, the educational Establishment met the crisis in numbers by lowering standards while raising classroom sizes. The children did not read as much or as well as their parents. They missed the discipline imposed on their parents by the Depression and service in the armed forces. They were exposed to drugs in a way unimaginable to their parents.

A major difference between Nixon's generation and the baby boomers was television. Unknown until after World War II, television had become ubiquitous by 1960, in the process changing habits and practices and leisure time to a degree and in ways that Nixon's generation, middle-aged before the television age, could never comprehend. The baby boomers spent more time watching television than they did in school, or in family activities, or in church, or at play, or studying, or doing anything else.

Television was rather like nuclear power. In the late forties, the heavy thinkers had prophesied that just as nuclear power would solve all the world's energy problems for all time, so would television enlighten and educate the masses in ways previously unimaginable. In the event, however, it was the gloom-and-doom sayers about nuclear power and television who were proved right. Much can be said about the effects of television, obviously, but it cannot be said that it produced an enlightened and educated citizenry. It did produce greed, and disenchantment with politics, and cynicism, while reinforcing the sense of self at the expense of community.

So there was substance to Nixon's conversation with Brezhnev about the "weakening of character" in the young. And Nixon was right to note that the phenomenon was producing a generation that was "almost totally obsessed with self, selfishness, and every kind of abstract idea." But his analysis of the cause—that "as people got more material goods they became less 'hungry,' lost their drive"—fell short of the mark.

Nixon failed to note the biggest difference of all between his generation and the baby boomers. It is simply stated. The boomers were born into a nuclear world. They had lived all their lives with the threat of instant extinction hanging over them, coupled with a sense of helplessness about when and for what cause the nuclear spasm would occur. Like television, this fundamental fact of living all their lives in a perpetual state of fear, not only about their own existence but the literal existence of life on the planet, was unique to the baby boomers. It certainly played some role in the creation of their sense of self and their insistence on instant gratification.

Not that they thought about it much, or that it was a conscious fear (except in periods of high tension, such as the Cuban missile crisis or the

October 1973 nuclear alert), but it was always there. How could it not have been, considering that the baby boomers, virtually every one of them, had gone through the experience in grade schools of hiding under their desks in practice alerts? Grade school children in the fifties were shown "civil defense" films in which a siren went off and, as children scrambled under their desks, a voice-over said, "Always remember, the flash of an atomic bomb can come at anytime, no matter where you may be, so duck and cover." They discovered, when they reached high school, that the power of the bombs they were trying to hide from would leave them all dead no matter where they tried to find protection—and if they did somehow survive the initial shock wave, they would find themselves in a world in which the living envied the dead.

And who was responsible for this threat hanging over everyone's heads? The scientists and technologists who made the bomb, of course, but even more the politicians who had been unable to reach any agreement on how to control, much less eliminate, the weapon.

Which brings us back to Nixon. He was one of the two most powerful politicians in the world. The other was Brezhnev. For the two of them to discuss the loss of character in the next generation without at least considering the effect of their own failure to achieve arms control was unfair of them.

For decades, they had been leading advocates of accelerating their country's strategic weapons stockpile. Back in 1956, when Soviet Premier Bulganin endorsed Adlai Stevenson's call for a nuclear test ban, Nixon had called Stevenson a "clay pigeon" for Soviet sharpshooters and compared him to Neville Chamberlain.[2] But, it must be immediately added, by no means was the failure to achieve arms control exclusively Nixon's or Brezhnev's fault—indeed by 1974, of all the world's leaders, they were trying the hardest to do something about the threat. They were, however, operating under severe constraints, some of them self-inflicted—their own ideologies, their own refusal to trust the other man, their own determination to hold onto power—but most of them caused by forces beyond their control. They were caught by a classic leadership contradiction; they could see clearly where the world ought to be headed, but they could not bring their own societies with them, indeed would have been thrown out of office had they tried to impose their vision on their countries.

In the same way, it is clearly unfair to blame all, or even most, of the problems created by the generation gap on Richard Nixon. He was not responsible for the creation of the television domination of the baby boomers' lives, nor for the war in Vietnam, nor for shortcomings of the educational Establishment in the fifties and sixties, nor for the move to the suburbs, nor for the rampant materialism. He did not create the "me" generation.

Had Nixon disappeared from the American political scene as a major player after 1962 the generation gap would still have been there, and young people would still have been cynical about politics, and using drugs, and thinking about "me" instead of "we."

Still, Nixon did contribute. Cynicism about the President was based in part on Lyndon Johnson's lies about Vietnam, but it was reinforced and dramatically strengthened by Richard Nixon's lies about Vietnam and Watergate. Divisiveness among the body politic came about in part because of Johnson's war in Vietnam, but it was reinforced and dramatically strengthened by Nixon, the man who all his life practiced the politics of divisiveness.

As to the mood of the country on the Fourth of July, 1974, Nixon must bear the ultimate responsibility. He was the one who set the whole Watergate scandal in motion, he was the one who had spent a year and a half defending himself through an active cover-up, he was the one who by refusing to resign when he knew he was guilty forced the nation to concentrate its attention all but exclusively on him. Had he resigned any time before July 1974, we could have spent the nation's 198th birthday celebrating instead of fighting among ourselves.

While his countrymen fought among themselves, the President sat in Key Biscayne, brooding over his fate. He had lost the power to govern, as signified by his inability to make Brezhnev a reasonable offer on arms control. He was hurting the Presidency, rather than sustaining it, as signified by the override of his veto of the War Powers Act. Yet he clung to the office. He was the ultimate "me" person.

CHAPTER SIXTEEN

THE COURT RULES—
THE HOUSE DEBATES
July 5–31, 1974

ON JULY 5, Nixon confessed in his diary that he had a "sinking feeling" in the pit of his stomach and that he was suffering through sleepless nights.

Such experiences were all but commonplace with Nixon. He had them before every crisis. A quarter of a century earlier on a number of occasions during the various ups-and-downs of the Hiss case, anxiety had all but overwhelmed him. So too at the time of the fund crisis of 1952, and when he heard in 1955 that Eisenhower had suffered a heart attack. They returned the next year, when Harold Stassen tried to drive him off the Republican ticket, and again in South America in 1958. He knew similar feelings in 1960, before the first debate with Kennedy, and on election night, when he felt the election was being stolen from him. When Lyndon Johnson announced the bombing halt on the eve of the 1968 election, Nixon's pulse raced, his stomach churned, and his nights were sleepless. This had happened numerous times during his Presidency, most notably just before he announced the Cambodian incursion, the bombing of Hanoi and the mining of Haiphong Harbor, and the Christmas bombing. Various episodes following the Watergate break-in, cover-up, and subsequent investigation had produced the familiar feelings.

Nixon was the oldest hand there was at dealing with crises. His physical symptoms notwithstanding, he was the best there was. Indeed, the churning stomach and the sleepless nights help him gear up.

In all his previous crises he had been able to draw on assets, beginning with a solid, all but unshakable constituency and a personal belief in the rightness of his actions. As he faced his last crisis, however, his assets had dwindled. His constituency was small, shaken and shrinking, and he knew that what he had done was, if not wrong, at least a bad mistake. To retain the support of his aides and family, he had had to lie to them about what he had known and done. His sole remaining real asset was his office. He swore to others, and to himself, that he would hold into it, no matter what, until two thirds of the senators voted guilty on impeachment charges. "Our only course of action is to keep fighting right through to the last," he noted in his diary.

Nixon knew that he was not the only one who would have to pay a price for his defiance. In his mind, "The whole purpose [of the Watergate investigation and impeachment attempt] of course is to discredit, destroy, harass everybody around the President." He had reason to believe that the campaign against him and those around him was working; Pat told him that day that Bebe Rebozo was "really depressed," and that Rose Mary Woods "has gone through hell."[1] Unmentioned but obvious was this: so had all his closest aides, not to mention his family.

Nevertheless he continued to make his decisions on his own, and to encourage his aides and allow his family to continue to defend him, without ever letting them in on his awful secret. Except for Haldeman, no one but Nixon knew what was on the June 23, 1972, tape. Not Julie Eisenhower, not Pat, not Ziegler, not Haig, not Rebozo, not Buzhardt, Garment, or St. Clair, all of whom were defending him at the risk of their own reputations. Not Ford, not the Republican congressmen, not the Southern Democrats, who were defending him at the risk of their own careers. Nixon, always the most isolated and self-centered of all the Presidents, had never been so isolated.

One prominent Republican who knew the President well told Elizabeth Drew that he had never known anyone in politics who was as tough as Nixon. "He is not bothered by things that would get to other men. There is no group he would listen to. No group. No one. Not his wife. Not Bebe. No one. He doesn't read the messages sent to him in the press. God, he's tough!"[2]

That toughness included a willingness to take a terrific pounding, and fight back. In all his previous crises, Nixon had not just taken it, but moved to the attack, launching counteroffensives that put him in control of events. The trouble in this last crisis was that he could not seize control of events. He had nothing with which to attack. While the country's attention centered on the compelling figure of Richard Nixon, the man himself could only watch, a spectator at a play in which others wrote the script and gave the directions, even though all the action revolved around him.

As a spectator, he was active, not in the sense of attempting to understand or analyze the deeper meaning of the play—evidently throughout the summer of 1974 he never discussed the substance of Watergate and related activities with anyone—but by doing what came more naturally to him, counting the votes. Kissinger noted that he spent hours doing "the arithmetic of the impeachment vote" and commented that "he was a man awake during his own nightmare."[3] His liaison aide with Congress, Bill Timmons, went over the count with him daily. They began with the House Judiciary Committee. The critical votes there were six so-called "swing" Republicans and three Southern Democrats. Timmons and Nixon agreed that if they could hold four of the Republicans and one of the Southerners, they had a chance at beating impeachment in the full House. Others told the President the same thing. He wanted to believe them. He was "encouraged but not overly optimistic." He found solace in the smallest things; when George Bush called to say that he would like Nixon to appear on a fund-raising telethon, Nixon regarded the call as a hopeful sign.[4]

Even if five or six of the swing votes held for Nixon, he anticipated losing in the Judiciary Committee. To soften the blow of an adverse vote, he and his aides worked to discredit the Committee in advance. Ziegler had already denounced the Committee on a number of occasions for its leaks and complained that it was stacked with liberals. In late June, Nixon's people had seized another opportunity to express outrage when Chairman Rodino was quoted as having told reporters that all twenty-one Democrats on the Committee were going to vote for impeachment. As the Committee was still hearing evidence, White House aide Kenneth Clawson demanded that Rodino be discharged because of his clear bias.

Actually Rodino had understood, from the beginning of the impeachment inquiry, how critical it was for him and his committee to be and to appear to be fair. He had worked diligently in that effort, and almost all observers agreed that he had succeeded. In this case, he had made an off-the-record remark during an informal discussion to the effect that he "thought" all the Democrats would vote for impeachment. After the Clawson demand, Rodino denied, from the House floor, that he had ever made or could have made the statement that the Democrats were going to vote to impeach, because he had never asked any member of the Committee how he or she would vote and hence could not know. Nixon was not convinced; he later accused Rodino of a "cover up."[5]

By July 8, Nixon was back in Washington. On that day, the Supreme Court heard arguments in *United States* v. *Nixon*. While his fate was being debated, Nixon met in the Oval Office with Ford. The President was in "one of his rambling moods." He did not mention the Supreme Court, nor the possibility of his leaving office and Ford taking over. Rather, he talked about inflation and other domestic issues, and the summit with Brezhnev.[6]

In the Supreme Court, St. Clair spoke for Nixon. He argued that the President's right to invoke executive privilege was absolute. Therefore he did not have to comply with the Special Prosecutor's subpoena. This ran counter to Nixon's own argument back in the Hiss case. Then Congressman Nixon had angrily denounced President Truman for withholding information from Congress. Nixon had said that Truman's action "cannot stand from a Constitutional standpoint or on the basis of the merits," for it would enable the President arbitrarily to deny Congress its lawful right to investigate wrongdoing in the executive branch.

Jaworski, in answering questions from the justices, did not cite Congressman Nixon. He did insist that executive privilege did not cover criminal activity. He asked a question of his own: "Shall the evidence from the White House be confined to what a single person, highly interested in the outcome, is willing to make available?" The answer could come only from the Supreme Court. Jaworski noted, "If there is any one principle of law that Marbury v. Madison decides, it is that it is up to the Court to say what the law is."[7]

Or, as Dwight Eisenhower put it, in a reference to a decision with which he disagreed (*Brown* v. *Topeka*), "I hold to the basic purpose. There must be respect for the Constitution—which means the Supreme Court's interpretation of the Constitution—or we shall have chaos."[8]

Nixon felt that the Court would end up voting along what he called political lines, meaning Republicans against Democrats. He had appointed four of the justices, but one of them, William Rehnquist, had removed himself because he had served in the Justice Department in the Nixon Administration.* That was why Nixon would not define what he meant by abiding by a "definitive" decision from the Court; he anticipated a 5 to 3 vote against him, and in that case could—in his own carefully chosen words—"*abide* by the Court's ruling without actually *complying* with it." He would offer edited, excerpted transcripts, rather than the tapes themselves.[9] That was, at best, a shaky scaffold on which to hang his future.

Even that might not be enough to save the Nixon Presidency. The Judiciary Committee evidently was going to recommend impeachment on the basis of evidence already in hand; the full House might go along. If Nixon went on trial before the Senate without complying fully with a Court order, the senators, as sensitive to the Court as Eisenhower, could well decide that he was guilty for refusing to comply.

The Supreme Court was critical in the crisis. This was exactly what the founding fathers had intended. The Constitution gave the justices lifetime tenure in order to free their minds from partisan considerations. The system had been in place for nearly two hundred years, and had not

---

*The other justices were: William Douglas (appointed by FDR), William Brennan (Ike), Potter Stewart (Ike), Byron White (JFK), Thurgood Marshall (LBJ), Chief Justice Warren Burger (Nixon), Lewis Powell (Nixon), and Harry Blackmun (Nixon).

failed the country. The people regarded the Supreme Court chamber as the center of gravity of the American system. With the tall marble columns on both sides of the room, the marble walls, the red-and-black marble floors, the burgundy carpets, the burgundy velour drapes, the justices filing in wearing their black robes, the voice calling out, "God save the United States and this Honorable Court," the scene rivaled the taking of the oath of office by a new President as a symbol of American democracy. Elizabeth Drew noted that people sat in the chamber hushed, "as if they were in fact in a temple."[10]

There was nothing Nixon could do to influence the justices. He was the most powerful man in the world, but in that chamber he was powerless.

That same July 8, Charles Colson went to jail. There was nothing Nixon would do about that, although he had the power to pardon. That same day, too, Ehrlichman was on the stand in his trial in the Ellsberg break-in. Nixon could have helped his former aide by turning over Ehrlichman's own notes of his meetings with the President, but he had refused to do so.

Also on July 8 the Dow Jones average declined 21 points, to its lowest point in three and a half years. Inflation was nearly 15 percent, and had become the nation's number-one worry. A Gallup Poll taken that week found that 48 percent of those surveyed named the inflation rate as the nation's paramount problem, followed by 15 percent who cited "lack of trust in government," and 11 percent who named "corruption in government" and "Watergate" as the principal areas of concern.[11]

The public was tired of Watergate and just wished that it—and Nixon—would go away. People were frightened by the highest inflation rate since 1946. They looked to their political leaders, the President most of all, to supply a solution. To try to think of one, and to escape Washington, Nixon decided to go to San Clemente.

BEFORE he could get away, he had to absorb another deluge of bad news. On July 9, the Judiciary Committee released eight transcripts its staff had prepared of Nixon's Watergate conversations. There were marked differences between the Nixon version and the Committee's transcript. The newspapers and television commentators played on these differences, which further undermined the President's credibility. Two days later, the Committee released the evidence John Doar had presented to its inquiry. There were more than four thousand pages, none of which did Nixon any good and much of which did him great harm. The headlines summarized the story: "PRESIDENT'S STATEMENT CONTRADICTED"; "PRESIDENT WITHHELD PART OF TAPE ON COVER-UP TALK"; "REBOZO LINKED TO $45,621 TO IMPROVE NIXON HOMES"; and so on.[12]

Nor could Nixon's lawyer help. Cross-examining John Dean before the Judiciary Committee, St. Clair attempted to discredit Dean by questioning his motives and calling him a liar. It did not work; even Republicans on the Committee said later that Dean had the better of the exchange. St. Clair dealt with the most damaging piece of evidence—Nixon's March 21, 1973, order to Dean to get the hush money to Hunt—with a denial. He said that Nixon never authorized hush money payments. He went on, "The president had no knowledge of an attempt by the White House to cover up involvement in the Watergate affair."[13]

How could he say such a thing? was the attitude of most Committee members, who had read what Nixon had said to Dean, and who knew that within hours of the meeting, the money had been paid.

The Ervin Committee released its final report. Predictably, it was scathing. It detailed the misuse of the IRS, the FBI, the CIA, and the Justice Department; it denounced the Plumbers; it hit Rebozo. In his summary, Ervin raised the question of whether the nation had had a genuine election in 1972. He charged that the first objective of the "various illegal and unethical activities" of the Nixon White House was "to destroy insofar as the Presidential election of 1972 was concerned the integrity of the process by which the President of the United States is nominated and elected."[14]

Rather than attempt to stand up to this tidal wave, Nixon tried to divert attention. He announced that he was going to deal with inflation head on and held a series of meetings in the White House to discuss how to do that. He called in leading businessmen and economists to open a "national dialogue." In ordinary times, a presidential initiative on the nation's number-one problem would have been the headline in the newspapers, the lead on the evening newscasts on television, and the subject of uncountable columns. But in July of 1974 the newspapers hardly had enough room to print all the Watergate stories and revelations. Nixon's inflation initiative was buried. He did not give up; he moved the meetings to San Clemente, where he intended to work on a major nationwide address on inflation.

ON July 12, Nixon, Pat, Ed, and Tricia flew on *Air Force One* to California. En route, they learned that Ehrlichman had been convicted of perjury and of conspiring to violate the civil rights of Daniel Ellsberg's psychiatrist. The news "deeply depressed" Nixon, who was struck by the "tragic irony" of Ellsberg going free while Ehrlichman went to jail.[15]

Nixon got one small boost that day. Vice President Ford, speaking in Santa Fe, referred to the thousands of pages of documents released by the Judiciary Committee and the Ervin Committee, and declared, "I think the evidence as a whole, the new evidence as well as the old evidence, clearly exonerates the President." He did not expect the President to be impeached, and he looked forward to Nixon's speech on inflation.[16]

The following morning, Ford flew to San Clemente, where he met with Nixon, Kenneth Rush, the counselor to the President coordinating economic affairs in the White House, Roy Ash, director of OMB, Herb Stein, chairman of the Council of Economic Advisers, and Ray Price, who was writing the inflation speech, to discuss the economy. It was clear to Ford that Nixon "wasn't as strong either mentally or physical as he had been before. I had a growing sense of his frustration, his resentment and his lack of a calm, deliberate approach to the problems of government. He complained bitterly how he was being mistreated by Congress and the press."[17]

A couple of days later, the public learned just how angry Nixon was, how deeply his resentments and hatreds ran, how little he understood the seriousness of the scandal that was scuttling his Administration, how unwilling he was to accept any personal responsibility. The occasion was a visit from Rabbi Korff. Korff had done an interview with Nixon some two months earlier and included it in a book he now presented entitled *The Personal Nixon: Staying on the Summit.* It showed Nixon at his worst, but neither Nixon, nor Korff, nor Nixon's advisers realized this fact. Ziegler, with great fanfare, called the reporters to the San Clemente press office and presented them with copies.

Korff had asked leading and goading questions; Nixon had replied with raw emotion. It was all in the book. Did the President feel that Haldeman, Colson, Ehrlichman, and other former aides could get a fair trial? "I would have to argue very strongly that the individuals who had been hauled publicly before committees and who also, in addition, have been slandered on television night after night through source stories and the rest, have had their chance for a fair trial destroyed."

Did Nixon feel that he had been treated fairly? Nixon said he had been treated with "savagery—well, we call it savagery, we will call it viciousness, sometimes libelous, so forth, of critics, et cetera et cetera, et cetera."

How did the Watergate scandal compare with Teapot Dome? Watergate, according to Nixon, would be seen by future historians as "the broadest but the thinnest scandal in American history, because what was it about?" No one of the men involved had received anything "in the way of financial reward for their service. Now, of course, I do not mean that crime can only be measured in terms of whether or not you were paid something. But when they say this is like Teapot Dome, that is comparing apples with oranges, and, shall we say, rather poor oranges too."

Why then did the press make such a big deal out of Watergate? Because, Nixon replied, "I am not the press's favorite pin-up boy. If it hadn't been for Watergate there would probably have been something else. So, now they have this . . . If I were a liberal Watergate would be a blip."

Would he consider resigning? "I have decided to go the distance to defend this office and to defend myself against charges of which I am wholly innocent."

Was he an anti-Semite, as people who had read his racial slurs on the transcripts charged? Nixon pointed to his appointment of Walter Annenberg as Ambassador to Britain and of Kissinger as Secretary of State to refute the accusation.

What about all those expletive deleteds? Nixon replied that if his critics "were to tape the conversations of Presidents that I have known, they wouldn't like their tone, either."

What would happen if he were impeached and found guilty? Nixon said such a development would have "devastating consequences" on foreign policy, would "jeopardize" world peace, and would have a "very detrimental effect on our political system for years to come."

In a transparent appeal to the Southern Democrats on the Judiciary Committee and in the Senate, Nixon said he was "very much concerned about what happens to the Republican party," that he wanted "good candidates" to win in November, "but however, if there are good Democrats, and I know many good Democrats, I will be for them."

How did Nixon feel about the investigations into his tax returns? He replied that he did not mind having them "gone over with a fine tooth comb" because "I have never cared much about money."

How did he stand up "under the kind of vilification and attack and savagery that has gone on for the past year and a half?" Inheritance, Nixon replied. "A strong mother, strong father . . . a strong family, all of whom stand like a rock against attacks when they are made.

"But in more personal terms, it gets down to what the Quakers call peace at the center. Peace at the center means that whatever the storms are, they may be roaring up or down, that the individual must have and retain that peace within him.

"The most important factor is that the individual must know, deep inside, that he is right. He must believe that. If, for example, these charges on the Watergate and the cover-up, et cetera, were true, nobody would have to ask me to resign. I wouldn't serve for one minute if they were true. But I know they are not true."

What did he think of the White House press corps? They "hate my guts with a passion," Nixon said. "But I don't hate them, none of them. . . . I can see in the eyes of them, not only their hatred but their frustration, and I, as a matter of fact I really feel sorry for them in a way, because . . . they should recognize that to the extent that they allow their own hatreds to consume them, they will lose the rationality which is the mark of a civilized man."

Why were the reporters so consumed with hatred? Vietnam, Nixon replied. "If I had bugged out of Vietnam, which they wanted, Watergate would have been a blip. They wouldn't have cared, but it is because I have not gone down the line with them that they care."

Could anything good come out of Watergate? Yes, Nixon replied: "A greater sense of responsibility on the part of the press, on the part of investigators and the rest, for the rights of individuals."

Korff had tried to persuade three New York publishers to print his interview. Rejected, he then created Fairness Publishers with money from his National Citizen's Committee for Fairness to the Presidency and printed 300,000 copies.[18]

That Nixon thought the widespread distribution of this stuff would help his cause illustrates how completely this once supremely realistic and practical politician had lost his political judgment.

Two days later Korff, back in Washington, presided over a $10-a-plate dinner at the Shoreham Americana Hotel. It was the opening session of his committee's five-day meeting. David Eisenhower attended, along with Senator Carl Curtis, Secretary of Commerce Frederick Dent, Pat Buchanan, speechwriter Reverend John McLaughlin, and other White House aides. Julie was there, to make a speech supporting her father. Nixon put in a telephone call to the gathering; he gave a pep talk, thanked Korff and the others for their efforts, and praised the group for supporting the office of the Presidency. The crowd chanted, "We love Nixon."[19]

OUT in San Clemente, Nixon continued to work on his inflation speech, and on his defense. He gave St. Clair some words of his own, from one of the tapes that had been subpoenaed but not turned over, to use in St. Clair's summation before the Judiciary Committee: Nixon to Haldeman, on March 22, 1973, "I don't mean to be blackmailed by Hunt—that goes too far." After the session, St. Clair told reporters that Nixon had "indicated it would be right to pay money to Hunt for humanitarian purposes."

The use of the excerpt from a subpoenaed but withheld tape, at the last day of the closed sessions, after the Committee had been examining evidence for ten weeks, produced a storm of criticism. Committee members described it as "outrageous," "incredible," and "practically an insult." And St. Clair's statement to the reporters hardly helped Nixon's cause, either.[20]

In his diary that day, July 18, Nixon wrote that "I began to think really about the whole impeachment process and very objectively and coldly." In fact, he continued to wallow in his illusions. He thought impeachment by the full House "possible although not probable." He felt the gamble of giving St. Clair one sentence out of a two-hour conversation had been a good one: "It is like a campaign. We have got to take some risks when everything is on the line."[21]

On July 19, John Doar summed up the evidence he had presented, then abandoned his neutral role to make a passionate appeal for the Committee to recommend impeachment. He talked of the President's "enormous crimes," and said he could not remain indifferent when Nixon committed "the terrible deed of subverting the Constitution." He gave the Committee staff-prepared articles of impeachment, twenty-nine in all. They centered on four allegations against Nixon: he had obstructed justice by participating in the cover-up; he had abused the powers of the Presidency by invading the civil rights of individuals and through misuse of government agencies; he had refused to honor subpoenas by the Judiciary Committee; he had committed fraud in connection with his income taxes and expenditure of public funds on his personal property.[22]

Nixon conferred with Ziegler, who then held a televised news conference. He called Doar a "partisan ideologue," who had proceeded in a "partisan, duplicitous, false way" and made a "total shambles of what would have been a fair proceeding." Rodino, according to Ziegler, had presented a false "picture of fairness." The whole thing was a "kangaroo court." Ziegler said he was speaking for the President.[23]

That night, Nixon made another diary entry. He resolved to remain resolute. "Cowards die a thousand deaths," he noted, "brave men die only once." With the Judiciary Committee vote coming on, and the Supreme Court decision on the tapes, he knew he faced as hard a month ahead as he had ever been through—"our Seventh Crisis in spades." He was sustained by two thoughts: that he was right, and that he was fighting "an assault on our entire system of government."[24]

Nixon spent the day of July 21 swimming, walking alone on the beach, brooding. That evening he attended a dinner in his honor at Roy Ash's lavish home in Bel Air, formerly W. C. Fields's home. Movie stars among the 150 guests added to the Hollywood glitter. After the champagne was poured, Ash offered a toast to the President. In his response, Nixon praised his Administration for its accomplishments, warned that the "structure of peace" he had built was "fragile," and reminded the group that it was terribly important that American leadership continue to be strong. "Apart from the man, the office of the presidency must never be weakened because a strong America and a strong American president is something which is absolutely indispensable" to world peace.

Growing personal, Nixon said people wondered how he could take it, how he could survive it, "how do you keep your composure, your strength, and the rest?" The answer was "a strong family . . . and a lot of good friends," people who stuck by him. "And I can assure you that no man in public life—and I have studied American history rather thoroughly—has ever had a more loyal group of friends . . . who have stood by him through good days as well as tough days than I have."[25]

Tricia recorded in her diary that it was a glorious affair. Watergate seemed "a million light-years away. . . . There was a glow of old about the entire evening."[26]

Nixon had friends back in Washington, too. That day, Rabbi Korff announced a three-day vigil of prayer and fasting by his followers on the Capitol steps.[27]

KORFF had no vote in either the Judiciary Committee or the Supreme Court, which was where Nixon needed help. Each body would be voting at the beginning of the last week of July. It was Richard Nixon's last election, the one that counted the most, the climax of his three decades in politics. In every previous campaign, he had been a man of furious activity in the last days; in this one, he stayed in San Clemente, a helpless observer.

He was losing support at a disastrous rate. Tom Railsback of Illinois, one of the swing Republicans on the Judiciary Committee, explained some of the reasons in an interview on July 22. Without indicating how he would vote, Railsback confirmed that he had been meeting regularly with the other uncertain Republicans on the Committee. They were all incensed, he said, over Nixon's noncompliance with the Committee's subpoenas. He feared that, "If the Congress doesn't get the material we think we need and then votes to exonerate, we'll be regarded as a paper tiger." Of course the group was bothered by the cover-up, but even more by the misuse of government agencies, especially the IRS.

Nixon's attempt to use the IRS to get his enemies bothered all the politicians, perhaps more than anything else that the President had done. One supposes they realized how vulnerable they were to such a vendetta. There is irony here. The Kennedys had used the IRS against Nixon, and others; one of Nixon's most consistent complaints to Haldeman was that the IRS would *not* cooperate with him and go after his enemies. Nixon was guilty of trying to misuse power with the IRS, but not of actually having done so. He was losing votes for something he had not done, but that had been done to him.

Railsback confessed that Nixon's attitude also disturbed him. He said that while he worried about the effect of impeachment on Pat and Julie, he did not have the same feeling about Nixon, because "he has not been contrite. He has not been remorseful; he has not been repentant. He has never admitted that he has made a mistake."[28]

On July 23, the day before the Judiciary Committee's televised hearings were scheduled to begin, Lawrence Hogan (R.-Md.), a conservative whose vote Nixon hoped he had, called a press conference to announce that he had decided to vote for impeachment. Hogan said that Nixon had "lied repeatedly" about Watergate, that the President had approved the payment of hush money, that he had "personally helped to orchestrate" the cover-up, and that unless he was driven from office, "government and politics will continue to be clouded by mistrust and suspicion." Hogan predicted that at least five other Republicans from the seventeen on the Committee would join him in recommending impeachment.[29]

Nixon, typically, cast doubts on Hogan's motives. Hogan was running for governor of Maryland; Nixon's spokesmen accused him of attempting to rescue a "faltering campaign" with his grandstanding act.[30] Perhaps the charge was accurate; if so, it hardly helped Nixon's cause that a conservative border-state Republican thought he could best help himself by attacking Nixon.

That afternoon, Nixon got even worse news. Timmons called to tell him that the three Southern Democrats on the House Judiciary Committee on whom he had counted—Walter Flowers of Alabama, James Mann of South Carolina, and Ray Thornton of Arkansas—were all lost.

"I was stunned," Nixon later wrote. He faulted his aides and blamed the bad news on poor tactics, rather than anything he had done. He told Haig that the staff decision to refrain from lobbying the members of the Judiciary Committee had caused the defections. He was determined to start lobbying now in an effort to try to get at least one of the Southerners back.

George Wallace owed Nixon some favors. Nixon had helped Wallace's brother with some IRS problems, and contributed heavily to Wallace's most recent campaign for governor. Presumably Wallace had some influence with Flowers. Nixon had Haig get Wallace on the phone.

It was 3:52 P.M. in California, 5:52 P.M. in Montgomery. Wallace said he could not hear the President very well, then complained that the call was unexpected.

Nixon made his request. Wallace replied that he had not examined the evidence, that he prayed for the President, that he was sorry that all this had come down on Nixon, but that he did not think it was proper for him to call Flowers, and besides Flowers might resent it.

Wallace rang off with a promise; if he changed his mind, he would call Nixon to let him know.

"I knew when I hung up the phone that he would not change his mind," Nixon later wrote.

As he replaced the receiver, at 3:58 P.M., Nixon turned to Haig and said, "Well, Al, there goes the presidency."

Haig would not give up. At his urging, Nixon called Alabama Senator James Allen to ask for help with Flowers. Allen said he could not do anything.

Still lobbying, Nixon called Joe Waggonner, the Louisiana Democrat who had promised him at least fifty Southern Democratic votes in the full House. Waggonner told the President he could hope to hold only between thirty and thirty-five of the Southerners. In that case, Nixon knew, he was going to be impeached by the full House.

In his diary, he tried to analyze the reason. He did not cite any of his own mistakes or actions; instead, he decided that he was going to be impeached because "the Democrats have made a command decision to get me out and Ford in and then tear him up and win in 1976."[31]

That night, Nixon tried to work on his inflation speech, but his mind wandered. Waves of despair and self-pity welled up in him. His options were down to resignation or impeachment, he felt; actually, those had been his only options for months. He had sworn innumerable times, in public and in private, that he would never, ever resign, but this night he began to reflect on the cost of impeachment, a Senate trial, and a guilty verdict.

It was not the cost to the nation that he worried about. Indeed, Haig had persuaded him that an extended trial in the Senate, divisive though it would surely be, was worth the price, because resignation "would mean a dangerously easy victory for the radicals—not just over me but over the system." The cost that concerned him was personal. If he continued the fight, and was found guilty and dismissed, he would lose his pension and the other perquisites that came to former Presidents. But if he resigned, "I could expect an onslaught of lawsuits that would cost millions of dollars and take years to fight in the courts."[32] Of course, that could also happen if he was impeached and found guilty, unless he pardoned himself, or Ford pardoned him.

He was sixty-one years old. One way or another, his active political career was about to end. He had a wife, and children, and sons-in-law, and grandchildren to think about. Not to mention the Republican Party. Not to mention his country. What he thought about was his reputation, his finances, life in retirement.

He was the most contradictory man. He prided himself on his ability to make the tough decisions—to stay after Hiss, to face the cameras to explain his secret fund, to go for the Republican nomination in 1968, Vietnamization, the bombing of Hanoi, the opening to China, détente with the Russians, and so many more. But the tapes had revealed a man who could be terribly indecisive.

So it was this night. He sat there, on the edge of the coast, looking out on the breakers of the Pacific Ocean, Price's draft of the inflation speech on his lap, along with his yellow legal pad containing his notes on the speech, in an agony of indecision. Resign or fight? He could not decide. If he fought, and if he lost in the Supreme Court—the decision was due in the morning—the tapes, including June 23, 1972, would go to the Special Prosecutor, and then be made public, and used in his Senate trial. In his heart, he knew what he had meant on June 23, but he also knew what he had said, and he knew what his prosecutors would do with what he had said. Resignation might save him this final humiliation.

But he was a proud man. He could not believe that he had done anything wrong, or anything for which his predecessors had not provided ample precedent. All that he had done was for the good of the country. Sure, he had made tactical mistakes in dealing with Watergate, but his enemies wanted to disgrace him not because of Watergate but because they hated him and his policies. Haig had reinforced his bedrock belief that resignation was an admission of guilt. By God, he was not guilty. He would never resign.

He drew a box in the upper-right-hand corner of his legal pad. In it he scribbled some names—Hogan, Railsback, Flowers, Waggonner. Below that he drew another box; in it he wrote, "12:01 A.M.—Lowest point in Presidency & S[upreme] C[ourt] to come."[33]

AT 8:30 the following morning, July 24, the news tickers in the San Clemente offices began clattering out the Supreme Court's decision in *United States* v. *Nixon*.

Chief Justice Burger, who wrote the judgment, read it in Court. He went through the history of the case, calmly and without emotion. He affirmed that it was the Court that decided what the law was. He cited grounds for a President's claiming executive privilege, including "the need to protect the confidentiality of the communications of a President with his aides and advisers." He declared that executive privilege "is Constitutionally based," a point that received scant attention because of what followed, but nevertheless a declaration that was of fundamental importance, as this was the first time the Supreme Court had spoken on the claim by Presidents of a doctrine of executive privilege. In practice, the Court's decision in *United States* v. *Nixon* wrote the words "executive privilege" into the Constitution.

Then Burger took away what he had given. The claim of executive privilege, he said, could not be used in criminal cases. The doctrine "does not mean that all material in the possession of a President is immune in all circumstances from judicial process." Nixon's claim must be weighed against the claims of "criminal justice." Therefore, by a vote of 8 to 0, the Court declared that Nixon had to turn over the subpoenaed tapes to the Special Prosecutor.[34]

Haig read that decision, then called Nixon—who had been up until 2:30 A.M. and was still sleeping—on the telephone.

"How are things going?" Nixon asked.

"Well, it's pretty rough, Mr. President. I didn't want to wake you until we had the complete text, but the Supreme Court decision came down this morning."

Haig's gloom prepared Nixon. "Unanimous?" the President asked.

"Unanimous. There's no air in it at all."

"None at all?"

"It's tight as a drum."[35]

Nixon dressed and began to confer with his lawyer and his aides. They discussed defiance, and ruled that out. They considered some form of partial compliance, such as handing over edited transcripts. They began calling Washington to test the idea. Nixon talked to some of his strongest supporters in Congress. They were dubious. Nixon had tried that before, with his own version of the tapes. His heavy-handed editing, his deletions, his transparent changes of words and meanings, all revealed when the tapes themselves were heard by the staff of the Judiciary Committee, had destroyed his credibility in such matters. No one would accept a Nixon-prepared transcript. It had to be the tapes themselves. In the afternoon that judgment was reinforced when Nixon received a telegram from eight Republican congressmen: "We have confidence that your affirmative response to this order will be consistent with the unparalleled significance of this development."[36]

As he could not defy, Nixon decided to do a damage assessment. He had Haig call Buzhardt in Washington. Nixon took the phone from Haig. In his deep, gravelly voice, he said, "There may be some problems with the June twenty-third tape, Fred," and asked Buzhardt to listen to it and make an evaluation.[37]

Buzhardt did, then called back to say the tape was the "smoking gun."* Haig told him to listen again. Buzhardt did. He called back to repeat what he had said. Haig told Nixon that the tape was apparently "embarrassing" but not totally "unmanageable." He said, "I think we can cope with it." St. Clair also thought it was manageable. Of course neither Haig nor St. Clair had heard it.[38]

Nixon spent the later part of the afternoon preparing a statement. Toward evening, St. Clair went to the Surf and Sand Hotel in Laguna Beach to read it to the reporters.

"While I am of course disappointed in the result," the statement said, "I respect and accept the Court's decision, and I have instructed

---

*On June 23, 1972, Haldeman told Nixon of Dean's plan to tell the CIA to tell the FBI to back off its investigation. "All right," Nixon replied. "Fine." Haldeman explained, "We're set up beautifully to do it." Nixon said, "Good deal. Play it tough. That's the way they play it and that's the way we are going to play it." He told Haldeman what to say to the CIA: "Don't lie to them to the extent to say there is no involvement, but just say this is sort of a comedy of errors, bizarre, without getting into it, [say] the President believes that it is going to open the whole Bay of Pigs things up again. . . . ' They should call the FBI in and say that we wish for the country, don't go any further into this case, period!" For the full context, see volume two of this work, pp. 568–69.

Mr. St. Clair to take whatever measures are necessary to comply with that decision in all respects." It continued, "I was gratified, therefore, to note that the Court reaffirmed both the validity and the importance of the principle of executive privilege—the principle I had sought to maintain."

After reading the statement, St. Clair pointed out that it would take time to prepare the tapes subject to the subpoena. An index and an analysis of the tapes would begin "forthwith." However, it would be a "time-consuming process." It might take as long as a month.

St. Clair concluded: "As we all know, the President has always been a firm believer in the rule of law. He intends his decision to comply fully with the Court's ruling as an action in furtherance of that belief."[39]

AT 7:45 P.M. Eastern time, the Judiciary Committee began its debate over the articles of impeachment. The proceedings were carried live on national television and radio.

Nixon and his friends characterized the debate as "demagogic theatrics," and charged that the Democrats were posturing "shamefully."[40]

It was mesmerizing. The Rayburn Building was filled with tension, frayed nerves, and fearful men. The members of the Judiciary Committee, ordinarily obscure, had the nation's almost complete concentration (between 35 and 40 million watched; of the four days of the debate, 90 percent of the American people heard or saw some part of it).[41] Some of the liberal Democrats seized the opportunity to indulge in self-serving moral pronouncements, but most members recognized the awesome nature of the moment and of their responsibilities. They spoke with eloquence, from the heart, in many cases with deeply felt pain.

Nixon did not watch the proceedings, a fact he made certain the people knew by having Ziegler announce it. Had he watched, he would have gotten some sense of the trauma he was putting his country through. Most members went back to basic principles, which they accused Nixon of subverting. The Southerners, representing districts where Nixon still had strong support, were especially emphatic and eloquent on this point.

Flowers, the man Nixon had hoped to hold, cited the Preamble to the Constitution: " 'We, the people of the United States,' and surely there is no more inspiring phrase than this—'We the People of the United States,' not we the public officials of the United States, not we the certified experts, or we the educators, or we the educated, or we the grownups over twenty-one or twenty-five, not we the privileged classes, or whatever, but just simply 'We, the people . . . ' We acting in our communities across the nation can pull our fragmented society together." Flowers said that the power of the Presidency "is a public trust. . . . If the trust of the people in the word of the man to whom they had given their highest honor . . . is betrayed, if the people cannot know that their President is candid and truthful with them, then I say the very basis of our government is undermined."[42]

Representative Barbara Jordan, a black congresswoman from Texas, took up Flowers's "We, the people" theme. She said that when the Constitution was written, "I was not included in that 'We, the people.' I felt somehow for many years that George Washington and Alexander Hamilton just left me out by mistake. But through the process of amendment, interpretation, and court decision I have finally been included in 'We, the people.' " She went through a list of Nixon's transgressions against the Constitution, then concluded, "My faith in the Constitution is whole, it is complete, it is total, and I am not going to sit here and be an idle spectator to the diminution, the subversion, the destruction of the Constitution."[43]

Caldwell Butler (R.-Va.) warned that "if we fail to impeach, we will have condoned and left unpunished a course of conduct totally inconsistent with the reasonable expectations of the American people . . . a course of conduct designed to interfere with and obstruct the very process which he is sworn to uphold; and we will have condoned and left unpunished an abuse of power totally without justification." He concluded with startling directness: "In short, power appears to have corrupted. It is a sad chapter in American history. But I cannot condone what I have heard; I cannot excuse it, and I cannot and will not stand still for it. The misuse of power is the very essence of tyranny."[44]

William Cohen (R.-Maine) dismissed the defense that there were precedents for Nixon's actions. "The answer is that democracy . . . may be eroded away by degree. Its survival will be determined by the degree to which we will tolerate those silent and subtle subversions that absorb it slowly into the rule of a few in the name of what is right."[45]

These scathing judgments were delivered by men and women who had heard ten weeks of testimony and examined thousands of pages of evidence. With the exception of Jordan, every one of the speakers knew that there was no political profit for them back among their constituents in impeaching Nixon. With no exceptions, every speaker wished with all his or her heart that this cup had not come.

Some who had also heard the evidence and examined the documents still supported Nixon, though on the narrowest of grounds—no specific crime had been committed by the President—and they waited until the Committee began considering the individual articles of impeachment to make their point.

Charles Wiggins (R.-Calif., representing Nixon's old district) and Charles Sandman (R.-N.J.) demanded specificity. Where was the smoking gun? "Isn't it amazing," Sandman asked, "that they [the proponents of impeachment] have so much but they are willing to say so little? Isn't it amazing? They are willing to do anything except make these articles specific." Delbert Latta (R.-Ohio) said, "A common jaywalker charged with jay-walking anyplace in the United States is entitled to know when and where the alleged offense is supposed to have occurred. Is the President of the United States entitled to less?"[46]

The key section of Article I to which the questions referred read: "Subsequent [to the break-in] Richard M. Nixon, using the powers of his high office, made it his policy, and in furtherance of such policy did act directly and personally through his close subordinates and agents, to delay, impede, and obstruct the investigation of such illegal entry; to cover up, conceal, and protect those responsible; and to conceal the existence and scope of other unlawful covert activities."

Wiggins demanded to know just when this "policy" began. When was it declared? Where was the evidence? His questions brought some consternation to the Democrats and sent Doar and his staff to scrambling for more evidence.

This was Nixon's most effective defense. Aside from the question of whether it was wise (as opposed to right) to drive him from office, it was the defense he had relied upon consistently. But had he been watching the debate, he would have winced each time Wiggins or Sandman or Latta demanded to know where was the evidence. Nixon knew where it was, and he knew it would be made public shortly. He knew that every time his defenders opened their mouths, they unwittingly made him more vulnerable.

ON July 25, as the Judiciary Committee debated, Nixon flew by helicopter to Los Angeles, then motorcaded to the Century Plaza Hotel, his headquarters in the final days of the 1968 campaign. In the hotel's Los Angeles room, 1,700 delegates to a conference on the economy sponsored by the California Chamber of Commerce applauded warmly as he stepped to the podium.

Skipping the ad-libbing with which he normally began a speech, Nixon plunged straight into his text: "I want to discuss today the major problem confronting America—inflation."

Nixon's aides had promised a major address. The speech was being broadcast nationally on television and radio. It gave Nixon an opportunity to announce some bold new program that would divert at least some of the attention from the impeachment debate. But he had nothing new to offer. No surprises, no innovations. Instead of giving people hope, or ideas, he gave them a lecture. He said that the root cause of inflation was that people wanted to consume more goods and services than they were willing to work and save for. He asked the people to display "patience," "spirit," and "sacrifice" in order to halt inflation. He called on the people to spend less money. He said people should work harder and spend less, that the government and corporations had been spending too much money on environmental control.

That line drew applause from the California businessmen. So did his promise of "a sweeping review" of the federal regulatory process. So did his promise that he would not "resort to the discredited patent medicine of wage and price controls," which he said would only create new economic distortions. (He had imposed the first mandatory peacetime wage and price controls in history on August 15, 1971; he had abandoned the policy in April 1974.)[47] That was all. The speech that Nixon had once hoped would save him, on which he had worked so many hours, was a bust.

The next day, Kissinger brought the West German foreign minister to meet Nixon. Kissinger was "shocked by the ravages just a week had wrought on Nixon's appearance. His coloring was pallid. Though he seemed composed, it clearly took every ounce of his energy to conduct a serious conversation. He sat on the sofa in his office looking over the Pacific, his gaze and thought focused on some distant prospect."

Much disturbed, Kissinger told Haig that afternoon that "the end of Nixon's Presidency was now inevitable." He said their responsibility was "to end the agony . . . and to bring about a smooth transition." An impeachment trial had to be avoided. Nixon had to be convinced that he must resign because the national interest dictated it, but it was not they who must convince him. That responsibility rested with senior Republicans, not with appointed aides.

Haig said he agreed, that he had come to the same conclusion.[48]

ON July 26, the Judiciary Committee debate ended. It had had a powerful effect on the American people. The televised proceedings, in the words of legal scholar Stanley Kutler, "had conveyed images of congressional conscientiousness, intelligence, and fair-mindedness."[49] They had educated the public about the meaning of impeachment, and had convinced a large majority that the process was legitimate and necessary. A Louis Harris Poll showed public opinion favored impeachment by 66 to 27 percent. That was up from 53 to 40 percent a week earlier.[50]

ON July 27, the Committee voted on the first article of impeachment, which charged Nixon with obstructing justice by engaging in a cover-up of the Watergate affair. The members voted to recommend impeachment to the full House by 27 to 11. Six of the seventeen Republicans joined all the Democrats in the majority.

Nixon was swimming in the ocean near San Clemente when the vote was cast. After dressing, he went to his office and wrote a statement for Ziegler to issue: "The President remains confident that the full House will recognize that there simply is not the evidence to support this or any other article of impeachment and will not vote to impeach. He is confident because he knows he has committed no impeachable offense."[51]

He had a quiet dinner that evening with his family, then went to his study to make a diary entry. Tricia had remarked to him, as they left the beach, that her mother was "really a wonderful woman." Nixon agreed. In his diary, he wrote, "She has been through a lot through the twenty-five years we have been in and out of politics. Both at home and abroad she has always conducted herself with masterful poise and dignity. But, God, how she could have gone through what she does, I simply don't know."[52]

Nixon sat up late that night, and the next. He feared that when St. Clair, Haig, and his other aides listened to the June 23 tape they would tell him, "We just don't think this is manageable." In that case, he would have to decide whether "to bite the bullet on resignation" or continue to fight until the full House voted to impeach, then resign. In other words, with the June 23 tape soon to emerge, he had finally decided he could not go through with a Senate trial. He had decided to resign; the question was when. That decision, he wrote, gave him "a feeling of calm and strength." The agony of indecision was over.[53]

He did not convey his decision to his aides, or his family, or prominent Republican supporters, much less to the nation. But he had made it. In his memoirs, he said the basis for the decision was the good of the country: the United States "simply could not afford to have a crippled President for six months."[54]

The decision made, his thoughts turned to the future. He wondered "whether I can sell a book or papers or what have you in order to have the funds that would be needed to maintain an adequate staff." He thought he would sell his home in Key Biscayne in order to have some cash on hand. Perhaps he would sell San Clemente, too.

He grew maudlin. "The sad thing," he wrote in his diary, "as Eddie says, is that the bad guys will have won."

He thought about what history would say of him. Kissinger had told him that his wife had said, "History in four years would look back on the President as a hero." Haig had said that "history will show me in the end to have been an outstanding President."[55]

With that consolation he went to bed.

THE following morning, July 28, Nixon and his family flew back to Washington. Pat's friend Helene Drown joined them. Nixon had never liked Mrs. Drown, could hardly stand to be in her presence, but Pat wanted her support and she came along.

She stayed for a week. Pat spent most of her time working on redecorating the Garden Room and the Queen's Room in the White House, replacing circa 1950 furniture with nineteenth-century American antiques. She also signed replies to the thousands of letters of support coming to the White House.

She was obviously going through an ordeal, but she kept her spirits up and retained her sense of humor. She told Drown that when reporters asked her about Watergate, "I just pretend I don't hear them. The next thing I know there will be the report that I'm getting deaf!"

Only on occasion would she complain, and then about the reporters, not the politicians who were impeaching her husband. "No matter what I do I can't win," she said to Drown. "If I give the press all the tidbits about people and issues, they would say I was talking too much. And if I give them nothing, they accuse me of having no opinions or being capable only of small talk."

The mood in the White House was tense, but Pat was determined not to give in to it. She concentrated on drapes and rugs, played gin rummy with Drown, listened to records. But she also worried, about morale, about her daughters, about her husband. Mrs. Drown told Julie, "She had to hold things together for all of you."

Julie, in her biography of her mother, wrote that she did not see it at the time, but later realized that "Mother was indeed the one holding it all together. In the pre-Watergate years she had seemed fragile. We had worried about her and wanted to protect her. Now she was the strongest of all."

Drown was the only one to whom she admitted her anguish. "Dick has done so much for the country," she said. "Why is this happening?" Mrs. Drown told Julie, "Your father never had a better admirer." Pat said to her on numerous occasions, "He always knows the right thing to say." She could get angry about a decision her husband made, "but always, overriding it all, was a tremendous respect of him . . . for the enormous problems he was dealing with."[56]

On July 29, a Monday, the Judiciary Committee took up Article II. It charged that Nixon had abused the powers of the Presidency. He had not taken care that the laws be faithfully executed, but had repeatedly engaged in conduct violating the constitutional rights of citizens. Among the specifics cited were the Plumbers, the wiretapping of reporters and NSC officials, and the misuse of the FBI and the CIA. But the first charge was the one that had the most appeal to the politicians, as well as being the most vulnerable to attack, and was therefore the most controversial. It charged that Nixon had "endeavored" to misuse the IRS. Not that he had done so, but that he had tried to do so.

Representative Wiggins was the most effective opponent of impeachment on the Committee, and he argued powerfully. "Just what is abusive conduct? I suggest that it is an empty phrase, having meaning only in terms of what we pour into it. It must reflect our subjective views of impropriety, as distinguished from the objective views enunciated by society in its laws." Article II, Wiggins charged, "would embed in our Constitutional history for the first time, for the very first time, the principle that a President may be impeached because of the view of Congress that he has abused those powers, although he may have acted in violation of no law."

He warned that by voting for Article II, the Committee would be "taking a step toward a parliamentary system of government in this country rather than that Constitutional system which we now have. We are . . . saying that a President may be impeached in the future if a Congress expresses no confidence in his conduct, not because he has violated the law but, rather, because that Congress declares his conduct to be abusive in terms of their subjective notions of propriety."

Wiggins concluded with the point Nixon had been trying to make for over a year, the need to preserve the powers of the office. "What standard are we setting for the Presidents in the future?" Wiggins asked. "How will any future President know precisely what Congress may declare to be an abuse, especially when they have failed to legislate against the very acts which they may condemn?"[57]

George Danielson (D.-Calif.) also rested his argument on the Constitution, but concentrated on the "take care" clause. "The offense charged in this article is truly a high crime and misdemeanor within the purest meaning of those words," he said. "The offenses charged against the President in this article are uniquely Presidential offenses. No one else can commit them. . . . Can anyone argue that if the President breaches his oath of office, he should not be removed?"[58]

William Hungate (D.-Mo.) said the article referred to "repetitive conduct." It was not a single act of Nixon's, not a "smoking gun," that had brought about this impeachment vote, but rather a pattern of abuse. The Committee would have to make a political as opposed to a criminal judgment, which was why the founding fathers had given the power to impeach to a political body. Hungate thought that Nixon's fellow politicians, being more knowledgeable about "the pressures and difficulties in public life" than ordinary citizens, were therefore more tolerant. "If only one violation had occurred, I would doubt that we should be here. Men are human. Humans are frail. But I think we discuss and consider here and see here a consistent disregard of the law."[59]

Late that day, the Judiciary Committee voted 28 to 10 to adopt Article II.

Nixon spent the day alone in the Lincoln Sitting Room of the White House, listening to the subpoenaed tapes (St. Clair, under pressure from Sirica, had promised to begin turning them over that week), reviewing related documents, noting sections he wanted withheld for national security reasons, and brooding.[60]

On July 30, the Committee adopted Article III by a vote of 21 to 17. It charged that the President had sought to impede the impeachment process by refusing to comply with eight Committee subpoenas for 147 tapes. By a vote of 26 to 12, it rejected Article IV, which charged that Nixon had usurped Congress's power to declare war in the 1969 secret bombing of Cambodia. By an identical vote, it rejected Article V, which dealt with Nixon's income taxes and government-paid improvements on his home.

That same day, St. Clair finally turned over to Sirica twenty of the tapes the Supreme Court had ordered Nixon to give to the Special Prosecutor. He did not include the June 23 tape. In a statement outlining claims of privilege, St. Clair contended that twenty-three segments totaling about forty-eight minutes were unrelated to Watergate and should not be transmitted from Sirica to Jaworski.

That day, St. Clair listened to the June 23 tape for the first time. He told Buzhardt that this was the smoking gun. What Nixon had said to Haldeman on June 23 so contradicted the arguments he had made before the Judiciary Committee that he (St. Clair) would become party to an obstruction of justice unless it was made public.[61]

Practically at the same time, Warren announced that Nixon would not resign even if the full House voted to impeach him.

THAT night, Nixon could not sleep. At 3:50 A.M. he took out his bedside note pad, wrote down the time, and began to list the pros and cons of resignation. He wrote for three hours.

He had listed the pros and cons of possible action before every crisis of his life. This last would be no different. Nothing was final until it was public. He convinced himself that he still had options; listing them would make them real.

This was the order: "What would be best for me?" After that came what would be best for his family, then for his friends and supporters, and finally what would be best for the country.

The strongest argument was that he had never been a quitter. To give up, to give in, to let his enemies win—never. His college football coach, Chief Newman, had told him, "Show me a good loser and I'll show you a loser."

The motto had served him well in the Hiss case, in the fund crisis, in the 1956 struggle to stay on the ticket with Ike, in South America in 1958, after the defeats in 1960 and 1962 campaigns, and so many times in his Presidency.

Never quit was not only the central theme of Nixon's political career, it was the core of his being.

That instinct was reinforced by other considerations. To quit would set a dangerous precedent. To quit would hurt his family and his supporters.

But there were compelling arguments for resignation. The country would be torn by a Senate trial that could take six months and would not even get under way until after the election, possibly not until January 1975. And the outcome was all but certain: "I would be defeated and dishonored, the first President in history to be impeached and convicted on criminal charges."

There was the Republican Party to think about. If he stayed in office, the 1974 election would be a referendum on Nixon and Watergate, and thus a catastrophe for the Republicans.

As dawn broke, Nixon made his decision. He turned the paper over and wrote on the back: "End career as a fighter."[62]

IT was July 31. The lead story in that morning's *Washington Post* showed that the editors had also been considering the pros and cons of resignation. It amounted to a piece of advice to Nixon. If the President was convicted by the Senate, he would lose the perquisites he would retain if he resigned: a pension of $60,000 per year, a stipend of $96,000 per year for staff salaries and allowances; free office space for himself and his staff; a widow's pension of $20,000 per year for his wife.[63]

Pat Buchanan floated an idea. He told reporters that Nixon "had not ruled out" a plan whereby he would ask the House to vote unanimously for his impeachment, without debate, so that he could be speedily tried in the Senate.[64]

That day, Haig read the transcript of June 23 for the first time. He called Kissinger to say it was urgent that he see him, and went to the State Department to consult. Haig told Kissinger that the smoking gun had been found; the June 23 tape left no doubt that Nixon was familiar with the cover-up and may have ordered it. What should he do?

Kissinger pointed out that the tape was bound to become public; someone in the Special Prosecutor's Office was sure to leak it. Haig should "ease Nixon's decision to resign." His task, "which no one else could carry out—was to give Nixon the psychological support to do the necessary."[65]

"Well, what do you think?" Nixon asked Haig when he returned to the White House.

"Mr. President," Haig replied, "I am afraid that I have to agree with Fred [Buzhardt] and Jim St. Clair. I just don't see how we can survive this one. . . . I think we have to face the facts, and the facts are that the staff won't hold and that public opinion won't hold either, once this tape gets out."

Ron Ziegler listened to the June 23 tape that afternoon. He too concluded that the situation was all but hopeless.[66]

Ken Clawson, who had not listened to the tape, was not giving up. He sent Haig a memo saying the White House should not assume impeachment by the full House. He urged that House Republicans get the message that they had "no easy loophole," that impeachment was bad for the country and destructive of the Presidency. "We should say flatly that no politician is going to get off the hook or shirk his duty in this matter."[67]

That day, John Ehrlichman was sentenced to twenty months to five years for conspiracy and perjury. He was the fourteenth of Nixon's former aides or associates to be convicted or plead guilty. Seven more had been indicted and still faced trial, including Haldeman.

Kissinger remarked, "In destroying himself, Nixon had wrecked the lives of almost all who had come into contact with him."[68]

That was hardly true. Kissinger was not destroyed by Watergate; if anything, his reputation was enhanced. So was Haig's. St. Clair and Buzhardt returned to their private law practices with no difficulty. Bush, Price, Ziegler, and other associates had successful post-Watergate careers. Speechwriters Buchanan and John McLaughlin became media stars. Safire became a leading columnist on the nation's number-one newspaper; it helped that he got out at the right time.

The men whose careers were badly damaged, if not destroyed, by Watergate were, above all, Haldeman, Ehrlichman, Mitchell, and Colson. These were the men Nixon had thrown to the wolves in his effort to save himself. They were also the men who had helped him to the top. Their loyalty cost them dearly.

The survivors were the men who joined Nixon at the top. Except for Bush, Buchanan, and Ziegler, they had little or no involvement in the re-election campaign. As a group, the survivors' loyalty to self transcended their loyalty to the President. As Nixon's Presidency came to an end, they set out to save themselves, at his expense.

CHAPTER SEVENTEEN

A RESIGNATION
FOR A PARDON?
August 1–6, 1974

ON THURSDAY MORNING, August 1, Nixon told Haig he had decided to resign. He was going to Camp David for the weekend to prepare his family. He would resign on Monday night, August 5, in a televised speech.

Haig thought it would be better if he resigned the following day, Friday the 2nd. The June 23 tape was going to Sirica even as Haig and Nixon talked. If Nixon resigned and left Washington before it was made public on Monday the 5th, the newspapers and television news programs would be so filled with accounts of Ford's inauguration and the transition that the impact of June 23 would be lessened.

Nixon said he would think about it; meanwhile he wanted Price to work on a resignation speech. In it, Nixon said, he would want to admit that he had made mistakes, but he did not want Price to write "a groveling mea culpa." His reason for resigning was the loss of his political support in Congress.

Further, Nixon instructed Haig to tell Ford that the President was "thinking of resigning," but without divulging when. Haig should impress on Ford the need for "absolute secrecy." The final decision, Nixon insisted, was his alone. He gave Haig a warning; if a group of Republican congressmen, or National Chairman Bush, or a delegation of Cabinet members began demanding his resignation, "my lifetime instincts of refusing to cave to political pressure might prevail."[1]

Haig met with Ford and later testified that he told Ford that Nixon was close to resigning. Ford should "be prepared to assume the presidency within a very short time."

But it seems there was more to it. Ford later testified that "It was his [Haig's] understanding from a White House lawyer that a President did have the authority to grant a pardon even before any criminal action had been taken against an individual."[2]

Haig has said that he ran through five options: Nixon could delay resignation, hoping that something might crop up to save him; Nixon could try to persuade the House to settle for a vote of censure; Nixon could pardon himself before resigning; Nixon could pardon the Watergate defendants, then pardon himself, then resign; or he could wait to be pardoned by his successor after resignation.[3]

The first two options were not feasible. The third, while legally possible, was politically impossible. It would raise a storm that would badly damage if not destroy the Republican Party's chances in the next election; it would be a confession of a guilt Nixon did not feel; it would make it impossible for him to rehabilitate his reputation. The same objections could be raised to the fourth option, and to the last one as well, though in a more muted way with regard to Nixon personally. Ford would then take the brunt of the storm.

Much has been written about this meeting, a good deal of it by men close to Nixon and Ford. The commentary consensus is that a deal was cut. But unless a tape recording emerges, or unless either Haig or Ford says something different from what they have already testified, no one can ever know for certain.

The situation invites speculation. First, while Nixon and Ford were close professional associates for more than a quarter century, they were not the sort of intimate friends who trust each other implicitly.

Second, Nixon owed Ford far more than Ford owed Nixon. Nixon had lied to Ford from January of 1973 onward as he insisted that he had no involvement in the Watergate cover-up; he had not just allowed but had encouraged Ford to make himself vulnerable by defending the President. While it is true that Nixon had chosen Ford to become Vice President, both men knew that circumstances rather than admiration, friendship, or trust dictated that choice. Further, there is no evidence that in October 1973 Nixon attempted to get Ford to agree that he would grant a pardon in return for the Vice Presidency. And Ford had said, in his confirmation hearings, that the American people would not "stand for" a pardon.

Third, it was the Vice President, not the President, who occupied a position of strength on August 1, 1974. Ford had widespread support from the public and from the Congress. Nixon did not. Nixon could not say, "Look, either you promise to pardon, or I'll never resign." The Presidency was not his either to give or to keep.

Fourth, it is necessary to recall what Bryce Harlow said to Ford in a discussion following the Haig-Ford meeting. Ford aide Bob Hartmann arranged a Harlow-Ford get-together because he wanted to convince Ford to tell Nixon that there could be no deal, or even the appearance of one.

It was better that the message come from Harlow, as he was close to Nixon while Hartmann was not.

Harlow told Ford, "It is inconceivable that [Haig] was not carrying out a mission for the President, with precise instructions, and that it is the President who wants to hear your recommendations and test your reaction to the pardon question. But the President knows that he must be able to swear under oath that he never discussed this with you and that you must be able to swear that you never discussed it with him."[4] Ford saw the point. At Hartmann's urging, he called Haig to say that he had no intention of recommending whether or not Nixon should resign. He added that nothing he and Haig had talked about (meaning the President's pardoning power) should be given any consideration whatsoever as indicating any intent on his part to involve himself in Nixon's resignation decision. Haig said he understood and agreed.[5]

This sounds to me more believable than the opposite conclusion, that Haig and Ford entered into a solid deal of pardon for resignation. My reading is that Nixon had thought the whole thing through (although no one can say for certain; as Hartmann has commented, "No man living can outguess Richard Nixon when it comes to figuring things out to the third, fourth, and fifth degree of indirection"[6]) and concluded that by far the greater risk was to have Haig ask straight out for a pardon agreement. That might have caused Ford to bristle, grow indignant, get angry, throw Haig out of his office, and set his feet in cement against a pardon.

It is often true in American politics that what is not said but that both sides can count on as being understood leads to a more solid agreement than what is promised.

Nixon could anticipate political developments. Looking ahead, he knew President Ford's problems in the late summer of 1974 would be many and difficult, and that the last thing the new President would want would be a flood of pre-Nixon-trial publicity, or a seismic struggle for evidence by the Watergate defendants. For his own good, for the good of the Republican Party, for the good of the country, Ford would want to avoid the orgy of Nixon-bashing that would accompany a Nixon indictment and trial.

Nixon could be confident that Ford would be aware that just picking a jury for a Nixon trial would dominate the headlines for weeks, perhaps months, and still might prove impossible. An actual trial would be even worse. As to what might be revealed in a trial, with hundreds of hours of unrevealed tapes and thousands of documents entered as evidence, again Nixon could count on Ford's shuddering at the mere thought of that happening just as he was trying to put his 1976 re-election campaign in motion.

It seems likely that Nixon knew that it was inevitable that Ford was going to have to pardon him, and he did not need to send Haig to see Ford to extract such a promise. Being Nixon, he could not help himself from manipulating and seeking reassurance. So he had sent Haig to see Ford, not to make a deal, but to make sure Ford knew that as President he would have the right to pardon even before an indictment. When Haig reported that Ford had been so informed, Nixon was satisfied.

No deal was struck, I believe. It was the structure of the existing situation, not the personalities of Nixon and Ford, nor any secret deals, that dictated developments.

As Haig was talking to Ford, Nixon was talking to Ziegler about the timing of the resignation. At Ziegler's urging, Nixon decided to wait until Monday, August 5. That would give his supporters a chance to read the transcript of June 23 (released on the 2nd to Sirica and to be made public on the 5th) and abandon ship before it hit the reef. Nixon spent the afternoon of the 1st going over Timmons's reports on how the voting shaped up and listening to the last group of tapes that had to be turned over to Sirica the following week. As Haig was reporting on his conversation with Ford, Warren was telling the White House press corps, "The President will not resign."

Bebe Rebozo flew up from Miami. At 7 P.M. he and Nixon went sailing up the Potomac on the *Sequoia*. Nixon told his friend he had decided to resign.

"You can't do it," Rebozo protested. "It's the wrong thing to do. You have got to continue to fight. You just don't know how many people are still for you."

Nixon told him about the June 23 tape. Rebozo thought it could not be as bad as Nixon said. He felt Nixon's staff had panicked. He urged Nixon to allow Russell Long (D.-La.) and other leading senators to listen to it and make their own evaluation.

It is hopeless, Nixon said. He asked Rebozo to back him up with the family. Rebozo said he would if Nixon would promise not to make an irrevocable decision until he had made one last effort to defend himself. Nixon agreed.[7]

FRIDAY, August 2, was hot and muggy. Judge Sirica sentenced John Dean to a prison term of from one to four years for his role in the conspiracy to cover up the Watergate break-in. Warren, reading to the press corps from notes presumably approved by Nixon, described the President as "an underdog" in the impeachment battle. Warren said, "We face an uphill struggle, but in a political struggle you have a chance to win." He added that Nixon would not resign.[8]

That afternoon, Haig and St. Clair showed Representative Wiggins the transcript of June 23. Wiggins read the transcript once, then again. "The guys who stuck by the President were really led down the garden path, weren't we?" he said bitterly.

Wiggins said the President had either to plead the Fifth Amendment or surrender the tapes to the Judiciary Committee immediately. St. Clair promised that the tapes would go to the Committee, soon. Wiggins read the transcript again and said if the President did not release it, he would; otherwise he would himself be a party to an obstruction of justice. Haig and St. Clair nodded but asked him to do nothing until Monday. Wiggins agreed. He could not see what Nixon could do to save himself. "Does he have another 'Checkers speech' on him?" he asked sarcastically.[9]

Haig reported to Nixon. The President knew that if he could not hold Wiggins, it was surely over. He decided to face up to the "painful task" of telling his family about the June 23 tape.[10]

He began with Julie. He called her into his EOB office. Wearing one of his soft cashmere smoking jackets, sitting in his favorite easy chair, he told her in a low, steady voice that he had no support left and would have to resign. Julie returned to the White House, where she called David, then Tricia and Ed Cox in New York, asking them to come at once. She found her mother in her bedroom and told her.

"But why?" Pat protested.

"He has to for his own good or he'll be impeached."

Mother and daughter embraced. Pat began to cry but quickly regained her composure. She called to cancel an order for a new set of china for the White House, then found some boxes and went to her bedroom. She began packing her belongings.[11]

The President went to the Lincoln Sitting Room. When Tricia arrived after flying down on the shuttle from New York, Julie told her. She went in to her father and found him in his armchair with his feet up on the ottoman, fussing with his pipe.

Nixon told her about June 23. He said it made his case hopeless. He would have to resign.

Tricia protested. She said that he must stay in office for the good of the country. She walked over to his chair, put her arms around him, kissed him on the forehead, and said, "You are the most decent person I know."

"I hope I have not let you down," he replied.

Pat, Julie, Bebe, David, and Ed joined them. Manolo brought in transcripts of June 23. The Eisenhowers and the Coxes left the room, David and Julie going one way down the hall, Ed and Tricia the other, to read. Pat stayed with her husband. She would not look at the transcript. He said to her, "I don't know what I'm going to do, but I know you will all stand behind me."

The youngsters returned. Julie, Tricia, and Ed had concluded that

Nixon's words on June 23 "could be taken one of two ways depending upon who was judging them." They were opposed to his resigning. David was not so sure.

Nixon insisted. It was wrong for the country to have a weak President. The Soviets might try something. His support was gone.

From Nixon's diaries and from the family, there is no mention of any apology on Nixon's part for having concealed the June 23 conversation from his family for a year and a half.

There was a silence which Nixon broke. "Was it worth it?" he asked.

Each assured him that it was. Pat said he should fight on. Then there was nothing left to say. Tricia wrote in her diary, "We left Daddy alone in his chair staring into the fire. Undoubtedly more telephone calls would be made and received long after we were gone."[12]

His family's strength stiffened Nixon's resolve. Now he decided that instead of resigning on Monday, he would release the June 23 tape and assess the reaction. He called Haig and told him that Price should stop working on a resignation speech and instead begin work on one explaining the June 23 tape, that would be delivered on Monday, as it was released.[13]

Price was upset. As deeply conservative as Buchanan, and smarter if less flamboyant, he had been—and would remain—Nixon's strongest supporter outside the family. But when he had read the transcript of June 23, he concluded the President had to resign, not because he was guilty but because of the appearance of guilt. He had been working on the resignation speech and was going to great lengths to keep it secret, a difficult task in a White House that had become, in Price's view, "a rumor factory, with many of the staff spending half their time scurrying around trying to pry out what was really happening, and the other half frantically gossiping about what they imagined might be happening."

Price argued with Haig about the decision only to discover that, "Everyone except me had flopped over." St. Clair, who had been strongly for resignation, now argued that a Senate trial would be an essential element in setting the constitutional precedent. The process should not be short-circuited. Haig has confessed that whenever Nixon changed his mind, so did he. Price found this understandable: "It was a difficult choice. There were principles in conflict. We were dealing in guesswork and uncertainty. The stakes were enormous. We were all under strain. Some mind changing was natural. But when I saw minds changing in unison, I was afraid the President was getting echoes of his own shifting moods, not independent advice." He made Haig promise that he would pass on to Nixon his own view that "There was no way for him to survive." The only way for him to leave with dignity was to leave now.[14]

Saturday, August 3, was a hot and humid day at Camp David. Nixon and his family flew by helicopter to the retreat at noon. His family was urging him to be strong. After a swim, Nixon went to the sauna. Ed came in, sat a few moments in silence, then turned to his father-in-law and said, "You have got to fight 'em, fight 'em, fight 'em." At dinner that evening, his family urged him to postpone his decision until after the June 23 tape was released.[15] Since Nixon had already decided to do that, he agreed readily.

SUNDAY, August 4. It was cloudy below Aspen Lodge, clear above. Nixon spent the morning working on a statement to accompany the release of June 23; he had decided against a prime-time speech, as that was a one-time opportunity, and he wanted to save it for a reply to the reaction to the tape.

Haig, Price, Buchanan, Ziegler, and St. Clair arrived early in the afternoon. Haig met privately with Nixon, then returned to the group to deliver the marching orders. Price should work with the others to produce a statement. Nixon would follow a "two-track" strategy. He would not foreclose resignation, he would preserve his options. He would release the tape, put the best face on it, and insist that he would continue to fight. In private, he would assess the reaction.

As the team worked on the statement, Haig and Ziegler were calling Nixon constantly, and taking his calls. They in turn made calls back to the White House, where they had their secretaries engaged in a piece of historical research, attempting to recreate a sequence of events. The question of timing was critical.

At issue was to establish when Nixon had first listened to the June 23 tape. He still insisted that he had not done so until late May 1974, but his own aides were suspicious. Ziegler, Haig, and St. Clair recalled that it was in early May that Jaworski had secretly proposed a deal—that if he were given eighteen of sixty-four subpoenaed tapes, he would not disclose that the grand jury had named Nixon an unindicted co-conspirator. After considering the proposal for two days, Nixon had turned it down. Had he listened to June 23 first? If so, his claim that he had not listened until late May, and that he had missed its significance when he did listen, was a lie.

The secretaries in Washington established the sequence. Jaworski had made his proposal on May 5. Nixon had checked out the tapes, including that of June 23, and had listened to them on May 6. He had rejected the proposal on May 7.

This was no secret. Jaworski possessed the White House logs that showed the sequence. Nixon had lied to Haig, St. Clair, Price, and Ziegler, along with everyone else. They now agreed that the President's statement was "going to have to say, somehow, that he had listened to the tape, and that even though it clearly contradicted his own public statements he had done nothing about it."[16]

Nixon resisted. He gave Haig a page of notes from his legal pad.

They posited a statement quite different: On July 6, 1972, when FBI Director Gray had told him that improper efforts were being made by the White House staff to get the FBI to limit its investigation, Nixon had written, "I asked him if he had discussed this matter with General Walters [of the CIA]. He answered—yes. I asked if Walters agreed with him. He answered—yes. I then told him to press forward with the investigation." According to Nixon's notes, "This clearly demonstrated that when I was informed that there was no national security objection to a full investigation by the FBI, I did not hesitate to order the investigation to proceed without regard to any political or other considerations." He concluded his notes by insisting that the investigation did proceed fully.[17]

The aides did not accept that explanation. They countered that it was not true, that it would be demolished by the politicians and the press, that Nixon could not survive the storm. Perhaps as important, these men wanted to protect themselves. They wanted Nixon to admit that he had never told them about June 23. If he did not, they would be subject to charges of conspiring to cover up.

"It's no use, Mr. President," Haig said. If Nixon did not admit that he had withheld evidence, "St. Clair and the other lawyers are going to jump ship, because they claim they weren't told about this beforehand and they based their case before the House Judiciary Committee on a premise that proved to be false."[18]

When Haig said to his boss, "It's no use," and said Price's statement had to stand, Nixon surrendered. "The hell with it," he said. "It really doesn't matter. Let them put out anything they want. My decision has already been made."[19]

Warren later denied that Nixon's decision to release the tape and issue the statement had been based on "any sort of ultimatum or anything like that" from St. Clair and the others.[20] Almost no one believed him.

Issuing that statement was Nixon's last mistake. He let his aides protect themselves, rather than him. Clearly he felt he had no choice, and he did not. He was exhausted, depressed, shaken. He could not think straight. He was torn by desire and emotion. He wanted to be free of the whole damned mess, forever, but he hated even the thought of resignation. His family wanted him to fight, which was what he wanted to do, but although he was ready to fight his enemies, he could not see how he could fight his aides.

He surrendered.

THE result was a statement that put the worst possible interpretation on the June 23 tape for Nixon, the best for his aides. Nixon's proposed alternative statement would have put the best possible interpretation on June 23, and might have slowed the rush toward resignation. It would not have saved his Presidency: he was right in thinking that he was doomed even without June 23. But it would have given his supporters an argument for his innocence, something to cling to.

The June 23 transcript and the statement answered Senator Baker's oft-quoted question, "What did the President know and when did he know it?" It left Nixon with virtually no support.

On Monday, August 5, Nixon returned by helicopter to Washington. He spent the morning with Haig, Price, and Ziegler in a last attempt to soften the statement. His aides would not budge. Simultaneously secretaries were preparing the transcripts of June 23 and other tapes for release, this time the entire transcript, not an edited version. That turned out to be a major PR mistake. As Nixon ruefully noted, "In the rush to produce copies of these [twenty-three] transcripts for distribution to the press, some personal references were carelessly and unnecessarily left in."[21]

At 4 P.M. the transcripts and the statement were distributed. The items that caught many readers' eyes first were some offhand remarks of Nixon's. On museums: "The Arts, you know—they're Jews, they're left wing." On appealing to Middle America: he wanted to have Tricia "ride a bus for 2 hours, do the cancer thing, do a park in Oklahoma." On speculation in the *lira:* "Well, I don't give a shit about the lira." On *Six Crises:* "It makes fascinating reading. . . . Actually, the book reads awfully well . . . reads like a novel. I want you [Haldeman] to reread it, and anybody else in the campaign. Get copies of the book and give it to each of them." Nixon on his old friend Herb Klein:"He just doesn't have his head screwed on. You know what I mean. He just opens it up and sits there with egg on his face. He's just not our guy at all is he?"[22]

The statement announced that the President was making public the transcripts of three conversations with Haldeman on June 23, 1972. It noted that on April 29, 1974, when Nixon had released edited versions of subpoenaed tapes, he had said that the materials being made available "will tell it all." But, he now confessed, when he had listened in May to some of the sixty-four additional tapes under subpoena, he "recognized that these presented potential problems. I did not inform my staff or my Counsel of it, or those arguing my case, nor did I amend my submission to the Judiciary Committee in order to include and reflect it." He explained that he had not done so because "I did not realize the extent of the implications which these conversations might now appear to have."

Then came two sentences the lawyers and aides had insisted upon: "As a result, those arguing my case, as well as those passing judgment on the case, did so with information that was incomplete and in some respects erroneous. This was a serious act of omission for which I take full responsibility and which I deeply regret."

Then there was a further admission: "Portions of the tapes of these

June 23 conversations are at variance with certain of my previous statements."

Next came a justification and clarification of sorts: Nixon had been concerned that the FBI investigation "might lead to the exposure either of unrelated covert activities of the CIA or of sensitive national security matters that the so-called plumbers' unit at the White House had been working on."

And yet another admission: "The June 23 tapes clearly show, however, that at the time I gave those instructions I also discussed the political aspects of the situation and that I was aware of the advantages this course of action would have with respect to limiting possible public exposure of involvement by persons connected with the re-election committee."

His review of additional tapes, he continued, had shown no other major inconsistencies with his previous statements, but "I have no way at this stage of being certain that there will not be others." He did not believe any further bombshells would explode, and he was giving all the tapes to Sirica, Jaworski, the House Judiciary Committee, and the Senate. And, of course, he was making all the transcripts public.

Finally, eleven paragraphs into the thirteen-paragraph statement, Nixon commenced his defense. "I recognize that this additional material I am now furnishing may further damage my case, especially because attention will be drawn separately to it rather than to the evidence in its entirety." He urged that two points be kept in mind. First, what actually happened. On his orders, the FBI did check with the CIA; the CIA had said none of its activities would be compromised by a full-scale investigation; he had then ordered the FBI to go ahead vigorously with the investigation; the FBI had done so.

Nixon asked readers to put the transcripts in perspective. "Whatever mistakes I made in the handling of Watergate, the basic truth remains that when all the facts were brought to my attention, I insisted on a full investigation and prosecution of those guilty." He gave his own judgment: "I am firmly convinced that the record, in its entirety, does not justify the extreme step of impeachment and removal of a President." He concluded with what seemed to promise that he would not resign: "I trust that as the constitutional process goes forward, this perspective will prevail."[23]

Nixon did not wish to hear the evening newscasters reporting his statement on the June 23 conversation. Nor did he want his family to "endure the ordeal." He gathered Pat, Julie, Tricia, David, and Rose Woods (Ed had returned to New York) for a dinner cruise on the *Sequoia*. None of them enjoyed those rides—Julie remarked that "being on the *Sequoia* was like bobbing along in a glass bottle"—but they went to please him. Coast Guard speedboats darted around them; reporters and photographers jammed every bridge they went under. "We were the subject of a death watch," Julie recalled.

Everyone made an effort to be lighthearted. They made small talk about the weather and a movie Julie and David had recently seen. Nixon could not be distracted. Someday, he told them, the experiences they were enduring would become more meaningful than painful "because we would see how they had brought us closer together."[24]

As the boat turned upstream to head home, Nixon went below and laid down in one of the staterooms. Pat told a worried Julie that her father's leg was still swollen and painful, and the doctors had urged him to keep it elevated as much as possible.

Nixon asked Woods to call Haig to get a report on the initial reaction to the statement and the transcripts. She came down to his stateroom to tell him that Haig had said, "Just tell him that this thing is coming about the way we expected."[25]

The reaction was the full catastrophe. The ten Republicans on the Judiciary Committee who had voted against recommending impeachment on every article were, one by one, reversing themselves. Sandman said, "It certainly changes my vote. This is devastating." Wiggins read a statement. His tone was one of cold rage. He demanded the President's resignation. He had difficulty controlling his emotions as he continued, "The magnificent career of public service of Richard Nixon must be terminated involuntarily." By sunset, all ten had said they would vote for Article I of the impeachment recommendation when it came before the full House, in effect making the Judiciary Committee vote to impeach unanimous.

Gerald Ford, who just the day before down in Mississippi had repeated his belief in Nixon's innocence, issued a statement saying that he had "come to the conclusion that the public interest is no longer served by repetition of my previously expressed belief that . . . the President is not guilty of an impeachable offense."[26]

Barry Goldwater kept his reaction to himself, but it was scathing. He felt that here "was the same old Nixon, confessing ambiguously, in enigmatic language, still refusing to accept accountability. It was, above all, an insincere statement, as duplicitous as the man himself."[27]

Why had Nixon gone through with this charade of testing the reaction before resigning? In his memoirs, he claims that he wished to give his friends and supporters an opportunity to disassociate themselves from his cause, to say publicly that they would vote to impeach so that they would be on the record when they faced the voters in November.

But perhaps there is another, more personal reason. Nixon's "test" exposed his isolation. With almost every politician in Washington who could get to a microphone denouncing him, he had a plausible reason to resign that did not involve a confession of wrongdoing or guilt.

That was one thing the statement accomplished for Nixon; it put the emphasis on the lies rather than the deeds. It allowed Republicans to say they would vote for Article I, the cover-up charge, while ignoring Article II, with its charge of abuse of power, and Article III, failure to cooperate with Congress in the impeachment inquiry. The howls of outrage from Republicans about lies carry less conviction when contrasted to their silence on Articles II and III. It was as if the lesson from Watergate would be, Don't cover up a break-in, and if you do, don't tape yourself while you do it, and if you do that, don't lie about it.[28]

Nixon had given his Republican and Southern Democratic supporters a plausible reason to abandon him; and they handed back an excuse to resign without confessing guilt.

IT was Tuesday, August 6. Nixon had instructed Haig the previous evening to call the Cabinet for a meeting in the early morning. Until he resigned, he later wrote, "I intended to play the role of President right to the hilt and right to the end."[29] It was an appropriate choice of words; he was reduced to playing at being President.

To begin with, he pretended to his Cabinet that he still had options, that he was wavering about what to do. He offered a list of reasons for not resigning. He reminded the members that the Presidency had experienced enormous trauma in the past decade, with the assassination of Kennedy and with Johnson "literally hounded from office." The institution must not sustain another "hammer blow" without a defense. Consequently, he must not resign, but would let the constitutional process run its course. To do otherwise "would be a regrettable departure from American historical principles."[30]

Vice President Ford was shaken by what Nixon was saying, and by the President's appearance. Clearly, Nixon had not been sleeping well, his complexion had turned sallow, and he lacked energy. He defended his record to them. "One thing I have learned is never to allow anybody else to run your campaign," he joked feebly. All Ford could think of was "how tired and drawn he seemed."[31]

Nixon asked the Cabinet for support. Not on Watergate—that would be too much, he knew—but on "the good things the Administration has done." The members should run their departments and sell their programs, get a little positive PR for the Administration.

Ford interrupted. "Mr. President," he said, "with your indulgence, I have something to say."

"Well, Jerry, go ahead."

"Everyone here recognizes the difficult position I'm in," he said. Ford spoke of his sympathy for Nixon and his family. "But I wish to emphasize that had I known what has been disclosed in reference to Watergate in the last twenty-four hours, I would not have made a number of the statements I made . . . I'll have no further comment on the issue because I'm a party in interest. . . . You have given us the finest foreign policy this country has ever had. A super job, and the people appreciate it. Let me assure you that I expect to continue to support the Administration's foreign policy and the fight against inflation."

"I think your position is exactly correct," Nixon responded. It seemed to Kissinger that Nixon had heard only the comment on inflation.

Nixon said he wanted to take up the most important issue confronting the nation—"inflation." He began by projecting policies for the next six months, including a meeting of top business, government, and labor people. Attorney General William Saxbe was dumbfounded. By his own testimony, Saxbe said, "Mr. President, don't you think we should be talking about next week, not next year?" According to Saxbe, Nixon looked around the table, no one said a word, and with that the President picked up his papers and left the room.[32]

According to Ford, Saxbe said, "Mr. President, I don't think we ought to have a summit conference. We ought to be sure you have the ability to govern."[33]

At this point the many different accounts of what happened in that meeting, both written and oral, told by the people who were there, diverge to the point that nothing can be certain, except that the tension in the room was as great as any of these men—all of them accustomed to high-stakes politics—had ever experienced.

Nixon had appointed every man in that room. Yet when he left office, they would stay on, at least as long as Ford wanted them.

George Bush had come close to telling Nixon to go, according to Kissinger, who recalled that Bush had pointed out that the Republican Party was in a shambles. Watergate had to be ended, before the November elections.[34] Ford remembered Nixon returning the discussion to the economy, only to be interrupted by Bush again. Watergate, and the resulting lack of public confidence in the Administration, the RNC chairman said, was affecting the economy.[35]

Finally, mercifully, the meeting came to an end.

Nixon returned to the Oval office. Kissinger joined him. Perhaps disturbed by the President's insistence that he would let the constitutional process run its course, Kissinger—who had earlier told Haig that neither of them must ever appear to be recommending resignation—now gave Nixon compelling reasons to resign. He said a Senate trial would take months, would "obsess the nation" and "paralyze our foreign policy," and would be "dangerous for our country" as well as "demeaning to the Presidency."[36]

Nixon later wrote, "I told him that I totally agreed with his appraisal. . . ." while Kissinger recorded that Nixon's reaction was to thank him for his views and promise to take them seriously.[37]

Kissinger had some good news that day. The Senate Foreign Relations Committee had voted unanimously to clear him of allegations that he misled the Committee during his confirmation hearings about his role in the 1969 wiretapping of government officials and newsmen. The State Department announced that the Secretary was "gratified" and "no longer sees any reason for resignation."[38]

St. Clair let it be known, indirectly, that he was instrumental in having the June 23 tape made public. He did not point out that after Sirica listened to and removed material unrelated to Watergate, it was going to go public anyway.[39]

Bob Haldeman was also scrambling to survive. Again there are some discrepancies in the memoirs and interviews with participants. According to Haldeman, he called Ziegler to say, "When it comes to the point that the President decides to resign, and I'm afraid it will, I want you to let me know before any announcement or final action is taken, because I want to talk to him once before it is too late."[40] According to Nixon, Haldeman called Haig to ask that Haig pass on a message: Haldeman was strongly opposed to resignation, but if resignation was Nixon's irrevocable decision, Haldeman recommended that Nixon grant the Watergate defendants a full presidential pardon as his last act in office. He should balance that act by granting amnesty for all Vietnam draft dodgers.[41]

Before Nixon could react, Rabbi Korff arrived for an appointment. Korff told the President, "You will be sinning against history if you allow the partisan cabal in Congress and the jackals in the media to force you from office."[42]

To Korff, Nixon laid into his enemies: "I know these people. When they detect weakness somewhere they would not hesitate to harden their position. If they want to put me behind bars, let them."[43] Korff later issued a statement from the Oval Office: "Unless there is an immediate outpouring of support addressed to the White House . . . it is my opinion and only my opinion he may resign in the national interest."[44]

Nixon did a vote count in the Senate with Timmons. Two days earlier they had felt the thirty-four votes needed to avoid conviction were in hand; now Timmons said there were only seven certain. He added that Goldwater wanted to see Nixon to tell him how hopeless the situation had become. Nixon told Haig to make an appointment for the following afternoon, and for Goldwater to bring Senator Scott and Representative Rhodes in on the meeting.[45]

Goldwater was in a rage. At a noon meeting of the Senate Republican Policy Committee, he growled, "There are only so many lies you can take and now there has been one too many. Nixon should get his ass out of the White House—today!"[46]

A message came. Goldwater was wanted on the telephone by the

White House. He excused himself, took up the receiver. An operator said Haig was calling from the Oval Office. When Haig picked up the phone, Goldwater heard a second click. He guessed it was Nixon, listening in. Haig asked how many votes Nixon had in the Senate.

No more than a dozen, Goldwater replied. It is all over, he snapped. "Al, Dick Nixon has lied to me for the very last time. And to a hell of a lot of others in the Senate and House. We're sick to death of it all."[47]

Public support for Nixon from his fellow politicians was almost non-existent. Of the 435 members of the House, only two—Otto Passman (D.-La.) and Earl Landgrebe (R.-Ind.)—had taken a public stand against impeachment. Of the one hundred senators, only one—Carl Curtis (R.-Neb.)—had made a public defense of Nixon. Out in California, Governor Ronald Reagan had called for resignation.

Nixon called Rose Woods into his office. He needed help with the family. "Tell them that the whole bunch is deserting now and we have no way to lobby them or keep them."

When Woods went off to seek out the family, Nixon took a legal pad and began making notes for his resignation speech. He called in Haig and Ziegler. "Things are moving very fast now." He would make his speech on Thursday night, August 8. "I will do it with no rancor and no loss of dignity. I will do it gracefully."

There was silence. Nixon broke it: "Well, I screwed it up good, real good, didn't I?"[48]

Haig went to his office and asked Price to join him.

"We'll need a thousand words," Haig said.

"He's finally decided?"

"Yes."

The speech should not be a *mea culpa,* nor a confession of guilt that Nixon did not feel, but a healing that would help rally the country behind Ford. Neither should it satisfy those "who crucified him, and are now trying to get him to say they were justified."[49]

Nixon went to the Lincoln Sitting Room and watched some news programs. Those politicians who were commenting on June 23 said they felt like they had been hit by a truck, that they had been betrayed, that they were shocked beyond words. They were unanimous that he should resign—now. There were some differences over whether or not Nixon should be granted amnesty.

Nixon sat in the Lincoln Sitting Room, working on his resignation speech, until 2 A.M. When he walked into his bedroom, he found a handwritten note from Julie on his pillow:

Dear Daddy—I love you. Whatever you do I will support. I am very proud of you.

Please wait a week or even ten days before you make this

decision. Go through the fire just a little bit longer. You are so strong!

I love you, Julie.

Millions support you.

Nixon wrote that "If anything could have changed my mind," Julie's note would have. But it was too late. He felt, "deep down in my heart and mind, that I had made the decision that was best for the country."[50]

CHAPTER EIGHTEEN

RESIGNATION
August 7–9, 1974

THE FINAL SCENE of the last act opened at 10:00 Wednesday morning, August 7, when Nixon entered the Oval Office. It lasted forty-eight hours. The author and protagonist of the drama—for he was now finally in command for the last act—called it a "Greek tragedy" that "had to be seen through until the end as fate would have it."[1] The audience was the 218 million people of the United States, and beyond them, the whole world.

The central character, stage manager, director in charge of casting, and author of the tragedy with its inevitable end, Nixon used his manifold talents as creator of make-believe to heighten suspense, build tension to an all but unbearable level, to justify his own actions, to manipulate his friends and family, and to confound his enemies. Beyond his need to justify what he was doing in a way that denied any moral shortcoming or criminal misconduct, Nixon aimed to stake out his claim as a great President, protect his pension, convince his audience that he was acting for the good of the country rather than the good of himself and was therefore truly tragic, defend his integrity, preach to the people, and give fair warning that he had no intention of retiring as a performer after the curtain came down. He succeeded in achieving the ultimate goal of every actor and of every playwright: he was mesmerizing.

On his desk was the first draft of his resignation speech, along with a covering memo from Price. The speechwriter said that he thought resignation was "sad" but "necessary." He hoped Nixon would "leave office as proud of your accomplishments here as I am proud to have been associated with you, and to have been and remain a friend. God bless you; and He will."[2]

422

Nixon took the draft to his office in the EOB. Crowds outside the iron fence surrounding the White House surged forward when he appeared; they were three, four, five deep. "Jail to the Chief!" many of them called out; others pressed their faces to the fence and just stared.

Nixon called Haldeman in California. "Bob," he opened, in a voice that Haldeman thought was tired and defeated, "I want you to know that I have decided I must resign."

"Is this a final decision?" Haldeman asked.

"There's no use fighting it any more," Nixon replied.

In that case, Haldeman said, "I'll do anything I can to help in carrying it out, although I personally oppose it." There was one point, however, he wanted to raise. "I firmly believe that before you leave office you should exercise your Constitutional authority and grant pardons to all those who have been or may be charged with any crimes in connection with Watergate. I think it's imperative that you bring Watergate to an end before you leave—for the sake of the country and especially for your successor." He added that amnesty for Vietnam draft dodgers would deflect criticism.

As Haldeman talked, Nixon later wrote, his mind wandered. He thought of the Haldeman of old, the "proud and brusque" chief of staff, now reduced to begging—or was he threatening?

Nixon did not give Haldeman a direct answer. Haldeman said he would send some written recommendations. Nixon assured him that he would think about a blanket pardon.[3]

Haldeman wrote the memo and called it in to his lawyers in Washington. They typed it up and got the document to the White House. Entitled "Notes for Consideration," it read, in part:

> On personal basis—better to close the chapter now than to have to sit by helplessly for the next several years and watch trials and appeals.
>
> Historically—would be far better to grant the pardon and close the door to such process than to let it run and have the trials become a surrogate impeachment. Also, history will look kindly on loyalty and compassion to subordinates caught in the web.
>
> Solves problems of potential prosecutor access to files and tapes by eliminating basis for further prosecution—also solves problem of defense forcing access to files.
>
> The only way to wipe the slate clean is to shut down the prosecution totally. . . . As long as it is there, there is a possibility of other things. . . .[4]

At one level, Haldeman's memo was straightforward, businesslike, and convincing. The points he made were logical, indeed obvious. At another level, Haldeman was simply continuing the cover-up, trying to protect Nixon—and himself—from whatever damaging material there was on the thousands of hours of unreleased tapes or the tens of thousands of documents in the files. On a third level, Haldeman was making a scarcely disguised threat. That "possibility of other things" line was ominous. It almost could be read as Haldeman threatening that he would send Nixon to jail if he did not get a pardon.

(When Nixon read the memo the following day, he rejected it coldly. Amnesty for the Vietnam draft dodgers was "unthinkable." He said that blanket pardon for Watergate defendants would cause a "hysterical" political reaction.[5])

Haldeman was not alone in raising the question of amnesty and blanket pardon; Ehrlichman joined him. Republicans in Congress, meanwhile, were discussing legislation that would grant the President immunity from prosecution if he should resign, while Democratic Senators Mansfield and Byrd were expressing their opposition to such a course and insisting that even if Nixon resigned, the impeachment process and trial in the Senate should go forward.[6] Haig discussed the possibilities with Nixon.

Nixon wanted no part of an immunity grant, either from the Senate or from the Special Prosecutor. He told Haig there should be no bargaining with Jaworski. He would not be "cajoled into resigning in exchange for leniency." He was not leaving office out of fear and he would take his chances on criminal prosecution.

"Some of the best writing in history has been done from prison," he told Haig. "Think of Lenin and Gandhi."

Haig said he had the impression that Jaworski would not prosecute Nixon if Nixon resigned. The President replied that, considering the way Jaworski had double-crossed him in the past, he found "little reason to feel reassured."[7]

After Nixon talked to Haldeman, Ed and Tricia Cox came to his EOB office to warn him that resignation would not bring an end to the nightmare. There would be trials and lawsuits. It was the point Haldeman had made. Ed and Tricia were afraid he would "wake up the morning after leaving office feeling he had made a terrible mistake by resigning."

They failed to change Nixon's mind, and left the office. A bit later, Ed returned, this time accompanied by David Eisenhower. Ed repeated his earlier warning. "I know these people," he said, referring to some of the young lawyers on Jaworski's staff. "They are smart and ruthless; they hate you. They will harass you and hound you in civil and criminal actions across this country for the rest of your life if you resign."

Nixon remained resolute. Among other things, he said he had to resign for the good of the party.

"You don't owe the party a damn thing," David exploded. "That was the way Granddad felt, and so should you. Do what you think is best for yourself, and what you think is best for the country."[8]

Nixon met with Price to go over the resignation speech. Price thought that although Nixon was showing the strain, he was nevertheless brisk and methodical. He handed Price an insert he had scrawled on the draft: "I have met with leaders of House and Senate, including my strongest supporters in both parties. They have unanimously advised me that because of Watergate matter, I do not and will not have support in Congress for difficult decisions affecting peace abroad and our fight against inflation at home, so essential to lives of every family in America."

In fact, he had not met with the leaders. He was scheduled to do so in an hour, at 5 P.M., although only the Republican leaders, Senators Goldwater and Scott and Representative John Rhodes, the House Minority Leader. But he knew what they were going to say; they were working from his script.

Price felt that Nixon was not only "pained by having to resign, but acutely embarrassed at doing it." In another handwritten marginal insertion, Nixon had written, "I have never been a quitter. To leave office is abhorrent to every instinct in my body." Nixon gave Price more instructions; he wanted to be certain, as a matter of precedent, that his resignation was perceived as the constitutional equivalent of having seen the process through. "One thing that is very important," he stressed to Price, "is basically a recognition that this *is* an impeachment."[9]

BUT of course it was *not* an impeachment, and he was *not* seeing the process through. He was resigning. By so doing, he was establishing the "Nixon precedent." Stephen Jones has predicted, "It is unlikely now that any President will ever be impeached or stand trial on impeachment charges. The 'Nixon option,' i.e., resignation and pardon, has become a precedent."[10]

Nixon was, in effect, substituting the British parliamentary system for the American system. That was the whole point of the elaborate minuet of the past week—the release of the June 23 tape, with its accompanying statement, the "assessment" of its impact, the upcoming meeting with Scott, Goldwater, and Rhodes, all of it. Nixon had made it clear that he lost his support in Congress. This amounted to a vote of "no confidence." Therefore, he could not govern. Therefore, he had to resign. Not because he was guilty of wrongdoing, either moral or criminal, but as a consequence of political fortune.

JUST before the Republican delegation came to the Oval Office, Nixon called Price again. He wanted to go over the point about his resignation being the equivalent of impeachment. Price said he thought he had found the wording. "And that's right!" Nixon exclaimed. "That six-minute conversation [of June 23]—Haldeman ran that CIA thing by me—it went by so fast that I didn't even pay attention. It was a stupid damn thing—but wrong."[11]

Steve Bull informed Nixon that the Republican delegation had arrived. The President told Bull to take them into the Oval Office. When Nixon arrived, walking over from the EOB, the three delegates were seated. Nixon pushed back his swivel chair, sat down, put his feet up on the desk, and began to reminisce about the past. He was bitter, hurt. He recalled men he had campaigned with who had turned on him. He said he remembered them well.

Suddenly he ended his soliloquy. He snapped at Rhodes that the situation was not good. Before Rhodes could reply, Nixon clumped his feet on the floor, wheeled his chair around, and faced Scott.

Scott turned to Goldwater. He said Barry would be the spokesman for the group.

Nixon stared at Goldwater. "Okay, Barry," he said, "go ahead."

"Things are bad," Goldwater said.

"Less than half a dozen votes?" Nixon asked, his voice dripping with sarcasm, his jaw jutted out, his eyes narrowed.

"Ten at most," Goldwater said. "Maybe less. Some aren't firm."

Nixon turned to Scott, who guessed there might be as many as fifteen. That was less than half Nixon needed to escape.

Goldwater thought he could see Nixon's blood pressure rising. "I took a nose count in the Senate today," Goldwater said. "You have four firm votes. The others are really undecided. I'm one of them." He was leaning toward voting guilty on Article II.

Nixon leaned over his desk toward Rhodes and asked, "Do I have any options?"

"I want to tell the people outside [the White House press corps] that we didn't discuss any options," Rhodes replied.

In a monotone, Nixon said he had no interest in a pardon. He would make his decision in the best interest of the country. He would do it without tears: "I haven't cried since Eisenhower died."

As the delegation left, Nixon said to Scott, "Now that old Harry Truman is gone, I won't have anybody to pal around with." He would be the only living ex-President.[12]

When the three visitors emerged from the White House, they were surrounded by reporters. They had expected it; had they wanted to avoid the press, they could have slipped out a side door. But they knew their roles and played them well. The playwright and director wanted them to keep up the suspense; they did.

"Whatever decision he makes," Goldwater said, "it will be in the best interest of our country. There have been no decisions made. We made no suggestions. We were merely there to offer what we see as the condition on both floors."

Scott said that they had told Nixon the situation was "gloomy," that it was "a very distressing situation." He asserted that "the President is in entire control of himself. He was serene and he was most amiable."

Goldwater was asked about immunity for the President. "The subject was not touched on," he replied. "The discussion was quite general in tone. We were fond old friends talking over a very painful situation."

Rhodes was asked whether the House would go ahead and vote on the articles of impeachment if Nixon resigned. He replied, "No useful purposes would be served by that."

Nixon's future was on the minds of many. In reply to one question, Attorney General Saxbe said that the question of granting immunity was in Jaworski's hands. Jaworski's office would not comment. On the evening news, NBC TV replayed the moment in Ford's vice presidential confirmation hearings in the Senate when he was asked whether he could pardon Nixon, and Ford had replied, "I don't think the public would stand for it."[13]

NIXON called Kissinger and asked him to come over. When the Secretary arrived, he found the President standing in the Oval Office, gazing at the Rose Garden through the bay windows. Nixon turned. He told Kissinger he had decided to resign. He wanted him to notify foreign governments, and to assure them that there would be no change in American foreign policy.

"Henry, you know that you must stay here and carry on for Jerry the things you and I have begun. The whole world will need reassurance that my leaving won't change our policies. You can give them that reassurance, and Jerry will need your help. Just as there is no question but that I must go, there really is no question but that you must stay."

Kissinger was struck by a feeling of great tenderness for Nixon. He put his arm around the President—perhaps the first time he had ever touched him, other than to shake his hand, in six years. He said, "History will treat you more kindly than your contemporaries have."[14]

NIXON walked to the residence. His family was waiting for him in the Solarium, the bright yellow and green room that was the family's favorite. Pat sat erect on the edge of the couch, her head high. She rose when her husband entered, came over to him, threw her arms around him, kissed him, and said, "We're all very proud of you, Daddy."

Nixon looked around the room. Deeply moved, he said, "No man who ever lived had a more wonderful family that I have."[15] This would be the last gathering of the family in the Solarium; this was an important scene; it should be recorded. For props, the dogs would be perfect. Nixon asked Manolo to bring them in. He did, and the dogs brought a laugh as they played and begged food.

There was a knock on the door. It was the official photographer, Ollie Atkins, camera in hand, smiling, ready to go to work.

Pat cringed. She told Atkins that no one really felt much like posing. Her husband corrected her. He said he had requested the photographs, "for history." Tricia got up and suggested that everyone stand together and link arms. Nixon very elaborately arranged them in place. Julie tried to hide partially behind her mother, because she was crying. Nixon told everyone to smile.[16]

It was obvious to Atkins that Pat and Tricia had also been crying, so he recalled, "I used a flash because the available light would have made it even more pathetic with the tears."

The family smiled for the camera through the tears. It was "the President's idea of what a picture should be," Atkins said. He snapped a photograph. At David's request, he took another. "I'm a blinker," David explained.[17]

Atkins turned away, by now in tears himself. Julie sobbed, threw her arms around her father, and said, "I love you, Daddy." Atkins quickly snapped another picture.

In his memoirs, Nixon wrote, "I still do not like to look at the pictures from that night. All I can see in them is the tension in the smiles, and the eyes brimming with tears."[18]

But Julie records, in her biography of her mother, that the pictures were under consideration for inclusion in Nixon's memoirs and that it was Pat who vetoed them. She told her daughter she hated those pictures, because "our hearts were breaking and there we are smiling."[19]

After Atkins left, the family had a quiet dinner together. "Mostly," Nixon wrote, "we ate in silence."[20]

AFTER dinner, Nixon went to the Lincoln Sitting Room, where he conferred with Ziegler on arrangements for his resignation speech the following night. They got into a reminiscing mood as they talked about the great swings they had known in the past two years and, in Nixon's words, "about how tragic it was that everything should end so suddenly and so sadly." Ziegler recalled Nixon's favorite line from Teddy Roosevelt, one the President had often used, about the "man in the arena." Nixon called Price, to tell him that Ziegler was going to try to find the full quotation so that it could be worked into the speech. He added that he had "made a few scribblings" on Price's latest draft and was sending Ziegler over with it. Finally, he said he wanted Price to add to the speech a "pledge" about his dedication to the nation in the future.[21]

At 9 P.M. Nixon called Kissinger and asked him to come over again. Kissinger found Nixon slouched in his easy chair, his legs on the settee, a yellow legal pad in his lap. They discussed foreign affairs, and reminisced about their years together. Nixon grew emotional, more so than he had at any other time during the final days. It was natural and inevitable that he should. It was in foreign affairs that he had made his bid for greatness. It was foreign affairs that had challenged him and fascinated him as domestic matters never could. It was in foreign affairs that he had been bold and innovative and successful. Kissinger had been his agent, his aide, his adviser in these triumphs.

Kissinger thought it a poignant moment. "At the close of his political career Nixon was left with the one associate about whom he was the most ambivalent, who made him uneasy even while counting on him to embody the continuity of his achievements."

The President went to the family kitchen and returned with the same bottle of brandy he and Kissinger had drunk from three years earlier, to toast the invitation to go to Peking.

Nixon wondered what history would say of him. Had he made a difference? Was the world a safer place because of him?

Kissinger assured Nixon, once more, that history would be kinder to him than his contemporaries, that history would recall his great achievements.

"It depends who writes the history," Nixon replied each time Kissinger repeated the point.

Would there be a criminal prosecution of ex-President Nixon? It was obvious to Kissinger that Nixon could hardly bear the thought "of the indignity of a criminal trial." Neither could Kissinger.

"If they harass you after you leave office," Kissinger blurted out, "I am going to resign as Secretary of State, and I am going to tell the world why!"

Finally, Kissinger prepared to leave. He recalled in his memoirs that he had been with Nixon for nearly three hours, but it could not have been that long, because the telephone logs show that Nixon had called him at 9 P.M. and that his next call—after Kissinger left—was at 10:35 P.M. In any case, Nixon walked with Kissinger down the hall toward the elevator. As they passed the Lincoln Bedroom, Nixon had an impulse. He asked Kissinger to go into the bedroom with him.

Nixon said he realized that Kissinger was not one to wear his religion on his sleeve; neither was he. He realized further that they had different religious beliefs. But he thought that deep down they had just as strong a belief in God.

Nixon said that every night, when he finished work, he would kneel briefly and pray silently. He asked Kissinger to pray with him now. They knelt and prayed.[22]

Nixon returned to the Lincoln Sitting Room. At 10:35 P.M. he called Price. His talk with Kissinger had reminded him of his accomplishments.

Now he wanted to make certain Price worked them into the resignation speech.

"There's just one thing," Nixon said in a melancholy and distant manner. "If you could add in—with regard to peace—the opening to China—that we started the process of limitation of nuclear arms—that we started a process of peace in the Middle East, which hasn't known peace for a thousand years."

Three minutes later, Nixon called Price again. He wanted a reference in the speech to ending the war in Vietnam.

Next Nixon called Kissinger, to ask that he not mention the scene in the Lincoln Bedroom to anyone. Kissinger already had, to his aides.

A half hour later, Nixon called to Price to warn him not to mention the triumphs "in a bragging way."

At 4:15 A.M., he called Price again. "I didn't want to bother you at night," Nixon said, "but I know you work at night. Is that all right?" He wanted some reference to the future, to follow the passages on what had been accomplished with a reminder of what still needed to be done.

Fifteen minutes later, he called again. "What I had in mind," Nixon said, "is a little liturgy—like this." And he spelled it out. "What I'm getting at," Nixon explained, "is reduction [of nuclear arms], not just limitation—so the terrible danger as we know it must not hang over the world." With millions of people around the world living in abject poverty, he wanted the speech to say that America's goal "should be to turn away from production for war so that all the people of the earth can live in peace, and can have an opportunity to enjoy the benefits of a decent life." He had other, similar sentiments he wanted to express.

This was pure Nixon. He was statesmanlike, sincere, and absolutely right on the mark as to America's true role in the world. He was boasting. He was attempting to turn attention away from the reason for his resignation to the cost to the country and the world of that resignation. He was crafting a speech that would make the transition smoother, one that could help begin the process of healing. As he sat there alone, in the early hours of his last full day as President, attempting to sum up his Presidency, he was at his best and at his worst.

At 4:45 A.M., he called Price to say he wanted the speech to set out a domestic goal, "prosperity without inflation, opportunity, not just for the few, but for all." The kind of prosperity that would make it possible for small businessmen like his father to succeed, the kind of opportunity that would allow poor boys like himself to rise to the top.

"Okay?" Nixon asked Price.

"Okay."

The last call came at 5:07 A.M. "I just wanted to say—on this one— don't run it by the NSC, or by Haig, or anyone. Just send it to me. You and I can work it out. On this one, I just want to say the things that are in my heart. I want to make this *my* speech."[23]

FOUR hours later, at 9 A.M., August 8, Nixon walked over to the Oval Office. He called Haig. He said he wanted to veto a $13.5 billion agricultural appropriations bill. It was inflationary, and he did not want to stick Ford with having to sign a veto on his first day in office. Haig brought in the bill, and Nixon signed his veto. He also appointed three federal judges, and accepted the resignations of an assistant secretary of transportation, a deputy director of the National Science Foundation, and a member of the Atomic Energy Commission. He appointed a chairman of the Combined Federal Campaign for the National Capital Area, and signed a message to the Congress transmitting the annual report on the Trade Agreements Program.

As Nixon performed these routine acts, his family was upstairs, sorting out items that would be sent into storage from those that would be shipped to San Clemente.

Nixon then wrote a letter to Arthur F. Sampson, administrator of the General Services Administration, which ran the National Archives. In it, he declared that no one should have access to his vice presidential papers without his personal permission until 1985. These were the papers he had given to the Archives in 1968 and for which he had taken the whopping deduction that got him into so much trouble. In the original deed of gift, Nixon had stipulated that access to the papers would be restricted only so long as he was President. (When the Archives announced the new regulations ten days later, there was a protest led by Ralph Nader's Tax Reform Research Group. It charged that the cover-up was continuing, that the public should have immediate access to the papers under the Freedom of Information Act, and that Nixon's attempt to postpone the date of access to the papers showed that he was still exercising rights of ownership. On March 22, 1978, Nixon removed the restriction and opened the bulk of his vice presidential papers to scholars.)[24]

At 10:48 A.M., Nixon had Steve Bull call Price to ask him to come to the Oval office right away. Price found Nixon sitting at his desk, at work on the latest draft of the speech. The President looked haggard and drawn, but he was thinking ahead. He hoped Price would come to California to work for him, "if he could somehow find the funds." Price said he would be glad to help. They made some changes in the speech. Nixon suggested a new opening; Price agreed.[25]

At 11 A.M., Price left and Ford entered. Nixon told Ford to sit down, then got straight to the point: "I have made the decision to resign. It's in the best interest of the country." He paused, then added, "Jerry, I know you'll do a good job."

Ford said he wished it had not come about in this way, but that he felt confident that he could do the job. They discussed details of the transition, and some of the problems Ford would face. Nixon urged him to strengthen NATO while striving to reach agreement with the Soviets on arms control. He hoped Ford would support a free and independent South Vietnam and Cambodia.

As to personnel in foreign policy, Nixon said the one man who was "absolutely indispensable" was Kissinger. If Ford let Kissinger get away, American foreign policy would soon be "in disarray throughout the world."

"Henry is a genius," Nixon went on, "but you don't have to accept everything he recommends. He can be invaluable, and he'll be very loyal, but you can't let him have a totally free hand."

In domestic affairs, Nixon urged Ford to keep up the fight against inflation, but warned him that wage and price controls were unwise. Nixon had tried them in 1971; he told Ford the controls had been "more harmful than helpful."

They talked about the appointment of a new Vice President. Nixon suggested Governor Rockefeller, but did not push the point. He also recommended that Ford retain Haig as chief of staff.[26]

HAIG and Ziegler came in, to discuss amnesty for the Vietnam draft dodgers and a blanket pardon for the Watergate defendants one last time. Nixon remained unalterably opposed. They talked about rumors sweeping through Washington about this or that deal Nixon had supposedly entered into with Jaworski. Nixon said it galled him "that people might think that my decision had been influenced by anything as demeaning as the fear of prosecution. . . . I did not care what else people thought as long as they did not think that I had quit just because things were tough."

His anger welled up. He let it out, volcanolike, all at once, in a single spasm of red hot lava.

"How can you support a quitter?" he bitterly asked Ziegler. He told a story about the time he was running a one-mile race in school, and there were fifty yards left and only two competitors running, with nothing at stake but next to last place. Still, he sprinted those last fifty yards.

"I have never quit before in my life," he cried out. "Maybe that is what none of you has understood this whole time. You don't quit."[27]

It was a remarkable scene. Why accuse Ziegler of never understanding, when Ziegler had spent six years doing everything he could to please his boss in every way possible?

The outburst showed, more clearly than anything else, how much he despised himself at that moment, and hated what he was doing.

You don't quit.

He had quit.

Dropped out of the race.

Walked out of the arena.

Abandoned the field to his enemies.

Oh, how he hated himself for violating all of his most deeply held principles, how he despised himself for running away, how furious he was with himself for having put himself in this position, and how natural for him, and how human, to take it out on Ziegler.

Slowly the eruption subsided. Rose Woods came in to get Nixon's last changes on his speech. She told the President his family wanted to be with him in the Oval Office that evening as he read his resignation speech, as a sign to the world that they were with him. He said that was out of the question—he would not be able to get through the speech if they were even nearby, much less in the room with him. He told Rose to tell the family to stay in the residence and watch the speech from there.[28]

AT 7:30 P.M. Nixon went to the EOB for a meeting with the congressional leaders. He wanted to inform them of his decision to resign. He had taken control of his emotions; he was determined to make it brief, businesslike, and dignified. He succeeded.

Nixon told the leaders of his decision. He thanked them for their support. Looking directly at Senator Mansfield, he said he had always respected them even when they opposed his policies—a sentiment that, if genuine, he had managed to hide for years. Mansfield puffed on his pipe without changing his dour expression. Nixon tried again: "Mike, I will miss our breakfasts together." Mansfield nodded, without enthusiasm. Nixon felt that Senator Eastland was the only man in the room "who seemed really to share my pain." The meeting ended.[29]

Nixon walked over to the Cabinet Room. There was a group of thirty-four congressmen plus three White House aides crowded together, waiting for him. He had invited them; they were his strongest supporters over the years. There were thirteen Republican senators, seven Republican representatives (not including Wiggins), four Southern Democratic senators, and ten Southern Democratic representatives. Nixon had invited a dozen others who had not come. Those who were there were the men with whom Nixon had worked for five and a half years, in his words, to "repeatedly beat back the Goliath of liberal Democrats and liberal Republicans" in Congress.

Representative Glenn Davis (R.-Wis.) wrote a memo the following morning describing the meeting.

"The President came in," Davis recorded. "He sat down, and then proceeded to talk on in a rambling fashion. He was under great emotional stress. Several times he stopped and was so choked up and there were just those moments of absolute silence. He was with us for about 20 minutes. He referred to us as his oldest and best friends in the Congress, expressed his appreciation for our coming, as he put it—just to say good-bye."

Nixon told them of his plans to leave the White House at 10 A.M. the next morning to fly to California. His resignation would be effective at noon.

Davis wrote, "He talked about his family; said they were unanimous in their opinion that he should stick it out and fight it through, but then he acknowledged that it was apparent that after the beginning of this week when the deterioration of his support became apparent and it was obvious as to what the likely outcome would be that he felt that the Nation needed a full-time President and a full-time Congress and that . . . was the basis for his decision to resign."

"The emotional level in the room," Nixon wrote in his memoirs, "was almost unbearable." When he saw men crying, he lost control, "and I broke into tears."

"I just hope that I haven't let you down," he recalled saying. Davis recorded his last line as "I hope you won't feel that I let you down."[30]

Nixon went to the small office next to the Oval Office, to look over the text of his speech and to be made up for television. Haig came in; he was concerned that the President might not be able to get through the broadcast.

"Al," Nixon reassured him, "I'm sorry I cracked up a bit in there, but when I see other people cry, particularly when they are crying for someone else rather than themselves, it just gets to me. I'll be all right now, so there's nothing to worry about."[31]

Lillian Brown, chief TV make-up artist for CBS News, Washington bureau, for twenty-eight years, and personal make-up artist for Kennedy, Johnson, Nixon, Ford, and Carter, did the make-up. She felt Nixon was a "basket case" when he sat down before the mirror, and she went to work. (Davis wrote that when Nixon left the Cabinet Room, "he was under such great emotional stress that it seemed unbelievable that he could pull himself together for the television speech.")

Brown worked quietly and efficiently. Her voice and her fingers were soothing. Nixon struggled for self-control. His willpower asserted itself. He began to talk, softly and slowly, about the beach in California. As Brown worked on his face, applying the special-formula make-up she had developed that would absorb his perspiration for up to one-half hour under the hot television lights, his composure returned.[32]

He was an old pro at television. He had faced the cameras a thousand times and more. In his first solo appearance, twenty-two years earlier, in the Checkers speech, he had faced a national audience. In his last solo appearance, he would face an international audience.

Television allowed him to speak directly to the people. Reporters could not question him, commentators would have to wait until he was finished to express their criticisms. He could say what he wanted, and to hell with the cynics and critics and sophisticated, sneering elite.

He loved surprises. Only he and Ray Price knew what he was going to say. A relative handful of others knew what he was going to do. Nearly everyone in the country expected him to resign, to be sure, but no one could count on it until he had said it.

This was the night. Nixon's drama had reached its climax. His audience knew how it was going to end, but was breathless to see how it was accomplished. Never before had the nation so completely concentrated its attention on one man.

AT 9:01 P.M., August 8, 1974, the red light on the camera facing Nixon's Oval Office desk went on, and he began to speak. He was calm. "This is the 37th time I have spoken to you from this office," the President said. On each occasion, he had done so in order to discuss some matter of national interest. Throughout his public life, he went on, "I have always tried to do what was best for the nation." So it was through "the long and difficult period of Watergate," when he had felt that it was his duty to preserve and complete the term of office to which the people had elected him.

"In the past few days, however, it has become evident to me that I no longer have a strong enough political base in the Congress to justify continuing that effort." So long as he had such a base, he said, he had felt strongly that it was necessary to see the constitutional process through to its conclusion; but with the disappearance of that base, "I now believe that the constitutional purpose has been served, and there is no longer a need for the process to be prolonged."

Nevertheless, he confessed, he would have preferred to carry through to the finish, "whatever the personal agony it would have involved, and my family unanimously urged me to do so. But the interests of the nation must always come before any personal considerations."

He had concluded that "because of the Watergate matter, I might not have the support of the Congress that I would consider necessary to make the very difficult decisions and carry out the duties of this office in the way the interests of the nation will require."

He had never been a quitter, he said, and to resign before his term was complete "is abhorrent to every instinct in my body." For the third time, he repeated that he had to do so for the good of the nation.

"Therefore, I shall resign the Presidency effective at noon tomorrow."

It was a carefully crafted opening. He was resigning for the good of the country, not to escape impeachment and trial, because he had lost his political base, not because of anything that he had done. He was not short-cutting the Constitution, but insisting that the constitutional process had been completed, because—although he did not say so directly—

resignation amounted to an acknowledgment that impeachment and a guilty vote were certain.

He turned to the future. He asked the people to support and help President Ford. It was essential "to begin healing the wounds of this nation, to put the bitterness and divisions of the recent past behind us. . . ." He hoped that by resigning he was hastening that healing process.

Returning to the past, Nixon said, "I regret deeply any injuries that may have been done in the course of the events that led to this decision. I would say only that if some of my judgments were wrong—and some were wrong—they were made in what I believed at the time to be the best interest of the nation."

Price had caught exactly the tone Nixon had wanted. He was not asking forgiveness. He was admitting manfully that he had made mistakes, mistakes of judgment, but his intentions had been good.

He thanked his supporters. "I leave with no bitterness toward those who have opposed me." He granted that his enemies only wanted what was best for the country, "however our judgments might differ."

After another plea for unity, he defended his Presidency. His Administration had ended America's longest war, and if his policies were continued it would be said of this generation of Americans that it not only ended one war but prevented future wars. He had opened to China. His administration had made friends with the Arabs and started the process of peace in the Middle East "so that the cradle of civilization will not become its grave." He had made crucial breakthroughs with the Soviet Union to limit nuclear arms, and established a new relation with the Soviets. At home, his Administration had brought peace and prosperity.

For more than a quarter of a century in public life he had fought for what he believed in. Sometimes he succeeded, and sometimes he failed, "but always I have taken heart from what Theodore Roosevelt once said about the man in the arena, 'whose face is marred by dust and sweat and blood, who strives valiantly, who errs . . . but who knows the great enthusiasms, the great devotions, who spends himself in a worthy cause, who at the best knows in the end the triumphs of high achievements and who at the worst, if he fails, at least fails while daring greatly.' "

He pledged that "as long as I have a breath of life in my body," he would continue to work for the causes he had been dedicated to throughout his public life, above all, to the cause of world peace. In assessing his contribution, he said he was confident "that the world is a safer place today . . . and that all of our children have a better chance than before of living in peace rather than dying in war" because of his efforts.

He concluded with a prayer: "May God's grace be with you in all the days ahead."[33]

The speech lasted sixteen minutes. It contained fifty-seven sentences. Eleven of the first twenty-five sentences dealt with his rationale for resigning. Six times he referred to the "personal sacrifice" he was making; five times he said he was resigning for the good of the country. His second main theme, the call to support Ford, took ten sentences.

In the latter half of the speech, twenty-two of the last thirty-two sentences were in praise of Richard Nixon and his Administration. Counting his assertions of his honorable motives, thirty-six of the fifty-seven sentences were devoted to self-justification of one sort or another.

Some 110 million watched, another 40 million listened, by far the largest audience ever for a political speech.[34]

THE first reaction Nixon heard came from Henry Kissinger, who was waiting for him in the corridor. "Mr. President," he said, "after most of your major speeches in this office we have walked together back to your house. I would be honored to walk with you again tonight."

As they walked past the Rose Garden, Kissinger said he thought that historically this would rank as one of the great speeches and that history would judge Nixon as one of the great Presidents.

A bit more realistically, Nixon responded with his standard reply, "That depends, Henry, on who writes the history."[35]

The President embraced his family, then began discussing the initial reactions to the speech. Most of the television commentators had expressed favorable reactions or, like Dan Rather, striven for evenhandedness. Some had praised him for the "healing" tone of the speech. Only Roger Mudd of CBS TV expressed criticism; Mudd said the President had evaded the issue and had not admitted his complicity in the coverup.[36]

Jaworski released a statement which said that bargaining regarding possible immunity from prosecution had played no part in Nixon's decision to resign. "There has been no agreement or understanding of any sort between the President and his representatives and the special prosecutor relating in any way to the President's resignation." He added that his office "was not asked for any such agreement or understanding and offered none."[37]

Television coverage, with comments from many politicians, lasted until well past midnight. So continuous and riveting was the drama that it appeared to be the last act in a national tragedy, as opposed to Nixon's personal tragedy. Ford set the tone and defined the mood when he said in brief televised remarks after the speech that Nixon's resignation was "one of the saddest incidents in U.S. history." George Bush also used the word "sad," then hastened to add that he did not mean to leave the impression of being "relieved."[38] Generally around the country the mood was one of relief or resignation.

Nixon did not watch the television, or hear the crowds. He had

Manolo bring him bacon and eggs in the Lincoln Sitting Room and began phoning friends and supporters around the country, saying to each he hoped he had not let him down. At 2 A.M., he went to bed, for the first time in forty hours.

HE woke at 6 A.M., August 9. He went to the Lincoln Sitting Room for a breakfast of corned beef hash and poached eggs. After eating, he took a yellow legal pad from his briefcase and began making notes for what he wanted to say to the Cabinet members and White House staff at the 9:30 A.M. farewell meeting in the East Room he had arranged.

Haig knocked and entered. Apologizing, but saying that it had to be done, Haig laid before Nixon a document that read: "I hereby resign the Office of President of the United States." It was addressed to Secretary of State Kissinger as the senior Cabinet member. Nixon signed, his last signature as a public official. Haig would deliver the letter to Kissinger later that morning, after Nixon and his family had departed the White House by helicopter.

When Haig left, Nixon had a thought for his farewell speech. He recalled something else that Teddy Roosevelt had written, and sent an aide to his EOB office to fetch a biography of T. R. When the aide returned with the book, Nixon quickly located the passage he wanted, and marked it.

Nixon called Haig for a final goodbye. Haig left a staff meeting dealing with the transition to return to the Lincoln Sitting Room. As he entered, he said, "To hell with the staff meeting. I would rather spend these last few minutes with you."[39]

It was a poignant moment. Haig had become Nixon's chief of staff less than eighteen months before; he had played no part in Nixon's triumphs; yet he was the only man left willing and able to help Nixon through this painful experience.

Nixon had spent his life in politics, knew every Republican and most Democrats by their first names, had known them for nearly three decades. Yet he did not have a single close friend among them. Even Senator Goldwater, who had stuck with Joe McCarthy to the end and beyond, continuing to defend and support McCarthy long after his death, and who had been a staunch supporter of Nixon throughout his career, had turned against him.

Haldeman was long gone, along with Ehrlichman, Mitchell, and Colson. Bob Finch had left the Administration years earlier. So had Herb Klein. Murray Chotiner was dead. Bill Rogers was back in New York. Nixon had not talked to his first running mate, Henry Cabot Lodge, Jr., in years, nor to his second, Spiro Agnew, in months. Mel Laird and Bryce Harlow had resigned. The men who had been closest to him as congressman, senator, Vice President, and President in his first term were all gone from his life.

He joined his family now, in the hallway, Pat in a pale pink and white dress, wearing dark glasses to hide the signs of two nights without sleep, and the tears. The residence staff was lined up, Manolo said, to say goodbye.

Nixon walked down the line. To those who literally served him, whether as waiters or valet or housekeepers, he was attentive and appreciative, and surprisingly spontaneous. The words came easily to him; they were heartfelt; they were right on the mark for the occasion; they were thoughtful and considerate.

Nixon told them he had been in the great palaces of Europe and Asia, that he had been a guest in many of the world's greatest and most famous homes. "But this," he said, indicating the White House, "is the best house because this house has a great heart, and that heart comes from those who serve it." He asked them to take the same special care of the new President that they had of him, proclaiming, "You're the greatest!" and then took care to shake hands with each of them.[40]

Steve Bull arrived to tell the family it was time to go down to the East Room for the final words of farewell. The family and aides crowded into the elevator so tightly that they could barely turn around. Bull, facing the door, began describing where each member would stand on the platform—the places were marked out—and where the cameras would be positioned.

When they heard the words "television cameras," Pat and Tricia became quite upset. "Oh, Dick," Pat cried in anguish. "You can't have it televised."

Television had intruded into Pat's private life ever since the Checkers speech. Now the monster was going to be present at this last moment, revealing the agony and ordeal. She was all but trembling in her anger, and breathing irregularly. Tricia was equally angry. It was too much, she said, after all the hurt television had caused them, that its prying eye should intrude on this last and most intimate moment of all.

Nixon, who had arranged for the cameras to be there, brushed his wife and daughter's objections aside. "That's the way it has to be," he said. "We owe it to our supporters. We owe it to the people."[41]

He did not mean his most personal supporters, his family, nor the staff and the Cabinet members who had stayed with him to the end (whose privacy was also being intruded upon by the television cameras). He meant rather that more abstract group, whose numbers were still in the millions, who had supported his policies, contributed to his campaigns, believed in his principles, believed in him.

He did owe them, although what it was and how it could ever be paid was difficult to say, and the need to explain himself yet once again over national television, as he had done so many times before, gave him the opportunity. Although the play had reached its climax the night before, with his resignation speech, he would use this last remaining opportunity to monopolize the national television networks for an encore.

The double doors to the East Room opened and the family entered. Nixon's Marine aide Jack Brennan announced, in his resonant voice, "Ladies and Gentlemen, the President of the United States of America and Mrs. Nixon, Mr. and Mrs. Edward Cox, Mr. and Mrs. David Eisenhower."

The words unleashed a thunder of applause. The guests rose to their feet—Buchanan, Price, St. Clair, Buzhardt, other aides and advisers, Kissinger, and the remainder of the Cabinet—as the Nixons, Coxes, and Eisenhowers moved to their assigned places on the raised platform. Pat defied the television dictators; she moved away from her marked position to stand closer to Tricia and Ed. She removed her dark glasses. Her husband moved to the podium.

As he did so, the applause intensified. Nixon caught Price's eye and smiled and nodded. He did the same with a few others that he picked out of the crowd. The applause went on. Many were weeping.[42]

Kissinger later described his feelings: "I was at the same time moved to tears and outraged at being put through the wringer once again, so that even in his last public act Nixon managed to project his ambivalence onto those around him."[43]

Nixon could not quiet the applause. Finally he started to speak, and the audience began to settle back into their seats. His eye caught the tears streaming down the face of Herb Stein. Nixon quickly averted his eye from Stein and locked it onto the camera, as a way of controlling his own emotions.

In his memoirs, Nixon said he welcomed the chance "to talk personally and intimately to these people who had worked so hard for me and who I had let down so badly."[44] But they were not in fact his audience, and he did not speak to them. He turned his full attention to the camera.

He began by saying the event was spontaneous, although he realized the press would report that it had been arranged. "We don't mind" what the press would say, he went on, "because they have to call it as they see it. But on our part, believe me, it is spontaneous."

He repeated the lines he had used earlier with the household staff about the White House being the best house, a house with a "great heart" that came from those who worked there.

He expressed a regret and made an awkward stab at a bit of humor: "I see so many on this staff that, you know, I should have been by your offices and shaken hands, and I would love to have talked to you and found out how to run the world—everybody wants to tell the President what to do, and boy, he needs to be told many times—but I just haven't had the time." But he wanted every person in the room to know that he or she was "indispensable."

Lillian Brown had not made him up for his appearance; the sweat was pouring from his brow. His lips were trembling. Still he plunged on.

"I am proud of this Cabinet," he said, and of everyone who had served in his Administration. "Sure, we have done some things wrong . . . and the top man always takes the responsibility, and I have never ducked it," but they could all be proud of one fact—no one in the Nixon Administration "ever profited at the public expense or the public till. . . . Mistakes, yes. But for personal gain, never. . . . I only wish that I were a wealthy man—at the present time, I have got to find a way to pay my taxes [laughter]—and if I were, I would like to recompense you for the sacrifices that all of you have made to serve in government."

He had some advice for young people: to be strong, to be willing to sacrifice, whatever they did. "There are many fine careers. This country needs good farmers, good businessmen, good plumbers, good carpenters."

The implied reference to Teapot Dome, and the words about careers, sent his mind back to his father.

"I remember my old man. I think that they would have called him sort of a little man, a common man. He didn't consider himself that way. You know what he was? He was a streetcar motorman first, and then he was a farmer, and then he had a lemon ranch. It was the poorest lemon ranch in California, I can assure you. He sold it before they found oil on it. [Laughter] And then he was a grocer. But he was a great man, because he did his job, and every job counts up to the hilt, regardless of what happens."

The paragraph demands comment. First of all, there is the vague "they" who are going around saying hurtful things about his father. Who are "they"? The liberal professors? The left-wing politicians? The reporters and television newsmen? The idle rich? The bureaucrats? The Establishment? At one time or another in his life, Nixon had expressed contempt and disdain for all these, and many other, categories of people. Whoever "they" were, they were integral to Nixon's thought process as well as to his speeches.

Typical, too, was Nixon's charge. It was not only false, it was absurd. No one had gone around the country whispering that his father was a nobody, just a common man. To the contrary, everyone who knew and commented on Frank Nixon agreed that he was a most uncommon man. But none, in their wildest imaginations, ever thought of Frank as a great man, and never before in any way had Nixon himself indicated that he thought so.

But there was a truth behind the exaggerations of filial piety, a truth instinctively understood by millions of the Americans in Nixon's audience. Frank Nixon had worked every day of his life; had never skipped out on a debt; his word was his bond. He had loved, cherished, and cared for his wife and sons; he had taken no handouts, accepted no charity; he had met his responsibilities. He had done all that with only four years of schooling and no sophisticated skills; with crushing medical bills and dogged bad luck.

Nixon was reaching out to a large portion of the American people when he said that his father was a great man. They understood he did not mean that Frank was a great individual, but rather that he was the kind of man who made America great. He was one of those faceless millions who did the work that built the country, without government help. He was the quintessential small businessman and farmer, a part of that large number who shared an ideology that emphasized hard work and no government interference in the free marketplace. It was that group, above all others, that Nixon sprang from, represented, identified with, and reached out to in his last speech as President.

Nixon moved from his father to his mother. "Nobody will ever write a book, probably, about my mother," he said. There was, perhaps, a bit of personal regret in the sentence, as Nixon had on occasion entertained the thought of writing such a book himself. "Well, I guess all of you would say this about your mother: my mother was a saint."

At first blush, another incredible assertion. Most people would *not* say that about their mothers, and most people would not *want* a saint for a mother. But Nixon went on to provide an example of Hannah Nixon's qualities and self-sacrificing life, as he recalled the years she spent in Arizona nursing her son Harold and four other tuberculosis patients, "and seeing each of them die, and when they died, it was like one of her own." And indeed, in interviews conducted with Nixon's family and neighbors, interviews done long before 1972, people who knew Hannah Nixon frequently used the word "saint" to describe her. The word naturally came to people's minds because Hannah did live her life for others, avoided squabbles, did her best to stay above the battle, radiated calm and love, and did all this in conditions not far removed from the frontier, with a loud, argumentative, domineering husband and five sons to raise.

Hannah was a saint in the same generic sense that Frank Nixon was a great man. Hannah was one of those tens of thousands of women who went West and helped build a civilization. Without them, without their sacrifices, without their religion, the task could not have been done.

After describing his mother, Nixon turned to Ed Cox, who was holding the biography of T. R., and took the book from him. As he pulled a pair of glasses from his coat pocket and put them on—the first time he had ever worn glasses in public—he tried one of his jokes: "As you know,

I kind of like to read books. I am not educated, but I do read books [laughter]."

He said he had a T. R. quote. He said he had been reading the biography the previous evening and had run across a diary entry Roosevelt had made when his young wife suddenly died. It was a moving description of Alice Roosevelt's beauty, her love, her joy, and her tragic death. The concluding sentence was: "And when my heart's dearest died, the light went from my life forever."

Nixon lowered the book and told his audience that although T. R. had written those lines when he was in his twenties, he had in fact gone on to a lifetime of service, "always in the arena, always vital." The light never went out, Nixon stated, not until the last breath, for those who had the self-discipline to live in the darkness a while, then turn it on again.

It was odd that Nixon could have given this speech without mentioning Pat, could have been so insensitive as to read another man's description of his wife. It made many of those present, and those watching on television, wince.

Nixon went on: "We think sometimes when things happen that don't go the right way; we think that when you don't pass the bar exam the first time—I happened to, but I was just lucky; I mean, my writing was so poor the bar examiner said, 'We have just got to let the guy through.' [laughter]—We think that when someone dear to us dies, we think that when we lose an election, we think that when we suffer a defeat, that all is ended. . . .

"Not true. It is only a beginning, always. . . ."

He was giving his promise that he intended to come back, to be resurrected one more time. He was no stranger to black despair or bitter defeat, had known them as intimately as he knew soaring hopes and glorious victory, and not even this lowest point was enough to destroy Richard Nixon. He would be back. As he had launched his second bid for the Presidency in his so-called "last press conference" in 1962, so now, twelve years later in his new "farewell speech" he was launching his next campaign, for resurrection and for the title of elder statesman.

T. R., as ex-President, had "served his country always in the arena, tempestuous, strong, sometimes wrong, sometimes right, but he was a man. And as I leave, let me say, this is an example I think all of us should remember.

"Greatness comes not when things go always good for you, but the greatness comes and you are really tested when you take some knocks, some disappointments, when sadness comes, because only if you have been in the deepest valley can you ever know how magnificent it is to be on the highest mountain."

Nixon had said the words many times, but never with greater poignancy or on a more memorable occasion. Less than two years earlier, he had been in possession of the strongest and broadest mandate the American people could give him, looking forward to reigning at the two-hundredth birthday of the United States, at which time he would take his rightful place alongside the great Presidents. Today, he was in seemingly utter and permanent disgrace, the only President forced to resign.

The words came from the innermost Nixon. They expressed his deepest belief, that true greatness lies more in the testing and the response to it, less in the result. It is the game, not the outcome, that matters. As a college football player, Nixon would stride up and down the sidelines, yelling encouragement at his teammates on the field, even when the score was USC 48–Whittier 0. As an adult he had much more contempt for the idle rich than he did for the student radicals, who at least were in the arena. In Nixon's world, greatness lay in giving your all on every play.

The President concluded with some advice: "Always give your best, never get discouraged, never be petty; always remember, others may hate you, but those who hate you don't win unless you hate them, and then you destroy yourself."[45]

It is noteworthy that in the second half of that sentence Nixon used six verbs. Three of them were "hate," a fourth was "destroy," a fifth was "win."

Tricia wrote in her diary that day that her father's words had "come from the heart" and were thus "unique." In her view, "at last the 'real' Nixon was being revealed as only he could reveal himself."[46]

Nixon paused and looked around the room. It was excruciating to look at him, impossible not to. He gave his farewell: "And so, we leave with high hopes, in good spirits, and with deep humility, and with very much gratefulness in our hearts. . . . Not only will we always remember you, not only will we always be grateful to you but always you will be in our hearts and you will be in our prayers.

"Thank you very much."[47]

THE crowd rose, cheering and applauding, as it had done when he entered the room fifteen minutes earlier.

Nixon walked with his family to the Diplomatic Reception Room, where the Fords were waiting for them. Nixon shook hands with Ford and wished him good luck.

Together, the Nixons and the Fords walked to the South Lawn. At the end of a scarlet carpet and a corridor of honor guards from the military services, an olive drab Marine helicopter stood waiting to take the President on his last ride from the White House out to Andrews Air Force Base.

"My heavens," Pat said, "they've even rolled out the red carpet for us. Well, Betty, you'll see many of these red carpets, and you'll get so you hate 'em."[48]

Julie kissed her father. David and Ford kissed Pat. Betty Ford kissed Nixon. Pat, Ed, and Tricia—along with Ziegler, Steve Bull, Jack Brennan, Manolo and Fina Sanchez—climbed into the helicopter (Julie and David were staying behind to oversee the packing).

At the last moment, just before boarding, Nixon reached out for Ford's hand, shook it warmly, and then touched Ford's elbow with his left hand, rather like a coach sending in a substitute. "Goodbye, Mr. President," he said.

Nixon mounted the steps to the helicopter. When he reached the top, he turned and jerked an awkward wave with his right arm. He was fighting back the tears. His mouth was turned down at the corners, his jowls sagged, his eyes narrowed.

In pain, but a proud man, he lifted both arms. He spread his first two fingers in his familiar "V-for-Victory" sign. His eyes opened, his head came up, his jowls lifted, and he broke into a huge smile. It was a moment etched forever into the memories of the millions who watched.

AT Andrews, a crowd had gathered. Nixon made no remarks, but as he climbed into *Air Force One* he gave another wave. On the plane Nixon sat alone. At twelve noon, as *Air Force One* cruised over Missouri, Nixon's resignation went into effect. Three minutes later, Ford completed the oath of office. Nixon did not watch or listen to the ceremony so he did not hear the new President's opening sentence of his inaugural address: "Our long national nightmare is over."[49]

CHAPTER NINETEEN

"THEY TOOK IT
ALL AWAY FROM ME"
August 9–September 8, 1974

AT NOON, Eastern time, August 9, 1974, *Air Force One* changed its call sign to SAM 27000. Nixon sat in silence in his padded swivel chair in his cabin office. Pat was alone in her small, private compartment, separated from her husband by a sliding partition.[1]

As the big jet made its final approach to the runway at El Toro Marine Base, Nixon looked out the window and saw a scene familiar to him. The parking lot was full, with hundreds of cars still trying to get in, and thousands of people waiting behind the fences along the runway. The plane touched down at 11:56 A.M. Pacific time. When it came to a stop, Nixon went to the open doorway. As the crowd began to cheer, he threw up his arms in the V-for-Victory salute. He descended the stairs, walked to the fence, and began shaking hands. Someone started singing "God Bless America." It caught on, and soon five thousand or more joined in a dissonant refrain. All along the fence, people were crying as they sang.

A voice called out, "Whittier's still for you, Dick." Nixon had planned to go straight to the waiting helicopter for the short flight to La Casa Pacifica, but on hearing the words of support, he decided to go first to the waiting battery of microphones. Slowly the singing died down, and he began to speak.

"Many statements have been made and this is not the time to bore you with another one," he began. "It is appropriate for me to say very simply this: having completed one task does not mean that we will just sit back and enjoy this marvelous California climate and do nothing." He said some more nice words about California, then about "this great plane" that had taken him to China, to Russia, to the Middle East, then about America being a nation with more freedom and more opportunity than any other. And finally, "I am going to continue to work for peace among all the world. I intend to continue to work for opportunity and understanding among the people in America."[2]

He had been through it so many times before, more times than anyone could possibly count—the arrival at the airport, the waiting crowd, the big smile and outstretched arms at the airplane door, working the crowd along the fence, the microphones, the speech praising the local weather, the promise to keep working for peace and freedom, the praise of America as number one—that the words came automatically to the old pro.

This time, however, apparently would be the last time.

Nixon and Pat, along with Tricia and Ed Cox, walked over to the waiting helicopter. It was an ordinary camouflage brown Marine Huey, the kind used in Vietnam, and it was a signal of Nixon's changed circumstances; in the past, he had flown from El Toro to La Casa Pacifica in a beautifully finished, white-topped helicopter with red-covered seats.[3]

The engine roared, the helicopter rose into the air, the crowd waved, cheered, and sobbed. Fifteen minutes later, it landed at the Coast Guard station adjoining La Casa Pacifica. The Nixons smiled at the Secret Service agents waiting, then got into a golf cart for the three-minute ride to their home.

Nixon went straight to the telephone. He called Haig, to demand that all of his records, papers, and the tapes be sent to San Clemente immediately.[4]

Thus began a struggle for the Nixon presidential materials and tapes. It was destined to last for seventeen years and more; at this writing, it still has not been resolved.

Two days earlier, in his Lincoln Sitting Room conversation with Kissinger, Nixon had wondered what history would say about him. Kissinger assured him that history would be kinder to him than his contemporaries. Nixon had replied, as he always did, "It depends who writes the history."

That was only partly true. It would also depend on the sources the historians had available to them. Knowing that, and knowing where the sources were and what was in them, Nixon's first act as a former President was to continue the cover-up. He wanted his tapes, his papers, his documents, so that he could decide what could be seen, and by whom, and when. Possession of the sources would allow him to dominate the writing of the history of his Administration. It would also provide him with essential and invaluable material for the writing of his own memoirs, which was one reason—perhaps the number-one reason—he had made the tapes in the first place.

In demanding the taped and written record of his Administration,

Nixon was within his rights. There was ample, indeed overwhelming, precedent. When George Washington returned to his home at Mount Vernon, he took his papers with him. So did his successors, and each of them was free to do with those papers whatever he wished. James Monroe, beset by debts in his old age, sold his. Martin Van Buren destroyed correspondence he deemed to be "of little value." Robert Todd Lincoln destroyed large parts of his father's papers, and held onto the rest. When he died in 1926, he gave the papers to the Library of Congress, but with the proviso that they remain closed until twenty-one years after his death; as a result, Abraham Lincoln's papers did not become available to the public and to scholars until 1947, eighty-two years after his death. Ulysses S. Grant sold his papers in what amounted to a public auction.

Theodore Roosevelt, William Howard Taft, and the widow of Woodrow Wilson all gave their papers to the Library of Congress, but the widows of Warren Harding and Calvin Coolidge did not (Mrs. Harding was eager to conceal as much as possible of her late husband's extramarital affairs). Herbert Hoover placed his papers in the Hoover Institution on the campus of his alma mater, Stanford University (in 1962 they were moved to the Hoover Library in West Branch, Iowa).

Franklin Roosevelt created the first Presidential Library, at Hyde Park, and established the method still in use—the library building was constructed with private funds, but the National Archives managed and maintained the building and its contents. This practice became law with the Presidential Libraries Act of 1955; that act gave the National Archives authority to accept any privately constructed structure housing presidential papers, and to provide the professional archivists to manage the collection. Truman established his library in Independence, Missouri; Eisenhower set his up in Abilene, Kansas. Kennedy's went to Boston, Johnson's to Austin.[5]

The Presidential Libraries Act carefully avoided any reference to the ownership of presidential papers. There had been arguments that the papers of an Administration should be public property, on the grounds that the President and his aides were doing the public's business at the public's expense. But the traditional private property claim remained in place, even though precedent from Theodore Roosevelt through Lyndon Johnson was strongly on the side of the President's papers being made available to the public and the scholarly community, and that they should be given to the government, not sold to private collectors.

From the time of his election in 1968, even before assuming office, Nixon had initiated a systematic collection of documents and papers with the view of their eventual transfer to a Nixon Library. A small team from the National Archives was attached to the White House for that purpose. But two events ensued that turned what had been a matter of concern only to archivists and scholars into a public controversy. One was Nixon's tax deduction for the donation of his vice presidential papers to the National Archives. The outrage that followed led to the introduction of bills in Congress—none of which had passed by August 1974—declaring papers produced by government workers in the course of government work to be public property.

The second event began on August 9, when Nixon called Haig and demanded that his papers, tapes, and other documents be sent to San Clemente immediately. The following day, Haig circulated a memorandum for the White House staff. "By custom and tradition," it began, "the files of the White House Office belong to the President in whose Administration they are accumulated. It has been the invariable practice, at the end of an Administration, for the outgoing President or his estate to authorize the depository or disposition to be made of such files." The memo instructed the staff to keep the papers of the Nixon Administration separate from those of the Ford Administration, and concluded with a statement from William Howard Taft, "The retiring President takes with him all the correspondence, original and copies, which he carried on during his administration."[6]

The process of getting Nixon's papers to him, or destroying documents, had already begun. After Ford took the oath of office on Friday, August 9, he had moved into an Oval Office that had been stripped clean. Bob Hartmann moved into the small adjacent office that Rose Mary Woods had used. It was, he noted, "heavy with the acrid smell of paper recently burned in the fireplace."[7]

BEFORE she left, Woods had turned to Marine Master Sergeant Bill Gulley, administrator of the White House military affairs office, in charge of most of the logistics of the Presidency, including communications and transportation. Gulley was a can-do, no-questions-asked Marine. Shortly before the resignation, Woods had told him that the President (Nixon) had some "personal things he wants done." On Friday morning, as Nixon was saying farewell to the Cabinet and White House staff, Gulley slipped into the family quarters and picked up eleven or twelve sealed boxes. From their heft, he guessed that they contained papers and documents. Without informing anyone on the staff, Gulley had the boxes trucked to Andrews Air Force Base and ordered them loaded onto an unmarked JetStar.[8]

As that was happening, a thirty-two-year-old lawyer on Ford's vice presidential staff, Benton Becker, walked past the Burn Room of the White House. He noted that it was so jammed with bags of paper waiting to be destroyed that the overflow was piling up in the corridor. The paper shredder was also working overtime. A week earlier, when Hartmann had been told that Nixon aides were "hauling suitcases and boxes out of here [the White House]," he had put Becker in charge of preserving the records so that there could be some continuity of government. So, on August 10, Becker on his own authority ordered the burning and paper shredding stopped.[9]

Late that night, however, Becker found three military trucks lined up outside the basement entrance to the West Wing, stuffed with boxes and file cabinets, about to depart for Andrews Air Force Base. When he learned what was happening, Becker told the Air Force colonel in charge, "This truck does not move."

"I take my instruction from General Haig," the colonel replied.

"Let's go see him right now," Becker retorted.

Haig was in his office. He claimed ignorance of what was happening and ordered the colonel to unload the trucks. To make certain that he did, Becker watched until the unloading was complete. "I had no illusions about Haig," Becker said in a 1983 interview, "and so I went outside and watched that son of a bitch unload."[10] He then told Hartmann what had happened; together they consulted with Phil Buchen, head of the Ford transition team. They agreed that the disposition of the papers was a decision that the new President would have to make, and that Becker had done the right thing.[11]

As to who ordered the removal, no one ever found out. It might have been Haig, or it could have been Gulley, or perhaps Nixon's military aide, Marine Colonel Jack Brennan (who was in San Clemente with Nixon). Whoever did it, it was part of a pattern. As Nixon's aides saw it, the White House was like an embassy or an infantry division headquarters being overrun by the enemy. The aides wanted to rescue what they could, destroy what they could not. The invaders, Ford's people, wanted to take the headquarters intact.

The principals in this unseemly but inevitable struggle were Al Haig and Bob Hartmann. Haig was retaining his office and his authority; Hartmann wanted to relieve him of both. There were many obvious reasons for Hartmann's attitude, but the most important was that he felt Haig's loyalty was to Nixon, not Ford. He called Haig and the other Nixon holdovers "the Praetorians." They continued to regard Nixon as the boss, and had the irritating, indeed, infuriating habit of referring to Ford as "Jerry." Of course, they were not acting exclusively for Nixon; as Haig and his friends took possession of or destroyed documents, they were protecting themselves as well.

OUT in San Clemente, Nixon spent the weekend in near seclusion. Bebe Rebozo and Bob Abplanalp joined him. He was close to a state of shock, unresponsive for the most part, making only an occasional phone call. It was a time to catch his breath, recover his composure. Ziegler and Brennan protected him.

On Sunday afternoon, August 11, Gulley showed up in a rented car.

He told Ziegler he needed to see Nixon, to give him something. Impossible, Ziegler replied. Gulley went in search of Steve Bull, who had also joined the small staff in San Clemente. He found Bull in his office, conferring with Brennan, and told them that he had a dozen cartons from the family quarters in the car that he wanted to give to Nixon. Further, he wanted them to know that there was a "shitload" of material at the White House, in the EOB, and in a government warehouse at Fort Meyer, Virginia. If Nixon wanted it, they would have to move quickly; Ford's people were already trying to lock the doors. Brennan and Bull saw the point and asked Gulley to return to Washington to begin shipping the stuff out immediately. Gulley said he would do it, using C-141s to transport the materials—each plane could carry 50,000 pounds.[12]

Gulley was right about the need for haste. As he started shipping stuff out to San Clemente "as fast as it fell into my hands, things that weren't yet under lock and key,"[13] the reporters began questioning Ford's press secretary Jerry terHorst about what was happening to Nixon's papers. He checked with Fred Buzhardt (still in charge in the White House legal office), who said the papers belonged to Nixon, based not on statute but on unbroken tradition. When terHorst passed that opinion on to the reporters, they wanted to know if the Special Prosecutor, Jaworski, concurred. TerHorst said he assumed so. But Jaworski immediately let it be known that his office had been merely "informed" of Buzhardt's ruling, not consulted, and did not concur.

That exchange put the heat on Ford. How could he possibly take the opinion of Nixon's lawyer on the question of ownership and possession of Nixon's papers and tapes at a time when Nixon's principal assistants were about to go on trial and Nixon himself might well be indicted? Ford therefore decided to name Phil Buchen a counsel to the President, and asked him to consult with everyone concerned—the Special Prosecutor, the White House legal office, and Nixon.

There were pressures coming from various directions. Nixon wanted his papers and had a strong claim to them. Ford wanted to get rid of them, and had no legal reason to hold onto them (there were no outstanding subpoenas against the papers). Ehrlichman, Haldeman, and Mitchell, about to go on trial, wanted access to them for their defense. Reporters wanted them for investigative stories. Beyond these and other specific claims, and beyond the fishing expeditions of reporters, there was the public's right to know what had happened in the Nixon Administration, including but not limited to Watergate. The public would never find out if Nixon got possession of the record—or so at least Nixon's enemies, most neutral observers, and even some of his friends assumed.

On August 15, terHorst announced Buchen's appointment and said that Buzhardt "has not yet resigned, but will resign." Simultaneously, Buchen met with Jaworski; they agreed that no Nixon papers would be shipped to California "pending further discussions." The temporary hold included all of Nixon's personal papers, tapes, and documents, "and not just those that might have a bearing on the Watergate affair." Buchen said that this development "in no way constitutes a denial that the materials are the personal property of the former President."[14]

Out in California, Nixon was beginning to realize the reality of his new position. Jack Brennan later said that it was during the first week of the exile that a deep sadness started to replace the sense of shock, a "sadness brought on by the sense of all that had been lost."[15] Or, as Nixon put it in a 1990 interview, "No one who has been in the Presidency with the capacity and power to affect the course of events can ever be satisfied with not being there."[16]

He hated being passive. For five and a half years he had been accustomed to making the decisions; now he was the recipient. Instead of acting, he was being acted upon.

He made repeated, and reportedly abusive, telephone calls to Haig, demanding his papers. Nixon was convinced that Ford was double-crossing him, reneging on a commitment to ship him his papers. Haig turned the pressure onto Ford. Becker recalled that "virtually every Nixon staff person that Gerald Ford inherited, and specifically referring to Alexander Haig, urged Ford . . . to send all of those documents, papers, and tapes back to their rightful owner." But Becker was opposed. In one Oval Office session between Becker, Ford, and Haig, he told the President that if he complied with Haig's demands, "history will record this as the final act of cover-up—there will be one hell of a bonfire in San Clemente."[17]

According to Gulley, enough material had already been flown out to start a hell of a bonfire—some 200 tons worth. Brennan, however, denies that anything like that amount arrived.[18] Whatever the quantity, and whatever the quality of those documents, what happened to them is a mystery.

There is another problem, namely, how on earth could Nixon have produced so many personal "papers"? The answer is that of course he did not, that these were the papers of his Administration. They included every document, almost, churned out in the White House from January 20, 1969, to August 9, 1974. They ranged from Haldeman's and Ehrlichman's handwritten notes of meetings with the President to copies of thank-you notes, birthday greetings, and the like, along with no one knows how many copies of such items as the daily News Summaries (which alone averaged fifty pages for each *day* of the five and a half years).

Gulley flew back to San Clemente. This time he had no trouble seeing Nixon. He found the former President looking ravaged. His eyes were red-rimmed and hollow, his demeanor was tense.

"What are those bastards going to do to me?" Nixon demanded.

"They're after your ass," Gulley replied. He said Hartmann and other Ford aides "are referring to you as a crook."

"I'm not going to deal with those . . . bastards," Nixon proclaimed. "I'm entitled to anything that any other former President is entitled to. Goddam, you know what I did for Johnson, and you know what I did for Ike and Truman, and goddam it, I expect to be treated the same way. When I travel, I expect military aircraft; I expect the same support I provided. I expect communications and medical personnel, everything they had. And, goddam it, you tell Ford I expect it."[19]

On August 20, Ford called Nixon on the telephone, but not to talk about his papers. Instead, the President—as a courtesy—wanted to give Nixon advance word on his selection of a new Vice President. It would be Nelson Rockefeller. Whatever feelings that news produced in Nixon, he said only that Rockefeller's name and experience in foreign policy would help Ford internationally. The extreme right wing of the Republican Party would be upset, Nixon concluded, but Ford should not worry about that because he could never please the reactionaries anyway.[20]

Two days later, Ford turned his attention to Nixon's papers. Tons of them, literally, were being packaged, boxed, and then stored on the fourth floor of the EOB. The Secret Service expressed a fear that the floor might collapse. Ford wanted to be rid of them, just as he wanted to be rid of Watergate, and come to that be rid of the problem of Mr. Nixon. He asked his Attorney General, William Saxbe, for an opinion; Saxbe said that tradition and precedent were clear, the papers belonged to Nixon, and he recommended that they be sent to California immediately.[21]

Adding to the pressure on Ford was the possibility of a grand jury indictment of Nixon, which would be followed by a subpoena for evidence. A Nixon indictment would do Ford no good, and much harm; a Nixon trial would be worse. Nixon, meanwhile, received a subpoena to give a deposition in a pending civil trial. "Do you think the people want to pick the carcass?" he plaintively asked a Republican congressman on the telephone.[22] A Gallup Poll taken that week showed 56 percent of the respondents favored a criminal trial for Nixon.[23]

There was talk of doing just that. A number of Jaworski's young assistants wanted to put Nixon in the dock with Ehrlichman, Haldeman, and Mitchell. In Nixon's view, "they were following the dictum . . . 'It is not enough to kill an adversary. He must first be dishonored.' "[24]

Senator Eastland went to see Jaworski. According to Jaworski, "He said he had just talked with Nixon, that Nixon had called from San Clemente. 'He was crying,' Eastland said. 'He said, "Jim, don't let Jaworski put me in that trial with Haldeman and Ehrlichman. I can't take any more." ' Eastland shook his head. 'He's in bad shape, Leon.' "[25]

On August 27, Nixon hired a new lawyer, Herbert J. Miller (St. Clair had returned to Boston shortly after the resignation). Miller had previously served as counsel for Kleindienst, the former Attorney General, and had earned a reputation as a plea bargainer, because after extended discussions with Jaworski he had made it possible for Kleindienst to plead guilty to a misdemeanor and receive a suspended sentence. Seymour Hersh reported in *The New York Times* that Miller's first goal "will be to try to persuade Leon Jaworski not to seek an indictment of Nixon."[26]

THE possibility of a pardon, which had always been in the back of the minds of all the participants in this drama, now became an acutely pressing subject. Democratic politicians, the Special Prosecutor's staff, the media, Sam Dash, and the public generally were all putting nearly irresistible pressure on Jaworski to indict Nixon. A commonly held view, at least the most often expressed view, was that Nixon should go to trial so that the public could learn "the truth about Watergate." This was held to be only fair, as his principal subordinates were already indicted (their trials were scheduled to begin on September 30). On August 22, the House Judiciary Committee released its final report; it detailed "clear and convincing evidence" that Nixon had obstructed justice thirty-six times, that he had "condoned, encouraged . . . directed, coached and personally helped to fabricate" perjury, and that he had abused power through misuse of such agencies as the FBI, CIA, and IRS. The report was approved by the full House by an astonishing vote of 412 to 3. Meanwhile the American Bar Association had approved without dissent a resolution at its national convention that the law must be applied impartially, "regardless of the position or status of any individual alleged to have violated the law." In short, the ABA wanted Nixon put on trial.

Two assumptions accompanied these views: first, that Nixon would be found guilty; second, that he would then be pardoned, on the grounds that almost no one wanted to see a former President put in jail. Another possibility, pardon before indictment, Ford had apparently ruled out at his confirmation hearing when he said that the American people would not stand for that.

But Ford had said that before he became President, before he learned that the nation's obsession with Nixon had not come to an end with the resignation, before he realized that great chunks of his valuable time would have to be wasted on questions concerning the past rather than dealing with the future. What to do about Nixon's papers and tapes was a bad enough problem; if Nixon were to be indicted, it would get worse; if Nixon were put on trial, it would tear the country apart, with who could say what consequences for the Ford Presidency (none would be good, that was certain).

On August 28, all this began to come to a head. Scheduled to hold his first news conference, Ford met with his aides to go over probable questions. At the top of the list were the disposition of Nixon's papers, and the possibility of a pardon. Leonard Garment, still on the White House staff, sent a memorandum to Haig and Buchen for the meeting. It was an impassioned plea for an immediate pardon. Garment cited Nixon's mental and physical condition, hinted that Nixon's life could be at stake, and warned that "unless the President himself takes action by announcing a pardon today, he will very likely lose control of the situation."

Garment's memo was accompanied by a draft presidential statement announcing a pardon, written by Ray Price. In justifying an immediate pardon, Price wrote, "there is no way that he [Nixon] could be given a fair trial by an unbiased jury."[27] Republicans had already been preparing the ground for a pardon. Senate Leader Hugh Scott had said Nixon had suffered enough. Rockefeller on national television said he agreed with Scott.

At Ford's news conference, Helen Thomas of UPI asked the first question. She wanted to know if Ford agreed with Scott and Rockefeller, "and specifically, would you use your pardon authority, if necessary?"

"I subscribe to that point of view," Ford answered, referring to the Scott/Rockefeller statements, but added that no charges had been made, and until a legal process had begun, "I think it is unwise and untimely for me to make any commitment."

Press commentary on these statements was friendly to Ford. The reporters read into his replies a definite intention to treat Nixon with compassion and to reserve the option of intervening, if need be, to spare him the ultimate humiliation of a prison cell. *The Washington Post*'s headline read: "PRESIDENT HINTS HE WOULD WEIGH PARDONING NIXON," qualified by a line in the lead story, "if charges are brought against him in the courts." *The New York Times* headline read: "FORD SAYS HE VIEWS NIXON AS PUNISHED ENOUGH NOW; PARDON OPTION KEPT OPEN."[28]

The following day, the need to act became urgent, as the Justice Department announced that a U.S. marshal had served two subpoenas on Nixon in San Clemente. The first called for his testimony as a defense witness at the request of Ehrlichman; the second called for his deposition in a civil suit growing out of a campaign rally (Nixon foes charged they had been illegally excluded). Those developments were pleasing to those who wanted to see Nixon harassed, but the Nixon-haters were infuriated by a request Ford made that day to the Congress for funds for Nixon to cover the cost of the transition. The amount he asked for was $850,000, and that was only a beginning. In addition, the GSA would maintain the office complex outside the gates of La Casa Pacifica indefinitely. Further, the GSA said Nixon was entitled to the services of "as many Federal

employees as he asks for to help during a six-month transition period."
In addition, by statute, the Secret Service would continue to guard Nixon.
None of these expenses were included in the $850,000 request.[29]

That same day, Haig told Ford that unless he moved quickly to
announce a full pardon for Nixon, the former President might suffer "a
personal and national tragedy."[30] Haig has denied saying this, as he has
denied any direct involvement in pushing Ford to issue a pardon at any
time. Why he is so insistent on his lack of involvement is something of
a puzzle—why on earth shouldn't he implore Ford to pardon his former
boss? As Bob Hartmann notes, what could be more natural or normal?[31]
Of course, there is this point: a pardon for Nixon was, in effect, a pardon
for Haig and whatever he may have done in the time he was Nixon's chief
of staff, about which we know very much less than we do about what
Haldeman, Ehrlichman, Mitchell, et al. were up to when they worked
for Nixon.

It is clear that Haig was in close telephone contact with Nixon
throughout this period. In addition, he was hearing from other members
of the Nixon family. Rebozo and Abplanalp had urged Julie, Tricia, Ed,
and David to contact Haig about Nixon's health. They had done so. After
Ford's news conference, David called the President from San Clemente.
He said his father-in-law was in a sorry physical and emotional state. One
moment Nixon was up, almost euphoric; the next he was down, depressed
and despairing. If something was not done, if the burden was not lifted,
David said, Nixon "might go off the deep end."[32] Implied but unsaid was
the question, how would Ford like it if there was a suicide? (There was
apparently little danger of that. A day later, Nixon entered into an agreement with agent Irving Paul "Swifty" Lazar; Lazar would find a publisher
for Nixon's memoirs, and would seek to obtain a $2 million advance.)[33]

On August 30, Gulley flew to San Clemente. Contrary to what the
White House was hearing from La Casa Pacifica, he found Nixon "a little
calmer. He was less formal, less tough-talking. I told him that the President and Mrs. Ford sent their best wishes to him and Mrs. Nixon, which
was a lie. But it had an effect on him."

Nixon wanted to talk. He said he had heard there was "a lot of
bitterness" in Washington. "I expect that," he went on, "but I want to
know specifically what their plans are. I want to know when I get my
papers. When do I get my personal effects?"

Gulley had no answers, but he was able to say that Ford had decided
Nixon should be sent briefing papers, intelligence evaluations, and the
like (as Nixon had done for Johnson, and Johnson for Eisenhower). Nixon
asked if he would have the use of military aircraft.

"I said no, that in fact there was a possibility he might have to pay
for the planes that had been used by and for him so far" to ship papers
to California. There had even been talk about making Nixon pay for the

use of *Air Force One* from Kansas City to El Toro on August 9, that is, for that part of the flight when he had been a private person.

"Well, if that's what the bastards want, I'll pay," Nixon said.

As the meeting was ending, Nixon said he wanted to give Gulley a memento. He asked Steve Bull to bring in a watch with the presidential seal. As he handed over the watch, Nixon said, "I really appreciate you being available. I'd like you to know that nothing more can hurt me, but associating with me can hurt those who do. You should always keep that in mind, because the media aren't going to let up on me. This is not going to satisfy them; they won't be satisfied until they have me in jail."[34]

SIMULTANEOUSLY, Ford was meeting in the Oval Office with Haig, Buchen, former Congressman and aide Jack Marsh, and Hartmann, to discuss a pardon. He told Buchen to do some research; if it turned out that he had the authority to pardon before an indictment, he was inclined to do so. Haig cleared his throat and asked to be excused. Ford waved him back down into his chair. The President then outlined his reasons: to avoid the degrading spectacle of a former President in the prisoner's dock in a criminal court; the difficulty, not to say impossibility, of meeting Supreme Court standards for an unbiased jury; the length of time that would be involved, with the Watergate obsession continuing; and finally, the obvious fact that if Nixon were convicted, whoever was President would certainly have to pardon him.

Then Ford made the inevitable, irrefutable point: "If eventually, why not now?"

Buchen said he could not argue with Ford's feelings about what was right, "but is this the right time?"

Ford returned to his basic point: "Will there *ever* be a right time?"

Haig said nothing, and left when Ford had to take a telephone call. To Hartmann, "it was obvious that Al wanted to be able to call upon the three of us as witnesses that he had not raised his voice as a pardon advocate."[35]

Buchen and Becker met with Nixon's lawyer Herbert Miller to discuss what would happen to Nixon's papers and tapes. They came up with a two-key solution: Nixon, or his agent, would hold one key, while Ford, or his agent, would hold the other. The agreement was that Nixon's papers and tapes would be shipped to a federal facility near San Clemente. Nixon and the government would share formal ownership. The written material would be available for court subpoenas for three to five years. Access would be limited to Nixon or his agents, but no originals could be removed. After five years, Nixon could dispose of them any way he pleased (presumably they would be deeded to the government for the Nixon Library, as prior presidential papers had been handled).

The tapes were another matter. For the first five years they would remain under government custody (i.e., the General Services Administration, or GSA, responsible for the Federal Archives and Records Service); only Nixon or his agent could listen to them; they could not be removed or destroyed. After five years, legal title would pass to the government, but Nixon could then direct the GSA to destroy some or all of them. Upon Nixon's death, or at the end of ten years, on September 1, 1984, all the original tapes automatically would be destroyed.[36]

From the point of view of Nixon's enemies, that was a sweetheart of a deal for the former President, allowing him to legally carry out the ultimate cover-up. From Nixon's point of view, he would be giving up a lot if he agreed—clear title to and possession of his own papers and tapes—and getting relatively little, as the material would still be subject to subpoena, open to any fishing expedition any prosecutor or court (or Jaworski) wanted to undertake.

Except that Nixon anticipated a presidential pardon. When that happened, Nixon would be immune from prosecution, and it would be difficult if not impossible to get at his papers via a subpoena.

The following day, September 4, Jaworski gave Buchen a letter in which he indicated he would not include Nixon in the upcoming Mitchell trial, but that the grand jury might go ahead and make a separate indictment of Nixon. If that happened, Jaworski warned, it would be nine months to a year, "and perhaps even longer," before the selection of a jury could begin. Given the anticipated difficulty in jury selection, it would be well into 1976 before a trial could start.[37] For Ford, for the Republican Party, for the nation, that would be a nightmare continued.

On Ford's instructions, therefore, Buchen let Miller know that Ford was considering a pardon. But there was a price: "I think it's important that there be a statement of true contrition from the former President. . . . I hope you would persuade your client to develop something that would tell the world, 'Yes, he did it, and he's accepting the pardon because he's guilty.' " Miller promised to get Nixon's reaction. He said he would go to San Clemente to do so, and asked that Becker accompany him.[38]

Ford met with Becker just before he left. Haig was present. In last-minute instructions, Ford authorized Becker to say, "It's not final, but in all probability, a pardon will be forthcoming." He should insist on a clear statement of contrition from Nixon.

"You'll never get it," Haig warned.

"Be very firm out there," Ford ordered, "and tell me what you see."[39]

EIGHT hours later, Miller and Becker were in San Clemente. Ron Ziegler met them. He said, "Mr. Becker, let me tell you this right now, President Nixon is not issuing any statement whatsoever regarding Watergate, whether Jerry Ford pardons him or not." Becker suspected Haig had telephoned to warn Nixon of what was coming.[40]

Becker threatened to turn around and leave. Miller succeeded in calming both men down, and they agreed to meet the next morning.

Over the next two days, Becker negotiated, primarily with Ziegler, over the deal that had already been struck with Miller on the tapes and papers. Not content with the major victory he had already won on the deal, Nixon now demanded final authority on granting access, plus a reduction from ten to five years in the time period before he was allowed to destroy the tapes. He got both concessions, inevitably, as Ziegler and Nixon knew (from Haig?) that Ford was in a hurry to grant the pardon.

With the compromise over Nixon's papers worked out, Becker and Ziegler went after a Nixon statement following a pardon. Ziegler offered a draft that dwelled on the pressures of the office of the President, on the necessity for reliance on the judgment and honesty of the White House staff, on the President's preoccupation with foreign affairs, and concluded by acknowledging only that Nixon should have delegated less authority.

When Ziegler asked Becker what he thought of it, Becker said the obvious, that *no* statement would be better than that. Ziegler met with Nixon, returned with a new version, heard Becker turn it down, and went back to Nixon. Two more times they went through the process, until Becker—still not satisfied—decided that the fourth draft was probably the best he was going to get from Nixon and said he would take it back to Washington for Ford to consider.

Then Becker asked to see Nixon. Ziegler at first refused, but Miller persuaded him it would do no harm.

Becker entered Nixon's small, bare office, and was shocked at the former President's appearance. "He looked terrible," Becker later reported to Ford. "He appeared to have aged and shrunken in the month since his resignation. His jowls were loose and flabby, and his shirt seemed to be too big for his neck. . . . His handshake was very weak."

Becker told Nixon he had reached an agreement with Miller and Ziegler on the papers and tapes. He went to the subject of pardon, and tried to explain to Nixon that the precedent was that acceptance of a pardon was an acknowledgment of guilt.

Nixon seemed uninterested. He asked Becker where he lived. Washington, Becker replied.

"How are the Redskins going to do this year?" Nixon asked.

"I really don't know, Mr. President," Becker replied. "We have some important things to talk about. Let's talk about them." Again he made the point that acceptance of a pardon constituted an admission of guilt.

"Uh-huh," Nixon replied.

After twenty minutes of listening to himself talk, Becker left. As he walked out to the driveway, Ziegler called him back. Nixon wanted to see him again.

"You've been a fine young man," Nixon told Becker. "You've been a gentleman. We've had enough bullies." His voice faltered, he looked away. Recovering, Nixon said, "I want to give you something. But look around the office. I don't have anything any more. They took it all away from me."

"That's all right, Mr. President," Becker said.

"No, no, no," Nixon went on. "I asked Pat to get these for me." He opened a desk drawer and pulled out two little boxes containing cuff links and a tie pin. "She got these out of my own jewelry box," Nixon said. "There aren't any more in the whole world. I want you to have them."

Becker got out of there as fast as he decently could, flew back to Washington, and reported to Ford.

"I'm not a medical doctor," he said, "but I really have serious questions in my mind whether that man is going to be alive at the time of the election."

"Well," Ford replied, "1976 is a long time away."

"I don't mean 1976," Becker said. "I mean 1974."[41]

In an interview ten years later, Becker said he found Nixon to be "an absolute candidate for suicide; the most depressed human being I have ever met, and I didn't think it was an act." He added that he conveyed that impression to Ford.[42]

Act or not, depressed or not, Nixon was moving fast to protect his reputation. He began working with Ziegler on a softening of his statement. When Becker discovered what was up in a telephone conversation with Ziegler, he told Ford, "I'm afraid if this continues, we'll be back to square one."

"We can't tolerate any weakened statement," Ford replied. "Call Ziegler back and tell him that." Becker did, and Nixon gave it up.[43]

He already had what he needed anyway, a statement that admitted no criminal action. Haig had it absolutely right; Nixon was never, ever, going to admit to a guilt he did not feel. In a September 5 interview with the Los Angeles Times, David Eisenhower expressed Nixon's view of the causes and meaning of Watergate. "Fifteen years hence the offense is going to look pretty small," David said. Nixon "simply acquiesced in the non-prosecution of aides who covered up a little operation into the opposition's political headquarters, which is a practice that was fairly established in Washington for a long time and that no one took that seriously."[44]

None of Nixon's predecessors were around to comment.

Even though he was not being forced to admit to any guilt, Nixon claimed to be reluctant to accept the pardon. Fifteen years later he called it "the hardest blow" he had to endure. He took it only after long talks with Miller had convinced him he was "utterly defenseless." He further claimed that he told Miller his first concern was that a pardon would "hurt Ford politically." Miller convinced him that while that was true in the short run, over the long term Ford would benefit from putting Watergate behind him.

Perhaps more telling was what Nixon described as "my desperate financial situation." Miller told him that attorneys' fees and the other costs of defending actions against him "would bankrupt me." (This from the man who had just been told by the most famous agent in America that his advance on his memoirs could reach $2 million.) Most telling was Miller's argument that "I had taken as much physically, mentally, and emotionally as I could and that I should accept the pardon for my own well-being and my family's as well." Besides, he could never get a fair trial.

According to Nixon, he allowed himself to be convinced that he should accept the pardon. "Next to the resignation," Nixon wrote in 1990, "accepting the pardon was the most painful decision of my political career." He added that the statement he issued at the time "accurately describes my feelings then and now."[45]

ON Sunday morning, September 8, Ford went on national radio and television from the Oval Office. There had been no prior announcement. After a short speech explaining his reasons, he read his pardon proclamation, granting Nixon "a full, free and absolute pardon . . . for all offenses against the United States which he . . . has committed or may have committed or taken part in during the period from January 20, 1969, through August 9, 1974." He then signed the proclamation.[46]

From San Clemente, Ziegler released Nixon's statement of acceptance. The former President said, "I was wrong in not acting more decisively and more forthrightly in dealing with Watergate, particularly when it reached the stage of judicial proceedings and grew from a political scandal into a national tragedy.

"No words can describe the depths of my regret and pain at the anguish my mistakes over Watergate have caused the nation and the Presidency—a nation I so deeply love and an institution I so greatly respect."

He expressed the "hope" that Ford's "compassionate act" would lift "the burden of Watergate" from the nation. He admitted that "others" believed he had acted illegally. He said he understood how his "own mistakes and misjudgments . . . seemed to support" that belief, and that he had dealt with Watergate in the "wrong way." That was a "burden I shall bear for every day of the life that is left to me."[47]

There was outrage both at the pardon and at Nixon's self-serving statement. Ford's Gallup Poll approval rating plunged in a month from 71 percent to 49 percent, the biggest single drop in the history of the poll. His press secretary and old friend Jerry terHorst resigned in protest, shocked that Ford would pardon Nixon "without getting in return a signed confession."[48]

Second-guessing began immediately, and still goes on. It was said that the surprise of the thing was what hurt most; the Sunday morning announcement, with no preparation, added to the inevitable impression that Ford had cut a deal with Nixon, a pardon for his resignation. It would have been preferable, some said, for Ford to have leaked his intention, giving Republicans a chance to line up behind a pardon. It would have been better had he brought Republican leaders into the Oval Office with him, to show support. It would have been better had he waited. It would have been better had he simply issued the pardon without a statement from Nixon, or indeed any contact with Nixon at all. It would have been better had he pointed out that Nixon's very acceptance acknowledged guilt, and that he knew that Nixon deeply regretted his wrongdoing. How could Nixon have denied that statement?

It would become the common wisdom that Ford cost himself the 1976 presidential election with the pardon. Perhaps. But then again, perhaps not. Perhaps Ford would not have received the Republican nomination without a pardon; recall that Reagan almost took it away from him anyway, then speculate on Reagan's chances had the convention met while Nixon, unpardoned, was on trial. And try to imagine what the 1976 campaign would have been like had it been conducted with Nixon in the dock.

In 1974, this author was one of those millions of Americans who were furious with Ford. Seventeen years later, I find the case for a pardon to be irrefutable. All the arguments that made Ford decide to pardon as soon as possible are accurate: the last thing the country needed was to continue to be torn apart by Richard Nixon; selecting a jury would have been virtually impossible; a Nixon trial would have dominated the headlines for months; had he been found guilty, whoever was President would have had to pardon him. "If eventually, why not now?"

Ford was both wise and courageous to pardon Richard Nixon. Whether he hurt or helped himself politically, we cannot know. In his memoirs, Ford quotes Winston Churchill: " 'Among the deficiencies of hindsight is that while we know the consequences of what was done, we do not know the consequences of some other course that was not followed'."[49]

A week or so after the pardon, Nixon telephoned the President. "Jerry," he said (no one except Pat *ever* called Nixon "Dick" when he was the President), "I know this is causing you great political difficulty and embarrassment, but I also want you to know that I'm appreciative and grateful." That was his only expression of thanks.[50]

•

ALMOST lost in the uproar over the pardon was the announcement of the compromise deal on Nixon's papers and tapes. Various lawyers representing various clients who had various interests in the tapes did notice, and they were horrified at the thought that Nixon would control the tapes, and could destroy them in five years. On Monday morning, they showed up in Washington seeking a temporary restraining order to stop the tapes from moving from Washington to San Clemente. Jaworski joined them. There were dozens of Freedom of Information Act requests for this or that portion of the tapes. The struggle for the tapes was not yet resolved, despite the pardon.

CHAPTER TWENTY

"THINGS ARE NOT WELL"
September 1974–May 1975

WHEN FORD ANNOUNCED the pardon, Nixon was on the road, driving from San Clemente to Rancho Mirage, California, southeast of Palm Springs. He told Pat, "This is the most humiliating day of my life." When Pat passed the remark along to Julie that evening, she added that for her it was the saddest day.[1]

Nixon had bargained for the pardon, and got it on his terms. It saved him immense amounts of money and problems. Yet it saddened him. The reason would appear to be that he realized it did not matter that he had not acknowledged guilt in his statement; he knew that his acceptance of the pardon nevertheless acknowledged guilt.

The Nixons were staying at Sunnylands, the estate of Walter Annenberg, the Ambassador to the Court of St. James. Annenberg was at home in Philadelphia, but his staff of thirty was present to see to the Nixons' needs. The place was more a principality than a mere estate. It stood on the corner of Bob Hope Drive and Frank Sinatra Drive on 220 acres of lush property made green by a recycled irrigation system, surrounded by 700 acres of desert "buffer" land. The main house contained 25,000 square feet of living space; the master bedroom had 2,000 square feet alone. Outside there was a 4,000-square-foot patio, a large swimming pool, artificial lakes, and a nine-hole golf course.[2]

All this splendor had little effect on Nixon. It was blazing hot, over 110 degrees; reporters and photographers hung around the place, telephoto lenses ready; a helicopter flew overhead, hoping for a photo opportunity. Nixon stayed inside.

That night, he had a stabbing pain in his lower abdomen on the left side. Dr. John Lungren, chief of staff at Long Beach Memorial Hospital and Nixon's longtime personal physician, was called to the estate. He discovered that Nixon's left leg was swollen to nearly three times its normal size, indicating the presence of a substantial clot in the leg, caused by a return of the phlebitis that had almost felled him back in June, in Egypt. Lungren warned Nixon that there was the potential of a life-threatening embolism and recommended strongly that he enter a hospital immediately. Nixon refused. Lungren then prescribed drugs to bring down the swelling and the wearing of a support stocking. He told Nixon to elevate the leg and stay off it.[3]

The next few days were terrifying to everyone near Nixon. He was depressed, unresponsive, in pain. On September 11, Ed Cox decided to make the public aware of the situation. He telephoned an Associated Press reporter. "This is something someone should talk about," he said. The family was concerned. Cox mentioned the recurrence of phlebitis. He said Nixon was reconsidering his announcement of the previous December that he would eventually give his San Clemente estate to the American people; Cox explained that he needed money.

Asked if the pardon had not cheered the former President, Cox said no. "He's still way down, very depressed. He is in a deep depression. . . . It's not that he's not sharp. He grasps things as quickly as ever. But the mental letdown plays on the physical problems. Each plays on the other and that cycle makes both worse."

Asked about the possibility of suicide, Cox replied, "You have to understand that [Nixon] is a very strong, very religious man. He wouldn't consider suicide because of his religious convictions, but I guess you never know."[4]

David Eisenhower also talked to the press. "Things are not well," he said. He reported that representatives of President Ford had sought "some kind of confession" before pardoning Nixon, and that he had refused: "He wasn't willing to concede anything." Asked whether Nixon accepted the White House view that guilt was implicit in his acceptance of a pardon, David replied that Nixon "views himself as an innocent man and continues to say so privately."[5]

On September 12, Nixon returned to San Clemente. Secret Service decoys managed to lure the reporters and photographers away, and he escaped without being seen. When the Nixons got home, the swelling was worse. Pat called Dr. Walter Tkach, a major general in the Air Force and Nixon's White House physician. Tkach flew out, phoned Lungren for his appraisal, then went to see Nixon. The swelling had reached dangerous proportions; Nixon was refusing to wear the support stocking. He was sullen and remote, apparently uncaring about his health.

"You have got to go to the hospital," Tkach ordered.

"If I go to the hospital," Nixon replied, "I'll never get out of there alive."

Tkach did not argue. Instead, he flew back to Washington, where he talked to reporters in a series of interviews. He said Nixon was "a ravaged man who has lost the will to fight." He was suffering from "severe physical strain and physical fatigue." His condition was "critical." He was heading for a heart attack. "The pardon did him no damn good," Tkach told Helen Thomas. "It will require a miracle for him to recover. I don't know if I can pull him through."[6]

Tkach's comments set off a speculative spree. Suicidal, most people seemed to think. Nixon's spirits surely were not lifted by news from Washington; Leon Jaworski had sent a subpoena to Los Angeles to be delivered to Nixon, commanding his appearance at the Watergate cover-up trial. Ehrlichman already had him under subpoena as a defense witness, so both sides wanted Nixon in the courtroom, to ask him a few questions about Watergate.

Judge Sirica, meanwhile, had rejected a motion that the trial of Haldeman, Ehrlichman, and Mitchell be postponed because of prejudicial publicity generated by Ford's pardon of Nixon. He did agree to set the trial date back three weeks. But at the same time, he made it clear that when the period was up the trial would go forward, with Nixon on the stand, whatever the state of his health.

KENNETH Clawson, a former *Washington Post* reporter who had taken Herb Klein's post as White House communications director, flew to San Clemente to see Nixon. He found the former President sitting behind his desk, his ailing leg propped atop it. Nixon apologized for not rising. "The damn sawbones say I've got to keep it elevated."

Seeing someone who had just arrived from the White House roused Nixon. He wanted the gossip. "Don't bullshit me now," he said. "What's going on? What's happening to you, the others? How are the new people?"

No good, Clawson said. The Ford people wanted to get rid of the Nixon holdovers, especially Haig. They were incompetent. They kept stressing how different they were from the Nixon people. They prided themselves on their small-town approach.

Nixon laughed. "Don't start quoting Sinclair Lewis to me again. After us, *Main Street* may be just what the doctor ordered."

Then he gave Clawson some advice. "I know you're feeling bitter, so am I. But we can't let it show, not now, possibly not ever. . . . Five years from now, then maybe, who knows?"

Clawson mentioned some of the good things Nixon had done, in foreign policy especially.

"They'll never give us credit for that," Nixon snapped. "We're out now, so they try to stomp us . . . kick us when we're down. They never let up, *never,* because we were the first real threat to them in years. And, by God, we would have changed it, changed it so they couldn't have changed it back in a hundred years, if only . . ." He broke off, stared out the window at the ocean.

He came back. He said he knew "what the game was all about and how to win it." He talked about being hungry, then remarked with deep bitterness: "What starts the process, really, are the laughs and snubs and slights you get when you are a kid. . . .

"You were a good athlete," Nixon went on, "but I was not, and that was the very reason I tried and tried and tried. To get discipline for myself and to show others that here was a guy who could dish it out and take it. Mostly, I took it. . . ."

Clawson interrupted. This time, he said, there was a difference.

"Yes," Nixon answered softly. "This time we had something to lose."

Clawson asked about the leg.

"They say it's very bad," Nixon replied. "But I've already told them to go to hell. I've told them I wasn't setting foot outside the wall around my property no matter what. They can cut off the damn leg, let it rot, or just wait for the clot to reach the end zone. I don't care."

Clawson couldn't think what to say. Nixon went on. "You've got to be tough. You can't break, my boy, even when there is nothing left. You can't admit, even to yourself, that it is gone. Now some people we both know think that you go stand in the middle of the bullring and cry, 'mea culpa, mea culpa,' while the crowd is hissing and booing and spitting on you. But a man doesn't cry.

"I don't cry. You don't cry."[7]

When Clawson left, Nixon, worried by the news that Ford's people were trying to run out the Nixon people, called the President. He asked about the state of the strategic arms limitation talks and expressed the hope that Kissinger would remain as Secretary of State. Ford said he hoped so too.[8]

On September 16, Dr. Lungren arrived at La Casa Pacifica to examine Nixon again. He found serious deterioration. The swelling was such that Nixon had difficulty putting on his pants. He was exhausted from the sharp, stabbing pain, and thus cranky and irritable. Lungren insisted that Nixon enter the hospital; Nixon finally agreed. At Long Beach Memorial, tests revealed a clot which had broken off in his leg and traveled to a lung. Lungren began heparin treatment—a slow drip of anticoagulant to shrink the clot. For five days, Nixon could not sleep because of the pain, the flashing light on the heparin apparatus, and its constant beep. Pat was at his side, to help in any way she could. She brought McDonald's hamburgers, and together they watched reruns of the TV western Bonanza.[9]

After a week, Nixon had recovered sufficiently to be spending long hours on the telephone. Ziegler gave a report to the press. "He is not having any psychiatric problems—not at all," he assured the reporters.

"He feels like anybody would feel after going through the uncertainty of the last 45 days. . . . Sometimes [he's] very reflective, sometimes looking ahead. But he is physically very fatigued and the events of the past months have caused him not to be in good spirits, to at times be in a low frame of mind. But this should not suggest that his mind is not acute or that he is not working or that the state of his mind is not a healthy state."[10]

There was some good news, the first in what must have seemed like ages. Lazar had sold the rights to Nixon's memoirs to Warner Paperback Library of New York, for a $2.5 million advance. The money would be paid in stages, as the writing progressed.

Inevitably, that announcement brought howls of protest from Nixon's critics. His aides were going on trial for their part in Watergate, and Nixon was getting rich writing about it. There were also suspicions that Nixon was faking his illness, to avoid having to testify in the Watergate trial.

On October 1, Lungren held a news conference. He said Nixon was better and would be going home soon, but there were still serious problems. He was "physically extremely fatigued" and would require at least a month of closely supervised recuperation. For three months he would have to avoid sitting, riding, or standing for prolonged periods, which meant that a flight to Washington for the trial was out of the question. As for taking a written deposition in San Clemente, that too would be impossible for at least three weeks. "There are a lot of doubting Thomases, the country is full of them," Lungren acknowledged. "But this is my honest conception of what I think could happen to him during his recovery period." [11]

Three days later, Nixon, smiling broadly and shaking the hands of hospital staff, was rolled out the door. "I feel great," he said, rising from his wheelchair to get into his car. "Just great."[12] He looked terrible. He had lost weight, his suit hung on him, his jowls were more prominent than they had ever been, giving his face a sagging appearance.

Nevertheless the doubting Thomases continued to doubt. Nixon filed a motion with Sirica, asking the judge to quash the subpoenas commanding his appearance as a witness. Sirica put the motions under seal and said they would remain under seal until he decided "what action I'll take, if any." The small, familiar cartoon figure of Puck the Penguin expressed the reactions of millions: "Somebody tell him he has the wrong foot up."[13] Meanwhile, the House voted 321 to 62 to cut the $850,000 transition expenses Nixon had requested to $200,000.

At the pyramid-shaped federal building in Laguna Niguel, the GSA had started work on a $100,000 vault to hold Nixon's papers and tapes in a place where they would be readily available to him. As envisioned, the vault could only be opened with two keys, one held by Nixon, the other by the GSA; this was part of the deal Nixon had struck with Ford.

This deal, as noted, worked out by Buchen and Becker with Nixon's lawyer Miller, had been challenged by lawyers, whose request for a restraining order had been granted.[14]

On October 3, the GSA said that because of mounting congressional opposition and the absence of any congressional authorization, it was holding up the work on the vault in Laguna Niguel. The next day, the Senate voted 56 to 7 to direct the Ford Administration to retain custody of Nixon's tapes and papers. The bill, which was sent on to the House, contained a flat prohibition against destruction of any Watergate tapes.[15]

Nixon spent most of the following two weeks in bed, coming into the living room only at dinnertime, eating from a TV tray placed to the side of his elevated left leg. Pat spent hours each day working in the garden, planting a colorful ground cover of purple gazanias and pink and white geraniums. Nixon, pleased to see her occupied, told her again and again how beautiful everything looked.[16]

ON October 11, jury selection for the Watergate trial was completed. Sirica then released legal papers filed by Ehrlichman and Haldeman. They contended that they had urged Nixon in the summer of 1972 to make "a full and complete disclosure" of the Watergate affair. They insisted that Nixon could testify to a variety of "unrecorded conversations" that would prove the truth of their assertion. Ehrlichman further contended that Nixon could testify about unrecorded conversations in which "instructions were given that all matters pertaining" to the Plumbers "were impressed with the highest security classification and were not to be revealed by any Government employee." He claimed he had advised Nixon to discontinue the prosecution of Ellsberg. He said that in yet another "unrecorded" conversation, on April 29, 1973, Nixon had acknowledged that Ehrlichman had tried to uncover the Watergate matter. Haldeman made similar claims. Both men wanted Nixon's testimony, plus tapes and documents.

Sirica also released Nixon's motion to quash the subpoena commanding his presence at the trial. Nixon argued that his health prevented his appearance; he further argued that the testimony and documents sought by Ehrlichman and Haldeman were covered by executive privilege.[17]

Three days later, Ehrlichman opened his defense by placing the blame for the cover-up squarely on Nixon. His lawyer, William Frates, told the jury that Nixon had covered up "to save his own neck." He said Ehrlichman had been "had" by Nixon.

"It's not easy for John Ehrlichman to make charges against a man he gave six years of his life to," said Frates, but he did it anyway. According to Frates, "Richard Nixon deceived, misled, lied to and used John Ehrlichman to cover up his own knowledge and actions." It was Nixon who had involved Ehrlichman in the cover-up, who had schooled him step by step in the techniques of stonewalling and obstruction of justice, who had directed all the crimes of which he stood accused and then left Ehrlichman "twisting slowly, slowly in the wind."[18]

It was clearly not in Nixon's interests to get into a witness box to answer questions from Ehrlichman's lawyer; come to that, he would do himself no good answering questions put by Jaworski. But Ehrlichman wanted him there, Jaworski wanted him there, Sirica wanted him there, and it would be fair to say that the reporters were eagerly anticipating his appearance.

Fortunately for Nixon, he had a perfect out. In mid-October, Dr. Lungren filed an affidavit with Sirica, stating that it was impossible to predict the duration of Nixon's need for therapy. However long it lasted, "the limitations on Mr. Nixon's physical activity will involve, first, the avoidance of prolonged periods of sitting, standing or walking which . . . might produce further clotting, and, second, the avoidance of any possible trauma which, given the coagulant therapy he will be receiving, could lead to hemorrhaging somewhere in the body." Lungren warned that if Nixon were compelled to testify, it "would pose a serious risk to his health."[19] Sirica was openly skeptical; he ordered Miller to prepare a complete medical report, hinting that if it were not convincing he would immediately demand Nixon's presence in his court, in a wheelchair if necessary.

Since the subpoenas issued to Nixon also demanded tapes and documents, he had to strike back. On October 17, he filed a suit in the Federal District Court, demanding that the GSA be ordered to comply with the agreement made between Buchen, Becker, and Miller; i.e., that the GSA send the Nixon Administration documents, papers, and tapes to California immediately. The suit contended that the agreement was legal, that the government had failed to enforce it, and that the documents were Nixon's personal property.

As the suit was being filed, President Ford was appearing before the House Judiciary Committee. He went to explain the pardon. It was an unusual, not to say unique, event, the first time a sitting President had made a formal appearance before a congressional committee (Lincoln had made an informal appearance). The session was televised. Ford assured the Committee, and the nation, "that there never was at any time any agreement whatsoever concerning a pardon to Mr. Nixon if he were to resign and I were to become President." That was the headline item. Less noticed by the press and public, but undoubtedly carefully, not to say painfully, noted by Nixon was Ford's promise that the Nixon papers and tapes "will not be delivered to anybody until a satisfactory agreement is worked out with the special prosecutor."[20]

Ford's refusal to comply with Nixon's demand received strong backing from the bench. On October 21, Judge Charles Richey of the Federal District Court (who had been of immense help to Nixon in the summer of 1972, when he delayed the Democrats' civil suit over the Watergate break-in until after the election) ordered a delay in implementing the agreement between Nixon and the White House for delivery of the materials to California. He did grant Nixon access to the material, but "for the sole purpose of preparing to testify in the Watergate criminal trial."[21]

In the House, meanwhile, consideration of the Senate bill that directed the Ford Administration to retain custody went to the printing subcommittee of the House Administration Committee. The chairman, John Brademas (D.-Ind.), felt that the Buchen/Becker/Miller agreement was "totally unsatisfactory." If Nixon ever got his hands on those tapes and papers, Brademas feared, as did many others, that he would destroy them. He was determined that Nixon would never get control of those materials.[22]

ON October 23, the struggle over the tapes became a secondary issue for Nixon. Dr. Lungren came to San Clemente to examine his patient. He was alarmed to find that despite the anticoagulant drugs, there was a new swelling. After telephone consultations with several specialists, he decided to hospitalize Nixon immediately. Nixon protested—when he came out of the hospital three weeks earlier he had told Pat he would never go to a hospital again—but Lungren overruled him.[23]

Radiological scans revealed that one of the main veins leading to the heart was almost blocked. As a result, the supply of blood to Nixon's left thigh was almost entirely shut off, raising the possibility of gangrene. X-rays of the thigh also showed evidence of several small clots, any one of which might break off. Drug therapy, the doctors hoped, would make surgery unnecessary.

But the drugs failed to reduce the swelling. On October 28 Lungren ordered a venogram, which showed a large new clot, some eighteen inches in length, about to break loose from the wall of the vein. Surgery was the only option. Fearful that Nixon would not agree, Lungren called Dr. Wiley Barker, chief of the surgical section at the UCLA Medical Center and an expert on venous diseases. He wanted Barker to study the venogram and then talk to Nixon.

Barker had been skeptical about Nixon's illness, but when he looked at the venogram, his doubts disappeared. The clot was one of the biggest he had ever seen. He went to Nixon's room.

"If you look at this clot cross-eyed," he told Nixon, "it will kill you."

"So, it's surgery, then?"

"If you want to go on living, it is."

Nixon smiled. "I can assure you about that. I've got too many things to do to go on being sick. Let's just get it out of the way."

"You know," said Barker as he prepared to go, "that venogram of yours is a classic. If you weren't who you are, I'd love to show it to my class."

Nixon smiled again. "I have a feeling that these X rays are going to belong to history anyway. Go ahead, use it."[24]

Surgery began at 5:30 A. M. It went well. When Nixon was wheeled out of the recovery room at 7 A.M., Pat was waiting for him. She sat next to his bed, feeding him little chips of ice with a spoon. He kept whispering "water" and his eyelids fluttered uncontrollably. Julie recorded that "he was so deadly white that Mother began to feel uneasy." Pat called Tricia, then Julie, asking them to come to California on the first available flight.

Two hours later, while propped on the edge of his bed, Nixon fainted and almost fell to the floor. Nurses caught him and rolled him back onto the bed. One of the nurses started slapping his face, calling to him: "Richard, wake up, Richard!" He barely regained consciousness, and knew it was neither Pat nor Lungren calling to him, because only his mother had ever called him Richard. Then he slipped back into a coma.

Pat was in a room two doors away, waiting with Rose Woods. She heard over the loudspeaker, "Emergency operating unit to seventh floor." There was only one patient on the seventh floor. She rushed to his room, where she saw six people around his bed with lifesaving equipment. Stunned, helpless, she turned and walked back to her room.

Nixon was unconscious and in cardiovascular shock. His blood pressure had dropped to 60 over 0 because of unexpected, massive internal bleeding. Four blood transfusions over a period of three hours pushed it back to normal.[25]

When he woke, he told Lungren that he was eager to go home. Lungren replied, "Listen, Dick, we almost lost you last night. You are not going to go home for quite a while."

Tricia and Julie had arrived. Together with Pat, they stayed by his side. When he woke again, he told Pat he didn't think he was going to make it. She gripped his hand and said, almost fiercely, "Don't talk that way. You have got to make it. You must not give up."[26]

He feared the worst. He asked Pat to get a notebook and pencil, as he wanted to dictate some last recollections. He talked for two hours, until Pat could not write any longer. Ziegler took over for her for another two hours, and then aide Frank Gannon for yet two more hours. He talked slowly, painfully. He was still connected to various life-support systems, nauseated, feverish. But he kept talking. He ranged over his life. He was reflective, even philosophical, except when he talked about Watergate—then he was bitter and combative. Gannon felt both privileged and terrified to be there.[27]

Slowly, over the next two days, he improved. The crisis passed.

COINCIDENTALLY, President Ford was in Los Angeles on a campaign trip on behalf of the 1974 Republican congressional candidates. There had been intense speculation in the press about whether or not he would go see Nixon. Ford's aides discussed the pros and cons and decided that if he did, the visit would put the pardon back on the front pages—on the eve of the election. They decided to recommend no visit.

"If there's no place in politics for human compassion," Ford said when he heard the recommendation, "there's something wrong with politics. I'm going to leave it to Pat."[28]

At 10 P.M. that night, October 31, he called Pat, who was staying with her daughters at Helene Drown's home, a half hour from Long Beach. He asked, "Would a visit help?"

"I can't think of anything that would help Dick more," Pat replied.[29]

Ford arrived the next morning. "Hi, Jerry," Nixon barely managed to say as he entered the room. Nixon's hair was tousled, his jowls were flabby, his arms—one of which was stuck with tubes and locked in a splint—were terribly thin. An air line extended from one of his nostrils, while a catheter protruded from his neck. Overhead a battery of emergency monitoring equipment blinked and flashed. He was deathly pale.

"Oh, Mr. President!" Ford could not help blurting out.

He regained his composure, and the two men tried to talk—about politics, naturally. Foreign policy and the upcoming election. "It looks like we're going to do fine," Ford lied.

There was a long silence. Finally, in a hoarse whisper, Nixon said, "My own situation is not too good. . . . I'm not feeling too well, but I'm going to make it."

"How are your nights?" Ford asked.

"None of my nights are too good."

After eight minutes, Ford prepared to leave. "Be well," he said. Nixon told him, "Mr. President, this has meant a lot to me. I'm deeply grateful." Outside the hospital, Ford told waiting reporters, "He's obviously a very, very sick man, but I think he's coming along."[30]

THE election results, four days later, were disastrous for the Republicans. Among the scores who were defeated were four members of the House Judiciary Committee who had voted against impeachment. There was other bad news. Rabbi Korff reported that the President Nixon Justice Fund had $9,325 in hand, that it owed $77,753 to Miller's law firm, and anticipated a bill for another $221,000 in legal fees.[31] Worse, it turned out that no one had bothered to buy health insurance for Nixon. He would have to pay his hospital bill from his own pocket.

On November 7, Miller handed Sirica an affidavit saying that Nixon would not be able to "participate" for at least two or three months in any "activity requiring substantial mental or physical effort." He could not possibly come to Washington for the trial, nor could he give a deposition in California. Sirica then announced that he was appointing a panel of three leading doctors to examine Nixon to determine whether he would be able to provide testimony, either in person or through deposition.[32]

On November 14, Nixon was allowed to go home. He had lost 15 pounds and looked tired and drawn. Five days later, the doctors appointed by Sirica showed up at La Casa Pacifica. Nixon, who had hoped for "a little relief from the merciless attacks of the critics," naturally resented having to undergo another examination, and the suspicions that lay behind the act. "So Sirica's three doctors came to San Clemente," he later wrote. "Each took turns poking and pinching and pulling and doing the other things that doctors do during an examination."[33]

The medical conclusion was that Nixon would not be capable of testifying at the Watergate trial before February 16, and he would not be able to testify by deposition at his home until January 6.[34] The Constitution guarantees a defendant the right "to have compulsory process for obtaining witnesses in his favor," but Sirica nevertheless declared that he wanted to wind up the trial by the first of the year. He was unwilling to wait and, over Frates's objections, ruled that Nixon's testimony would not be necessary.

So, due to the illness that almost took his life, Nixon escaped having to comment in public on Watergate. He did make some private remarks. Bill Gulley saw him in San Clemente. Watergate came up. Nixon said, "I really feel compassion for John Mitchell. These poor people who are now literally going bankrupt trying to defend themselves." He went on, "There's no question that Watergate happened. There's no question that it shouldn't have happened. But a lot of innocent people are being dragged into this, and a lot of reputations are ruined."

Gulley found it "strange" that whenever "Nixon speaks of Watergate it's always as a thing detached from him. It's never in the context of something he was involved in. He always speaks of it as if it were something over there—in that corner. . . . He'd say, 'God. What the country has gone through with this Watergate business.' It's always in that vein, as if it had nothing to do with him."[35]

On November 26, Rebozo and Abplanalp came to La Casa Pacifica to talk finances. They advised Nixon to sell his Key Biscayne properties, and said they would form a non-profit foundation that would buy them, at a substantial profit for Nixon. Abplanalp later told the Philadelphia *Sunday Bulletin* that Nixon had to sell in order "to stay within his means. For the first time in years, Mr. Nixon has become conscious of what it costs to live. And it's been our idea to help him make up a budget he could live with. We're not talking about a welfare case; we're simply talking about shrinking his holdings, making it easier for him to make both ends meet." Abplanalp said Nixon's projected income, from his pension and royalties from his writing, was $200,000 per year. The Key Biscayne properties would bring in between $750,000 and $1 million; Nixon had purchased them five years earlier for $250,000.[36]

That was a handsome profit. Nixon needed the money, partly to pay his bill at Long Beach Memorial Hospital ($23,000), partly for legal fees incurred in defending himself against various lawsuits, current and expected (projected at $500,000), partly to make further payments on his back taxes (he still owed $148,081 on the illegal deduction of the gift of his vice presidential papers, plus back income taxes due the state of California totaling more than $75,000). In addition, there were the costs of maintaining La Casa Pacifica, where the taxes alone amounted to $37,300 per year.

Congress had cut back drastically on his transition allowance, leaving him with but $60,000 to pay his staff, which amounted to twenty-two, including drivers, secretaries, stewards, and senior aides such as Ziegler and Brennan. Further, there were his telephone expenses—Nixon, always networking on the phone, made more than two hundred long-distance calls in the few days before Christmas. That practice, Abplanalp said, would have to stop, but he must have known it would not.

That sounds like a big staff, and a lot of calls. But the expense of being a former President is tremendous. As one example, Nixon had received more than 1 million pieces of mail since his resignation. Volunteers from an Orange County Republican club were helping to process it, but still there were heavy costs.[37] And, of course, all those legal fees. In his 1990 memoirs, Nixon wrote that he had spent "over $1.8 million in attorneys' fees to defend myself against . . . suits and to protect my rights that were threatened by government action."[38]

MOST of that money went to the "protect my rights" area; Nixon incurred the cost as a part of the never-ending struggle to retain control of his papers and tapes. In December, the House had passed and Ford had signed the Senate bill that then became the Presidential Records and Materials Preservation Act of 1974. The act did not openly challenge the concept of private property in the records of a former President, but it did order that the government obtain "complete possession and control" of Nixon's presidential materials. It entrusted the National Archives with custody and the authority to determine their use. Specifically, Congress recognized the need "to provide the public with the full truth, at the earliest reasonable date, of the abuses of governmental power popularly identified under the generic term 'Watergate.' " The act directed the Archives to process and open the records to scholars "at the earliest reasonable date."[39]

Whatever the cost, Nixon was determined to challenge the act, which he characterized correctly as treating him differently from all other Presidents. Nixon's suit eventually reached to the Supreme Court. On June 17, 1977, by a vote of 7 to 2 (Burger and Rehnquist dissenting), the Court upheld the act. Still, over the next seventeen years, Nixon fought to prevent implementation of the law, using various highly expensive legal devices.

Right after Christmas 1974, testimony in the Watergate trial ended and the case went to the jury. Nixon never was compelled to testify under oath about Watergate. He would tell his side of the story of Watergate in his own time, on his own conditions. Whether he told the truth or not, we cannot know unless and until the remainder of the tapes and documents are opened.

THE nearly five months since Nixon's return to California had been tumultuous. He had been pardoned for any and all crimes he may have committed, and he had avoided having to appear in court. But he had also nearly lost his life. He had taken a severe financial beating. He apparently had lost control of his presidential papers and tapes. According to Julie, "Christmas 1974 was the lowest point in my father's life."[40]

On New Year's afternoon, as Nixon was watching the Rose Bowl on television, the jury in the Watergate trial came in. The verdict was guilty. Haldeman and Mitchell were stoical, announcing their intention to appeal. Ehrlichman was bitter. "If I had known Nixon was taping my conversations," he said, "I would have acted differently." It was those tapes, played in court, that had convicted Ehrlichman and the others.[41]

Nixon refused public comment. Ziegler told reporters, "President Nixon is deeply anguished by Watergate, and that these men, who were among his closest aides, and their families, have suffered so much, and that their lives have been so tragically touched by Watergate."[42] Nixon had anticipated a guilty verdict, and had anticipated that Sirica would impose a heavy sentence. The judge gave three years for each of the defendants.

Anticipated or not, the convictions and sentences had a big impact. Nixon went once more into a deep depression. He found it difficult to sleep and had to be encouraged to eat. He kept to himself.[43] Pat held him together. As David Eisenhower later put it, "She was the mainstay." Nixon recalled, "I'm told I was more dead than alive. Pat was there. . . . If it hadn't been for her, I might not have survived. . . . Pat's devotion kept me alive—I doubt if I would have made it without her."[44]

They ate their evening meal together, watching *Bonanza,* but they did not sleep in the same bed. "Nobody could sleep with Dick," she explained. "He wakes up during the night, switches on the light, speaks into his tape recorder or takes notes, it's impossible."[45]

For January 9, 1975, his sixty-second birthday, she organized a surprise birthday party. She called Rebozo, and Abplanalp, and reporter

Victor Lasky. They arrived in mid-afternoon; Pat met them in her gardening clothes, took them to Nixon's office, and opened the door. Nixon's jaw dropped in surprise. "Well, goddam!" he exclaimed.

The party that followed was a success, with gag gifts and drinks and songs. Nixon had a heaping silver bowl of caviar, a gift from the Shah, brought out. "Eat, eat," he urged. "The Shah won't like it if you don't." Nixon told the guests of the birthday greetings he had received, from Chou En-lai, Ronald Reagan, President Ford, and others. He offered a toast: "Never dwell on the past. Always look to the future."[46]

Three days later, however, Ziegler told the Los Angeles *Times* that he was "fed up" with the abuse he said Nixon was taking. He said Nixon had become the target of vindictiveness. "It's the first American political exile," he said. "You only have to be here to sense it is exile—the abandonment by friends, the isolation, the vindictiveness of some in Washington, including some in Congress and some in the Ford White House." He described Nixon as "certainly a beaten man."[47]

That was not accurate. He was still recovering, he was 10 pounds underweight, he was depressed, but he was far from beaten. He continued his decades-old practice of networking with the mighty over the telephone. He received a few prominent visitors. Secretary of State Kissinger came in January to discuss foreign policy. Barry Goldwater dropped in. He later told reporters they had discussed the possibility of Nixon's returning some day to "the political arena, not as a candidate but as a party spokesman.

"We discussed whether he would be accepted back into the party's affairs," Goldwater said, "and I told him I thought he would be." It would depend on his health, of course, and, "It's not going to happen the day after tomorrow, or next month or even next year, but as time goes on I think Watergate will gradually be put behind us.

"And I have a suspicion that as time goes on he'll be available for the Republican party."[48]

On February 9, the six-month transition period ended. Nixon had to let go of most of his staff, including Ziegler. Teams of GSA workers dismantled the prefabricated modules that had been the working quarters for the staff. Nearly all the telephone lines were disconnected, including the one that had linked La Casa Pacifica directly to the White House.

On February 19, Nixon ventured out of San Clemente for the first time in three months to drive to Sunnylands, for a week-long visit with Walter Annenberg. He had recovered sufficiently to play a bit of golf, though he had to quit after two holes. There was a party, with lots of famous people—Ronald and Nancy Reagan, Bob and Dolores Hope, Herman Kahn, Frank Sinatra and Barbara Marx, Freeman Gosden, Leonard Firestone. Spiro Agnew, a houseguest at Sinatra's neighboring estate, did not attend.

Nixon told some jokes, engaged in some gossip, offered a toast. He praised Annenberg and his wife, and the estate. He too had once lived in a big house with many rooms, Nixon said. "When you are on top, it is filled with all your friends. Afterward, you don't need a house so large." He thanked those present for sticking with him even when he was down. That word "down" hung in the pause, until he added: "Let me assure you—I'm not out."[49]

His friends were helping to see to that. The mortgage on La Casa Pacifica was paid off, by persons unknown. A group calling itself the Nixon Historical Association was preparing to purchase the Key Biscayne homes and preserve them as historical sites. The group had rented office space in Rebozo's Key Biscayne Bank.[50]

Nixon's physical health was improving, thanks to an improbable and unexpected discovery. He found he enjoyed playing golf. He had never been very good at the game, nor had he liked it very much. During his Presidency he played only a dozen or so times. But in San Clemente, he wrote, "golf became my lifesaver." He began to play every day, with Jack Brennan as his partner. He shot 125 on his first full round, and almost quit on the spot. But the challenge intrigued him. He stuck with it, and soon broke 100. As Brennan was a retired Marine colonel, they usually played at the Camp Pendleton course. Along with an occasional swim, the exercise helped him put on weight and improve his condition generally.[51]

He had an idea on how to improve his finances. In early March he had dinner with Paul Presley, the owner of the San Clemente Inn, and Johnny Grant, a Los Angeles television personality. He brought up a fund-raiser that Bob Haldeman had devised. Haldeman had sold two hours of televised conversation to CBS TV for $100,000. Mike Wallace had conducted the interview. Haldeman stonewalled ("I don't know what happened" in Watergate); it was not much as a show; but it sure helped pay Haldeman's legal fees. Nixon told Presley and Grant that he knew some people objected to interviewing for a fee, but wondered how it was different from accepting royalties for writing a book. Anyway, CBS had paid Lyndon Johnson and Eisenhower for interviews.

Grant and Presley got together with Rabbi Korff to begin exploratory talks with the networks. But their asking price was too high, $250,000, and the negative publicity about the interview-for-hire with Haldeman had made the networks leery. Nothing came of it.[52] Korff went to Dallas to raise money for the President Nixon Justice Fund. On arrival, he told reporters that the $175,000 initial payment Nixon had received on his advance for his memoirs from Warner Books had been spent, that the $200,000 in transition expenses allocated by Congress was gone, and Nixon had less than $2,000 in his bank account.[53]

He still had his rich friends, however, and the rest of the $2.5 million advance coming to him when he wrote his memoirs, plus his determination, pride, and will. He was much too smart, and much too weak, to begin an active, public comeback so soon after his disgrace. But, long term, he was damned if he was beaten. To prepare the way, he entered into an agreement with the regents of the University of Southern California. He would establish his presidential library on the USC campus, and donate his papers to it, pending the outcome of his suit challenging the constitutionality of the Presidential Records and Materials Preservation Act. The agreement was the result of weeks of negotiation between Nixon's lawyers and USC President John Hubbard.

Hubbard could have made the announcement to the regents and the press himself, but Nixon insisted on meeting with the regents to inform them. Not only that, he allowed a member of the press to attend, the first time he had faced a reporter since August 1974. Annenberg hosted the affair at Sunnylands; the reporter was twenty-one-year-old Kari Granville, editor of *The Daily Trojan*, USC's student newspaper.

"I'm feeling fine," Nixon told her. "Luckily, this doesn't affect the brain. Mentally, I'm O.K."

Granville reported that he told the regents that the presidential papers that would be deposited in the library "will include those famous tapes you've heard so much about." He wanted the library to have a China wing, a Russia wing, and a wing dedicated to memorabilia of the First Lady and First Family. "He acted as though his place in history was guaranteed by foreign affairs," she wrote. "It was almost as though he were still President. He didn't mention Gerald Ford at all."

Nixon neither drank nor sampled the hors d'oeuvres, but he had something personal to say to each of the thirty guests he greeted in a receiving line. His favorite topics were Brezhnev and football, particularly the USC Rose Bowl champion team. Granville reported that he "showed signs of nervousness as he mingled with the guests, but those who have known him said his habit of directing his eyes downward occasionally was a characteristic Nixon always carried with him."[54]

AT the end of April, NVA armored units, driving Soviet-built tanks, knocked down the gates of the presidential palace in Saigon. William Safire, who had written speeches for Nixon in the first term, and had since joined *The New York Times* to write a column, was visiting Nixon in La Casa Pacifica that day. He found Nixon in good spirits and health. "The haunted, hunted look of the final days in the White House-turned-bunker is gone. He is ruddy from the California sun, the hand holding the coffee cup is steady." But he was struck by the juxtaposition of La Casa Pacifica with the refugee camp for South Vietnamese at Camp Pendleton. To Safire, it seemed that the former President and the refugees, "who had been locked together throughout his Presidency, wound up abandoned on the same doorstep."

There was a considerable difference, of course; the Los Angeles *Times* had pointed to it in a cartoon that day. A Vietnamese refugee, bowl in hand, stands at the door of La Casa Pacifica: "We're your Camp Pendleton neighbors, Mr. Nixon; may we borrow a cup of rice?"[55]

At the time, Nixon made no comment—not even putting out any "it is known that he believes" leaks—on the transformation of Saigon to Ho Chi Minh City. There was no criticism of Ford or Kissinger, not even of Congress. Nor was there any mention, at the time, of his new neighbors. In 1990, he did comment; he wrote that as he and Brennan drove to the golf course, they passed the camp housing thousands of refugees. "Every time we drove by their camp, I was saddened by the thought that had I survived in office, they might not have suffered this tragic fate."[56] He never stopped to say hello or to ask if there was anything he could do for them.

SAFIRE entitled his column "Report from Elba." Was the image intended as a threat, or a promise? Elba was the site of Napoleon's first exile; when he escaped from it, first hundreds, then thousands, then tens of thousands of Frenchmen rallied to him, and many of them died for him in the subsequent Battle of Waterloo.

NIXON was not ready to end his own, self-imposed exile, but he did urge Pat to get out. The occasion was the dedication of the Patricia Nixon Elementary School in her hometown of Artesia (renamed Cerritos). She did not want to go. She hated making any kind of public appearance, especially alone. But she went.

Julie asked her why. She explained that Dick had pleaded, "You just have to go, Pat." She said, "I went for him."

In her remarks at the dedication, Pat Nixon said, "I'm proud to have the school carry my name. I always thought that only those who have gone had schools named after them. I am happy to tell you that I'm not gone—I mean not really gone."[57]

CHAPTER TWENTY-ONE

A TRIP TO CHINA
June 1975–March 1976

By JUNE 1975, ten months after his resignation, Nixon's health was slowly improving. He was 10 pounds below his normal weight of 164; he looked worn-out, exhausted; his nose was more prominent and his jowls more pendulous; he walked with a limp most of the time; his leg was still painful except when propped up. But he was getting better every day, just as he was bringing down his golf score. He was sleeping up to twelve hours a night, far more than at any other time in his adult life, and a source of irritation to him, as he resented wasting so much time in bed.

Every weekday morning, he walked the 300 yards down the driveway at La Casa Pacifica, past unkempt, sun-yellowed lawns—once kept bright green by the GSA gardeners, now neglected—through the south gate onto the Coast Guard's Navigational Aid Station to the single-story office buildings that were once the heart of the Western White House. Now he worked with one or two aides, mostly on his memoirs. But even if the army of aides was gone, he dressed as he had at the White House, a dark suit, white shirt, muted tie, black shoes.

At the end of the working day, Nixon walked back to his home and took a short swim in the pool. Then it was time to start his regular networking with friends and associates around the country. He would spend an hour or two on the phone, reminiscing, seeking advice, giving advice, discussing business. Then it was a quiet dinner with Pat, and some television, unless Julie and Tricia were there, or Rebozo or Abplanalp. Other more or less regular visitors included John Mitchell, Ron Ziegler, Billy Graham, and Frank Sinatra.

Pat spent her days working with the one remaining gardener, pruning and trimming the rose bushes, planting ground cover, pulling weeds. She

481

wore colorful pants suits and seemed more cheerful than she had been in years. "Gardening became my Mother's salvation," Julie later wrote. "That first year in San Clemente, Mother went through four pair of heavy canvas garden gloves."[1] She almost never went out; her trip to Cerritos was her only solo public appearance in the first five and a half years after the resignation.

Her apparent good spirits masked a deep depression. In May 1975, Julie sent her an airplane ticket to Washington as a Mother's Day gift. Pat called her daughter: "Why don't you come out here?"

Julie replied that she did not want to leave home while David was studying for his law school exams.

"You have only one person to take care of there," Pat rejoined, "but two broken people here."[2]

But her husband was only down, not broken. "Our day," Nixon assured an old friend that summer, "will come again."[3]

Not any time soon, however. There was to be more humiliation first. Faced with possible disciplinary action by the state bar of California, Nixon tried to resign his bar membership. It was not accepted, because his letter of resignation failed to mention that he was the subject of a disciplinary investigation. Nixon had to write a second letter, which began: "I, Richard M. Nixon, against whom an investigation is pending, hereby resign as a member of the State Bar of California." He got off easier with the Supreme Court, which allowed him to resign as a lawyer entitled to practice before it on the ground that he had not practiced law for several years and did not intend to do so in the future. But in New York, the state bar rejected his resignation because he had not admitted any wrongdoing. (That same month, the Massachusetts bar readmitted Alger Hiss, without forcing Hiss to first acknowledge his guilt of the crime of which he had been convicted.)[4]

Pat, near despair as bad news piled up, about family finances, about old friends and associates going off to prison, about new embarrassments for her husband, blurted out one morning, "Dick, I don't know how you keep going." He answered her: "I just get up in the morning to confound my enemies."[5]

In fact, he had more positive goals. He was obsessed with a desire for a historic rehabilitation of his own reputation and that of his Administration—which was the main reason, far more important than the money, he was working so hard on his memoirs—and he was eager to get involved in politics again. Not in a public way, of course—that was out of the question, at least for the present—but as a behind-the-scenes role player in the 1976 presidential contest, and as a contributor to the making of foreign policy. After so many years at the center of the action, he was impatient.

He had always been an addict of inside information, the secret stuff, the goods on this or that senator or this or that foreign leader, the plans of this or that candidate. Now he was reduced to reading the newspapers and a once-a-week intelligence briefing, and occasional materials from the National Security Council. This was thin gruel but apparently the most he was going to get from the Ford White House.

He was restless in his self-imposed exile. Except for trips to the Camp Pendleton golf course, he hardly ever left La Casa Pacifica. He had not been out of the United States for over a year, the longest period without foreign travel since 1947. Thomas Brown, who did a profile on "The Exile" for *The New York Times Magazine* in the summer of 1975, noted that "virtually everyone who has been in recent contact with Nixon remarks on his desire to travel abroad." He had received many invitations to visit, including one from Brezhnev, another from Mao, a third from the Shah of Iran, and a fourth from King Hussein of Jordan.[6]

But it was too early for that. A foreign trip would have exposed Nixon to the media in a way that he was not yet ready to handle. His friends, however, thought he should be getting started on his comeback. Nixon insisted on planning his exit from isolation carefully. At the end of May, he called Rebozo, Abplanalp, and John Mitchell to La Casa Pacifica for a strategy meeting. They urged him to move East, back to New York, to the center of the action. In New York, he would have greater communication with national and international leaders, and access to the world press. It would be a repeat of 1963, when he started a comeback after losing the governor's race in California by moving to New York.[7]

When word of this advice leaked, Russell Baker commented that the possibility of Nixon coming to New York reminded him of "the opening of 'The Bride of Frankenstein,' in which the battered Karloff, supposedly destroyed in the burning of the old mill, emerges unscorched from a convenient cellar and sets forth on another romp. Nixon has more lives than Lazarus."[8]

Nixon countered Baker's ridicule with another leak to test the waters. "A former White House associate" told *The New York Times* that Nixon was making plans for a trip to Europe in the near future, "as a private citizen combining pleasure and fact finding." The informant said that Nixon had spoken to him of a desire to go abroad "and do what I can as a private citizen to help solidify the cause of peace." According to the source, Nixon believed that with the appearance of his memoirs, which he hoped to complete within a year, people would see his Administration in "a truer historical perspective." His achievements in foreign affairs would "overshadow the misjudgments of Watergate."[9]

By early August, the flow of visitors to San Clemente was increasing. In most cases, they had something to say to the press when they emerged, presumably with Nixon's blessing if not his urging. The main theme was that Nixon was taking an active interest in Republican Party politics, spending hours on the telephone "talking 1976." Ronald Reagan, with the support of many old Nixon hands, including Pat Buchanan, was challenging Ford for the nomination. Nixon's visitors declared that the former President felt it was impossible to take the nomination away from Ford. Further, "He [Nixon] feels strongly that any right-wing revolt centering largely upon foreign policies which President Ford inherited from him, and has generally kept intact, would not only be a gift to the Democrats but would turn the party back toward obsolete and dangerous isolationism with serious consequences for the nation and the cause of world peace."[10]

Nixon called Hugh Scott, John Rhodes, Barry Goldwater, Strom Thurmond, and others to urge them to take firm steps to curb the growing conservative criticism of Ford. Much of that criticism centered on Ford's recent trip to the European Security Conference in Helsinki, Finland, where he had signed a human rights accord. Reagan and his friends viewed the trip as just short of a sellout to Communism; Nixon saw it as an essential sequel to his own policy of détente with the Soviets. Nixon was reportedly making frequent calls to Kissinger to urge him to stay the course. By letting his visitors leak these sentiments to the press, Nixon was making sure the word got out to the party as a whole.

David Eisenhower also did some leaking that summer. In the August issue of *McCall's* magazine, David offered some intimate glimpses of his father-in-law. "Mr. Nixon had a trait of being almost boyish about the Presidency," David wrote. "He had a hard time believing where he was. He was so excited about it that he shared it with me, almost carelessly. He invited you to be a decision-maker, to play the game."

They often discussed Watergate, David said, "very objectively and dispassionately." Nixon "spoke of it, well, in a kind of third person way, as if it was something that was happening down the street."[11]

On the first anniversary of his resignation, Nixon was described by a "former staff member" as "a rejuvenated and impatient man." Nixon felt "the emotionalism is fast draining out of Watergate," and believed that more and more people were looking upon him as a man who may have made serious errors of judgment but who did his best in the national interest. His spirits were high, thanks in part to the more than 2 million letters he had received in the past year, 95 percent of which were said by a former aide to carry messages of "sympathy, respect, and gratitude."[12]

THAT same day, August 9, Nixon met with David Frost to discuss a multipart television interview arranged by Nixon's agent, Swifty Lazar. The major networks had turned Lazar down on the idea of Nixon's selling his memories for television, either because the price was too high (Lazar had asked $750,000) or on the grounds that they did not want to pay for news. But Frost had come to Lazar with a proposal, and in June they had reached an agreement. Frost would get twelve two-hour sessions with Nixon, enough material for four ninety-minute shows. Nixon would have no editorial control. Frost would put together the financing and sell the program as an independent producer. Nixon agreed these would be exclusive interviews, and that his memoirs would be published no earlier than three months after the airing of the interviews. In return, Nixon would get $600,000 plus 20 percent of any profits.[13]

Frost came to San Clemente to sign the contract. Jack Brennan, who had recently resigned his commission to work full time for Nixon, met him. He took Frost to Nixon's office. Frost, during small talk, mentioned an item in that day's newspaper about Brezhnev.

Nixon responded, "Communism stifles art. There is little important art you can cite from Communist countries. Solzhenitsyn is not nearly as impressive as Tolstoy."

For the next six hours Nixon and his lawyers went over the contract. When all was settled, Frost handed over a check for the first payment, in the amount of $200,000.[14]

Frost announced the deal at a news conference the following day. *The New York Times* editors were outraged. In an editorial, the newspaper demanded, "Is 'executive privilege' for sale to the highest bidder?

"After refusing to appear before Congressional committees, and the Federal courts in Watergate-related cases, former President Nixon has now made a deal to 'tell all' in a series of telecasts that will be filmed now and shown after the 1976 elections." Noting Frost's assertion that "no subject, including Watergate, has been barred," the *Times* suggested that if Nixon had decided the time for full disclosure had come, a better forum would be a congressional committee or a grand jury.[15]

WHAT Nixon still wanted from Congress, however, was not an opportunity to tell his side of Watergate, but the return of his papers, tapes, and other documents. He needed them to write his memoirs and to prepare for the Frost interviews; he demanded them because they were his private property and had an incalculable value. On August 19, his lawyers issued a formal challenge to the act of Congress seizing his papers. The lawyers contended that Congress had sat in judgment of Nixon and "found him guilty and then punished him" by seizing the papers. They asserted that he owned the 42 million documents and more than 5,000 hours of tape recordings generated while he was in the White House.

In an accompanying statement, Nixon released a deposition taken from him by lawyers representing the government, which was the defendant in the suit. They had asked some obvious questions, such as how it could be that 42 million documents were Nixon's personal property. As an example, they had wanted to know how much of his time had been spent in personally preparing written documents.

The Presidency, Nixon replied, was a burdensome office. Lincoln and Jefferson wrote their own speeches, he pointed out, but few Presidents in the twentieth century had done so. As a point of historical fact, he said, "I have spent more of my time preparing my own speeches and other public statements than any President since Woodrow Wilson." That was as close as he came to explaining how it was that those 42 million documents were his property.

Once he got his property back, Nixon promised, he would review the material "expeditiously" in order to make it available to scholars in the Nixon Library at USC. First, however, it would have to be screened by himself, his wife, or his daughters, in order to make "the delicate judgments with regard to what is private and what is personal and what is political and what is embarrassing, what is national security." All such categories would remain under seal.

There might not be much left after the application of such criteria by the Nixon family, and there was no guarantee as to what Nixon meant by "expeditiously." The government lawyers had asked if he had a time period in mind "within which to make full disclosure of all the Watergate matters?"

A. No.
Q. Do you expect it to be longer than five years?
A. I can't tell until I see how big the task is.
Q. How long do you expect it will take for you and the members of your family to review all the tapes, Mr. Nixon?
A. I don't know.

Nixon had gone on to explain that he was not suing for the return of his papers and tapes for his own purposes, but to protect future Presidents. He said that the "principle of confidentiality, which I realize is not in vogue these days in many quarters, is indispensable for making great decisions."[16]

The sitting President, or at least his Justice Department, would have none of that argument. The Justice Department entered the case with a brief that contended Congress had a rational basis for believing that Nixon "would not be a trustworthy custodian, even temporarily," for the papers and tapes, and that the federal court should reject Nixon's suit. It cited the 18½-minute gap in one White House tape, and the glaring discrepancies between transcripts of the tapes prepared by the White House and those produced by the Special Prosecutor and the House Judiciary Committee.[17] On January 7, 1976, the federal court would uphold the law, saying that Congress had had "an adequate basis for concluding that Mr. Nixon might not be a wholly reliable custodian of the materials." Nixon appealed.[18]

•

THIRTEEN months after his resignation, Nixon made his first public appearance. He picked an odd setting. It was a charity golf tournament for a retarded children's home, held at the La Costa Country Club of Carlsbad, California. There was nothing wrong with the course, nothing exceptional about the cause, but his hosts and playing companions were hardly the sort one expected to find playing golf with a former President. The hosts were the officers of the International Brotherhood of Teamsters; his playing companions included Frank Fitzsimmons (a prime suspect in the disappearance and presumed murder of Jimmy Hoffa ten weeks earlier), Allen Dorfman (a convicted felon who would later be executed gangland-style), Anthony Provenzano (New Jersey Teamster leader later convicted of murder), and others of that ilk.

At the first tee, Nixon declined an offer of a box of golf balls; instead, he pulled out his own box with a dozen balls inscribed with his signature and the presidential seal. "Here," he said, handing it to Fitzsimmons, "give these to the poorest golfers in the tournament. Somebody might want one."

Nixon whacked one down the fairway. It shanked into the rough on the right. He hit another. It hooked into the rough on the left. Another shank, another hook. There was a mob of reporters looking on; Nixon announced, "Those were for practice; this is for real." Then he knocked one down the middle of the fairway. He ended by shooting 92 on the par 72 course.[19]

Once again, the editors of *The New York Times* criticized him, this time for playing with Fitzsimmons and his "mobster associates." The editorial said that Nixon "seemed deliberately . . . to raise anew all the unanswered questions about his relations with Frank E. Fitzsimmons and the scandal-stained International Brotherhood of Teamsters."[20] Nixon's day on the golf course got wide and unflattering coverage; it just seemed inexplicable to most reporters and editors that Nixon would make his first public appearance with such a crowd. People had to wonder what Nixon owed the Teamsters.

Perhaps stung by the criticism, perhaps surprised by it, Nixon retreated to La Casa Pacifica, not to emerge for three months.

He did let selected reporters and photographers in, to do feature stories on his life in retirement. *Time* magazine did a color layout; *Newsweek* had the smiling faces of Mr. and Mrs. Nixon on its cover, with a story on his "new life." Obviously the nation's fascination with the Nixons had not ended with the resignation, but just as clearly few if any of his old enemies were ready to forgive. He was going to have to plan his comeback appearances more carefully. He needed friends to help; unfortunately many of his stateside friends were either in prison, or under indictment, or under suspicion, and he did not feel free to visit his friends in Russia, China, and Iran.

He had other friends in high places in foreign countries who owed him favors. Few foreign leaders could make much sense out of Watergate, and certainly did not feel that Nixon had betrayed them or his trust.

The obvious place to go was the scene of his greatest triumph. He had been preparing for it ever since the resignation. On the wall of his office there was a picture of Nixon with Mao and Chou En-lai. He had decorated his home and office in an Oriental motif. He was reading Chinese history. Mao had written an invitation, and had called on the telephone when Nixon was hospitalized to tell Nixon he considered him one of the greatest statesmen in history, and to say Nixon was welcome anytime.[21]

Any overseas trip, whether to China or Europe, would be easier and more profitable if Nixon had advance approval and an advance briefing from the Secretary of State. That official, it happened, now worked for Ford, and in any case Kissinger, like Nixon, was not known for loyalty to old friends. The Chinese were displeased by Ford's signing the Helsinki Accords, which like the American right wing they saw as too accommodating to the Soviet Union. In July, the Chinese government had sent an urgent invitation from Mao to Nixon to come talk. Nixon had called Kissinger to say he wanted to go, perhaps in September, but Kissinger was against it. Ford had not yet gone to China, and if Nixon were to go before the President, it would embarrass the new Administration. A disappointed Nixon agreed to wait and to consult Kissinger before making any plans.[22]

Nixon's relations with Kissinger, never relaxed, were now more strained than ever. In mid-October, when Kissinger was at a dinner party in Ottawa, a microphone was left open at the speakers' table, and Kissinger's chit-chat with his hosts was recorded on a tape in the press room. On the subject of Nixon, Kissinger said, "He was very good in foreign policy [but] he was a very odd man. . . . He is a very unpleasant man. He was so nervous. It was such an effort for him to be on television. He was an artificial man in the sense that when he met someone he thought it out carefully so that nothing was spontaneous, and that meant he didn't enjoy people.

"People sensed that. What I never understood is why he became a politician. He hated to meet new people. Most politicians like crowds. He didn't."[23]

The remark caused much comment. It moved Bill Safire to write a gossipy column on the ever-fascinating Nixon-Kissinger relationship. Safire reported that at the recent Vladivostok summit, Kissinger had sought to tout Ford at Nixon's expense, saying that Nixon "would never look Brezhnev in the eye." He recounted other Kissinger cracks, then revealed that Nixon had sent a warning to Ford of "the danger of Kissinger hubris, and the need to cut him down to mere superstar size." Safire wrote that

Kissinger had called Nixon with "profuse apologies" after the Ottawa tape episode, but nevertheless, "Mr. Nixon's friends let it be known" that Nixon was keeping a sharp eye on Kissinger's responses to inquiries about the 1969 wiretapping of NSC members. "If Dr. K tries to pass the buck on everything to Mr. Ex.," Safire warned, he would be in big trouble.[24]

The little games Nixon and Kissinger played with each other, usually through a third party, went on. In November, Ford went to China. In late December, David and Julie went to China, where they had a private audience with Mao. The Chairman extended a personal invitation for a Nixon visit. Now that Ford had made his trip, Nixon felt free to accept. But with the primary season about to begin in the United States, and with Reagan challenging Ford (and leading him in the polls in New Hampshire, where the first primary would take place on February 24), Nixon decided to say nothing to Ford or Kissinger about his trip until the last possible moment, and then only after the Chinese had made a formal announcement.

He did tell Gulley, at the Annenberg estate in January 1976. "Now that Ford's been to Russia and China, I can go again," he said. As to the upcoming primary, Nixon remarked, "Jerry's got New Hampshire anyway, this won't hurt him; and it's better if I go now than closer to the election."[25] Then Nixon called Ford to say that he would stay out of the public eye until after the November election.[26]

On February 2, Kissinger visited Nixon at La Casa Pacifica. They discussed foreign policy. Nixon mentioned that someday he would like to return to China, but there was nothing in his tone to indicate he would be going any time soon.

Three days later, the Chinese government announced that Nixon would be flown to Peking on a special Chinese airliner on February 21, the fourth anniversary of his first visit to China, and just three days before the New Hampshire primary. Ford's National Security Adviser, Brent Scowcroft, and his chief of staff, Dick Cheney, along with other aides, were furious. "Nixon's a shit," said Scowcroft, who almost never swore. Ford was astounded. The timing could not have been worse, Nixon had lied to him; it was unbelievable.

Nixon made a bad situation worse when he called Kissinger to claim that the Chinese had given him only thirty-six hours advance notice. Nixon could not possibly have expected Kissinger to believe that. Perhaps he hoped Kissinger could convince Ford that such was indeed the case. Kissinger, however, told Ford that the Chinese did not do business that way.[27]

Ford kept his outrage to himself. Other Republicans did not. Barry Goldwater said on the Senate floor that the Justice Department should consider prosecuting Nixon under the provisions of the Logan Act, which bars private citizens from negotiating with foreign countries. "If he

[Nixon] wants to do this country a favor," Goldwater added, "he might stay over there."[28]

In his *National Review* column, William Buckley called Nixon a "pariah." He warned the Chinese that "Richard Nixon is not the leader of anything at all these days. He has less influence on the Republican Party than [sportscaster] Howard Cosell." Buckley felt that "the spectacle of Nixon, wining and dining with the nabobs in the oriental palaces while Howard Hunt rots in jail and Mitchell and Ehrlichman and Haldeman live broken lives trying to pay their lawyers' fees, will aggravate sentiments of injustice that can only be exercised at the expense of Gerald Ford."[29]

Joseph Kraft in his *Washington Post* column called the trip "a sleazy act, thoroughly typical of the qualities which earned him the sobriquet Tricky Dick."[30] Mary McGrory felt that "any other man might have delayed the many-squalored thing. . . . Sure, Gerald Ford spared him indictment, trial, possible prison and even admission of anything graver than 'errors in judgment.' But what has he done for him lately?"[31]

David Broder broke his own promise never again to write about Nixon: "The utter shamelessness of the man—his willingness to exploit and corrupt every institution and relationship of which he has ever been a part—has become so blatant that one would think it would not require comment . . . There is nothing, absolutely nothing he will not do in order to salvage for himself whatever scrap of significance he can find in the shambles of his life."[32]

This outburst of outrage may have surprised Nixon, but it did not tempt him to cancel the trip. It did force him to explain himself. He did so through the column of his friend Safire, in the form of a statement he authorized Safire to print: "In 1972, I went to the People's Republic of China because I concluded that a new and constructive relationship between the U.S. and the P.R.C. was indispensable . . . I believe that this relationship is, if anything, more important today than it was four years ago. I look forward to the opportunity of seeing again the leaders and the people of the P.R.C." Safire then went on to explain that the trip had nothing to do with a resurrection of Nixon, but was intended to place a seal of approval on Chou En-lai's successor, Hua Kuo-feng (Chou had died recently of cancer). Nixon was doing Mao a favor by making it possible for Hua Kuo-feng, as his first public act, to greet Nixon, which would have the effect of making Hua legitimate.[33]

Other interpretations stressed the need by the Chinese for American aid, without explaining how Nixon could get it for them. Still others were even more convoluted, that despite Nixon's supposed support for Ford, he really wanted Reagan to win. Few made the obvious point: there was no other place Nixon could go that would give him so much publicity, so much attention, so much respect (at least from the hosts, if not from Americans), or launch his comeback so spectacularly.

On February 20, Nixon, accompanied by Pat, Brennan, two communications specialists, a fifteen-member Secret Service contingent, and a medical corpsman, flew in a Chinese Boeing 727 to Peking. That was as nothing compared to the crowd that had flown with him four years earlier, but there were some reminders of old times. *The New York Times* and many other newspapers carried a front-page photo of Nixon and Pat, with two of their Chinese hosts. (Ford's picture, as he and Betty campaigned in New Hampshire, was on page 11.) The *Manchester Union Leader*, New Hampshire's largest paper and a staunch supporter of Reagan, carried a series of editorials on the Nixon trip. One described it as a "miserable way" for Nixon to repay Ford.[34]

Ford was besieged with questions about the trip. His response was that private citizen Nixon had a right to go wherever he wanted, whenever he wanted. He insisted that Nixon had received no special briefing, did not carry any messages, and would not be debriefed when he returned. Kissinger undercut him; the Secretary told reporters that "we will, of course, wish to learn about the nature and the result" of the meetings when Nixon returned.

THERE were no bands at the Peking airport, no television cameramen. The world had changed considerably since he had last stood on that runway, four years earlier. Vietnam was now one country, Communist-ruled. The SEATO had folded up, ironically holding its last ceremony while Nixon was in the air over the Pacific. Chou En-lai was dead. Nixon had been forced to resign his power. The bright promise of the first Nixon trip had not been realized; the United States still had not recognized China, there had been only a slight increase in trade between the two countries, there was no military alliance, nor any prospect of significant improvement.

A cynic, or a conservative, might well ask what if anything had been gained by Nixon's "opening to China." William Buckley did ask. His answer was, nothing good for the United States. In his view, the fruits of Nixon's opening were: "We lost a major war for the first time in our history; made a mockery of the whole notion of Vietnamization; established a detente" that allowed the Soviets to take the lead in strategic weapons while imposing their will in Angola, and "dismembered the NATO alliance."[35]

Buckley's list of horrors put the blame in the wrong place. They all would have happened whether or not Nixon had gone to China in 1972. His trip had been purely symbolic. It had solved no problems, found no solutions. What had made it noteworthy was the fascination of watching

Richard Nixon hobnobbing with Mao and Chou. So again in 1976, although the television networks had not sent over their crews, the newspaper reporters were there, and suddenly Nixon was back. Nearly every daily paper in America had a photograph of Dick and Pat in China on the front page, many of them for each day of the week they were in the country. For the first time since the pardon and his illness, Nixon was the major news story, even as the presidential campaign was getting hot. He gave many toasts at many banquets; his every word was scrutinized for its significance; hidden meanings were found in the most commonplace remarks; it was as if he were still President.

Nixon had a wonderful time. "Wow," he said as he walked through the door of State Guest House No. 18, where he had stayed in 1972, "What memories this brings back."

There were meetings with Prime Minister Hua Kuo-feng, Foreign Minister Chiao Kuan-hua, and with the Chairman himself. As he so loved to do in foreign countries, Nixon got out to visit with the people on the street. It happened on the day of the New Hampshire primary; the following morning, *The New York Times* gave its headline to Ford, who had won a narrow victory over Reagan, and to Jimmy Carter, the Georgia ex-governor who had won the Democratic primary, but the two front-page pictures were of Nixon in China, mixing with the people. The top picture showed a skeptical Nixon arguing with a Chinese official from Tsinghau University in Tiananmen Square. The cut line said the official was explaining to Nixon the student posters criticizing "capitalist roaders" in government. The sign behind them ordered: "Fiercely Criticize the Reemergence of the Demoniacal Rightist Wind."[36]

The farewell banquet at the Great Hall of the People was as lavish as the one in the same place four years earlier. It was the first ever held there for a private citizen. Nixon's toasts were as grandiose as if he were still President. Quoting one of Mao's famous sayings, he declared, "Nothing is hard in this world if one dares to scale the heights.

"We did scale the heights, but there is more work to be done. We shall not fail. We must not fail, because of the young people we saw at the university today. China will not fail and the United States will not fail." This was interpreted by the reporters as a slap at Ford and Kissinger for their failure to move relations with China forward.[37]

From Peking, the Nixons traveled to south China, where they were greeted by tens of thousands of cheering Chinese citizens on the streets of Canton. At a tractor factory, he tried to pedal a foot-powered thresher, but was unable to do it alone. A Chinese worker helped and as the two men pedaled, Nixon said, "Ah—Chinese and Americans working together."

That was too good a line to let go of. At the banquet that night, Nixon said, "With both of us with our feet on the pedal, it went twice as fast.

The Chinese people are a great people. And the American people are a great people. And together we can do great things, even greater things."[38]

On February 29, Nixon bid farewell to his many Chinese friends and flew back to Los Angeles. It had been a spectacular trip, a successful trip, an exhausting trip, a rewarding trip. Nixon had gotten himself back on the front pages in a positive way, reminded his fellow Americans that no matter what they thought about him, he was honored and respected abroad, and made himself once again an insider (he was the only Westerner to have talked privately to the new Chinese Prime Minister).

The payoff came a few days later. Kissinger called. The Secretary apologized for not having come in person. He explained that it would embarrass Ford. Nixon said nothing. Kissinger then asked for a complete accounting of Nixon's trip, a debriefing. Nixon agreed to provide a written report. He was on his way back.[39]

CHAPTER TWENTY-TWO

THE FINAL DAYS
AND
THE '76 ELECTION
April–December 1976

AT THE BEGINNING of spring 1976, Simon and Schuster published Bob Woodward and Carl Bernstein's account of *The Final Days*, the denouement of the Watergate scandal. It covered Nixon's last months in office and his resignation. It was unfriendly to Nixon and to his Administration. It was based on uncited and unverifiable sources; it contained long quotations from spoken conversations that were either recalled with unbelievable accuracy or else were made up by participants (it was impossible to tell which); it was gossipy; it was sensational and dramatic.

It infuriated Nixon, his family, and his supporters. It was so spectacularly successful that two weeks after publication Simon and Schuster raised the price for the third printing of the fastest-selling book it had ever published from $10.95 to $11.95.[1] In the entire history of publishing in America, this was the first time any firm had ever raised the price of a book in the year, much less the month, that it was printed.

By the end of the second week the book had been reprinted again, bringing the total number in print up to 427,000. Simon and Schuster sold the paperback rights to Avon Books for $1,550,000, a record for a nonfiction book.[2]

Woodward and Bernstein were good reporters. The story they told was filled with high drama and low skulduggery; it purported to give an insider's account of the biggest political event of the century; the hype was skillful and successful. Of course the basic reason for the phenomenal reception of *The Final Days* was the fascination nearly everyone, nearly everywhere, had with Richard Nixon.

The subject of the book was portrayed as dangerously unstable. Woodward and Bernstein had him drinking heavily. According to *The*

Final Days, Nixon went around talking to the portraits on the walls of the White House. In a climactic scene, Nixon and Kissinger fell to their knees to pray, and supposedly Nixon broke down and sobbed. Pat Nixon, Woodward and Bernstein claimed, was a secret and heavy drinker. They wrote that the couple had not had sexual relations in fourteen years.

Nixon wanted to sue. He consulted several lawyers who convinced him that proving deliberate libel in the United States was difficult; a suit and trial would only give the book more publicity while costing a fortune.

Nixon made no public statement on the book. Julie Eisenhower hotly denied the description of her mother. "The nebulous, weak figure of *The Final Days* is not my mother," she said. In August of 1974, Pat was "a courageous and strong woman." As evidence, Julie cited Pat's heavy schedule of public events and travel in America and abroad. She pointed out that "this was hardly the schedule of a reclusive, heavy drinker" preoccupied with her own problems and oblivious to her responsibilities or the needs of her family.[3]

Haldeman denied that Nixon ever drank heavily. Kissinger said that the account of his meeting with Nixon the night before the resignation was "distorted and inaccurate" and showed "an indecent lack of compassion." Rabbi Korff, who was just gearing up for another fund-raising campaign for Nixon's legal fees, reported that funds were drying up as a result of the book. He added that Nixon was depressed by what the book said, and by the way the public seemed to accept it as true.[4]

The movie version of *All the President's Men*, Woodward and Bernstein's book on the prelude to Watergate, came out simultaneously with *The Final Days*, to the great benefit of both. Bill Safire was enraged by this double whammy against his old boss. He asked why there was such a market for this "journalfiction," and decided, "the answer is the need of many people to cover up their guilt feelings. Now that the nation has learned that the power-abuses of the Kennedy-Johnson era were greater both in scope and intensity than even the worst excesses of the Nixon years . . . there is a requirement for a heavy dose of reassurance that it was right to strike Nixon down." Safire was especially upset at Woodward and Bernstein's "jeers and snickers" at Nixon's falling to his knees to pray to God for "some answer to why he could not be allowed to fulfill his dream of being the world's peacemaker."[5]

Of course, Nixon would be able to give his version of what happened in his memoirs, and in a way Woodward and Bernstein had done him a favor by building the potential audience. The public was eager to read what he had to say for himself. Three months after *The Final Days* appeared, *The New York Times* purchased newspaper and magazine serialization rights to the memoirs for an undisclosed, but very large sum. Sydney Gruson, executive vice president of The Times Company, said, "Nixon's personal account of Watergate and the events leading to his resignation; detente with Russia; the reopening of contact with China; the Vietnam War . . . all will be of immense interest." William Sarnoff, chairman of Warner Publishing, Inc., the publisher, said he had read parts of the manuscript and found them to be "an intensely moving, personal memoir of events and emotions that could be told only by the man who experienced them."[6]

In addition to the further advance payment on his memoirs, Nixon gathered in some large cash sums in the first half of 1976. He sold his two homes in Key Biscayne for $710,000. He had purchased them in 1969 for $253,000, and had paid the GSA $92,000 in 1972 for improvements considered personal. The considerable profit he realized led the editorial writers of The New York Times to remind the public that back in April 1974, Nixon had promised to pay the government the $432,787 in back taxes plus interest that the IRS said he owed after it had rejected his deduction of $576,000 for his vice presidential papers. He had paid $284,706, but still owed $148,081. As the three-year statute of limitations had run out, he was under no legal obligation to pay up, but the Times editors felt that, in view of his handsome profit on the Key Biscayne sales, he should do so.[7]

But Nixon had big expenses to go with his big income. There were lawyers' fees, as he continued to challenge the constitutionality of the law seizing his presidential papers. There were salaries for Brennan and other aides. There were salaries for the researchers helping him on his memoirs. There was a big monthly bill to the telephone company to be paid, and continuing medical expenses. Nixon did not pay up on the back taxes.

He was spending most of his time, in the spring and early summer of 1976, working on his memoirs. He took a break for the Fourth of July weekend. On Friday, the 2nd, he and Pat dined with friends at a restaurant. The next night they attended a $76-a-couple bicentennial dinner dance in the Grand Ballroom of the Newport Beach Marriott.[8] On the 4th, they drove to Palos Verdes for a small party in honor of Julie's twenty-eighth birthday at the home of Jack and Helene Drown. That evening, Pat was quiet and withdrawn, but Nixon was in a talkative mood. His subject was the way Ford had seized, or failed to seize, the opportunity afforded him by the bicentennial celebration. Nixon had wanted with all his heart to preside over America's two hundredth birthday party, as the apex of his own forty years in politics. It must have pained him to watch Ford assume the role that was rightfully his. He got some pleasure from criticizing Ford's performance.

"Ford missed a good chance," Nixon told David Eisenhower and Benjamin Stein, who had been a young speechwriter for Nixon. "How many speeches did he give? Seven? Ten? However many it was, it was too many. He just flew all over giving speeches and putting wreaths on things. Now does anyone remember anything that Ford said?"

No one present did. "That's exactly the point," Nixon said. "He had a chance to make a speech that everyone in the country would watch and remember. He should have said, a week before July Fourth, 'Look, I'm going up to Camp David to work on this speech.' He didn't actually have to work on it. He could go swimming or do anything. But people would have thought he was working on it. Then he could have given it and he could have locked up the nomination right then or there. Or am I wrong?"

David said he was right. "Then why didn't Ford do it?" Nixon asked. "Didn't he have anyone telling him he should do it?"⁹

Ford himself was quite pleased with the way the weekend had gone. He summed it up nicely when he recalled watching television that evening. The networks had covered his various appearances, then shown clips of people around the nation celebrating in various ways two hundred years of freedom. Recalling the mood of the country two years earlier, Ford told himself, "Whatever happens with the nomination and the election, you've done a good job, Jerry."¹⁰

Nixon commented on the upcoming election to Eisenhower and Stein. "It has to be Mondale," he said of the Democrats, referring to Minnesota Senator Walter Mondale. "He's a liberal. He's from the Midwest. He looks good on the tube."

Television, Nixon explained, was "what it's all about. How you come across on the tube."

Someone said Senator John Glenn of Ohio came across on the tube. Nixon said Glenn was dumb. He thought Senator Muskie was too old. Another Democratic candidate, Governor Jimmy Carter, had been in the Navy, so he "might be good" on defense.

Through the summer, via Gulley, who was still making regular visits from Washington to San Clemente, Nixon was offering Ford his advice. When he read a critical remark by Betty Ford about Nancy Reagan, he told Gulley to tell Ford not to antagonize Mrs. Reagan. "Nancy Reagan runs Ronald Reagan," Nixon explained. "She's a very strong woman, and if you make her angry, you're never going to pull this guy into camp, and Ford's really going to need Reagan after the convention. . . . He just cannot afford to alienate Nancy. . . . Nancy Reagan's a bitch, a demanding one, and he listens to her."¹¹

Gossip and catty remarks about candidates' wives were far short of real involvement. To get back into politics in a meaningful way, Nixon was going to have to provide some explanation of Watergate. He was doing just that, in his memoirs, on which he was working nearly full time. He would have to exercise some patience, and be willing to start once again at the bottom, with local appearances at local events for local causes. He scheduled his first public political event for July 12. He would speak at a fund-raising party for Representative Charles Wiggins, who represented his old district and who had been one of his chief defenders on the House Judiciary Committee, but who had turned on him after reading the transcript of the June 23, 1972, tape. It would be held in Yorba Linda, Nixon's birthplace.

Five days before the event, Nixon got some bad news. He shared it with Pat, warning her that the big story the next day would be his disbarment in New York. He had earlier tried to resign from the New York Bar, as he had done from the bars of California and the U.S. Supreme Court, but New York would not accept his resignation because Nixon had not acknowledged that he could not successfully defend himself against charges brought by the New York Bar Association that he had obstructed justice and concealed evidence in the Watergate affair. In a 4-to-1 opinion, the Appellate Division of the State Supreme Court sustained the charges. Nixon was found guilty of violating the Code of Professional Responsibility; this was the first time Nixon had been found guilty by an official party of charges relating to Watergate.[12]

PAT was spending the morning reading *The Final Days*, which she had borrowed over her husband's protest from one of the secretaries. Because Manolo and Fina Sanchez were on vacation, she spent the afternoon housecleaning. The work left her exhausted. She barely managed to change into a swimsuit for a late afternoon dip with Dick, David, and Julie, then rested at the shallow end while they swam. At dinner, she was able to eat only a few bites of the meal Julie had prepared and afterward she could barely walk to her room. An hour later, Julie went to ask her mother if she wanted to watch a TV show. She found her lying on her bed, fully clothed, sound asleep.

In the morning, shortly before seven o'clock, Pat went to the kitchen to make coffee. She tried to open a new can, using her left hand, and found she couldn't do it. When Nixon came in a few minutes later, he found her struggling with the top of a grapefruit juice bottle. He noticed immediately that the left corner of her mouth was drooping and that her speech was slurred. He guessed at once that she had had a stroke. Not wanting to frighten her, he drank his juice, then said he was going to his office. Instead, he woke Julie and told her, "I think your mommy's had a stroke."

While Julie tried to convince her mother to lie down, Nixon called Dr. Jack Lungren, described the symptoms, and at Lungren's request called for a doctor from Camp Pendleton. The doctor arrived at ten and after a quick exam said Mrs. Nixon had had a "tiny stroke." Her blood pressure was markedly elevated—175 over 110. Nixon called for an ambulance. Pat protested. She said she was merely tired and needed some rest. When her husband insisted, she packed a small suitcase and, when the ambulance arrived, climbed into it herself.[13]

Julie and Nixon rode with her for the 40-mile trip to Long Beach

Memorial Hospital. "My God," Pat said to Julie, "this shouldn't be happening to me."[14]

She never got sick. Or tired. Or depressed. She never had time. A couple of years earlier, David had told an interviewer, "I . . . worry about her because she never lets any of us know what troubles her. She is a shoulder to everyone—but whose shoulder does she lean on?" She blamed herself for the stroke. She told Julie, "I'm so angry with myself—getting ill."[15] "I keep everything in," she once told an interviewer. "I never scream . . . If I have a headache, no one knows about it . . . If I were dying, I wouldn't let anyone know."[16]

This time, she was defenseless. She told the head nurse of intensive care at Long Beach Memorial, who had cared for her husband twenty months earlier, "Connie, I'm beat. I'm through." She never expressed such sentiments to her family.

During his wife's first two weeks in the hospital, Nixon devoted himself to her. He picked out mail to bring her—over a million letters of sympathy and good wishes arrived—and flowers, along with news and gossip. He fussed over Tricia and Julie, worried about what they were eating and if they were getting enough sleep.

He drove to the hospital each morning. He entered Pat's room with a bounce in his step and a smile on his face. After kissing her on the cheek, he said immediately, "Well, let me feel your grip." Pat could barely lift her left hand, but she would grit her teeth and try to grasp his fingers. Each day she got a little stronger. Nixon sat by her bed and read some of the telegrams, letters, and editorials he had selected. Fifteen minutes of this left her exhausted, and he would leave.

Adversity had brought out a new tenderness in Nixon. His concern and love for her was obvious. Before the resignation, he had shunned any public display of affection. The couple had entered a new stage in the partnership, more caring, more concerned, more loving, and Nixon had been more willing to show it. Now, when he was ready to deepen their relationship, he had to face the fear of losing her. He could help bring her back with his encouragement, but recovery was up to her.

She knew it, and she never thought of quitting. Her therapy exercises were painful, and she wanted no witnesses to her struggle. But when she realized how desperately her family needed to see signs of progress, she would let them watch as she did "the steeple," the laborious process of joining the fingers of her left hand with those of her right. She would break into a sweat from the effort, but she did it. She later told Julie that another exercise, climbing three steps in the therapy room, was "the hardest thing I have ever done physically."[17]

Pat Nixon later told a reporter, "I had to become a child again so I could learn to use my arm and hand. I had to put blocks in square spaces and pegs in round holes, just as though I were a child."[18]

Nixon was the first to feel confident that she would make it. "That determination and fire in her eyes I've seen so often in difficult moments in the past is coming back," he said while she was still in the hospital. "I think this is going to be a determining factor."[19]

As she had so often in the past, Pat cheered up those around her. "I think Mrs. Nixon is very amazing in the spirit she has taken," Dr. Lungren told a news conference. "Her attitude is very refreshing. Many patients are very despondent, they feel life is all over, they give up the fight. She's done none of this."[20] Within three weeks, she was home. Not yet recovered, but on the way.

OF course, Nixon had to cancel his appearance for Wiggins in Yorba Linda. While he was absorbed with his wife, the Democrats met and nominated Carter. A month later, the Republicans met in Kansas City. The party had five times nominated Nixon for national office, but not once was his name mentioned in the convention, not once. A brief reference to his China policy had been dropped from the party platform. Rabbi Korff was incensed. He attempted to get signatures on a petition condemning the platform committee for deleting the reference, but without success. "People speak of events like the open door to China as if they were done by a phantom," he complained.[21]

Nixon nevertheless stayed with the Republicans. He was almost as intensely interested in the '76 convention as he had been in the previous seven. As always, he wanted to manipulate. In this case, what he wanted to manipulate was the choice of Ford's running mate. He had stayed publicly neutral on the Ford-Reagan struggle, even though Reagan had campaigned on a platform of attacking détente, attacking the Panama Canal Treaty (which Nixon had endorsed and Ford supported), and pledging to rid the nation of Henry Kissinger as Secretary of State. R. W. Apple of *The New York Times*, like many others, found Nixon's neutrality inexplicable, considering what Ford had done for Nixon and what Reagan was saying about Nixon's policies.[22] Perhaps Nixon thought Reagan would take the nomination away from Ford, and did not want to alienate him. Who can say? But with regard to the second spot, Nixon was very much involved, or at least tried to be.

His candidate was his old friend John Connally. He employed his usual methods—networking on the telephone with party leaders around the country, leaking his feelings to the press via friends, dropping hints, making suggestions. A "Republican leader" from Orange County, identified as a "friend" of Nixon, told one reporter that Nixon was "deeply concerned" over Ford's choice of a running mate. Nixon, the friend said, had been "disheartened" when he learned that Connally's stock was dropping in Kansas City. Nixon made a series of calls to Kansas City, to tell delegates that "Without a man of Mr. Connally's forceful personality, political skill and vote-getting ability to offset Jimmy Carter's strength among Southern voters, Ford could not win in November." Nixon tried to get through to Ford on the telephone, but the President would not talk to him. Without consulting Nixon, Ford selected Senator Robert Dole of Kansas as his running mate.[23]

Two days after the convention ended, Gulley flew to California to see Nixon. "It was as if he had just been waiting for me, waiting to roll up his sleeves," Gulley remembered. "The minute I walked in he said, 'O.K. Now we know who our guy is, we know who their guy is. Let's go to work.' Those were his exact words."

He told Gulley the point spread in the polls, favoring Carter, was false. He had instructions for Gulley to carry to Ford's chief of staff, Dick Cheney. They were about what to do "with this guy in this state and that guy in that state. He went into personalities, which ones had to be contacted and why. I was writing notes furiously to take back to the White House, and he was going without stopping for breath."

Throughout the campaign, Nixon sent advice to Ford. There were pages on how to debate, points to remember. Points like what to wear, where to stand, make sure to be rested, how to react if Carter turned mean (be sad, not angry), get in some "spontaneously" funny lines. The suggestion were about how Ford should conduct himself; Nixon did not offer advice about content.[24]

Ford acted on some of this advice. In his most famous and embarrassing moment in the Ford-Carter debates, he looked sincere and sure of himself and presidential as he declared, "There is no Soviet domination of Eastern Europe." He rejected other Nixon suggestions. Repeatedly, Nixon demanded to know whether Ford had followed up on the contacts he had provided in various cities and states. Gulley would reply that to the best of his knowledge, Ford had done so.

"Well, goddamn it, I checked, and he hasn't," Nixon would explode, "and the guy is getting pissed."[25] Nixon had told Ford to use John Mitchell in New Jersey and Missouri. "He knows more about those two states than anybody around. He can be useful behind the scenes, but it's got to be covert." Ford did not use Mitchell. Nixon advised him to keep Hartmann out of California, because "the Republicans in California hate him." Hartmann worked California. Nixon told Ford to give up on New York, not waste any time there, because Carter was going to ride in on Pat Moynihan's coattails. Ford made a major effort in New York.

"Don't worry about what you say about Nixon," Nixon told Gulley to tell Ford. "Murder me. I understand. Remember, Carter scares the hell out of me. Scare the hell out of the American people about Carter's foreign policies; bear down on it. He'll come close to making us a number two power."

"An international incident can be useful to Ford," Nixon advised.

"But be careful how you use it. If an international situation blows up, dramatize it. He's the President. Of course if it comes out I suggested it, they'll say, 'Nixon says start a war.' "

"Kissinger's talking too much about black Africa," Nixon said. "It's pissing off the red-necks. The Negro vote's lost; don't let it lose you the white votes. The Democrats have the Negroes and the Jews, and let them have them—in fact, tie them around their necks."[26]

These were the politics Nixon had worked with great success in 1946, in 1950, in 1952, and again in 1968 and 1972. But it did not suit Gerald Ford. He made up lots of ground, almost passed Carter in the last days, but in the end was sunk by the weight of having been appointed by Nixon and having pardoned Nixon. He lost a close one: in the exit polling conducted by the Republicans, 7 percent of those who voted for Carter gave as the reason Ford's pardon of Richard Nixon. A few years later when asked if he would have done it again, Ford thought a moment, then replied, "I think I still would have." [27] Nixon had no public comment on the election, then or later.

There was much he could have said, as in any close election. Most speculation centered on the effect of the pardon, with a majority concluding that it cost Ford the election. Nixon's trip to China with its attendant publicity reminded voters of who had put Ford into the White House, and who had pardoned Nixon. But before concluding that it was Nixon's lack of gratitude, his refusal to do the decent thing and stay out of sight until after the election, that caused Ford's defeat, recall some of Ford's blunders, most especially the "no Soviet domination" line. How many voted for Carter because of that gaffe? Recall, too, double-digit inflation, and that winning re-election in all of the world democracies was difficult in the mid-seventies, in the wake of the oil shock.

It is not provable that Nixon cost Ford the 1972 presidential election. It is obvious that Nixon hurt the man who had done so much for him.

CHAPTER TWENTY-THREE

SELLING MEMORIES,
WRITING MEMOIRS
1977

THE 1976 PRESIDENTIAL CAMPAIGN had given Nixon an opportunity to help shape the future. He had been looking forward, rather than backward. But for the next year and a half he would engage himself in explaining the past, his actions as President, most of all his defense of all that Watergate now included. It was emotional and exhausting work, but highly profitable, in the double sense that he was well paid for providing his self-defense on the cover-up, and he was able to make his case without having to face cross-examination.

Nixon seems to have known the truth of George Orwell's observation, "To control the present is to control the past. To control the past is to control the future." He must also have been aware that out-of-work politicians cannot control the present, but that there is much they can do to shape the future's perception of the past.

There are many methods, and between 1977 and 1990 Nixon used every one of them. The two most important were his continuing struggle to control the basic documentary record and to tell his story in a compelling way. That Nixon was not completely successful in reversing the public perception of his role in the Watergate scandal was less because of a lack of skill or dedication, more a consequence of the difficulty of the task. But however hard the row he set himself to hoe, he never allowed himself to get discouraged, he never quit digging away, and he continued to reap great benefits from his work.

His most effective effort was control of the documentary record. Written memoirs and oral histories (interviews) help the historian go beyond the contemporary accounts of events to understand what happened and why, but they can never be conclusive: memory is always inaccurate and usually self-serving. That is why the historian insists on seeing the full written record, on examining all the documents (and in Nixon's case listening to all the tapes) before attempting to come to a final judgment. That is also the reason historians never regard their work as "definitive." They know that there are always documents yet to be discovered that will add to our knowledge and change our view of the past.

Nixon's ability to control the documentary (and taped) record of his Administration was sharply limited by the Presidential Records and Materials Preservation Act of 1974. It gave physical possession, although not ownership, of the papers and tapes of the Nixon Administration to the National Archives. The only important document Nixon had in his own possession was his diary, said to be 10,000 typescript pages in all.

The uniqueness of Nixon's situation was highlighted in the third week of January, the day before Carter's inauguration, when nine truckloads of Ford's White House documents were taken to the University of Michigan, where Ford planned to establish his presidential library. This event gave Nixon a reason to challenge the 1974 law, and he did so immediately. On January 25, his lawyers filed a brief with the Supreme Court saying that Nixon had been singled out as an unreliable custodian of the record of his Administration. "Congress may not enact a statute that applies to a single individual and subjects him or her to treatment different from or worse than others receive, entirely on the basis of legislative judgment or blameworthiness," the brief said. The law provided that the National Archives would make the decision as to which of the materials were private, and which should be made available to scholars. Nixon's lawyers argued that this arrangement violated Nixon's constitutional right to privacy. "There is simply no precedent for such a wholesale seizure of and search through an individual's papers," the brief concluded.[1]

Three days after the brief was filed, the U.S. Court of Appeals for the District of Columbia ruled, 2 to 1, that Nixon had to yield tapes in civil as well as criminal cases. It had already ruled that tapes that were played to the jury in the Watergate trials of Mitchell, Haldeman, Ehrlichman, and others had to be made available for public sale and broadcast, a ruling Nixon was challenging in the Supreme Court. On January 28, the appeals court ruled in favor of Representative Ronald Dellums (D.-Calif.) and 1,200 persons arrested in the May Day 1971 demonstrations at the Capitol. Dellums and the others had asked for all tapes of conversations at the White House from April 16 through May 10, 1971, at which the demonstrations were discussed. There were a half dozen additional similar civil suits pending.[2]

In April, the Supreme Court began hearing arguments in the case. In their questions, the justices expressed concern about the justification for the 1974 bill and misgivings about the possibility that the statute could lead to unauthorized public disclosure of confidential government information. They were also worried about Nixon's regaining control over purely personal materials, such as tape recordings of conversations with his wife. On three occasions, Chief Justice Burger wondered whether if the bill were upheld the Congress would be able to pass statutes impounding papers of Supreme Court Justices when they left office. That line of questioning gave Nixon hope that the justices would strike down the bill.[3]

The General Services Administration, the parent organization of the National Archives, was meanwhile trying to get from Congress some workable guidelines on the manner in which Congress would allow scholars and the public to have access to the Nixon papers and tapes, as mandated by the Presidential Records and Materials Preservation Act. Three earlier attempts to create acceptable regulations had failed. If the Court upheld the bill, whatever regulations were approved would certainly be challenged by Nixon and other members of his Administration. Donald Young, a counsel for the GSA, remarked, "We're going to have lawsuits for a long, long time. I think Nixon will be dead and gone long before this thing is finally resolved."[4]

In San Clemente, at the beginning of 1977, Nixon suspended work on his memoirs in order to prepare for the Frost interviews. Taping was scheduled to begin on March 23. He began cramming and rehearsing with his chief researchers, Ken Khachigian (a former White House speechwriter), Diane Sawyer (former assistant to Ron Ziegler), and Frank Gannon (also from Ziegler's office). The procedure was similar to a pre-news conference briefing: Nixon's aides would ask him likely questions and he would practice his answers. The questions were predictable—Cambodia, the Christmas bombing, Brezhnev and détente, the China opening, civil rights, civil liberties, Watergate—and Nixon, thanks to his work on his memoirs, was on top of all of them, except Watergate, the section of his memoirs he had not yet written. So to most possible questions Nixon knew exactly what he wanted to say and could concentrate on how he would say it. In any area where he had uncertainty, he would call the man most directly involved for more information; he made a number of calls to Kissinger.

The interviewing was done at a private home on Monarch Bay, six miles north of San Clemente, that Frost had rented. Frost's first question was one that he said "almost every American and people all over the world want me to ask. They all have their questions, but one of them in every case is, 'Why didn't you burn the tapes?' "

Nixon, who certainly must have been prepared for the question, managed to appear surprised (to Frost he appeared to be "numbed"). He gave a rambling twenty-minute answer, beginning with the taping system he had inherited from Lyndon Johnson. He made some obvious points:

"The tapes in many respects contradicted the charges that had been made by Mr. Dean," and that to burn the tapes "would have been an indication that I felt there were conversations on there that demonstrated that I was guilty." In what was almost an aside, delivered in such a low-key way that it has gone unnoticed (in the sense that fourteen years later Frost's question was still the one most asked about Nixon and Watergate), Nixon told the flat-out, bottom-line truth: he said he had to "admit in all candor" that he had not believed "that they were going to come out."

Had Frost pursued the point, Nixon most likely would have given an explanation of the doctrine of executive privilege, contended that the tapes should have been covered by the doctrine, and possibly pointed out that the Johnson and Kennedy libraries had extensive tape recordings of White House conversations that had not been made public. Had Frost pressed a bit harder, Nixon might have made the most critical point of all: that there were some exculpatory statements he had made on those tapes. Frost could have pointed out that only Nixon and Haldeman knew a tape recorder was running as the cover-up conversations took place.

In the years since the Frost interviews, Nixon has said countless times that his biggest mistake was *not* destroying the tapes. It always gets a laugh (initiated by Nixon as he delivers the line). It was in March of 1977, in the Frost interviews, that he got started on this line of defense. He said he should have burned them, not for personal reasons, but for the sake of future Presidents, who might not get honest opinions from advisers who feared they were being taped. Then he made a point that he has often repeated: "As a matter of fact, if the tapes had been destroyed, I believe it is likely I would not have had to go through the agony of the resignation." He is almost certainly right about that.

Nixon said the damning remarks recorded on tape were taken "out of context." (Of course, so were his exculpatory statements.) People did not realize that when he ordered Dean to pay hush money to Hunt, he was merely exploring "options" or "playing the devil's advocate." Then there were those "expletives deleted," which were embarrassing and "disappointed a lot of my friends, although I must say, it is not the first time that it's occurred."[5]

This first exchange set the pattern for most of what followed. With some important exceptions, Frost asked obvious questions, then permitted Nixon to give rambling and self-serving answers. It made for good television—what could be more fascinating than Nixon on Nixon? Even the camera crew, ordinarily inured to anything short of an earthquake taking place on the other side of the lens, were caught up in a sense of being present at history in the making.

Of course, it was not history in the making; it was Nixon making big money by telling a potentially huge audience some of the highlights from his forthcoming memoirs, giving his side of the story, defending himself and his Administration. Frost wanted to know how Nixon could justify falsifying reports about the bombing of Cambodia. Nixon compared his action to Ike on the eve of D-Day: "And, ah, Eisenhower, and his commanders, ah, of course, had all kinds of stories put out deliberately, ah, which were false, in terms of where we might attack and so forth. And then they went into Normandy. Ah, in this case, the bombing had to be secret for the reasons we did."[6]

Nixon defended the Christmas bombing against Frost's charge that the agreement the North Vietnamese signed in January was only "slightly" better than the accord already reached in October. The January agreement was "substantially" better.

Did Nixon think he could have saved South Vietnam in May 1975? Nixon thought not, because of the War Powers Act and the bombing cut-off legislated by Congress effective August 15, 1973. Still, if Congress had met its responsibility and provided the funds Ford requested for ARVN in the spring of 1975, the South Vietnamese would have "had the necessary equipment" and "I believe they could have held on." Nixon went on:

> "Had the Congress kept its commitments, the commitments we had made to South Vietnam, then we wouldn't even be discussing this esoteric question . . .
>
> FROST: But, nevertheless, Congress didn't keep us in Vietnam.
>
> NIXON: As a matter of fact, the Congress lost it. And that's the tragedy and they have to take the responsibility for it."[7]

Frost noted that had it not been for the Vietnam War there would have been less domestic discord and thus less of a need for the Nixon Administration to engage in "so-called abuses of power. . . . In that sense, someone has said—I wonder if you agree—that in that sense, perhaps, you were the last American casualty of the Vietnam War."

Nixon's face seemed to Frost to become "a mask of pain." He paused, drew a breath, and spoke: "A case could be made for that, yes. Ah, there isn't any question but that in the conduct of the war I made, ah, enemies who were, from an ideological standpoint, ah, virtually, ah, well, paranoiac, I guess. . . . But the action, and many of them I took with great reluctance, but recognizing I had to do what was right, the actions that I took in Vietnam: one, try to win an honorable peace abroad, and two, to keep the peace at home. . . . That was, of course, not easy to do, in view of the dissent and so forth, that we had. And so, it could be said that I was, ah, if I, that I was one of the casualties, or maybe the last casualty in Vietnam. If so, I'm glad I'm the last one. . . ."[8]

That was certainly heartfelt as well as painful, probably as painful to Nixon supporters and to Nixon enemies as to Nixon himself. Frost got other striking lines from the interview. He went into covert activities, then asked about the Huston Plan.

"Well," said Nixon, "when the President does it, that means that it is not illegal."

That would become one of the most quoted lines from the interviews; it shocked Frost, and most viewers. But Nixon's elucidation, long since forgotten, made a case for his assertion: "If the President, if, for example, the President approves something, approves an action because of the national security or, in this case, because of a threat to internal peace and order of significant magnitude, then the President's decision in that instance is one that enables those who carry it out to carry it out without violating a law. Otherwise they're in an impossible position."[9]

Much of the twenty-six hours of interviewing consisted of old familiar stuff. Nixon on the media: "The greatest concentration of power in the United States today is not in the White House; it isn't in the Congress and it isn't in the Supreme Court. It's in the media. And it's too much. . . . It's to much power and it's power that the Founding Fathers would have been very concerned about. . . . There is no check on the networks. There is no check on the newspapers."[10]

Frost asked about Mrs. Nixon. Nixon said her recovery from the stroke was almost complete. "But it hasn't been easy, and particularly let me say, I've mentioned the stories that have been written, and some written by, ah, some book authors"—Nixon pretended he could not remember the names of Woodward and Bernstein, looked at the ceiling for guidance, and then gave up—"and so forth, which reflected even on her, on occasion, what her alleged weaknesses were. They haven't helped, and, as far as my attitude towards the press is concerned, I respect some, but [for] those who write history as fiction on third-hand knowledge, I have nothing but utter contempt. And I will never forgive them. Never!

"All I say," he went on, "is Mrs. Nixon read it [*The Final Days*], and her stroke came three days later. I didn't want her to read it, because I knew the kind of trash it was, and the kind of trash they are."[11]

As the interviews went on, Frost continued to draw Nixon out, sometimes in revealing ways. He got what previous reporters seldom had from Nixon, a bit of raw emotion. He was not an antagonistic interviewer, although he and his staff had done extensive research and he did ask some tough and a few searching questions.

The test was Watergate. The show was promoted as the "only public trial Nixon will ever have."[12] It was hardly a trial. Frost was not a prosecutor, Nixon did not have a lawyer present, there was no formal cross-examination, no judge to rule on out-of-order questions, and so forth. Frost was more interested in putting on a good show than he was in discovering the truth. Still, it was the only time Nixon answered questions, in public, about Watergate. And the interview did provide some memorable moments.

Nixon claimed he was not guilty of criminal activity in the cover-up, because his motive was not criminal. Frost quoted to him sixteen statements from his "cancer on the presidency" conversation with John Dean in which Nixon gave orders to pay Howard Hunt the hush money he was demanding, or indicated that he knew the money was being paid and agreed to it. (Some samples: "Let me put it frankly: I wonder if that doesn't have to be continued?"; "That's worth it, and that's buying time"; "Hunt has at least got to know this before he's sentenced"; "We have no choice"; and so on.)

"Let me stop you right there," Nixon cut in. "Right there. . . . You were reading there out of context, out of order." He insisted that because he had refused to grant clemency, he was not submitting to blackmail. And he claimed that no money had been paid to Hunt "as a result of a direction given by the President for that purpose."[13] That last clause stuck in his mind; he used it again thirteen years later, in his book *In the Arena*, when he wrote that his accusers never quoted his "that would be wrong" statement about clemency, and "ignored the even more crucial fact that no payments were made as a result of that conversation."[14] He did not deny that money was paid (within six hours, in fact) *after* his talk with Dean; he simply denied that it was paid *as a result* of that talk. In other words, Nixon told Dean to see to it that the money was paid, quick; Dean saw to it that the money was paid, quick; but the money was not paid "as a result of that conversation."

Frost did try to push:

Here's Dean, talking about this hush money for Hunt; talking about blackmail and all of that: I would say that you endorsed, or ratified it. But let's leave that to one side—
NIXON: I didn't endorse or ratify it.
FROST: Why didn't you stop it?
NIXON: I had no knowledge of the fact that it was going to be paid.

Then he admitted that it was "possible" he had made a "mistake" in not stopping it.[15]

With regard to Bob Haldeman and John Ehrlichman, Nixon agreed that "I can be faulted," because "I defended them too long. Maybe I tried to help them too much." He said, "I think the great story as far as a summary of Watergate is concerned, and I, ah, did some of the big things rather well, I screwed up terribly in what was a little thing and became a big thing. But I will have to admit I was not a good butcher." The reason was, "When it comes to people, you know, I feel for 'em. And when you let your feelings, your heart get in the way of your head, that's when you make mistakes. And that's what I did."[16]

It was preposterous for Nixon to claim that his only mistake had been in trying to protect his friends, that his fatal flaw was a lack of ruthlessness. Haldeman and Ehrlichman were only the first he threw to the wolves when his pursuers started to close in on him, and the firing had come early, before the revelation of the taping system and before the Special Prosecutor had been confirmed. But whatever the facts, Nixon stuck with his defense; in his 1990 book *In the Arena* he wrote, "Some have said my major mistake was to protect my subordinates."[17] That "some have said" is of course a favorite Nixon formulation; others say his major mistake was to order a cover-up, then as soon as the going got hot to fire the men he had ordered to carry out the cover-up.

Frost wanted to know if Nixon would not go beyond the word "mistakes" in explaining Watergate.

"Well, what word would you express?" Nixon asked.

Frost's sense of timing was good. He knew he had reached a climactic moment. To heighten the drama, Frost picked up his clipboard from his lap and tossed it onto the floor beside his chair. "Since you asked me that heart-stopping question," he said, there were three things he wanted Nixon to say, things he thought the American people wanted to hear. One was that there had been more than mistakes, there had been wrongdoing. Second, people wanted to hear him admit that he abused power. "And thirdly—I put the American people through two years of agony and I apologize for that." He warned that unless Nixon said these things, "you're going to be haunted for the rest of your life."

Nixon started off with the mistakes. He had made "horrendous ones . . . ones that were not worthy of a President . . . ones that did not meet the standards of excellence that I had always dreamed of as a young boy." He had lied. "And for all those things, I have a very deep regret."

With conviction and defiance, he went on: "People didn't think it was enough to admit mistakes. Fine. If they want me to get down and grovel on the floor, no. Never. Because I don't believe I should."

He was not blaming anyone else for his downfall. "I brought myself down. I gave them a sword. And they stuck it in. And they twisted it with relish. And, I guess, if I'd been in their position, I'd have done the same thing."[18]

Who could question that observation?

Frost tried to return to the Dean-Hunt hush money. Whatever Nixon's motives, wasn't it true that he was, "to put it at its most simple, a part of a cover-up at times?"

No, "because I did not have the motive required for the commission of that crime." He had not committed an impeachable offense. The House would have indicted him, he admitted, had he not resigned, but "I might have won" in the Senate. "But, even if I'd won in the Senate by a vote or two, I would have been crippled and . . . in any event, for six months the country couldn't afford having the President in the dock." So he resigned for the good of the country, and thus "I have impeached myself."

Frost asked, "How do you mean, 'I have impeached myself'?"

"By resigning. That was a voluntary impeachment."

Nixon quickly introduced a new theme. When Dean had told him there was a cancer on the Presidency, and that Haldeman, Ehrlichman, Mitchell, and Dean had engaged in an illegal cover-up, "I will admit that I started acting as a lawyer for their defense. I was not prosecuting the case." Rather than acting as the chief law-enforcement officer in the United States, "to the extent that I did not meet that responsibility . . . [it was] in trying to advise Ehrlichman and Haldeman and all the rest as to how best to present their cases, because I thought they were legally innocent, that I came to the edge.

"And under the circumstances, I would have to say that a reasonable person could call that a cover-up."[19] He had tried too hard to protect his friends, and in doing so, "I let the American people down. And I have to carry that burden with me for the rest of my life.

"My political life is over.

"I will never yet, and never again, have an opportunity to serve in any official position. Maybe I can give a little advice from time to time . . .

"I did not commit a crime, an impeachable offense. . . .

"I made so many bad judgments, the worst ones, mistakes of the heart rather than the head, as I pointed out.

"But, let me say, a man in that top judge . . . top job, he's gotta have a heart.

"But his head must always rule his heart."[20]

Nixon said later that the Frost interviews "proved to be the major ordeal of my stay in San Clemente." He agreed to make the broadcast "not by choice but by necessity,"[21] A commercial venture had turned into an encounter. Perhaps the most emotional moment came at the very end, when Frost asked him to describe his feelings following the resignation and the pardon.

Nixon said he had been "emotionally and physically and mentally fagged out. I know a lot of people—and I can understand it—say, 'Gee whiz, it just isn't fair, you know, for an individual to be . . . ah . . . get off with a pardon simply because he happens to have been President, and when another individual goes to trial and maybe has to serve a prison sentence for it.' I can understand how they feel. I can only say that no one in the world, and no one in our history could know how I felt. No one can know how it feels to resign the presidency of the United States. Is that punishment enough? Oh, probably not. But whether it is or isn't, as I have said earlier in our interview, we have to live with not only the past but the future. And I don't know what the future brings, but whatever it brings, I'll still be fighting."[22]

THE first program aired the night of May 4, 1977. It attracted an audience of between 45 and 50 million, making it the most-watched news interview in the history of television and one of the highest-rated news broadcasts ever.[23]

The remaining four programs drew somewhat smaller but still substantial audiences, more viewers than most of the entertainment programs, and they all created new headlines. Nixon was back on the front pages. He had made $540,000. He had made the best case for himself that could be made. He had infuriated his enemies, delighted his friends. He had vowed that whatever happened, "I'll still be fighting." He was coming back.

ONE month after the last Frost program was on the air, Nixon took a heavy blow from the Supreme Court. By a 7–2 vote (Burger and Rehnquist dissenting), the Court ruled that the Presidential Records and Materials Preservation Act was constitutional, on the grounds that Nixon was "a legitimate class of one," subject to special treatment by Congress.

On August 9, 1977, the third anniversary of Nixon's resignation, the GSA moved 1,800 boxes of material, containing the tapes and the most sensitive files of Nixon's aides, from the EOB to the National Archives, where they were placed "in a vault within a vault within a vault," a specially constructed steel enclosure in a vault of the Archives.[24]

The Court ruling on the presidential papers complicated the research process for Nixon's memoirs. But the 1974 law did not deny Nixon access to the documents of his Administration, and Gannon went to Washington and brought back thirty thousand photocopied pages from the files. In addition, Nixon had a large clipping collection that dated back to 1946 to work with, and his aides had conducted dozens of supplementary interviews. Further, Nixon had his own diary to draw on as he wrote, plus his daughters' diaries. Working with this mass of documentation, Nixon had dictated some 1.5 million words. He was taking elaborate security precautions with the manuscript, locking it every night in a vault.[25]

"The decisive factor in my decision to write my memoirs," Nixon later declared, was "mental recovery." Writing the memoirs "was an enormous mental challenge requiring the full use of all my creative abilities." He believed, "Writing a book is the most intensive exercise anyone can give to his brain," and the process "provided the therapy that was needed for a full spiritual recovery, by enabling me to put Watergate behind me."[26]

By March 1977, the manuscript was growing to unmanageable size. Warner Books, a paperback reprint house, had little experience editing original manuscripts. Warner's president, Howard Kaminsky, solved that problem by selling for $225,000 the hardcover rights to Grosset & Dunlap, a major New York publisher. Grosset put its vice president and editorial director, Robert Markel, in charge of editing. He flew to San Clemente and took five full days to read the manuscript. He was pleased with what he read, but insisted it had to be cut.

Gannon was opposed. "This is a seamless story," he protested. "If you are going to know any of it, you have to know all of it."

Yes, Markel replied, "but you also have to be able to lift it."

A meeting was arranged between Nixon, his staff, and representatives from Warner and Grosset. Markel insisted on cuts. Khachigian and Gannon began arguing. Kaminsky suggested the possibility of publishing a condensation first, to be followed by a multivolume history of the Nixon Presidency.

Nixon, who had listened but not spoken, at last declared, "You can cut and cut and cut, and finally all you have left is the bones." But, he added sadly, "that's okay with me."

They discussed the book's reception. Nixon was certain that the reviewers would give him the shaft. One of the Grosset editors disagreed; he thought reviewers would bend over backward to be fair.

"You don't know this crowd," Nixon interjected. "*I* know them. There is no way, *no way*. It is all going to be negative."[27]

A month later, at another session with Markel, Nixon said that however the critics judged it, he was determined to make it readable. "That's important," he said. "I want people to read it. I want them to understand."

In the summer of 1977, a team of Grosset copy editors came to San Clemente to copy-edit and trim the manuscript by two thirds. Nixon's staff, the copy editors, Nixon himself began working six and even seven days a week, up to twelve hours a day. He was in his office by seven, checking the previous day's revisions and deletions, scribbling his comments in the margin, dictating new material. After a light lunch and short nap, he would take a swim, then go back to work. After dinner he read, usually history, most often a biography or the memoirs of great men. De Gaulle's memoirs were his favorite.

At his doctor's insistence, he did get a bit of exercise. He would take King Timahoe on long walks on the beach, and twice a week play golf with Brennan.[28]

Diane Sawyer was the staff expert on Watergate. She read extensively in the record, conducted interviews with Haldeman and Ehrlichman, among others, and prepared a "flow-chart" tracing day by day the events of June 1972 to August 1974. When Nixon read it, in late July, he told her, "You know, this is the first time I've really understood everything that happened."[29]

IN October, Nixon broke away from his monklike existence long enough to give his first political speech since his resignation. The occasion was a Republican fund-raising $500-a-couple buffet at a private oceanfront home in Corona Del Mar. Nixon spoke off the cuff to about one hundred people. He said that Orange County Republicans needed to find young, attractive candidates. He pointed out that a "fighting spirit" was more important to a political candidate than money. The treasurer of the Lincoln Club, a conservative Republican organization in Orange County that Nixon had recently joined and sponsor of the buffet, characterized Nixon's remarks as "a pep talk to workers in the field."[30] Who better than Nixon at that task?

January 9, 1978, was Nixon's sixty-fifth birthday. He and Pat, Julie and David, and Jack Brennan went to one of Nixon's favorite restaurants, the El Adobe in San Juan Capistrano, for dinner. A surprise guest was waiting for them, Bob Abplanalp. They ate chili releno, beef enchilada, Spanish rice and refried beans; there was a cake with sixty-five candles. "Everyone kidded him about being eligible for Social Security and Medicare," Brennan told a reporter. "He said he'd refuse Social Security."[31]

Hubert Humphrey called with birthday wishes. The two old rivals talked for fifteen minutes. It was obvious that Humphrey was tired. His voice was slurring and Nixon could tell he was in considerable pain from the cancer that was taking his life. When he hung up, Nixon called Brennan into his office. "He's only got a few days," Nixon said. "I don't care what it takes, but I'm going to his funeral. Start working on it."

Humphrey died two days later. After clearing his appearance with Muriel Humphrey, who said she would be "honored" to have him present, Nixon flew by commercial jet to Washington.[32] Brennan managed to keep the flight a secret, so reporters and television crews waited in vain to capture his return to the capital. Pickets at Dulles Airport, carrying familiar signs ("Honk If You Think He Is Guilty," "End the War") also missed him.[33]

Ordinarily, when former Presidents come to Washington they stay in a government-owned red-brick townhouse on Lafayette Square, but President Carter had not extended an invitation to Nixon. Instead, Nixon stayed with the widow of a former California judge in her northern Virginia estate.

He was gloomy and depressed, whether by Humphrey's death or his return to Washington, or both, who could say? He was apprehensive about a gathering of the VIPs scheduled for the morning of January 15 at Senator Howard Baker's office. They were to wait there for the proper moment to enter the Rotunda in the Capitol. Nixon told Brennan to call Baker to beg off, but Baker insisted that he come.[34]

He arrived, unnoticed, accompanied by Brennan and Tricia, about 10:30 A.M. Waiting for him in Baker's office were President Jimmy Carter, former President Gerald and Betty Ford, Henry Kissinger, and Nelson Rockefeller. It was an awkward moment. Ford broke the tension by walking over, sticking out his hand, and saying, "Good to see you, Mr. President."

They compared golf scores, vying as to whose was worse. Then the others came up, to shake hands. They all called Nixon "Mr. President."

"You as mean as ever, Henry?" Nixon asked.

"Yes," Kissinger answered, "but I don't have as much opportunity as before." They exchanged notes on memoir writing.

Photographers persuaded Carter to join Ford and Nixon for a group picture. Carter managed a smile; Nixon looked grim. Ford, standing between them, gazed off into space.

The service was tearful and emotional. Nixon stood straight and stiff, then sat, folded his hands in his lap, laced and replaced his fingers as he looked straight ahead. When it was over he spoke briefly to Muriel Humphrey, then slipped out a side door. Within hours, he was back in San Clemente.

According to Linda Charlton of *The New York Times,* "he was indisputably the celebrity of the morning." Even though he said not one word to the press or the public, and showed no emotion, even though there was another former President and the current President present, most eyes were on him most of the time.[35]

CHAPTER TWENTY-FOUR

"I'M OUT!"

1978

IN HIS MEMOIRS, published in early 1978, Nixon made his case in a readable if unreliable book. Despite the outpouring of words on Watergate and Vietnam, which dominate the work, there is no revelation, no new information; there are no insights, there are only defenses. And there are lies. Nixon wrote of his March 21, 1973, conversation with John Dean, "I had not finally ordered any payments to be made to defendants, and I had ruled out clemency." He quoted himself as having written in his diary, the evening of June 23, 1972 (the day he told Haldeman to tell the CIA to tell the FBI "don't go any further into the case, period"), "I emphasized to Haldeman, we must do nothing to indicate to Pat Gray or to the CIA that the White House is trying to suppress the investigation." When he published that supposed diary entry, he knew the tape was public knowledge. He asserted that no one from the White House approached the CIA to request that it turn off the FBI investigation, except John Dean, who had acted on his own. Nixon gave a convoluted explanation of his role in the Ellsberg break-in. "I do not believe I was told about the break-in at the time. . . . Ehrlichman says that . . . he told me about it after the fact in 1972. I do not recall this, and the tapes of the June–July 1972 period indicate that I was not conscious of it then, but I cannot rule it out."

He left out a great deal. Readers were spared what promises he made to the Chinese in 1972 about Formosa, and treated to the details of small talk with Mao. The same with Brezhnev.

Contradictory as always, this man who guarded his privacy quoted extensively from his daughters' diaries in times of great emotional stress.

There were many positive features to the memoirs. He was con-

516

vincing in defending détente and the need to open to China. His assess-
ments of foreign leaders were usually good and sometimes brilliant. He
was especially worth reading on Mao, Khrushchev, and Brezhnev.

He was brutally direct in describing his associates. Kissinger, he
wrote, was "Machiavellian, deceitful, egotistical, arrogant, and insulting."
Rogers was "vain, uninformed, unable to keep a secret, and hopelessly
dominated by the State Department bureaucracy." But, "I valued both
men for their different views and qualities."

Overall, *RN: The Memoirs of Richard Nixon* was a classic example
of Nixon at work, setting out to make everything perfectly clear, leaving
everything opaque.

THE publication of his memoirs, a relatively warm reception from the
critics, impressive sales, the return to the headlines, all helped to trans-
form Nixon from recluse to man on the go. He was campaigning again,
to become America's elder statesman; and another goal, which could be
achieved only after his death, to go down as one of the great Presidents.
On May 20, he hosted a party at La Casa Pacifica to mark publication
day. He gave Pat, Tricia, and Julie the first three copies of the book. He
urged them to start at the beginning and read through to the end. (Pat
went straight to Watergate. But she told Julie the next morning she had
gone back to the beginning of the book because it made her sick to see
how much of it was given over to Watergate. She said, "He'll never get
any credit for anything he says on the subject anyway. I wanted him to
just state frankly that he didn't know, that no one knows, the full story
of Watergate.")[1]

A week later Nixon threw a gala party that was pure joy for him. His
guests were three hundred POWs, accompanied by wives and children,
celebrating the fourth anniversary of their release from North Vietnam.
Pat decked the patio with flowers; there were six bars set up around the
pool; there were buffet tables laden with Mexican-style hors d'oeuvres.
Nixon gave each POW an autographed copy of his memoirs. Air Force
Major General John Flynn, as spokesman, told him, "Sir, we have a debt
of eternal gratitude to you. We wish you the best. God bless you, sir."

That same week, Nixon accepted an invitation to dedicate a $2.7
million recreation center in Hyden, Kentucky, a town of about five
hundred residents. The money for the center had come from Nixon's
revenue-sharing program; the locals intended to name the center after
Nixon. The event was scheduled for July 2. It would be his first public
speech since August 9, 1974.

About one thousand people were at the airport with signs: "Nixon's
the One for 1980," "Now More Than Ever," and "We Are Grateful." A
four-piece high school band struck up "Hail to the Chief."

There was a microphone, and there was Nixon, and it was just as if the previous four years never happened. Nixon thanked the folks for coming out "on a Saturday afternoon, [when you] could be listening to a baseball game—that's what I do, incidentally—or football, if it's on, maybe going fishing or something." Instead they came to the airport to stand in the hot sun to greet him, and "I really appreciate your coming out."

He talked about trips to Kentucky in the past, and the glories of the state, its racehorses and its jockeys, its hospitality. Pointing to the young men in the crowd, Nixon declared, "I'm just thankful today that after the longest, most difficult war in America's history that we were able to end it, bring our POW's home and end the draft, so that you young men will not have to fight abroad."

Then it was off for the Appalachia Motel in Hyden, where Happy Chandler, former governor and commissioner of baseball, was waiting. (No active Kentucky Republicans had found it possible to be present.)[2]

At noon the following day, Nixon rode in a motorcade through town. The limousine was a 1956 Cadillac borrowed from an Ohio businessman for the occasion. It had been built for Ike and was the same car in which Secret Service agents were riding behind Kennedy in Dallas the day he was assassinated.

In the Nixon Center, a crowd of four thousand gathered. There were two thousand more outside. Nixon sat through an hour of introductions and when his turn finally came, he was drenched in sweat. That was nothing new to him, and he swung into his speech like the old pro that he was.

The forty-two-minute address was vintage Nixon. He warned of "the threat of conquest without war," of "aggressors who go under borders, promise liberation and deliver dictatorships," and he said of the United States that "no other nation in the world today has the power to save freedom, not only for ourselves but for others."

He managed to remind the audience that "I've been to more than 90 countries."

He drew wild applause when he said, "I believe in freedom of information, but I think it's time we quit making heroes of people who take secret foreign policy documents and print them in the newspapers."

He signed off with "God bless America."

After, he signed autographs and soaked in adulation.

Then it was off in Bob Abplanalp's private jet to Memphis, where he spent an hour in the airport lounge signing more autographs and shaking hands with supporters, before boarding a commercial flight to California.[3]

ON August 15, 1978, in San Clemente General Hospital, Julie gave birth to a daughter, named Jennie Elizabeth Eisenhower. The following day, Nixon wrote a note to his first grandchild. It concluded, "Whatever you do, wherever you go, and whatever you become, we shall always be proud of you—RN."

In September, an old friend and major supporter of Nixon, Elmer Bobst, died. Bobst had asked that Nixon deliver a eulogy. Nixon agreed to go to New York. Unlike his first trip back to Washington, for Humphrey's funeral, this time he let the press know when and where he would arrive. The reporters were there to do their interviews; Nixon was ready to give them some front-page copy.

President Carter was at that moment meeting with Sadat and Menachem Begin at Camp David. "I hope it does resolve in a lessening of tensions in the area," Nixon said of the summit, "and that the talks establish a negotiating framework." He pushed himself. He was in New York, he said, not just for the Bobst memorial service, but to sign a contract for a new book with his publishers at Warner. He hoped to produce a book "that will be read by the opinion makers," and promised that it would be "politically controversial." But he assured the reporters that by no means did that mark any re-entry into the political arena.

He stayed in the largest suite in the Waldorf Towers. He walked the four blocks from his hotel to the Warner Communications Building in Rockefeller Center. Accompanying him was a Secret Service entourage that resembled the one he had when he was still President.[4]

Back in California, invitations began to flow in. The first that Nixon accepted was from the American Legion in Biloxi, Mississippi, to give an address on Armistice Day. He flew east in Abplanalp's jet, stopping in Dallas for an enthusiastic airport reception, then flying on to Shreveport, Louisiana, to spend the night with his old ally Representative Joe Waggonner.

At the Shreveport airport, he worked a crowd of five hundred or so and noted that he was "the only natural born citizen over 35 who cannot run for President." That was because the Constitution said no man could be elected President more than twice. But "I will continue to speak out on foreign policy and domestic problems as they relate to the future of our country."

When a group began chanting, "Keep coming out, Dick, keep coming out," he smiled, raised his hand, and said, "Don't worry, I will. I guarantee you this is not the last of my public appearances. This is just one of many I plan in the future. Officially, you can say, 'I'm out!' "[5]

Nixon's "I'm out!" was too much for the editors of The New York Times. The words, they wrote, "imply that he has bravely and silently endured a heavy sentence." Where and when? And what about Bob Haldeman, who was still in prison? And what about John Mitchell, who ditto? "We wonder just how 'in' those gentlemen think Mr. Nixon has been.

"More grating still is that 'Officially.' The implication is that, beyond the formal pardon issued by President Ford, a merciful Judge Nixon has now ruled that a manly Defendant Nixon deserves to be 'out.' "[6]

But in the Deep South, the long-term love affair with Dick Nixon continued. In Gulfport, Nixon attended a reception at the Broadwater Beach Hotel organized by Fred LaRue, the Mississippi Republican who had delivered hush money to the Watergate burglars and served six months in prison for it. Every prominent Republican in the state was at the reception, held in a congressional district that had given Nixon 87 percent of its vote in 1972.

The Mississippi Coast Coliseum in Biloxi was jammed for Nixon's speech. He called for a stronger CIA and FBI, for the defense of freedom, for "putting the government on a diet," for support of "the real spirit of America." He said that around the world, "the Communists are on the offensive and the non-Communist nations are on the defensive." He claimed that "the Soviets are moving faster than we are."

Nixon had been to the Mississippi Gulf Coast in 1969, following Hurricane Camille, which had devastated the area. He had made millions in federal disaster relief available. Now he leaned into the microphone to recall Camille. "Some of the skeptics were saying it would take 25 years, if ever, for the area to come back. But as I shook hands and I spoke to you, I had a very different opinion. I knew that there was a spirit no hurricane could possibly break. I said to some, 'You can come back, and, when you do, I'll come back to see what you've done.' "

He paused, and smiled broadly, and allowed the anticipation to build. Then he said, "You've come back, and I've come back," and the applause and shouts all but lifted the roof off the Coliseum.[7]

LATER that month, Nixon made an overseas trip. *Dossiers de l'Ecran,* French television's top-rated weekly show, had invited him to France, and the Oxford Union, the student debating society, had proposed a debate at Oxford University.

He arrived in Paris on November 26, set up headquarters at the Ritz, stayed four days, received visitors—including the Supreme Allied Commander, Europe, General Al Haig—and gave interviews. The television show was a success. It opened with a forty-minute documentary on his career. It barely mentioned Watergate and concluded with Frank Sinatra singing "My Way." Then for three hours he answered call-in questions. Ninety percent of the callers were friendly, and Nixon answered their questions with aplomb.

The reviews were sensational. *"Quel homme!"* ("What a man!") *Le Figaro* declared in a headline. One reporter commented, "It's too bad he can't run for President of France. He would win hands-down."[8]

At the Oxford Union, on November 30, there were difficulties. Labour Party MPs, leftist trade union leaders, and American students denounced his visit and organized an anti-Nixon demonstration. When he arrived at Oxford, several hundred demonstrators greeted him with shouts and curses.

Inside the hall, as the president of the Union introduced Nixon, the crowd outside chanted, "Nixon go home!" Sensing the president's embarrassment, Nixon put him at ease by opening with the observation that the demonstrators made him feel right at home.

He answered questions for two hours. Almost all of them were friendly; Nixon handled them well. He praised Carter for the Camp David agreement, predicted peace in the Middle East, told a story of brinksmanship involving himself and Brezhnev, and said of Watergate, "Some people say I didn't handle it properly, and they're right. I screwed it up. And I paid the price. Mea culpa. But let's get on to my achievements. You'll be here in the year 2000, and we'll see how I'm regarded then."

One of the few hostile questions concerned Cambodia. Was he sorry he ordered the "invasion" in 1970? He replied that he only wished he had done it sooner, and added that to accuse the United States of "invading" the North Vietnamese-occupied areas of Cambodia was like accusing the Allies of "invading" German-occupied France in 1944.

A student asked Nixon about his future plans. He grew emotional. "So long as I have a breath in my body," he replied, "I am going to talk about the great issues that affect the world. I am not going to keep my mouth shut. I am going to speak out for peace and for freedom." He paused. His voice seemed to break slightly as he added, "My political life is over."

Recovering, he went on: "Let me just make one thing clear. I'm not just going to fade away and live the good life in San Clemente, listening to the waves and playing golf. If I did that, turned my mind off, I would be dead mentally in a year, and physically, too."[9]

From London, Nixon flew to New York, where he took up residence for ten days at the Waldorf-Astoria. Pat flew East from California to join him; Julie and Jennie were also there, and Ed and Tricia lived in the city, so the family was together for Christmas shopping. Spiro Agnew was also staying in the Waldorf-Astoria, but the two men did not get together.[10]

Nixon granted an interview to Nick Thimmesch, a syndicated columnist who had been a political aide. Thimmesch was startled at the change in his old boss. The last time he had seen Nixon, a couple of years earlier, he had seemed exhausted and depressed. Now he was healthy, invigorated, full of fight.[11]

"A man is not finished when he is defeated," Nixon told Thimmesch. "He is finished when he quits. My philosophy is that no matter how many times you are knocked down, you get off that floor, even if you are bloody, battered, and beaten, and just keep on slugging—providing you have something to live for. . . . You've got to learn to survive a defeat. That's when you develop character."

Thimmesch was writing an article for *The Saturday Evening Post* on Nixon's thinking on foreign affairs. The United States should maintain military superiority over the Soviets; a SALT II agreement that only maintained instability was a danger, and a bad agreement was worse than none at all. He said that although he applauded Carter's "fine rhetoric on human rights," he did not approve of the policy. "Did anybody suggest that . . . we are going to say to [the Saudis], 'Look, boys, until you unveil the women—the Shah of Iran has already done that—we won't buy your oil?' H—no!

"We can criticize, but the bottom line is to keep friends of the United States. I don't approve of kicking our friends in public, like the Argentineans and the Brazilians. The Latins are proud, and they're going to tell us, 'Up yours.'

"Where are the human rights in China? Are we going to change our policy on China because they don't have human rights? H—no!"

Nixon said that the Shah was authoritarian, while Marcos in Manila had a military government, "but do you want Communism out there? Those are authoritarian states, but they don't threaten their neighbors and they are our friends. Totalitarian Communist states do threaten their neighbors and they are not our friends."[12]

Here was a new-old Nixon, abandoning détente, embracing the ideas of the New Right. He sounded more like himself in the 1950s than as President. He kept his hard line when he invited a group of selected journalists up to his suite for an interview. They were all on the right. Nixon said he favored a "good" SALT II treaty, but rather than accept a bad one he would press ahead with development of advanced weapons systems. He would insist that SALT II permit the deployment of the MX mobile missile and not place any limitations on the cruise missile. He said the Soviets were cautious, but wanted global control short of war. "They don't want war, but they want the world."

America's principal problem, Nixon said, was its "leadership class." He heaped scorn on top corporate management: "Brezhnev could swallow most of these corporate types in one gulp." He would rather see George Meany in any negotiation with Brezhnev. He was scornful of the college and university professors, the media, the bureaucracy. He said the clergy had lost its nerve and now prattled about flaws in American society rather than paying attention to international realities.

"Nixon today gives the impression of being much more hard-line on relations with the Soviets than he was as President," William Buckley wrote in *National Review*. "In his attitude toward the established leadership class he now seems to have much in common with the kind of criticism being offered by the 'New Right.' "[13]

The Nixons flew home to California for Christmas. On December 20, his former chief of staff was released on parole from Lompoc Federal Prison, after eighteen months as a prisoner. While Haldeman was in Lompoc, Nixon had written, called on the telephone, tried to maintain contact. That became increasingly difficult after the Frost interviews. Nixon's depiction of himself as a man done in because he was too loyal to his subordinates, along with his blaming Haldeman, Ehrlichman, and Mitchell for the cover-up, had been too much for Haldeman. He got even in a book he wrote in prison, published in 1978 by Times Books, entitled *The Ends of Power*. He charged that Nixon ordered the break-in at Ellsberg's psychiatrist's office, that it was Nixon, probably, who had erased the eighteen and a half minutes of incriminating tape, who put together the cover-up plan.

Nixon stopped writing letters and making phone calls to Lompoc.

But that Christmas time, Nixon called Haldeman in Los Angeles. "Merry Christmas," Nixon said when Haldeman answered, "and welcome back."

They talked, easily and smoothly. Nixon discussed his travels and the new book he was writing. Haldeman said he was thinking of going into business on his own; Nixon offered to put him in touch with friends who could help. He invited Haldeman to drop by whenever he could; he wanted to hear Haldeman's views on the current political scene.

Haldeman, pleased with the reconciliation, began putting out the word—at first quietly and carefully, later rather stridently—that his co-writer, Joseph Di Mona, was responsible for all the bad things *The Ends of Power* said about Nixon. By 1990, Haldeman was repudiating the book altogether and planning to write another one, this time by himself, telling the truth.[14]

CHAPTER TWENTY-FIVE

THE REAL WAR
1979–1980

ADORED IN PARIS, applauded in Oxford, Nixon still had vocal critics in Washington. In mid-January 1979, after the White House announced that Nixon had accepted President Carter's invitation to a state dinner for Chinese Deputy Prime Minister Deng Xiaoping, there was a barrage of complaints.

Actually, Carter had not wanted to invite Nixon. Just a month earlier he had established formal diplomatic relations with China, but was having major policy differences with the Chinese government over conflicting views on Soviet intentions and the wisdom of concluding a new arms limitation treaty. Bringing Nixon into this delicate situation, to the dismay of the liberals whose support he had to have to get SALT II ratified, was not his idea. But the Chinese government had insisted that Nixon be invited, and threatened that if he were not, Deng would visit him in San Clemente. Carter gave in.[1]

When Nixon's limousine pulled up at the White House gate, there were several dozen demonstrators there, protesting his return. One group carried a large white banner that read, "Nixon: You Belong in Prison. Not in the White House."

Inside, Nixon went up to the family quarters, where Carter introduced him to Deng. Then, with Vice President and Mrs. Walter Mondale on one side, Representative and Mrs. Thomas P. O'Neill on the other, Nixon descended the grand staircase to the room where he had said goodbye to his staff on August 9, 1974. Mrs. O'Neill had told Carter she would refuse to attend the dinner until she was assured she would not be seated at Mr. Nixon's table, but she managed a smile when they met.

At Nixon's table in the State Dining Room the guests were National

Security Adviser Zbigniew Brzezinski; Fang Yi, a Chinese deputy prime minister; Ambassador to China and Mrs. Leonard Woodcock; and Richard Holbrooke, assistant secretary of state for Asian affairs. Nixon was relaxed. When the Marine Corps string ensemble began to play, he remarked, "You know they're playing the same songs, the songs they played when I was here." Brzezinski asked him which world leaders he most admired. "You won't catch me naming them," Nixon laughed, "because each one is different." Then he began to name them. De Gaulle. Mao. The Shah of Iran. He paused. Fang Yi leaned forward. "And Chiang Kai-shek."[2]

The following morning, Nixon had a two-and-a-half-hour private meeting with Deng, after which it was announced that he would visit Peking again that summer. Then he had lunch with John Mitchell, who had been released from prison two weeks earlier. Unlike Haldeman and Ehrlichman, Mitchell had never uttered one word critical of Nixon, not even after it was disclosed that Nixon had suggested to his aides that they set Mitchell up to take full responsibility for the cover-up. Nixon had been in contact with Mitchell by telephone over the past couple of years; a mutual friend told a reporter, "The world doesn't know it, but they're still good friends."[3]

Before departing for New York to visit Tricia, who was in the seventh month of her first pregnancy, Nixon drove to Arlington Hospital in Virginia to visit another old friend, Bryce Harlow, who was recovering from an attack of emphysema.[4] A return to the White House, a meeting with two of China's leaders, an invitation to Peking, chats with Mitchell and Harlow, a visit to Tricia—altogether a most satisfying trip.

Back home, Nixon returned to his writing. Sixty-six years old, he was showing his age in his graying hair, but he had a California tan, walked briskly, had no fat on him, and was cheerful and upbeat in his demeanor and carriage. He was working as hard as any professional writer; up before five, he wrote until noon. For relaxation, he would take an afternoon swim, plus a daily two-mile walk. In the evenings, he liked to listen to baseball games while autographing books or answering mail. He also enjoyed driving north on the freeway to attend California Angels baseball games. Ray Price had rejoined him, to help on the book. It was hard-hitting stuff on foreign policy, very hawkish, quite congenial to Price. Nixon thought of the book as a *cri de coeur*. He wanted to warn against Moscow's aggressiveness, and criticize Carter for "trying to preserve detente at almost any cost." He felt it was "critically important . . . to restore American strength and leadership."

In short, he was back in business at the same old stand, criticizing the Democrats for being soft on Communism and neglectful of the nation's defense. That it was his own policies Carter was trying to maintain evidently gave him not the slightest pause.

Writing "does not come easily to me." He found it to be "a major effort." It took him months to develop first outlines and to dictate first drafts. "In editing later drafts," he wrote, "I would sometimes take a full day to craft a sentence to convey a precise thought or to formulate a memorable line." No prose writer who ever lived could possibly believe such a claim, but then Nixon could count on it that the vast majority of his readers had never written a book, and would be mightily impressed by the thought of the author wracking his brains through an entire day, just to get one sentence right for their benefit.[5]

Bill Safire paid a visit. He, Price, and Nixon talked their craft. Nixon said he had another book in the back of his mind, one about the giants he had known: Eisenhower, De Gaulle, Adenauer, Dulles, and others. They talked politics. Nixon was supporting John Connally for the Republican nomination in 1980, but he was giving his views on foreign policy to any candidate who asked. "Reagan is a good listener," Nixon said, "and not just for show."

Returning to the subject and purpose of the book he was working on, Nixon said that 1980 would be a critical election (of course, he had said—and felt—that about every presidential election from 1948 on). "If the U.S. chooses a President who will not stop the present drift toward Soviet strategic superiority," he told Safire, "the Chinese—survival-minded above all—will move toward rapprochement with the Soviet Union." Grimly, shaking his head, he growled, "Which would be most ominous."

Was Carter keeping him informed? Nixon said the President had offered him a briefing on SALT II. A twinkle came into his eye. He laughed. He could read treaties, Safire wrote, and had declined the briefing. He wanted amendments, improvements. He indicated to Safire that if Kissinger issued a statement that was interpreted to mean Nixon was supporting the treaty, make no mistake—Nixon would let his opposition be known, loudly and clearly.[6] This from the man who, when he began his second term in January 1973, had made SALT II the centerpiece of his foreign policy, the culmination of his Administration's achievements.

ON March 14, 1979, in New York Hospital, Tricia gave birth to a son, named Christopher Nixon Cox. Pat had been with her during the preceding week; Dick flew out to meet his new grandson. As a grandfather, Nixon showed a side of himself he had suppressed for decades. He took genuine, spontaneous pleasure in his grandchildren. He could play with them for hours on end without getting itchy to get back to work; he bounced them on his knee, goo-gooed and baby-talked to them; bought them toys and clothes; and for once, and at last, just plain enjoyed himself.

Adding to his happiness was his wife's recovery. "Pat's great these days," he told Nick Thimmesch, who was doing an article on her for *McCall's* magazine. "She's totally well. She has no health problems at all any more." She loved the ocean, and he felt that her work in the garden, pruning, trimming, and transplanting, was good therapy for her.

Nixon told Thimmesch he wanted to see Pat get credit for her accomplishments. He felt the world had not given her the recognition she deserved. A great lady like Pat should be honored, he said, and he was taking soundings on how that could be done. If it was going to be done, it would have to be done without Pat's cooperation. "My mother doesn't want any attention," said Julie. "She just wants people to leave her alone." On occasion she and Helene would have lunch in the Beverly Wilshire's La Bella Fontana room, where the management found them a discreet corner table. Sometimes she would wear a wig.[7]

IN New York City, where people were more accustomed to celebrities, wigs would not be necessary. Plus, Pat wanted to be closer to Tricia and Christopher. Plus, La Casa Pacifica was really too small a home for the Nixon life style, with insufficient room for overnight guests. Plus, Nixon was getting restless. He wanted to get back to where the action was. And Abplanalp and Rebozo were pressing the Nixons to move, and offering to help them make the transition. When Pat told Julie of her plan to move to New York, Julie expressed surprise. Pat explained to her, "We're just dying here slowly."[8]

On May 24, Brennan announced that the Nixons had sold La Casa Pacifica for an undisclosed sum (estimates ran to $2 million) to a group of Orange County businessmen.[9] News of the sale brought howls from the Nixon-watchers. Editorial writers wanted to know what about Nixon's promise to give the place to the United States, and what about all the money the GSA spent on Nixon's home (supposedly, $703,367)?

Nixon disdainfully refused to comment. For the active politicians, however, especially Democrats, this was much too tempting a target to pass up. The House voted to withhold $60,000 from Nixon's allowances unless and until he paid the government back for improvements at San Clemente.[10]

The Senate moved into the action. It passed a "sense of the Senate" resolution urging Nixon to pay for such items as $6,600 for a gazebo, $2,300 for a flagpole, $13,500 for a heating system, $217,006 for a lighting and electronic system, $137,623 for landscaping, and other items such as a fire hydrant and a railway safety signal.[11]

Nixon struck back. On September 6, the day after the Senate resolution, Nixon wrote to the GSA. Brennan released the letter to the press. Nixon said that the Secret Service had insisted on "certain additions and alterations to my property." It had since been falsely stated by certain politicians that these changes were in fact improvements that had nothing to do with security. Except for the flagpole, that was absolutely untrue.

"Consequently, I hereby request that all items in question be removed and that the property be restored to its original condition within 60 days.

"I am forwarding my check in the amount of $2,300 to the United States Treasury by express mail today to cover the cost of the flagpole."[12]

Nixon was also having problems in his attempt to purchase a home in New York City. His and Pat's first choice had been a $750,000 Madison Avenue co-op, but residents complained of the attention and security problems Nixon's presence would bring and blocked the sale. Their next selection was a $925,000 Fifth Avenue co-op, but as one resident, Mrs. George Leisure, told a reporter, "Everyone signed against them. Money's not enough here."

The story had New York in a dither. The *Times* ran a major article on the exclusive co-ops along Fifth, Madison, Park, and Lexington avenues. All built before 1929, they were restricted—no Jews or Catholics. But a broker remarked that "Today, Jews and Irish and Iranians who have gone to the right schools can get in many buildings, but they'd better have a net worth of $10 million. But I'm not so sure that a Texan could, even if he had $10 million."[13] Nixon did not have $10 million (his net worth was more like $3 million), and he attracted attention, so he was rejected.

Eventually, Nixon was able to purchase for $750,000 a three-story, brick and gray-stone townhouse on East 65th Street, between Lexington and Third avenues, only seven blocks from Tricia, Ed, and Christopher. The eminent Judge Learned Hand had lived there for fifty years. Nixon was not sorry about the apartment deals falling through. "We don't want neighbors that close," he declared. "It's hard to ride in the elevator with people. Maybe you don't want to say hello."[14]

The new home had four bedrooms, a wood-paneled library, seven baths, six fireplaces, and a small garden (fifteen by twenty feet) in back. The next-door neighbor was David Rockefeller; Theodore H. White, the author, lived across the street; Ashraf Pahlavi, the twin sister of the Shah, lived nearby on Park Avenue.[15]

On the other side of the garden wall lived Arthur Schlesinger, Jr., biographer of both Jack and Robert Kennedy and an intellectual font for liberal Democrats for four decades. Schlesinger had been on John Dean's enemies' list, and damn proud of it. He noted wryly that up at Harvard, he had John Kenneth Galbraith over the back fence. "Now I have ended up with Richard M. Nixon." When Schlesinger's young son was playing on the fence one day after the Nixons moved in, the Secret Service shooed the child away. Professor Schlesinger told the agents his boy had been playing on that fence for more than a year, then gave them a lecture on freedom and democracy.[16]

On July 13, Nixon flew down to Cuernavaca, Mexico, to visit the deposed Shah of Iran, to assure him that "millions of Americans in the

U.S. are still his friends." They spent a day together at the Shah's villa, comparing notes on their respective exiles. The Shah was bitter about Carter, who was refusing him admittance to the United States; Nixon told him to keep fighting.

At an airport news conference, Nixon got after Carter on his policy toward two old friends, the Shah and General Somoza. "One principle that I have followed," he said, "is that whether it's in Vietnam or it's in Iran, you don't grease the skids for your friends. If the United States does not stand by its own friends we are going to end up with no friends." Carter had recently called on Somoza to resign. Nixon deplored that action, and added, "I think it is crucial that every possible step be taken to make sure that a Castro-type government does not come to power in Nicaragua because that would be a threat to every free nation in the Western hemisphere."[17]

On Labor Day, just before leaving La Casa Pacifica, the Nixons hosted a combination birthday party for John Mitchell and a nostalgic reunion for many of his aides from the days in power. Some 250 guests turned out, including Dwight Chapin, Rose Mary Woods, Herb Klein, Ron Ziegler, Robert Mardian, Ray Price, Gerald Warren, Ben Stein, and Bill Safire. Noticeable by their absence were Bob Haldeman and John Ehrlichman.

Spirits were high. The gloom, depression, and desperation they had all felt the last time they were together were gone. "It's been five years," Steve Bull said. "You look back and people are lifting up their heads again." John Mitchell told the group, "We who have served in the Nixon Administration can be proud of some monumental accomplishments, although that's not to say we didn't run into a few skids along the way."

Nixon, in introducing Mitchell, referred to what he called the "character, loyalty and guts" of his former Attorney General. "John Mitchell has friends and he stands beside them."[18]

Two weeks later, Nixon was off for China. Ed Cox and Jack Brennan, plus a contingent of Secret Service agents, accompanied him. The Chinese gave two banquets in his honor, but with less pomp and circumstance than during his earlier visits. "There is an old Chinese proverb that applies very well in this situation," said one Chinese leader when giving a toast: "When drinking the water, don't forget those who dug the well. We don't forget our friends."[19]

In his toast, Deng said that the establishment of relations between China and the United States was in the interests of "world peace and the struggle against hegemonism" (the Chinese code word for the Soviet Union's adventurism).[20] Nixon declined to talk to reporters about his discussions with Deng; rumors had it that he was negotiating for access to Chinese oil reserves for American oil companies. According to one unnamed source, who talked to journalist Robert Sam Anson for his book

Exile, Nixon had been offered "fantastic sums" in return for using his contacts in China, but turned down all such offers. "He didn't want to do anything to screw up his relationship with the Chinese," said the source. "Besides, by then, he didn't need the money."[21]

The final page proofs of Nixon's new book, which he titled *The Real War*, arrived at the end of the year, just as the Nixons completed packing and began their move to New York. He and Pat went down to Key Biscayne, to stay with Rebozo, while he corrected them. He handed them back to the publisher the day he arrived in New York to live: February 14, 1980.

He immediately plunged into the job of promoting his book. He gave an exclusive interview to the San Clemente *Sun-Post*, which was printed in mid-February and widely quoted. He announced that the New York Times Syndicate had bought the serial rights, with the first installment to be syndicated in mid-April, and said, "The great advantage about writing a book like this, as one not seeking political office, is one can be totally objective."[22] In March, he made a trip to Paris, to consult with his European publisher, then on to Africa, to visit the Ivory Coast—tried and true ways of getting his name in the newspapers and on television.

The Real War, published on May 1, was a best-seller on both sides of the Atlantic. In France and England, the entire stock of copies sold out within a week. In the United States, it went to the top of *Time* magazine's best-seller list.

The Real War had an apocalyptic, alarmist message, more suitable to the early fifties than the late seventies. Nixon wrote, "We find ourselves confronted with a choice between surrender and suicide—red or dead."[23] He listed the countries that had gone Communist since 1974, and it was like the maps of the early fifties in elementary schools, showing the red tide sweeping across the world. He asked if America could make it to the twenty-first century, and said the chances were 50–50.

The Real War was essentially a highly selective history of the Cold War. Nixon's method was to collect the harshest quotations and cite the nastiest events to support his thesis—which was that World War III began even before World War II ended, and that World War III was "the first truly total war."[24] He pasted the quotes and the events together without historical context or analysis, and tied them up with blood-curdling chapter titles, such as "No Time to Lose" and "No Substitute for Victory." The book was full of slogans, but noticeably absent were the slogans he had used when he was in power: "A generation of peace," "An era of negotiations," and "A new world order."

Instead, there was anticipation of what was coming in American politics. "It may seem melodramatic to treat the twin poles of human experience represented by the United States and the Soviet Union as the equivalent of Good and Evil, Light and Darkness, God and the Devil," he wrote, "yet if we allow ourselves to think of them that way, even hypothetically, it can help clarify our perspective on the world struggle."[25] This was some three years before Reagan called the Soviet Union an "evil empire," and showed how quickly the author of détente could tell which way the tide was moving and swim with it—indeed, get ahead of it.

Much of *The Real War* was taken directly from his memoirs. So much, in fact, that Nixon was rather like the Ancient Mariner, tugging at the nation's sleeve, trying to tell his story one more time, even as the nation wanted to get on to the wedding and into the future. He managed to work in a defense of every major and most of the minor acts of his Administration, admitting only two mistakes—imposing wage and price controls in 1971 (but Congress made him do it) and raising expectations too high after his 1972 Peking and Moscow summits. This last was part of a tortuous, convoluted attempt to explain why détente was good in the early seventies but bad for the beginning of the eighties.

He struck back at his domestic enemies with all his old bitterness. Vietnam, he said, was "one of the crucial battles of World War III." After "years of fighting the war the wrong way and losing," he wrote, the "best and the brightest" decided "there was no way we could win the war and that we should get out. . . . What they really meant was that since *they* could not win in Vietnam, they automatically assumed that nobody could. Arrogant even in defeat, with the guilt-ridden carping they poisoned an already disillusioned American public and frustrated all the military and political efforts we made in Vietnam to win the war. Now, shocked by the bloodbath in Cambodia and the tragic plight of the boat people fleeing from 'liberated' South Vietnam, they frantically thrash about trying to find someone to blame. All they have to do is look in the mirror." He accused the liberals of sabotage in Vietnam, and said that "like the blood on Lady Macbeth's hand," that spot would never out.[26]

Aside from the American liberals, the book was a diatribe on the Soviet Union, as opposed to an attack on Communism. The Chinese were a great people with great leaders and a great future and just plain great. The Soviet Union, by contrast, "has threatened, blustered, connived, conspired, subverted, bribed, intimidated, terrorized, lied, cheated, stolen, tortured, spied, blackmailed, murdered—all as a matter of deliberate national policy."[27] (The reviewer for *Pravda* wrote, "One can hardly believe one's eyes when reading this mad raving, to put it mildly."[28])

Trade with the Soviet Union would only strengthen our enemies, said the man who made granting the Soviets most-favored-nation status one of his top priorities when he was President, and so should be avoided. Trade with China was good, because it would draw China into a Western orbit. "That is why we are justified in giving MFN status to China and denying it to the Soviet Union. The Soviet Union threatens us; China, as of now, does not."[29]

In *The Real War*, as in his memoirs, Nixon took every opportunity to remind the public of how many countries he had visited, how many foreign leaders he had met, how long he had been a world leader. It was remarkable how many great and shrewd men had confided their most brilliant insights to him; "as so-and-so told me" preceded dozens of quotations. Among those so cited were (a partial list): Konrad Adenauer, Aneurin Bevan, Charles Bohlen, Chester Bowles, Leonid Brezhnev, William Buckley, Nikolai Bulganin, Chiang Kai-shek, Whittaker Chambers, Winston Churchill, Charles de Gaulle, Deng Xiaoping, John Foster Dulles, Dwight Eisenhower, Andrei Gromyko, Herbert Hoover, Lyndon Johnson, John Kennedy, Nikita Khrushchev, Henry Kissinger, Alexei Kosygin, Douglas MacArthur, Harold Macmillan, André Malraux, Mao Zedong, Georges Pompidou, Anwar el-Sadat, the Shah of Iran, Edward Teller, Margaret Thatcher, Sir Robert Thompson (his favorite, with ten quotes), Harold Wilson, and Zhou Enlai.

Sometimes, these men said things to Nixon they never said to anyone else. Ike, according to Nixon, felt that "the U.S. restraint of Britain, France, and Israel when they were trying to protect their interest in Suez [in 1956] was a tragic mistake."[30] Nixon felt Eisenhower's actions were a mistake, and often said so, but Ike did not—or at least, not to anyone other than Nixon. To this author, and many other interviewers and friends, Ike vehemently defended his policy.

Putting it all together, Nixon said it was time to go over to the offensive in World War III. According to Nixon, "We can afford a vastly increased defense effort—if we *decide* to. We can postpone desirable social goals in order to ensure survival—if we *decide* to. We can carry the twilight war to the enemy—if we *decide* to."[31]

The Real War was Nixon's foreign-policy platform for the 1980 campaign. It was exactly what the right wing of the Republican Party, and its leader, Ronald Reagan, wanted to hear. In the 1980 campaign, the incumbent President was a Democrat, and thus fair game.

As for Nixon, the former President had four role models for guidance. Herbert Hoover had been vicious in his attacks on Franklin Roosevelt from the time he left the White House until his death. Harry Truman had sniped at Ike and spoken for Adlai, but generally refrained from criticizing the President on foreign policy. Eisenhower had contented himself with generalizations in criticizing Kennedy and Johnson on domestic policy, and never said a word against them on foreign policy. Johnson had seldom criticized Nixon on domestic policy and actively supported him on foreign policy.

During Carter's first three years in office, Nixon had been generally supportive, especially of Carter's efforts to broker a peace between Israel and Egypt. Carter's crisis, the seizing of the American Embassy in Tehran and the holding of hostages, gave Nixon a perfect opportunity for carping criticism, but he resisted the temptation and expressed qualified support for the President's policy of seeking a peaceful resolution of the crisis. But, like most Americans, by the spring of 1980 he was growing restless. In early April, while on a book promotion tour in Europe, he told an interviewer that the time had come for the President to "stop giving warnings and take action." When Carter did so a week later, ordering a commando raid that ended in an embarrassing disaster, Nixon told reporters in West Berlin that he "certainly support[ed] what President Carter did in making his decision to try to rescue the hostages."

Two weeks later, during an interview with Barbara Walters on ABC TV, Nixon termed further military action "an empty cannon at this time," and proposed that the United States "provide a carrot for negotiation by offering the Iranians massive economic assistance"—in other words, offer a ransom. But he was critical of Carter for showing too much concern for the hostages.

He tried to explain: "I think that one of the major errors that President Carter made at the outset was to indicate that his primary, and, in fact, it seemed to me, his only concern at the beginning, was the lives and safety of the hostages. They are important. But the moment you do that, you are inviting blackmail. They know you'll pay any price in order to save those lives and we could never do that."[32]

The dying Shah, meanwhile, finally found refuge in Egypt, where Sadat admitted him. On July 27, 1980, he died. The State Department issued an almost insulting statement—"His death marks the end of an era in Iran, which all hope will be followed by peace and stability"—and the White House announced that no special representative would be going to the funeral.[33]

Nixon, angry, found a way to express his feelings: within hours of the Shah's death, he boarded an airliner bound for Cairo and the Shah's funeral. Ed Cox and thirteen Secret Servicemen accompanied him. Of course this made the papers, thus embarrassing Carter.[34]

He had left in such a hurry, taking the first plane available, a TWA flight, that he found himself on the leg from Paris to Cairo in tourist class, exposed to the stares of his fellow passengers and suffering cramps in his phlebitic leg. When he debarked in Cairo, he was in a furious mood. He told a group of waiting reporters that Carter's handling of the Shah was "one of the black pages of American foreign policy history." It was "shameful [that] the Administration didn't even have the grace to point out that he had been an ally and friend of the United States for 30 years." After a pause, he added, "I think President Sadat's guts in providing a home for the Shah in his last days at a time when the U.S. turned its back on one of its friends is an inspiration to us all."[35]

The following day, in the funeral procession, Nixon walked at Sadat's left, with King Constantine, the former monarch of Greece, on Sadat's right. The crowds were large, but nothing to compare to the crowds Nixon and Sadat had drawn in the spring of 1974. Still, they were large enough to evoke what must have been bittersweet memories.

Back in the States, it was back to campaigning. When *The New York Times* declared that Independent candidate John Anderson had more foreign-policy experience than Reagan, Nixon wrote a letter to the editor. "In checking the record," he said, "I find that in fact Governor Reagan made four official trips abroad at the request of the White House between 1969 and 1973." He listed the sixteen countries Reagan had visited, then added, "I can attest to the fact that he was well-received and conducted his meetings with major foreign policy leaders with intelligence, skill and judgment."[36]

On Labor Day, he granted an exclusive interview to journalist Marguerite Michaels for *Parade* magazine. He claimed that he had had "very good talks" with Reagan. "I think he values my foreign policy judgment," which was understandable, as "I've traveled more miles and known more leaders than anyone since World War II. I have a deep sense of where the world should go." He would not campaign actively for Reagan, because "all that Watergate crap would get dragged in," but who knew what might happen after Reagan won the election? "Maybe" there would be a place for Nixon, "something like a counselor or negotiator." In any case, "I will be available for assistance and advice."[37]

When the interview was published, early in October, a senior Reagan aide said, in reference to Nixon's speculation that there might be a place for him, that Nixon "was hallucinating." An embarrassed Reagan called Nixon to apologize. Reagan said he had demoted the aide and assured Nixon that he was glad to have his advice, and was willing to say so publicly. Nixon told Reagan to go easy on the aide. These things happen in campaigns. He understood.[38]

In the second week of September, Nixon was on the NBC "Today" show every morning, being interviewed by Teddy White, commenting on the campaign. He portrayed himself as the senior statesman above the fray, analyzing the campaign rather than participating in it or favoring one candidate over the other. He said Carter was "very tough, very shrewd," and had a staff that was "ruthless." Carter, said Nixon, would "use the Presidency to the hilt" to win re-election. "They're a tough bunch, believe me, these Georgia boys. They may play softball down in Plains, but they play hard ball in the country."

Still he thought Reagan would win. Carter's weakness was "his record, his deeds. Reagan's weaknesses are his words, and when you run against words, I think the one that is weak on deeds is going to lose." And he ticked off the states Reagan would carry—and got all of them right.[39]

He hardly spent all his time working for Reagan. Mainly, he worked for money, or for his reputation, or both. He signed a new contract with Warner Books, with a whopping advance, for a series of portraits of the great men he had known. He granted an occasional interview, carefully selecting from the twenty or so requests he received each week. One went to thirty-three-year-old Bob Greene, a columnist for the Chicago *Sun-Times*. Greene had gotten Nixon's attention by writing a letter saying that he wanted to talk to Nixon about Nixon for the same reason as "an eight-year-old wants to go to Disney World."[40]

Greene was an adroit and intelligent interviewer. He got Nixon to talk about subjects he usually avoided. Psychoanalysis, for example. Nixon said he was different from other men, more distant, reserved. "You've got to retain a curtain," he explained. "A President must not be one of the crowd. He must maintain a certain figure." He was a fatalist, he said. Other old men worried about heart attacks, cancer, and the rest. "But I never get morbid about it. I never worry about it. I just figure that every day may be the last." He had no desire to be "buddy-buddy" with anyone, not even Rebozo. He was a formal man. He always wore a coat and tie, even when he was writing, even when he was alone. For another example, Rebozo always called him "Mr. President."

"You mean," asked Greene, "that when you and Rebozo were out on a fishing boat, in casual clothes, and he wanted to offer you a beer, he actually said, 'Would you like a beer, Mr. President?' "

"Yep," Nixon replied. "That's right. That's the way." Others might want to sit with a close friend "and, you know, just spill your guts. Not me. No way.

"I don't allow my feelings to get hurt. If I had feelings I probably wouldn't have even survived."

He talked about his life since resignation. "Somebody who has served as President," he said, "there is nothing else that he can do." Then he described some of the many things he was doing. No cocktail parties— "a cocktail party is an invention of the devil"—but a lot of sports, a lot of writing, a lot of reading. "If I wake up at night," however, "I don't read anymore. Reading does not put me to sleep, it stimulates me. And I cannot go to sleep if I have music on, because I concentrate on the music."[41]

FROM the time of his resignation until late in 1980, Nixon had been entangled in some fifty lawsuits, many of them frivolous, or done for publicity purposes or to harass the former President. He had incurred almost $1 million in legal expenses in defending suits seeking damages.

He had successfully fended off efforts to compel him to testify in court in as many as twenty cases. But on October 29, in the Federal District Court in Washington, D.C., he made a voluntary appearance.

The occasion was the trial of two former FBI officials, W. Mark Felt, former acting associate director, and Edward S. Miller, former chief of the Bureau's intelligence division. They were charged with violating the civil rights of members of the radical Weather Underground by authorizing break-ins of the suspects' homes during 1972 and 1973. They admitted that they had given authorization; their defense was that they had done so in the name of national security. Since their indictment, two and a half years earlier, Nixon had followed the case closely and contributed money to their defense. He had offered to testify on their behalf, but fearing his impact on a largely black jury in Washington, the defendants' attorneys had declined. The prosecution had been happy to oblige, however, and Nixon appeared as a nominal witness for the government.

When he appeared to take the oath, protesters representing former antiwar activists and the Black Panther Party, victims of the Bureau's' intelligence programs, shouted charges of "thief" and "liar" at Nixon, and called him a "war criminal" who "committed genocide." They were removed from the courtroom by federal marshals.

In his testimony, Nixon described the concerns he had as President. He explained that he had been eager for the Bureau to find the Weathermen fugitives because there was "hard evidence" that some members of the group had collaborated with foreign governments and because their violent protests impeded his efforts to end the war. He was never asked, and did not say, whether he had approved the break-ins that Felt and Miller were accused of authorizing. He did acknowledge that he had approved the so-called Huston Plan on July 23, 1970, authorizing federal agents to conduct "surreptitious entries." He had done so, he explained, on the basis of his inherent authority to order warrantless searches to gather foreign intelligence information in cases involving national security. He argued that when a President authorized illegal entries "for good cause, what would otherwise be unlawful or illegal becomes legal." He added that he had rescinded approval for the plan four days after approving it because of objections from J. Edgar Hoover, but said that he "did not intend my revocation of what is called the Huston plan to be a prohibition" on the use of warrantless searches.

Nixon said repeatedly that the threat posed by subversives and terrorists, such as the Weathermen, was magnified by the fact that the United States was at war at the time. He pointed out that there had been more than forty thousand bombings, bomb scares, and bomb threats in his first year in office alone. Bombings killed twenty-three people and injured hundreds, causing $20 million in property damage. Therefore he felt it was "essential to strengthen our capacity" to catch the terrorists before they killed more "innocent people."[42]

Nixon's testimony did not help the defendants. Felt and Miller were found guilty and sentenced to pay fines of $5,000 and $3,500 respectively. They appealed, and the next year Reagan granted them presidential pardons. Nixon sent each man a bottle of champagne, with an accompanying note: "Justice ultimately prevails."[43] A cynic might have some doubts about justice prevailing, but presidential pardons certainly did.

The smashing Republican victory on November 4 brightened Nixon's already good mood. So did the publication of a mass-market edition of *The Real War* by Warner Books. In late November, Nixon wrote an introduction for the paperback. He said the challenge he described in the book continued, "but I am confident that President Reagan and the members of his administration will have the vision to see what needs to be done and the courage to do it." But they would need public support for the sacrifices the people would have to make, and that support depended on public understanding. "That is why I hope this book will be widely read."[44]

With the new mood in the country, and a new Administration coming to power in January, Nixon decided that despite the Supreme Court decision, he would try once again to overthrow the 1974 Presidential Records Act. On December 18 he filed suit in the Federal District Court in Washington, alleging that he had been deprived of the "exclusive enjoyment, control and use" of the materials of his Administration held by the National Archives. The suit also demanded the return of materials unrelated to his performance as President, such as communications with family members and friends. It further asserted that no other former President had been subjected to such treatment and contended that his constitutional rights to privacy, speech, and freedom of association had been violated.[45]

"You don't quit," Nixon had told Ron Ziegler on his last day in the White House. So long as he had a breath left in his body, Richard Nixon would never quit.

CHAPTER TWENTY-SIX

COURTING HISTORY
1981–1984

"RICHARD NIXON is back," Julie Baumgold opened her article on Nixon's life in the city for *New York* magazine. "He's out walking the early-morning streets. Signing autographs at Yankee Stadium. On television. At '21.' At Luchow's. At David K's. At Windows on the World. In Central Park. On 57th Street. He's ready to see Norman Podhoretz and Irving Kristol. Ready to talk. Grant access. Open the door. Be heard from again."

He had come to New York before when he needed to resurrect himself, to begin again, and in many ways the early 1980s were similar for him to the early 1960s. He was making big money, although this time from his writing rather than a law practice; he was traveling; he was pontificating; he was a magnet to the press and television newscasters; he was shameless in the way he courted men of power; he was full of energy and determination. He was reinventing himself, creating another new Nixon, this one the senior statesman, source of original ideas to solve old problems in foreign affairs.

He was up at 5 A.M., to get his exercise for the day before the city woke up. He would take a two-mile walk, up Third Avenue and back on First, dressed in his business suit. Joggers would stare, do a double take. At 7 A.M. the Secret Service agents drove him to his fifteen-room office at 26 Federal Plaza, on Foley Square. Paid for by the government, the office was behind an unmarked door, totally anonymous, until the door was opened on a bonanza of Atkins color photographs of Nixon on the walls. Six people worked for him there, including Ray Price. His private office had seven American flags, a desk, a few chairs and two upholstered couches, separated by a coffee table. He ate his lunches there—a tin of salmon with a little mayonnaise and Rykrisp—signed mail, dictated, gave interviews, read. He went every day of the week when he was in town, Saturdays and Sundays being his favorites, as no one else was there.[1]

Still, he wasn't entirely comfortable in the office. At the conclusion of a two-hour interview with columnist Richard Reeves, Nixon got up to show him out. He tripped on an electric wire leading to a lamp, recovered, went to the door, grasped the knob, opened the door, said, "Well, here we are," and then realized he had opened the door of his closet.[2]

At least he was learning to laugh a bit at his own fabled awkwardness. Bragging about his year-old grandson Christopher, he told Baumgold that the boy was "not much on the talking side but very mechanical—he can put anything together. He has a cash register. It takes three motions to run it. *I* can't do it."[3]

He and Pat went to see Tricia, Ed, and Christopher three or four times a week. Every two or three weeks they would drive down the Jersey Turnpike to Berwyn, Pennsylvania, to see Julie, David, Jennie, and Alex Richard, the Eisenhower's second child, born October 12, 1980. The Eisenhowers had moved to the Philadelphia area from California shortly after the Nixons left San Clemente. They had become a writing couple; Julie was doing a biography of her mother, while David was working on what his publisher was touting as the "definitive" biography of his grandfather.

After a half decade in near seclusion, Nixon was very much in circulation. Typically, he claimed the opposite. "We've already had the best dinners, been to the best homes," he said. "We've seen them all." He had not returned to New York to see and be seen. He and Pat, he said, never went to parties. But they did, often, with such prominent New Yorkers as Arthur Sulzberger, Roone Arledge, Michael O'Neill, Henry Kissinger, George Steinbrenner, Roy Cohn, Midge Decter and her husband Norman Podhoretz, and many others. It was all a part of the carefully scripted comeback—swapping stories, jokes, political gossip, and occasionally insights.

He hosted dinners—stag, intimate, off-the-record affairs for the opinion makers. Herb Stein, Hugh Sidey, Alan Greenspan, Arthur Burns, Bill Safire, Len Garment, publishers, reporters, politicians were his guests. The dinner was invariably Chinese. (Nixon's love affair with China was ongoing. His home was decorated in a Chinese motif; his house servants were a Chinese couple; his bookcases carried works on Chinese history, Chinese art, Chinese politics.) After dinner, the party adjourned to the living room, where Nixon served glasses of *mao-tai* and demonstrated the Chinese manner of toasting. He would regale the group with talk, usually political stories from his own experiences—although never, ever, Watergate.[4] He was utterly fascinating. Hugh Sidey, who dined with the great and the near-great on a regular basis, confessed that for all the predictability of an evening with Nixon, all the bad jokes, all the self-serving stories, he would rather sit at Nixon's table than any other.[5]

Nixon usually ended the evening around 10:30 P.M. with an announcement, "Well, I promised to get so and so to the local house of ill repute by eleven, so I guess we ought to call it a night," followed by that awful "ha, ha, ha" laugh of his.[6]

He claimed he did not see the "trendies," the "Beautiful People." They were a part of "Henry's crowd." He said that it all but broke Kissinger's heart when the trendies turned on him because of Vietnam. "They were his people. Harvard. He moved with that crowd. He doesn't have that many friends among the hawks. But he doesn't give up. He sees the [trendies] all the time. He's pretty tenacious."[7]

So was the former President a pretty tenacious man. He kept after the media with a will and an energy that was awesome. He had not come to New York to rest. "People who want a quiet life, unchallenged, should not live here," he said. "It's the fastest track in the world."[8] He made dozens of speeches annually before prestigious organizations at home and abroad (he never took an honorarium for a speech). He wrote books. He wrote columns and op-ed pieces for *Time*, *Newsweek*, *The New York Times*, *The Wall Street Journal*, the London *Sunday Times*, the Washington *Times*, and the Los Angeles *Times* syndicate. He gave background, off-the-record talks to editorial boards for all the big newspapers, the news magazines, and the television networks. He did television interviews with such media stars as Pat Buchanan, Bryant Gumbel, Peter Jennings, Morton Kondracke, Ted Koppel, Bernard Shaw, Tom Brokaw, John Chancellor, Chris Wallace, Larry King, and others. ("On reflection," he wrote in 1990, "I am still not sure it was worth appearing on these programs because television is essentially an entertainment and not an educational medium.")[9]

It was worth it. He was listened to, got quoted, forced the big-time columnists to write about him again, without dragging in Watergate. David Broder was reporting on his political statements. So was Hugh Sidey, and of course Bill Safire, and others.

Nixon cultivated young writers, such as R. Emmett Tyrrell, editor of *The American Spectator*, and the up-and-comers on *Time* and the other magazines. "They are hard to identify," he told Baumgold, "but there are ten or fifteen. It's difficult for them to come to California, but easy here," which was yet another good reason to live in New York.[10]

Nixon wanted more than respect and rehabilitation. He wanted influence. He had encouraged Haig to make an ill-conceived run for the Presidency in the maneuvering of 1979, then taken to talking him up for Secretary of State. He told one of his dinner groups that Haig "is the meanest, toughest, most ambitious son of a bitch I ever knew. He'll make a great secretary of state." After Reagan's election, Nixon got on the telephone, calling senators, Reagan aides, anyone with influence with the

President-elect. Six weeks after the election, Reagan called him to say he had all but decided to name Haig Secretary of State. What did Nixon think? Nixon thought it was a brilliant choice.[11]

In Haig's confirmation hearings, Democratic senators on the Foreign Relations Committee wanted to know what role Haig had played in arranging a "deal" for the Nixon pardon by Ford. Haig protested, vehemently. Unconvinced, some of the senators began demanding evidence—such as the tapes. Nixon called Senator Jesse Helms (R.-N.C.) to assure him that there was nothing on the tapes incriminating to Haig. "Absolutely not," Nixon told Helms. "And I should know more about those tapes than anyone else."[12] Of course, the taping system had been removed a couple of months after Haig became Nixon's chief of staff, and long before Ford became Vice President. Haig was confirmed, 15 to 2.

How much influence Nixon had on Haig, or Reagan, with whom he was also in telephone contact, cannot be said. The strong supposition is, not much.

IN the middle of 1981, after eighteen months in their townhouse, the Nixons moved to the suburbs. For $1 million, they purchased a modern fieldstone and redwood home on four-and-a-half wooded acres in Saddle River, New Jersey. It was less than an hour's commute to his office, in a community of successful New Yorkers—executives, bankers, lawyers, and brokers. Initially, they planned to hold onto their townhouse. Nixon aide Nick Ruwe (a former advance man, he had taken Brennan's place when Brennan went into private business) told reporters it was uncertain how they would split their time. "That's totally up in the air," he said. "They've both been having a ball in New York. They're just crazy about New York."[13]

One month later, they sold the townhouse, in what the New York Daily News called "the sweetest real estate deal since the Indians sold Manhattan Island for $24," to the Syrian Mission to the United Nations, for $2.6 million, more than three times what they had paid for it two years earlier.[14] Had it been known that Brennan headed a Washington-based company called Global Research International, that John Mitchell was in the business with him, that the business was selling military supplies to foreign governments, that Nixon sometimes served as an intermediary by providing letters of reference to such customers as Nicolae Ceausescu of Romania, that Saddam Hussein of Iraq was one of Global Research's biggest customers—had all this been known, why then the Daily News and other newspapers might have raised more than an eyebrow. They might have put some investigative reporters to finding out what prompted the Syrians to pay such a price.

But none of this was known until 1990, when a lawsuit brought out the information. It seemed that Global Research had sold Iraq $181 million worth of uniforms (with Spiro Agnew involved as an intermediary), that Global received an $8.7 million commission, that the uniforms were made in Romania, and that Nixon provided a letter of reference at Brennan's request. On May 3, 1984, he wrote Ceausescu, "I can assure you that Colonel Brennan and former Attorney General John Mitchell will be responsible and constructive in working on this project with your representatives." He closed by relaying "warm personal regards to you and Mrs. Ceausescu."

In a letter to Ceausescu of October 31, 1986, Nixon wrote, "My good friend John Mitchell told me recently that the contract . . . was complete, and I wanted to let you know how highly Mr. Mitchell spoke of the diligence of the Romanian workers." Miami-based arms dealer Sarkis Soghanalian served as Hussein's agent. He said Nixon also called Ceausescu for Global. "He was their angel. He was, of course, introducing Brennan and everybody else." More than uniforms were involved; in 1985, Global sold Iraq, through Soghanalian, twenty-six McDonnell Douglas-Hughes helicopters for $27.4 million. Global evidently had trouble collecting from Soghanalian, which was what the 1990 lawsuit that brought this material to light was about.[15]

Whether Nixon received a fee for his actions is not known. Whether he helped Brennan with other customers is not known. Rumors were rife, but then rumors had always been rife about Richard Nixon and his doings. One had it that Nixon had interceded on behalf of Atlantic Richfield with the Chinese to secure drilling rights in China; a friend of Nixon's had sworn that it was not so and asserted that Nixon did not need money.[16]

HE certainly was making big money, from his books, and he could have been making much more if he had charged for his speeches. He certainly was spending big money, great sums on his lawyers, on his travels, on his homes. Through the 1980s, he certainly was meeting with many world leaders, especially in the Third World, especially those who were customers for the arms merchants. Because Nixon was Nixon, the circumstances gave rise to suspicion, but there is no proof that Nixon did more than write a couple of letters for Brennan and Mitchell, who were men who had served him loyally and well, men to whom he owed many favors. And if he did charge a fee for providing contacts and introductions and letters of reference, that is not a crime.

Right after Labor Day 1981, the Nixons moved to Saddle River. Nixon took off on a business trip, to Europe, accompanied by Rebozo, Ruwe, and about twenty-five other people, including Secret Service and secretaries. He left it to Pat to organize the move. So she packed the books, the clothes, and the family treasures, supervised the movers, sent a few things to Tricia, got a few things back from Tricia and Julie, redecorated the new home (Chinese landscapes on the walls), and more. Dennis Murphy, of Murphy Brothers Moving and Storage, told reporters that Mrs. Nixon spent a whole week packing. "She packed 200 cartons of books and about 30 boxes of personal items and all their clothes. She kept the books in order according to his own system." Murphy said the Nixons had "about five times as many clothes as most people have," plus an extensive wine cellar, three hundred to four hundred bottles. When the van arrived in Saddle River, Murphy related, he had to order Pat not to move the cartons. "I told her she'd have to stop or get a union card."[17]

That same summer of 1981, Duke University President Terry Sanford came to Nixon with a proposal. Sanford was a former Democratic governor of North Carolina. He knew that Nixon's project of establishing his presidential library at USC had languished, and he wanted the Nixon papers for Duke. He said Duke would donate the land for a library-museum and raise the $25 million construction cost from private contributions.

Nixon liked the idea. Duke had provided the scholarship that made it possible for him to go to law school, and although the faculty had embarrassed him in 1954 (when the trustees announced they were giving an honorary degree to the law school's most famous graduate, a faculty body voted against it and Nixon then declined to come), that was the faculty, not the university. He told Sanford to get a firm proposal from the trustees.

Sanford decided first of all to get the history department's endorsement. He met with the professors, expecting them to be delighted at the prospect of having readily available to them the papers of the central figure in American politics for the previous four decades. But like other politicians turned academics before and since, Sanford learned he had a lot to learn about professors. The history department wanted no part of Mr. Nixon and his papers. One member, Peter Wood, pontificated, "I am deeply concerned that this could have a lasting, negative affect on teaching, research and morale and general respect for Duke University."[18]

Things got worse, as the professors guarded their purity at the expense of their research and responsibilities. One said that to allow a Nixon library on the campus "would link the name of a great university forever to that of one of our worst Presidents."[19] The faculty met as a whole (five hundred strong) to debate the issue. Assistant Professor Sydney Nathans, a recent Johns Hopkins history Ph.D., was passionate in his opposition. "It would be an archival 'Treasure of the Sierra Madre.'" he said. "We will not possess it. It will possess us."[20]

Political scientist James David Barber was caustic in his contempt. "You don't have to hate Nixon to worry about linking up with him and his friends in a long and deep relationship," he said. Barber was disdainful: "I don't want to spend the rest of my life at this place correcting the record regarding Nixon. As of now, I say it's broccoli and I say to hell with it."[21] Thus the spirit of scholarship in the political science department at Duke.

Eventually, the Duke Academic Council voted 35 to 34 not to build a Nixon library. Various small towns then offered to provide a home for the Nixon papers; in April 1983, Nixon chose San Clemente, and by early 1984 architectural drawings had been completed and fund raising started. Former Nixon Administration official John C. Whitaker, serving as executive director of the Richard M. Nixon Presidential Archives Foundation, set a goal of $25 million and announced that the library would be privately run—that is, unlike all other presidential libraries, it would not be operated by the National Archives. Nor was it going to have the Nixon papers, which would by law stay in Washington with the Archives. What it would have was Nixon memorabilia, a research center specializing in studies of the free enterprise system, conference rooms, and a hotel, restaurant, and other tourist facilities around it, in a Spanish-colonial motif.[22]

ON October 6, 1981, President Sadat was assassinated. Nixon told Haig he was going to go to the funeral; so did Carter and Kissinger. The Secret Service warned against Reagan's attending and, as other heads of state were going, this might seem a slight, so Haig proposed that all three former Presidents go together.

So it came about that Nixon, Ford, and Carter gathered at the White House for a reception hosted by Reagan. It was a stiff, formal, awkward affair. Nixon helped break the tension among them when the former Presidents were swinging over the White House in the helicopter taking them to Andrews Air Force Base, by looking down and commenting, "I kind of like that house down there." He smiled at Carter and Ford. "Don't you?"

They flew to Egypt accompanied by Kissinger, Secretary of Defense Caspar Weinberger, Senator Percy, Chairman of the Foreign Relations Committee Senator Thurmond, and other congressmen. The former Presidents talked about their relations with Sadat, about Middle East politics, about their presidential libraries and the books they were writing, about life after the White House. Despite herself, Rosalynn Carter was impressed by Nixon. She told a fellow passenger he was more charming than she'd imagined, indeed he was almost nice.[23]

In Cairo, the dignitaries, from all over the world, gathered in a staging area for the funeral procession. The former Presidents arrived sitting in an armor-plated limousine flown in from Washington. Seeing them in a noticeably erect posture, Percy quipped, "My, aren't we looking upright." Nixon tapped his chest. "It's this," he said, referring to the bullet-proof vest he was wearing under his shirt. Percy, who was not so equipped, remarked, "I'm walking behind you."[24]

The procession went past the reviewing stand where Sadat had been gunned down. The bullet holes had not been patched, the bloodstains were still on the floor.

After the ceremonies, Nixon flew by the Royal Saudi jet to Jidda, where he attended a banquet hosted by King Khalid and Crown Prince Fahd and talked about arms sales to the Saudis. Then it was on to Amman, and another banquet with King Hussein as host. Next stop Tunis, for a meeting with President Habib Bourguiba. Then Fez, Morocco, for talks with King Hassan and a news conference. Finally, Paris, where he stayed at the Crillon Hotel and, through the American Embassy, issued a statement.

He said the leaders he had met with supported the proposed $8.5 billion sale of Airborne Warning and Control System planes (AWACS) and other military equipment to Saudi Arabia. He said the United States should promote peace in the Middle East but "until the Camp David process is completed, should not negotiate with the P.L.O." He said Libyan leader Muammar el-Qaddafi "is more than just a desert rat. He is an international outlaw. Directly or indirectly he threatens every friend of the United States and the West," and called for a boycott of Libyan oil.[25]

Nixon's views got respect and attention. *Time* devoted a full page to his thoughts and called him "the world's unique and ubiquitous elder statesman without portfolio."[26] His old nemesis *The Washington Post* wrote of "Nixon's redemption" and said the trip had furthered his "rehabilitation." Haynes Johnson, one of the paper's top reporters, noted that "there was both a poignancy and a fascination at seeing him standing at attention with the other presidents on the steps of that plane. . . . God knows what hurts he must hold inside, or what thoughts his return to that ceremonial public duty must have prompted. . . . [But] here he was, back in the full glow of the presidential spotlight as an official state funeral emissary. . . . What great repatriation, what ultimate way back from Elba, than to perform as a peacemaker?"[27]

Senator Robert Dole (R.-Kans.) lightened it up a bit shortly thereafter, when he was presiding at the Gridiron Club. Referring to the photographs of the three former Presidents together, which had filled the newspapers, Dole asked: "Did you see the pictures? There they were, See No Evil, Hear No Evil, and Evil."[28]

IN the fall of 1981 Warner Books came out with Nixon's fourth book, entitled *Leaders*. It got a reception similar to that of *The Real War*— worldwide newspaper syndication by The New York Times Company,

British and Japanese and French editions; scornful, even devastating reviews in the major outlets; praise in the small-town press; strong sales.

Nixon had written the book with the help of Ray Price and a cadre
of "bright undergraduates" Price enlisted to prepare monographs, reading
lists, and other research tools for Nixon. The model for the book was
Winston Churchill's *Great Contemporaries,* written shortly before the
war, when Churchill was out of government. To qualify for inclusion in
Nixon's study, a leader had to meet two tests. First, "I had to have known
them—which did not eliminate many, since I had known every major
postwar leader except Stalin." Second, "they also had to have made a
difference—by building their nation, by saving it, or by moving the world
in some other singular way." There was another quality that many of the
leaders he chose to write about shared: "Each had returned from the
wilderness to lead his nation out of a moment of supreme crisis."[29]

This was a point almost all reviewers mentioned, that the book told
a great deal more about Nixon and his values, feelings, and philosophy
than it did about anything else. In a book of short biographies of Churchill,
de Gaulle, Douglas MacArthur, Konrad Adenauer, Khrushchev, Chou
En-lai, Brezhnev, and others, the remarkable thing was that the personality who dominated the book was Richard Nixon's. No praise of himself
embarrassed him—he included it all. The picture section included photos
of Nixon with Churchill, de Gaulle, Adenauer, Khrushchev, Brezhnev,
and the others. The quotes were primarily "as he said to me on this
occasion."

Still Nixon, as always, could surprise. In an introduction to a paperback version, he asked, "what else set these leaders apart?" and answered, "none of [them] ever commissioned a public opinion poll."
Imagine Nixon picking out that point to praise! But he did, explaining
that leaders stand out "because of their ability to *change* the national
mood or to take an unpopular issue and make it popular."[30]

Surprising, too, was that he wrote a book about leaders he had known
and did not include Dwight Eisenhower. At first, that made Ike's younger
brother Milton angry; but on reflection Milton decided it was just as well,
because "I hate the association of the name Eisenhower with the name
Nixon."[31] Nixon's explanation was that he had written about only one
American, MacArthur, and he wrote about MacArthur primarily in his
relationship with postwar Japan.

His cast was revealing. When dealing with foreign potentates he was
far more relaxed and successful than when dealing with domestic problems. His own more pleasant memories were for the days in Paris, Bonn,
Moscow, and Peking, rather than Washington. He was full of praise for
foreigners, derogatory about most Americans: "Some leaders are masters
of intrigue, spinning webs of deception, planting suggestions that the
unwary will take as promises, wheeling and dealing, constantly, even

compulsively, plotting and maneuvering. For Lyndon Johnson this was second nature. FDR was a master at it." Not Golda Meir, with whom he compared himself.[32] Eisenhower's strength was that he was a good delegator. There was a nice little thrust in his continuing verbal duel with his old National Security Adviser and Secretary of State: Kissinger, Nixon wrote *en passant,* was "seldom . . . lavish in his praise of people who are out of earshot."[33]

Nixon's capsule biographies contained nothing new in the way of information or insights (even the personal anecdotes, and especially the best ones, had already appeared in his memoirs, and many were repeated in *The Real War*). Much of the book consisted of rambling comments on leadership. Courage, intelligence, ambition, egotism, foresight, dignity, charisma, were described at too great length. There were contradictions: a real leader should never look back, but he should learn from his mistakes. Qualities most would think essential to leadership were not on Nixon's list, including virtue, but the most noticeable absent quality was that of teacher. The great leaders in a democracy—Churchill, Washington, Jefferson, Lincoln, Teddy Roosevelt—are first of all great teachers. But that thought seemed not to have occurred to Nixon.

To Nixon, great leaders were not necessarily good men. He cited Peter the Great, Julius Caesar, Alexander the Great, and Napoleon as examples. Nor were great leaders men who "raised statecraft to a higher moral plane. Rather, we are talking about those who so effectively wielded power on such a grand scale that they significantly changed the course of history for their nations and for the world."[34]

NIXON's road back to respectability had many obstacles on it, not all of them put up by the Democrats or his other old enemies. In their 1980 convention, as in 1976, the Republicans had not mentioned the name of the man they had nominated five times. In February 1981, when Nixon attended his first fund-raiser outside California, the leading Republicans in the state, Ohio, were absent. The dinner had been held in Columbus; Nixon was the guest of honor; Republican Governor James Rhodes, the state chairman, and the state's entire Republican congressional delegation stayed away. The county chairman delivered a caustic criticism: "It's like inviting your former mistress to your family Christmas dinner."[35]

But as Nixon had said to Gulley after the Frost interview, "There are four, four and a half million Nixon Nuts out there, that no matter what I do, it wouldn't make any difference to them. They'd still support me." Gulley had commented, "He called those hard-core supporters 'the nutty fringe,' but he feels there are enough of them so that they can't be ignored by other Republican politicians. Nixon feels the party can't afford to alienate them."[36]

The Sadat funeral and the attendant publicity made Nixon more in demand. He made speeches, attended more fund-raisers, granted television interviews, held news conferences, the works. One of the interviews was with Diane Sawyer, now co-host of the CBS "Morning News," and in it he discussed, briefly, Watergate, for the first time since the Frost show. Noting that the tenth anniversary of the Watergate break-in was approaching, Sawyer asked him what it meant to him now.

"It happened a long time ago," Nixon answered. "I've said everything I—I can on the subject. I have nothing to add, and I'm looking to the future rather than the past."

Sawyer wanted more. "A lot of people say . . . that you never just said 'I covered up and I'm sorry.' "

Nixon replied that "I've covered all that in great, great detail" in the memoirs and on the Frost broadcast. "I've said it all, and I'm not going to say anything more in the future."

Still Sawyer pressed. "Do you think about it when you're just sitting alone?"

"Never," Nixon snapped. "No. . . . I'm not going to spend my time just looking back and wringing my hands about something I can't do anything about."[37]

He would look back, however, to celebrate his triumphs. That fall four of his old advance men, led by Ron Walker, put together a reunion in Washington to mark the tenth anniversary of the great victory in the 1972 election. It was a weekend-long affair, held at the Marriott Hotel in Washington, with a huge blue banner that read WELCOME CLASS OF '72. Many of the old gang were there, including Mitchell, Kissinger, Buchanan, Colson, Warren, Ziegler, and Rose Woods. Haldeman canceled at the last minute; Safire and Sawyer were invited but did not attend; Ehrlichman failed to respond to the invitation; Dean was not invited, but commented that he was "surprised that the school for scoundrels would hold a class reunion."

The man himself was there, shaking hands, smiling, joking, ebullient. Walker lauded him as "one of the greatest statesmen the world has ever known." Woods spoke of her boss as "the most honorable man this country ever produced," which triggered a standing ovation. Nixon gave a speech, praising advance men, the Republican Party, and his former aides. He concluded with a reading from Teddy Roosevelt's "Man in the Arena" speech, the part about the man who "at the best, knows in the end the triumphs of high achievements and who, at the worst, if he fails, at least fails while daring greatly, so that his place shall never be with those cold and timid souls who know neither victory nor defeat."

He took off his reading glasses. The teary-eyed group leaned forward. "None of you are timid souls," Nixon said.

Someone started singing "God Bless America." Nixon joined in. He went to the piano and banged out another verse. He played "Happy

Birthday." He asked for requests, then played "Let Me Call You Sweetheart."

"More," his old aides called out. "More."[38]

By the late winter of 1983, Nixon was becoming more critical of Reagan,
letting it be known in his interviews, background briefings, and occasionally in his columns for the newspapers that unremitting hostility toward the Soviet Union was a misguided policy. He did not denounce
Reagan's military buildup or the mounting deficits, but he was letting it
be known that he was unhappy, that he feared Reagan was following the
advice of *The Real War* too closely.

In late February, he was guest of honor at a stag dinner at the home
of Senator Mark Hatfield (R.-Ore.), who had been a leading critic of
Nixon's Vietnam policy and who had his doubts about Reagan's confron-
tational attitude toward the Soviet Union. Several big businessmen were
in the group, which also included former Senator Fulbright.[39]

Word of the dinner leaked, and it led Safire to write a blistering
piece about Nixon. Why was he criticizing his old boss, Safire asked
himself, and answered: "Because he is now the darling of the new de-
tenteniks, the hotly desired guest of the morning shows and Op-Ed pages,
and the guru of the Hatfields and Percys. Conventional wisdom is revisionist, and now hails Mr. Nixon as all-wise on foreign policy; I think his
latest writing is accommodationist and wrong-headed."[40]

For Safire, worse was to come. Over the Independence Day weekend
of 1983, Nixon began work on a new book, entitled *Real Peace*. It was
short, only 107 pages ("shorter is frequently better," Nixon wrote in his
introduction to the paperback edition, "because shorter texts are usually
more powerful and always more read"); still, for a man who claimed to
sometimes take a full day to get one sentence right, he finished with
remarkable speed—five weeks later the book was done. So urgent was
its message, so anxious was Nixon to get it into the hands of the policy
and opinion makers, that he decided to publish it himself, at his own
expense, thus skipping the editorial process and thereby having the book
published six months sooner.[41]

In late August, Nixon mailed bound page-proof copies of *Real Peace*
to American and foreign leaders and journalists, some 115 in all, including
Reagan, the new Secretary of State, George P. Shultz, Kissinger, Bill
Buckley, Hugh Sidey, and Howard K. Smith. In a covering letter, Nixon
announced that by September 10 he would be sending seven hundred
hardcover copies to "a selected number of Government officials and opinion leaders in the United States and abroad."

The title implied a criticism of Reagan, but Nixon denied the implication. In a postscript to his covering letter, he wrote: "Before you
conclude that I am a fallen away hawk, I suggest you read particularly

my comments on El Salvador!"[42] On El Salvador he said both the hawks and the doves were wrong; the hawks wanted to send only military aid, while the doves wanted to send only economic aid, when both were essential. The "fundamental truth" was that in El Salvador, as throughout the developing world, the people "cannot have progress without security, and they cannot have security without progress."[43]

Sending out the bound page proofs proved to be a good idea. Nixon got favorable blurbs from many of the recipients (making *Real Peace*, he later wrote, "my most critically acclaimed book") and an auction in the New York publishing world for the book. The New York Times Syndication Sales Corporation bought the newspaper rights, then sold the book to Little, Brown.

In his introduction, Nixon said he had always wanted to approach writing an entire book as if it were a long speech: "I wanted it to have the impact of a book but with the clarity, simplicity, and immediacy of a spoken address."[44] Those were contradictory goals, and he had made a dreadful mistake. *Real Peace* was a string of generalizations and quips that were suitable to a political speech but lacking substance; simplistic assertions, given in short, snappy sentences that would have wowed an audience in a speech, made the author look superficial when read on page after page.

"The United States wants peace; the Soviet Union wants the world." As always, Nixon set up straw men to bludgeon down: "Some, out of desperation or supreme naivete, have suggested that an international authority be established to banish nuclear weapons and make sure they are never built again." Who those "some" were, he did not say. But he ridiculed them: "That the disarmists would propose some outlandish 'world government' shows that most of them, to put the most charitable light on the matter, are living in a dream world."[45]

Nixon not only made a mistake in trying to use cheer lines from a speech to make a book, he made another when he decided to skip the editing process. The result was (in William Gibbs Macadoo's characterization of Warren Harding's speeches) an army of pompous phrases marching over the landscape in search of an idea.

What the idea was could not be found. Was Nixon being critical of Reagan or not? Did he think substituting confrontation for negotiation was wise? What was his opinion of the massive military buildup Reagan was conducting? No one could tell.

"There can be no real peace in the world unless a new relationship is established between the United States and the Soviet Union," was the opening sentence of the book. That seemed straightforward enough, as did his assertion that "The time is ripe for a deal."[46] Yet the Communists were on the march. Over 100 million people around the world had been lost to the West since Nixon left office in 1974. The Communists could not be trusted. Yet Communism had lost its appeal, and the Soviet leaders did not want a nuclear war. Yet they were aggressive, and it was critical for the United States to restore the military balance before it was too late and freedom was snuffed out around the world.

What it all came down to, Nixon wrote, was that "to keep the peace and defend our freedom, we need to adopt a policy of hard-headed detente." He explained that "hard-headed detente is a combination of detente with deterrence."[47]

So there it was—Nixon was simultaneously a detentenik and a Reaganite. Whatever one's position on specific foreign and military policy debates, you could find a Nixon quote in *Real Peace* to support it.

NIXON spent the winter of 1983–84 traveling, promoting his latest book, writing a new one, giving interviews, contributing op-ed pieces, and otherwise working in the opinion-making business. He insisted on being taken seriously, and he was; on being respected, and—for the most part, by most people—he was. He was making certain that his place in history, if not assured, was at least improving.

To that end, he spent thirty-eight hours with Frank Gannon, one of the assistants on his memoirs, videotaping an "electronic memoir." Historic Video Productions produced the memoir and sold it worldwide; Nixon was reported to have received $1 million from the deal.

CBS TV bought the American rights. Gannon provided the network with two and a half hours of tapes, from which CBS producers selected ninety minutes to show on "American Parade" and "60 Minutes" on April 8, 10, and 15, 1984. Professional reporters were unhappy that CBS paid $500,000 for interviews conducted by a former Nixon aide who had been an employee of the J. Walter Thompson advertising agency. The network brushed the critics aside. "They are remarkable interviews of a forthcoming nature which we have not seen before," declared Ed Joyce, president of CBS News. Don Hewitt, executive producer of "60 Minutes," added, "I saw a Richard Nixon I never saw before."

Hewitt did not say where he had been for the past couple of decades. No serious Nixon-watcher saw a new Nixon, although there were some disclosures—though not about Nixon. One was that Lyndon Johnson had placed microphones in the reception area outside the Oval Office "so he could listen to what people were saying about him before they came inside." Another was that Johnson had installed recording equipment under the bed in the White House living quarters. Generally, however, it was the old Nixon saying the usual things: "It's the responsibility of the media to look at government—especially the President—with a microscope. I don't argue with that, but when they use a proctoscope, it's going too far." Watergate "was wrong, stupidly handled."[48] But it would be carping to criticize him for making money telling his story one more time.

At the beginning of spring, Nixon flew to California, to spend a week at the Annenberg estate and to see to his more permanent place in history, as he spent a day touring the site selected in San Clemente for his presidential library. He held a news conference, at which he assured reporters that "all the records will be here." Even Watergate? "The Watergate episode, of course, is part of the history of the times."

On May 9, 1984, he spoke to the American Society of Newspaper Editors in their Washington convention. It was a triumph. "I have no enemies in the press whatsoever," he declared. He even had some journalists who were friends. But, "when they give it to me, I give it back, in kind, and that's just the way it's going to be." The editors loved it.

He got into foreign policy and gave the editors something to write about when they got back home. He called for the development of a new relationship with the Soviet Union, replacing confrontation with "detente, peaceful competition, a Cold Peace.

"The United States wants to reduce tension and the Soviet Union needs to reduce tension."

Lest he be mistaken for a dove, he quickly added a call for increased military spending in order to "restore" the United States to equality with the Soviet Union in strategic and conventional arms.

When he finished, the editors rose to their feet to give him nearly a full minute of enthusiastic applause.[49] Quite a contrast to his last appearance before a press group (the Associated Press Managing Editors Association, in Orlando, Florida, in November 1973), when he had told a stunned and hostile audience, "I am not a crook."

THE summer of 1984 was a good one for Nixon. He signed a contract with Arbor House—which outbid both Little, Brown and Warner Books—for a history of the American effort in Vietnam. He traveled, made speeches, got on the telephone to offer advice to the men in power in Washington, attended baseball games, spoke out on the state of the world and America's role in it, entertained, made sure he was seen and heard, got his name in the papers and on the television newscasts.

Not everything was perfect. Pat's health was poor. In 1983, she had had a mild stroke, her second. It had not caused a paralysis nor left her with any speech problems, but it did leave her weaker. The Nixons considered moving back to the city; they put their Saddle River home up for sale and made a bid on a co-op apartment. Nixon explained, "It's a question of whether she wants the burden of a big house. In the case of someone who has had a stroke, you must always worry about a fall."[50] But they decided to stay put. On the Fourth of July, 1984, Pat was admitted to the New York Hospital for treatment for a pulmonary infection. Her attitude toward these illnesses, Julie wrote, was "ignore the discomfort and don't give in."

She was leading a very private life. Her husband entertained a steady stream of politicians, writers, and businessmen, but she seldom made an appearance at his dinners. That summer, she declined the Secret Service protection provided for former First Ladies. She had only the most limited contact with outsiders and felt it was a waste for the government to go to the expense of twenty-four-hour security. She preferred her privacy. Her world revolved around her passion for reading and her home. Although her health prevented her from gardening as much as she wanted, she enjoyed living in the country. Julie recalled her remark the previous October: "Julie, even though it is fall and the flowers are almost gone, it is still so beautiful. The leaves make a garden in the sky."

Henriette Wyeth Hurd, of the famous Wyeth family, painted Pat's portrait. She worked on it for five weeks, and later gave Julie a word portrait that was as sensitive and illuminating as her painting. Hurd wrote that Pat almost never alluded to her troubles, although she did once say of Watergate, "it was completely terrible." When they broke to eat, Hurd noted "the way she puts the plates down at lunch so that the design immediately meets your eye; the little bouquets of flowers—they are a great comfort to her." Pat "loves beauty and the care of things and caring for others. The care of their lives means a tremendous amount to her. A home to your mother is like playing a piano, a painting. She can arrange things so they give beauty. She makes a theater of her own and takes an aesthetic delight in her house. She can't do it with life itself but the house is something she has control over."

On June 20, 1984, Julie gave birth to her third child, a girl, named Melanie Catherine. Pat could play with the grandchildren by the hour. A favorite game was "shoe store," in which all Pat's shoes were lined up in the bedroom. Nixon, too, enjoyed his grandchildren to the fullest extent possible. Julie reported that "it is not uncommon to receive a phone call from my father's secretary announcing, 'The President is on the phone.' " He was not calling for Julie or David, but for Jennie, Alex and, later, Melanie.[51]

AUGUST 9, 1984, was the tenth anniversary of Nixon's resignation. In the preceding week the newspapers carried stories about it, and discussed what had happened to Nixon and his aides since. Anthony Lewis, the leading liberal columnist, recalled the way Nixon had "lifted his arms in that grotesquely inappropriate V, climbed into the helicopter and was gone from our national life."

But, of course, he was not gone, Lewis wrote. Nixon "has spent these 10 years feverishly working to rehabilitate himself, using what he always thought mattered more than substance: the P. R. route. His strategy has been to talk and write about the higher things, refusing always to discuss Watergate, and thus to make the country forget his criminality."[52]

Veteran reporter John Herbers, who had been covering Nixon for decades for *The New York Times,* did an anniversary piece. "A decade later he has emerged at 71 years of age as an elder statesman, commentator on foreign and domestic affairs, adviser to world leaders, a multimillionaire and a successful author and lecturer honored by audiences at home and abroad."

Herbers noted that Nixon had taken to comparing himself to Herbert Hoover. Nixon was quoted as saying that Hoover had been "viciously vilified, deserted by his friends and maligned by his enemies, but in the twilight of his life, [he] stood tall over his detractors." Nixon also liked to quote from another former wanderer in the wilderness who came back, Charles de Gaulle (who was quoting Sophocles): "One must wait until the evening to see how splendid the day has been." Of course, Herbers noted, Hoover had only been accused of bad policies, not criminal acts.[53]

By the tenth anniversary of Watergate, Nixon had come a long way in rehabilitating himself. He had won back the respect, if not the hearts, of most Republicans and not a few Democrats. That there were millions who were not prepared to forgive him was, in large part, his own fault. All he had to do was say eight words, in three sentences, to win the respect and even the affection of the vast majority of his countrymen: "I covered up. It was wrong. I'm sorry."

He desperately wanted that respect, that affection, that full rehabilitation, but he would never say those words. There is a curious parallel here with Alger Hiss. Hiss desperately wanted rehabilitation, and he could have had it by saying, "I spied and I was wrong." He could have added that he had done it for what he regarded as a good cause rather than a self-serving cause, to help the anti-Fascist forces. But Hiss would never say those words; like Nixon, he was too proud. Both Nixon and Hiss had a preoccupation with their own image, and that image precluded them from admitting to any transgression; indeed, through their actions both men escalated the transgression. Hiss escalated by his denials and then his challenge to Chambers to repeat his allegation outside the privileged halls of Congress and then through his civil lawsuit for defamation. Nixon did the same thing by his references to the nonexistent Dean Report and by asserting he was innocent before anyone had charged that he was guilty.

A further irony. Both men were done in by the existing physical evidence of their own words, i.e., the four notes in Hiss's handwriting and the typed Baltimore documents, and the Watergate tapes. The two men were destroyed by their own creations.[54]

CHAPTER TWENTY-SEVEN

ELDER STATESMAN
1985–1990

THE SECOND HALF of the ninth decade of the twentieth century was a golden time for Nixon, climaxed by the celebration of his fiftieth wedding anniversary and the opening of the Richard Nixon Library and Birthplace. In that half decade he published three books, all best-sellers; he appeared on the most prestigious television programs; he gave advice to politicians, words of wisdom to editors, quips to reporters; he traveled at a pace that left younger men pleading for a breather; he met with the most powerful men in the world and gave them advice on how to conduct themselves and their affairs; he attended the major sports events, where he attracted more TV cameras than celebrities from Washington, Wall Street, or Hollywood; his photograph was back on the cover of the weekly news magazines; he used his notoriety as the only President to resign his office to draw attention to himself. Without admitting to any wrongdoing, much less apologizing, he managed to rehabilitate himself.

Nixon recreated himself through a carefully crafted campaign featuring hard work, willpower, luck, brass, and political skill. As to luck, there was the Reagan Presidency. After eight years of Reagan, millions of former Nixon opponents found themselves wishing they had Nixon back. And that came after four years of a Carter Presidency that most Americans regarded as, at best, inept.

For a man who had been close to death in his early sixties, Nixon in his seventies was in remarkably good condition. That was not just luck, of course; he stayed in shape by smoking and drinking moderately, watching his diet, keeping busy, taking care of himself. He suffered some of the ills that old flesh is heir to, including a skin cancer (removed in 1985), an extremely painful case of the shingles in 1985, a short hospitalization for the flu in 1986, prostate surgery in 1987, and a treatment for heart-rhythm disturbance in 1990, but none had been life-threatening.

He carried his age well. His hair was grayer but also fuller. His jowls seemed somehow more pendulous, his nose was somehow more prominent, more of a ski slope than ever, and the bags under his eyes were more noticeable. There was a sag to his body that emphasized his bent shoulders and the beginnings of a pot belly. His step might be slower, but it was firm. His smile could still lift his face and light up a room. He dressed as carefully and conservatively as always. Altogether he looked like what he strove to be, a respected, wise, dignified older man.

His mental health was better. He was living a relaxed life appropriate to his age. A doting grandfather, he saw more of his grandchildren than he had of his own children. He almost never went out at night. He was up at 4:30 or 5 A.M. to begin his day with a two-mile walk. He worked as hard on his books as on his reputation.

He invited younger reporters to Saddle River for dinner. No matter how cynical they thought they were, nor how liberal, they were awestruck to be in his presence, in his home, drinking his wine, hearing his stories. No one could resist leaning forward to catch every word when the ex-President would begin, "As de Gaulle told me . . ." or, "So Ike lets out a yelp and . . ." or, "That was the time Khrushchev took me aside to say . . ." The reporters felt they were in the presence of history, and they were naturally impressed.

And they were impressed further when, later in the evening, Nixon pontificated on the state of the world, on how the President was doing in foreign policy, on what the Chinese or Russians were up to. They loved it when he grew cynical and started making cracks about the Democrats, about their publishers, about the television newscaster superstars, even about some Republicans. They listened intently to his predictions, and they agreed among themselves that he was certainly the most fascinating man of his time.

Older reporters were not immune to it.[1] But it was the youngsters, the up-and-coming, that Nixon worked to cultivate. They were flattered even when they had to pay the price of listening to Nixon's jokes. When Strobe Talbott and John Stacks were interviewing Nixon for *Time* in 1987, Nixon asked photographer Eddie Adams to come in to take some pictures. Adams was the Associated Press photographer who had taken one of the most famous photos of the Vietnam War, the execution of a Viet Cong captive by Colonel Loan on the streets of Saigon during the Tet Offensive of 1968. As Adams was setting up, Nixon told him, "What we should do is put out a contract on Khomeini." After a pause, he delivered his punch line—"Eddie, you can take the picture." He followed it with a big "Ha, ha!"[2]

Reporters who spent their working days recording the bromides of working politicians found Nixon's very cynicism refreshing. In 1988, Roger Rosenblatt of *Time* magazine got both an invitation to dinner ("And then the President entered, smiling like a baby, and [we] all rushed to welcome him into the room") and a private interview (as Rosenblatt set his tape recorder on the table, Nixon remarked, "That's one of those *new* tape recorders. They're so much better than the *old* tape recorders"). Nixon gave him a string of quotable observations. Referring to the upcoming Democratic Convention in Atlanta, he said that Jesse Jackson "will have his way with the platform, and the candidate will ignore the platform. That's the way it happens."

As to the voters, Nixon observed that "the media go on about the 'undecided voter.' Ha! Undecided voter. That's bullshit. Believe me, people decide about politics early on. You take the average guy. You know? Sipping beer and eating his pretzels. He's worrying about who he should vote for?" Try getting a quote like that out of George Bush, or Michael Dukakis, or Walter Mondale, or the old Nixon.

About his own recovery, Nixon used the word "renewal," and then explained to Rosenblatt, "Americans are crazy about renewal."[3]

As to any effort on his part to create a "new Nixon," however, that he hotly denied. "It has not been a deliberate program," he said in 1986 when asked about his comeback, "and I am frankly surprised at the extent to which there seems to be an audience for what I have to say." Then he immediately made it perfectly clear that he understood why there was so much interest: people came to hear him speak or bought his books, or read his interviews, "Because they say, 'What makes this guy tick?' They see me and they think, 'He's come back' or 'He's risen from the dead.' "[4]

In 1986, Nixon had his recently hired administrative assistant, thirty-one-year-old John Taylor, begin sending regular Nixon updates to the press corps. In the first issue, Taylor noted that in 1985 Nixon had received almost five hundred invitations for speeches or requests for interviews. He had published his sixth book and taken a month-long trip around the world that included a luncheon given on the India-Pakistan border by the Khyber Rifles and a helicopter flight to the Pegu Pagoda in Burma "where he rang the same ceremonial bell he had rung on his first visit in 1953."[5]

In 1985, Nixon had given up his Secret Service protection; Taylor told reporters that the motive was solely to save the government money (an estimated $3 million per year).[6] Nixon was more honest; he wanted more personal freedom. He got his best thinking done on his morning walks, and "When you're with Secret Service they walk with you and a car comes behind. If you're going to be thinking, you've got to walk alone."[7] Three years later, he said he had found that discontinuing the Secret Service protection "improved the quality of my trips. . . . I now had the freedom I wanted to go anywhere in the world without the very efficient but nonetheless very intrusive presence of the Secret Service."[8] In place of the agents, he hired a combination driver and security guard.

Taylor made sure that the American people knew that Nixon, unlike the other former Presidents, was saving them money by paying for his own security. When the Associated Press put out a dispatch on Nixon's release from the hospital in 1986, after his bout with the flu, it stated that he was accompanied by the Secret Service. Taylor immediately demanded a correction.[9]

Taylor's job was to be on the watch for misstatements about Nixon, and there were so many of them. When Hugh Sidey mentioned in his column that Nixon had ordered an air brush to eliminate the martini glasses that appeared in Ollie Atkins's photographs of the family on the last evening in the White House, Taylor sent a rebuttal to *Time* magazine. When this author wrote in a *New York Times Book Review* review of a biography of Adlai Stevenson that Nixon had lied about Stevenson, Taylor sent in a long letter to the *Times* insisting that Nixon had done no such thing. (Nixon had said that Stevenson "leaped to the defense of the arch-traitor of our time, Alger Hiss." What Stevenson had done was reply to a question in a written deposition. The question was what was Hiss's reputation so far as Stevenson was aware. Stevenson had replied with one word, "Good.")[10]

IN early 1985 Nixon published *No More Vietnams*, a history of the war in Vietnam, 1945–75, a gloating "I told you so" description of his own policies in Vietnam, and a prescription for the future. As history, the book is a curious mixture of genuine insight, honest evaluation, irresponsible diatribe, and sour grapes, marred as always by too many metaphors ("By allowing the Ho Chi Minh Trail to become a freeway for Hanoi's invasion, we put Ho Chi Minh in the driver's seat in the Vietnam War").[11] Typical, too, were strings of statistics without citations that were impossible to check, accompanied by statements without names or sources ("It is estimated that between 300,000 and 500,000 [North Vietnamese] peasants either committed suicide or died as a result" of Ho's policies).[12]

The book opens with "The Myths of Vietnam." Nixon lists twenty-two myths, in some cases with telling effect, for example, the myths that the Buddhist protest in 1962 resulted from religious repression, that Tet in 1968 was a military defeat for the U.S. Army, and that it was a calculated American policy to bomb civilian targets. But most of the myths he "discovered" were exactly that, *his* discoveries. It was a myth, he wrote, to believe and say that "The Viet Cong won the hearts and minds of villagers through humanitarian policies," without informing his readers who had ever thought or said such a thing. Other straw men on his list of myths were: "Most American soldiers were addicted to drugs, guilt ridden . . . and deliberately used cruel and inhumane tactics," and "Life is better in Indochina now [in 1985] that the United States is gone."[13] Who had ever said such a thing?

As history, the book is contentious and shrill. The American antiwar movement was "a brotherhood of the misguided, the mistaken, the well-meaning, and the malevolent." Still, it was not the "decisive factor" in the failure to win the war. That responsibility rested with Kennedy and Johnson, who "began and escalated the war," but "did not give the American people victories and did not effectively explain the justice of what we were fighting for."[14] Indeed, every President who dealt with Vietnam, from Truman to Ford, had blundered, except himself.

He ascribed terrible motives to his enemies. The doves had argued that the war was unwinnable; they had done so because "they reasoned that if the Vietnam War proved unwinnable, then all battles against totalitarian aggression were unwinnable."[15] The doves were pacifists who wanted totalitarianism.

The responsibility for the final debacle in Vietnam was clearly with Congress. Not, be it noted, with Nixon's friends in Peking and Moscow, the men he had met with in 1972, the keys to peace, the linkage he and Kissinger had worked so hard to bring about. One might have thought Nixon would have been furious with the Chinese and Russians for giving the NVA the firepower to overrun South Vietnam. As for Hanoi demanding more supplies after the cease-fire, Nixon wrote: "Moscow and Peking demurred, saying that it was a hopeless and wasteful effort to keep sending arms that would later be destroyed through American bombing. But after Congress cut off the possibility of future bombing in June 1973, there was no longer any reason for restraint. Moscow and Peking had been willing to help us contain Hanoi—but only if we were determined to do so as well."[16] So Peking and Moscow were off the hook, and Congress was back on.

The last chapter, "Third World War," was a plea for greater involvement in Central America, essentially a think piece supporting Reagan's policy of military aid for the Nicaraguan contras. The thrust was that the United States should not be deterred from becoming involved in Central America because of the "Vietnam Syndrome." To those who were saying the United States should stay out, Nixon was replying that the lesson of Vietnam was not that the United States should stay out of such places from now on, but that we should not fail again.

No More Vietnams was praised by conservative publications such as *National Review* and the Chicago *Tribune*, panned by *The Washington Post* and *The New York Times*, and had substantial sales. Its message—that we were right to fight in Vietnam, that it was a noble cause, and that we won only to have the victory thrown away by a chicken Congress—found a receptive audience. If that argument came close to the Nazi charge of "stab in the back," that was not Nixon's fault, nor was he alone in writing revisionist history. What was regrettable was that he could write such a big book on such an important subject, one in which he had played a leading role from 1954 to 1969 and *the* leading role from 1969 to 1973, without once asking himself difficult questions.

No More Vietnams was published on the tenth anniversary of the fall of Saigon. Four months later, on the fortieth anniversary of the dropping of the atomic bomb on Hiroshima, *Time* magazine printed an 8,000-word interview with Nixon. He reviewed the nuclear arms race, then said he had come close to using the weapons on a number of occasions in Vietnam; again in October 1973, when Brezhnev threatened to intervene unilaterally in the Mideast; again in 1970, when it appeared that the Soviets might "jump the Chinese"; and in 1971, during the India-Pakistan War, when "the Chinese were climbing the walls" and it looked like they might intervene to stop India. Had they done so, Nixon said, "and the Soviets reacted, what would *we* do? There was *no question* what we would have done."

The unnamed *Time* reporter was impressed. "He frowns and shrugs," he wrote of Nixon. "In rapid succession he looks perplexed, annoyed, engaged. . . . He is in high gear now. He does not sound like a man out of office. . . . The only way out is arms control, but 'arms control must not be sought as a goal in itself. Far more important is our political understanding of the Soviets.' For Nixon, this is where things get interesting, where the country gets interesting.

" 'You see,' " Nixon said, 'I'm not talking about *winning*. I'm talking about the world as it is. The rivalry between the U.S. and the Soviet Union can be managed but not eliminated. That's the kind of world we live in.' "[17]

Great copy. A wonderful mixture of insider history and realistic pronouncements on current and future problems. No wonder reporters clamored for interviews.

It was as it had always been, Nixon wrote four years later: "While they liked me even less than before, I was news. Like moths to a flame, reporters cannot resist reporting a good news story."[18]

He gave them plenty of good stories. He wrote an article on summitry for *Foreign Affairs*. He stopped in at a crowded Burger King in New Jersey and was besieged by autograph seekers. In 1986 he made *Rolling Stone's* list of "Who's Hot: The New Stars in Your Future."

In April 1986, Nixon wowed the American Newspaper Publishers Association. When he finished explaining the world situation, the publishers gave him a standing ovation. Asked what lessons Watergate held for him, he replied with his one-liner: "Just destroy all the tapes."

The camera clicks reached a crescendo when he shook hands with

Katharine Graham of *The Washington Post* and shared a friendly laugh with her. Graham was so impressed that she ordered her editor to put a smiling picture of Nixon on the cover of the *Post*-owned magazine *Newsweek*, with a headline reading: "HE'S BACK; THE REHABILITATION OF RICHARD NIXON." The issue carried a six-page article on Nixon's resurrection, accompanied by twelve photographs and an additional three-page interview entitled "The Sage of Saddle River." He had some cutting remarks about Kissinger, about George Bush ("He may not be a strong leader"), about the CIA, about the Establishment. He had praise for Reagan, and himself. On his own place in history, he said that "Without the Watergate episode I would be rated, I should think, rather high. Without it. But with it, it depends on who's doing the rating." He then explained that scandals only affect a President's popularity when there are simultaneous economic problems, and "we really got the triple whammy" from inflation, food shortages, and the Yom Kippur War with the resulting oil embargo.[19] In short, vintage Nixon, made especially delectable by the fact that his old nemesis Graham was paying for the ink, the paper, and the distribution.

NIXON enjoyed the publicity; but he wanted more. He would have loved to have had power, but he was realistic enough to realize that was impossible. He did want influence. To that end, he set out to capture the mind of Ronald Reagan, but in Reagan's first term the President had paid little attention. Détente was out, confrontation was in. In his second term, Reagan began to soften toward the Soviets, and as he did so Nixon was there to give advice.

There had been no summit meeting in Reagan's first term. As the second term began, however, there was some interest on Reagan's part on getting together with the new Soviet leader Mikhail Gorbachev, who was eager for such a meeting. Nixon sent Reagan a long memorandum telling him that "a quickie, get-acquainted summit would be immensely popular," but warning that "it will do far more harm than good."[20]

Eventually, a summit was set up for Geneva in November 1985. Reagan sent his National Security Adviser, Robert McFarlane, to Saddle River for advice. The President also called personally for further counsel. Nixon guarded his access carefully. When Reagan floated the idea of calling in Ford, Carter, and Nixon for a pre-summit seminar, Nixon did some research into Ford's and Carter's schedules, found a date they could not make, and named that as the only time he could show up. The idea died.[21]

This activity was little more than Reagan being kind to Nixon. The President set his own agenda, made his own decisions. He was polite about informing Nixon, but did not consult him. "I talk to him [Reagan] quite regularly," Nixon told *Newsweek*, then admitted that "Usually he calls me from Camp David, usually after he has had one of these, you know, tough decisions." *After*. For example, Reagan called *after* he had ordered an air strike on Tripoli with the aim of killing Libyan leader Colonel Muammar el-Qaddafi.[22]

In July 1986, Nixon approached Reagan from another direction, Moscow. He made a trip to the Soviet Union and got himself invited to a private session with Gorbachev in the Kremlin. He found himself impressed by Gorbachev's "charisma, his intellect, and his decisiveness," but what impressed him most was Gorbachev's "absolute self-confidence." Nixon judged Gorbachev to be "just as tough as Brezhnev but better educated, more skillful, more subtle, and not as obvious while making the same points. Brezhnev used a meat ax in his negotiations. Gorbachev uses a stiletto." Extending the metaphor, Nixon added, "But beneath the velvet glove he always wears, there is a steel fist."[23]

On his return to the United States, Nixon sent Reagan a twenty-six-page memorandum on the meeting. Someone—could it have been Nixon?—gave a copy to *Time* magazine's Strobe Talbott, who reprinted it a year later along with an exclusive interview with Nixon.

The memo showed Nixon attempting to explain Reagan and Gorbachev to each other, coaxing them toward accommodation, acting as honest broker. He had told Gorbachev that the Soviets could do business with Reagan precisely because Reagan was a conservative, and he had told Reagan that a major strategic arms deal was possible and could be obtained with only minor concessions on Reagan's cherished Strategic Defense Initiative (SDI) antimissile program. Nixon quoted Anatoly Dobrynin as telling him that Gorbachev was "politically very strong, and President Reagan should seize the opportunity to deal with him." Endorsing that view, Nixon told Reagan he found Gorbachev to be "either the greatest actor the political world has produced or . . . a man totally in charge with the power and ability to chart his own course."

Nixon's memo was flattering to Reagan. Nixon said he had told Gorbachev that Reagan was "enormously popular," which meant he could get Senate approval of any arms agreement he entered into. "I told [Gorbachev] that after President Reagan left office, he would [continue to] be enormously popular and would have a great influence on public issues due to his incomparable communication skills. It was, therefore, very much in Gorbachev's interest that President Reagan have a stake in a new, improved U.S.-Soviet relationship which he would have initiated. This would ensure that he would strongly support his successor's efforts to carry out the Reagan initiatives. On the other hand, failure to reach agreement while President Reagan is in office might run the risk of developing a situation where President Reagan might become a powerful critic."

Gorbachev seemed impressed. "I don't believe anything I said during the conversation had a greater impact on him," Nixon wrote.

Nixon told Reagan of Gorbachev's forceful objections to SDI. He reported that Gorbachev "said it was simply a myth that the Soviet Union opposed SDI because they feared the enormous cost to their economy. He went on to say that his opposition to SDI was not based on his fear of its military potential or of our technological edge. . . . His major objection to SDI [was] if it went forward there would be a massive spiral in the arms race." He urged Reagan to consider a strategic arms deal that would protect America's right to continue "purposeful research in SDI while trading restrictions on deployment for reductions in Soviet missiles."

Scattered through the memo were the kind of grace notes that Nixon knew Reagan liked to read: "I sensed that Gorbachev's attitude toward the President and the First Lady was one of genuine affection. His last words to me as I was leaving his office in the Kremlin were, 'Give my warmest regards to President Reagan and to Lady Nancy.' "[24]

A month after receiving Nixon's memo, Reagan went to the summit, in Reykjavik, Iceland, where to the dismay of his aides he and Gorbachev agreed on the elimination of all nuclear weapons and the missile systems to deliver them, and further agreed that this process of disarmament was to be completed in ten years. These agreements in principle, however, then had to be scrapped when Reagan refused to accept Gorbachev's demand that the United States give up its SDI program.

IN 1987, Nixon did more traveling, more speaking, more hosting of dinner parties, more writing. He had a new publisher, Simon and Schuster. He finished the book he was working on, *1999: Victory Without War*, on his seventy-fifth birthday, January 9, 1988.

1999: Victory Without War was the best and worst of Nixon. He described the book as "the product of a lifetime of study and on-the-job training in foreign policy,"[25] and wrote it as a how-to guide for whomever was elected President in November. To that end he made two particularly significant contributions, both deeply imbedded in his long career in foreign policy. First, he tried to persuade right-wing Republicans to support negotiations with the Soviet Union on arms control and a low-keyed management of the competitive relationship. Second, he sought to arouse Democrats and Republicans alike to reject the temptations of isolationism and to face the complex challenges of the twenty-first century with a rekindled spirit of internationalism.

In pursuit of those goals he wrote a long, sensitive section on Gorbachev, with equal stress on his personality and his problems. There was some good analysis, and some typical Nixonian hardheaded realism: "We must always remind ourselves that the purpose of the Gorbachev reforms is not to move toward more freedom at home or toward a less threatening foreign policy abroad, but rather to make the communist system work better."[26]

He denounced extremists in the United States, inventing some new words to describe them as he did so. The "superdoves," he said, had been the "dominant influence" in the Carter Administration, and they were naive. When they controlled policy, "war became more likely, not less." At the opposite extreme were the "superhawks," who dominated the Reagan Administration. They were "unrealistic," and as naive in their own way as the superdoves, because they believed total victory was possible.[27] Nixon did not: "We must recognize that there are no permanent victories in the American-Soviet struggle."[28] The middle ground Nixon advocated called for a "comprehensive policy that combines deterrence, competition, and negotiation."[29]

There were some excellent predictions: "Eastern Europe today is ripe for positive peaceful change. . . . Since World War II, the tectonic plate of Soviet imperialism has been pushing against that of Eastern European nationalism. These forces have produced tremors in the past, but unprecedented pressures will build up along the fault line in the 1990s. Without genuine reform, a political earthquake in Eastern Europe is inevitable in the years before 1999."[30]

There were some bad predictions: "The Kremlin . . . cannot pull out its 120,000 troops [in Afghanistan] without precipitating a collapse of the communist government in Kabul. . . . Moscow has the potential power to prevail. But at the current rate victory will not come for at least twenty years."[31] And, contradicting what he wrote earlier about change in Eastern Europe, he predicted that "the Soviet Union will do whatever is necessary—including a brutal military invasion—to suppress an insurgency seeking to liberate one of its satellites in Eastern Europe."[32]

Contradiction was becoming a problem for Nixon, because he was doing so much writing on the same subject. He wrote that as President, he was "well aware that our highly successful summit meeting in 1972 might spawn euphoric expectations among the American people. Even though I knew I stood to benefit politically from such euphoria, I tried to tamp it down and to keep our successes in perspective."[33] But in *The Real War*, he had written, "Creation of a willowy euphoria is one of the dangers of summitry. During my administration excessive euphoria built up around the 1972 Peking and Moscow summit meetings. I must assume a substantial part of the responsibility for this. It was an election year, and I wanted the political credit."[34]

Nixon also got himself into contradictions as a result of his never-ending search for colorful imagery: "An ebb follows every tide in history," he said in opening a paragraph. No problem there. But he ended the paragraph with a warning; if the United States did not support freedom fighters in Nicaragua, Afghanistan, and elsewhere, "this red tide will never ebb."[35]

Nixon gave endless advice. With regard to the Iran-Iraq War, for example, he wrote: "We should seek a solution that provides peace without victory."[36] The phrase was Woodrow Wilson's, and it had a better ring to it than "victory without war" when applied to Iran-Iraq. Nixon was not willing to apply it to U.S.-Soviet relations, however. There, again contradicting his earlier statement, he said he wanted victory.

This led to another problem: he never made clear the logic by which he viewed the Soviet Union as the source of the world's evil while at the same time considering China as one of the great hopes for the future. Both were Communist powers, with bad ideologies and unworkable policies, but while the Soviet Union had to be defeated, "In the twenty-first century the Sino-U.S. relationship will be one of the most important, and most mutually beneficial, bilateral relationships in the world."[37]

Overall, the trouble with *1999: Victory Without War* is that Nixon was a speechmaker rather than a book writer. He advocated good, sensible policies, but he did so with cheer lines from speeches without providing the kind of detailed analysis necessary to back them up. His rhythm was all wrong. He was repetitious. He had certain favorite lines that were sure to appear in each of his books. "America wants peace; the Soviet Union wants the world" . . . "While the United States and the Soviet Union can never be friends, they cannot afford to be enemies" . . . "The Great Wall of China is very thick. [A variation on this one began 'The walls of the Kremlin are very thick.'] It is difficult enough to be heard when you are inside the wall. It is impossible to be heard when you are outside the wall" . . . "[With regard to the Third World] At least the communists talk about the problems. Too often we talk only about the communists."

But of course Nixon did not set out to please literary critics, or academic historians. He wanted to make a little money, he wanted to strengthen his reputation as a foreign-policy pundit, he wanted to share his experience and practical idealism, he wanted to have an impact on the next President. He achieved these goals, and took a pardonable pride in so doing.

Publication day was April 10, 1988. To mark it, Nixon appeared on a special hour-long version of the NBC News program "Meet the Press," then went on a nationwide author's tour. He took the opportunity to comment on the presidential election, while denying that he was trying to make a political comeback or to promote sales of his book. "It isn't comeback," he said, nor was he speaking out "in order to be well thought of." Rather, his purpose was "to get the message across."

He was highly quotable on the candidates. "The best politics is poetry rather than prose," he said. "Jesse Jackson is a poet. Cuomo is a poet, and Dukakis is a word processor." After the Iowa caucuses in February, he said Vice President Bush had "insufficient drive," but after Senator Dole's campaign collapsed in New Hampshire, Nixon declared that Bush had "really come into his own."[38]

He was exercising care in what he said. As elder statesman, he had to be a quiet oracle, no longer the strident partisan. He knew he could not endorse a candidate, that to do so would cross the line and make him a liability. He could endorse a policy, and he could give private advice. The Republican candidates came to him for suggestions and insights, partly to flatter him, partly because they would have been fools not to find out what Nixon thought. More often, he called the candidates to offer unsolicited advice. Either way, he kept his hand in.[39]

He had learned that admitting to mistakes made him more believable, so on "Meet the Press" he admitted to two mistakes. The first was no surprise—it was that he had not been tough enough in dealing with the North Vietnamese. "I would say the major mistake I made as President was one—this will surprise you—was not doing early in 1969 what I did on May 3 of 1972 and on December 15, of 1972, and that was to bomb and mine North Vietnam." It had not been his fault. "I wanted to do it. I talked to Henry Kissinger about it, but we were stuck with the bombing halt that we had inherited from the Johnson Administration, with Paris peace talks." He had not trusted the peace talks; "Just like the cease-fire talks down there in Nicaragua, I didn't trust them at all. And they proved to be, of course, phony," as presumably the Nicaragua talks would prove to be. He did not explain why he was stuck with Johnson's policy, what prevented him from exercising his best judgment, but he did say that if he had gone ahead with the bombing and mining, "we would have ended the war in Vietnam in 1969 rather than in 1973. That was the biggest mistake of my Presidency."

On Watergate, he pointed out that in 1972 he had gone to China, established détente, and ended the Vietnam War. "Those were the big things. And here was this small thing, and we fouled it up beyond belief. It was a great mistake. It was wrong, as I've pointed out again and again.

"It was a small thing, the break-in, and break-ins have occurred previously in other campaigns as well. At that point, we should have done something about it. We should have exposed it, found out who did it, rather than attempting to contain it, to cover it up. It was the cover-up that was wrong, and that was a very big thing; there's no question about it at all."

Chris Wallace of NBC TV asked him to comment on current affairs. On the Iran-contra affair, Nixon said the error was not breaking the law by the Administration; rather, "the fatal flaw in the policy was selling arms to Iran, period, because it is not in the interest of the United States, or of Israel, for that matter, to have Iran win this war."

What should the United States do about Panama's dictator Manuel Noriega, indicted on drug trafficking charges in the United States? Nixon replied that it would be a mistake to use force. "Noriega is an irritant to us," he explained, "but we want to remember that in getting rid of that irritant, we don't want to cause much greater difficulties." Sending in America's armed forces "could produce an adverse reaction throughout Central America."[40]

AT the 1988 Republican Convention, Nixon's name was once again not mentioned. The elder statesman still did not have a party. His recovery was still incomplete.

Bush won the November election easily. As President, he adopted foreign policies that aroused neither Nixon's enthusiasm nor ire. His relationship with Nixon was rather like Reagan's had been—ready to listen, ready to please where it did not cost anything, not eager for much in the way of public association.

During Bush's first year in office, revolutionary change swept through East Europe. The Soviet Union was beset by internal problems nearly as bad as those of the early Stalin years, and as it had done then, so in 1989 did it look inward. It pulled its troops out of Afghanistan, it destroyed missiles and tanks, it began withdrawing from Eastern Europe, it made no effort to retain the Berlin Wall or to block the reunification of Germany. On these and many other issues, Gorbachev acted the opposite of the way Nixon had confidently predicted in his writings and pronouncements since 1985 (Gorbachev was first of all a Communist; Communists were always expansionists; he would use the Red Army before allowing any Warsaw Pact nations to break away; etc.). *Time* magazine, quite swept away by the scope of the whole thing, named Gorbachev its "Man of the Decade." The best Nixon had ever gotten from *Time* was one half the "Man of the Year" award (he shared it with Kissinger for 1972).

If Nixon had been wrong about Gorbachev, at least he had the satisfaction of seeing Communism collapse in East and Central Europe. He had supported "Captive nations" resolutions ever since he came to Washington in 1947; he had gone to Hungary at Christmastime, 1956; he had told Khrushchev to his face that the Soviet Union was enslaving people across twelve time zones; he had denounced the Berlin Wall the day it went up; he had always supported Radio Free Europe and the Voice of America; he had done as much as any politician in the Western world could do to bring freedom to the captive peoples.

Nixon could not fully enjoy the momentous developments in Europe in the fall of 1989, because of events in China in June of that year. Since his trip to China in 1972, Nixon's relationship with the Chinese leadership had grown and deepened. The Chinese had stood by him when almost no one else would. He had made four trips to the country after his resignation; his opening to China stood out as *the* greatest achievement of his Presidency; his reputation rested on it ultimately; the Chinese in the 1980s had instituted economic reforms that brought rapid improvement. Nixon, in his latest book, had given Chinese leaders high praise, and expressed even higher hopes for the future of U.S.-Chinese relations.

But in June 1989, following a Sino-Soviet summit and restoration of relations (which Nixon had insisted could never happen), the Chinese government ordered the Chinese Army to massacre Chinese students protesting for democracy in Tiananmen Square in Peking. The world was outraged and sickened.

Nixon was deeply disturbed, as much by the reaction to the event as to the event itself. Congress, backed by the American people, wanted nothing to do with the butchers of Tiananmen. Republicans and Democrats demanded that the Bush Administration break off all relations, impose wide-ranging sanctions, and isolate the Chinese as a punishment. Nixon wanted to "restore momentum to one of the most important bilateral relationships in the world." So did Bush, who had once been Ambassador to China. In July, the President secretly sent a delegation headed by National Security Adviser Brent Scowcroft to Peking to patch things up as best he could. Bush did not consult Nixon, did not even inform him.

Nixon, meanwhile, decided to go on his own, to do what he could, even though "virtually all of my close friends urged me not to go. They predicted that my critics would hammer me unmercifully for appearing to try to salvage the China initiative by tipping glasses with those who had ordered the Tiananmen crackdown less than five months before."[41]

There certainly was a great deal more at stake than Nixon's reputation, and it certainly was true that Nixon had a privileged status in China that allowed him to say things others could not. Before leaving, in October, he consulted with Bush and Scowcroft. In China, he had over twenty hours of one-on-one meetings with China's top leaders. He was blunt, telling Deng Xiaoping, "I have watched Sino-U.S. relations closely for seventeen years [a nice piece of arithmetic and a bit of rewriting of history, as it implied that Nixon had paid no attention to China before 1972]. There has never been a worse crisis than now in those relations." He had come, he made clear to Deng and other leaders, to help improve those relations, but he insisted on telling them facts they did not want to hear. At one banquet, he said in his toast that differences over the massacre were "huge and unbridgeable," and asked if China would "turn away from greatness and consign itself to the backwater of oppression and stagnation?" In another toast, he warned that "many in the United States, including many friends of China, believe the crackdown was excessive and unjustified" and that it had "damaged the respect and confidence which most Americans previously had for the leaders of China." He said that the massacre had been a great tragedy, and that "another tragedy would be the death of a relationship and of policies that have served so well."[42]

Upon his return, Nixon met with Bush. The President had already decided to take a long view and Nixon gave him full support. In a new book he was then writing, Nixon offered the reasons: China was a nuclear power; it was a key player in regional conflicts in Asia and the Middle East; it was a potential trading partner; it would be a critical factor in dealing with global environmental problems; and so forth. None of this was in any way original or exceptional, but not very many politicians were saying such things publicly in 1989. But as Nixon, ever the realist, pointed out: "As much as we might not like it, we must accept the fact that our relations to other countries should be determined primarily by what they do outside, not inside, their borders." He also warned that "in our efforts to punish the leaders of China, we would punish the people of China even more," a principle he had failed to follow in Chile in 1970, but a good principle nevertheless.[43]

Nixon sent a written report to a bipartisan group of congressional leaders. *Time* reprinted parts of it. With regard to the massacre and its meaning, Nixon said that "the gap between us [Americans and Chinese] is totally unbridgeable." He explained that every Chinese leader "insisted that the suppression of the demonstrations was necessary and justified. They believe the American reaction was an unacceptable intrusion in their internal affairs."

"One top Chinese leader told me," Nixon wrote in a passage that was as self-descriptive of Nixon since 1974 as it was of the Chinese since Tiananmen, "that any colleague who humiliated China in the world community by acting contrite did not deserve to be in office. Contrition may be an attractive characteristic in soap-opera stars, but not in leaders of great nations such as China."

But never mind that the Chinese were not going to apologize, Nixon told the U.S. politicians. *Realpolitik* dictated that America and China re-establish good relations. There were geopolitical reasons, and economic ones. ("China will provide a huge market for the advanced industrial countries. Do we want to rule ourselves out and leave that potential market to the Japanese and the Europeans?") He urged that the United States eliminate economic sanctions, resume government financial assistance to those who wanted to invest in China, resume financing of major Chinese projects by the World Bank, and re-establish high-level contact with the government. He concluded with his "the Great Wall of China is very thick" image.[44]

•

AFTER telling the congressmen things no active politician would have risked saying—those things that only the elder statesman can say—Nixon returned to Saddle River and his work on his next book. He had a new office, within walking distance of his home, saving him the daily two-and-a-half-hour commute. The government paid $137,000 in rent for the office; Nixon got another $173,000 to pay for his staff of three people. In addition, he received $115,000 a year as his presidential and congressional pensions.[45]

The book he was working on, published in early 1990, was entitled *In the Arena: A Memoir of Victory, Defeat and Renewal*. The memoir section was brief. He told, again, the story of his trip to China in 1972, and followed it with the story of his last day in the White House. He dealt with his period of self-imposed exile in San Clemente, and gave a short account of his activities since moving to New York. That took seventy-five pages. The remaining three hundred pages were taken up with thoughts about such subjects as reading, speaking, privacy, enemies, silence, causes, and so on—thirty subjects altogether. His purpose in writing the book, he said, was to comfort those who had suffered losses; he felt they would benefit by seeing what he had gone through. Of course, what he had suffered was unique; as he told *Time* magazine in an interview accompanying excerpts from the book, "No one had ever been so high and fallen so low."[46]

Nixon did himself a disservice in the Watergate section of *In the Arena*. It was the usual Nixonian response to Watergate, shrill and self-pitying. He listed the twelve "myths" of Watergate. The first, and "most blatantly false," was that he ordered the break-in. The second and "most politically damaging" was that he ordered the payment of hush money to Hunt and the others. The third and "most serious" was that he ordered the CIA to obstruct the FBI investigation. The fourth and "most preposterous" was that he or someone on his staff erased eighteen and one-half minutes of incriminating conversation from the tapes. The fifth and "most one-sided" was that he illegally had the IRS audit Larry O'Brien's tax returns—it was not illegal, he pointed out, to get wealthy people to pay their taxes. The sixth and "most hypocritical" was that he "sold" ambassadorships to major contributors.

The seventh and "most personally disturbing" was that he deliberately lied in press conferences and speeches about the cover-up. The eighth and "most widely believed" was that he ordered illegal wiretapping and surveillance. The ninth was that he ordered the break-in to the office of Daniel Ellsberg's psychiatrist. The tenth and "most ridiculous" was that he was the first President to tape conversations in the White House.

The eleventh and "most unfair" was that he made money out of being President. The twelfth and "most vicious" was that he had "tried" to cheat on his income taxes.[47]

With regard to the first "myth," the truth was that no one had ever charged him with ordering the break-in. With regard to the second, on twelve separate occasions in the March 21, 1973, tape he had ordered Dean to get the money to Hunt. With regard to the third, he had ordered the CIA to tell the FBI to back off. With regard to the fourth, fifth, and sixth myths, Nixon was on solid ground.

With regard to the seventh myth, he had said many things in his press conferences in 1973 and 1974 that he knew to be lies, the most famous being his assertion that John Dean had made a report that indicated no one in the White House was involved. Thirteen years earlier he had admitted on the Frost interview that "in some of the statements and press conferences and so forth . . . I want to say right here and now, I said things that were not true."[48] With regard to the eighth myth, Nixon had ordered wiretaps, but there were precedents set by the Kennedy and Johnson administrations. With regard to the ninth, he had admitted to Ehrlichman that he knew in advance about the Ellsberg operation.

With regard to the tenth myth, he was absolutely right; and with regard to the eleventh, he had a case, but he did sell his property in San Clemente at a big profit. With regard to number twelve, backdating a deed of gift to circumvent the tax laws is illegal.

In his first claim, he appeared to be making an admission: "In retrospect, while I was not involved in the decision to conduct the break-in, I should have set a higher standard for the conduct of the people who participated in my campaign and administration. I should have established a moral tone that would have made such actions unthinkable. I did not. I played by the rules of politics as I found them. Not taking a higher road than my predecessors and my adversaries was my central mistake. For that reason, I long ago accepted overall responsibility for the Watergate affair. What's more, I have paid, and am still paying, the price for it."[49]

It was a perfect Nixonian statement. Accepting "overall" responsibility denied specific responsibility. His "confession" blamed Kennedy, Johnson, Truman, Roosevelt, and Eisenhower for setting bad examples.

"Some have said," he wrote, citing his favorite source, "some," "that my major mistake was to protect my subordinates."[50] Who could he mean? Almost all his subordinates had gone to prison, after he had thrown them off his sinking ship.

Had Nixon left out that Watergate section, *In the Arena* would have avoided the blast that came from reviewers, almost all of whom concentrated almost exclusively on Watergate. This made him furious. When he concluded his deal with *Time* for the excerpt and interview, he had to agree to no editorial control. (He did get his photo on the cover, for the sixty-seventh time, easily the record.)[51]

In the Arena was in many ways his best book since the memoirs. It was often quite interesting and informative. Nixon on the subject of reading is well worth reading, as is Nixon on silence, memory, and others. He is especially good on old age, and it is heartwarming to hear him say (Simon and Schuster issued a tape recording of Nixon reading excerpts of his book): "Two thousand years ago, the poet Sophocles wrote, 'One must wait until the evening to see how splendid the day has been.' There is still some time before the sun goes down, but even now, I can look back and say that the day has indeed been splendid. . . . It has been my good fortune to have lived a very long and a very full life."[52]

The book also contained Nixon's reactions to the 1989 upheavals in Central and Eastern Europe and the Soviet Union, and his recommendations on how to respond. Not for Nixon any "Gorbymania." He subjected Gorbachev to a fairly detailed analysis, which was sometimes original and always wary without being hostile. He hoped the reforms would bring about a democratic, open-market Soviet Union, but warned that "if they give Gorbachev's faltering Communist system the jolt it needs to begin to catch up with the West, in the next century we may well face a strong, more confident, more dangerous adversary." Nixon advised maintaining a strong nuclear deterrent and a watchful attitude.

He wanted no part of offering American economic assistance to the Soviets until they had fulfilled six conditions: a free-market economy, a fully independent East Europe, a reduction in Soviet conventional forces, a verifiable START agreement, an end to Soviet support for Cuba and other client states, and finally the adoption of a political system that respected human rights and was based on free elections.[53]

To most Americans, those seemed reasonable conditions. A number of congressmen cited them in the spring of 1990, when Gorbachev visited the United States and asked for aid, as reasons to refuse. President Bush also cited them.

So Nixon was still there in his old age, setting conditions, influencing policy. If he was no longer in the arena, he was more involved than any former President had been since Teddy Roosevelt. He was still playing. "In geopolitics the game never ends," he wrote. "There is no point at which all sides cash in their chips. No victory is ever permanent and no defeat irredeemable."[54] Words to live by, as Nixon had, all his life.

•

ON March 8, 1990, Nixon returned to Washington, to speak to the House Republican Conference, to meet with senators seeking re-election to give them advice, and to hold a news conference. He strode through the corridors of Congress regally. He exuded good humor. Congressional aides in their early twenties turned out by the dozens to crowd the corridors; they applauded and cheered. He was late for his news conference because so many lawmakers, lobbyists, staff members, and reporters wanted to have their picture taken with him. Newt Gingrich, the House Republican whip, several times called it an "extraordinary experience." Senator Dole pronounced him "rehabilitated."

In the news conference, Nixon was relaxed and eminently quotable. When a reporter called him "Mr. Gorbachev," he laughed and said, "I've been called worse." Asked about the Iran-contra scandal and Reagan's recently released videotaped testimony in which he had said he could not recall much about any of these events, Nixon replied with some double entendres. Reagan was not a crook, he said. He followed with another straight-faced use of a memorable Watergate phrase: "How this man, who is 79 years of age, could not have made more mistakes and forgotten more I don't know. I think that President Reagan was not trying to dissemble. He was not trying to cover up."

Was he at peace with himself? "I'll save that for the next conference. I know that I'm getting older and the press seems to be getting younger."

Generally he kept the conference on the subject of foreign policy. He said Poland's efforts at free-market reform "must not fail," and that it was up to the United States to assure "the victory of freedom" as Communist power crumbled. He opposed economic aid to the Soviet Union. He approved Bush's overtures to China: "If the United States does not play a role in China, who does that leave among the major powers? It leaves the Soviet Union and Japan. Does anyone think the Soviet Union is going to export human rights to China? And anyone that thinks Japan is going to export democracy to China must be smoking pot."

At the height of the excitement, a Republican senator's aide scurried out of Dole's office to grab colleagues for picture-taking with Nixon. "He's doing great," the excited young man called over his shoulder. "He's back."[55]

He was, and he had done it without taking "the easy way." There had never been a gesture of contriteness. The people yearned for him to ask for forgiveness, so that they could forgive, but he would not. Hell would freeze first.

IN 1990, sixteen years after his resignation, he continued to block access to large portions of his papers and the great bulk of the tapes. Meanwhile, through his memoirs and other writings, and through his comments in news conferences and at speeches, he became the first and most important revisionist of the Nixon Administration. His special topic was Watergate. By 1990 he had successfully created an impression that the only thing he and his Administration had ever done that was wrong was Watergate, and that Watergate was not much more than an inexplicable break-in followed by a badly managed but completely understandable attempt to cover up. His biggest mistake, he said, was not burning the tapes.

So many believed him that his version became the standard perception of Watergate. By 1990 people born after 1965 asked of Nixon, "What did he do that was so terrible?" They had read about Jack Kennedy and the womanizing, about Bobby Kennedy and the wiretapping, about Lyndon Johnson and his use of the FBI; they had lived through the Reagan Administration and Iran-contra; they were living through and paying for the savings and loan scandal. No wonder they wanted to know what Nixon had done that was so terrible.

Nixon was clever enough to stay out of partisan politics. He realized that, at least before 1990, his endorsement or any attempt to manipulate the party convention would hurt rather than help any Republican candidate, and that campaigning for the nominee was out of the question. Harry Truman could speak out for Stevenson, Ike could speak out for Goldwater, but Nixon could not speak out for Ford or Reagan.

Nixon was also careful to stay out of the arena on domestic political issues. He was not outspoken on abortion, or on flag burning, or other divisive internal issues. Given his lifelong tendency to seek a middle-ground compromise on domestic controversies, had he been foolish enough to speak out he would have alienated the hard core of his support, conservative Republicans.

What Nixon did not do was a factor in his comeback, but what he did do was more important. The self-imposed exile in San Clemente was critical. It was his time in the wilderness, the paying of penance. When he emerged to begin his active campaign for elder statesman, he hit exactly the right note, using the Frost show to tell his story to a mass audience, using his memoirs to tell his story to a somewhat smaller but politically more significant audience. Of course this would not have worked had he not had a hell of a story to tell, or had he not told it in a gripping way.

Once out in the open, he was brilliant in picking his spots for campaign appearances. To begin in Hyden, Kentucky, was a master stroke; Biloxi, Mississippi, was a natural follow-up; going to Oxford University was absolute genius. Those old standbys, foreign trips, served him well.

He was bold enough, and shrewd enough, to go before his former tormentors for speeches and questions and answers—the reporters, the editors, the publishers, he took them all on. And they loved it, he gave them great copy. His private dinner parties for the reporters and columnists were something new and highly profitable to him.

His own writing was the most important ingredient in his comeback. Except for that section on Watergate in *In the Arena,* he concentrated on foreign affairs, past, present, and future. He had much to say, and some of it he said well. In the process he managed to make the indisputable point that among the world leaders of the second half of the twentieth century, he was the American who knew more of them than anyone else, and he was the American who was most admired, by friend and foe alike.

What had seemed impossible in the summer of 1974 had happened by the summer of 1990. Nixon was respectable, even honored, certainly admired. As with his earlier comebacks and successes, there was no mystery or miracle involved. He had planned the campaign, and executed it, carefully and wisely. He had assessed his assets and faced his liabilities; he had used the former well and managed to avoid the latter.

It helped, of course, that he lived so long. Passions cooled, he mellowed, his enemies died off. He was not, after all, remotely like Hitler or Stalin, a man to be forever loathed. Americans want to be proud of their Presidents, and Nixon was one of them. He had done some good, some bad, as they all had. Sixteen years after his resignation, he had finally fought his way out of Purgatory. He was like the others, like Roosevelt and Truman and Eisenhower and Kennedy and Johnson. In July 1990, like them he got his own library.

CHAPTER TWENTY-EIGHT

THE LAST LAUGH
July 19, 1990

THEY BEGAN descending on the house Nixon had been born in, the one Frank Nixon built, the night before the dedication of the Richard Nixon Library and Birthplace. By 6 A.M. on the morning of July 19, 1990, there were thousands of people standing in line, waiting to join in the midday celebration and to welcome Dick Nixon home to Yorba Linda.[1]

Four Presidents of the United States were present for the ceremonies, which were marked by Hollywood hype. Nixon advance men had done their work—banners, streamers, helicopters, cops, massive publicity, loud speakers, Secret Service, limos, movie stars, and the rest. One local radio announcer called it the Olympics of politics, then thought of a better analogy, the Oscar of politics. There were more than one thousand reporters present, plus television cameramen and broadcasters from around the world. Some of the biggest names in the news business were there, including R. W. Apple of *The New York Times*, Tom Brokaw of NBC TV, and Barbara Walters of ABC TV.

Major figures from the Nixon Administration came to honor their boss, including Haldeman, Woods, Ziegler, Safire, Buchanan, Bob Finch, Maurice Stans, and William Simon, along with four Secretaries of State, William Rogers, Henry Kissinger, George Shultz, and Alexander Haig. Other celebrities included Bob Hope, Gene Autry, Billy Graham, and Norman Vincent Peale.

It was the first time four Presidents had appeared together in public (the only other time four Presidents were together was in the Oval Office in 1981, when Ford, Carter, and Nixon attended the private reception hosted by Reagan before they flew off to Sadat's funeral). It was the first time ever that four First Ladies were together. It was Pat Nixon's first public appearance in ten years.

There were some sour notes, beginning with the absence of those who had not been invited, including John Ehrlichman, John Dean, Gordon Liddy, Howard Hunt, and Donald Segretti. No Nixon function could be complete without protesters, but the signs were new—not "Free Alger Hiss," or "Tricky Dick," or "Send Checkers Back to Texas," or "Dump Nixon," or "Nixon Go Home," or "End the War," or "Stop the Bombing," or "Pay Your Taxes," or "Jail to the Chief," or any other of the anti-Nixon slogans from his past. Instead, the pickets demanded federal support for AIDS research and abortion rights, causes that seemed light-years away from Nixon's career and served as a reminder of how long he had been in American politics.

There were the inevitable controversies that surrounded any event in which Nixon was involved. The executive director of the Nixon Library, lawyer Hugh Hewitt, had announced that Bob Woodward and others like him ("irresponsible journalists") would not be able to use the research materials. An immediate uproar of protest at this attempt to censor through control of access to the material forced Hewitt to back down, at least to the extent of explaining that all "qualified and responsible" researchers would be admitted. He did not say who would pass the judgment, or on what basis.

It did not matter anyway, as the "library" did not exist. Except for books written by Nixon for sale in the gift shop, this was a library without books or documents. Hewitt said that in a year or so, the research room would be open, with selected copies of some of the materials held by the Nixon Presidential Materials Project of the National Archives in Alexandria, Virginia.

Nixon did not use the word "Presidential" in the formal title on the facade of the building. His library did not qualify under the terms of the 1955 Presidential Libraries Act, which authorized the National Archives to accept and then administer any privately constructed structure housing presidential papers. Far from turning his papers over to the National Archives, Nixon was at war with the agency, as he had been for sixteen years. Unlike his predecessors and successors, Nixon did not want to make the record of his Administration available to scholars and the public through the professional archivists of the National Archives; instead he continued the struggle he had begun the minute he arrived in San Clemente on August 9, 1974, to take control of and keep under seal his documents and tapes. His lawsuits and challenges designed to prevent the National Archives from opening his record precluded giving control and administration of his library to the Archives.

Typical of Nixon, he turned this extreme negative—that he alone of modern Presidents would have to pay for the administration of his library from private funds—into something positive. First, he had chosen the director. Second, the director could decide what documents to make available. Third, the director could decide who got to use the materials. Fourth, the library could be used for Republican fund-raisers and other private functions.

Fifth and best of all, Nixon was able to put a spin on the situation that gave him a lovely PR line. The publicity surrounding the opening stressed that Nixon's was the only "Presidential Library" to be built with and maintained by private funds. Of course, *all* presidential libraries are built with private funds and Nixon's was not a presidential library. Further, Nixon claimed that his motive in running the library with private funds was to save the taxpayers money. He specifically denied that keeping control of what documents were available or who could use them was any part of his motive.

So where he should have blushed, he boasted. Like Hoover, Roosevelt, Truman, Eisenhower, Kennedy, Johnson, Ford, Carter, and Reagan, he had the prestige of a presidential library, but unlike them he would not have professional archivists opening his record to examination. In the process of becoming, finally, the equal of all other former Presidents, he had managed to pass them by. His was the last laugh.

Although the word "museum" appears nowhere on the building, what was dedicated on July 19 was a Richard Nixon museum. Its purpose was to glorify the man. Built at a cost of $25 million—$2 million of that reportedly donated by Nixon personally—it was a magnificent museum. High-tech audio and visual displays traced his life from his birth in 1913 to his 1989 visit to China. One small section covered Watergate—complete with heavily edited tapes of three Watergate conversations, in which a voice-over commentary explained how it was that the "smoking gun" tape of June 23, 1972, was not really a "smoking gun," and otherwise tried to convince listeners that Watergate had been a partisan effort by Nixon's foes to reverse the results of the 1972 election.

The theme of the museum was Nixon the world leader, the builder of peace, the great President, perhaps the greatest of the twentieth century. The commentary on the display on his November 3, 1969, "Silent Majority" speech (played continuously on a large color television screen) asserted that it "remains the milestone against which all other presidential addresses are judged." Critics wondered what had happened to the Gettysburg Address.

Overall, the museum told the story of a boy from a tiny house built by his father (and beautifully restored, a delightful period piece) on the wrong side of the tracks on the wrong coast of the country, who became the dominant American politician and one of the major world leaders of the twentieth century.

Each President gave a short address. Gerald Ford offered some reminiscences of his association with Nixon in Congress in the late forties, praised him for his courage, and called him the man responsible for the collapse of Communism in Europe. Reagan said the world was a "safer and better place because of Nixon" and thanked God that he was once again a "major player in world politics." Bush called Nixon the "quintessence of middle America," a man who "loved America's good, quiet, decent people," and concluded: "History will say of you, 'Here was a true architect of peace.'"

Thus was Nixon finally welcomed back into the Republican Party. For years Ford, Reagan, and Bush had ignored him in public (while increasingly seeking his advice in private). Since 1974 his name had not been spoken at a Republican National Convention. Now the crowd could not get enough of it. Indeed, it appeared all but certain that if the Orange County audience had been asked which of the four Presidents on the podium was the greatest President, Nixon would have won in a landslide.

As Bush introduced Nixon, the crowd rose for a standing ovation. Nixon stood at the mike, as proud and as happy and self-satisfied as he had ever appeared. He smiled, he waved, and the crowd roared for more.

"I've been introduced to literally thousands of audiences all over the world," he said. "This is the first time I've ever been introduced by a President of the United States."

He had indeed given thousands of speeches, even if he had forgotten the ones when Ike had introduced him, and on this occasion he drew on some of the best of them, using lines that had been tried and were guaranteed to work.

He noted the presence of Pat, Nancy Reagan, Barbara Bush, and Betty Ford, commenting that "there is no more important a position or a career that a woman could have than to be a First Lady, the wife of the President of the United States." He and Pat had seen many wonderful places, and had enjoyed many memorable experiences, "but nothing we have ever seen matches this moment, to be welcomed home again so warmly on this day by our friends in California."

He hoped all those present, and the millions watching on television, would visit the library. The past was interesting but "it is important only insofar as it points the way to a better future."

Unlike Ford, Reagan, and Bush, he spoke without notes, which led to a fumble when he said he was born "in this little house, 71 years ago." He stumbled again in the next paragraph: "Looking back over the years, when I think of what has happened in those 70 years. . . ." He corrected himself, noting it was "77 years," and then returned to familiar ground: "I remember that 70 years ago in that little house, I used to lie in bed. I'd hear the train whistle in the middle of the night, and I would dream of places far away that I'd hoped to visit someday. I never dreamed that I would ever have the opportunity to visit over 80 countries."

Nixon assured the audience that the United States was still number one in the world, that "without the leadership of the United States, peace and freedom could not survive in this world." He said his generation had saved the world from Communism, and urged young people to set an even greater goal, to make the world safe for freedom.

He said, "It's a long way from Yorba Linda to the White House," a line that brought many nods and some tears.

His own emotions all but overwhelmed him as he spoke to the young people in the audience. "I believe in the American Dream because I have seen it come true in my own life." He hoped their dreams would also come true, but warned that they would suffer disappointments in life, and grow discouraged.

"It is sad to lose," said the man who knew, "but the greatest sadness is to travel through life without knowing either victory or defeat. Always remember that only when during your lifetime you are involved in a cause greater than yourself, can you be truly true to yourself."

He gave a triumphant wave. The band played "God Bless America" and the audience sang. Some fifty thousand red, white, and blue balloons ascended into the sky. He was home. In the museum behind him, he was staking out his claim to greatness.

NIXON IN RETROSPECT

NIXON WILL NEVER be called Richard the Great. He was a sometimes brilliant, frequently successful, often flawed leader, but never a great leader. Greatness as a leader was what he dedicated his life to attaining. He came close, but in the end it eluded him.

In his old age, Nixon wrote about the qualities of greatness in a leader. He asserted that virtue was not one of them. What lifted great leaders above the rest, he believed, was that they were "more forceful, more resourceful," shrewder. They combined intelligence, courage, hard work, tenacity, judgment, "and a certain measure of charm" with insight, foresight, and a "willingness to take the bold but calculated risk." The great leader must want the job and be willing to pay the price. "Above all, he must be decisive."[1] That was a somewhat accurate self-description. Yet, even with those qualities, Nixon was not a great leader.

Nixon had many of the characteristics of Alexander the Great as he is described by John Keegan in his masterful work, *The Mask of Command*. Keegan raises the question of who the "inner," the "essential," the "real" Alexander was, and comments:

> It is a question that can perhaps be answered about no human being. But it is particularly inappropriate in Alexander's case. In his life, the private and public self, thought and action, reflection and execution, so entwine and interpenetrate that the one cannot be disentangled from the other. Like a great actor in a great role, being and performance merged in his person. His life was lived upon a stage—that of court, camp and battlefield—and the unrolling of the plot which he presented to the world was determined by the theme he had chosen for his life.[2]

581

What Nixon did best, most consistently, throughout his career was to act. Act in the double sense of direct political action and of acting the lead role in a play. He was both the man in the arena and the man on the stage. He had a willingness to endure toil and dare dangers. He was always a participant. But he was also always an actor, observing the effect of his performance. "Most of the great leaders I have known were accomplished actors," he wrote in his retirement, "though only de Gaulle candidly admitted it. Like the great stage performers, they played their public role so well that they virtually became the parts that they created."[3]

Nixon was also the playwright, setting the stage, manipulating the characters, and trying to dictate the plot. Of course he could not; the characters and plot often escaped his control.

As Keegan notes so perceptively, even Alexander could not control events. When his army in India wanted to go home, he could not stop it. He could, and did, stage a melodrama that gave him a chance to strut and elicited a grand if grotesque display of the army's love for him. But it ended with the army's getting its way. Alexander recognized the limits to his rule.

Nixon often failed to see the limits. He did not understand that real power lies with the people and their perceptions. Power to Nixon was manipulation, inside information, polls, favors, trade-offs, bribes, public relations, smears, and intimidation. Power was publicity rather than policy. But legitimate power in a democracy is bound by tradition. Power is possibility created by potential but limited by custom, mores, a sense of what is right and what is wrong. Franklin Roosevelt's greatest political failure, his attempt to pack the Supreme Court, illustrates the point. So does Nixon's attempt to cover up Watergate.

Nixon knew that to be a great leader, he had to set a great goal, and he did so. It was world peace. The phrase was one he used too often; it was a concept he sometimes abused, and yet it *was* the cause to which he dedicated his life. Not always effectively, not always wisely, not always selflessly, but always.

How could it have been otherwise? Recall that in 1972, at the time of Nixon's re-election, the United States had been involved in a foreign war for seventeen of the fifty-nine years of his life, and in the Cold War for twenty-seven years. For eighteen years after 1972 the United States was at peace, and the Cold War had been declared over. He deserves some of the credit, first for his contributions over the decades to the containment of Communism, then for his promotion of détente. In his own mind, he has not gotten it. It is characteristic of Nixon to feel neglected. He was, after all, a man who was nominated five times by his party for national office, and who won four of the ensuing elections, but still felt life had not treated him fairly.

If no success was ever great enough, no defeat was final. "He is a cork," Bryce Harlow has observed. "Push him down and he pops right back up. . . . He verges on being indestructible." If he ever had a heart attack, Harlow quips, he would breathe into his own mouth and resuscitate himself. He had a remarkable ability to turn negatives into positives: his total inexperience in government when in 1946 he first presented himself for public office; the fund crisis of 1952; the loss to Kennedy in 1960; the California governor's race of 1962, when he was shot down and left for dead. He was apparently annihilated by Watergate, and his enemies thought they were dancing on his grave. Each time he had come back. As Harlow put it, "There is no apparent way to stop Nixon."[4]

How did he keep coming back? First, Nixon was tough, the toughest man in American politics in his day. The insults of his political opponents, the accusations of the investigative reporters cut him deeply, and he bled freely, but he always recovered. The source of that toughness lay in the struggles of his early years, tempered by the struggles of his middle years, hardened by the struggles of his White House years. He never expected life to be easy, and it never was; he never expected to have anything given to him, and it never was.

Second, he was so disciplined and worked so hard. Politics was more than his work, more than his avocation, more than his hobby; politics was his life. "One has the feeling that he's thinking all the time," Elliot Richardson said of him.[5] Bob Hartmann's line about no man living being able to outguess Nixon speaks to Nixon's cunning, to the reach of his brain and the power of his memory, but also to his dedication to the job at hand, his habit of looking at a situation or a problem from every possible perspective, and his practice of never stopping thinking.

Third, he knew so much. This was a consequence of being constantly at work. When he wasn't gathering in information on his travels, or on the lecture or campaign trail, or on his telephone network, he was reading. He did not read for pleasure, but to learn. He was the last American President to do serious reading. In an interview with columnist Bob Greene in the early eighties, Nixon said that his great concern for his grandchildren's generation was that television had replaced reading. "There are so many good books out there to read," Nixon said. "It is something people have lost if they sit in front of the tube and turn off their minds. . . . My best advice to any young person moving up is: Read more, look at television less."[6]

Fourth, he took risks. He was willing to subject himself to ridicule, rebuff, rejection, to gain power. He explained to Greene that he knew many able people, men with intelligence, mystique, charisma, "who stopped at Congress. Who never went to the Senate. Never went on to become governor. Who stopped at that level.

"Because they didn't want to risk a safe seat. The moment people begin to think of how they can be secure, they are never going to make it clear to the top.

"You've got to take great risks and lose if necessary. And maybe lose twice or three times and keep coming back. That's the secret."[7]

Whenever Nixon got going on self-description or self-analysis, he talked about risk taking. The other theme was struggle. It was struggle that gave life meaning, not victory, but struggle. Victory was sweet, surely, but it had a downside; victory gained meant struggle ended. Thus Nixon's habitual reaction to victory was depression.

He identified with those who struggled far more than he did with those who merely won. That was why he cherished his contacts with Mao and Chou En-lai and Charles de Gaulle and felt a unique affection for them. The praise he most treasured was Mao's remark that *Six Crises* "wasn't a bad book." He explained to David Frost that Mao and Chou "being part of the Long March, you can see why a comeback means so much more than inheriting the job or being elected to the job and getting it rather easily, and then doing it. Because it's struggle that appeals to them. It's triumphing over adversity. It's climbing to the summit, and not being on the summit."

In a later interview with Frost, Nixon expanded on the theme. "To me," he said, "the unhappiest people of the world are those in the watering places, the international watering places . . . drinking too much, talking too much, thinking too little. . . . They don't know life. Because what makes life mean something is purpose. A goal. The battle. The struggle. Even if you don't win it."[8]

Most losing candidates react to defeat by quitting public life. Nixon reacted to the humiliation of being forced to resign the Presidency by thrusting himself back into the arena.

Fifth, he came back because he had so much pride he could never accept defeat, never crawl off and hide. That pride was a source of strength, but it was also a weakness, as it kept him from saying that he had done wrong. All his political life he scorned "the easy way," which upon examination almost always proved to be the way of the weak, of the liberal, or of the uninformed—in his view. But after August 9, 1974, he really did reject "the easy way." He could have resurrected himself much sooner, become the elder statesman earlier, had he admitted his wrong-doing in the cover-up and apologized for it. The American people wanted to forgive him, but he would not let them. His pride kept him from saying what he insisted was not true, that he had committed acts for which he needed forgiveness. He did not want forgiveness, nor sympathy, nor understanding; he wanted respect. Slowly, over the decade and a half following his resignation, he earned that respect the hard way, Nixon's way.

•

THIS analysis of his public stance presents Nixon in a near-noble cast. But there was more to the man than a politician who could rebound. There were, after all, reasons why he was defeated so often. His personality contained negative aspects to contrast to his pride, his toughness, his willingness to take risks, his self-discipline.

To Eisenhower's secretary Ann Whitman, Nixon "seems like a man who is acting like a nice man rather than being one." When they handed out charm, Nixon said he would pass. He was not, one of his college classmates remarked, the kind of man you would want to go backpacking with; his cousin, novelist Jessamyn West, said he "wasn't a little boy that you wanted to pick up and hug." His body movements were awkward; his laughter forced; his smile, large and appealing from a distance, seldom seemed spontaneous.

Nixon was a stuffed shirt. No one ever saw him relaxed in blue jeans and T-shirt. He wore a coat and tie when alone working on a speech or book, or reading, or listening to music. There are many stories and there are photos of him walking on the beach in coat and tie, wearing dress shoes, the surf rolling over his feet. There is a photo of him hosing down his roof in Los Angeles in 1961, as a grass fire burns in the hills above. He has on a long-sleeved white shirt, tie, suit pants, dress shoes.

Nixon was an old-fashioned square. The first time he smelled marijuana smoke was in the early eighties. His taste in music ran to the classics and love ballads; he had no interest in rock or folk music. He was an aficionado of football and baseball, but did not read novels. Aside from watching and reading about sports, as Alexander Butterfield told the House Judiciary Committee, "He had no hobbies."

Nixon was fearful of spontaneity and needed orderliness. He desired perfection and was preoccupied with appearances. Butterfield described him as a "detail man" and gave examples: "The President was concerned with whether the shades were closed or open. Social functions were always reviewed with him, the scenario. . . . He debated whether we should have a U-shaped table or a round table. . . . He was very interested in meals and how they were served . . . in whether or not salad should be served. . . . Ceremonies, he was interested in the details of the drive up the walkway, whether the military would be to the right or left, which uniforms would be worn by the White House Police, whether or not the Secret Service would salute the Star Spangled Banner and sing. . . . We had some paintings put in the west lobby and he wanted us to log in the comments made about each painting to see how popular it might be to guests who were awaiting appointments in the lobby. . . . He spent a lot of time on gifts—gifts for congressional leaders, gifts for people who came into the Oval Office. He actually looked at the inventories of cuff links and ash trays and copies of *Six Crises,* and such things as that."[9]

Bill Safire said of Nixon that he "can don a personality by opening a door." With George Shultz, Nixon could be the concerned leader striving for free markets and more personal liberty; with Len Garment, he was a supporter of the arts; with Bob Finch, a political analyst and older brother; with Ray Price, he played Woodrow Wilson brooding over the fate of the nation; with Cap Weinberger or Herb Stein he was Herbert Hoover; with Bryce Harlow, he played Eisenhower; with John Mitchell, he was FDR, the political wheeler-dealer; with Chuck Colson he was Harry Truman, profane and tough, socking it to the opposition. Safire concludes, "When he didn't want to be anybody but himself, he sent for Bebe Rebozo."[10]

It is a mark of how many different Nixon personas there were that when the transcripts of the Nixon-Haldeman-Ehrlichman-Mitchell conversations were made public, many men who had had intimate contact with Nixon over long periods of time—Safire, Steve Hess, Maurice Stans, Shultz, Harlow, and others—were shocked. *They* had never heard Nixon talk like that.

The tapes revealed a man who seldom told a joke or encouraged one. He had a problem with his sense of humor. David Frost gives an example. He and Nixon were exchanging small talk before one of the interviews. Frost mentioned an item in that day's paper about Brezhnev.

"I would not like to be a Russian leader," said Nixon, shaking his head. "They never know when they're being taped."

No smile. No sudden realization of what he had said, followed by a genuine, or even a self-conscious laugh. Nothing.[11]

He seemed infected by self-pity. This trait was reinforced by the facts of his life—he had so much for which to pity himself. There was his youthful poverty. His two most important political opponents were John F. Kennedy and Nelson Rockefeller. Where he had to beg campaign funds from rich men, they were rich men.

Nixon overdid his boyhood experiences to elicit sympathy. He told the story of the pony he wanted but never got so often that reporters turned it into a joke. Hugh Sidey relished the time he watched Marshal Tito and President Nixon in the tiny bedroom of Tito's boyhood home. Nixon got going on the pony story; Tito cut him off: "We had eleven kids who were in this room."[12]

WHAT made Richard Nixon what he was? How could a man who had so much talent, brains, ambition, and success feel so insecure, so snubbed, so unrewarded? It is not insignificant that with all the words expended on him, Nixon himself has provided the most insightful analysis. He was reminiscing at San Clemente with Kenneth Clawson shortly after his resignation.

"What starts the process, really," Nixon explained, "are the laughs and snubs and slights you get when you are a kid. Sometimes it's because you're poor or Irish or Jewish or ugly or simply that you are skinny. But if you are reasonably intelligent and if your anger is deep enough and strong enough, you learn that you can change those attitudes by excellence, personal gut performance, while those who have everything are sitting on their fat butts. . . . [When you get to the top] You find you can't stop playing the game the way you've always played it because it is a part of you and you need it as much as you do an arm or a leg. So you are lean and mean and resourceful and you continue to walk on the edge of the precipice because over the years you have become fascinated by how close to the edge you can walk without losing your balance."[13]

With Nixon, the anger ran so deep it never left him. He was the angriest American President.

Hugh Sidey described Nixon's view of himself: "Born clumsy, not very good looking, to parents who were overworked, overburdened, harsh. Confronted by poverty, by a society that was wealthy and did not much care about him. Ridiculed in early life and always. Yet there was a fierce talent beneath all that. He kept everything—resentment and talent. He understood that his success depended on him developing his mind and at least to some degree getting along in society. But he never abandoned his black impulses to lash out at the world which had made him kind of lumpy and uncoordinated and denied him warmth and security."[14]

He was a man who could not trust others, and had no real friends. Nearly everyone who worked closely with Nixon has commented on this. Eisenhower told Ann Whitman that he couldn't understand how a man could go through life without friends.

Nixon had hundreds of associates, thousands of acquaintances. Most of these people admired him, and many of them appreciated the opportunities he had opened up for them. But only a handful ever really liked him. Bryce Harlow felt that "people didn't like him for the simple reason that he didn't like people."[15] Henry Kissinger wrote that "Nixon had no truly close friends," and remarked on his "congenital inability ever to confide totally in anyone."[16] Barry Goldwater told Nixon in 1973, "No one . . . I know feels close to you," and Goldwater knew every prominent Republican in the country.[17]

Even with Rebozo and Abplanalp, there was distance. Nixon told Bob Greene, "I never wanted to be buddy-buddy. Not only with the press. Even with close friends. I don't believe in letting your hair down, confiding this and that and the other thing—saying, 'Gee, I couldn't sleep, because I was worrying about this or that and so forth and so on.'

"I believe you should keep your troubles to yourself. . . . Some people are different. Some people think it's good therapy to sit with a close friend and, you know, just spill your guts."[18]

Nixon thought of such people as weak. Others would regard them as normal and feel that it must be a terrible thing to go through life without at least one intimate friend, one person from whom you have no secrets, one person for whom you have an unquestioning love, whose shortcomings and sins are forgiven, a person whom you trust totally and whose love you take for granted and toward whom your own loyalty is complete. Aside from Pat and his daughters, with whom he found some semblance of this in his last defeat, Nixon had no such person.

Kissinger wrote that "even [Nixon's] intimates lived with the consciousness that they might be abandoned or dropped if it served some inscrutable purpose." It happened to nearly everyone who was close to him, although not to Kissinger.

Kissinger described Nixon's personality in his memoirs:

Painfully shy, Nixon dreaded meeting new people; only the anonymity of large, approving crowds could make him feel secure. Fearful of rejection, he constructed his relationships so that a rebuff, if it came, would seem to have originated with him. Fiercely proud, he could neither admit his emotional dependence on approbation nor transcend it. Deeply insecure, he first acted as if a cruel fate had singled him out for rejection and then he contrived to make sure that his premonition came to pass.[19]

WHY was Nixon unable to trust? Why was it difficult for him to love? These often asked questions have produced a variety of answers, but most of them come down to one thing. According to Harlow, "I suspect that my gifted friend somewhere in his youth, maybe when he was very young or in his teens, got badly hurt by someone he cared for very deeply or trusted totally—a parent, a relative, a dear friend, a lover, a confidante. Somewhere I figure somebody hurt him badly, and from that experience and from then on he could not trust people."[20]

Hugh Sidey recalls a remark Kissinger made to him shortly before Nixon's resignation: "Can you imagine what this man would have been had somebody loved him?"

"What do you mean?" Sidey asked.

"Had somebody in his life cared for him," Kissinger replied. "I don't think anybody ever did, not his parents, not his peers." After a pause, Kissinger added, "He would have been a great, great man had somebody loved him."[21]

The theme of the unloved boy is central to the numerous psychobiographies of Nixon. It was all Hannah's fault, for spending too little time with Richard, too much time with Harold. It was all Frank's fault, for spending too much time at work, too little with his son. Frank did not love Richard enough, so Richard could not love.

This author has many problems with that analysis. Who can say how much love is enough? Who can say that Nixon's childhood was in any way so exceptional that it scarred him for life? What son ever had a father who loved him enough? What successful man ever had a mother who was loving enough, forgiving enough, understanding enough? Frank Nixon spurred his son, disciplined him, made him work, demanded more of him. This helped make Richard ambitious, eager to show his parents what he could do; it is hard to see how it made him incapable of love. Besides, he loves Pat, Tricia, and Julie, and they love him.

"A man's character is his fate," according to the Greek philosopher Heraclitus. Nixon had gifts in abundance—brains, acceptably nice looks, good health, a marvelous memory, knowledge, superb acting ability and stage presence, a faithful family, awesome willpower, among others. Indeed, he had nearly every gift that the gods could bestow. The one that he most lacked was character. Virtue comes from character. That is why Nixon despised virtue, and railed against it.

Another quality that he lacked was an ability to respect others. In 1986 Harlow spoke to the point, admitting that he could not explain it: "The President went through, and it is probably still in him, a process of some kind that made him disrespect people. I don't know whom he respects even now—really really respects."[22]

Nixon put himself first, always. First, last, and in between. In his poem *Chief Joseph of the Nez Percé*, Robert Penn Warren has Joseph wanting to continue the fight against the U.S. Cavalry, to preserve his own honor and self-respect. But Joseph asks himself, "What right had I/ To die—to leave sick, old, young, women—merely to flatter/My heart's pride?" And then Joseph has a flash of insight. He decides to surrender, explaining, "A true chief no self has."

Richard Nixon was not a true chief. He could no more "no self have" than he could bring himself to love, trust, and respect the American people.

He did have respect for many foreign leaders, most of all Chou and Mao, Churchill, and de Gaulle. Above all, de Gaulle, who was a model and inspiration for Nixon. The theme of coming back from adversity had an obvious appeal to Nixon, but there was more depth to it than that. Nixon wrote about de Gaulle in *Leaders* with great affection, but also with insight.

"He acted a part," Nixon wrote, "playing a role he himself created in a way that fit only one actor. Even more, he fashioned *himself* so that he could play it. He created de Gaulle, the public person, to play the role of de Gaulle, personification of France." Nixon quoted de Gaulle, approvingly, to the effect that "a leader must choose between prominence and happiness. . . . A leader must endure strict self-discipline, constant risk taking, and perpetual inner struggle." Nixon noted, again approvingly, that de Gaulle allowed no one to get close to him, and shunned the friendship of his colleagues. He "transferred away any aides who had worked with him for a long time in order to reduce the risk that they would become too familiar with him."[23]

Nixon once told Bill Gulley, "The minute you start getting familiar with people, they start taking advantage."[24] As good a place as any, better than most, to begin to understand Richard Nixon is to read his remarks about Charles de Gaulle, as the quotation in the preceding paragraph makes obvious. How accurate Nixon was in portraying the deep and complex character of de Gaulle is a separate subject. But in describing his hero as a self-created man, a man of self-discipline, a risk taker, an aloof man who underwent perpetual inner struggle, Nixon was surely giving us an excellent self-portrait.

He had heroes from the American past, but how well he understood them is another matter. Had he understood them, he could never have made the incredible statement in *Leaders* that "virtue is not what lifts great leaders above others."[25] What would George Washington say of that? Thomas Jefferson? Abraham Lincoln? Nixon's own twentieth-century heroes, Theodore Roosevelt and Woodrow Wilson?

Franklin Roosevelt said the Presidency is pre-eminently a place of moral leadership. In a free, open, and democratic society, politics is above all an education process. The leader leads through persuasion and consent. Nixon tried to lead through surprise and manipulation.

Secrecy and surprise are the enemies of democracy. Open, informed, and prolonged debate are the supporting pillars of democracy. Nixon loved secrecy and surprise, and he scorned the give and take of democratic discussion. The three actions for which he was proudest—ending the war in Vietnam, opening to China, establishing détente with the Soviets—were achieved through secret, closed discussions. Nixon argued that without secrecy, he could not have done what he did. That may be. But perhaps, too, had he involved the people and their representatives in the policy-making process, there might have been some support for South Vietnam in 1975; there might have been some staying power to détente; there might have been peace in the Middle East.

Had Nixon engaged in public debate, education, and persuasion, he could have been a great President. As it is, he doesn't even rate as a good one. He is the only President who resigned his office, the only one forced to accept a pardon for his deeds. This will never be forgotten. Two hundred years from now, when he will get only a paragraph or two in a high school American history text, the first sentence will begin: "Richard

Nixon, thirty-seventh President, resigned his office because of the Watergate scandal."

The passage will go on to note his opening to China, his pioneering efforts at establishing détente, and his role in ending the American involvement in Vietnam. Depending on what happens in the first generation of the twenty-first century, he could be seen as a pivotal figure in world politics of the post-World War II era, the man who prepared the way for the ending of the nuclear arms race and of the Cold War. It might go the other way and fault him for a failure to seize the opportunity and use American power in 1973 to impose an enforceable peace on Israel and the Arabs. It all depends on how things turn out, and the judgment on Nixon will shift with every major upheaval in world politics.

What will not shift is that spot that will not out, the Watergate cover-up, resignation, and pardon. Even that spot, however, will look different as time passes; indeed, it already does, as the Iran-contra scandal of 1986 and various other scandals of the Reagan Administration put Watergate in a somewhat different perspective.

On the domestic side, Nixon has no claim to greatness. He can point to might-have-beens, but not accomplishments. The great Presidents are the ones who bring about permanent changes that directly affect every American: in the twentieth century, Teddy Roosevelt and conservation, Woodrow Wilson and the Federal Reserve System, Franklin Roosevelt and Social Security, Dwight Eisenhower and the Interstate Highway System, Lyndon Johnson and Medicare. Nixon might have achieved that level of accomplishment in a number of areas, such as welfare reform, or national health insurance for all, or government reorganization, or revenue sharing, but in each case he failed.

His failures, like his successes, are relative. In this regard it is well to recall that four of the seven Presidents who served in the tumultuous period between the onset of the Depression and the end of the Vietnam War (1929–75) were judged to be failures by their contemporaries. Herbert Hoover, Harry Truman, Lyndon Johnson, and Richard Nixon had all fallen to such a point that when they left office, three out of four voters disapproved of the way they were doing their job. John Kennedy was in office for too short a period to allow for any meaningful assessment, so it appears that only Roosevelt and Eisenhower were judged competent by their fellow citizens. That illustrates a number of points: the difficulties of the times; the high expectations people have of the President; the unfairness of contemporary judgments, among others. But it also shows that Nixon's place in history is likely to go up as time goes by, just as Hoover's and Truman's have risen. History is apt to be kinder than contemporaries, as passions cool, perspective is gained, new events cast new light on old actions.

•

NIXON wanted to be judged by what he accomplished. What he will be remembered for is the nightmare he put the country through in his second term, and for his resignation.

Was the country better off because of his resignation? What was gained, and what was lost, from the nineteen months of national preoccupation with Richard Nixon and Watergate?

It cannot be said that justice was done, not when Nixon's men went to prison for carrying out his wishes, orders, and instructions, and he did not. Nor can it be said that his resignation was punishment enough, because of his insistence that he resigned as a result of losing his political base rather than as a consequence of wrongdoing.

In the years since his resignation he has admitted only that he made mistakes. It is inappropriate to forgive a man who insists that he did nothing to be forgiven for; it is difficult to extend sympathy to a man who put the country through a nineteen-month agony on the grounds that if he resigned merely as a result of demands that he do so, it would change the American system from a presidential one to a parliamentary one, and who then resigned because of those demands.

But neither can it be said that Nixon was guilty of unique crimes for which he deserved singular punishment. The cover-up was not unique, nor was the payment of hush money, nor the attempt to use the FBI and the CIA and the Justice Department to obstruct justice. There was ample precedent for most of these actions, as there was for the break-in at Dr. Fielding's office, the placing of wiretaps on reporters and NSC officials, the surveillance techniques, or the dirty tricks in the 1972 campaign; there were ample precedents for the ITT scandal, the milk fund, the bombing of Cambodia, the attempted use of the IRS to get his enemies, and Nixon's personal enrichment through improvements on his homes in California and Florida. Nor have these and other illegal practices come to an end since 1974. It is inexcusable to dismiss such activities with a shrug and a "that's just the way it is" attitude; one can and should deplore them. But it would be wrong to think they started and ended with Nixon. Two wrongs do not make a right, not even in politics, but they do make a precedent.

The aftermath of Watergate did bring changes. For the historian, one of the most important was the Presidential Records and Materials Preservation Act of 1974, which preserved his papers and tapes with the National Archives.

Another direct legislative result of Watergate was the Privacy Act of 1974, which extended the provisions of the Freedom of Information Act passed in the Johnson Administration. The new law permitted individuals to see personal information in their federal agency files, and to correct or amend the information. This has been helpful to individuals under attack, but scholars who have used the Freedom of Information Act in attempts to study federal agencies have discovered that the FBI, CIA, DOD, and others can use national security to effectively emasculate the documents. The scholars get the documents, but only after delays that sometimes run into years, and even then they are censored, with sentences, whole paragraphs, and sometimes entire pages blanked out.

In 1978, Congress passed the Ethics in Government Act. It too was a direct result of Watergate, as it established a legal basis for the office of special prosecutor. It required financial disclosures by executive and judicial branch officials (although not by members of Congress) and restrained the "revolving door" through which public officials moved into the private sector on leaving office, using their knowledge and contacts for private gain. The law required the Attorney General to investigate possible violations and to report to a three-judge panel whether the charges were unfounded or whether the judges should appoint a special prosecutor. That prosecutor could not be removed except by impeachment or conviction of a crime. The bill passed both houses overwhelmingly. It has been used on a number of occasions in the past decade, with mixed results. It has been amended, and strongly challenged. Three former Attorneys General (including Benjamin Civiletti, of the Carter Administration) have criticized it.

Another result of Watergate was the War Powers Act of 1973, passed over Nixon's veto. Whether that bill is a good thing or not remains a subject of bitter debate. Nixon's successors have felt constrained by it and complained about it. But, in general, they have still found it possible to shoot first, explain later.

Because of Watergate, Congress passed some campaign reform bills. Their effect has been minimal at best. Most citizens would agree with the generalization that campaigns have become dirtier, more negative, and more driven by money since 1974 than they were before.

In general, Watergate gave Congress an opportunity to exercise more impact than it had in the first three decades following World War II, in foreign as well as domestic affairs. Beyond the War Powers Act, there was congressional exposure of some of the activities of the CIA by the Church Committee in the Senate. The Church Committee hearings had no direct relationship to Watergate, but they happened because of a general atmosphere created by Watergate. They resulted in the release of a great deal of information and documents about the CIA, and new legislation that had some effect on constraining CIA activities; whether this was good or bad is also a subject of debate.

In December 1974, Congress also passed the Jackson-Vanick Amendment to the trade bill, which denied most-favored-nation status to the Soviet Union as punishment for various limitations on emigration. Whether Nixon could have blocked passage or not we cannot know; we do know that the amendment was of no immediate help for the cause of Jewish emigration while it did much harm to Soviet-American relations, just as Nixon warned.

Watergate gave the nation a press corps that was encouraged to do more investigative reporting, concentrating on the personalities and personal lives of politicians rather than policy. Various politicians who could be said to have had good policies but bad morals have suffered as a consequence; perhaps the nation has benefited as a consequence, although this author doubts it.

Watergate strengthened the Democratic hold on Congress. The 1974 election was as disastrous for the Republicans as the 1964 election. Because of the skill of Congress in protecting incumbents, the Democrats have held onto most of those gains. They bid fair to retain their hold on Congress well into the twenty-first century.

Watergate strengthened the public's cynicism about politics. Obviously Nixon's Democratic predecessors in the 1960s made major contributions to this development, but it reached a peak in 1973–74. Since then, it has continued, perhaps gotten worse; it is certain that voter participation has gone down in every election and shows no signs of being reversed.

Watergate gave the doctrine of executive privilege a constitutional standing, as a result of the written decision in *United States v. Nixon*. Presidents since Nixon have used the doctrine, most successfully Reagan in the aftermath of the Iran-contra affair. Overall, however, it is clear that the principal results of Watergate in legislative, political, and media affairs have weakened the office of the Presidency. The kind of freewheeling powers exercised in foreign affairs by Presidents Roosevelt, Truman, Eisenhower, Kennedy, and Johnson have not been available to Presidents Ford, Carter, Reagan, and Bush. The restraints are sometime subtle, sometimes blatant, sometimes partisan, but they evidently are permanent.

For well over a year, Richard Nixon stayed in office, fighting overwhelming odds. Aside from his insistence that he was doing so because he was not guilty, his principal justification for putting the nation through such agony was his determination not to weaken the office of the Presidency. But by holding on so long, he weakened the office of the Presidency. Perhaps this is a good thing. Perhaps not. But it certainly is one of the lasting results of Watergate.

THE number-one immediate result of Watergate was to force Richard Nixon to resign. This brought intense satisfaction to millions of Nixon's foes and dismay to millions of Nixon's supporters. Whether it was good for the country or not is a legitimate subject for discussion.

What was lost when Nixon resigned? No definitive answer is possible, as we can never know what he might have accomplished had he stayed in office free of his Watergate woes. We do know what he was proposing. His opponents dismissed those proposals as transparent attempts to wriggle out of Watergate, and perhaps his motives were base; nevertheless he selected the policies he wanted to emphasize and encourage, they bore his personal stamp, and they held great promise.

The first thing that was lost through Nixon's resignation, according to his supporters, was the chance for a free South Vietnam. Had Nixon stayed in office in full exercise of his powers, the argument goes, when the NVA launched its spring offensive in 1975 he would have sent back the American bombers and provided the ARVN with the resupply it required to throw back the invaders, just as he supplied Israel in October 1973. With Nixon's help, the government in Saigon would have defeated the offensive and survived.

"We won the war in Vietnam, but lost the peace," Nixon wrote ten years after the fall of Saigon. "All that we had achieved in twelve years of fighting was thrown away in a spasm of congressional irresponsibility."[26]

My own view is that Congress was never going to give Nixon the money to resume the bombing or to resupply the ARVN, and that the government of President Thieu was incapable of reforming itself sufficiently to improve the ARVN to the point that it could hurl back the NVA. Still, had Watergate never happened and had Nixon stayed in office, he would have been in a better position to extract some funds from Congress to support President Thieu in 1975 than Ford and Kissinger were. That is another way of saying that Nixon's policy of Vietnamization at least gave Thieu and the ARVN a chance. By no means was it exclusively his fault that they failed to seize it.

Because Nixon resigned, the full promise of his opening to China has not been realized.

Because Nixon resigned, the full promise of détente with the Soviet Union has not been realized. The era of cooperation Nixon had sought to inaugurate was replaced by a decade and a half of confrontation. The superpowers spent those fifteen years snarling at each other, spending stupendous sums on ever more destructive and less needed weapons, enormously increasing the costs and the risks of the Cold War. What began to happen in the late eighties, as first Reagan and then Bush embraced Gorbachev, could have happened in the mid-seventies. SALT II, still unratified as of this writing, could have been in place long ago.

Because Nixon resigned, a chance for a comprehensive Middle East peace was lost. Not much of one, perhaps, but at least equal to the chance of South Vietnam surviving.

Because Nixon resigned, his program for an energy policy that would lessen American dependence on foreign oil was abandoned.

Because Nixon resigned, the Republican Party moved to the right, bringing a majority of the voters in the country along with it. Watergate discredited Nixon personally while dealing a blow to the "middle ground" that he had pre-empted in the 1960s between the Rockefeller and Goldwater forces. When Nixon resigned, the conservatives were free to criticize his policies, which they did. William Buckley bitterly assailed Nixon for the "humiliating defeat" in Vietnam, for a budget deficit "larger than any Democrat ever dared to endorse," and for the "baptism of detente" with its attendant naïve talk of the "peace-loving intentions of the Communist superpower." Other conservatives damned Nixon for surrendering strategic superiority to the Soviets, for dismantling the Navy, and for expanding Lyndon Johnson's Great Society.[27]

Conservatives charged that Nixon had betrayed their cause and ignored "the Mandate of 1972." In their view, Nixon won so decisively over McGovern because of the social issues, big spending by big government, "radicalism," and "permissiveness." But the re-elected Nixon had pandered to the liberals, because of his cynical judgment that the conservatives had no choice but to support him.

When Ford continued Nixon's more moderate policies in defense, taxation, and spending, conservatives continued to complain that the mandate of 1972 was being ignored. In May 1975, Ronald Reagan condemned Ford for a projected $51 million budget deficit. The next year, Senator James Buckley and Pat Buchanan led a revolt against President Ford, calling for an "open convention." They and their allies almost managed to win the 1976 nomination for Reagan. Ford's defeat by Carter gave the conservatives unchallenged control of the Republican Party. This led to major changes in American politics, government, economic affairs, foreign policy, and much more, after Reagan won the 1980 election.

Because Nixon resigned, his proposal not just to maintain but to expand the Basic Education Opportunity Act and the student loan program died. Who can count how many American youngsters were deprived of their chance at higher education as a result?

Because Nixon resigned, the welfare reform he proposed that was so badly needed died. So did his program providing health insurance for all Americans. Who can measure the misery endured by millions of poor Americans as a result?

It was Nixon's advocacy of such programs as student loans and grants and national health insurance for all that most infuriated conservatives like the Buckley brothers. As did the liberals, the conservatives always assigned to Nixon the worst motives; in this case, the conservatives charged that Nixon was trying to pander to the liberals to save his own skin. That hardly seems fair. By the time he was pushing these proposals, in early 1974, Nixon knew that he had *no* liberal supporters left. He knew his fate rested with the conservatives in Congress. Nevertheless he made the proposals. Would it be too much to suggest that Richard Nixon, who grew up in near-poverty conditions because of the crushing medical expenses his family had to pay and who could attend college only on scholarship, made these proposals because he believed in them?

Because Nixon resigned, revenue sharing died. This came just at the time the cities were losing their factories and tax bases. The result was visible poverty in the cities, in the form of homeless men, women, and children, such as had not been seen in America since the Depression.

Because Nixon resigned, his program for a broad and badly needed reorganization of the federal government—his "New American Revolution"—died.

Because Nixon resigned, what the country got was not the Nixon Revolution but the Reagan Revolution. It got massive, unbelievable deficits. It got Iran-contra. It got the savings and loans scandals. It got millions of homeless, and gross favoritism for the rich.

None of that was any part of the proposed Nixon Revolution. When Nixon resigned, we lost more than we gained.

NOTES

The following abbreviations are used throughout the Notes:

NPMP—Nixon Presidential Materials Project, Alexandria, Virginia
NS—News Summaries, found in Nixon Presidential Materials Project.
PP—Public Papers of the President, Government Printing Office, Washington, D.C.

CHAPTER ONE

1. Washington *Star-News*, 11/9/72.
2. *New York Times*, 12/21/72.
3. Kissinger, *White House Years*, 1402–6.
4. Klein, *Making It Perfectly Clear*, 364–65.
5. Kissinger, *White House Years*, 1407.
6. Woods to Nixon, 11/12/72, NPMP.
7. *New York Times*, 11/10/72.
8. *Ibid.*, 11/21/72.
9. Colson oral history, NPMP.
10. Kissinger, *White House Years*, 1411–12; Nixon, *Memoirs*, 718.
11. Haldeman memo, 11/10/72.
12. *Ibid.*, 11/12/72.
13. Nixon to Haldeman, 11/15/72, NPMP.
14. NS, 12/16/72.
15. Colson oral history, NPMP.
16. *New York Times*, 11/13/72.
17. Nixon to Haldeman, 11/17/72, NPMP.
18. Ehrlichman notes, 11/28/72 and 12/7/72, NPMP.
19. *Ibid.*, 11/28/72.
20. *Ibid.*, 12/8/72.
21. *New York Times*, 11/22/72.
22. Haldeman notes, 11/15/72.
23. Colson oral history, NPMP.
24. Haldeman memo, 11/18/72.
25. Ehrlichman notes, 11/28/72, NPMP.
26. Colson oral history, NPMP.
27. Price, *With Nixon*, 196–97.
28. *PP* (1972), 1150–51.
29. Ehrlichman papers, 11/28/72, NPMP.
30. Haldeman memo, 12/10/72, NPMP.
31. Nixon, *Memoirs*, 762.

32. *Ibid.*, 763.
33. Ehrlichman notes, 11/28/72, NPMP.
34. Nixon, *Memoirs*, 770.
35. Timmons to Ehrlichman, 11/18/72, and Kehrli to Colson, 12/12/72 and 12/13/72, all with Nixon notations, NPMP.
36. Nixon, *Memoirs*, 733.
37. Haldeman notes, 3/26/73, NPMP.
38. Colson/Hunt telephone conversation, 11/13/72, transcript and tape in NPMP.
39. Colson oral history, NPMP.
40. Nixon, *Memoirs*, 777.
41. *Ibid.*, 774.
42. Lukas, *Nightmare*, 273–79.
43. Dean, *Blind Ambition*, 148–49.
44. *New York Times*, 12/5/72.
45. Lukas, *Nightmare*, 261.
46. Haldeman, *The Ends of Power*, 177.
47. *Ibid.*, 178–79.
48. The interview was reprinted in the *New Republic*, 12/16/72.
49. Colson oral history, NPMP; Hersh, *The Price of Power*, 612.
50. Nixon, *Memoirs*, 719.
51. Kissinger, *White House Years*, 1417.
52. *Ibid.*, 1419; Nixon, *Memoirs*, 721.
53. Nixon, *Memoirs*, 721; Kissinger, *White House Years*, 1420.
54. Nixon, *Memoirs*, 722.
55. *Ibid.*, 723.
56. *Ibid.*
57. *Ibid.*, 723–24.
58. Hung and Schecter, *The Palace File*, 137.
59. Kissinger, *White House Years*, 1426.
60. Hersh, *Price of Power*, 617.
61. Zumwalt, *On Watch*, 412–15.
62. Nixon, *Memoirs*, 724.
63. *Ibid.*
64. *Ibid.*, 726.
65. Ehrlichman notes, 12/5/72.
66. Kissinger to Haldeman for President, 12/5/72, NPMP.
67. Nixon to Kissinger, 12/6/72, NPMP.
68. Kissinger to Nixon, 12/7/72, NPMP.
69. Nixon to Kissinger, 12/7/72, NPMP.
70. Nixon, *Memoirs*, 732–33.

CHAPTER TWO

1. Nixon, *Memoirs*, 733–34.
2. Ibid., 732.
3. Kissinger, *White House Years*, 1449.
4. Haldeman notes, 12/26/72, NPMP.
5. Kissinger, *White House Years*, 1449.
6. Nixon to Kissinger, 12/15 and 12/16/72, NPMP.
7. NS, 12/15/72.
8. Kissinger, *White House Years*, 1450–51.
9. Nixon, *Memoirs*, 737.

10. Kissinger, *White House Years*, 1459.
11. *Ibid.*, 1455.
12. *Ibid.*, 1459–60; Nixon, *Memoirs*, 737.
13. Nixon, *Memoirs*, 737.
14. *Washington Post*, 12/19–12/24/72; *The New York Times*, 12/19–12/24/72.
15. Nixon, *Memoirs*, 738.
16. *Ibid.*, 734.
17. *Ibid.*, 738.
18. *Ibid.*, 736.
19. *PP* (1972), 1157.
20. NS, 12/19/72.
21. Haldeman notes, 12/31/72.
22. Colson papers, NPMP.
23. Nixon, *Memoirs*, 740; Frost, *"I Gave Them a Sword,"* 137.
24. *The New York Times*, 12/27/72.
25. Nixon, *Memoirs*, 741; Kissinger, *White House Years*, 1458; Hersh, *Price of Power*, 627–28; Hung and Schecter, *Palace File*, 143.
26. Nixon, *Memoirs*, 741.
27. Timmons to RN, quoting Jackson, with RN notes, 1/3/73, NPMP.
28. Nixon, *Memoirs*, 742.
29. Haldeman notes, 1/4/73, NPMP.
30. Hung and Schecter, *Palace File*, 144.
31. Nixon remarks, 1/5/73, in Press Secretary files, NPMP.
32. Nixon, *Memoirs*, 743–44; Kissinger, *White House Years*, 1462.
33. Haldeman summary notes, 5/7/73, NPMP.
34. Nixon, *Memoirs*, 745; Colson oral history, NPMP.
35. Dean, *Blind Ambition*, 180.
36. Transcript, 1/8/73, NPMP.
37. *The New York Times*, 1/9/73.
38. RN note, 1/10/73, Haldeman papers, NPMP.
39. Kissinger, *White House Years*, 1464; Nixon, *Memoirs*, 746.
40. Hung and Schecter, *Palace File*, 146.
41. Eisenhower, *Pat Nixon*, 355–56.
42. Haldeman notes, 1/12/73, NPMP.
43. Haldeman summary notes, 5/7/73, NPMP.
44. *Ibid.*
45. Nixon, *Memoirs*, 747–48; Kissinger, *White House Years*, 1468.
46. Hung and Schecter, *Palace File*, 148.
47. Kissinger, *White House Years*, 1469.
48. *Ibid.*, 1470.
49. Haldeman memo, 1/19/73, NPMP.
50. *PP* (1973), 13–15.
51. Nixon, *Memoirs*, 756.
52. *Ibid.*, 754.
53. Nixon *Memoirs*, 757; Kissinger, *White House Years*, 1475.
54. Haldeman notes, 1/12/73, NPMP.
55. Nixon to Haldeman, 1/25/73, NPMP.
56. Cole to Nixon, 1/26/73, NPMP.
57. Haldeman notes, 1/27/73, NPMP.
58. Haldeman memo, 1/30/73, NPMP.
59. NS, 1/30/73.
60. NS, 2/15/73.
61. NS, 3/14/73.

62. NS, 3/12/73.
63. *PP* (1973), 55–56.
64. NS, 2/13/73.
65. NS, 1/30/73.
66. NS, 1/30/73.
67. NS, 2/12/73.
68. NS, 2/26/73.
69. *PP* (1973), 205–6.
70. Nixon to Kissinger, 3/4/73, NPMP.
71. Nixon to Kissinger, Rogers, and Richardson, 3/10/73, NPMP.
72. NS, 3/8/73.
73. Haldeman memo, 2/9/73, NPMP.

CHAPTER THREE

1. Nixon, *Memoirs*, 770.
2. *Ibid.*
3. Nixon to Ehrlichman, 3/4/73, NPMP.
4. *New York Times*, 1/28/73.
5. Haldeman notes, 1/24/73, NPMP.
6. *New York Times*, 2/12/73.
7. Nixon to Ehrlichman, 3/14/73, NPMP.
8. NS, 3/19/73.
9. NS, 3/15/73.
10. *New York Times*, 3/11/73.
11. NS, 2/5/73.
12. Haldeman memo, 3/7/73, NPMP.
13. Nixon to Haldeman, 3/12/73, NPMP.
14. Falk to Nixon, with Nixon notes, 2/22/73, NPMP.
15. RN talking paper, 3/5/73, NPMP.
16. *PP* (1973), 54.
17. Nixon, *Memoirs*, 861.
18. Ehrlichman notes, 2/12/73, NPMP.
19. Nixon notes on Haldeman to Nixon, 2/22/73, NPMP.
20. NS, 3/3/73.
21. Haldeman notes, 2/28/73, NPMP.
22. Nixon notes to Buchanan on a memo from Scowcroft to Staff Secretary, 3/17/73, NPMP.
23. Buchanan to Nixon, 3/11/73, NPMP.
24. Quoted in Kehrli to Gergen, 2/15/73, NPMP.
25. Nixon to Haldeman, 3/4/73, NPMP.
26. *PP* (1973), 60–61.
27. Haldeman summary notes, 5/7/73, NPMP.
28. Nixon, *Memoirs*, 778.
29. Transcript, 2/16/73, NPMP.
30. Transcript, 2/28/73, NPMP
31. New York Times, *The White House Tapes*, 69–92.
32. Nixon to Ziegler, 3/15/73, NPMP.
33. *New York Times*, 2/15/73.
34. *Washington Post*, 2/8/73.
35. *Ibid.*, 2/8/73.
36. *Ibid.*, 2/14/73.

37. Haldeman to Julie Eisenhower, 3/3/73, NPMP.
38. NS, 2/12/73.
39. Schoenebaum, *Profiles of an Era,* 26.
40. *Ibid.,* 510.
41. NS, 2/7/73.
42. *New York Times,* 3/1/73.
43. *PP* (1973), 160–61.
44. *Ibid.,* 185–86.
45. NS, 3/13/73.
46. New York Times, *White House Tapes,* 92–122; Transcript, 3/1/73, NPMP.
47. *PP* (1973), 203–4, 211.
48. Nixon, *Memoirs,* 784.
49. *Ibid.,* 514.
50. Transcript, 3/17/73, NPMP.
51. Transcript, 3/20/73, NPMP.
52. New York Times, *White House Tapes,* 126–31.
53. Nixon, *Memoirs,* 791.

CHAPTER FOUR

1. Transcript, 3/21/73, NPMP; Nixon, *Memoirs,* 800; Dean, *Blind Ambition,* 194–210; transcripts, 2/14/73, 2/23/73, NPMP.
2. Nixon, *Memoirs,* 799.
3. Transcript, 3/21/73, NPMP.
4. *Ibid.*
5. Nixon, *Memoirs,* 799; transcript, 4/26/73, NPMP.
6. Transcript, 3/22/73, NPMP.
7. Haldeman, *Ends of Power,* 241; Dean, *Blind Ambition,* 211.
8. Transcript, 3/22/73, NPMP; Dean, *Blind Ambition,* 211–12.
9. Transcript, 3/22/73, NPMP.
10. Haldeman, *Ends of Power,* 199.
11. Haldeman notes, 3/24/73, NPMP; Haldeman, *Ends of Power,* 246–47; Dean, *Blind Ambition,* 217–23.
12. *New York Times,* 3/24/73.
13. Dean, *Blind Ambition,* 213.
14. Haldeman notes, 3/26/73, NPMP.
15. *New York Times,* 3/27/73.
16. NS, 3/26/73.
17. *PP* (1973), 234–38.
18. *New York Times,* 3/30/73.
19. Transcript, 3/27/73, NPMP.
20. Haldeman summary notes, 5/7/73, NPMP.
21. Ehrlichman notes, 3/30/73, NPMP.
22. *New York Times,* 3/31/73.
23. Ehrlichman, *Witness to Power,* 373; Haldeman, *Ends of Power,* 249; Nixon, *Memoirs,* 812.
24. *New York Times,* 3/25/73 and 4/1/73.
25. Kissinger, *Years of Upheaval,* 319.
26. *Ibid.,* 315; Hung and Schecter, *Palace File,* 163.
27. Kissinger, *Years of Upheaval,* 311; Hung and Schecter, *Palace File,* 163.
28. *New York Times,* 4/3/73.

29. Haldeman, *Ends of Power*, 250–51.
30. Ehrlichman notes, 4/4/73, NPMP.
31. Nixon, *Memoirs*, 814–15.
32. Ehrlichman, *Witness to Power*, 374.
33. Nixon, *Memoirs*, 813.
34. Ehrlichman, *Witness to Power*, 374–75.
35. Nixon, *Memoirs*, 813–14.
36. Ehrlichman, *Witness to Power*, 375.
37. Nixon, *Memoirs*, 815.
38. Ehrlichman, *Witness to Power*, 375.
39. Ehrlichman notes, 4/11/73, NPMP.
40. *Ibid.*, 4/13/73.
41. Ehrlichman, *Witness to Power*, 376.
42. *New York Times*, 4/12/73.
43. Nixon, *Memoirs*, 818.
44. Transcripts, 4/19/73, 4/20/73, and 4/26/73, NPMP.
45. Transcript, 4/14/73, NPMP.
46. *Ibid.*
47. *Ibid.*
48. Nixon, *Memoirs*, 823.
49. Transcript, 4/14/73, NPMP.
50. Nixon, *Memoirs*, 826.
51. Transcript, 4/14/73, NPMP.
52. *Ibid.*

Chapter Five

1. Transcript, 4/15/73, NPMP.
2. New York Times, *White House Tapes*, 446–75.
3. *Ibid.*, 476–84.
4. Nixon, *Memoirs*, 827; Henry Petersen interview by Stanley Kutler, in Kutler, *The Wars of Watergate*, 301.
5. Nixon, *Memoirs*, 827.
6. Haldeman, *Ends of Power*, 258–59.
7. New York Times, *White House Tapes*, 491.
8. Haldeman, *Ends of Power*, 259–60.
9. Ehrlichman, *Witness to Power*, 382; Ehrlichman notes, 4/15/73, NPMP.
10. Dean, *Blind Ambition*, 259–60; New York Times, *White House Tapes*, 492.
11. Dean, *Blind Ambition*, 260–64; Drew, *Washington Journal*, 89.
12. *New York Times*, 4/16/73.
13. New York Times, *White House Tapes*, 538.
14. Transcript, 4/16/73, NPMP.
15. Transcript, 4/16/73, NPMP; Dean, *Blind Ambition*, 265–67; Haldeman, *Ends of Power*, 202; Dean, *Blind Ambition*, 263.
16. New York Times, *White House Tapes*, 523–29.
17. *Ibid.*
18. *Ibid.*, 538–86.
19. *Ibid.*, 586–600.
20. *Ibid.*, 601–7.
21. *Ibid.*, 607–15.
22. *Ibid.*, 616–19.

23. *Ibid.*, 620–22.
24. *Ibid.*, 665–95.
25. *PP* (1973), 298–99.
26. Nixon, *Memoirs*, 831; *New York Times*, 4/19/73; transcript, 4/17/73, NPMP.
27. New York Times, *White House Tapes*, 709–42.
28. Haldeman notes, 4/18/73, NPMP.
29. *New York Times*, 4/20/73.
30. Transcript, 4/19/73, NPMP; Haldeman, *Ends of Power*, 263–65. Ehrlichman, *Witness to Power*, 406–07.
31. Nixon, *Memoirs*, 836–38.
32. Haldeman notes, 4/23/73, NPMP.
33. Nixon, *Memoirs*, 840.
34. Moynihan to Nixon, 4/22/73, NPMP.
35. Transcript, 4/25/73, NPMP.
36. Haldeman, *Ends of Power*, 268.
37. Transcript, 4/25/73, NPMP.
38. Haldeman, *Ends of Power*, 69–71.
39. Transcript, 4/25/73, NPMP; Haldeman, *Ends of Power*, 272–75.
40. Transcript, 4/25/73, NPMP.
41. Nixon, *Memoirs*, 843; transcript, 4/25/73, NPMP.
42. Transcript, 4/26/73 (two meetings), NPMP; Haldeman, *Ends of Power*, 281–287.
43. Nixon, *Memoirs*, 845–46.
44. Ehrlichman notes, 4/29/73, NPMP.
45. *Ibid.*; Haldeman, *Ends of Power*, 292–94; Nixon, *Memoirs*, 846–47.
46. Ehrlichman, *Witness to Power*, 390; Nixon, *Memoirs*, 847; "Top Aide Tells How Nixon Sold Him Out," *New West*, May 23, 1977.
47. Kissinger, *Years of Upheaval*, 102–03.
48. Richardson, *The Creative Balance*, 4–5.
49. Haldeman notes, 4/30/73, NPMP.
50. *PP* (1973), 328–33.
51. Nixon, *Memoirs*, 850.
52. Richard Nixon, "Memo to President Bush: How to Use TV." *TV Guide*, 1/14/89.

Chapter Six

1. Nixon, *Memoirs*, 854.
2. *New York Times*, 5/2/73.
3. *Ibid.*, 5/1/73.
4. *Ibid.*, 5/2/73.
5. Los Angeles *Times*, 5/2/73.
6. *New York Times*, 5/2/73; Haldeman, *Ends of Power*, 296.
7. *New York Times*, 5/2/73.
8. Ehrlichman, *Witness to Power*, 406–7.
9. Kissinger, *Years of Upheaval*, 109; Morris, *Haig*, 224; Gulley, *Breaking Cover*, 145.
10. Gulley, *Breaking Cover*, 146.
11. *New York Times*, 5/3/73 and 5/4/73.
12. *Ibid.*, 5/4–5/8/73.
13. *Ibid.*, 5/8/73.

14. *Ibid.*, 5/9/73.
15. *Ibid.*
16. Nixon, *Memoirs*, 857.
17. *New York Times*, 5/8/73.
18. Nixon, *Memoirs*, 857; Richardson, *The Creative Balance*, 38.
19. *New York Times*, 5/11/73.
20. *Ibid.*
21. Gulley, *Breaking Cover*, 239.
22. *PP* (1973), 523–26.
23. *New York Times*, 5/11–5/12/73.
24. *Ibid.*, 5/15/73.
25. *Ibid.*, 5/16/73.
26. *Ibid.*, 5/17/73.
27. *Ibid.*, 5/18/73.
28. Richardson, *The Creative Balance*, 38.
29. Nixon, *Memoirs*, 910.
30. *Ibid.*, 910–11, 873.
31. Haldeman, *Ends of Power*, 300–2.
32. *New York Times*, 5/23/73.
33. *PP* (1973), 547–53.
34. *New York Times*, 5/23/73.
35. Nixon, *Memoirs*, 865.
36. *PP* (1973), 555–63; *New York Times*, 564–65.
37. Nixon, *Memoirs*, 866–67; *PP* (1973), 564–65.
38. Nixon, *Memoirs*, 868–69.
39. Timmons to Nixon, 4/13/73, NPMP.
40. Timmons to Nixon, with Nixon notation, 5/10/73, NPMP.
41. *New York Times*, 5/26/73.
42. Lukas, *Nightmare*, 350.
43. *Ibid.*, 356–57.
44. Harris to Nixon, with Nixon notation, 5/15/73, NPMP.
45. Woods to Nixon, 5/14/73, NPMP.
46. *PP* (1973), 584–87.
47. Chicago *Tribune*, 6/3/73.
48. Nixon, *Memoirs*, 872.
49. *New York Times*, 5/30/73.
50. *Washington Post*, 5/29/73.
51. *Ibid.*, 5/31/73 and 6/1/73.
52. *New York Times*, 6/1/73.
53. *Ibid.*, 6/3/73, and *Washington Post*, 6/3/73.
54. Nixon, *Memoirs*, 874.
55. Haldeman, *Ends of Power*, 302–3.
56. *Ibid.*, 198–201.
57. Transcript, 6/4/73, printed in *Washington Post*, 7/21/74.
58. *New York Times*, 6/5/73.
59. *Ibid.*, 6/6/73.
60. *Ibid.*
61. *Ibid.*, 6/7/73.
62. *PP* (1973), 577–83; *New York Times*, 6/9/73.
63. *New York Times*, 6/8/73 and 6/10/73.
64. *Ibid.*, 6/15/73.
65. Cole, "Talking Points," 6/14/73, NPMP, summarizing the Nixon-Agnew meeting.

CHAPTER SEVEN

1. Kissinger, *Years of Upheaval*, 124.
2. Ibid., 202.
3. *Ibid.*
4. *Ibid.*, 211–12.
5. *Ibid.*, 210.
6. Ambrose, *Rise to Globalism*, 272.
7. *Ibid.*, 273; Kissinger, *Years of Upheaval*, 220–21.
8. Kissinger, *Years of Upheaval*, 137.
9. *Ibid.*
10. Garthoff, *Detente and Confrontation*, 321–22.
11. Kissinger, *Years of Upheaval*, 176–77.
12. *Ibid.*, 319.
13. *Ibid.*, 324.
14. *Ibid.*, 355.
15. Nixon, *Memoirs*, 875.
16. Garthhoff, *Detente and Confrontation*, 325.
17. *Ibid.*, 326.
18. Nixon, *Memoirs*, 875.
19. Kissinger, *Years of Upheaval*, 249.
20. Nixon, *Memoirs*, 876.
21. Kissinger, *Years of Upheaval*, 253.
22. Ehrlichman notes, 4/18/73, NPMP.
23. Ehrlichman notes, 4/20/73, NPMP.
24. Stern, *Water's Edge*, 81–82.
25. Nixon to Haig, 7/7/73, NPMP.
26. Garthoff, *Détente and Confrontation*, 329.
27. *Ibid.*, 334.
28. Kissinger, *Years of Upheaval*, 291.
29. Nixon, *Memoirs*, 878–79.
30. Garthoff, *Détente and Confrontation*, 333.
31. *Ibid.*, 334–35; Nixon, *Memoirs*, 881.
32. Nixon, *Memoirs*, 881.
33. *Ibid.*, 882; Kissinger, *Years of Upheaval*, 294.
34. Kissinger, *Years of Upheaval*, 294.
35. Nixon, *Memoirs*, 882.
36. Gordon Chang, "JFK, China, and the Bomb," *Journal of American History*, March 1988, 1287–1310.
37. See Nixon notes on Timmons to Nixon, 6/21/73, NPMP.
38. Nixon, *Memoirs*, 882–83.
39. Kissinger, *Years of Upheaval*, 299.
40. *Ibid.*
41. *PP* (1973), 609.
42. *Ibid.*, 621–22.
43. Kissinger, *Years of Upheaval*, 359.

CHAPTER EIGHT

1. Goldwater, *Goldwater*, 262.
2. *New York Times*, 6/26/73.
3. *Ibid.*

4. *Ibid.*
5. Nixon, *Memoirs,* 890.
6. *Ibid.,* 893.
7. *Ibid.*
8. *New York Times,* 6/27/73.
9. *Ibid.*
10. *Ibid.*
11. *Ibid.,* 6/28/73.
12. *Ibid.*
13. *Ibid.*
14. *Ibid.*
15. *Ibid.*
16. *Ibid.,* 6/29/73.
17. Haldeman, *Ends of Power,* 305–6.
18. Scott Armstrong, "Friday the Thirteenth," *Journal of American History,* March 1989, 1237.
19. *New York Times,* 6/30/73.
20. *PP* (1973), 632–35.
21. *New York Times,* 7/3/73.
22. *Ibid.,* 7/5/73.
23. *PP* (1973), 636–38.
24. *New York Times,* 7/8 and 7/9/73.
25. Haldeman, *Ends of Power,* 305.
26. *New York Times,* 7/11 and 7/12/73.
27. Nixon, *Memoirs,* 898–99.
28. *New York Times,* 7/13 and 7/14/73.
29. *Ibid.,* 7/17/73.
30. Donald Sanders, "Watergate Reminiscences," *Journal of American History,* March 1989, 1231.
31. Armstrong, "Friday the Thirteenth," 1240.
32. David Thelen, "Conversations with Alexander P. Butterfield," 1253.
33. Sanders, "Watergate Reminiscences," 1232–33.
34. Nixon, *Memoirs,* 900.
35. Dean, *Blind Ambition,* 332.
36. Lukas, *Nightmare,* 381; Price, *With Nixon,* 245.
37. Price, *With Nixon,* 245.
38. Ambrose, *Eisenhower,* II, 203.
39. *New York Times,* 7/17/73.
40. Nixon, *Memoirs,* 900.
41. Woodward and Bernstein, *The Final Days,* 58.
42. Haldeman, *Ends of Power,* 205.
43. Nixon, *Memoirs,* 901.
44. Haldeman, *Ends of Power,* 205.
45. Nixon, *Memoirs,* 902–3.
46. *Ibid.,* 903.
47. Ervin to Nixon, 7/17/73, NPMP.
48. Nixon to Ervin, 7/23/73, NPMP.
49. *New York Times,* 7/18/73.
50. *PP* (1973), 647–53.
51. *Ibid.,* 655–57.
52. Herschensohn to Nixon, with Nixon commentary, 7/23/73, NPMP.
53. NS, 7/23/73.
54. *New York Times,* 7/24/73.

55. NS, 7/25/73.
56. NS, 7/26/73.
57. *PP* (1973), 668–70.
58. NS, 7/27/73.
59. NS, 7/27/73.
60. *New York Times*, 7/30/73.
61. *Ibid.*, 7/25–7/28/73.
62. *Ibid.*, 7/31/73.
63. Haldeman, *Ends of Power*, 306.

CHAPTER NINE

1. *New York Times*, 8/1/73.
2. *Ibid.*
3. *Ibid.*, 8/2/73; *Washington Post*, 8/1/73.
4. *PP* (1973), 673–75.
5. *New York Times*, 8/5–8/10/73.
6. *PP* (1973), 686.
7. *New York Times*, 8/16/73.
8. Nixon, *Memoirs*, 913.
9. *Ibid.*; Witcover, *A Heartbeat Away*, 144.
10. Goldwater, *Goldwater*, 263–64.
11. Morris, *Haig*, 245–46.
12. *Washington Post*, 8/14/73.
13. Agnew, *Go Quietly . . . or Else*, 34.
14. *Ibid.*, 22.
15. Goldwater, *Goldwater*, 265.
16. Witcover, *A Heartbeat Away*, 146; Nixon, *Memoirs*, 913.
17. Agnew, *Go Quietly*, 102–3.
18. *Wall Street Journal*, 8/7/73.
19. Agnew, *Go Quietly*, 109–11; Nixon, *Memoirs*, 823, 914; *New York Times*, 8/10/73.
20. Agnew, *Go Quietly*, 113.
21. Nixon, *Memoirs*, 914–45.
22. NS, 8/3/73.
23. *New York Times*, 8/10/73.
24. *PP* (1973), 691–97.
25. Nixon, *Memoirs*, 905.
26. *New York Times*, 8/17/73.
27. *Ibid.*; *Washington Post*, 8/16/73 and 8/17/73.
28. *New York Times*, 8/17/73.
29. *Ibid.*
30. *Ibid.*
31. Nixon comments on Haig to RN, 8/21/73, NPMP.
32. Lang and Lang, *The Battle for Public Opinion*, 83.
33. *New York Times*, 8/21/73.
34. Agnew, *Go Quietly*, 130.
35. *PP* (1973), 710–24.
36. Buzhardt, et al., to RN, 8/22/73, with RN notation, NPMP.
37. *Washington Post*, 8/23/73.
38. Kissinger, *Years of Upheaval*, 415–17.
39. *Ibid.*, 418–19.

40. *New York Times*, 8/21/73.
41. Kissinger, *Years of Upheaval*, 422–23.
42. *New York Times*, 8/26/73.
43. Kissinger, *Years of Upheaval*, 431.
44. *PP* (1973), 815–16.
45. Kissinger, *Years of Upheaval*, 432.
46. Los Angeles *Times*, 8/28/73.
47. *New York Times*, 8/30/73.
48. *Ibid.*
49. *Ibid.*, 8/31/73.
50. Agnew, *Go Quietly*, 140–41.
51. Nixon, *Memoirs*, 915.
52. Witcover, *A Heartbeat Away*, 145.
53. *PP* (1973), 732–42.
54. Drew, *Washington Journal*, 7.
55. *Washington Post*, 9/5/73; *New York Times*, 9/7/73.
56. *New York Times*, 9/12/73; author's experience working with Nixon's papers.
57. *New York Times*, 9/9/73.
58. *Washington Post*, 9/11/73.
59. *New York Times*, 9/12/73.
60. *PP* (1973), 752–54.
61. Weinberger to RN, with RN notation, 9/14/73, NPMP.
62. Buzhardt, et al., to RN, with RN comments, 9/7/73, NPMP.
63. *New York Times*, 9/14–9/16/73.
64. Agnew, *Go Quietly*, 157–58.
65. Nixon, *Memoirs*, 916.
66. *Washington Post*, 9/22/73.
67. *Ibid.*, 9/25–9/27/73; Agnew, *Go Quietly*, 164–67; Nixon, *Memoirs*, 916–17.
68. *PP* (1973), 822.
69. *Washington Post*, 9/27/73; *New York Times*, 9/27/73.
70. *New York Times*, 9/27/73.
71. Eisenhower, *Pat Nixon*, 378.
72. *New York Times*, 9/30/73.
73. Nixon, *Memoirs*, 972.
74. *New York Times*, 9/27/73; *Washington Post*, 10/5/73.
75. *PP* (1973), 838–44.
76. *Ibid.*, 837.
77. Nixon, *Memoirs*, 920.

Chapter Ten

1. Nixon, *Memoirs*, 922.
2. *New York Times*, 9/23 and 10/4/83.
3. Price, *With Nixon*, 250.
4. Nixon, *Memoirs*, 920.
5. Kissinger, *Years of Upheaval*, 454, 468.
6. *PP* (1973), 848.
7. Nixon, *Memoirs*, 922.
8. *Ibid.*, 922–23; Agnew, *Go Quietly*, 197–98.
9. Hartmann, *Palace Politics*, 21.
10. Richardson, *The Creative Balance*, 38.
11. Woods to Nixon, 10/10/73, NPMP.

12. Nixon, *Memoirs*, 924; Kissinger, *Years of Upheaval*, 496; Zumwalt, *On Watch*, 434.
13. Golan, *The Secret Conversations of Henry Kissinger*, 45–61.
14. Zumwalt, *On Watch*, 435; see also Garthoff, *Detente and Confrontation*, 369–70.
15. Nixon, *Memoirs*, 924.
16. Zumwalt, *On Watch*, 434.
17. Nixon, *Memoirs*, 925–26.
18. Quoted by Seymour Hersh in "The Pardon," *The Atlantic Monthly*, August 1983, 21.
19. Ford, *A Time to Heal*, 102.
20. Hartmann, *Palace Politics*, 19.
21. Ford, *A Time to Heal*, 104.
22. *Ibid.*, 103.
23. The ballots are in NPMP; see also Woods to Nixon, 10/12/73, and Ford to Nixon, 10/11/73, in *ibid*.
24. Ford, *A Time to Heal*, 73.
25. Haldeman interview.
26. Hersh, "The Pardon," 58.
27. Kissinger, *Years of Upheaval*, 514.
28. Drew, *Washington Journal*, 41.
29. Hersh, "The Pardon," 56.
30. Ford, *A Time to Heal*, 105.
31. Hartmann, *Palace Politics*, 26–27; *PP* (1973), 868–69.
32. Nixon to Krogh, 10/7/73, NPMP.
33. *New York Times*, 10/13/73.
34. Kissinger, *Years of Upheaval*, 510.
35. Nixon, *Memoirs*, 926–27; Kissinger, *Years of Upheaval*, 514–15.
36. Kissinger, *Years of Upheaval*, 537.
37. Nixon, *Memoirs*, 929.
38. *Ibid.*, 928.
39. *Ibid.*, 929.
40. Kutler, *The Wars of Watergate*, 402.
41. Richardson, *The Creative Balance*, 39.
42. Kissinger, *Years of Upheaval*, 534–35; Nixon, *Memoirs*, 930.
43. Nixon, *Memoirs*, 931.
44. *New York Times* and *Washington Post*, 10/19–10/22/73.
45. Nixon, *Memoirs*, 932.
46. *New York Times* and *Washington Post*, 10/18 and 10/19/73.
47. *PP* (1973), 887–88.
48. *New York Times*, 10/20/73.
49. Kissinger, *Years of Upheaval*, 547–48; Nixon, *Memoirs*, 933.
50. Kissinger, *Years of Upheaval*, 546.
51. Garthoff, *Détente and Confrontation*, 371.
52. Kissinger, *Years of Upheaval*, 550–51.
53. *Ibid.*, 552.
54. *New York Times*, 10/21/73.
55. Richardson interview, Boston *Globe*, 9/9/84.
56. Richardson, *The Creative Balance*, 44; Nixon, *Memoirs*, 934; *PP* (1973), 890.
57. Morris, *Haig*, 251.
58. Richardson, *The Creative Balance*, 44.
59. *New York Times*, 10/21/73.
60. Richardson, *The Creative Balance*, 46–47.

61. *New York Times*, 10/21/73.
62. Nixon, *Memoirs*, 935.
63. Drew, *Washington Journal*, 53.
64. Nixon, *Memoirs*, 935.
65. *New York Times*, 10/21/73.
66. Drew, *Washington Journal*, 53.
67. Lang and Lang, *The Battle for Public Opinion*, 102.
68. *Ibid.*, 103–4.
69. Nixon, *Memoirs*, 935–36.
70. Drew, *Washington Journal*, 53.
71. Garthoff, *Détente and Confrontation*, 371–72; Kissinger, *Years of Upheaval*, 569.
72. *New York Times*, 10/22/73.
73. *Ibid.*
74. *Washington Post*, 10/22/73.
75. *New York Times*, 10/22/73.
76. *Ibid.*
77. Lang and Lang, *Battle for Public Opinion*, 109.
78. Drew, *Washington Journal*, 67.
79. *Ibid.*, 69.
80. Eisenhower, *Pat Nixon*, 392.
81. *New York Times*, 10/24/73.
82. Nixon, *Memoirs*, 936; Kissinger, *Years of Upheaval*, 569.
83. Nixon, *Memoirs*, 937.
84. Stein to Nixon, 10/24/73, NPMP.
85. *PP* (1973), 893.
86. Garthoff, *Détente and Confrontation*, 375.
87. Nixon, *Memoirs*, 938.
88. Kissinger, *Years of Upheaval*, 579–80.
89. Nixon, *Memoirs*, 938.
90. Kissinger, *Years of Upheaval*, 585.
91. Morris, *Haig*, 257.
92. Zumwalt, *On Watch*, 448.
93. O'Neill, with Novak, *Man of the House*, 253–54.
94. Nixon, *Memoirs*, 941.
95. Kissinger, *Years of Upheaval*, 608–9.
96. *New York Times*, 10/26/73.
97. Kissinger, *Years of Upheaval*, 598–99.
98. Lang and Lang, *Battle for Public Opinion*, 106.
99. Eisenhower, *Pat Nixon*, 390.
100. *New York Times*, 10/27/73.
101. *PP* (1973), 896–905.
102. Eisenhower, *Pat Nixon*, 385.
103. Bush to Haig, 10/29/73, NPMP.
104. *New York Times*, 10/30/73.
105. *Ibid.*, 10/31/73.
106. *Ibid.*, 11/4/73.
107. *Ibid.*, 10/29/73.
108. Nixon, *Memoirs*, 943–44.
109. Woods to Nixon, 11/1/73, NPMP.
110. Sirica, *To Set the Record Straight*, 182.
111. *New York Times* and *Washington Post*, 11/1 and 11/2/73.
112. Nixon, *Memoirs*, 943.

113. *Ibid.*, 945.
114. *New York Times*, 11/2/73.

Chapter Eleven

1. Drew, *Washington Journal*, 100–1.
2. *Ibid.*, 99; *New York Times*, 11/4/73.
3. *Time*, 11/12/73 (printed and distributed 11/5/73).
4. Drew, *Washington Journal*, 88.
5. *New York Times*, 11/6/73.
6. Kutler, *Wars of Watergate*, 429; Woodward and Bernstein, *Final Days*, 25–30; Nixon, *Memoirs*, 946.
7. Nixon, *Memoirs*, 946.
8. *New York Times*, 11/3/73.
9. *Ibid.*, 11/4/73.
10. *Ibid.*, 11/7/73.
11. *Washington Post*, 11/8/73.
12. *PP* (1973), 916–22.
13. *Washington Post*, 11/9/73.
14. *New York Times*, 11/8/73.
15. *PP* (1973), 929–33.
16. *New York Times*, 11/10 and 11/11/73; Nixon, *Memoirs*, 948.
17. *New York Times*, 11/15/73.
18. Drew, *Washington Journal*, 113.
19. *New York Times*, 11/16/73.
20. Nixon, *Memoirs*, 948–49.
21. *PP* (1973), 934–41.
22. *Ibid.*, 946–64.
23. Drew, *Washington Journal*, 121.
24. Nixon, *Memoirs*, 957.
25. *Ibid.*, 963.
26. *Ibid.*, 952.
27. Ambrose, *Nixon*, I, 29.
28. Nixon, *Memoirs*, 288.
29. Lang and Lang, *Battle for Public Opinion*, 115.
30. Nixon, *Memoirs*, 972.
31. *New York Times*, 11/22/73; *PP* (1973), 966, 972.
32. Lang and Lang, *Battle for Public Opinion*, 120.
33. Nixon, *Memoirs*, 950.
34. *New York Times*, 11/22/73.
35. Lang and Lang, *Battle for Public Opinion*, 120.
36. *New York Times*, 11/27/73.
37. *Ibid.*, 12/7/73.
38. *Ibid.*
39. Sirica, *To Set the Record Straight*, 198.
40. Nixon, *Memoirs*, 951–52.
41. Haldeman, *Ends of Power*, 207.
42. *New York Times*, 11/27/73.
43. Garment to Nixon, 11/24/73, NPMP.
44. *PP* (1973), 973–75.
45. Schoenebaum, *Profiles of an Era*, 386.

46. *PP* (1973), 975.
47. Drew, *Washington Journal*, 143.
48. Ford, *A Time to Heal*, 111–12; Hartmann, *Palace Politics*, 80.
49. Ford, *A Time to Heal*, 112–13.
50. *New York Times*, 12/9/73.
51. *PP* (1973), 1005–7.
52. Lang and Lang, *Battle for Public Opinion*, 121.
53. *New York Times*, 12/9/73.
54. Lang and Lang, *Battle for Public Opinion*, 121.
55. *Washington Post*, 12/13 and 12/18/73.
56. *Ibid.*, 12/20/73.
57. *Christianity Today*, 12/22/73.
58. *Christian Science Monitor*, 12/19/73.
59. Goldwater, *Goldwater*, 267–70.
60. Zumwalt, *On Watch*, 459–60.
61. Nixon, *Memoirs*, 968.
62. Eisenhower, *Pat Nixon*, 395–96.
63. *Ibid.*, 398.

Chapter Twelve

1. *New York Times*, 1/10/74; Morris, *Haig*, 269.
2. *New York Times*, 1/2/74.
3. Stripling to Woods, with RN notation, 1/7/74, NPMP.
4. *New York Times*, 1/7/74.
5. *Ibid.*, 1/10/74.
6. Nixon, *Memoirs*, 970.
7. *New York Times*, 1/9/74.
8. *PP* (1974), 5–6.
9. Nixon, *Memoirs*, 988.
10. Kissinger, *Years of Upheaval*, 885.
11. Nixon, *Memoirs*, 971.
12. *Ibid.*, 975.
13. *Washington Post*, 1/16/74.
14. *New York Times*, 1/16/74.
15. *Washington Post*, 1/23/74.
16. *Ibid.*, 1/23/74.
17. Kissinger, *Years of Upheaval*, 371.
18. *New York Times*, 1/4/74.
19. Nixon, *Memoirs*, 982.
20. Kissinger, *Years of Upheaval*, 852.
21. *PP* (1974), 12–15.
22. Washington *Star-News*, 1/24/74.
23. *Washington Post*, 1/21/74.
24. Ford, *A Time to Heal*, 116.
25. *New York Times*, 1/22/74.
26. Leon Jaworski oral history, The Texas Collection, Baylor University.
27. Kutler, *Wars of Watergate*, 448.
28. *New York Times*, 1/31/74.
29. Zumwalt, *On Watch*, 479–80.
30. *PP* (1974), 46; Nixon, *Memoirs*, 978.

31. *PP* (1974), 47–55.
32. Garment to Nixon, with enclosure and RN notation, 2/7/74, NPMP.
33. *PP* (1974), 101–3.
34. *Ibid.*, 140.
35. *New York Times*, 2/6/74.
36. *Ibid.*, 2/7/74.
37. *Ibid.*, 2/6/74.
38. *Ibid.*, 2/13/74.
39. *Ibid.*
40. *Ibid.*, 2/14/74.
41. *Ibid.*, 2/15/74.
42. *Ibid.*, 2/19/74.
43. Harlow to Nixon, with RN notations, 2/16/74, NPMP.
44. Nixon motivational notes for Cabinet meeting, 2/21/74, *ibid.*
45. *PP* (1974), 199–207.
46. *Ibid.*, 210–12; Nixon's handwritten draft is dated 2/26/74 and is in NPMP.
47. *PP* (1974), 215–22.
48. *Ibid.*, 229–40.
49. Nixon, *Memoirs*, 990.
50. *New York Times*, 3/12/74.
51. Buchanan to Nixon, 2/26/74, NPMP.
52. *PP* (1974), 245–51.
53. Kissinger, *Years of Upheaval*, 914.
54. Eisenhower, *Pat Nixon*, 399–400.
55. *Ibid.*, 403.
56. *Ibid.*, 401–2.
57. Drew, *Washington Journal*, 179, 185.
58. *Washington Post*, 3/13/74.
59. *New York Times*, 3/13/74.
60. *PP* (1974), 261–76.
61. *Ibid.*, 279–82.
62. Eisenhower, *Pat Nixon*, 404.
63. *New York Times*, 3/20/74.
64. *PP* (1974), 284–98.
65. *Ibid.*, 298–302.
66. Nixon, *Memoirs*, 993.
67. Los Angeles *Times*, 3/23/74.
68. *New York Times*, 3/24/74.
69. *PP* (1974), 303–5.
70. *Ibid.*, 306–13.
71. *Ibid.*, 316–23.
72. *Ibid.*, 325–27.
73. *Washington Post*, 3/27/74.
74. Drew, *Washington Journal*, 214.
75. *New York Times*, 4/4/74.
76. *Ibid.*, 4/3/74.
77. *Washington Post*, 4/3/74.
78. *New York Times*, 3/31/74.
79. Hartmann, *Palace Politics*, 114–16.
80. *New Republic*, 4/13/74.
81. *New York Times*, 4/3/74.

Chapter Thirteen

1. *New York Times*, 4/1 and 4/4/74.
2. *PP* (1974), 336.
3. Quoted in *The New York Times*, 4/9/74.
4. *Washington Post*, 4/5/74.
5. *New York Times*, 4/11/74.
6. *PP*, (1974), 337–38.
7. *New York Times*, 4/11/74.
8. *Washington Post*, 4/12/74.
9. Woodward and Bernstein, *Final Days*, 124–25.
10. Nixon, *Memoirs*, 998–99.
11. Todd, *The White House Transcripts*, a pamphlet privately printed in 1974; for a shorter version, see Todd, "The Nixon Transcripts," in *Discovery: Research and Scholarship at the University of Texas*, vol. 1, no. 2, December 1976.
12. Jeff Shepard interview.
13. Nixon, *Memoirs*, 994.
14. *New York Times*, 4/26/74.
15. *PP* (1974), 379–88.
16. *New York Times*, 4/29/74.
17. Price, *With Nixon*, 264.
18. *PP* (1974), 389–97.
19. *New York Times*, 5/2/74.
20. *Ibid.*
21. Drew, *Washington Journal*, 253.
22. *PP* (1974), 404–9.
23. Nixon, *Memoirs*, 996.
24. *Washington Post*, 5/7/74.
25. *Ibid.*, 5/10/74.
26. *New York Times*, 5/2/74.
27. Hearst papers, 5/5/74.
28. Chicago *Tribune*, 5/9/74.
29. Omaha *World-Herald*, 5/7/74.
30. Los Angeles *Times*, 5/10/74; Cleveland *Plain Dealer*, 5/10/74.
31. Eisenhower, *Pat Nixon*, 407.
32. *New York Times*, 5/10/74.
33. Lang and Lang, *Battle for Public Opinion*, 126.
34. *Ibid.*, 127.
35. Nixon, *Memoirs*, 997–98.
36. *Ibid.*, 999–1001.
37. Hartmann, *Palace Politics*, 120–21.
38. Drew, *Washington Journal*, 273.
39. *Ibid.*, 275; *Washington Post*, 5/12/74.
40. Eisenhower, *Pat Nixon*, 408–9.
41. Drew, *Washington Journal*, 272–73.
42. *New York Times*, 5/6/74.
43. *Washington Post*, 5/11/74.
44. Ford, *Time to Heal*, 121–22.
45. Washington *Star-News*, 5/6/74.
46. *New York Times*, 5/14/74.
47. *PP* (1974), 442–45.
48. *Ibid.*, 449–50.

49. Ken Cole to Nixon, with RN notation, 5/17/74, NPMP.
50. Haig to Nixon, with RN notation, 5/19/74, NPMP.
51. *PP* (1974), 452.
52. Greensburg *Tribune-Review*, 5/14/74.
53. Nixon to Chapin, 5/15/74, NPMP.
54. Nixon, *Memoirs*, 1001.
55. *New York Times*, 5/17/74.
56. *Ibid.*, 5/14/74.
57. *Ibid.*, 5/15/74.
58. *Ibid.*, 5/20/74.
59. Drew, *Washington Journal*, 279.
60. Julie Eisenhower to Nixon, 5/15/74, NPMP.
61. Ford, *Time to Heal*, 121.
62. *New York Times*, 5/21/74.
63. *Ibid.*, 5/31/74.
64. *PP* (1974), 450–51.
65. *New York Times*, 5/23/74.
66. *Washington Post*, 5/25/74.
67. Drew, *Washington Journal*, 283.
68. *New York Times*, 6/4/74.
69. Ford, *Time to Heal*, 122.
70. Nixon, *Memoirs*, 1003–5.
71. Los Angeles *Times*, 6/6/74.

CHAPTER FOURTEEN

1. *PP* (1974), 472.
2. Nixon, *Memoirs*, 1005–6.
3. *New York Times*, 4/21/74.
4. Kissinger, *Years of Upheaval*, 1111.
5. *PP* (1974), 463.
6. Kissinger, *Years of Upheaval*, 1092.
7. Nixon, *Memoirs*, 1006.
8. *New York Times*, 6/8/74.
9. *Ibid.*, 6/11/74.
10. *PP* (1974), 478–81.
11. *New York Times*, 6/7/74.
12. *PP* (1974), 475–77.
13. Nixon, *Memoirs*, 1007.
14. *Ibid.*, 1007–8.
15. *Ibid.*, 1008.
16. *New York Times*, 6/10–6/11/74; *Washington Post*, 6/10/74.
17. Kissinger, *Years of Upheaval*, 1117.
18. Nixon, *Memoirs*, 1009.
19. Kissinger, *Years of Upheaval*, 1119.
20. *Washington Post*, 6/12/74.
21. Kissinger, *Years of Upheaval*, 1120–21.
22. Nixon, *Memoirs*, 1009.
23. *Ibid.*, 1010.
24. Kissinger, *Years of Upheaval*, 1125.
25. Nixon, *Memoirs*, 1010.

26. Kissinger, *Years of Upheaval*, 1126.
27. *PP* (1974), 497.
28. Nixon, *Memoirs*, 1011.
29. *PP* (1974), 485–87.
30. *Ibid.*, 487–91.
31. Nixon, *Memoirs*, 1011.
32. *PP* (1974), 493–94.
33. *Ibid.*, 503–5.
34. Kissinger, *Years of Upheaval*, 1125.
35. *PP* (1974), 507–8.
36. Kissinger, *Years of Upheaval*, 1135.
37. Nixon, *Memoirs*, 1013–14.
38. *New York Times*, 6/17/74.
39. Kissinger, *Years of Upheaval*, 1136.
40. *PP* (1974), 518–23.
41. Kissinger, *Years of Upheaval*, 1137.
42. Nixon, *Memoirs*, 1017.
43. *PP* (1974), 539.
44. Nixon, *Memoirs*, 1018.
45. *Ibid.*
46. *Ibid.*, 1022–23.
47. *New York Times*, 6/22/74.
48. Nixon, *Memoirs*, 1019.
49. *Ibid.*, 1020–21.
50. Kissinger, *Years of Upheaval*, 983.
51. Nixon, *Memoirs*, 1024.
52. Kissinger, *Years of Upheaval*, 1151–52.
53. Garthoff, *Détente and Confrontation*, 412–13.
54. Kissinger, *Years of Upheaval*, 1157–58.
55. *Ibid.*, 1157.
56. Nixon, *Memoirs*, 1024–25.
57. NSC meeting notes, 4/1/60, Eisenhower Library, Abilene, Kansas.
58. Zumwalt, *On Watch*, 506.
59. *Ibid.*, 498, 507–10.
60. Garthoff, *Détente and Confrontation*, 409.
61. Nixon, *Memoirs*, 1026.
62. Kissinger, *Years of Upheaval*, 1161.
63. Nixon, *Memoirs*, 1027.
64. *New York Times*, 6/27/74.
65. *PP* (1974), 551.
66. Nixon, *Memoirs*, 1027.
67. *PP* (1974), 553–54.
68. Nixon, *Memoirs*, 1027; Kissinger, *Years of Upheaval*, 1163–64.
69. Nixon, *Memoirs*, 1028–29; Kissinger, *Years of Upheaval*, 1168.
70. Eisenhower, *Pat Nixon*, 414; *New York Times*, 6/30/74.
71. Nixon, *Memoirs*, 1030–31.
72. *Ibid.*, 1032.
73. *Ibid.*, 1032–33.
74. *Ibid.*, 1034.
75. *Ibid.*, 1036.
76. Garthoff, *Détente and Confrontation*, 433–34.
77. Nixon, *Memoirs*, 1036.

78. *New York Times*, 6/27/74.
79. Garthoff, *Détente and Confrontation*, 434–35.
80. *PP* (1974), 578–82.

CHAPTER FIFTEEN

1. Nixon, *Memoirs*, 1033.
2. Ambrose, *Eisenhower*, II, 350.

CHAPTER SIXTEEN

1. Nixon, *Memoirs*, 1040–41.
2. Drew, *Washington Journal*, 314.
3. Kissinger, *Years of Upheaval*, 1181.
4. Nixon, *Memoirs*, 1042.
5. Lang and Lang, *Battle for Public Opinion*, 144; Nixon, *Memoirs*, 1041.
6. Ford, *Time to Heal*, 123.
7. *New York Times*, 7/9/74.
8. Ambrose, *Eisenhower*, II, 409.
9. Nixon, *Memoirs*, 1043 (RN's italics).
10. Drew, *Washington Journal*, 307.
11. *New York Times*, 7/14/74.
12. *Ibid.*, 7/10–7/13/74.
13. *Ibid.*, 7/12/74.
14. *Washington Post*, 7/14/74.
15. Nixon, *Memoirs*, 1045.
16. *New York Times*, 7/13/74.
17. Ford, *Time to Heal*, 123.
18. *New York Times*, 7/17/74; Rabbi Korff, *The Personal Nixon*.
19. *PP* (1974), 595–97.
20. *New York Times*, 7/19/74.
21. Nixon, *Memoirs*, 1047–48.
22. *Washington Post*, 7/20/74.
23. *New York Times*, 7/20/74.
24. Nixon *Memoirs*, 1048.
25. *PP* (1974), 600–6.
26. Nixon, *Memoirs*, 1049.
27. *New York Times*, 7/22/74.
28. Drew, *Washington Journal*, 327.
29. *New York Times*, 7/24/74.
30. Price, *With Nixon*, 314; Nixon, *Memoirs*, 1050.
31. Nixon, *Memoirs*, 1050–51.
32. *Ibid.*, 1051.
33. Price, *With Nixon*, 320.
34. *New York Times*, 7/25/74.
35. Nixon, *Memoirs*, 1051.
36. Kutler, *Wars of Watergate*, 513; Nixon, *Memoirs*, 1052.
37. Morris, *Haig*, 289.
38. Nixon, *Memoirs*, 1052.
39. *New York Times*, 7/25/74.
40. Drew, *Washington Journal*, 343.

41. Lang and Lang, *Battle for Public Opinion*, 168.
42. Drew, *Washington Journal*, 342–43.
43. *Ibid.*, 349–50.
44. *Ibid.*, 346–47.
45. *Ibid.*, 348.
46. *Ibid.*, 356.
47. *PP* (1974), 606–14.
48. Kissinger, *Years of Upheaval*, 1196–97.
49. Kutler, *Wars of Watergate*, 531.
50. *New York Times*, 8/3/74.
51. *Ibid.*, 7/28/74.
52. Nixon, *Memoirs*, 1053.
53. *Ibid.*, 1053–54.
54. *Ibid.*, 1054–55.
55. *Ibid.*
56. Eisenhower, *Pat Nixon*, 416–17.
57. Drew, *Washington Journal*, 370.
58. *Ibid.*, 371.
59. *Ibid.*
60. *New York Times*, 7/30/74.
61. Nixon, *Memoirs*, 1055.
62. *Ibid.*, 1056.
63. *Washington Post*, 7/31/74.
64. *New York Times*, 8/1/74.
65. Kissinger, *Years of Upheaval*, 1198.
66. Nixon, *Memoirs*, 1057.
67. Clawson to Haig, 7/31/74, NPMP.
68. Kissinger, *Years of Upheaval*, 1198.

Chapter Seventeen

1. Nixon, *Memoirs*, 1057–58.
2. Hersh, "The Pardon," 58.
3. Lukas, *Nightmare*, 545.
4. Hartmann, *Palace Politics*, 21.
5. *Ibid.*, Ford, *A Time to Heal*, 13.
6. Hartmann, *Palace Politics*, 21.
7. Nixon, *Memoirs*, 1058–59.
8. Drew, *Washington Journal*, 387.
9. Lukas, *Nightmare*, 547; Nixon, *Memoirs*, 1059.
10. Nixon, *Memoirs*, 1059.
11. Eisenhower, *Pat Nixon*, 417–18.
12. *Ibid.*, 419–20; Nixon, *Memoirs*, 1060–61.
13. Nixon, *Memoirs*, 1061.
14. Price, *With Nixon*, 327–30.
15. Nixon, *Memoirs*, 1062.
16. Price, *With Nixon*, 333–35.
17. Nixon, *Memoirs*, 1062.
18. *Ibid.*
19. *Ibid.*, 1063.
20. *New York Times*, 8/7/74.
21. Nixon, *Memoirs*, 1063.

22. *New York Times,* 8/6–8/7/74.
23. *PP* (1974), 621–23.
24. Eisenhower, *Pat Nixon,* 420; Nixon, *Memoirs,* 1063.
25. Eisenhower, *Pat Nixon,* 421; Nixon, *Memoirs,* 1064.
26. Drew, *Washington Journal,* 390.
27. Goldwater, *Goldwater,* 275.
28. Drew, *Washington Journal,* 396.
29. Nixon, *Memoirs,* 1064.
30. *Ibid.,* 1065.
31. Ford, *Time to Heal,* 18–19; Lukas, *Nightmare,* 558.
32. Kutler, *Wars of Watergate,* 542–43.
33. Ford, *Time to Heal,* 21.
34. Kissinger, *Years of Upheaval,* 1203.
35. Ford, *Time to Heal,* 21.
36. Kissinger, *Years of Upheaval,* 1205.
37. Nixon, *Memoirs,* 1066.
38. Drew, *Washington Journal,* 399.
39. *Ibid.*
40. Haldeman, *Ends of Power,* 311; Haldeman interview.
41. Nixon, *Memoirs,* 1067.
42. *Ibid.*
43. Lukas, *Nightmare,* 560.
44. *New York Times,* 8/8/74.
45. Nixon, *Memoirs,* 1067.
46. Lukas, *Nightmare,* 559.
47. Goldwater, *Goldwater,* 276.
48. Nixon, *Memoirs,* 1067–68.
49. Price, *With Nixon,* 339.
50. Nixon, *Memoirs,* 1069–70.

CHAPTER EIGHTEEN

1. Nixon, *Memoirs,* 1072.
2. Price, *With Nixon,* 339–40.
3. Nixon, *Memoirs,* 1071; Haldeman, *The Ends of Power,* 312–13.
4. Lukas, *Nightmare,* 566.
5. Nixon, *Memoirs,* 1079.
6. *New York Times,* 8/8/74.
7. Nixon, *Memoirs,* 1080.
8. *Ibid.,* 1071–72.
9. Price, *With Nixon,* 340.
10. Stephen Jones, "Was Richard Nixon Guilty?" *Journal of the Oklahoma Bar Association,* 265.
11. Price, *With Nixon,* 340.
12. Goldwater, *Goldwater,* 278–79; Nixon, *Memoirs,* 1073.
13. Drew, *Washington Journal,* 403–5.
14. Kissinger, *Years of Upheaval,* 1206–7; Nixon, *Memoirs,* 1073.
15. Nixon, *Memoirs,* 1075.
16. Eisenhower, *Pat Nixon,* 424.
17. Lukas, *Nightmare,* 564.
18. Nixon, *Memoirs,* 1075.
19. Eisenhower, *Pat Nixon,* 424.

20. Nixon, *Memoirs*, 1075.
21. *Ibid.*, 1076; Price, *With Nixon*, 341.
22. Nixon, *Memoirs*, 1076–77; Kissinger, *Years of Upheaval*, 1207–10. Kissinger was not so sure they knelt.
23. Price, *With Nixon*, 341–44.
24. *PP* (1974), 623–26; Lukas, *Nightmare*, 565; *New York Times*, 8/18/74; Nixon to Sampson, 3/22/78, NPMP.
25. Price, *With Nixon*, 344–45.
26. Ford, *Time to Heal*, 28–29; Nixon, *Memoirs*, 1078–79.
27. Nixon, *Memoirs*, 1080.
28. *Ibid.*
29. *Ibid.*
30. Glenn Davis memo, 8/9/74, Davis Papers, Wisconsin State Historical Society; Nixon, *Memoirs*, 1082.
31. Nixon, *Memoirs*, 1082.
32. Lillian Brown interview; Glenn Davis memo, 8/9/74.
33. *PP* (1974), 626–29.
34. Lang and Lang, *Battle for Public Opinion*, 192–93.
35. Kissinger, *Years of Upheaval*, 1212; Nixon, *Memoirs*, 1084.
36. Lang and Lang, *Battle for Public Opinion*, 193.
37. *New York Times*, 8/9/74.
38. Lang and Lang, *Battle for Public Opinion*, 199.
39. Nixon, *Memoirs*, 1086.
40. *Ibid.*, 1086–87.
41. Eisenhower, *Pat Nixon*, 426; Nixon, *Memoirs*, 1087.
42. Eisenhower, *Pat Nixon*, 427; Price, *With Nixon*, 349.
43. Kissinger, *Years of Upheaval*, 1213.
44. Nixon, *Memoirs*, 1088.
45. *PP* (1974), 630–32.
46. Nixon, *Memoirs*, 1088.
47. *PP* (1974), 632.
48. Ford, *Time to Heal*, 39.
49. Eisenhower, *Pat Nixon*, 429.

Chapter Nineteen

1. Eisenhower, *Pat Nixon*, 429.
2. Ibid., 429–30; Anson, *Exile*, 22–23.
3. *New York Times*, 8/11/74.
4. Benton Becker remarks, at the Hofstra Nixon conference.
5. For a thorough discussion, see Raymond Geselbracht, "The Four Eras in the History of Presidential Papers," *Prologue* (quarterly publication of the National Archives), vol. 13, no. 1, 1983, 37–42.
6. *Ibid.* See also Francis Heller, "American Law, Presidential Papers, and Memoirs," a paper prepared for the Conference on Political Memoirs, University of British Columbia, September 21–24, 1989.
7. Hartmann, *Palace Politics*, 173.
8. Gulley, *Breaking Cover*, 9–10; Anson, *Exile*, 27–28.
9. Hartmann, *Palace Politics*, 161, 187–88.
10. Hersh, "The Pardon," 72.
11. Anson, *Exile*, 31; Hartmann, *Palace Politics*, 195–96.
12. Anson, *Exile*, 28.

13. Gulley, *Breaking Cover*, 229.
14. *New York Times*, 8/17/74.
15. Brennan interview.
16. RN interview, *Time* magazine, April 9, 1990.
17. Becker remarks at the Hofstra Nixon conference; Hersh, "The Pardon," 72.
18. Brennan interview.
19. Anson, *Exile*, 31–32.
20. Ford, *Time to Heal*, 146.
21. *Ibid.*, 164.
22. Kutler, *Wars of Watergate*, 556.
23. *New York Times*, 9/2/74.
24. Nixon, *In the Arena*, 19–20.
25. Hersh, "The Pardon," 73.
26. *New York Times*, 8/28/74.
27. Hersh, "The Pardon," 73–74.
28. *Washington Post*, 8/29/74; *New York Times*, 8/29/74.
29. *New York Times*, 8/30/74.
30. Hartmann, *Palace Politics*, 256.
31. *Ibid.*
32. Anson, *Exile*, 46.
33. *Ibid.*, 34.
34. Gulley, *Breaking Cover*, 230–31.
35. Hartmann, *Palace Politics*, 258–61.
36. *Ibid.*, 248; Ford, *Time to Heal*, 165.
37. Ford, *Time to Heal*, 167–68.
38. *Ibid.*, 165–66.
39. Ford, *Time to Heal*, 168; Hersh, "The Pardon," 76.
40. Hersh, "The Pardon," 76.
41. Ford, *Time to Heal*, 168–72; Becker remarks at Hofstra Nixon conference.
42. Kutler, *Wars of Watergate*, 562.
43. Ford, *Time to Heal*, 173.
44. Los Angeles *Times*, 9/5/74.
45. Nixon, *In the Arena*, 21.
46. Ford, *Time to Heal*, 178.
47. *New York Times*, 9/9/74.
48. Kutler, *Wars of Watergate*, 564.
49. Ford, *Time to Heal*, 160–61.
50. *Ibid.*, 181.

Chapter Twenty

1. Eisenhower, *Pat Nixon*, 433.
2. *New York Times*, 9/14/74.
3. Anson, *Exile*, 61–62.
4. *New York Times*, 9/12/74.
5. *Ibid.*, 9/13/74.
6. Anson, *Exile*, 62; *New York Times*, 9/15/74.
7. Kenneth Clawson, "A Loyalist's Memoir," *Washington Post*, 9/9/79.
8. *New York Times*, 9/24/74.
9. Eisenhower, *Pat Nixon*, 433–34.
10. Anson, *Exile*, 70.

11. Los Angeles *Times*, 10/2/74.
12. *Ibid.*, 10/5/74.
13. Eisenhower, *Pat Nixon*, 434.
14. Leon Friedman interview.
15. *New York Times*, 10/4–10/15/74.
16. Eisenhower, *Pat Nixon*, 434, 438.
17. *New York Times*, 10/12/74.
18. *Ibid.*, 10/22/74.
19. Anson, *Exile*, 74.
20. *New York Times*, 10/18/74.
21. *Ibid.*, 10/22/74.
22. John Brademas interview.
23. Eisenhower, *Pat Nixon*, 434; Nixon, *In the Arena*, 22; Anson, *Exile*, 75.
24. Anson, *Exile*, 77.
25. Eisenhower, *Pat Nixon*, 434–35.
26. Nixon, *In the Arena*, 23.
27. Anson, *Exile*, 80.
28. *Ibid.*, 81.
29. Eisenhower, *Pat Nixon*, 436.
30. *Ibid.*, 82–83.
31. *New York Times*, 10/31/74.
32. *Ibid.*, 11/9/74.
33. Nixon, *In the Arena*, 24.
34. *New York Times*, 11/30/74.
35. Gulley, *Breaking Cover*, 240.
36. Philadelphia *Sunday Bulletin*, 12/8/74.
37. Anson, *Exile*, 92–93.
38. Nixon, *In the Arena*, 20.
39. For a full discussion of this most fascinating business (at least to archivists and historians), see Ray Geselbracht's excellent article, "The Four Eras in the History of Presidential Papers," *Prologue*, vol. 13, no. 1, 1983.
40. Eisenhower, *Pat Nixon*, 437.
41. *New York Times*, 1/2/75.
42. *Ibid.*, 1/3/75.
43. Anson, *Exile*, 85.
44. Winzola McLendon, "Pat Nixon Today," *Good Housekeeping*, February 1980, 128–29.
45. Lester David, "Pat Nixon's Life Story: 'I Gave Up Everything I Ever Loved . . . ' ", *Good Housekeeping*, August 1978, 87.
46. Anson, *Exile*, 88.
47. Los Angeles *Times*, 1/12/75.
48. *New York Times*, 1/29/75.
49. Anson, *Exile*, 99–100.
50. *New York Times*, 2/21/75.
51. Nixon, *In the Arena*, 30–31.
52. Anson, *Exile*, 101.
53. *New York Times*, 4/1/75.
54. Thomas M. Brown, "The Exile," *New York Times Magazine*, 8/3/75; *New York Times*, 4/24/75.
55. *New York Times*, 5/5/75; Los Angeles *Times* 5/5/75.
56. Nixon, *In the Arena*, 31.
57. Eisenhower, *Pat Nixon*, 441.

Chapter Twenty-One

1. Eisenhower, *Pat Nixon*, 438.
2. *Ibid.*, 443.
3. Los Angeles *Times*, 8/8/75.
4. *New York Times*, 5/27/75, 6/24/75, 9/20/75, 10/1/75.
5. Eisenhower, *Pat Nixon*, 439.
6. Brown, "The Exile."
7. Los Angeles *Times*, 5/30/75.
8. *New York Times*, 6/3/75.
9. *Ibid.*, 6/8/75.
10. *Ibid.*, 8/9/75.
11. *Ibid.*, 7/23/75.
12. *New York Times*, 9/9/75.
13. Frost, *"I Gave Them a Sword,"* 18–21.
14. *Ibid.*, 27–30.
15. *New York Times*, 8/12/75.
16. *Ibid.*, 8/21/75.
17. *Ibid.*, 9/14/75.
18. *Ibid.*, 1/8/75.
19. Anson, *Exile*, 117–19.
20. *New York Times*, 10/13/75.
21. Anson, *Exile*, 122.
22. *Ibid.*, 122–23.
23. *New York Times*, 10/17/75.
24. *Ibid.*, 10/20/75.
25. Gulley, *Breaking Cover*, 265.
26. Ford, *Time to Heal*, 360.
27. Hartmann interview; Ford, *Time to Heal*, 360.
28. Anson, *Exile*, 126–27.
29. *National Review*, 3/19/76.
30. *Washington Post*, 2/17/75.
31. Quoted in Anson, *Exile*, 127.
32. *Washington Post*, 2/25/75.
33. *New York Times*, 2/9/75.
34. *Ibid.*, 2/21/76; Manchester *Union Leader*, 2/15/76.
35. *National Review*, 3/19/76.
36. *New York Times*, 2/26/76.
37. *Ibid.*, 2/26/76.
38. *Ibid.*, 2/29/76.
39. *Ibid.*, 3/4/76.

Chapter Twenty-Two

1. *New York Times*, 4/11/76.
2. *Ibid.*, 4/13/76.
3. *Ibid.*, 5/17/76.
4. *Ibid.*, 3/30/76 and 5/1/76.
5. *Ibid.*, 3/29/76.
6. *Ibid.*, 6/16/76.
7. *Ibid.*, 7/29/76.
8. Anson, *Exile*, 138.

9. *Ibid.*, 139; Benjamin Stein, "Richard Nixon Goes to a Party," *Esquire*, November 1976.
10. Ford interview.
11. Gulley, *Breaking Cover*, 248.
12. *New York Times*, 7/9/76.
13. Eisenhower, *Pat Nixon*, 447–49.
14. McLendon, "Pat Nixon Today."
15. Eisenhower, *Pat Nixon*, 452.
16. Nick Thimmesch, "The Unsinkable Pat Nixon," *McCall's*, April 1979.
17. Eisenhower, *Pat Nixon*, 451.
18. Thimmesch, "The Unsinkable Pat Nixon."
19. McLendon, "Pat Nixon Today."
20. *New York Times*, 7/10/76.
21. Anson, *Exile*, 147.
22. *New York Times*, 6/6/76.
23. *Ibid.*, 8/19/76; Anson, *Exile*, 148.
24. Gulley, *Breaking Cover*, 249–50.
25. Anson, *Exile*, 149.
26. Gulley, *Breaking Cover*, 264.
27. Anson, *Exile*, 150.

CHAPTER TWENTY-THREE

1. *New York Times*, 1/26/77.
2. *Ibid.*, 1/29/77.
3. *Ibid.*, 4/21/77.
4. *Ibid.*, 6/5/77.
5. Frost, *"I Gave Them a Sword,"* 93–95.
6. *Ibid.*, 113.
7. *Ibid.*, 139.
8. *Ibid.*, 142.
9. *Ibid.*, 183–84.
10. *Ibid.*, 191.
11. *Ibid.*, 193.
12. From the dust jacket of Frost's book.
13. Frost, *"I Gave Them a Sword,"* 238–41.
14. Nixon, *In the Arena*, 34.
15. Frost, *"I Gave Them a Sword,"* 241–42.
16. *Ibid.*, 261–63.
17. Nixon, *In the Arena*, 41.
18. Frost, *"I Gave Them a Sword,"* 266–69.
19. *Ibid.*, 270–71.
20. *Ibid.*, 270–72.
21. Nixon, *In the Arena*, 43.
22. Frost, *"I Gave Them a Sword,"* 302.
23. *New York Times*, 5/5, 5/6, 5/13/77; Anson, *Exile* 168–69.
24. *New York Times*, 8/10/77.
25. Anson, *Exile*, 172–73.
26. Nixon, *In the Arena*, 33.
27. Anson, *Exile*, 174–75.
28. *Ibid.*, 176–77.
29. *Ibid.*, 180.

30. Los Angeles *Times*, 10/8/77.
31. *New York Times*, 1/11/78.
32. *Washington Post*, 1/16/78; Anson, *Exile*, 184.
33. *New York Times*, 1/16/78.
34. Anson, *Exile*, 184.
35. *New York Times*, 1/16/78; Anson, *Exile*, 185.

Chapter Twenty-Four

1. Eisenhower, *Pat Nixon*, 456.
2. *New York Times*, 7/2/78; Anson, *Exile*, 192–93.
3. *New York Times*, 7/3/78.
4. Los Angeles *Times*, 9/14/78.
5. *New York Times*, 11/11/78.
6. *Ibid.*, 11/14/78.
7. *New York Times*, 11/12/78; Anson, *Exile*, 196–97.
8. Anson, *Exile*, 198–99.
9. *Time* magazine, 12/11/78; *New York Times*, 12/1/78; Anson, *Exile*, 199–200.
10. *New York Times*, 12/4/78.
11. Anson, *Exile*, 201.
12. Thimmesch, "Richard Nixon Speaks His Mind."
13. *National Review*, 12/22/78.
14. Haldeman interview; Anson, *Exile*, 202–7.

Chapter Twenty-Five

1. Jack Brennan interview.
2. Anson, *Exile*, 207–8; *New York Times*, 1/30/79.
3. *New York Times*, 2/2/79.
4. *Ibid.*, 1/31/79.
5. Nixon, *In the Arena*, 72–73.
6. William Safire, "Return from Elba," *New York Times*, 7/26/79.
7. Thimmesch, "The Unsinkable Pat Nixon"; Anson, *Exile*, 210.
8. Eisenhower, *Pat Nixon*, 458.
9. *New York Times*, 5/25/79.
10. *Ibid.*, 7/19/79.
11. *Ibid.*, 9/6/79.
12. Los Angeles *Times*, 9/7/79.
13. *New York Times*, 9/4/79.
14. Julie Baumgold, "Nixon's New Life in New York," *New York* magazine, 6/9/80.
15. Anson, *Exile*, 212.
16. Schlesinger interview.
17. *New York Times*, 7/14/79.
18. *New York Times*, 9/4/70; Los Angeles *Times*, 9/4/79.
19. Anson, *Exile*, 215.
20. *New York Times*, 9/19/79.
21. Anson, *Exile*, 214.
22. San Clemente *Sun-Post*, 2/13/80.
23. Nixon, *The Real War* (Touchstone edn., 1990), 4.
24. *Ibid.*, 19.

25. *Ibid.*, 314.
26. *Ibid.*, 96, 114–15, 122.
27. *Ibid.*, 4.
28. *New York Times*, 5/20/80.
29. Nixon, *The Real War*, 211.
30. *Ibid.*, 79.
31. *Ibid.*, 297.
32. Anson, *Exile*, 223–24.
33. *Ibid.*, 224.
34. *New York Post*, 7/28/80.
35. *Washington Post*, 7/29/80.
36. *New York Times*, 7/17/80.
37. Marguerite Michaels, "Why Nixon Believes We're Losing the Race on Land, on Sea, and in the Air," *Parade*, 10/5/80.
38. Anson, *Exile*, 230.
39. *New York Times*, 9/8/80; Anson, *Exile*, 228.
40. Anson, *Exile*, 236.
41. Greene, *Cheeseburgers: The Best of Bob Greene*, 142–59.
42. *New York Times*, 10/30/79.
43. Anson, *Exile*, 235.
44. Introduction to the Warner Books edition of *The Real War* (1981).
45. *Washington Post*, 12/19/80.

CHAPTER TWENTY-SIX

1. Baumgold, "Nixon's New Life in New York."
2. Richard Reeves interview.
3. Baumgold, "Nixon's New Life in New York."
4. Anson, *Exile*, 218.
5. Hugh Sidey interview.
6. Anson, *Exile*, 219.
7. Baumgold, "Nixon's New Life in New York."
8. *Ibid.*
9. Nixon, *In the Arena*, 74.
10. Baumgold, "Nixon's New Life in New York."
11. Anson, *Exile*, 239–40.
12. *Washington Post*, 1/25/81.
13. *New York Times*, 6/12/81.
14. *New York Daily News*, 7/23/81.
15. *U.S. News and World Report*, 6/4/90.
16. Anson, *Exile*, 214–15.
17. *New York Times*, 9/6/81.
18. *Ibid.*, 8/16/81.
19. *Ibid.*, 9/30/81.
20. *Ibid.*, 9/1/81.
21. Anson, *Exile*, 245.
22. *New York Times*, 2/5/84.
23. Anson, *Exile*, 253.
24. *Time* magazine, 10/26/81.
25. *New York Times*, 10/18/81.
26. *Time* magazine, 11/2/81.
27. *Washington Post*, 10/13/81.

28. Robert Dole interview.
29. Nixon, *Leaders* (Touchstone edn., 1990), xii.
30. *Ibid.*
31. Milton Eisenhower interview.
32. Nixon, *Leaders*, 284.
33. *Ibid.*, 218.
34. *Ibid.*, 3.
35. *New York Times*, 2/19/81.
36. Gulley, *Breaking Cover*, 246.
37. Anson, *Exile*, 264.
38. *New York Times*, 11/8/82; Anson, *Exile*, 272–73.
39. *New York Times*, 3/1/83.
40. *Ibid.*, 4/14/83.
41. Nixon, *Real Peace* (Touchstone edn., 1990), 10.
42. *New York Times*, 9/1/83.
43. Nixon, *Real Peace*, 88.
44. *Ibid.*, 9–10.
45. *Ibid.*, 21, 27.
46. *Ibid.*, 15, 33.
47. *Ibid.*, 36–37.
48. *New York Times*, 3/13 and 3/14/84.
49. *Ibid.*, 5/10/84.
50. *Ibid.*, 1/25/84.
51. Eisenhower, *Pat Nixon*, 458–60.
52. *New York Times*, 8/2/84.
53. *Ibid.*, 8/5/84.
54. Thanks to Steve Jones for bringing this comparison to my mind.

CHAPTER TWENTY-SEVEN

1. Hugh Sidey interview.
2. John Stacks interview.
3. *Time* magazine, 4/25/88.
4. *Newsweek*, 5/19/86.
5. *New York Times*, 2/28/86.
6. *Ibid.*, 3/13/85.
7. *Newsweek*, 5/19/86.
8. Nixon, *In the Arena*, 50.
9. *New York Times*, 2/8/86.
10. *New York Times Book Review*, 9/3/89.
11. Nixon, *No More Vietnams* (Touchstone edn., 1990), 169.
12. *Ibid.*, 245.
13. *Ibid.*, 142.
14. *Ibid.*, 111–13.
15. *Ibid.*, 117–18.
16. *Ibid.*, 121.
17. *Time* magazine, 7/29/85.
18. Nixon, *In the Arena*, 75.
19. *Newsweek*, 5/19/86.
20. *Ibid.*
21. *Ibid.*
22. *Ibid.*

23. Nixon, *1999: Victory Without War* (Touchstone edn., 1990), 66–67.
24. *Time* magazine, 11/30/87.
25. Nixon, *1999: Victory Without War*, 323.
26. *Ibid.*, 45.
27. *Ibid.*, 58–60.
28. *Ibid.*, 131.
29. *Ibid.*, 62.
30. *Ibid.*, 36.
31. *Ibid.*, 36.
32. *Ibid.*, 130.
33. *Ibid.*, 189.
34. Nixon, *The Real War*, 266.
35. Nixon, *1999: Victory Without War*, 131.
36. *Ibid.*, 120.
37. *Ibid.*, 246.
38. *New York Times*, 4/15/88.
39. *Ibid.*
40. *Ibid.*, 4/11/88.
41. Nixon, *In the Arena*, 61.
42. *Ibid.*, 63.
43. *Ibid.*, 65.
44. *Time* magazine, 11/20/89.
45. *New York Times*, 9/22/88.
46. *Time* magazine, 4/9/90.
47. Nixon, *In the Arena*, 34–39.
48. Frost, *"I Gave Them a Sword,"* 268.
49. Nixon, *In the Arena*, 41.
50. *Ibid.*
51. James Stacks interview.
52. Nixon, *In the Arena*, 368.
53. *Ibid.*, 321.
54. *Ibid.*, 325.
55. *New York Times*, 3/9/90.

CHAPTER TWENTY-EIGHT

1. This chapter is based on the author's personal observation. He got in line at 5 A.M.

EPILOGUE

1. Nixon, *Leaders*, 330–31.
2. Keegan, *The Mask of Command*, 50–51, 90.
3. Nixon, *Leaders*, 327.
4. Kenneth W. Thompson, ed., *The Nixon Presidency*. Vol. VI of *Portraits of American Presidents*, 6–7.
5. *Ibid.*, 151.
6. Greene, *Cheeseburgers*, 155–56.
7. *Ibid.*, 151.
8. Frost, *"I Gave Them a Sword,"* 28.
9. Butterfield's testimony in *Impeachment of Richard M. Nixon, President of the United States, Report of the Committee on the Judiciary, House of Representatives.*

10. Safire, *Before the Fall*, 603.
11. Frost, *"I Gave Them a Sword,"* 28.
12. Thompson, *The Nixon Presidency*, 306.
13. Clawson, "A Loyalist's Memoir."
14. Sidey to author, 2/27/90, author's possession.
15. Thompson, *The Nixon Presidency*, 9.
16. Kissinger, *Years of Upheaval, 1101.*
17. Goldwater, *Goldwater*, 262.
18. Greene, *Cheeseburgers*, 149–51.
19. Kissinger, *Years of Upheaval*, 1101.
20. Thompson, *The Nixon Presidency*, 9.
21. Sidey to author, 2/27/90, author's possession.
22. Thompson, *The Nixon Presidency*, 16.
23. Nixon, *Leaders*, 43, 70–71.
24. Gulley, *Breaking Cover*, 238.
25. Nixon, *Leaders*, 348.
26. Nixon, *No More Vietnams*, 165.
27. Kutler, *Wars of Watergate*, 577.

BIBLIOGRAPHY

Agnew, Spiro. *Go Quietly . . . or Else*. New York: William Morrow, 1980.

Ambrose, Stephen E. *Eisenhower: The President*. Vol. II. New York: Simon and Schuster, 1984.

————. *Rise to Globalism: American Foreign Policy Since 1938*. New York: Penguin Books, 1985.

Anson, Robert Sam. *Exile: The Unquiet Oblivion of Richard M. Nixon*. New York: Simon and Schuster, 1984.

Armstrong, Scott. "Friday the Thirteenth." *Journal of American History*, March 1989.

Baumgold, Julie. "Nixon's New Life in New York." *New York* magazine, June 9, 1980.

Brown, Thomas. "The Exile." *New York Times Magazine*, August 3, 1975.

Chang, Gordon. "JFK, China, and the Bomb." *Journal of American History*, March 1988.

Clawson, Ken. "A Loyalist's Memoir." *The Washington Post*, September 9, 1979.

David, Lester. "Pat Nixon Today," *Good Housekeeping*, February 1980, 128–29.

Dean, John W. III. *Blind Ambition*. New York: Simon and Schuster, 1976.

Drew, Elizabeth. *Washington Journal*. New York: Random House, 1975.

Ehrlichman, John. *Witness to Power: The Nixon Years*. New York: Simon and Schuster, 1982.

Eisenhower, Julie Nixon. *Pat Nixon: The Untold Story*. New York: Simon and Schuster, 1986.

Ford, Gerald. *A Time to Heal*. New York: Harper & Row, 1979.

Frost, David. *"I Gave Them a Sword": Behind the Scenes of the Nixon Interviews*. New York: William Morrow, 1978.

Garment, Leonard. "The Hill Case." *The New Yorker*, April 17, 1989.

Garthoff, Raymond L. *Détente and Confrontation: American-Soviet Relations from Nixon to Reagan*. Washington, D.C.: The Brookings Institution, 1985.

Geselbracht, Raymond. "The Four Eras in the History of Presidential Papers." *Prologue*, vol. 13, no. 1, 1983.

Golan, Matti. *The Secret Conversations of Henry Kissinger*. New York: Quadrangle, 1976.

Goldwater, Barry M., with Jack Casserly. *Goldwater*. New York: Doubleday, 1988.

Greene, Bob. *Cheeseburgers: The Best of Bob Greene*. New York: Atheneum, 1985.

Gulley, Bill, with Mary Ellen Reese. *Breaking Cover*. New York: Simon and Schuster, 1980.

Haldeman, H. R., with Joseph Di Mona. *The Ends of Power*. New York: New York Times Books, 1978.

Hartmann, Jerry. *Palace Politics: An Inside Account of the Ford Years*. New York: McGraw-Hill, 1980.

Heller, Francis. "American Law, Presidential Papers, and Memoirs," paper for Conference on Political Memoirs, University of British Columbia, September 21–24, 1989.

Hersh, Seymour M. "The Pardon." *The Atlantic Monthly*, August 1983.

———. *The Price of Power: Kissinger in the Nixon White House*. New York: Summit Books, 1983.

Hung, Nguyen Tien, and Jerrold L. Schecter. *The Palace File*. New York: Harper & Row, 1986.

Jones, Stephen. "Was Richard Nixon Guilty?" *Journal of the Oklahoma Bar Association*, Oklahoma City, Winter issue, 1978.

Keegan, John. *The Mask of Command*. Harmondsworth, Middx.: Penguin Books, 1988.

Kissinger, Henry. *White House Years*. Boston: Little, Brown, 1979.

———. *Years of Upheaval*. Boston: Little, Brown, 1982.

Klein, Herb. *Making It Perfectly Clear*. Garden City, New York. Doubleday, 1980.

Korff, Rabbi Baruch. *The Personal Nixon: Staying on the Summit*. Boston: Fairness Publishers, 1979.

Kutler, Stanley I. *The Wars of Watergate: The Last Crisis of Richard Nixon*. New York: Alfred A. Knopf, 1990.

Lang, Gladys Engle, and Kurt Lang. *The Battle for Public Opinion: The President, the Press, and the Polls During Watergate*. New York: Columbia University Press, 1983.

Lukas, J. Anthony. *Nightmare: The Underside of the Nixon Years*. New York: The Viking Press, 1976.

McLendon, Winzola. "Pat Nixon Today." *Good Housekeeping*, February 1980.

Michaels, Marguerite. "Why Nixon Believes We're Losing the Race on Land, on Sea, and in the Air." *Parade*, October 5, 1980.

Morris, Roger. *Haig, the General's Progress*. New York: Seaview Books, 1982.

Murray, Robert K., and Tim H. Blessing. "The Presidential Performance Study: A Progress Report." *Journal of American History*, December 1983.

New York Times. *The White House Tapes*. New York: The Viking Press, 1974.

Nixon, Richard M. *1999: Victory Without War*. New York: Touchstone, 1990.

———. *In the Arena: A Memoir of Victory, Defeat and Renewal*. New York: Simon and Schuster, 1990.

———. *Leaders*. New York: Touchstone, 1990.

———. "Memo to President Bush: How to Use TV." *TV Guide*, January 14, 1989.

———. *The Memoirs of Richard Nixon*. New York: Grosset & Dunlap, 1978.

———. *No More Vietnams*. New York: Touchstone, 1990.

———. *The Real War*. New York: Touchstone, 1990.

———. *Real Peace*. New York: Touchstone, 1990.

O'Neill, Thomas P., with William Novak. *Man of the House: The Life and Political Memoirs of Speaker Tip O'Neill*. New York: Random House, 1987.

Price, Raymond. *With Nixon*. New York: The Viking Press, 1977.

Public Papers of the President (1972–1974). Washington, D.C. Government Printing Office.

Richardson, Elliot. *The Creative Balance: Government, Politics, and the Individual in America's Third Century*. New York: Holt, Rinehart and Winston, 1976.

Rovere, Richard. "Richard the Bold." *New York* magazine, June 19, 1978.

Safire, William. *Before the Fall*. Garden City, New York. Doubleday, 1975.

Sanders, Donald. "Watergate Reminiscences." *Journal of American History*, March 1989.

Schoenebaum, Eleanora. *Profiles of an Era: The Nixon-Ford Years*. New York: Harcourt Brace Jovanovich, 1979.

Sirica, John J. *To Set the Record Straight*. New York: W. W. Norton, 1979.

Stein, Benjamin. "Richard Nixon Goes to a Party." *Esquire*, November 1976.

Stern, Paula. *Water's Edge: Domestic Politics and the Making of American Foreign Policy*. Westport, Conn.: Greenwood Press, 1979.

Thelen, David. "Conversations with Alexander P. Butterfield." *Journal of American History*, March 1989.

Thimmesch, Nick. "Richard Nixon Speaks His Mind." *The Saturday Evening Post*. March 1979.

———. "The Unsinkable Pat Nixon." *McCall's*, April 1979.

Thompson, Kenneth W. *The Nixon Presidency*. Vol. VI of *Portraits of American Presidents*. University Press of America, 1987.

Todd, William. "The White House Transcripts." *Discovery: Research and Scholarship at the University of Texas*, Vol. 1, no. 2, December 1976.

Witcover, Jules, and Richard M. Cohen. *A Heartbeat Away*. New York: The Viking Press, 1974.

Woodward, Bob, and Carl Bernstein. *The Final Days*. New York: Simon and Schuster, 1976.

Zumwalt, Elmo R., Jr. *On Watch*. New York: Quadrangle, 1976.

MANUSCRIPTS

The Nixon Presidential Materials Project (NPMP) in Alexandria, Virginia, is the basic documentary collection of the Nixon Administration. NPMP also holds the tape recordings made in the Oval Office, Nixon's EOB office, the Cabinet Room, and over the telephone. Fifty hours of these tapes, covering Watergate-related conversations and used in various trials of Nixon subordinates, are available to scholars. The Glen Davis Papers at the Wisconsin State Historical Society, Madison, Wisconsin, were also used.

NEWSPAPERS

Boston *Globe*
Chicago *Tribune*
Christianity Today
Christian Science Monitor
Cleveland *Plain Dealer*
Greensburg *Tribune-Review*
Los Angeles *Times*
Manchester *Union Leader*
The New York Times
Omaha *World-Herald*
San Clemente *Sun-Post*
The Wall Street Journal
The Washington Post
Washington *Star-News*

INTERVIEWS

Benton Becker
John Brademas
Jack Brennan
Lillian Brown
Charles Colson (NPMP)
Robert Dole
Milton Eisenhower
Gerald Ford
Leon Friedman
H. R. Haldeman
Leon Jaworski
        (The Texas Collection, Baylor University)
Steve Jones
Richard Reeves
William Safire
Jeff Shepard
Hugh Sidey
John Stacks

ACKNOWLEDGMENTS

ON AUGUST 8, 1974, Moira and I were visiting my father in Whitewater, Wisconsin. That evening, Richard Nixon came on national radio and television. We anticipated a resignation announcement. The expectation made it impossible for us to be together, as we had such different feelings about the man. My father, like my late mother, had been a strong Nixon supporter ever since the Hiss case. Moira had worked for Nixon in the 1960 campaign but had withdrawn her support because of his failure to end the Vietnam War. Ever since the Hiss case, I had been a Nixon critic. We did not want to expose to each other the powerful, all-but-overwhelming emotions that were sure to accompany his resignation speech, so that evening—and again the following morning as Nixon said good-by to his Cabinet and staff—I went out in the driveway to listen on the car radio, while Moira listened on the kitchen radio, and Dad watched on the television in the living room.

Dad died seven years later, still unable to fathom how I could be so sensible about Eisenhower, so unreasonable about Nixon. As for Moira and me, the intensity of our feelings about Nixon continued, but became more complex and mixed after 1982, when we embarked on an eight-year voyage of discovery seeking to understand and evaluate the man.

She has been with me the whole way—suggesting, advising, consulting, helping with the research, providing insights. She is precious to me, beyond description. It is with the greatest pleasure, therefore, that I acknowledge first of all that I could not possibly have begun, much less completed, this voyage without her.

The funny thing is, the more she got to know Richard Nixon, the less she liked him, while as for me, well, in volume one I developed a grudging admiration for the man (he had been right on the Hiss case, while I had been wrong; he was outstanding in his support for the Marshall Plan and for civil rights; he served Ike well and faithfully as Vice President), in volume two I came to have a quite genuine and deep admiration for many of his policies (détente and China most of all, but others as well),

635

and in volume three I found, to my astonishment, that I had developed a liking for him. That is not easy to do, as he doesn't really want to be liked—he wants to be admired, respected, and obeyed—and he does do awful things. But I like him as a family man, and because he never gives up and is always true to himself. Of course, many of the qualities that make him what he is are negative—his self-centeredness, his partisanship, his anything-to-win methods, his anger, among others—but he is being himself as he acts them out.

So my second acknowledgment goes to Richard Nixon. I have lived with him for up to ten hours per day, almost every day, for seven years, and never once got bored.

Third, thank you to Alexander Butterfield. He told the truth.

The staff at the Nixon Presidential Materials Project in Alexandria, Virginia—including Clarence Lyons, Jim Hastings, Joan Howard, Maarja Krusten, Frederick Graboske, Nick Lemann, Richard McNeill, Ray Geselbracht, Sue Ellen Stanley, among others—have been indispensable. They are also friendly and helpful, characteristics I have encountered with the people working for the National Archives over the past thirty-five years. They are all professionals of the highest degree of competence.

As to the Richard Nixon Library and Birthplace in Yorba Linda, California, I was in line at 5 A.M the day it opened (July 20, 1990) and was thus the first person to enter the building with a purchased ticket. Unfortunately, the only books in the "library" were by Richard Nixon (*In the Arena*), Julie Eisenhower (*Pat Nixon*), and David Eisenhower (*Eisenhower at War*). They were for sale in the gift shop. There were no manuscripts or tape-recorded conversations available for scholarly research. The library is, in fact, a museum.

During the time I've been engaged in researching and writing about Nixon, I've received much-appreciated and wonderfully generous support from my home institution, the University of New Orleans. I especially want to thank Chancellor Greg O'Brien, Vice-Chancellor Gordon Mueller, and my department chairman, Dr. Gerry Bodet. They are all friends, I am glad to say; I'm distressed to have to add that I owe each of them more than I can ever repay. So too with UNO.

Mrs. Carolyn Peterson Smith, the secretary at the Eisenhower Center at UNO, typed the first twenty chapters, working from yellow legal pads covered with cross-outs and handwritten additions. For the remaining chapters, I switched to a computer. I made many mistakes; she guided and corrected me; she is a gem.

My staff at the Eisenhower Center gave me the peace of mind that allowed me to concentrate on Nixon by carrying forward the work of the Center—including the various conferences it sponsored but most of all the project to collect the oral histories of the junior officers and enlisted men of D-Day—in an exemplary manner. Associate Director

Gunter Bischof, Assistant Director Ron Drez, and student workers Marissa Ahmed, Tracy Hernandez, and Maria Andara worked harder than they should have had to do so that I could finish the Nixon biograpy. The D-Day project is very dear to my heart and I cannot thank them adequately for keeping it going, indeed flourishing, for these past years.

My agent, John Ware, was as always superb. I've been with John for fifteen years and seven books now, which speaks for itself.

Michael Beschloss provided insight, information, and encouragement. He it was who convinced me to expand from two to three volumes, and to not stop with Nixon's resignation, as I was sorely tempted to do, but to go on to cover the period 1974–1990.

When Alice Mayhew talked me into writing a biography of Richard Nixon, she thought she was going to get a one-volume work. She reluctantly agreed to two volumes, and even more reluctantly to three. She puts a staggering amount of time into her line editing, all to my benefit. During the period of the Nixon volumes, the Mayhew assistants I worked with were Henry Ferris, now senior editor at Houghton Mifflin, Ann Godoff, now a senior editor at Random House, and David Shipley, now assistant editor of the Op-Ed page of *The New York Times*. Ari Hoogenboom did the work on this volume with the kind of professional competence I've come to expect from the young people working for Alice.

My daughter, Mrs. Stephenie Ambrose Tubbs, did the newspaper and magazine research for this volume, as she had done for the previous two volumes. She has an M.A. in history from the University of Montana, a keen sense of what is important, a good eye for the colorful anecdote, a cheery disposition, and a fine sense of humor. She would send me immense stacks of copies of newspaper stories and magazine articles; I could count on her brightening the task of going through them by making hand-written comments, too often sarcastic, but often right on the mark. As just one example, somewhere she found a piece entitled "Richard Nixon's Favorite Bird." She made a copy, then scribbled beside the headline, "The Phoenix."

The errors are mine. They are present in spite of, rather than because of, Stephenie and all the others who helped.

STEPHEN E. AMBROSE
The Cabin
Dunbar, Wisconsin

Eisenhowerplatz
Bay St. Louis, Mississippi

Army War College
Carlisle, Pennsylvania
August 1988–August 1991

INDEX

и